SOCIAL COMPARISON

Contemporary Theory and Research

SOCIAL COMPARISON

Contemporary Theory and Research

Edited by

JERRY SULS
The University of Iowa

THOMAS ASHBY WILLS
*Ferkauf Graduate School of Psychology, and
Albert Einstein College of Medicine*

LEA LAWRENCE ERLBAUM ASSOCIATES, PUBLISHERS
1991 Hillsdale, New Jersey   Hove and London

Copyright © 1991 by Lawrence Erlbaum Associates, Inc.
All rights reserved. No part of this book may be reproduced in any form, by photostat, microform, retrieval system, or any other means, without the prior written permission of the publisher.

Lawrence Erlbaum Associates, Inc., Publishers
365 Broadway
Hillsdale, New Jersey 07642

Library of Congress Cataloging-in-Publication Data

Social comparison : contemporary theory and research / edited by Jerry Suls and Thomas Ashby Wills.
    p. cm.
  Includes bibliographical references.
  ISBN 0-8058-0549-4.—ISBN 0-8058-0550-8 (pbk.)
  1. Social psychology. 2. Self-evaluation. 3. Self-respect.
I. Suls, Jerry M. II. Wills, Thomas Ashby.
HM251.S671157   1990
302—dc20   90-31062
                                                                               CIP

Printed in the United States of America

10 9 8 7 6 5 4 3 2 1

Contents

Contributors   xi
Introduction   xiii

PART I: GENERAL MODELS OF SOCIAL COMPARISON

1. **A Brief History of Social Comparison Theory**
   Ladd Wheeler   3

   Informal Social Communication   4
   Social Comparison Theory   5
   Criticisms   6
   Schachter's Contributions   7
   The Rank-Order Paradigm   8
   The Case for Dissimilarity   11
   Adaptive Versus Hedonic Forces   12
   Attitude Versus Ability Similarity   13
   General Versus Specific Similarity   14
   Modeling as Social Comparison   14
   Attribution and Social Comparison   16
   Downward Comparison   18
   In Memoriam   18
   References   19

2. **Serving Self-Relevant Goals Through Social Comparison**
   Joanne V. Wood and Kathryn L. Taylor   23

   Serving Goals Through Social Comparison   24
   When Do Self-Evaluation Versus Self-Enhancement Goals
       Dominate Social Comparisons?   40
   Conclusion   45
   References   46

3. **Similarity and Self-Esteem in Downward Comparison**
   Thomas Ashby Wills   51

   Similarity and Self-Esteem in Downward Comparison   51
   The Theory of Downward Comparison   52

Comparison Differential and Subjective Well-Being   56
Level Effects and Dimensional Comparison   62
Effects of Downward Comparison   64
Downward Comparison and Self-Esteem   67
General Discussion   72
Acknowledgments   74
References   74

4. **Changing Patterns of Comparative Behavior as Skills Are Acquired: A Functional Model of Self-Evaluation**
Diane N. Ruble and Karin S. Frey   79

Phases of Self-Related Skill and Knowledge Acquisition   81
Implications for Age-Related Predictions and Findings   92
Motivational Implications   100
Conclusions   104
Acknowledgments   107
References   107

5. **Emotion in Social Comparison and Reflection Processes**
Abraham Tesser   117

The Self-Evaluation Maintenance (SEM) Model   118
Emotion as a Marker of SEM Processes   125
The Emotional Experience of Comparison and
   Reflection Processes   132
Emotion as a Mediator of SEM Behavior   137
Summary   143
Acknowledgment   144
References   144

PART II: SOCIAL COGNITION AND SOCIAL COMPARISON

6. **The Uniqueness Bias: Studies of Constructive Social Comparison**
George R. Goethals, David M. Messick, and Scott T. Allison   149

Social Comparison Theory and Perceptions of Social Reality   150
Studies of Perceived Consensus: Overestimations
   and Underestimations   157
The Uniqueness Bias: On Being Better Than Average   159

Reality-Constrained Self-Deception: The Role of
  Behavioral Specificity in the Uniqueness Bias   162
The Uniqueness Bias in Other Populations   166
Gender and Uniqueness   168
The Link to Self-Esteem and Depression   169
Constructive Social Comparison and the Uniqueness Bias   171
Acknowledgments   173
References   173

7. **Social Projection and Attitudinal Certainty**
   Norman Miller, Sharon Gross, and Rolf Holtz   *177*

   An Unspoken Half of Social Comparison Theory: Social
     Projection as a Source of Certainty   178
   Research on the Effects of Social Projection   184
   The Effects of Attitudinal Certainty on Projection   196
   The Relation Between Projection and Social
     Comparison Processes   199
   Conclusion   204
   Acknowledgments   205
   References   205

8. **Self-Esteem and Intergroup Comparisons: Toward a Theory of Collective Self-Esteem**
   Riia Luhtanen and Jennifer Crocker   *211*

   The Role of Self-Esteem in Prejudice and
     Intergroup Comparisons: Review of Theories   212
   A Paradox of Self-Esteem and Ingroup Bias   214
   Personal or Collective Self-Esteem   221
   Unresolved Issues   225
   Campus Racism: The Role of Personal and Collective
     Self-Esteem   231
   Acknowledgments   232
   References   232

PART III: SPECIFIC MODELS OF COMPARISON

9. **Responses to Upward and Downward Social Comparisons: The Impact of Esteem-relevance and Perceived Control**
   Brenda Major, Maria Testa, and Wayne H. Bylsma   *237*

   Esteem-Relevant Social Comparisons   241

viii   CONTENTS

        Perceived Control over Comparison Discrepancies   244
        Review of Relevant Research   249
        Summary and Conclusions   255
        References   257

10.   **Social Comparison Processes in Envy and Jealousy**
       Peter Salovey   261

       Envy and Jealousy as Dispositions, Feelings,
         and Situations   262
       Social Comparison and Self-Definition: The Antecedents
         of Envy and Jealousy   268
       Social Consequences of Envy and Jealousy   274
       Social Comparison, Envy, and Jealousy in Sociocultural
         Context   278
       Conclusions   280
       Acknowledgments   281
       References   281

11.   **When Social Comparison Goes Awry: The Case of Pluralistic Ignorance**
       Dale T. Miller and Cathy McFarland   287

       The Puzzle of Pluralistic Ignorance   288
       Pluralistic Ignorance and the Social Comparison
         Process   289
       The Breeding Grounds for Pluralistic Ignorance   291
       Toward a Theory of Pluralistic Ignorance   296
       Empirical Evidence   298
       Discussion   303
       Acknowledgments   310
       References   310

PART IV: APPLIED MODELS OF SOCIAL COMPARISON

12.   **Downward Comparison and Coping With Threat**
       Frederick X. Gibbons and Meg Gerrard   317

       Downward Comparison and Subjective Well-Being   322
       Downward Comparison and Coping Outcome   330

Active Downward Comparison and Social
   Distancing   335
Summary and Conclusions   340
Conclusion   341
Acknowledgment   342
References   342

13. Comparisons, Justice, and the Internment of Japanese-Americans
Donna Nagata and Faye Crosby   347

Denial of Personal Disadvantage   353
Lessons   362
Acknowledgment   364
References   365

14. Social Comparison and Coping With Major Medical Problems
Glenn Affleck and Howard Tennen   369

Social Comparisons in Rheumatoid Arthritis   370
Social Comparisons by Mothers of Medically Fragile
   Infants   375
Social Comparisons Among Women With Impaired
   Fertility   380
Summary and Conclusions   389
Acknowledgments   391
References   391

PART V

15. Commentary: Neo-Social Comparison Theory and Beyond
Thomas Ashby Wills and Jerry Suls   395

Similarity and Social Comparison   395
How Do Comparison Goals Shift?   397
Consequences of Comparison   400
Do People Strive for Uniformity or Uniqueness?   402
To What Degree Is Comparison Motivated by
   Uncertainty?   404
Do People Avoid Comparison?   406

x CONTENTS

    New Directions   408
    References   409

Author Index   413

Subject Index   429

Contributors

Glenn Affleck   Department of Psychiatry, University of Connecticut Health Center, Farmington, Connecticut 06032.

Scott Allison   Department of Psychology, University of Richmond, Richmond, Virginia.

Wayne Blysma   Department of Psychology, State University of New York at Buffalo, Buffalo, New York 14260.

Jennifer Crocker   Department of Psychology, State University of New York at Buffalo, Buffalo, New York 14260.

Faye Crosby   Department of Psychology, Smith College, Northampton, Massachusetts 01063.

Karin Frey   Experimental Education Unit, University of Washington, Seattle, Washington 98195.

Meg Gerrard   Department of Psychology, Iowa State University, Ames, Iowa 50011.

George R. Goethals   Department of Psychology, Williams College, Williamstown, Massachusetts 01267.

Frederick X. Gibbons   Department of Psychology, Iowa State University, Ames, Iowa 50011.

Sharon Gross   Department of Psychology, University of Southern California, Los Angeles, California 90007.

Rolf Holtz   Department of Psychology, Lamar University, Beaumont, Texas 77710.

Riia Luhtanen   Department of Psychology, State University of New York at Buffalo, Buffalo, New York 14260.

Cathy McFarland   Department of Psychology, Simon Fraser University, Burnaby, British Columbia, Canada V5A 1S6.

CONTRIBUTORS

Brenda Major   Department of Psychology, State University of New York at Buffalo, Buffalo, New York 14260.

David M. Messick   Department of Psychology, University of California at Santa Barbara, Santa Barbara, California 93106.

Dale T. Miller   Department of Psychology, Princeton University, Princeton, New Jersey 08544.

Norman Miller   Department of Psychology, University of Southern California, Los Angeles, California 90007.

Donna Nagata   Department of Psychology, Smith College, Northampton, Massachusetts 01063.

Diane N. Ruble   Department of Psychology, New York University, Six Washington Place, New York, New York 10003.

Peter Salovey   Department of Psychology, Yale University, New Haven, Connecticut 06520.

Jerry Suls   Department of Psychology, University of Iowa, Iowa City, Iowa 52242.

Kathryn L. Taylor   Department of Psychology, State University of New York at Stony Brook, Stony Brook, New York 11794.

Abraham Tesser   Institute of Behavioral Research, University of Georgia, Athens, Georgia 30602.

Maria Testa   Department of Psychology, State University of New York at Buffalo, Buffalo, New York 14260.

Howard Tennen   Department of Psychiatry, University of Connecticut Health Center, Farmington, Connecticut 06032.

Ladd Wheeler   Department of Psychology, University of Rochester, Rochester, New York 10027.

Thomas Ashby Wills   Department of Epidemiology and Social Medicine, Albert Einstein College of Medicine, 1300 Morris Park Avenue, Bronx, New York 10461.

Joanne V. Wood   Department of Psychology, University of Waterloo, Waterloo, Ontario, Canada N2L 3G1.

Introduction

Assessment of abilities, opinions, and overall feelings of self-worth, are commonly acknowledged to be influenced by how one's attributes compare with those of other people. In contemporary social psychology, this process is known as *social comparison* or *interpersonal comparison*, but, of course, the idea goes back to the classic Greek philosophers and probably before that. The assessments that are the consequence of comparison create affect, contribute to decision making about goals, and direct future actions. It is one thing, however, to observe that self-assessments are relative in nature, but quite another to describe and explain how comparisons are made, with whom, and how they influence self-evaluations and subsequent behavior. One of the major tasks of social scientists in the last 80 or so years has been to uncover the specifics of this process.

Research on attitude formation by Theodore Newcomb, on conformity by Solomon Asch, and on reference groups by Ray Hyman, among others, provided evidence of the impact of interpersonal comparisons, but a systematic theory of the comparison process was lacking until the early 1950s. Drawing from his and Kurt Lewin's earlier research on group communication and group influence, Leon Festinger (1954) provided such a theory. It has served as the major point of departure in the last 35 years for a long line of social psychological research. For some, the theory has been a continuing source of fascination, for others obsession, and for still others irritation. Independent of the specific reactions it produces, one index of the importance of a scientific theory is the degree to which it engages other scientists. By that criterion alone, Festinger's theory stands as one of the landmarks of social psychology.

In charting the history of the study of comparison processes, one can discern four phases. The first represents the publication of Festinger's theory and the subsequent research of Stanley Schachter in the 1950s on affiliation. A second generation of research involves refinements of the theory, extensions, and the development of new research paradigms. This research was presented in Latane's *Journal of Experimental Social Psychology* Supplement in 1966 and was composed mainly of social psychologists who trained or were strongly influenced by Schachter and Willerman while they were at the University of Minnesota. In the mid-1970s, a third generation of researchers was represented by the contributors to the Suls and Miller (1977) volume on comparison processes. Now, a fourth generation of research is evident, indicating the continued vitality and importance of comparison theory for the field of social psychology.

Several factors have contributed to the continued interest in social comparison. First, research using an attributional approach to comparison, introduced formally by Goethals and Darley in the 1970s, has led to a new understanding of the dimensions among which people compare. Second, the relevance of theory and research in other areas, notably social cognition and the psychology of the self, to comparison processes has become increasingly appreciated. The role of self-enhancement processes has transformed what some may term the *cold cognitions* emphasis of classic comparison theory that focused on accurate self-assessment, to concerns about *hot cognitions* in research that considers how social comparisons reduce negative affect and maintain self-esteem. Third, concepts from social comparison theory have been tested in naturalistic settings with persons who have experienced negative life events, such as physical illness or stigmatizing conditions. This work has extended considerably the scope and coverage of social comparison research.

This volume presents the most recent developments in this field of study. As described in the chapters that follow, the theory has gone through several iterations, taken on new problems and research paradigms, and reached out to other social-psychological areas of study. Some of this research addresses questions that are logical extensions of Festinger's theory; some considers questions that derive from entirely different ways of construing the comparison process from Festinger's original approach. Although all questions are not settled, the work presented here shows how far the original social comparison theory has evolved and suggests where we are likely to find the next insights.

The book is organized into five major sections. The first part consists of five chapters describing general models of the comparison process. The section begins with a survey chapter of the theory's progress from 1954 to the late 1970s by Ladd Wheeler, one of the pioneers in this area. Each of the subsequent chapters focuses on a different but central aspect of comparison: (a), the role of goals in comparison behavior; (b), the direction that comparison takes; (c), how the priority and use of comparison information changes with level of skill; and (d), effects of comparison on emotion. Part II considers the extension of social comparison processes to important problems in social cognition. In this section, we see examinations of the role of consensus estimation, the effects of projection on attitude certainty, and the role of comparison processes in ingroup bias. Part III provides new insights on how comparison applies to social psychological phenomena. The chapters consider factors that influence whether people compare upward or downward, factors influencing perceptions of envy and jealousy, and an analysis of how perceptions of personal deviance result from aberrations of the comparison process. Part IV involves recent developments in which social comparison theory has been tested in applied settings. This work provides new evidence concerning the use of comparison in coping with psychological and medical problems, and how comparison bears on questions of social justice and inequity. Finally, Part V provides a commentary in which the contributions are critically reviewed, some general questions raised, and suggestions for future study are provided.

Jerry Suls
Thomas Ashby Wills

I GENERAL MODELS OF SOCIAL COMPARISON

This section begins with a history of the development of comparison theory. Ladd Wheeler describes the roots of Festinger's thinking and then reviews major developments through the early 1980s.

The subsequent chapters in Part 1 present recent revisions, amplifications, and reinterpretations of comparison theory. A major focus of Festinger's original statement was on self-evaluation: the process of learning one's accurate standing. In Chapter 2, Wood and Taylor discuss how social comparison is relevant to other goals in addition to self-evaluation. Futhermore, rather than compare with persons who are similar or somewhat better off (a major prediction of Festinger's), Wood and Taylor describe how people may deviate from that pattern by comparing along dimensions on which they know they will fare better, or even create or fabricate comparison sources for themselves.

In Chapter 3, Thomas Wills summarizes the basis of downward comparison theory, in which people encountering threats to self-esteem may compare with others who are worse off in order to improve subjective well-being. The chapter provides a detailed analysis of how choices of comparison targets and the outcome of the comparison process may be influenced by particular types of similarity between the self and the other. A major point of discussion is how dispositional self-esteem bears on the comparison process.

In Chapter 4, Diane Ruble and Karin Frey describe how a skill acquisition model can provide a better undertanding of how and when social comparisons are important. The authors propose that interest in comparison depends on the level of skill development in the domain in question, and provide a general perspective that helps to reconcile apparently disparate patterns of comparison behavior.

Chapter 5, by Abraham Tesser, discusses his Self-Evaluation Maintenance model. This model describes the circumstances when people are positively or negatively affected by the results of social comparison, and delineates how they respond to each type of comparison. Tesser also discusses a companion process—reflection—describing conditions in which people may gain increased self-esteem from basking in the reflection of another's accomplishments. The emphasis of the chapter is on the effects of comparison and reflection on emotion, a topic that has not been considered in most social comparison models.

1 A Brief History of Social Comparison Theory

Ladd Wheeler
University of Rochester

Social comparison theory (Festinger, 1954a, 1954b) has a most peculiar history. Pictorially, this history is like the tracks of a squirrel in my snow covered backyard. The tracks zig zag unpredictably and then disappear near an elm, to next be seen near a maple, or the tracks may be obscured by those of other squirrels, or rabbits. In this chapter, I follow the tracks and draw the bigger trees through 1977, with a few additional comments about the early 1980s.

The theory was published between Festinger's theory of informal social communication (1950) and his theory of cognitive dissonance (1957). With each successive theory, Festinger attempted to subsume the previous one. Indeed, social comparison theory quite nicely subsumed the informal social communication theory, the major difference being that comparison theory included abilities as well as opinions, and comparison theory was more individually oriented. That is, the communication theory stressed the power of the group over the individual, whereas the comparison theory emphasized individuals using others to fulfill their own need to know. The attempt to subsume comparison theory under dissonance theory was strained and unconvincing, largely because other people were not necessary to the latter theory. The shift across the three theories was clearly toward an individualistic focus.

INFORMAL SOCIAL COMMUNICATION

In trying to understand social comparison theory, it is essential to review the earlier theory of informal social communication. Pressures toward uniformity of opinion in a group exist because of the need for social reality and the need for group locomotion. Communications arising from pressures toward uniformity are instrumental—intended to influence the person communicated to. Pressures to communicate:

1. increase with perceived opinion discrepancy in the group,
2. increase with the relevance of the opinion to group functions, and
3. with the cohesiveness of the group (resultant of all the forces acting upon the members to remain in the group).

Pressures to communicate to a particular person in the group:

1. increase with the opinion discrepancy between the communicator and that person,
2. decrease with the perception that the person is not a member of the group or is not wanted as a member of that group, and
3. increase with the perception that communication is likely to change the person in the desired direction.

The amount of change in opinion resulting from having received communication:

1. increases with pressures toward uniformity in the group,
2. increases with the resultant force for the recipient to remain in the group, and
3. decreases to the degree that the opinion is anchored in other groups or serves important need satisfying functions for the person.

The tendency to change the composition of the psychological group (pushing members out of the group):

1. increases as the perceived discrepancy in opinion increases and
2. increases as the cohesiveness of the group and the relevance of the issue to the group increases.

This is a relatively simple and very plausible theory. Everything in it is consistent with the treatment of opinions in social comparison theory, although there are some differences in wording and emphasis. The far greater ambiguity of social comparison theory as stated in *Human Relations* (Festinger, 1954a) is due largely to the addition of abilities, which led to the substitution of "comparison" for "communication."

This substitution is necessary because one cannot change a person's ability or one's own ability through talk. Instead one must compete or cooperate or cease comparison in order to achieve uniformity. Also, it is not uniformity one wants; the unidirectional drive upward motivates one to be slightly better than others. Finally, the whole reason for uniformity is different for opinions and abilities. For opinions, uniformity is an indication that one is correct. For abilities, uniformity is an indication that one is capable of doing the same things that others can do.

We see, then, that the 1954 theory is far more complicated than the 1950 theory; the cost of creating a more general theory was great in terms of the intellectual demands on the consumers.

SOCIAL COMPARISON THEORY

Social comparison theory (Festinger, 1954a) was cast in the form of nine hypotheses, eight corollaries, and eight deviations. Fortunately, Festinger summarized the major points in the 1954 Nebraska Symposium on Motivation (Festinger, 1954b).

> We started out by assuming the existence of a motivation to know that one's opinions are correct and to know precisely what one is and is not capable of doing. From this motivation, which is certainly non-social in character, we have made the following derivations about the conditions under which a social comparison process arises and about the nature of this social comparison process.
>
> 1. This social process arises when the evaluation of opinions or abilities is not feasible by testing directly in the environment.
> 2. Under such circumstances persons evaluate their opinions and abilities by comparison with others.
> 3. This comparison leads to pressures toward uniformity.
> 4. There is a tendency to stop comparing oneself with others who are very divergent. This tendency increases if others are perceived as different from oneself in relevant dimensions.
> 5. Factors such as importance, relevance and attraction to a group which affect the strength of the original motivation will affect the strength of the pressure towards uniformity. (p. 217)

Note that there is no mention of the unidirectional drive upward in the case of abilities (although there was a passing reference in the text), perhaps because Festinger thought this might be culturally determined (Festinger, 1954a, p. 125), and he wanted, in Nebraska at least, to make more universal statements. Or perhaps he did not mention the unidirectional drive because there was little evidence for it other than earlier studies showing that the level of aspiration is set slightly higher than a reported group average (Lewin, Dembo, Festinger, & Sears, 1944). In view of these facts, it is interesting that so much research has been directed to the question of upward versus downward comparison.

CRITICISMS

Nissen (1954), in commenting on the Nebraska paper, was delighted that Festinger had used the drive to know as his basic concept. He, too, believed this to be a primary drive common to man and animals. He disagreed, however, that the drive to know should lead to pressure to uniformity.

1. Having an ability greatly divergent from others is valuable knowledge, even if not precise, and those with outstanding ability often work hard to make that ability even more divergent from others.
2. Many people do not believe that opinion agreement implies correctness and may in fact conceitedly interpret opinion divergence as evidence of correctness.
3. Changing one's opinion to agree with the group does not increase knowledge.

Nissen interpreted the experiments Festinger discussed as evidence of a gregariousness drive that "should be especially strong towards members of the species having the same skin color, stature, opinions, abilities, and so on" (p. 223).

Deutsch and Krauss (1965) also criticized the theory.

1. Similarity to a comparison other isn't necessary. "Self-location on a scale of ability may be aided by knowing something about the extreme positions on the scale as well as knowing where one stands relative to others who are similar" (p. 67).
2. The need for similarity is given very strong motivational properties when in fact "people frequently seek out variety, novelty, and difference in their social encounters" and these things are as important in gaining self-knowledge as is comparison with similar others (p. 67).
3. The need to know may not lead to comparison but vice versa. It is only after people compare and find differences that they need to evaluate their opinions or abilities.

I return to some of these criticisms later. The important thing to note here is that social comparison theory went nowhere. Singer (1966) noted that:

> In brief, social comparison theory was an interesting suggestion put forth a decade ago with one solid finding supporting it (Hoffman et al., 1954) and, in the interim, studies using it as a point of departure but essentially concerned with other phenomena (e.g., Schachter, 1959) have utilized the theory. Moreover, this fallow period has not occurred because the theory was so tightly drawn that no additional work needed to be done. Quite the contrary, *questions about its specifics can be raised readily.* (p. 104, italics added)

Arrowood (1986) was more blunt in saying that "social comparison theory as stated in 1954 was really a masterpiece of ambiguity" (p. 279) and that this ambiguity had created a rocky road for the theory. Another reason for the fallow period is that Festinger and his students orphaned the theory and adopted dissonance theory. The baby was nourished through this difficult time by the research and teaching of Stanley Schachter.

SCHACHTER'S CONTRIBUTIONS

Schachter's (1959) work on affiliation is well known, although it was only Wrightsman's (1960) dissertation that really tied the work to social comparison theory. Wrightsman manipulated anxiety and then had subjects wait, either together or alone. There was greater homogenization of anxiety in the together conditions (talk and not talk) than in the alone condition, and this was taken as evidence of two manifestations of pressures to uniformity—the tendencies to change self and change others. There was also evidence for the third manifestation—the tendency to cease comparison with those who are extremely divergent from oneself. In the together conditions, homogenization was greater in those groups with intermediate initial anxiety ranges than in those groups with wide initial anxiety ranges.

During the next few years a number of investigators attempted to refine the evidence concerning emotional comparison. Cottrell and Epley (1977) summarized these studies:

> The results of studies to date seem to point to the conclusion that fear elicits affiliation. The evidence is much less certain that ambiguous emotional states lead to affiliation and that affiliation is for purposes of reducing a state of uncertainty about one's emotional reactions. A second postulated product of affiliation, fear reduction, is well established, although studies have not clearly identified the mechanism through which fear reduction takes place. There is convincing evidence for a modeling process in which the subject imitates the calm responses of a companion. The evidence is much less convincing for the conclusion that the simple physical presence of a companion is sufficient to diminish fear.
>
> On all points, there is a need to clarify existing constructs, particularly those surrounding the notion of uncertainty of emotional reactions. Further em-

pirical research is needed to support assertions of the theory, some of which rest on very modest empirical support. (p. 66)

Schachter's second[1] and perhaps larger contribution to social comparison theory was a year-long graduate seminar he taught at the University of Minnesota through 1960 in which he covered the material from Lewin and his students from the beginning to the present. It was very difficult to complete that course without developing a keen interest in social comparison. After all, the theory had been written at the University of Minnesota, much of the empirical work had been done there, and Schachter had been involved in all this for years. Schachter, like Festinger, perceived the essence of the theory to be pressures toward uniformity, and movement toward uniformity (such as homogenization of anxiety ratings) was taken as evidence of social comparison processes. In the late 1950s and early 1960s, however, Schachter's students began to ask other questions. They wanted more direct evidence for such theoretical statements as "Given a range of possible persons for comparison, someone close to one's own ability or opinion will be chosen for comparison" (Festinger, 1954a, p. 121, Corollary IIIA). Furthermore, they were concerned with the ambiguity of the unidirectional drive upward. If one wanted to be better than others, should one compare downward to assure being better, or should one compare upward to compete for the better position?

THE RANK-ORDER PARADIGM

To investigate such questions the group of students at Minnesota developed what has come to be known as the rank-order paradigm. Subjects are given rank-order information about a group in which they are tested for something, they are given their own numerical score, and they are asked to select (on the basis of rank) one person in the group whose numerical score they would like to see. This technique allows questions to be asked about direction of comparison (up or down) and about similarity (adjacent ranks or extreme ranks).

In the first of these studies (Wheeler, 1962, 1966), subjects were tested in groups of seven for their ability to profit from a special psychology seminar they would be required to take if chosen for it. The seminar was described in such a way as to create a high or low motivation to be selected. Subjects were told that they occupied the middle rank, and they were given the approximate scores of the top and bottom ranks. By far the strongest

---

[1] Some would also mention Schachter's two-factor theory of emotion (Schachter & Singer, 1962). However, he immediately realized that social comparison was just one means by which arousal could be labeled (Schachter & Wheeler, 1962), and the research went in a different direction.

result was that comparison choices were of others who had higher scores. This effect was stronger under high motivation than low motivation, and combining these two conditions, choice of adjacent ranks was more frequent than choice of other ranks. Finally, those who believed themselves to be more similar in score to the person immediately above them in the rank order than to the person below them were more likely to compare upward. In short, the experiment provided evidence for upward comparison and for comparison with similar others.

Hakmiller (1962, 1966) immediately set out to demonstrate downward comparison. Subjects were tested in groups of six for the personality trait "hostility toward one's parents," described as very negative (high threat) or as somewhat positive (low threat). Subjects were told that the purpose of the experiment was to cross-validate a paper-and-pencil test of hostility (the MMPI) with a more precise test (galvanic skin responses to TAT slides). Subjects were given a rank ordering predicted by the MMPI in which the subject was at the fifth rank, low on hostility. The more precise test was then given, and the subjects were told that they had quite a high hostility score. In short, they were given unexpectedly negative information about themselves in the high-threat condition. The predominant comparison choice in the high-threat condition was of the person predicted by the MMPI to be the most hostile. Although this was comparison upward in the rank order, it was psychologically downward comparison with someone expected to be worse off than the subject herself. Hakmiller called this *valuational* as opposed to *evaluational* comparison.

I have gone into some detail about these two experiments because, with them, the upward/downward comparison controversy was empirically joined. The Hakmiller experiment is frequently cited and often described as a "classic" demonstration of downward comparison under threat. The two experiments also extended comparison theory to personality traits. In attempting to reconcile the two experiments, Thornton and Arrowood (1966) used the same paradigm to test the hypothesis that "people compare with others thought to be better off than themselves *if* they can assume similarity to others in that direction" (p. 41). The hypothesis was not supported, and in explaining why, the authors argued that social comparison is motivated by both self-evaluation and self-enhancement. "The self-evaluative end is satisfied through comparison with a . . . positive instance of the attribute in question. The self-enhancing end is satisfied through goal approach on the irreality level—here, through comparison with someone better off than oneself" (p. 46). Note that self-enhancement is used here to refer to upward comparison, although it has come to refer to downward comparison (one of the quirks in our progress). The positive instance hypothesis was taken from studies of concept attainment, the idea being that one can understand an attribute better by looking at someone who has it rather than someone who doesn't. This was quite similar to Festinger's (1954b) argument that comparing one's ability to a similar other tells us what we can do, while comparison to a dissimilar other doesn't.

These three experiments were published in a Supplemental issue of the *Journal of Experimental Social Psychology* (*JESP,* Latané, 1966), along with six other empirical articles on social comparison theory, done almost entirely by former Minnesota students and their current students. The issue also contained a social comparison bibliography (Radloff & Bard, 1966), showing that from 1955 to 1965, 32 articles or books had appeared "for which social comparison theory appears to have had a major or important role in either the formulation of a study or the interpretation of its results" (p. 111). That was a small number, and we all hoped that the Supplement would draw overdue attention to the theory.

In fact, the rank-order papers did generate some research (Arrowood & Friend, 1969; Friend & Gilbert, 1973; Gruder, 1971; Gruder, Korth, Dichtel, & Glos, 1975; Wheeler et al., 1969; Wilson & Benner, 1971). The results of these and related studies were summarized by Gruder (1977):

> Persons want to find out how they stand—and that their standing is respectable. In order to do this, they want very much to learn about the highest-scoring other, apparently because he or she represents the most uncertainty and is, therefore, important in interpreting the meaning of any other position on the dimension. They are also interested, for the same reason, in the other who best represents a definition of the dimension, the "positive instance." And they want to compare themselves with others who are better off than they are on the dimension, presumably to allow them to assess the extent to which they are similar to these fortunate others. Finally, persons prefer to compare themselves with others who are similar to themselves on dimensions other than the one being evaluated.[2] (pp. 37–38)

This summary was in Gruder's chapter in the book on social comparison processes edited by Suls and Miller (1977), the next major development

---

[2] Note that Gruder did not conclude that people compare themselves to others who are similar on the comparison dimension itself, although this is a straightforward prediction from social comparison theory and could easily have demonstrated using the rank-order paradigm. I think that this is a curious historical accident. Wheeler (1966) told subjects that the top score in the group was between 550 and 600 and the bottom score, between 25 and 75. Virtually all subsequent researchers did the same. Gruder, Korth, Dichtel, and Glos (1975) made the highest score even more ambiguous by (a) varying the certainty that the highest score was indeed between 550 and 600 (2 chances in 10 vs. 9 chances in 10) or (b) increasing the range of the score to between 500 and 600. In addition, most of the experiments had conditions in which no information at all was given about the extreme scores. As a result, subjects have always been very interested in the extreme scores, obscuring the expected interest in similar scores. However, in the two cases more conducive to comparison with similar others, such comparison was significantly greater than chance (Gruder, 1971, Range condition of Exp. 1; Wheeler et al., 1969, Range condition, choice of score).

in social comparison theory after the Supplement (Latané, 1966). Perhaps the best way to continue this history is to comment on a selection of the contributions in the Suls and Miller book, as this highlights developments between 1966 and 1977.

THE CASE FOR DISSIMILARITY

Mettee and Smith (1977) argued that, in many cases, dissimilar others are preferred for comparison. There are two reasons for this: (a) affective consequences are blunted when comparing with dissimilar others, and (b) dissimilar others are often better sources of information.

Generally, those who are similar to us in a variety of ways are better references with respect to self-evaluation information, just as Festinger proposed. Because of this, affective consequences are more potent when comparing with a similar other. If comparison with a similar other provides unfavorable information about the self, it is more painful than unfavorable information obtained through comparison with a dissimilar other—who can simply be dismissed as irrelevant. Taylor and Mettee (1971) found that an obnoxious similar other was disliked more than a dissimilar obnoxious other, even when subjects had been assured that they did not possess the obnoxious trait. (See also Cooper & Jones, 1969; Novak & Lerner, 1968.) Mettee and Wilkins (1972) found derogation of a slightly superior ability other and indifference toward a very superior ability other. Mettee and Riskind (1974) conducted an experiment in which subjects were either substantially or marginally outperformed and their better-performing partners were either promoted to a noncomparable higher ability level or remained classified at the same ability level. The partner who was substantially outperforming the subject and was promoted to a higher ability level was liked significantly more than any of the other partners, presumably because this partner was noncomparable and nonthreatening after the promotion.

The evidence that dissimilar others are a better source of information was largely from the rank-order studies we have already considered. Mettee and Smith argued that when people know their own score and rank, they already possess much of the information available through comparison with similar others, and that comparison with the highest rank gives important information about the range of scores. They also argued that there are *affective* reasons for comparing with the best off other in the rank-order studies. In an essentially noncompetitive situation in which individuals are more concerned with the favorability of their characteristic ability level than with their performance (which the individual basically knows), comparison with someone better off allows identification with this person and self-enhancement of perceived ability level. As opposed to identification, contrast is most likely to occur when people are competing in performance and perceive themselves and others whose performance is just above or just below their own as being at the same characteristic level on the underlying attribute. In this case, people are likely to compare to someone they have outperformed.

There seems to be a contradiction between saying that dissimilar others are a better source of information than similar others, but that affect is blunted when comparing to dissimilar others. This can probably be resolved by stating that *sometimes* dissimilar others are better sources of information, and when that is true, affect is not blunted. In the usual case, dissimilar others are poorer sources of information, and affect is blunted.

ADAPTIVE VERSUS HEDONIC FORCES

The next contribution of the 1977 Suls and Miller book that I consider is that of Brickman and Bulman, who argued that people are motivated to avoid social comparison, as well as to seek comparison. They are so motivated because: "If two people compare themselves on a valued dimension, the chances are that one will be superior and one will be inferior. Someone will feel bad, and both parties or the collectivity must be concerned with coping with these negative feelings" (p. 152).

> Adaptive pressures push people to seek social comparisons as one form of useful information that they can use to improve themselves. To this end, comparison with similar others is more valuable than comparison with dissimilar others, since more valid inferences can be made from similar others. Comparison with superior others, although painful, is more valuable than comparison with inferior others, since more useful information may be acquired by observing superior others. Hedonic pressures push people to avoid social comparisons as [sic] situations in which one party or the other will feel bad, threatened by inferiority or insecurity, sensitivity or insensitivity, shame or guilt, loss of uniqueness or sense of deviance. To this end, comparison with dissimilar others is more valuable than comparison with similar others, since less valid inferences can be made from dissimilar others. Comparison with inferior others, although less useful, has greater hedonic value than comparison with superior others. (p. 179)

This was the first extensive attempt to call attention to the costs of social comparison. We are not given a calculus for determining whether adaptive or hedonic forces will prevail, but we may guess at the calculus from four unpublished experiments that were presented:

1. Subjects anticipated greater enjoyment of discussions in which disclosure of scores was asymmetrical or nonreciprocal than of discussions

in which disclosure was symmetrical or reciprocal. This demonstrates avoidance of social comparison when people must interact with one another.
2. Subjects in a minority position anticipated enjoyment of a discussion when they were superior, but wanted to avoid discussion when they were inferior. Subjects in a majority were indifferent. This demonstrates avoidance of comparison when people are self-conscious, anxious, or sensitive.
3. Satisfaction with own state was greater after comparison with a *superior* other who was either of the same generation but of a dissimilar background or of a previous generation and of a similar background. This demonstrates that being inferior in a competitive situation makes people feel bad, but may be encouraging when the situation is noncompetitive.
4. Subjects were more satisfied when they and their partner each received a high and a low score on two tests (regardless of whether they received the high score on the same or different tests) than when both received average scores on the same two tests. This was meant to demonstrate the problems of equality, but the results of the nine-condition experiment were not very supportive.

Although this research is of interest, it really does not demonstrate avoidance of comparison. Because of hedonic forces, people may not anticipate enjoyment of comparison, and they may not feel good after certain comparisons, but adaptive forces may cause them to compare anyway. After all, they cannot know the results of a comparison until it is made.

ATTITUDE VERSUS ABILITY SIMILARITY

Miller and Suls (1977) contributed to the book with six unpublished studies on people's preferences for work partners as a function of similarity of abilities and attitudes. Miller and Suls summarized the results as follows:

1. Individuals of superior ability are chosen for cooperative interactions (partners), while similar-ability others are preferred for competitive situations (opponents).
2. The degree of superiority preferred in a partner is a function of various factors associated with the affiliative situation. Two such factors, the size of the interacting group and the prospect that the outcome of the group interaction will be evaluated, implicate the operation of defensive comparison, which tempers the desire for a partner of superior ability.

3. Preferences for partners of superior ability are subsumed by the introduction of another factor of relevance to the interaction: attitude similarity. When both attitude and ability dimensions are salient to the evaluated group effort, individuals prefer high-ability others whose attitudes are similar to theirs. Partners whose attitudes are dissimilar are uniformly nonpreferred, regardless of ability level.
4. Partner preferences only partially match individuals' eventual satisfaction with an interaction. Partners of superior ability are actually satisfying when they possess similar attitudes but noticeably dissatisfying when they hold dissimilar attitudes. Satisfaction seems high with a similar-ability partner, regardless of attitude similarity. Thus it appears that some measure of similarity, whether it be ability or attitudinal, ensures a satisfying interaction (p. 121).

It is not surprising that people prefer superior ability others in a cooperative situation, because the team would likely do better. It is surprising, however, that defensive concerns exist even in a cooperative situation, reducing choice of superior others when the work is to be evaluated and when the group is small, both making comparison more salient. Adding attitude similarity to the studies was very instructive, because attitudinally dissimilar others were avoided regardless of their ability level. The only time ability similarity was important was for competitive situations.

GENERAL VERSUS SPECIFIC SIMILARITY

These results were nicely supplemented by Castore and DeNinno (1977), who presented five studies on choice of discussion partners who varied on general and situation-related attitudinal similarity. Across the studies, there was a clear tendency to prefer those with generally similar attitudes. This is partially explained by the fact that situation-related similarity was distorted in the direction of general similarity. The results supported a prediction logically derived by Israel (1956): Given two orthogonal dimensions along which similarity can be evaluated for a choice of a comparison other, similarity will be evaluated in terms of more general, as opposed to situation-specific, aspects of similarity.

MODELING AS SOCIAL COMPARISON

Berger's (1977) contribution was a social comparison analysis of modeling or imitation. The translation of modeling into social comparison is as follows:

1. Observers have a need to evaluate their abilities and a need to evaluate their performance in a given situation.
2. The performance of a model can provide information that is relevant to such evaluations (i.e., attributional or instrumental relevance).
3. Social comparisons involve particularistic standards, standards related to personal characteristics that the model and the observer have in common. This dependence upon a model with similar, or nearly similar, characteristics is a form of identification when it produces imitative performances.
4. Observers imitate the similar model's performance when it represents the best available standard for observers to accurately evaluate either an ability that they have in common with the model or the appropriateness of their instrumental behavior and/or its consequences in a given situation (p. 214).

The meat of Berger's argument concerns similarity–dissimilarity between model and observer, because various studies have suggested that dissimilarity between the model and observer may lead to more imitation than similarity does (Goethals, 1972; Goethals & Nelson, 1973; Wheeler & Levine, 1967). Berger argued that these studies involve universalistic rather than particularistic standards (Parsons, 1949) and are therefore not really social comparison. If people compare their running time to the performance of all people, they are using a universalistic standard, and the fact that other people are involved does not make it a *social* comparison. If, however, they compare their performance to others of the same age, that is a particularistic comparison and is social comparison. According to Berger, it is implicit with social comparison theory that comparison involves selection of a person on the basis of some specific characteristic that the person has in common with the individual making the comparison.

Stotland and his associates had provided evidence that observer-model similarity enhances imitation (Burnstein, Stotland, & Zander, 1961; Stotland & Canon, 1972; Stotland & Patchen, 1961; Sotland, Zander, & Natsoulas, 1961). However, Stotland and Canon (1972) said that this was due to the *generality of similarity schema*—the cognitive rule that people who are alike in one way are usually alike in others. The Stotland position would be that any similarity between the observer and the model should increase imitation, whereas social comparison theory suggests that the similarity must be related to the characteristic that is being evaluated. There is some evidence for both positions, and Berger suggested that it may depend upon the "realm of relevance" (Festinger, 1954a, pp. 132–133). When the realm of relevance is wide, as it would be when observer-model generality is based on multiple characteristics, there would be considerable generality as predicted by the schema position; when the realm of relevance is narrow, as it would be when similarity is based on only one characteristic, it would be necessary that the characteristic be specifically related to the behavior to be modeled. This analysis is clearly relevant to the results of Castore and DeNinno (1977) discussed earlier, and to the findings of Zanna, Goethals, and Hill (1975) that same-sex comparisons are preferred even when the opposite sex is superior. Gender implies similarity on multiple characteristics.

ATTRIBUTION AND SOCIAL COMPARISON

The last contribution to the 1977 book I discuss is that of Goethals and Darley (1977), an attributional approach to social comparison. In a commentary chapter in that book, Wheeler and Zuckerman (1977) considered this chapter to be the most original and important because it tied social comparison theory to Kelley's (1967) attribution model.

Students of social comparison theory had for years been concerned with the relationship between two statements in the original theory (Festinger, 1954a): Corollary III-A was that "Given a range of possible persons for comparison, someone close to one's own ability or opinion will be chosen for comparison." Hypothesis VIII was that "If persons who are very divergent from one's own opinion or ability are perceived as different from oneself on *attributes consistent with the divergence*, the tendency to narrow the range of comparability becomes stronger." The first statement implies that we will compare with others who are similar on the attribute to be evaluated, whereas the second implies that we will compare with others who are similar on attributes related to, and predictive of, the attribute to be evaluated. Although it was unknown to most of us (because we did not read *Sociometry*), Patchen (1961) argued that we must take secondary dimensions into account, because "comparisons on this primary dimension cannot be made in a cognitive vacuum" (p. 138). Patchen proposed an equity-like relationship between "my earning/his earning" compared to "my position on dimensions related to earnings/his position on dimensions related to earnings." (Other assertions about the importance of related attributes were made by Wheeler et al., 1969, and Wilson, 1973.) Although the Goethals and Darley emphasis on related attributes was not new, it was exciting and romantic because it introduced two of our old flames to one another. In the case of abilities, Goethals and Darley claimed that people will compare themselves to others who are similar on related attributes. If we compare to others who are advantaged on related attributes, we are likely to perform less well than they, but this must be discounted in our attributions about our ability because of the others' advantaged status (another plausible cause). The same argument holds if we compare to others who are disadvantaged on related attributes. If, on the other hand, the unexpected happens and we outperform advantaged others or underperform disadvantaged others, attributions about our ability will be augmented (the presence of inhibitory causes). Note the implication that although we should choose to compare to others who are similar on related attributes, there may be more psychological impact as a result of comparing to others who are dissimilar on related attributes.

In the case of opinions, it is necessary to distinguish between beliefs (a potentially verifiable assertion about the true nature of an entity) and values (liking or disliking an entity). It is only a belief that can be correct or incorrect, and evidence for correctness is that the belief is entity-based rather than person-caused. Agreement with someone similar on related attributes, or disagreement with someone dissimilar on related attributes, would be discounted because of the possibility of person-causation. On the other hand, agreement with someone dissimilar on related attributes, or disagreement with someone similar, would be augmented because of the increased likelihood of entity-causation. Thus, a person should compare to both similar and dissimilar others when evaluating beliefs. When evaluating values, which have no truth value, anything a dissimilar other says will be discounted, and anything a similar other says will be taken seriously.

In 1977, there was not much evidence for this attributional recasting of social comparison theory. Goethals and Ebling (1975) found that subjects chose comparison to others with similar values when trying to decide which of two people they would prefer as a friend. Reckman and Goethals (1973) found that there was more comparison with dissimilar others when subjects were trying to make accurate judgments about another person than when they were trying to determine if they found the other person likable.

Some subsequent work should be mentioned, however. Gastorf and Suls (1978) found greater evaluation certainty when subjects compared with others similar on related attributes. Suls, Gastorf, and Lawhon (1978) found that subjects chose to compare with same-sex and same-age others in evaluating performance, regardless of which groups excelled. Suls, Gaes, and Gastorf (1979) found that subjects chose to compare against same-sex or combined-sex norms regardless of which group excelled and also when sex was not mentioned as being related to performance. Feldman and Ruble (1981) reported similar results. Miller (1984) compared subjects who had strong self-schemas with respect to gender to aschematic subjects. Schematic subjects made same-sex performance comparisons whether gender was related to performance or not; aschematic subjects made same-sex comparisons only when performance was related to gender. Wheeler, Koestner, and Driver (1982), using a modification of the rank-order paradigm, found that subjects compared their performance to others who had the same amount of practice on the task, but only when performance was related to practice. Wheeler and Koestner (1984) found that subjects wanted to know the amount of practice given to others who were similar to them in performance, but only when practice was related to performance. Miller (1982) found that female subjects chose to compare to others from the same college, but only when college was related to performance. However, subjects chose to compare with similarly physically attractive others regardless of the relationship or lack of it between attractiveness and performance. The related attributes hypothesis cries for more research and theory.

DOWNWARD COMPARISON

The last contribution mentioned is the paper by Wills (1981) on downward comparison. I need not say much about it, because Wills has a chapter in this book. I mention it because it was a landmark paper, causing a shift from concerns about accurate self-evaluation to concerns about self-enhancement, not in the original sense used by Thornton and Arrowood (1966)—attempting to identify with superior others—but rather in the sense of focusing on those who are worse off. "Even a hawk is an eagle among crows," typifies this new view. There were certainly precursors to Wills' paper—Hakmiller (1966), of course, and also Goethals and Darley (1977), who argued that when protecting one's self-esteem is important, the individual has more to gain from comparing with those who are disadvantaged on related attributes—but it was the response to Wills' paper that produced what one might call "neo social comparison theory," which is illustrated in most of the following chapters.

IN MEMORIAM

Leon Festinger died on February 11, 1989 of liver cancer. (He arranged for it to be announced at his Memorial Service that it was *not* lung cancer, probably to prove that continuing to smoke Camels had not been a mistake.) Earlier that day he won $2.50 from Stan Schachter at backgammon and insisted on being paid immediately. He loved games—from pinball at MIT to cribbage, chess, Go, and backgammon—and thinking was a game that required changing content to avoid being in a rut: statistics, animal behavior, decision processes and motivation, social psychology, perception, archeology, and finally, medieval history. Although he left the field of social psychology in 1964, his style and brilliance continue to afford us an upward comparison.

REFERENCES

Arrowood, A. J. (1986). Comments on "Social Comparison Theory: Psychology from the Lost and Found." *Personality and Social Psychology Bulletin, 12*(3), 279–281.

Arrowood, A. J., & Friend, R. (1969). Other factors determining the choice of comparison other. *Journal of Experimental Social Psychology, 5,* 233–239.

Berger, S. M. (1977). Social comparison, modeling, and perseverance. In J. M. Suls & R. L. Miller (Eds.), *Social comparison processes: Theoretical and empirical perspectives* (pp. 209–234). Washington, DC: Hemisphere.

Brickman, P., & Bulman, R. J. (1977). Pleasure and pain in social comparison. In J. M. Suls & R. L. Miller (Eds.), *Social comparison processes: Theoretical and empirical perspectives* (pp. 149–186). Washington DC: Hemisphere.

Burnstein, E., Stotland, E., & Zander, A. (1961). Similarity to a model and self-evaluation. *Journal of Abnormal and Social Psychology, 62,* 257–264.

Castore, C. H., & DeNinno, J. A. (1977). Investigations in the social comparison of attitudes. In J. M. Suls & R. L. Miller (Eds.), *Social comparison processes: Theoretical and empirical perspectives* (pp. 125–148). Washington, DC: Hemisphere.

Cooper, J., & Jones, E. E. (1969). Opinion divergence as a strategy to avoid being miscast. *Journal of Personality and Social Psychology, 13,* 23–30.

Cottrell, N. B., & Epley, S. W. (1977). Affiliation, social comparison, and socially mediated stress reduction. In J. M. Suls & R. L. Miller (Eds.), *Social comparison processes: Theoretical and empirical perspectives* (pp. 43–68). Washington, DC: Hemisphere.

Deutsch, M., & Krauss, R. M. (1965). *Theories in social psychology.* New York: Basic Books.

Feldman, N. S., & Ruble, D. N. (1981). Social comparison strategies: Dimensions offered and options taken. *Personality and Social Psychology Bulletin, 7,* 11–16.

Festinger, L. (1950). Informal social communication. *Psychological Review, 57,* 271–282.

Festinger, L. (1954a). A theory of social comparison processes. *Human Relations, 7,* 117–140.

Festinger, L. (1954b). Motivation leading to social behavior. In M. R. Jones (Ed.), *Nebraska symposium on motivation* (Vol. 2, pp. 191–218). Lincoln, NE: University of Nebraska Press.

Festinger, L. (1957). *A theory of cognitive dissonance.* New York: Row, Peterson.

Friend, R. M., & Gilbert, J. (1973). Threat and fear of negative evaluation as determinants of locus of social comparison. *Journal of Personality, 41,* 328–340.

Gastorf, J. W., & Suls, J. (1978). Performance evaluation via social comparison: Performance similarity versus related-attribute similarity. *Social Psychology, 41,* 297–305.

Goethals, G. R. (1972). Consensus and modality in the attribution process: The role of similarity and information. *Journal of Personality and Social Psychology, 21,* 84–92.

Goethals, G., & Darley, J. (1977). Social comparison theory: An attributional approach. In J. M. Suls & R. L. Miller (Eds.), *Social comparison processes: Theoretical and empirical perspectives* (pp. 259–278). Washington, DC: Hemisphere.

Goethals, G. R., & Ebling, T. (1975). *A study of opinion comparison.* Unpublished manuscript, Williams College, Williamstown, MA.

Goethals, G. R., & Nelson, R. E. (1973). Similarity in the influence process: The belief-value distinction. *Journal of Personality and Social Psychology, 25,* 117-122.

Gruder, C. L. (1971). Determinants of social comparison choices. *Journal of Experimental Social Psychology, 7,* 473–489.

Gruder, C. L. (1977). Choice of comparison persons in evaluating oneself. In J. M. Suls, & R. C. Miller (Eds.), *Social comparison processes: Theoretical and empirical perspectives* (pp. 21–42). Washington, DC: Hemisphere.

Gruder, C. L., Korth, B., Dichtel, M., & Glos, B. (1975). Uncertainty and social comparison. *Journal of Research in Personality, 9,* 85–95.

Hakmiller, K. L. (1962). *Social comparison processes under differential conditions of ego-threat.* Unpublished doctoral dissertation, University of Minnesota, Minneapolis, MN.

Hakmiller, K. L. (1966). Threat as a determinant of downward comparison. *Journal of Experimental Social Psychology, 2*(Suppl. 1), 32–39.

Hoffman, P. J., Festinger, L., & Lawrence, D. H. (1954). Tendencies toward group comparability in competitive bargaining. *Human Relations, 7,* 141–159.

Israel, J. (1956). *Self-evaluation and rejection in groups. Three experiments and a conceptual outline.* Uppsala, Sweden: Almqvist & Wiksell.

Kelley, H. H. (1967). Attribution theory in social psychology. In D. Levine (Ed.), *Nebraska symposium on motivation* (Vol. 15, pp. 192–240). Lincoln, NE: University of Nebraska Press.

Latané, B. (1966). Studies in social comparison—Introduction and overview. *Journal of Experimental Social Psychology, 2*(Suppl. 1), 1–5.

Lewin, K., Dembo, T., Festinger, L., & Sears, P. S. (1944). Level of aspiration. In J. McV. Hunt (Ed.), *Personality and behavior disorders* (Vol. 1, pp. 333–378). New York: Ronald Press.

Mettee, D. R., & Riskind, J. (1974). Size of defeat and liking for superior and similar ability competitors. *Journal of Experimental Social Psychology, 10,* 333–351.

Mettee, D. R., & Smith, G. (1977). Social comparison and interpersonal attraction: The case for dissimilarity. In J. M. Suls & R. L. Miller (Eds.), *Social comparison processes: Theoretical and empirical perspectives* (pp. 69–102). Washington, DC: Hemisphere.

Mettee, D. R., & Wilkins, P. D. (1972). When similarity "hurts": Effects of perceived ability and a humorous blunder upon interpersonal attractiveness. *Journal of Personality and Social Psychology, 22,* 246–248.

Miller, C. T. (1982). The role of performance-related similarity in social comparison of abilities: A test of the related attributes hypothesis. *Journal of Experimental Social Psychology, 18,* 513–523.

Miller, C. T. (1984). Self-schemas, gender, and social comparison: A clarification of the related attributes hypothesis. *Journal of Personality and Social Psychology, 46* (6), 1222–1229.

Miller, R. L., & Suls, J. M. (1977). Affiliation preferences as a function of attitude and ability similarity. In J. M. Suls & R. L. Miller (Eds.), *Social comparison processes: Theoretical and empirical perspectives* (pp. 103–124). Washington, DC: Hemisphere.

Nissen, H. W. (1954). Comments on Professor Festinger's paper. In M. R. Jones (Ed.), *Nebraska Symposium on Motivation* (Vol. 2, pp. 219–223). Lincoln, NE: University of Nebraska Press.

Novak, D. W., & Lerner, M. J. (1968). Rejection as a consequence of perceived similarity. *Journal of Personality and Social Psychology, 9,* 147–152.

Parsons, T. (1949). *Essays in sociological theory.* New York: Macmillan.

Patchen, M. A. (1961). A conceptual framework and some empirical data regarding comparisons of social rewards. *Sociometry, 24,* 136–156.

Radloff, R., & Bard, L. (1966). A social comparison bibliography. *Journal of Experimental Social Psychology, 2*(Suppl. 1), 111–115.

Reckman, R. F., & Goethals, G. R. (1973). Deviancy and group-orientation as determinants of group composition preferences. *Sociometry, 36,* 419–423.

Schachter, S. (1959). *The psychology of affiliation.* Stanford, CA: Stanford University Press.

Schachter, S., & Singer, J. E. (1962). Cognitive, social, and physiological determinants of emotional state. *Psychological Review, 69,* 379–399.

Schachter, S., & Wheeler, L. (1962). Epinephrine, chlorpriomazine, and amusement. *Journal of Abnormal and Social Psychology, 45,* 121–128.

Singer, J. E. (1966). Social comparison—Progress and issues. *Journal of Experimental Social Psychology, 2*(Suppl. 1), 103–110.

Stotland, E., & Canon, L. K. (1972). *Social psychology: A cognitive approach.* Philadelphia: Saunders.

Stotland, E., & Patchen, M. (1961). Identification and changes in prejudice and in authoritarianism. *Journal of Abnormal and Social Psychology, 62,* 265–274.

Stotland, E., Zander, A., & Natsoulas, T. (1961). Generalization of interpersonal similarity. *Journal of Abnormal and Social Psychology, 62,* 250–256.

Suls, J. M., Gaes, G. G., & Gastorf, J. W. (1979). Evaluating a sex-related ability: Comparison with same-, opposite- and combined-sex norms. *Journal of Research in Personality, 13,* 294–304.

Suls, J. M., Gastorf, J., & Lawhon, J. (1978). Social comparison choices for evaluating a sex- and age-related ability. *Personality and Social Psychology Bulletin, 4,* 102–105.

Suls, J. M., & Miller, R. L. (Eds.) (1977). *Social comparison processes: Theoretical and empirical perspectives.* Washington, DC: Hemisphere.

Taylor, S. E., & Mettee, D. R. (1971). When similarity breeds contempt. *Journal of Personality and Social Psychology, 20,* 75–81.

Thornton, D., & Arrowood, A. J. (1966). Self-evaluation, self-enhancement, and the locus of social comparison. *Journal of Experimental Social Psychology, 2*(Suppl. 1), 40–48.

Wheeler, L. (1962). *Desire: A determinant of self-evaluation through social comparison.* Unpublished doctoral dissertation, University of Minnesota, Minneapolis, MN.

Wheeler, L. (1966). Motivation as a determinant of upward comparison. *Journal of Experimental Psychology, 2*(Suppl. 1), 27–31.

Wheeler, L., & Koestner, R. (1984). Performance evaluation: On choosing to know the related attributes of others when we know their performance. *Journal of Experimental Social Psychology, 20,* 263–271.

Wheeler, L., Koestner, R., & Driver, R. E. (1982). Related attributes in the choice of comparison others. *Journal of Experimental Social Psychology, 18,* 489–500.

Wheeler, L., & Levine, L. (1967). Observer-model similarity in the contagion of aggression. *Sociometry, 30,* 41–49.

Wheeler, L., Shaver, K. G., Jones, R. A., Goethals, G. R., Cooper, J., Robinson, J. E., Gruder, C. L., & Butzine, K. W. (1969). Factors determining choice of a comparison other. *Journal of Experimental Social Psychology, 5,* 219–232.

Wheeler, L., & Zuckerman, M. (1977). Commentary. In J. Suls & R. Miller (Eds.), *Social comparison processes* (pp. 335–357). Washington, DC: Hemisphere.

Wills, T. A. (1981). Downward comparison principles in social psychology. *Psychological Bulletin, 90,* 245–271.

Wilson, S. R. (1973). Ability evaluation and self-evaluation as types of social comparisons. *Sociometry, 36,* 600–607.

Wilson, S. R., & Benner, L. A. (1971). The effects of self-esteem and situation upon comparison choices during ability evaluation. *Sociometry, 34,* 381–397.

Wrightsman, L. S., Jr. (1960). Effects of waiting with others on changes in the level of felt anxiety. *Journal of Abnormal and Social Psychology, 61,* 216–222.

Zanna, M. D., Goethals, G., & Hill, J. (1975). Evaluating a sex-related ability: Social comparison with similar others and standard setters. *Journal of Experimental Social Psychology, 11,* 86–93.

2 Serving Self-Relevant Goals Through Social Comparison

Joanne V. Wood
University of Waterloo

Kathryn L. Taylor
State University of New York at Stony Brook

People compare themselves with others for a variety of reasons; graduate students may determine their relative standing in classes so as to evaluate their capabilities; aspiring ballet dancers may emulate the techniques of principal dancers; cancer patients may remind themselves of others whose circumstances are worse so as to lift their own spirits. Although Festinger (1954) proposed his theory of social comparison as a theory of opinion and ability evaluation, researchers recognized early in the history of social comparison that comparisons may serve other goals. People may compare themselves with others to evaluate their emotions (Schachter, 1959), their personality traits (Thornton & Arrowood, 1966), and ultimately their selves, rather than their specific attributes. As Singer (1966) said, "When a person asks "How much X do I have?" he is also asking "What sort of person am I for possessing that much X?" (p. 105).

Although Festinger (1954) emphasized accurate self-evaluation as the goal of social comparison, researchers have increasingly recognized that social comparisons may serve other goals. This increasing recognition is bringing about dramatic changes in contemporary thinking about social comparison, changes in both the view of the social comparison process and the view of the social comparer (see Wood, 1989, for a review).

We focus on two main questions in this chapter. First, how do individuals make social comparisons so as to achieve their goals? We focus on comparisons involving personal attributes such as abilities and personality traits. Second, when do particular goals dominate social comparison processes?

Before addressing these questions, we describe Festinger's original theory and what he said or implied about the purpose of social comparison.

Festinger (1954) proposed that humans have a drive to evaluate their opinions and abilities. He emphasized that these evaluations must be accurate because, to function effectively, people's opinions must be on the mark and their judgments of their own capacities and limitations must not be mistaken. Festinger went so far as to state that, "the holding of incorrect opinions and/or inaccurate appraisals of one's abilities can be punishing or even fatal in many situations" (p. 117). There is evidence that people are interested in achieving an accurate self-evaluation (Raynor & McFarlin, 1986; Trope, 1986). Trope, for example, has shown that when subjects are presented with a choice among tasks that vary in their capacity to diagnose levels of ability, they tend to select tasks that promise to be most diagnostic of their abilities. Moreover, they often pick diagnostic tasks even when the outcome is likely to be unfavorable (see Trope, 1986, for a review).

Festinger also described another goal that influences comparisons, namely a "unidirectional drive upward" that operates for abilities. In Western culture, people not only wish to evaluate their abilities, they also wish to improve them. Research on achievement motivation (Atkinson & Raynor, 1974) and observational learning (Bandura, 1986) attests to widespread interest in self-improvement.

Festinger's emphasis on accurate self-evaluation as the goal of social comparison and on the "unidirectional drive upward" portrayed the individual as facing up to his or her honest self-assessment and perhaps as aiming to better the self. However, since the late 1970s, research has increasingly emphasized self-enhancement motives—motives aimed at protecting or enhancing one's self-esteem. People are biased in their self-evaluations; they often harbor unrealistically positive views of themselves. Rather than always seeking an unbiased self-evaluation, they often bias information in a manner that is self-serving (Taylor & Brown, 1988).

SERVING GOALS THROUGH SOCIAL COMPARISON

How may individuals make social comparisons to serve these goals? When researchers have investigated the ways in which goals guide comparison processes they have focused on the comparison targets that people select. For example, they have studied the circumstances under which people compare with "upward" targets—others who are superior to themselves. Although this work has been extremely valuable, we argue that the social comparison literature has overemphasized the selection of comparison targets.

One reason for this statement is that the literature has not fully appreciated two other components of the comparison process that influence target selection: the nature of the dimension under evaluation and the dimensions that surround the dimension under evaluation. The "dimension under evaluation" is the specific attribute—such as friendliness, intelligence, or personal wealth—that is the focal attribute under consideration. In the case of self-evaluation, for example, it is the attribute on which one is trying to determine where one stands relative to others. The nature of the dimension under evaluation varies in several ways, such as in its familiarity and in its importance to the individual, and these variations are critical determinants of target selection.

The literature has not fully appreciated that comparisons also occur on surrounding dimensions—dimensions other than the focal dimension under evaluation. For example, when researchers evaluate their productivity, they may not only compare the number of their publications (the dimension under evaluation) with those of other researchers; they also may take into account other dimensions, such as how long the others have been doing research, the nature of their research, and the quality of the journals in which they have published.

A second sense in which the literature has overemphasized target selection is that it has failed to recognize that there are avenues for achieving one's goals through social comparison other than the selection of a comparison target. Several comparison processes may lead to outcomes that satisfy comparison goals. The outcomes that serve each goal are: For self-evaluation, the comparisons that are most useful are those that are most informative about one's own standing on the dimension under evaluation; for self-improvement, the most useful comparisons are those that teach one how to perform better or that motivate one to do better on the dimension; for self-enhancement, the comparisons that are the most useful are ones that make one feel better about the self or one's circumstances. We illustrate ways in which individuals may reach these outcomes by means other than selecting a particular comparison target; they may use other components of the comparison process, such as the nature of the dimension under evaluation and the surrounding dimensions.

First, however, we review the ways in which individuals may select comparison targets to achieve their goals. We discuss target selections on the dimension under evaluation, and then target selections on surrounding dimensions.

Target Selections on the Dimension Under Evaluation

Self-Evaluation. Festinger (1954) proposed that when one is seeking an accurate self-evaluation, the most informative comparison target is similar to oneself. When comparison others' abilities appear to be very different from one's own, one cannot appraise one's own ability precisely nor assess how stable that ability is. Festinger provided the example of novice chess players, who could not determine their skill precisely by comparing their games with those of master players.

Precisely what Festinger meant by similar others is unclear (e.g., Suls, 1977). Similarity may be defined in terms of proximity along the specific dimension under evaluation. For example, when the chess player compares with the master player, he or she is comparing with someone dissimilar on the dimension under evaluation. However, similarity also may be defined in terms of dimensions that surround the specific dimension under evaluation. For example, the chess player may compare with other players who have been playing chess about the same length of time. We consider first the former meaning of similarity because it concerns the dimension under evaluation.

A large number of studies suggest that individuals trying to evaluate themselves on some attribute compare themselves with others who are similar on that attribute (e.g., Wheeler, Koestner, & Driver, 1982). However, whether or not a similar other is the most informative target appears to depend on how familiar one is with the attribute. When individuals are unfamiliar with the dimension under evaluation, they seem to be very interested in comparing with others who are dissimilar. It has been shown that when subjects know their own score on a test but do not know what the range of scores is, they are especially interested in learning the scores of the highest scoring person and the lowest scoring person (e.g., Friend & Gilbert, 1973; Wheeler et al., 1969). Although these persons are extremely different from the subject, they may be uniquely informative for two reasons. First, extremely different others may exemplify the characteristic under evaluation, which may be helpful if one is unfamiliar with that characteristic (Arrowood & Friend, 1969; Thornton & Arrowood, 1966). New graduate students seeking to understand what is expected of them may compare themselves with a more senior graduate student who is called exemplary by the faculty and other students. Second, extremely different others may help one to define the range of possibilities on the dimension (Singer, 1966). Defining this range may be necessary before one can locate one's own position on the dimension (Wheeler et al., 1969).

Indeed, people appear to be interested in obtaining any information they can about the distribution of others' standings on the dimension under evaluation (e.g., Brickman & Berman, 1971). It seems likely that knowing one's own score may have little meaning by itself; one may need to know where others stand on that dimension to have a context for interpreting one's own score. Thus, individuals are clearly interested in comparing with others who are different from themselves along the dimension under evaluation, perhaps as an initial step toward self-evaluation (cf. Wheeler & Zuckerman, 1977).

When subjects are familiar with the dimension under evaluation, however, they appear to seek comparisons with others who are similar. Once subjects know of the range of scores, they choose to see the scores of others who are close to themselves in the rank-order of scores (e.g., Wheeler et al., 1969). Similarly, Trope's (1979) studies suggest that when individuals evaluate an ability, they tend to choose tasks that are diagnostic of that ability within their own ability range. That is, a highly able person tends to choose a task that will discriminate between high ability levels; a person low in ability chooses a task that will discriminate between low ability levels. Although dissimilar others may be particularly informative when individuals are unfamiliar with the dimension under evaluation, then, the range of relevant comparison others appears to narrow as individuals become more aware of their own standing. Thus, Festinger's (1954) similarity hypothesis seems to hold true for comparisons along the dimensions under evaluation only when the dimension is familiar.

These points are summarized in Table 2.1, which also summarizes other strategies relevant to each of the comparison goals.

Self-Improvement. The comparison targets that serve self-improvement are those that teach one how to perform better or that motivate one to do better on the dimension. Comparisons with others who are superior to or better off than oneself, called *upward comparisons,* may do both: One may learn from others who are more skilled (Berger, 1977), and one may be inspired by their example (Brickman & Bulman, 1977). Indeed, many researchers have interpreted upward comparisons as reflecting achievement motives, or what Festinger (1954) called the "unidirectional drive upward." Consistent with this view, there is evidence that people who are highly motivated to achieve a goal (Wheeler, 1966) and Type A individuals, who are hard-driving and competitive (Gastorf, Suls, & Sanders, 1980), are especially likely to make upward comparisons.

The most sought after comparison target in social comparison studies thus far appears to be upward. Many studies demonstrate that people tend to compare with others whose scores are better than their own (e.g., Arrowood & Friend, 1969; Wheeler & Koestner, 1984). When comparing with the extremes of the dimension, their first choice is the most positive extreme (e.g., Arrowood & Friend, 1969), and even when they compare with similar others, they compare with those whose scores are similar but slightly better, rather than slightly worse (e.g., Wheeler et al., 1969). A naturalistic example of upward comparisons comes from the study of bridge players in which most players wanted to compare their strategies with those of better players (Nosanchuk & Erickson, 1985).

Evidence that upward comparisons lead to self-improvement comes from a study by Seta (1982), who showed that subjects' performance on a task

TABLE 2.1
Comparison Strategies That Serve the Goals of Self-Evaluation,
Self-Improvement, and Self-Enhancement

Goal	Target Choice for Dimension Under Evaluation	Target Choice for Surrounding Dimensions	Other Strategies
Self-evaluation	On familiar dimensions—others who are proximal on the dimension On unfamiliar dimensions—others who are dissimilar on the dimension	Others who are similar on related attributes help one to interpret one's own standing on dimension under evaluation Comparisons with others who are similar on even unrelated attributes have special impact	
Self-improvement	Upward comparisons—with others who are superior	Similar others have more impact	
Self-enhancement	Downward comparisons—with others who are inferior or less fortunate, especially when dimension is desirable or self-relevant Similar comparisons if no downward available On uncontrollable dimensions, avoidance of downward comparisons	Assume similarity when others are superior on dimension under evaluation and are not competitors "Bask in reflected glory" of similar other's success (on non self-relevant dimensions)	Imagine comparison targets who are inferior Avoid unfavorable comparisons Manipulate surrounding dimensions (e.g., attribute another's superiority to related attributes) Select dimensions on which one is superior

improved when they were in the presence of someone whose performance was slightly better. In addition, the modeling literature indicates that when people are exposed to models who are successfully performing a desired behavior, their own behavior improves (Bandura, 1986).

It seems plausible that another target on the dimension under evaluation could serve self-improvement goals. Specifically, downward comparisons with inferior others may teach one about what not to do. However, we know of no evidence for this possibility. There has been much less research explicitly devoted to self-improvement as a goal of social comparison than to the other comparison goals. This is surprising, given that Festinger (1954) mentioned the upward drive in the original theory, and given that upward comparisons seem to be such popular comparison targets.

Self-Enhancement. On the dimension under evaluation, a comparison target who is inferior often makes one feel better about oneself. Such targets are called *downward comparisons.* A study by Hakmiller (1966) provided the first evidence of downward comparisons. When he told subjects that they were high in "hostility to one's parents" (which was described in very negative terms), they chose to see information about others who had even more hostility than themselves, and in that sense were inferior and in the "downward" direction (Hakmiller, 1966).

In 1981, Wills offered a theoretical analysis of downward comparison. He proposed that when people experience misfortune or threat, they frequently compare themselves with someone who is inferior or less advantaged, in an attempt to feel better about themselves or their situation. He reviewed a great deal of evidence on topics ranging from hostile aggression to humor to support this thesis. Downward comparisons may operate by reminding threatened individuals of how their circumstances might have been worse. When one's own circumstances are contrasted with circumstances that are worse, one may feel less threatened (Taylor, Wood, & Lichtman, 1983).

Since Wills' (1981) paper, research on downward comparisons has mushroomed. Laboratory evidence that threat leads to downward comparisons has continued to accumulate, and several field studies of people coping with various stressors have indicated that they make downward comparisons (e.g., Affleck, Tennen, Pfeiffer, Fifield, & Rowe, 1987). For example, in an interview study, the vast majority of breast cancer patients spontaneously compared themselves with others who were less fortunate than they (Wood, Taylor, & Lichtman, 1985). One woman said "At first [the scar] was gross. . . . Now I don't think it's so bad, especially after you've seen my friend; she just had two radiation implants put in" (Wood et al., 1985, p. 1176). Downward comparisons appear to improve one's mood or enhance self-esteem (Affleck & Tennen, chapter 14, this volume; Crocker & Gallo, 1985; Gibbons, 1986; Morse & Gergen, 1970).

Further evidence of the usefulness of downward comparison targets is provided by studies in which subjects are asked to rate themselves compared with other people. These studies suggest that people typically are motivated to see themselves as superior to others. On dimensions that are desirable, people tend to rate themselves as superior to others (Alicke,

1985; Brown, 1986). They appear to underestimate the degree to which others possess these desirable traits and overestimate the degree to which others possess undesirable traits (Campbell, 1986).

Research on downward comparison has brought about fundamental changes in the social comparison literature in the last few years: It has changed the thrust of social comparison theorizing from self-evaluation to self-enhancement; and it has increasingly moved data collection from the laboratory to the field.

Although the downward comparisons seem to be the most promising route toward self-enhancement, it is not the only one. If there is no one worse off than oneself, one may nonetheless find consolation in others who are similar (Wills, 1981). When people have undesirable characteristics, such as strong fears, they overestimate the number of people who share their flaws (Suls & Wan, 1987). Schachter's (1959) work on affiliation also points to this interest in similar comparison others; when people were frightened by the prospect of electric shock, they chose to wait with others who were also awaiting electric shock (Cottrell & Epley, 1977). Wills (1981) has interpreted these findings in terms of downward comparison; people who are threatened may prefer to compare with less fortunate others, but they will affiliate with others who are equally unfortunate if no less fortunate others are available. As Coates and Winston (1983) speculated, this need for "miserable company" may be part of the attraction of support groups (cf. Gibbons & Gerrard, this volume).

The Role of the Nature of the Dimension Under Evaluation in Self-Enhancement. How is it that either downward comparisons or similar comparisons (with others who are similarly flawed or who share one's fate) may result in self-enhancement? Which particular target is most self-enhancing appears to depend on the nature of the dimension under evaluation. One aspect of the "nature of the dimension" is its desirability: When a dimension is desirable, the self-enhancing comparison choice is someone who is inferior to oneself. When the dimension is undesirable, such as difficulty making friends, comparisons with others who are similar may be self-enhancing, although the ideal comparison other may be someone who has even more difficulty making friends.

Another aspect of the nature of the dimension under evaluation that determines whether or not a target is self-enhancing is the dimension's self-relevance, or how important it is to one's self-definition. Comparisons along self-relevant dimensions appear to have more impact than comparisons that are not self-relevant. Tesser and his colleagues have accumulated a great deal of evidence that suggests that another person's success is distressing when it involves a dimension that is central to one's own self-definition (Pleban & Tesser, 1981; Tesser & Campbell, 1982; Tesser, Millar, & Moore, 1988; see also Salovey & Rodin, 1984). Because inferiority on such dimensions is so painful, people should be especially likely to prefer downward comparison targets on self-relevant dimensions. It appears that they do. The tendency to see oneself as highly talented and to underestimate others' talents is especially pronounced on dimensions that one regards as personally important (Campbell, 1986; Marks, 1984). Tesser's research even suggests that people may try to hinder the performance of others, thereby ensuring a downward comparison, on self-relevant dimensions (e.g., Tesser & Smith, 1980).

In contrast, similar comparison others do not appear to be the targets of choice on self-relevant dimensions. Although they may be consoling when one has an undesirable characteristic, on self-relevant dimensions similar others may threaten one's sense of identity (Brickman & Bulman, 1977; Fromkin, 1972).

Recently, Major, Testa, and Bylsma (chapter 9, this volume) have identified another aspect of the nature of the dimension under evaluation that may determine whether a comparison target is self-enhancing, namely, whether or not a dimension is controllable. A comparison with someone who is superior to oneself may not be as disappointing as the usual upward comparison when one thinks that one has the potential to control or influence one's standing on the dimension under evaluation. On controllable dimensions one may be able to improve one's situation and possibly even achieve the same status as the superior other. Similarly, downward comparisons may not be self-enhancing when one thinks that one has little control over the dimension. For example, if cancer patients believe that they have little control over their cancer, comparisons with other patients whose disease is progressing will be threatening rather than comforting (Wood et al., 1985). Downward comparisons in this case signify that one's own fate may be like that of less fortunate others.

Summary. Individuals may serve their comparison goals by choosing targets of comparison along the dimension under evaluation. Which target will serve one's goal depends on the nature of the dimension under evaluation—its familiarity, desirability, self-relevance, and controllability. When the goal is self-evaluation on an unfamiliar dimension, a very informative comparison choice is someone who is extremely different from oneself. When the dimension is familiar, however, one may fine tune one's self-evaluation by comparing with others who are very similar on that dimension. Self-improvement goals seem to be served best by upward comparisons. When one has an unfavorable characteristic, one may self-enhance by reminding oneself of others who are similarly flawed. Even better is a downward comparison—someone who possesses even more of the undesirable characteristic. Downward comparisons are especially desirable on self-relevant dimensions. On uncontrollable dimensions, however, a downward comparison may be threatening rather than self-enhancing.

Thus far we have considered individuals' choices of comparison targets along a single dimension—the very dimension on which they are trying to ascertain their own standing in the case of self-evaluation, or trying to better themselves in the case of self-improvement. One may well ask whether individuals typically confine their comparisons to the specific dimension under evaluation. The answer appears to be no, and in the next section we consider target selections along dimensions other than the specific dimension under evaluation.

Target Selections on Dimensions that Surround the Dimension Under Evaluation

Self-Evaluation. Several researchers have argued that people make more informative comparisons by also considering dimensions that are related to the dimension under evaluation (Suls & R. L. Miller, 1977). To borrow an example offered by Zanna, Goethals, and Hill (1975), a swimmer evaluating his or her swimming speed would consider not only other swimmers' swimming speed—the dimension under evaluation—but also dimensions that are related to swimming speed, such as the others' age, experience, and recent swimming practice. Rather than compare with someone whose speed was similar, the swimmer would compare with someone who was similar on these related dimensions (Goethals & Darley, 1977). Such dimensions are referred to as *related attributes,* and they are informative because they permit one to make a less ambiguous attribution for one's own performance. For example, if one swims slower than someone who has been swimming for many more years, one can draw no conclusions about one's swimming ability, but if one swims slower than others who have been swimming about the same length of time, one might conclude that one's own swimming ability is poor. By reducing ambiguity, comparisons with others who are similar in related attributes permit one to draw clearer conclusions about one's own ability.

Many studies confirm the importance of related attributes. First, when individuals have the opportunity to consider attributes that are related to the dimension under evaluation, they prefer to compare themselves with others who are similar on those dimensions (e.g., Miller, 1982; Wheeler et al., 1982; Zanna et al., 1975). Second, people who already have information about their relative standing on the dimension under evaluation still desire information about related attributes (Wheeler & Koestner, 1984). Third, comparisons with others who are similar on related attributes appear to have more impact on one's evaluations than comparisons with others who are dissimilar (e.g., Gastorf & Suls, 1978).

Related attributes seem to be useful in serving the goal of self-evaluation because they permit one to better understand the meaning or implications of one's standing on the dimension under evaluation. A great deal of evidence has accumulated in the last several years, however, that suggests that individuals are interested not only in related dimensions; they seek to compare with others who are similar on dimensions that are unrelated to the dimension under evaluation as well (see Wood, 1989, for a review). For example, when the dimension under evaluation was logical reasoning, subjects chose to compare with others who were similar in physical attractiveness, even though attractiveness was perceived to be unrelated to logical reasoning (Miller, 1982).

Why would individuals be interested in dimensions that are unrelated to the dimension under evaluation? Several possible explanations have emerged (Wood, 1989). One very promising view is that of Miller, Turnbull, and McFarland (1988), who suggested that comparison targets who are similar in related and unrelated attributes serve different interests. Comparison targets who are similar on related attributes help one to gain an accurate evaluation of one's standing on some attribute "relative to other people in general" (p. 908). Comparison targets who are similar on dimensions that are unrelated to that attribute help individuals to determine how their standing compares with those of "others with whom they identify or feel a bond" (p. 909), which is important to their self-worth. How one's ability compares with that of a friend may matter a great deal more than how it compares with a stranger's ability, not because one gains a more accurate self-evaluation, but because one's emotional ties with the friend give the comparison more impact.

Evidence concerning related and unrelated attributes suggest that individuals are interested in "surrounding dimensions," dimensions other than the dimension under evaluation. Research by Tesser and his colleagues has been especially illustrative of the importance of surrounding dimensions. Their studies indicate that comparisons with others who are "close," that is, who are similar on any of several dimensions such as age, gender, race, college major, or personality have more impact on one's self-evaluation than do comparisons with dissimilar others (see Tesser, 1986, for a review). Comparisons that show one to be inferior on the dimension under evaluation are especially painful, and comparisons that show one to be superior on that dimension are especially pleasurable, when the comparison other is "close" on surrounding dimensions (cf. Brickman & Bulman, 1977). For example, Tesser, Millar, and Moore (1988, Study 3) found that subjects were most distressed by their failure on a task that was personally important to them when a friend performed better than they did. These surrounding dimensions also appear to be important to self-improvement and self-enhancement, although there is less evidence pertaining to these goals.

Self-Improvement. Research on observational learning suggests that people are most likely to imitate another person's behavior on a specific dimension when that person is similar on other dimensions (see Bandura, 1986, for a review). Once again the similarity between the observer and the model may be important even when it occurs on a dimension that is objectively unrelated to the imitated dimension. For example, people with phobias who observe models approach a feared stimulus are more likely to imitate that approach behavior when the models are similar rather than dissimilar in gender and age, even when gender and age "do not really affect how well one can perform the feared activities" (p. 404).

Self-Enhancement. One also may focus on surrounding dimensions to achieve self-enhancement. It has long been recognized that upward comparisons present a dilemma; although they provide an example for people to emulate, they also make individuals aware of their own inferiority. Wheeler (1966) proposed that highly motivated persons—those most likely to make upward comparisons—are spared of feelings of inferiority because they assume that they are similar to the superior person. If one assumes that one is generally similar to a superior person, one may even be encouraged by the comparison rather than deflated. Aspiring novelists may feel encouraged by the knowledge that a Pulitzer Prize winner (an upward comparison) attended the same creative writing program (similarity on a surrounding dimension).

Tesser's (chapter 5, this volume) research points to another way in which one may enhance the self by making use of surrounding dimensions when one is selecting comparison others. If one chooses to compare with someone who is successful and also "close" on surrounding dimensions, one may "bask in reflected glory" (as long as the other's superiority is not on a dimension that is very important to one's self-definition).

Summary. Clearly, targets who are similar on dimensions that surround the dimension under evaluation are important in achieving comparison goals. These surrounding dimensions apparently form the context for and lend meaning to comparisons along the specific dimension under evaluation. In the case of related attributes, the meaning that similar others provide is clear: They are predictive of where one should be on the dimension under evaluation, so they help one to interpret one's relative standing along that dimension (Goethals & Darley, 1977). When those surrounding dimensions are not related to the dimension under evaluation, their meaning is not clear (Wood, 1989). For whatever reason, they seem to carry implications about where the individual should or could be on the dimension under evaluation. For example, when phobics observe models who have conquered their phobias and who are similar in age, they may be inspired by the implication that they, too, will overcome their phobia. Similarly, when someone from one's own hometown is more successful than oneself in one's chosen occupation, one may feel deflated because this comparison somehow implies that one should have been more successful.

Summary of Target Selections

It seems clear that target selection is not as simple as it is sometimes characterized. Comparisons occur on more than just a single dimension at a time, and the targets of choice are often not similar others. Instead, which target an individual selects depends on his or her comparison goal, the nature of the dimension under evaluation, and the dimensions that surround the dimension under evaluation. It is important to note that Festinger (1954) acknowledged these two latter parameters to some extent; he recognized that the self-relevance of the dimension under evaluation and the relatedness of other dimensions were important to the comparison process (Wood, 1989). Despite significant exceptions (e.g., Goethals & Darley, 1977; Tesser, 1986), later researchers, for the most part, have not systematically evaluated the implications of these two parameters.

Other Comparison Strategies

Although the research reviewed thus far points to several factors that determine whether a target will serve one's goal, it is also true that there are means of achieving one's goals through social comparison other than the selection of comparison targets. Other strategies include imagining comparison targets, avoiding comparisons, manipulating surrounding dimensions, and selecting comparison dimensions. These strategies are largely aimed toward the goal of self-enhancement: They all involve manipulating the comparison process so that the comparison comes out in a particular way, namely so that the outcome is favorable to the self. To ensure this outcome, one must exert influence on the comparison process. In contrast, when one is aiming for a truly unbiased self-evaluation, several comparative outcomes may be informative, and hence there is little need to manipulate the comparison process. Manipulating the process would likely lead to a biased rather than unbiased outcome.

Imagining Comparison Targets. If no suitable comparison target is available among one's personal contacts, one may imagine one. For example, in the breast cancer study previously described, many respondents appeared to "manufacture normative standards of adjustment" (Taylor et al., 1983). They seemed to fabricate comparison others, or at best, to generalize from second-hand information about one or two people who had an especially difficult time adjusting. For example, one woman said, "I have heard, second hand, that some of them, many years down the road, are still not over it. . . . There are women who don't ever reach this point [that I have]" (Wood et al., 1985, p. 1174). Although these women were comparing themselves with others, they seemed to be comparing not with specific other women but with hypothetical others. These hypothetical others always seemed to be adjusting less well than the respondent. Taylor et al. (1983) argued that such comparisons permitted the respondents to feel good about their own adjustment. We observed a similar phenomenon among the husbands of these breast cancer patients. When they described how supportive they had been of their wives, many men compared themselves with other men who are not so loving. We called these "mythical-men" comparisons, because very few men leave their wives if they contract breast cancer.

People also may imagine comparison targets when they are assessing their own risk for disease and other misfortunes. Most people assess their own risk as lower than average (Weinstein, 1980). One way that they may maintain their illusions of invulnerability is by comparing themselves with imaginary others who are especially vulnerable. Perloff and Fetzer (1986) found that when subjects assessed their risk for heart disease, they compared themselves with people who had weight problems and a family history of heart disease. In comparison with such high risk individuals most people emerge favorably, and they may assure themselves that they are at low risk for heart disease.[1]

Some of the findings described earlier also may involve a process of imagining comparison targets. When individuals have an undesirable characteristic and overestimate the numbers of others who share it (i.e., perceiving false consensus), they may be fabricating comparison others. Sherman, Presson, and Chassin (1984) provided subjects with feedback regarding whether they had successfully or unsuccessfully selected a "real" suicide note from a choice of two notes. When subjects thought they had failed to select the correct note, they overestimated the number of others who picked the same note that they had; but when they thought they had succeeded, they did not. These subjects may have imagined comparison others responding the way they had, or, as Suls and Wan (1987) argued, they may have "projected" these characteristics onto others. Similarly, when people say they are far superior to most of the population on some

---

[1] However, it is possible, as Perloff and Fetzer (1986) pointed out, that the "representativeness heuristic" (Kahneman & Tversky, 1973) may account for respondents bringing to mind high risk individuals; respondents may not have been attempting to feel less threatened. Regardless of the mechanism generating these comparisons, the result is that people arrive at a comparison that is favorable for the self.

(i.e., perceiving false uniqueness), they may be imagining a nameless mass of people who are inferior.

How do we know these judgments are distortions of the truth? Maybe people are accurate when they estimate that others are not talented on the dimensions on which they themselves are talented. Campbell (1986) investigated this issue by comparing each respondent's estimates of others' standings on dimensions with the estimates of the rest of the sample. She found that, compared with others' estimates, people tended to underestimate others' abilities and overestimate their own abilities on dimensions that they valued. Although these findings concern individuals' judgments about others' attributes rather than these others' actual attributes, the fact that there were discrepancies between most respondents' estimates and those of the rest of the sample indicates that somebody must have been distorting. Several findings indicate, then, that people may concoct comparison targets when no other targets are available who suit their comparison purpose.

Avoiding Comparison Targets. Another strategy is simply to avoid comparisons altogether (Brickman & Bulman, 1977). When individuals believe that their ability is particularly low or when they are threatened in some other way, they tend to avoid comparisons with others who are superior (e.g., Friend & Gilbert, 1973; Pyszczynski, Greenberg, & LaPrelle, 1985; Smith & Insko, 1987). After subjects had received information that they had failed, they appeared to avoid information about others who had succeeded and to seek information about others who had failed (Pyszczynski et al., 1985). Similarly, when individuals think that their inferiority will be made public, they are much less likely to interact with superior others (Smith & Insko, 1987; Wheeler et al., 1969; Wilson & Benner, 1971). More generally, norms seem to develop that serve to restrict social comparisons; it is uncommon, for example, for faculty members to regularly exchange their curriculum vitae (Brickman & Bulman, 1977).

Dramatic examples of avoiding comparisons were described by respondents in the breast cancer sample. Many women dropped out of breast cancer support groups or even changed the times of their appointments with the physician to avoid seeing others in the waiting room: "I went to a Cancer Society meeting one evening . . . and I realized how many women had *both* breasts removed. Until that time, it had never occurred to me. And I've never gone back to another meeting, because I had nightmares that night" (Wood et al., 1985, p. 1176).

One may not only avoid comparisons behaviorally, one may avoid comparisons cognitively. Martin (1986) offered a striking illustration of how poor people may avoid comparisons with wealthy persons, even when reminders of affluence are salient. When an Appalachian woman was asked by a friend about the amount of money she was earning, she replied: "I am very content; I have more than my neighbors." Her friend continued, "What about the people on 'the hill'?" (This was a wealthy residential area, clearly visible from the [woman's] frontyard.) She answered, "My life is here. I don't think about them" (p. 217).

Manipulating Surrounding Dimensions. One may call on the dimensions that surround the dimension under evaluation to achieve one's comparison goal. To soften the blow of a comparison with another person who is far superior, individuals may point out the differences between themselves and the superior person on attributes that are related to the dimension. An academic who learns that another person in the field has 300 publications may feel better knowing that the other person obtained his or her doctorate much longer ago, that his or her research is easier to conduct, and so forth. One may attribute the other's superiority to these differences in related attributes (Brickman & Bulman, 1977). Another example comes from the breast cancer research, in respondents' reactions to comparisons with "supercopers," famous women whom the media present as adjusting extremely well to their breast cancer (Wood et al., 1985). Respondents seemed to regard such comparisons as irrelevant. One said: "They're very prominent women. They're very well-to-do. They're married. I could not relate to that." By perceiving superior others to be dissimilar, one may "take some of the sting out of defeat or inferiority" (Brickman & Bulman, 1977, p. 162; see also Mettee & Smith, 1977).

One even may try to create dissimilarity on surrounding dimensions. Tesser's research has indicated that when individuals discover that another person who is "close" (similar on surrounding dimensions) is superior to themselves, they often attempt to reduce closeness (Tesser, 1986). They may spend less time with the other (Tesser, 1980), physically distance themselves (Pleban & Tesser, 1981), or derogate the other by making unfavorable ratings of the other or even rating the other as inferior to the self (Tesser, Campbell, & Smith, 1984; also Salovey & Rodin, 1984). All of these strategies create physical or psychological distance from the comparison other, thereby reducing closeness and creating dissimilarity. One may manipulate surrounding dimensions, then, either by focusing on dissimilarity in related attributes or by reducing closeness. These strategies may permit one to dismiss unfavorable comparisons as irrelevant to one's self-esteem.

Selecting Comparison Dimensions. Individuals may not only select comparison targets, they may select the dimensions on which they will compare. Taylor et al. (1983) termed this strategy *dimensional comparison*. This involves selectively focusing on attributes on which one appears advantaged. Examples may be drawn from the breast cancer study, in which the majority of respondents spontaneously mentioned a dimension on which they were luckier than other women. For example, women who had lumpectomies compared themselves to women who had more disfiguring surgeries. The object of the comparison in this case is not a disadvantaged person but a dimension of comparison (in this case, degree of disfigurement) on which the comparer is relatively better off. Another example is that many married women compared themselves favorably to single women, saying that they were luckier because they had more support.

What is striking about these dimensional comparisons is that they virtually always involved a dimension on which the respondent was advantaged rather than disadvantaged (Wood et al., 1985). Even women who were dying described ways in which their circumstances were better than that of other women (e.g., they were surrounded by loved ones, whereas many others were not). Although these women could have compared with women who had never had breast cancer, and although some dimensions on which they were disadvantaged loomed very large, they emphasized the dimensions on which they were superior. If one is careful about one's comparison dimensions, one may enjoy favorable comparisons quite frequently.

Evidence of selecting comparison dimensions also emerges from studies that have permitted subjects a choice of tasks. Tesser and Campbell (1980) reported that subjects selected tasks at which they were not only talented, but more talented than other people. In addition, people tend to evaluate others on the dimensions that they themselves value (Lewicki, 1983). Because these dimensions also tend to be the ones on which they believe they are talented, individuals "thereby virtually [assure] a favorable self-other comparison" (Taylor & Brown, 1988, p. 195).[2]

A strategy that is related to selecting comparison dimensions is to redefine the importance of a dimension. Tesser and his colleagues have found that when individuals learn that another person is superior to the self on a dimension that they hold dear, they may at times redefine that dimension

---

[2] This evidence that people select dimensions for comparison on which they are superior to others presents an interesting contradiction with evidence that people often choose to compare with superior others. A resolution to this contradiction may rest on the circumstances under which people make upward comparisons. The study by Tesser and Campbell (1980), in which subjects received feedback about how their performance on tasks compared with that of another person, then selected another task to work on, may have stirred subjects' competitive feelings. People are less likely to compare with superior others under competitive conditions (e.g., Miller & Suls, 1977). In addition, people may appear to make more or fewer upward comparisons, depending on the measure one uses. The studies indicating that people evaluate themselves more favorably than others involve "comparative rating" measures, whereas the evidence cited earlier about upward comparisons involve selection measures. Later we discuss the differences between these measures.

as less central to the self (Tesser, 1986; Tesser & Campbell, 1980). For example, Tesser and Campbell (1980) demonstrated that subjects lowered their ratings of the personal importance of "social sensitivity," or of "aesthetic judgment" after they had performed less well than another on that dimension.

Summary: Serving Goals Through Social Comparison

Comparison processes involve much more than the selection of a comparison target. To achieve self-enhancement one may not only make downward comparisons (or similar comparisons if one has an unfavorable characteristic), one may imagine an inferior target, manipulate surrounding dimensions, select a dimension on which one is advantaged, or simply avoid comparisons entirely. Thus, people need not depend on having a particular target available who will serve their goal; they may concoct a target in their imagination or focus on dimensions rather than specific other individuals (Taylor et al., 1983).

The comparison process appears to be far more malleable than the traditional social comparison literature has assumed. This new view of the comparison process is emerging through the recent focus on self-enhancement in social comparison. Dimensional comparisons illustrate how this focus changes the picture of the comparison process. Recall that for the goals of self-evaluation and self-improvement we stated that the most useful comparisons are those that are most informative about one's own standing on the dimension under evaluation, and that help one to improve oneself on the dimension under evaluation, respectively. Both of these goals imply a dimension under evaluation; self-enhancement does not. Self-enhancing comparisons are simply those that make one feel better about oneself or one's circumstances; the dimension under evaluation is not constrained (Taylor et al., 1983). For example, if dancers discover that their talent is fading, they may console themselves by comparing along the dimension under evaluation with other dancers who are inferior, but they also may choose to compare along other dimensions; they may emphasize that they are better parents or better gardeners than others. Research on self-enhancement is revealing that the comparison process is far more flexible than previously thought.

WHEN DO SELF-EVALUATION VERSUS SELF-ENHANCEMENT GOALS DOMINATE SOCIAL COMPARISONS?

Given the importance of goals in directing social comparisons, a critical issue for contemporary social comparison theory is which motive is dominant at any particular time. Research that has addressed this question has focused mostly on the relative importance of self-evaluation versus self-enhancement. A strong consensus has emerged: "Although self-evaluation is an important goal for a person facing a new situation, self-enhancement appears to become more important when [the] situation presents a specific threat to self-esteem" (Gruder, 1977, p. 37). However this conclusion deserves reexamination. Recent research raises two questions about the conflict between self-evaluation and self-enhancement.

Do Persons Who Are Low in Self-Worth Make Downward Comparisons?

According to Wills' (1981) downward comparison theory, people who are chronically threatened or chronically low in self-esteem are especially likely to make downward comparisons because they are most in need of self-enhancement. Research supports this idea with respect to chronic threat. When a group experiences chronic low status or deprivation, its members tend to overevaluate their group or disparage other groups (see Wills, 1981, for references). However, recent evidence suggests that some individuals most in need of self-enhancement may not make downward comparisons.

Although people with low self-esteem often rate the self higher than the other, they do so to a lesser degree than people with high self-esteem (Brown, 1986; Campbell, 1986), even when their self-esteem is threatened (Crocker, Thompson, McGraw, & Ingerman, 1987). Studies of mildly depressed people, who are often low in self-esteem, yield similar findings. Whereas nondepressed college students appear to consistently rate themselves as superior to others, depressed students do not; sometimes depressed persons perceive themselves to be equal to others and sometimes they see themselves as inferior to others (Alloy & Ahrens, 1987; Brewin & Furnham, 1986; Campbell, 1986; Kuiper & MacDonald, 1982; Tabachnik, Crocker, & Alloy, 1983). This research not only conflicts with Wills' (1981) proposal, it also conflicts with studies that suggested that low self-esteem persons are more likely to make downward comparisons (Friend & Gilbert, 1973; Smith & Insko, 1987; Wilson & Benner, 1971). How may these contradictions be reconciled?

One possible explanation hinges on differences in the dependent measures used (for a review of methods in social comparison research, see Wood, 1990). The studies that suggest that low self-esteem or depressed people make fewer downward comparisons have used "comparative rating" measures (e.g., Crocker et al., 1987), which involve explicitly rating oneself relative to others. For example, college women who had high self-esteem but who were members of a low status sorority rated other sororities more negatively than their own sorority to a greater degree than did women with low self-esteem (Crocker et al., 1987, Study 2). In contrast, studies that suggest that low self-esteem or depressed persons make more downward comparisons have used "selection" measures (e.g., Friend & Gilbert, 1973), which involve seeking information about others. For example, depressed people whose moods were temporarily worsened wanted to see information about someone who was even more miserable (Gibbons, 1986).

These measures may capture different meanings of social comparison. To make a downward comparison on a comparative rating measure, one must claim that one is more talented or accomplished than another. Such claims should come more naturally to persons with high self-esteem than to persons with low self-esteem who "avoid making exaggerated or strongly positive claims for themselves" (Baumeister, Tice, & Hutton, 1989). In contrast, making a downward comparison on a selection measure does not require one to claim superiority; it requires only seeking information about others who promise to be inferior. Thus, low self-esteem persons may be capable of selecting downward comparisons when they may be reluctant to claim that they are superior on a comparative rating.

Recently we conducted a study to examine this possible explanation for the discrepant findings concerning self-esteem (Wood, Taylor, Michela, & Gaus Binkley, in preparation). To manipulate threat to self-esteem, we exposed subjects to a favorable or unfavorable comparison with a supposed "other subject." We then asked subjects to make comparative ratings, and we also presented a selection measure which provided an opportunity for them to seek further comparisons with this same person. Specifically, we asked subjects to choose further tests for both the other person and themselves to take; when they chose the same tests for both the self and other, we interpreted that as choosing to compare; if they chose different tests, we interpreted that as avoiding comparisons. A self-enhancing comparison choice on this selection measure would involve avoiding comparisons when one has failed and seeking further comparison when one has succeeded. We predicted that on the comparative rating measure high self-esteem persons would make more pronounced self-enhancing comparisons than would low self-esteem persons. Although our predictions regarding high self-esteem persons were more complicated, we expected on the basis of past research (e.g., Friend & Gilbert, 1973), that low self-esteem persons would make self-enhancing comparison choices on the selection measure.

Our results partially supported these predictions. On the comparative rating measure, high self-esteem persons rated themselves as superior to the "other subject" to a greater degree than did low self-esteem persons. However, they were no more likely to do so when they were threatened than when they were not. The absence of an effect of threat makes it unclear whether the comparative ratings resulted from self-enhancement motives. They may have stemmed from a preexistent conviction on the part of high self-esteem persons that they are superior to others.

[margin note: Or the S's were not really threatened]

Our results concerning the selection measure were more clear-cut because we obtained an interaction between self-esteem and threat. Low self-esteem persons made comparison choices that appeared to be self-enhancing. After they had received information that they were superior to the other—when subjects could expect that further comparisons would also be favorable—low self-esteem persons chose to compare further with the "other subject." In contrast, after they had learned that they were inferior—when they could expect that further comparisons would be unfavorable—low self-esteem persons made fewer comparisons with the "other subject."

High self-esteem persons did not exhibit this pattern of comparison selections; they made more comparisons after failure than after success. We speculated that they refrained from comparing with the other subject when they had succeeded because, unlike low self-esteem persons, they are accustomed to feeling superior to others, and hence may have had little interest in comparing further with someone who was clearly inferior. They seemed to compare after failure on dimensions on which they would restore their superiority (see Wood et al., in preparation, for more discussion).

These results support our argument that the contradictory findings involving self-esteem may be attributable in part to differences in dependent measures. On comparative rating measures, which involve making a judgment regarding oneself relative to others, low self-esteem may appear to be making fewer (or less pronounced) downward comparisons than high self-esteem persons. In contrast, on selection measures, which do not require a claim of one's superiority, low self-esteem persons seem to be quite capable of making comparison choices that benefit their self-esteem.

Is Threat Necessary to Activate Self-Enhancement Motives?

The idea that threat is a necessary precursor to downward comparison has become a well-accepted fixture of current social comparison theory (Gruder, 1977; Wills, 1981). However, some evidence challenges this idea. Wood et al. (1985) examined the threat hypothesis by correlating several hypothesized indicators of threat (such as prognosis) with downward comparisons among breast cancer patients. Although women closer in time to their surgery were more likely to make downward comparisons, the results otherwise failed to support the prediction that downward comparisons increase with threat. There were several possible reasons for this failure, including the possibility that objective sources of threat (e.g., type of surgery) may not match patients' perceptions of what is threatening (Wood et al., 1985).

Other evidence also challenges the threat hypothesis. As described earlier, studies suggest that people have a general tendency to compare themselves favorably to others; they rate themselves as having more positive attributes and fewer unfavorable attributes (e.g., Alicke, 1985; Suls & Wan, 1987). Most of these studies did not involve circumstances of threat. Although people sometimes respond to threat by making even more pronounced self-enhancing comparative ratings (Crocker et al., 1987; Sherman et al., 1984), the evidence that people may make downward comparisons even when they are not threatened suggests that there may be a general tendency—not just a threat-induced tendency—to see the self more favorably than others (at least among persons high in self-esteem). How may these findings be reconciled with the threat hypothesis?

One possible resolution is that the threat hypothesis is correct, but that threat is prevalent in everyday life. People are subjected to many potential insults to self-esteem all day long; they are confronted continually with others who are more beautiful, more articulate, and more accomplished. To defend against this onslaught of unfavorable information, people may marshall self-enhancing comparisons frequently. However, the idea that individuals are nearly constantly under threat is likely to violate many researchers' conception of what constitutes "threat."

Another possible resolution again involves dependent measures. Most of the studies that suggest that nonthreatened people compare downward involve comparative ratings (e.g., Alicke, 1985; Campbell, 1986), whereas studies involving selection suggest that threatened people make downward comparisons but that nonthreatened people do not (e.g., Friend & Gilbert, 1973; Hakmiller, 1966). As we suggested earlier, comparative ratings and selection measures may not always correspond with each other. Comparative ratings involve making a judgment regarding oneself in relation to another; selection measures do not.

Because comparative ratings involve judgment they are more ambiguous (Wood, 1990). They may reflect the sum total of the comparisons one has made in the past. If one is surrounded by inferior others, one may rate oneself as superior to most people. However, one's judgment also may be influenced by such factors as one's current mood and one's self-esteem. One also may use comparative ratings to derogate others in an attempt to enhance the self (e.g., Crocker et al., 1987). When people rate themselves as superior to others, then, that does not necessarily mean they have come to that judgment by making a preponderance of downward comparisons in the past. If these same people were presented with a selection measure they may well select upward comparisons, as people tend to do when they are not threatened (Gruder, 1977). Similarly, when people choose to compare themselves with inferior others on selection measures, that does not necessarily mean that they would rate themselves as superior to others on comparative ratings. More research aimed at understanding comparative ratings, and more studies that employ both types of measures at once, in both threat and nonthreat conditions, are needed.

Given the experimental evidence that argues for the threat hypothesis, it would be premature to conclude that threat is not important. Threat does appear to magnify the tendency to make self-enhancing comparisons (e.g., Sherman et al., 1984). However, the evidence that threat may not be a necessary precondition for downward comparison merits reconsideration of the threat hypothesis. Threat may merely heighten a prevailing tendency to make downward comparisons.

CONCLUSION

We have considered two questions involving goals that may be served by social comparison. First, what comparative strategies do people use to serve their goals? Although researchers have increasingly recognized the variety of motives that drive social comparison, this recognition is just beginning to reveal the complexities these goals introduce into the comparison process. Although the literature has emphasized the selection of comparison targets it appears that there are many other comparative strategies that individuals may use to achieve their goals, many of which do not involve a specific, living-and-breathing comparison target at all.

In addition to presenting a more complex and malleable view of the comparison process, recent research is portraying the social comparer as strikingly different from the portrait drawn by Festinger (1954). Festinger characterized the individual as largely rational and unbiased, aiming for an accurate self-evaluation. Not only does the individual appear to be driven by interests in self-enhancement, the individual appears to be very active when drawing comparisons. Although the literature has emphasized that the individual is selective, it has viewed the individual's capacity to be selective as constrained by whatever comparison targets are available.

Because some comparison strategies do not require a comparison target, the individual may exert far more influence on the comparison process than most past research has indicated (Wood, 1989). People may bend and shape the comparison process into a variety of forms to serve their goals. Indeed, social comparison often may be a process of constructing social information rather than of passively receiving it; as Goethals (1986) has said, people may fabricate and ignore social reality when making social comparisons (Wood, 1989).

Recognizing that the individual is very active leads to the second question that we addressed, which concerns when particular goals dominate social comparison processes. Recent research challenges the prevailing wisdom concerning self-evaluation versus self-enhancement motives. People who seem to be most needy of self-enhancement may not make self-enhancing comparisons, especially on comparative rating measures; and second, threat may not be necessary to activate self-enhancement motives.

REFERENCES

Affleck, G., Tennen, H., Pfeiffer, C., Fifield, J., & Rowe, J. (1987). Downward comparison and coping with serious medical problems. *American Journal of Orthopsychiatry, 57,* 570–578.

Alicke, M. D. (1985). Global self-evaluation as determined by the desirability and controllability of trait adjectives. *Journal of Personality and Social Psychology, 49,* 1621–1630.

Alloy, L. B., & Ahrens, A. H. (1987). Depression and pessimism for the future: Biased use of statistically relevant information in predictions for self versus others. *Journal of Personality and Social Psychology, 52,* 366–378.

Arrowood, A. J., & Friend, R. (1969). Other factors determining the choice of a comparison other. *Journal of Experimental Social Psychology, 5,* 233–239.

Atkinson, J. W., & Raynor, J. O. (Eds.) (1974). *Motivation and achievement.* Washington, DC: Hemisphere.

Bandura, A. (1986). *Social foundations of thought and action: A social cognitive theory.* Englewood Cliffs, NJ: Prentice-Hall.

Baumeister, R. F., Tice, D. M., & Hutton, D. G. (1989). Self-presentational motivations and personality differences in self-esteem. *Journal of Personality, 57,* 547–579.

Berger, S. M. (1977). Social comparison, modeling, and perseverance. In J. M. Suls & R. L. Miller (Eds.), *Social comparison processes: Theoretical and empirical perspectives* (pp. 209–234). Washington, DC: Hemisphere.

Brewin, C. R., & Furnham, A. (1986). Attributional versus preattributional variables in self-esteem and depression: A comparison and test of learned helplessness theory. *Journal of Personality and Social Psychology, 50,* 1013–1020.

Brickman, P., & Berman, J. J. (1971). Effects of performance expectancy and outcome certainty on interest in social comparison. *Journal of Experimental Social Psychology, 7,* 600–609.

Brickman, P., & Bulman, R. J. (1977). Pleasure and pain in social comparison. In J. M. Suls & R. L. Miller (Eds.), *Social comparison processes: Theoretical and empirical perspectives* (pp. 149–186). Washington, DC: Hemisphere.

Brown, J. D. (1986). Evaluations of self and others: Self-enhancement biases in social judgments. *Social Cognition, 4,* 353–376.

Campbell, J. D. (1986). Similarity and uniqueness: The effects of attribute type, relevance, and individual differences in self-esteem and depression. *Journal of Personality and Social Psychology, 50,* 281–294.

Coates, D., & Winston, T. (1983). Counteracting the durance of depression: Peer support groups for victims. *Journal of Social Issues, 39,* 169–194.

Cottrell, N. B., & Epley, S. W. (1977). Affiliation, social comparison, and socially mediated stress reduction. In J. M. Suls & R. L. Miller (Eds.), *Social comparison processes: Theoretical and empirical perspectives* (pp. 43–68). Washington, DC: Hemisphere.

Crocker, J., & Gallo, L. (1985, August). *The self-enhancing effect of downward comparison.* Paper presented at the meeting of the American Psychological Association, Los Angeles, CA.
Crocker, J., Thompson, L. L., McGraw, K. M., & Ingerman, C. (1987). Downward comparison prejudice and evaluations of others: Effects of self-esteem and threat. *Journal of Personality and Social Psychology, 52,* 907–916.
Festinger, L. (1954). A theory of social comparison processes. *Human Relations, 7,* 117–140.
Friend, R. M., & Gilbert, J. (1973). Threat and fear of negative evaluation as determinants of locus of social comparison. *Journal of Personality, 41,* 328–340.
Fromkin, H. L. (1972). Feelings of interpersonal undistinctiveness: An unpleasant affective state. *Journal of Experimental Research in Personality, 6,* 178–185.
Gastorf, J. W., & Suls, J. (1978). Performance evaluation via social comparison: Performance similarity versus related attribute similarity. *Social Psychology, 41,* 297–305.
Gastorf, J. W., Suls, J., & Sanders, G. S. (1980). Type A coronary-prone behavior pattern and social facilitation. *Journal of Personality and Social Psychology, 38,* 773–780.
Gibbons, F. X. (1986). Social comparison and depression: Company's effect on misery. *Journal of Personality and Social Psychology, 51,* 140–148.
Goethals, G. R. (1986). Fabricating and ignoring social reality: Self-serving estimates of consensus. In J. M. Olson, C. P. Herman, & M. P. Zanna (Eds.), *Relative deprivation and social comparison: The Ontario Symposium* (Vol. 4, pp. 135–158). Hillsdale, NJ: Lawrence Erlbaum Associates.
Goethals, G. R., & Darley, J. M. (1977). Social comparison theory: An attributional approach. In J. M. Suls & R. L. Miller (Eds.), *Social comparison processes: Theoretical and empirical perspectives* (pp. 259–278). Washington, DC: Hemisphere.
Gruder, C. L. (1977). Choice of comparison persons in evaluating oneself. In J. M. Suls & R. L. Miller (Eds.), *Social comparison processes: Theoretical and empirical perspectives* (pp. 21–41). Washington, DC: Hemisphere.
Hakmiller, K. L. (1966). Threat as a determinant of downward comparison. *Journal of Experimental Social Psychology,* (Suppl. 1), 32–39.
Kahneman, D., & Tversky, A. (1973). On the psychology of prediction. *Psychological Review, 80,* 237–251.
Kuiper, N. A., & MacDonald, M. R. (1982). Self and other perception in mild depressives. *Social Cognition, 3,* 223–239.
Lewicki, P. (1983). Self-image bias in person perception. *Journal of Personality and Social Psychology, 45,* 384–393.
Marks, G. (1984). Thinking one's abilities are unique and one's opinions are common. *Personality and Social Psychology Bulletin, 10,* 203–208.
Martin, J. (1986). The tolerance of injustice. In J. M. Olson, C. P. Herman, & M. P. Zanna (Eds.), *Relative deprivation and social comparison: The Ontario Symposium* (Vol. 4, pp. 217–242). Hillsdale, NJ: Lawrence Erlbaum Associates.
Mettee, D. R., & Smith, G. (1977). Social comparison and interpersonal attraction: The case for dissimilarity. In J. M. Suls & R. L. Miller (Eds.), *Social comparison processes: Theoretical and empirical perspectives* (pp. 69–101). Washington, DC: Hemisphere.
Miller, C. T. (1982). The role of performance-related similarity in social comparison of abilities: A test of the related attributes hypothesis. *Journal of Experimental Social Psychology, 18,* 513–523.
Miller, D. T., Turnbull, W., & McFarland, C. (1988). Particularistic and universalistic evaluation in the social comparison process. *Journal of Personality and Social Psychology, 55,* 908–917.
Miller, R. L., & Suls, J. M. (1977). Affiliation preferences as a function of attitude and ability similarity. In J. M. Suls & R. L. Miller (Eds.), *Social comparison processes:*

Theoretical and empirical perspectives (pp. 103–123). Washington, DC: Hemisphere.

Morse, S., & Gergen, K. J. (1970). Social comparison, self-consistency, and the concept of self. *Journal of Personality and Social Psychology, 16,* 148–156.

Nosanchuk, T. A., & Erickson, B. H. (1985). How high is up? Calibrating social comparison in the real world. *Journal of Personality and Social Psychology, 48,* 624–634.

Perloff, L. S., & Fetzer, B. K. (1986). Self-other judgments and perceived vulnerability to victimization. *Journal of Personality and Social Psychology, 50,* 502–510.

Pleban, R., & Tesser, A. (1981). The effects of relevance and quality of another's performance on interpersonal closeness. *Social Psychology Quarterly, 44,* 278–285.

Pyszczynski, T., Greenberg, J., & LaPrelle, J. (1985). Social comparison after success and failure: Biased search for information consistent with a self-serving conclusion. *Journal of Experimental Social Psychology, 21,* 195–211.

Raynor, J. O., & McFarlin, D. B. (1986). Motivation and the self-system. In R. M. Sorrentino & E. T. Higgins (Eds.), *Handbook of motivation and cognition: Foundations of social behavior* (pp. 315–349). New York: Guilford.

Salovey, P., & Rodin, J. (1984). Some antecedents and consequences of social-comparison jealousy. *Journal of Personality and Social Psychology, 47,* 780–792.

Schachter, S. (1959). *The psychology of affiliation.* Stanford, CA: Stanford University Press.

Seta, J. (1982). The impact of comparison processes on coactors' task performance. *Journal of Personality and Social Psychology, 42,* 281–291.

Sherman, S. J., Presson, C. C., & Chassin, L. (1984). Mechanisms underlying the false consensus effect: The special role of threats to the self. *Personality and Social Psychology Bulletin, 10,* 127–138.

Singer, J. E. (1966). Social comparison—progress and issues. *Journal of Experimental Social Psychology,* (Suppl. 1), 103–110.

Smith, R. H., & Insko, C. A. (1987). Social comparison choice during ability evaluation: The effects of comparison publicity, performance feedback, and self-esteem. *Personality and Social Psychology Bulletin, 13,* 111-122.

Suls, J. M. (1977). Social comparison theory and research: An overview from 1954. In J. M. Suls & R. L. Miller (Eds.), *Social comparison processes: Theoretical and empirical perspectives* (pp. 1–19). Washington, DC: Hemisphere.

Suls, J. M., & Miller, R. L. (Eds.). (1977). *Social comparison processes: Theoretical and empirical perspectives.* Washington, DC: Hemisphere.

Suls, J., & Wan, C. K. (1987). In search of the false-uniqueness phenomenon: Fear and estimates of social consensus. *Journal of Personality and Social Psychology, 52,* 211–217.

Tabachnik, N., Crocker, J., & Alloy, L. B. (1983). Depression, social comparison, and the "false consensus" effect. *Journal of Personality and Social Psychology, 45,* 688–699.

Taylor, S. E., & Brown, J. (1988). Illusion and well-being: A social psychological perspective on mental health. *Psychological Bulletin, 103,* 193–210.

Taylor, S. E., Wood, J. V., & Lichtman, R. R. (1983). It could be worse: Selective evaluation as a response to victimization. *Journal of Social Issues, 39,* 19–40.

Tesser, A. (1980). Self-esteem maintenance in family dynamics. *Journal of Personality and Social Psychology, 39,* 77–91.

Tesser, A. (1986). Some effects of self-evaluation maintenance on cognition and action. In R. M. Sorrentino & E. T. Higgins (Eds.), *Handbook of motivation and cognition: Foundations of social behavior* (pp. 435–464). New York: Guilford.

Tesser, A., & Campbell, J. (1980). Self-definition: The impact of the relative performance and similarity of others. *Social Psychology Quarterly, 43,* 341–347.

Tesser, A., & Campbell, J. (1982). Self-evaluation maintenance and the perception of friends and strangers. *Journal of Personality, 50,* 261–279.

Tesser, A., Campbell, J., & Smith, M. (1984). Friendship choice and performance: Self-evaluation maintenance in children. *Journal of Personality and Social Psychology, 46*, 561–574.

Tesser, A., Millar, M., & Moore, J. (1988). Some affective consequences of social comparison and reflection processes: The pain and pleasure of being close. *Journal of Personality and Social Psychology, 54*, 49–61.

Tesser, A., & Smith, J. (1980). Some effects of friendship and task relevance on helping: You don't always help the one you like. *Journal of Experimental Social Psychology, 16*, 583–590.

Thornton, D. A., & Arrowood, A. J. (1966). Self-evaluation, self-enhancement, and the locus of social comparison. *Journal of Experimental Social Psychology*, (Suppl. 1), 40–48.

Trope, Y. (1979). Uncertainty-reducing properties of achievement tasks. *Journal of Personality and Social Psychology, 37*, 1505–1518.

Trope, Y. (1986). Self-enhancement and self-assessment in achievement behavior. In R. M. Sorrentino & E. T. Higgins (Eds.), *Handbook of motivation and cognition: Foundations of social behavior* (pp. 350–378). New York: Guilford.

Weinstein, N. D. (1980). Unrealistic optimism about future life events. *Journal of Personality and Social Psychology, 39*, 806–820.

Wheeler, L. (1966). Motivation as a determinant of upward comparison. *Journal of Experimental Social Psychology*, (Suppl. 1), 27–31.

Wheeler, L., & Koestner, R. (1984). Performance evaluation: On choosing to know the related attributes of others when we know their performance. *Journal of Experimental Social Psychology, 20*, 263–271.

Wheeler, L., Koestner, R., & Driver, R. E. (1982). Related attributes in the choice of comparison others: It's there, but it isn't all there is. *Journal of Experimental Social Psychology, 18*, 489–500.

Wheeler, L., Shaver, K. G., Jones, R. A., Goethals, G. R., Cooper, J., Robinson, J. E., Gruder, C. L., & Butzine, K. W. (1969). Factors determining the choice of a comparison other. *Journal of Experimental Social Psychology, 5*, 219–232.

Wheeler, L., & Zuckerman, M. (1977). Commentary. In J. M. Suls & R. L. Miller (Eds.), *Social comparison processes: Theoretical and empirical perspectives* (pp. 335–357). Washington, DC: Hemisphere.

Wills, T. A. (1981). Downward comparison principles in social psychology. *Psychological Bulletin, 90*, 245–271.

Wilson, S. R., & Benner, L. A. (1971). The effects of self-esteem and situation upon comparison choices during ability evaluation. *Sociometry, 34*, 381–397.

Wood, J. V. (1989). Theory and research concerning social comparisons of personal attributes. *Psychological Bulletin, 106*, 231–248.

Wood, J. V. (1990). *A critical analysis of measures of social comparison: Implications for theory and research*. Manuscript submitted for publication.

Wood, J. V., Taylor, K. L., Michela, J. L., & Gaus Binkley, V. (1990). *Social comparison following threat: Two types of comparisons and dispositional self-esteem*. Manuscript in preparation.

Wood, J. V., Taylor, S. E., & Lichtman, R. R. (1985). Social comparison in adjustment to breast cancer. *Journal of Personality and Social Psychology, 49*, 1169–1183.

Zanna, M. P., Goethals, G. R., & Hill, J. F. (1975). Evaluating a sex-related ability: Social comparison with similar others and standard setters. *Journal of Experimental Social Psychology, 11*, 86–93.

3 Similarity and Self-Esteem in Downward Comparison

Thomas Ashby Wills
Ferkauf Graduate School of Psychology, and
Albert Einstein College of Medicine

SIMILARITY AND SELF-ESTEEM IN DOWNWARD COMPARISON

The theory of social comparison was originated by Leon Festinger in a series of papers published in 1954 (Festinger, 1954a, 1954b). Since that time it has been a continuing influence in social psychology. The ideas proposed by Festinger were nurtured in seminars at Minnesota (see Goethals, 1986) and studied directly in paradigms that included affiliation preferences (Schachter, 1959) and social comparison choices (Wheeler, 1966). The basis for the theory was consolidated in an issue edited by Latane (1966), which led to additional studies on comparison choices (e.g., Brickman & Berman, 1971; Gruder, 1971; Wheeler et al., 1969; Wilson & Benner, 1971). The potential of social comparison theory was further realized by Suls and Miller (1977), including attention to the theory of related attributes (Goethals & Darley, 1977) and the costs of social comparison (Brickman & Bulman, 1977). Research has extended this body of theory (Feldman & Ruble, 1981; Gastorf & Suls, 1978; Wheeler, Koestner, & Driver, 1982). In these and other areas, work on social comparison has continued to advance our understanding of how persons use social information for conceptualizing the self and arriving at perceptions of their own adjustment.

The theory of social comparison encompasses principles for describing the process of *upward comparison* (i.e., comparing with a person who is better off than the self) and the process of *downward comparison* (i.e., comparing with a person who is worse off than the self). Festinger's (1954a) theory focused on social comparison to obtain evaluation of one's abilities, and posited that this type of comparison would be guided both by a general principle of similarity (comparing with persons who are close to one's own level on the attribute) and a unidirectional drive upward (within the range of comparisons, choosing persons who are slightly better off than the self). I refer to this aspect of comparison processes as upward comparison because it involves comparison with others whose performances are better than those of the self. This chapter is intended as a continuation of previous work on downward comparison (Wills, 1981). First I summarize the basis of downward comparison theory and the current support for downward comparison principles. Then I address some issues in downward comparison theory, with a focus on the role of similarity and self-esteem in downward comparison. In a final section I take stock and outline directions for further research.

THE THEORY OF DOWNWARD COMPARISON

The theory of downward comparison began with an interest in the theories of prejudice, aggression, and bad news in newspapers (Wills, 1974). Consideration of the relation of social comparison principles to various aspects of sociopsychological research led to the belief that downward types of social comparison were implicated in these processes. Formal development of this theoretical approach (Wills, 1981) led to the statement of the basic principle of downward comparison, which posits that subjective well-being can be enhanced through comparison with a less fortunate other. The theory suggested that this occurs in situations where a person is distressed and the objective situation is not readily ameliorable through instrumental action. The postulate was that a person could then increase his or her subjective well-being through comparison with a less fortunate other. My conception of subjective well-being was of short-term variation in mood, as would be assessed by a subjective-tension rating. Whether downward comparison could lead to long-term changes in self-concept was not specifically considered.

The formal theory of downward comparison did not deny the validity of upward comparison. My thinking was that Festinger's principles clearly were correct for certain situations, such as comparisons of intellectual ability under relatively neutral conditions. The situations in which upward comparison would be demonstrated, however, were situations in which the individual may not have much personal stake in the outcome of the comparison. The question has been whether the same type of comparison would obtain when persons were not sure that the comparison outcome would be favorable to themselves, such as when a person is not performing well, or does not have a high position in the socioeconomic ladder, or does not perceive a high probability of achieving the higher status of an upward comparison target. My view was that in such conditions, persons would be more likely to engage in downward comparison.

The theory thus proceeds from the proposition that downward comparison exists, that it can be employed to enhance subjective well-being, and that downward types of comparison would most likely be observed in situations where a person's self-esteem or physical well-being was threatened. Two versions of the downward comparison process are posited: one in which an individual enhances subjective well-being by comparing with a person who is worse off than the self (downward comparison), another in which subjective well-being may be enhanced by comparison with a person who is also experiencing problems but is at essentially the same level as the self (*lateral comparison*). Lateral comparison and downward comparison are theoretically distinct processes and may have different consequences, although this point has not been extensively pursued in empirical research. Additional postulates are that downward comparison will be more prevalent among persons with chronically low self-esteem, and that downward comparison tends to be directed at target groups that are societally defined as low status, a corollary that was intended to address some of the phenomena of social prejudice. Finally, it is posited that people are ambivalent about downward comparison because it presents some conflict with normative prescriptions. This corollary suggests that there will be some lack of concordance among people's attitudes and behavioral choices in comparison situations, and downward comparison may sometimes be pursued in a manner that is not clearly labeled as comparison.

Support for the Theory

Initially, the support for the principles was largely indirect, as downward comparison had not been presented as a formal theory. Hakmiller's (1966) classic study provided evidence of downward comparison in a choice situation, with Friend and Gilbert (1973) and Wilson and Benner (1971) providing corroborative evidence, but the majority of social comparison studies showed exclusively upward comparison. There was some evidence for tension reduction when subjects were allowed to compare with less fortunate others, both in studies of fear-affiliation (Amoroso & Walters, 1969; Kiesler, 1966) and studies of projection (Bennett & Holmes, 1975; Burish & Houston, 1979). Finally, a study of outcome distributions in groups (Brickman, 1975) exemplified the ambivalence that persons have about downward comparison. In groups that included a member whose outcomes were worse off than those of the self (i.e., a downward comparison differential), subjects reported better subjective well-being; but they also reported on other measures that they regarded this condition as less fair than conditions where outcomes were more equally distributed. Recent research has provided increased support for the theoretical principles and is summarized in the following sections (for detailed review see Wills, in press).

Existence of Downward Comparison. The phenomenon of downward comparison has been demonstrated in field studies with several types of populations. These include cancer patients (Wood, Taylor, & Lichtman, 1985), mentally retarded adolescents (Gibbons, 1985; Harter, 1985), fire victims (Thompson, 1985), arthritis patients (Affleck et al., 1987, 1988; Blalock, Devellis, & Devellis, 1989; Devellis et al., 1990), mothers of premature infants (Affleck et al., 1987), with some qualifications, physically handicapped adults (Schulz & Decker, 1985), and college professors (Cansler & Stiles, 1981). The studies show a particular preference among distressed persons for comparison with persons (usually other patients) who have a more severe condition or are not coping as well with the condition. This work is discussed in detail in other chapters.

Threat and Comparison. Studies with a variety of populations have shown that when subjects are stressed or threatened, there is a tendency to shift from upward to downward comparison. Shifts in comparison preferences occur because of comparison publicity (Smith & Insko, 1987) and in studies with failure feedback, where threatened subjects show a preference for information about others who did worse than themselves and an avoidance of information about persons who did better (Pyszczynski, Greenberg, & LaPrelle, 1985; cf. Frey & Stahlberg, 1986). Comparison preferences of young children were directly assessed by Levine and Green (1984) in a performance situation and results showed that when performance was declining, children's preferences shifted toward comparison with others whose performance was inferior. A study by Amabile and Glazebrook (1982) also showed a negative shift in social perceptions as the comparison situation worsened.

Comparison and Subjective Well-Being. The postulate that downward comparison will enhance subjective well-being has been demonstrated in several contexts. In laboratory studies by Gibbons (1986) and Gibbons and Gerrard (1989), subjects who were prescreened on depressive mood were given an opportunity to choose from a range of statements about others, representing either positive or negative affect. Results showed that those who were depressed preferred to read negative statements, and that a downward comparison experience produced an enhancement of mood state. A field study by Heath (1984) examined the content of newspaper reports of crime in 36 cities, and found that residents of cities whose newspaper reported a high level of crime in other cities showed less fear of crime, a result that apparently derived from a comparison process. The field results were subsequently replicated in a laboratory study with controlled variables, which showed the same results and strengthened the causal interpretations derived from the field data. Diener (1984) and Emmons and Diener (1985) have discussed evidence on the relation of social comparisons to life satisfaction, and Affleck and Tennen (chapter 14, this volume) provide detailed discussion of evidence on subjective well-being in studies with medical patients.

Self-Esteem and Comparison. The linkage of self-esteem to comparison processes has been indicated in several types of studies. In studies of direct comparison choice several studies have shown a shift toward downward comparison choices among persons low in self-esteem; this has been found for comparisons of ability (Smith & Insko, 1987) and personality attributes (Friend & Gilbert, 1973; Wilson & Benner, 1971). Laboratory studies of the impact of comparison on subjective well-being (Gibbons, 1986; Gibbons & Gerrard, 1989) showed that individuals who scored high on depressive symptomatology were more likely to prefer downward comparison choices, and that change in well-being after downward comparison occurred primarily for these persons. In studies based on comparative ratings of self and others, results are more complex. Tabachnik, Crocker, and Alloy (1983) had depressed and nondepressed subjects make ratings of personality attributes for themselves and the typical college student, and compared these with independent prevalence figures. Results indicated that both groups showed a self-enhancing tendency in social perceptions, but this tendency was more pronounced among the depressed. In studies with interpersonal relations, it has been found that persons with low self-esteem are more likely to engage in self-enhancement through indirect comparisons of own group with outgroup (Brown, Collins, & Schmidt, 1988) and through derogation of sources of social evaluation (Baumgardner, Kaufman, & Levy, 1989).

Social Perception. In addition to studies of actual comparison choices studies of social perception have also suggested that perceptual processes are influenced by social comparison concerns. For example, social perception in a threatened population was studied by Sherman, Presson, and Chassin (1984) in a laboratory paradigm where subjects were given success versus failure feedback and then asked to estimate the proportion of persons who would fail. Results showed that subjects who failed overestimated the percentage who would fail. Relevant control conditions in this and another study (Sherman, Presson, Chassin, & Agostinelli, 1984) indicated that the shift was attributable to a self-enhancement mechanism, not simply attributive projection from one's own behavior. A study of fearful persons by Suls and Wan (1987) also found that those who were distressed by a particular fear markedly overestimated the prevalence of that fear in comparison to actual population figures: The authors suggested that such perceptions make persons feel better about themselves because they indicate that many others have the same problem (i.e., a lateral comparison process). Other studies with nonthreatened populations have found that persons tend to perceive themselves as having fewer undesirable attributes and more desirable, controllable attributes than the typical person (Alicke, 1985) and to have abilities that are rare in the population (Campbell, 1986; Marks, 1984; Marks & Miller, 1987), findings that are consistent with a self-enhancement mechanism.

To summarize, recent studies have provided more direct support for the postulates of downward comparison theory. Downward comparison has been demonstrated with several paradigms and in several different populations, including clinical samples. A linkage between situational threat and downward comparison has been demonstrated, and specific tests have shown enhancement of subjective well-being as a result of downward comparison. A relationship between self-esteem and comparison choices has been indicated in several studies. Finally, linkage of comparison processes to social perception has been suggested in several paradigms, such as Sherman et al. (1984), where esteem threat led to altered perceptions of social consensus.

While recent research has extended the base of support for downward comparison principles, some aspects of the theory have not been developed. This is the purpose of the following sections, which address some issues that have not been extensively investigated. First, I consider the relative effects of lateral comparison versus downward comparison, and the effect of downward comparison differential on subjective well-being. Next, I consider the issue of similarity in downward comparison. I then consider the role of self-esteem in downward comparison and the theoretical effects of downward comparison on various outcome dimensions.

COMPARISON DIFFERENTIAL AND SUBJECTIVE WELL-BEING

Downward Comparison and Lateral Comparison

In considering the relation between comparison differential and net gain in subjective well-being, the first issue is the relative preference for downward or lateral comparison. In both cases it is assumed that the focal person is experiencing a problem on at least one dimension. Downward comparison is defined as comparison with a target who is worse off on at least one dimension. Lateral comparison is defined as comparison with one who is also experiencing problems, but is at the same level as the self on a given dimension. The question can be posed, which type of comparison is more effective?[1]

The question seems to break down into two subissues. The first is whether there is an overall primacy of downward comparison over lateral comparison. I think there might be some reluctance to engage in downward comparison because of the general ambivalence people feel about this type of comparison. On balance, a small downward comparison would seem to be preferred over lateral comparison because, other things being equal, there should be more gain from comparison differential than from comparison equality. The only question here is whether, in naturalistic settings, things typically are equal; the presence of related attributes and personality similarity are additional factors that could drive the comparison in other directions. The basic prediction is a simple one: preference for downward over lateral comparison. Currently there is little empirical evidence on this question, so direct tests would seem warranted.

Satisfaction Enhancement Versus Deviance Reduction. A second issue is whether the effects of lateral and downward comparison occur on the same dimensions. It is possible that downward comparison may influence ratings of life satisfaction because it provides direct evidence that the self is better off than the target; but strict downward comparison may not influence self-perceptions because it does not address the relative standing of the self in the population (Suls, 1986). In contrast, lateral comparison may influence some types of self-perceptions because it provides direct evidence that there are many others with the same problem; thus, feelings of deviance may be reduced. Each type of comparison could influence subjective well-being through effects on life satisfaction or deviance reduction, but through different mechanisms. Thus, it might be useful to include standard measures of life satisfaction with measures tapping the individual's perception of being different (in an undesirable manner) from most others, or perception of the frequency of his or her own attributes in the population.

General Similarity and Downward Comparison

The next question assumes a downward comparison and asks whether the magnitude of the comparison differential is linearly related to change in subjective well-being. As the discrepancy in status between the self and

---

[1] For clarification, it is useful to contrast the concept of lateral comparison with Festinger's concept of comparison with similar others. Festinger's (1954a) model assumes that persons are doing relatively well and wish to compare with others who are doing well (in order to improve their performance). The situation is somewhat different for lateral comparison, where the focal person is doing relatively poorly and is motivated to compare with others who are having problems.

the other becomes greater (i.e., the other is increasingly worse off), is there a linear increase in subjective well-being? I do not posit a linear effect. The general prediction is that a moderate comparison differential will produce the greatest net gain in subjective well-being.

The argument is that at a small comparison differential, the net gain from the comparison is small. At a moderate comparison differential, there should be substantial change in subjective well-being because comparing provides direct evidence that the self is better off than the other. As the comparison differential becomes large, however, other factors become relevant. Observing distress in another person may evoke empathic concerns (Eisenberg & Fabes, in press), and normative prescriptions also support empathic concern (Berkowitz, 1972). At high levels of status differential these tendencies may override comparison processes. In addition, the overall visibility of the comparison as seen by the self qua observer might make persons increasingly uncomfortable with downward comparison at large differentials.[2] Thus, the prediction is a quadratic effect, with positive net gain when the comparison differential is small to moderate, but negative outcomes occurring when the comparison differential exceeds a certain point. This is diagrammed in Fig. 3.1A.

Outgroup Comparisons. One moderating factor is posited. The preceding discussion assumes comparison with others who are members of groups reasonably similar to the self, in the sense of universalistic comparison posited by Miller (Miller, Turnbull, & McFarland, 1988). However, when comparison with an outgroup is being pursued, or when competition with the comparison target is in effect (conditions that are likely correlated) the effect may change. I am not sure whether a strict linear effect would obtain as there must be boundary conditions for comparison with outgroups. The prediction would be that the reflection point in the function is shifted, so that a larger differential in comparison with the outgroup is accepted before discomfort begins. This is diagrammed in Fig. 3.1B. Other moderating factors (e.g., centrality of the dimension, competitive versus cooperative relationship between groups) might further moderate the shape of the function, but are ignored here in the interest of simplicity.

---

[2] The concept is that downward comparison is often effected in a manner to obscure the fact that a comparison is being pursued, as in the case of some types of humor (see Wills, 1981). In the case of humor, the visibility of the comparison as perceived by the audience (i.e., observers) is posited to be a factor in the impact of a humor stimulus (e.g., a joke). In the case of a comparison made by the self, the person also serves as his/her own observer; if the visibility of the comparison becomes too great, then discomfort ensues because the self qua observer begins to note public consciousness concerns.

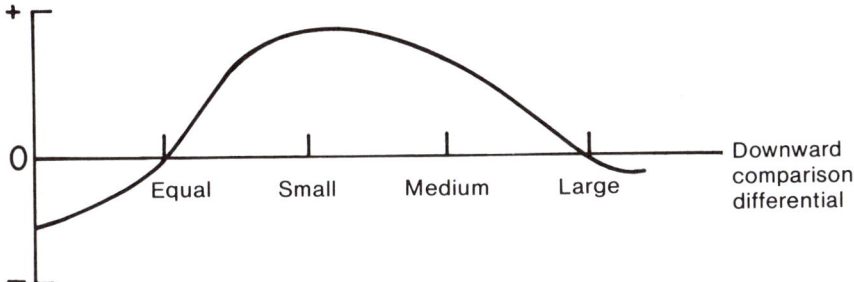

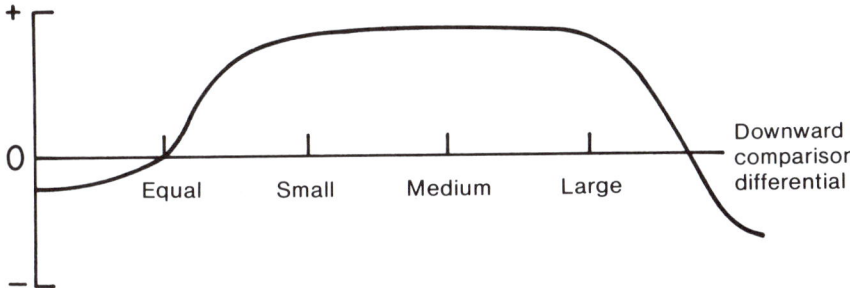

FIG. 3.1. Comparison differential and net gain.

Principle of Mixed Elements

Given that a downward comparison is being pursued, a further question concerns factors that influence the outcome of comparison. The question is, should there be a preference for downward comparison with a person who is similar to the self on dimensions such as personality, or on related attributes such as sex or age?

To derive a basic hypothesis I proceed from what I term the principle of *mixed elements* in comparison. The assumption is that a potential downward comparison situation presents the self with two elements of information: fate similarity and future similarity. Fate similarity is the present case (i.e., the person is worse off than the self at the present time). Future similarity is the person's assessment of the probability that he or she could become like the target person. The two elements should be relatively independent for typical life situations, and presumably would have different implications for the change in the focal person's subjective well-being.

TABLE 3.1
Mixed Elements in Downward Comparison

A. Fate Similarity and Future Similarity

	Future Similarity	
	Low	High
Fate Similarity		
worse off	+	−
much worse off	+ +	− − −

B. Fate Similarity and Personality Similarity

	Personality Similarity	
	Low	High
Fate Similarity		
worse off	+	+ ?
much worse off	+ +	− −

Note: Symbols within cells indicate net change in subjective well-being. A + indicates positive change in well-being, a − indicates negative change in well-being. A + + or + + + indicates larger positive changes, a − − or − − − indicates larger negative changes.

To the extent that *fate similarity* is dissimilar (i.e., the target person is worse off than the self) the net gain in subjective well-being would be greater than when the current status of the self and other is similar. There must be boundary conditions on this. Observing a target person suffering a horrible, gruesome fate seems unlikely to make a typical person feel better about him or herself because empathic concern would override any potential increment from comparison. The expectation is that net gain will be greatest when the fate similarity of the target is moderately similar to the self. This is the same basic argument previously advanced for the effect of comparison differential with other factors being equal.

With *future similarity* the argument is somewhat different. If the comparison situation conveys information suggesting that the probability of becoming like the target person is high, presumably there would be negative change (i.e., anxiety would be increased). If future similarity is low, the prediction is that there will be a net increase in well-being. This prediction is illustrated in Table 3.1A. It is evident from the table that there should be some situations where downward comparison will result in a decrement in subjective well-being.

What about personality similarity? My hypothesis is that future similarity and personality similarity have some implicit linkage (i.e., people tend to believe that if they are similar to another, they are likely to have the same fate as the other). For example, if a person employed on Wall Street observes someone who is very similar to the self hauled into court after being caught red-handed in insider trading and stock market manipulation, this seems unlikely to make the focal person feel sanguine about his or her own future. (There will be some situations where the linkage is not logically necessary, for example, the occurrence of cancer or heart disease to another person would not carry any necessary connotation of personality similarity.) In general, the postulate is that when personality similarity is low downward comparison will produce an increase in subjective well-being, but when personality similarity is high the effect of downward comparison will be negative. This is diagrammed in Table 3.1B. For the cell where personality similarity is high but the other is only slightly worse off the prediction is more arguable. My view is that there would be some increase in subjective well-being because the effect of personality similarity is somewhat weaker than the effect of future similarity.[3]

A further elaboration of this model could consider varying degrees of fate similarity or personality similarity (low, moderate, high) as in the previous consideration of comparison differential. In addition, the three-way interaction between fate similarity, future similarity, and personality similarity could be considered. These topics may be premature, however, as tests of the two-way interactions would seem the necessary preliminary steps for extending the theory.

Locus of Other's Attributes. A corollary of the postulates about fate, future, and personality similarity concerns the focal person's attributions about the *locus* of the other person's condition. Given that the comparison target is worse off than the self, there are several important attributional questions than can be posed concerning the reason (Weiner, 1985). If the target's unfortunate situation appears to be caused by low ability, this might produce different comparison effects than when the unfortunate situation is attributed to external factors. Assuming that people generally perceive themselves as more competent than typical others, downward comparison may produce an increase in subjective well-being in the first condition, but

---

[3] I would think that the distribution will be negatively skewed. Even persons who are quite dissimilar in personality to the self would still have some effectiveness as downward comparison targets. This is different from Festinger's thinking on self-evaluation, which posits that comparison with a very dissimilar other is not useful for determining the level of one's own attributes. For downward comparison, however, accurate determination of relative standing is not the issue; the question is whether there is a comparison differential that is favorable to the self. An unresolved question is whether effective comparison requires some element of identification with the other, in the sense of Miller et al.'s (1988) construct of particularistic comparison.

a decrease in the second condition. Or, if the comparison target is similar to the self and is worse off because of attributes that are perceived as relatively unchangeable, the element of future similarity may become involved and comparison may have a negative effect on subjective well-being (cf. Major et al., this volume). In contrast, if the comparison differential occurs because of changeable factors (e.g., low effort) then the comparison situation may be somewhat altered because future similarity is minimized. This yields another prediction: The outcome of downward comparison will be influenced by the perceived attributes of the comparison target. It is not clear whether the locus, stability, or controllability of attributes would have the most impact on comparison outcome, and this suggests a question for further research.

To summarize, the discussion suggests some complexity to the process of downward comparison. Given a typical downward comparison situation most comparison differentials are posited to be effective to some extent, and the outcome of the comparison process is not closely linked to the magnitude of the comparison differential. I suggest that the information in a comparison situation contains mixed elements of fate similarity and future similarity, and that the outcome of the comparison process will be strongly affected by the balance of information concerning these two elements. Derivations from the mixed-elements principle further suggest some properties of the target person that will affect the outcome of a downward comparison process.

LEVEL EFFECTS AND DIMENSIONAL COMPARISON

Another theoretical issue concerns how the comparison process is influenced by a person's absolute level on the continuum of subjective well-being. The general expectation is that the propensity for downward comparison increases as subjective well-being decreases (Wills, 1981, 1983), and evidence previously discussed is consistent with this proposition. There is another issue raised by the interaction between the *propensity* for comparison and the *availability* of comparisons. This derives from a consideration of how absolute level shapes the availability of downward comparisons. A hypothesis about level effects is diagrammed in Table 3.2.

The argument is that those with the greatest motivation for downward comparison have the lowest availability of comparisons, and vice versa. At a high level of well-being (Point A in the table) persons potentially have a large range of downward comparisons available but their motivation for comparison is relatively weak, and the large discrepancy between self and other would push toward the boundary conditions of the fate similarity effect (Fig. 3.1), where the comparison differential is sufficiently large that reactions to comparison may be minimal or negative. The suggestion is

TABLE 3.2
Level Effects

Subjective Well-being Continuum

[Diagram: vertical scale from High to Low with Middle marked. Four vertical range bars labeled A (upper), B (upper-middle), C (lower-middle), and D (lower), each showing the range of possible comparisons.]

Note: Length of lines indicates range of possible comparisons for persons at different points on well-being continuum (A, B, C, D).

that persons around mid-scale (particularly Point B) would have the most effective range of comparisons available, but their motivation for self-enhancing comparisons is only moderate. For persons with low well-being (Point D in the table) there is something of a quandary because the motivation for comparison is strong but the available range of comparisons is restricted by floor effects. Assuming the need for self-enhancement is active, there is a particular coping problem for these persons if they try to make a downward comparison on the given dimension. It is possible that for these persons, lateral comparison will be an effective mode, and this suggests the prediction that lateral comparison will be observed for this group. Note, however, that the model here assumes comparison on a single dimension.

The alternative model is that this comparison issue is resolved by what Wood et al. (1985) have termed *dimensional comparison.* They observed that medical patients evidenced a number of comparisons made with people with similar status (i.e., other cancer patients) but who were worse off than they on another dimension (e.g., family support). That is, instead of making a downward comparison on the original dimension, the patients shifted to another dimension. The point is that this is not just another type of comparison, but may be a necessary aspect of downward comparison when pursued as a coping process.

Dimensional comparison may also be derivable from the personality principle. Shifting to another dimension of comparison on which the focal person is worse off may decrease perceived personality similarity (because the self is now different from the other on two dimensions, not one). Hence, the net gain is increased because the personality similarity principle is operative.[4] It is possible that dimensional comparisons are particularly effective because they involve separate contributions from (a) level effects and (b) similarity effects, and it may be possible to determine the contribution of each mechanism in a laboratory study.

A point worth noting is that these postulates emphasize the flexibility of the downward comparison process. If comparison on one dimension is constrained the person can easily shift to another dimension. Further, cognitive processes may be invoked in some cases. For example, if personality for available targets is too similar, some distancing from the target may occur. This would increase the effect of the downward comparison. Again there is a contrast with upward comparison, which is quite restrictive in its operation, whereas downward comparison is in theory more flexible.

EFFECTS OF DOWNWARD COMPARISON

What are the effects of downward comparison? Given that a downward comparison is pursued, what dimension(s) of self-appraisal or subjective well-being are altered? In upward comparison the effects of comparison are posited to be quite specific, that is, a person compares to evaluate a specific ability, and confidence or certainty about that dimension is presumably increased. Festinger did not explicitly postulate what consequences certainty would have for coping, adaptation, self-esteem, and so on, but the presumption is that accurate self-evaluation is adaptive in some sense. With downward comparison the situation is more complex because the theoretical postulates are less restrictive. Following, I discuss how particular outcome dimensions may be affected.

---

[4] In fact the anecdotes presented in Wood et al. (1985) suggest this. Several of the respondents emphasize that they are different from the target person because of the dimensional difference.

Negative Affect Postulate

The basic principle of downward comparison posits that subjective well-being will be enhanced through comparison with a less fortunate other. The definition of *less fortunate other* is one who is experiencing negative mood. The original sense of the postulate was that contemporaneous mood would be changed, and that a person's mood state would be better after the comparison. Affect of course has at least two dimensions: positive and negative (Diener, 1984; Watson & Tellegen, 1985). The presumption is that it is primarily the negative affect that is changed. Comparison with a less fortunate other would not seem to increase positive affect in any obvious way, because this typically derives from positive social interaction and perceptions of the self, conditions that do not seem characteristic of the situations where downward comparison is typically observed. The prediction is that negative affect is reduced because the perceived negativity of one's own situation is at least temporarily altered through comparison. This postulate is consistent with the situations where tension reduction has been directly observed (Amoroso & Walters, 1969; Bennett & Holmes, 1975; Burish & Houston, 1979; Hakmiller, 1966; Kiesler, 1966).

Life Satisfaction

Comparison also may affect life satisfaction. The downward comparison process may involve a comparison in which the focal person compares his or her life situation with that of another person. Such comparison is feasible because (with the level-effect restrictions noted above) such comparison is accessible for a substantial part of the population. Further, life situation (i.e., house, car, garage, family, neighborhood, income, occupation) is a relatively stable attribute. Unlike comparisons based on contemporaneous affect, comparisons based on life situation might have a more enduring effect on perceived life satisfaction. There are some data which suggest that this effect occurs (Brickman, Coates, & Janoff-Bulman, 1978; Dermer, Cohen, Jacobsen, & Anderson, 1979). Note that with comparison based on a relatively stable attribute, linkages with other stable self-attributes, such as self-esteem, may theoretically begin to occur.

Optimism

Can downward comparison produce an increase in positive dimensions? I think it is possible. One candidate is optimism. I think that this effect (i.e., downward comparison increasing optimism) would depend on a combination of conditions: personality similarity is high, and the information suggests that the comparison other's unfortunate state is temporary. A corollary is that the comparison dimension involves an attribute that is controllable. Given a particular set of downward comparison conditions, the comparison process might then produce an increase in the focal person's optimism about his or her own future, although the effect might be specific to the dimension of comparison, not broadly generalized as in comparison based on life satisfaction.

Note that the dimension of stability or controllability is again introduced. This was not present in the original theory except from the focal person's standpoint. It was posited that downward comparison would occur only when the person was experiencing a problem that was not easily changed. It is plausible that problem stability has a significant effect with respect to target choice and outcome of comparison. If two downward comparison targets are provided representing controllable and uncontrollable problems respectively, the prediction is that there will be a preference for the former comparison.

This is possibly reflected in the anecdotal reports from field studies with medical patients. One of the common reports from respondents in these studies is that they perceive they are coping better with the illness than are others (see Affleck & Tennen, chapter 14, this volume; Wood, chapter 2, this volume). Note that the reports do not reflect the perception that the comparison person (who has the same illness) is not coping with the problem; such a comparison might invoke negative future similarity, and hence be threatening. Note also that it may be particularly serviceable to make comparisons about one's own coping ability, because the standards are flexible. A comparison that showed exactly the same level of adjustment could produce a favorable comparison because the self is perceived to have a more severe problem or less favorable environmental conditions, which gives the person more to cope with.

Motivation

A related issue is whether downward comparison may increase coping motivation. Comparison theory has typically focused on perceiving one's own attributes from either a self-evaluation or a self-enhancement standpoint. There has been less attention to issues of motivation. But motivation may be crucial for coping processes (Wills, 1987). The theoretical procedure here is less clear. In upward comparison theory the postulate is that upward comparison will increase coping motivation because persons compare with a better-off other and are motivated to achieve the (higher) level of the target. However there are grounds for believing that upward comparison may tend to be avoided by some persons, particularly when distress is elevated (Brickman & Bulman, 1977).

The argument is that downward comparison may be related to motivation. The postulate is that comparison-oriented coping is stage-linked, related to motivation at early stages of the coping process. This is in agreement with models of coping which suggest that in early stages of coping with a stress, the primary goal is to minimize distress and activate coping (Lazarus & Folkman, 1984). The function of downward comparison for reducing distress may be most relevant at this stage of coping. Being able to control distress through downward comparison may increase perceived coping ability and hence increase motivation for further coping, and choice of appropriate comparisons may influence a person's optimism. *Appropriate* here means a comparison that involves the right combination of characteristics, particularly with regard to controllability and future similarity.

As coping proceeds, in theory there should be a shift toward upward comparison. Persons become less concerned with obtaining comforting information about the self and become more concerned with evaluating the success of their own coping efforts relative to the general population (or their reference group within the general population). A reduced level of distress and a greater level of confidence about one's coping ability make it easier to start engaging in upward comparisons, which would be somewhat uncomfortable but may be necessary for further progress in coping. Note also that a failure to shift from downward to upward comparison might be a prognostic indicator of poor outcome.

DOWNWARD COMPARISON AND SELF-ESTEEM

The first issue is the relation between self-esteem and use of downward comparison. A second issue is the more general relation between self-enhancing perceptions and social comparison processes.

Self-Esteem and Downward Comparison Choices

The original conception held that downward comparison functions as a self-enhancement mechanism and that motivation for use of comparison-oriented coping would be stronger among persons with lower self-esteem. The reasoning was that if downward comparison is evoked by acute stress, then it should also be evoked by chronic stress. The assumption was that a poor self-image serves as a chronic stressor, which tends to arouse negative affect and hence prompts coping efforts.[5] Coping here means either

---

[5] An alternative view is that depressive cognitive processes represent a breakdown in esteem maintenance because they focus on negative aspects of the self and pessimism for the future (e.g., Kuiper, MacDonald, & Derry, 1983; Pyszczynski & Greenberg, 1987; Segal, 1988; Swallow & Kuiper, 1988). Whether clinical depression results from a breakdown in self-protection processes is an interesting question which is beyond the scope of this chapter.

lateral comparison, dimensional comparison, or downward comparison, all of which involve the choice of a particular comparison target. The converse prediction was that since high self-esteem, in theory, derives from self-acceptance and satisfaction with one's self-attributes, there should be little need for self-enhancement among persons with high self-esteem.

Currently there are two bodies of evidence that bear on the relationship between self-esteem and social comparison. First is a group of studies that have presented subjects with an opportunity to make choices of target persons and examined how comparison choices varied as a function of self-esteem. These studies, involving comparisons of ability and personality attributes, have consistently shown a downward shift in comparison choices among persons with lower self-esteem (Friend & Gilbert, 1973; Smith & Insko, 1987; Wilson & Benner, 1971). Similar findings are obtained in studies where subjects are blocked on depressive symptomatology (Gibbons, 1986; Gibbons & Gerrard, 1989), which show depressive subjects preferring downward comparison choices. This body of evidence supports the postulate that downward comparison will be employed as a coping strategy by low self-esteem persons.

Another group of studies uses a paradigm in which subjects do not make actual comparison choices, but instead make evaluative ratings of (a) the self and (b) others, on various dimensions of ability and personality. Findings in these studies show that across dimensions, the rating differential (self–other) is generally positive and is greater for those subjects who are high in self-esteem (Crocker, Thompson, McGraw, & Ingerman, 1987; Tabachnik, Crocker, & Alloy, 1983); that is, persons tend to perceive themselves as better than others, and this tendency is greatest for persons with high self-esteem. These data have been interpreted as disconfirming downward comparison theory because they show those with high self-esteem perceive a greater differential between themselves and others (e.g., Crocker et al., 1987). Analogous findings from studies of uniqueness where samples are blocked on self-esteem (Goethals, chapter 6, this volume; cf. Campbell, 1986) show persons in the high-esteem group evidencing a greater tendency to perceive their own positive attributes as distinguished from those of the general population. These data have been interpreted as reflecting greater use of self-enhancement processes by persons with high self-esteem.

In dealing with these apparently discrepant bodies of evidence, beyond noting that they involve completely different paradigms it is perhaps useful to briefly discuss the concept of self-esteem. A basic proposition is that in adult samples self-esteem is based on an extended history of performances and social relationships which become incorporated into an organized self-schema (see Lewicki, 1983; Markus & Kunda, 1986). In this context, low self-esteem is presumed to derive from a history of relatively poor performance and some relatively unfavorable social relationships. This presumably is what measures of generalized self-regard are indexing (i.e., the perception that one has a relative lack of abilities or personal attributes that are valued in the general population). Measures of self-esteem applied to persons with this kind of self-perception will then produce data indicating that the person feels he or she is not as competent as others in instrumental or social domains.

Applying this discussion to the literature, I suggest that studies with different paradigms are asking different questions. One is: Do persons with low self-esteem rate themselves as superior to other persons? Another is: Do persons with low self-esteem engage in self-enhancing comparisons? If one asks the first question the answer will necessarily be negative because low self-esteem persons will respond (in some sense rationally) that they are inferior to others. However, this is unrelated to the question of whether persons with low self-esteem engage in self-enhancing comparisons. The implication is that quite different results will be produced by a given study, depending on which question is addressed (see also Wood, chapter 2, this volume).

A specific example is provided by Tabachnik et al. (1983), the only study to include both a rating differential and another measure. This study employed groups of college students selected through prescreening to be high versus low on depressive symptomatology. Subjects made ratings of themselves as well as average college students on various personality attributes, and data were also obtained from an independent random sample of students. One analysis of these data focused on the rating differential (self–other) in the original sample. These data indicated that compared to nondepressed subjects, the depressed subjects rated themselves higher on negative attributes and lower on positive attributes, consistent with the original classification of depression. In rating others the depressed subjects perceived other persons as having more negative attributes and fewer positive attributes, consistent with a projection process (Miller et al., chapter 7, this volume; cf. Suls & Wan, 1987). The self–other difference scores indicated that high self-esteem persons perceived their own relative status in more favorable terms.

Another analysis involved comparison of data from the original sample with self-ratings from the independent sample, which indexes accuracy of perceptions. There was a general tendency for inaccuracy because all subjects overestimated the percentage of college students who were characterized by negative attributes and underestimated the percentage who were characterized by positive attributes (i.e., a self-enhancement bias). However, a significant interaction indicated that this effect was stronger among depressed subjects. These data, then, indicate that self-enhancement through biased social perception is stronger among those who are depressed.

These considerations lead to the suggestion that low self-esteem persons will employ self-enhancement mechanisms that are indirect. Because of their level of instrumental or social performance it is difficult for them to engage in direct self-aggrandizement but it is possible to engage in indirect forms of self-enhancement that rely upon selection of worse off targets or biasing of perceptions of other persons. These mechanisms are psychologically easier because they utilize existing targets (or perceptions) and do not require the person to expend energy on the improvement of positive attributes. This perspective accommodates the studies by Brown et al. (1988) and Wood et al. (chapter 2, this volume), which suggest that low-esteem persons engage primarily in indirect forms of self-enhancement, as well as the studies previously discussed that show selection of downward comparison targets to be more prevalent among persons with lower self-esteem.

The further question is that if low-esteem persons engage in downward comparison, why doesn't this make them eventually comparable to high-esteem persons? Although this question is not easily answered, one possible resolution is that other things being equal, comparison-oriented coping may have its primary effect for subjective well-being but not for self-concept because the information value of upward and downward comparisons is different. To the extent that self-concept is rooted in information from actual performances, coping that focuses exclusively on subjective well-being rather than change in behavior will lead, in the long run, to maintaining a low level of self-esteem. If performance and adjustment don't change, then self-concept is unlikely to change.

General Comparison Processes

A more general issue is whether social comparison processes have a role in the formation of stable aspects of self-concept. Persons potentially have both upward and downward comparisons available. If interested in upward comparison, they can find better-off similar others, or engage in range-seeking to determine where they stand relative to the general population. If interested in downward comparison, they can find comparison targets with whom they compare favorably. The theoretical paradox is that (a) upward comparison can alter self-concept because of the high information value of the comparison, but upward comparisons may tend to be unfavorable to the self; whereas (b) downward comparisons will be favorable to the self, but may have less impact on self-concept because of their lower information value (Wills, in press). The question is, what is the balance of upward and downward comparison in prevailing conditions, and how does this relate to formation or maintenance of self-concept?

In theory there are three possible resolutions of this issue. One is that people avoid upward comparison entirely; this seems unlikely because if it were true, self-understanding and eventual action would become divorced from reality. A second is that persons alternate upward comparison and downward comparison. They pursue upward comparison when they need to determine their standing on a particular attribute and the situation suggests that the outcome will be positive. They will pursue downward comparison when insecure or threatened on a particular dimension and comparisons are available that produce a net gain in subjective well-being. This formulation seems plausible.

A third model, which may coexist with the second, is that there is a memory effect. Persons engage in both upward and downward comparison but there is a memory differential for comparisons that are favorable to one's self-image. In this model, persons continually engage in both types of comparison but there is a bias in long-term storage for occasions in which the comparison was favorable to the self. Thus, over the long term a stable comparison differential will develop such that the self is perceived to have more favorable and fewer negative attributes than other people (cf. Alicke, 1985; Campbell, 1986; Marks, 1984). The suggestion is that at the micro level there are a variety of favorable and unfavorable comparison experiences (Tesser, chapter 5, this volume) but at the macro level there is a storage advantage for the former. Over the long term, this effect would contribute to the general perception that the self is superior to others (Taylor & Brown, 1988).

Is this model consistent with other evidence on self-related information processing? There is evidence that persons are more likely to encode information when it concerns central dimensions of self-concept (Greenwald, 1980; Lewicki, 1983) and that processing of self-related information is pursued with reference to an organized self-schema (e.g., Markus & Kunda, 1986; Sande, Goethals, & Radloff, 1988). There is a preference for positive versus negative information about the self (e.g., Andersen & Williams, 1985; Strube & Roemmelle, 1985; Swann, Griffin, Predmore, & Gaines, 1987). Thus the basis for a memory differential is there. Under ordinary conditions comparisons may be relatively inactive, in which case self-related constructs are not much affected. In times of stress or uncertainty, comparison processes may shift toward downward comparison to favor maintenance of self-esteem in the face of challenges from the environment. Hence the product is a self-concept that is relatively positive and relatively stable.

There is one major problem for this formulation. This is whether persons generally prefer information that is favorable to the self-concept or that is consistent with the self-concept. If the latter, the prediction is that persons with a negative self-concept will seek and prefer negative information about the self because it is consistent with their self-concept (Swann et al., 1987). At present the generality of self-consistency versus self-enhancement is unresolved, and discussion continues among the proponents of alternative views.

From this point one could go in several directions. Research could aim to test whether downward comparison has any impact on self-concept. It could be interesting to determine the balance of upward and downward comparisons in everyday life, or to test for a memory differential in comparison outcomes. Alternatively, one could ask whether depression develops because of an inappropriate use of upward comparison (Swallow & Kuiper, 1988). All of these seem interesting questions which would have some bearing on problems of self-evaluation and adjustment.

GENERAL DISCUSSION

I have summarized current evidence on downward comparison and suggested some further questions about comparison processes and outcomes. One basic question is whether there is a preference for downward comparison over lateral comparison, and this issue is still largely unresolved. Another issue is the role of similarity in downward comparison. I have suggested that there are mixed elements in the comparison process, which may influence comparison in different ways. These could be examined for their separate and interactive relations to comparison outcomes. I consider level effects in comparison and suggest implications for the phenomenon of dimensional comparison, which is derived in several ways. I suggest some ways in which comparison outcome may be influenced by attributes of the comparison target. Finally, I consider the relation between social comparison and self-esteem, both on an immediate and long-term basis.

Mixed Elements in Comparison

One conclusion of this chapter is that the effects of similarity in downward comparison are complex. The social comparison process, in theory, presents several different types of information, which bear on the current fate similarity of the self and the target; the prospect of the self becoming like the target in the future; and the overall personality similarity between the self and the comparison person. These three elements of fate similarity, future similarity, and personality similarity probably have different consequences for the downward comparison process, and, depending on the combination of elements, the outcome of comparison may be positive or negative in its effects for subjective well-being. Thus the downward comparison process is not necessarily a simple phenomenon, and precise specification of outcomes may depend on measurement of the individual elements in a comparison.

Upward Comparison

There are still some unanswered questions about upward comparison. It is known that in relatively neutral situations people tend to compare with others who are somewhat better off than the self, both on the focal dimension and on related attributes (e.g., Gastorf & Suls, 1978; Goethals & Darley, 1977; Feldman & Ruble, 1981; Wheeler, Koestner, & Driver, 1982). But there is still little knowledge about the typical mix of upward and downward comparisons in prevailing naturalistic conditions. Because measuring repeated comparisons in natural settings presents some challenges, this is not an easy question to answer, but the results would be informative (see Wills, 1987).

Additionally, one can still ask what happens in upward comparison? While the phenomena of upward comparison and range-seeking have been demonstrated in elegant designs, to what use do people put the information and how does it fit into their overall coping goals (see Wood, this volume). Do people, for example, use upward comparison to set goals for self-improvement, or to strengthen the belief that they (a good person) are like the upward target (a good but slightly better person), (cf. Singer, 1966; Wheeler, 1966)? It would be helpful to get more data on the consequences of upward comparison on various dimensions, which would have some bearing on these questions.

A corollary is that there is still little understanding of the affective consequences of upward comparison. The expectation from a reading of social comparison theory would be that upward comparison will have generally positive affective consequences (because of accurate self-understanding, increased certainty, etc.). But Tesser's studies (chapter 5, this volume) show that comparison with a better off other may have negative affective consequences. This raises some questions about what is happening in upward comparison, and suggests a need for more attention to the outcome of the comparison process and the question of how persons combine (or alternate) upward and downward comparisons in daily life. A following question is: What will happen at the societal level as current social forces tend to turn personal relationships into competitive ones (Hornung & McClullough, 1981; Sanders & Suls, 1982)?

Downward Comparison

I have noted that the basic postulates of downward comparison have consistent support. At the same time, the process of downward comparison is not well understood. There is no specific evidence on whether there is a preference for lateral comparison over downward comparison. Further research on such questions would help to better understand how comparison processes in general, and downward comparison in particular, really operate. Another aspect not well understood is the consequences of downward comparison. From a perusal of the literature one could find opinions that downward comparison is either constructive, destructive, or neutral in its consequences for adjustment; but currently there is little evidence on the subject. Because downward comparison seems to be a response with substantial prevalence in some settings, there would seem to be a need for greater understanding of its consequences. Elaboration of methodological issues relevant for strong tests of this issue is beyond the scope of the present chapter, but is discussed in other papers (See Affleck & Tennen, chapter 14, this volume; Wills, 1987; Wood, chapter 2, this volume).

A final issue is whether a model of self-enhancement through downward comparison has utility for approaching phenomena that have not usually been construed in social comparison terms, such as hostile humor, gossip, aggression, vandalism, and effects of media on social behavior (Wills, 1986). Pursuit of questions about how social comparison theory applies to these phenomena could be an interesting endeavor.

ACKNOWLEDGMENTS

Versions of this chapter were presented at the Conference on Coping with Loss Experiences, Trier, West Germany, and in the symposium "Current Perspectives on Social Comparison" at the meeting of the American Psychological Association, New Orleans. Thanks to Hans Werner Bierhoff, Frederick Gibbons, Jerry Suls, Bernard Weiner, and Ladd Wheeler for their comments on a draft of this chapter.

REFERENCES

Affleck, G., Tennen, H., Pfeiffer, C., & Fifield, J. (1988). Social comparisons in rheumatoid arthritis: Accuracy and adaptational significance. *Journal of Social and Clinical Psychology, 6*, 219–234.

Affleck, G., Tennen, H., Pfeiffer, C., Fifield, J., & Rowe, J. (1987). Downward comparison and coping with serious medical problems. *American Journal of Orthopsychiatry, 57*, 570–578.

Alicke, M. D. (1985). Global self-evaluation as determined by the desirability and controllability of trait adjectives. *Journal of Personality and Social Psychology, 49*, 1621–1630.

Amabile, T. M., & Glazebrook, A. H. (1982). A negativity bias in interpersonal evaluation. *Journal of Experimental Social Psychology, 18*, 1–22.

Amoroso, D. M., & Walters, R. H. (1969). Effects of anxiety and socially mediated anxiety reduction on paired-associate learning. *Journal of Personality and Social Psychology, 11*, 388–396.

Andersen, S. M., & Williams, M. (1985). Cognitive/affective reactions in the improvement of self-esteem. *Journal of Personality and Social Psychology, 49*, 1086–1097.

Baumgardner, A. H., Kaufman, C. M., & Levy, P. E. (1989). Regulating affect interpersonally: When low esteem leads to greater enhancement. *Journal of Personality and Social Psychology, 56,* 907–921.

Bennett, D. H., & Holmes, D. S. (1975). Influence of denial and projection on anxiety associated with threat to self-esteem. *Journal of Personality and Social Psychology, 32,* 915–921.

Berkowitz, L. (1972). Social norms, feelings, and other factors affecting helping and altruism. In L. Berkowitz (Ed.), *Advances in experimental social psychology* (Vol. 6, pp. 63–108). New York: Academic Press.

Blalock, S., DeVellis, B., & DeVellis, R. (1989). Social comparison among individuals with rheumatoid arthritis. *Journal of Applied Social Psychology, 19,* 665–680.

Brickman, P. (1975). Adaptation level determinants of satisfaction with equal and unequal outcome distributions in skill and chance situations. *Journal of Personality and Social Psychology, 32,* 191–198.

Brickman, P., & Berman, J. J. (1971). Effects of performance expectancy and outcome certainty on interest in social comparison. *Journal of Experimental Social Psychology, 7,* 600–609.

Brickman, P., & Bulman, R. J. (1977). Pleasure and pain in social comparison. In J. M. Suls & R. M. Miller (Eds.), *Social comparison processes: Theoretical and empirical perspectives* (pp. 149–186). Washington, DC: Hemisphere.

Brickman, P., Coates, D., & Janoff-Bulman, R. (1978). Lottery winners and accident victims: Is happiness relative? *Journal of Personality and Social Psychology, 36,* 917–927.

Brown, J. D., Collins, R. L., & Schmidt, G. W. (1988). Self-esteem and direct versus indirect forms of self-enhancement. *Journal of Personality and Social Psychology, 55,* 445–453.

Burish, T. G., & Houston, B. K. (1979). Causal projection, similarity projection, and coping with threat to self-esteem. *Journal of Personality, 47,* 57–70.

Campbell, J. D. (1986). Similarity and uniqueness: Effects of attribute type, relevance, and self-esteem. *Journal of Personality and Social Psychology, 50,* 281–294.

Cansler, D. C., & Stiles, W. B. (1981). Relative status and interpersonal presumptuousness. *Journal of Experimental Social Psychology, 17,* 459–471.

Crocker, J., Thompson, L. L., McGraw, K. M., & Ingerman, C. (1987). Ingroup bias and evaluations of others: Effects of self-esteem and threat. *Journal of Personality and Social Psychology, 52,* 907–916.

Dermer, M., Cohen, S. J., Jacobsen, E., & Anderson, E. A. (1979). Evaluative judgments of aspects of life as a function of vicarious exposure to hedonic extremes. *Journal of Personality and Social Psychology, 37,* 247–260.

DeVellis, R., Holt, K., Renner, B., Blalock, S., Blanchard, L., Cook, H., Koltz, M., Mikow, V., & Harring, K. (1990). The relationship of social comparison to rheumatoid arthritis symptoms and affect. *Basic and Applied Social Psychology, 11,* 1–18.

Diener, E. (1984). Subjective well-being. *Psychological Bulletin, 95,* 542–575.

Dovidio, J. F., & Gaertner, S. L. (1983). Race and help-seeking. In B. M. DePaulo, A. Nadler, & J. D. Fisher (Eds.), *New directions in helping (Vol. 2). Help-seeking* (pp. 285–302). New York: Academic Press.

Eisenberg, N., Fabes, X. (in press). Empathy and prosocial behavior. *Review of Personality and Social Psychology, 12.*

Emmons, R. A., & Diener, E. (1985). Factors predicting satisfaction judgments. *Social Indicators Research, 16,* 157–167.

Feldman, N. S., & Ruble, D. N. (1981). Social comparison strategies: Dimensions offered and options taken. *Personality and Social Psychology Bulletin, 7,* 11–16.

Festinger, L. (1954a). A theory of social comparison processes. *Human Relations, 7*, 117–140.
Festinger, L. (1954b). Motivation leading to social behavior. In M. R. Jones (Ed.), *Nebraska symposium on motivation* (pp. 191–223). Lincoln: University of Nebraska Press.
Frey, D., & Stahlberg, D. (1986). Selection of information after receiving more or less reliable self-threatening information. *Personality and Social Psychology Bulletin, 12*, 434–441.
Friend, R. M., & Gilbert, J. (1973). Threat and fear of negative evaluation as determinants of locus of social comparison. *Journal of Personality, 41*, 328–340.
Gastorf, J. W., & Suls, J. (1978). Performance evaluation via social comparison: Performance similarity vs. related-attributes similarity. *Social Psychology, 41*, 297–305.
Gibbons, F. X. (1985). A social-psychological perspective on developmental disabilities. *Journal of Social and Clinical Psychology, 3*, 391–404.
Gibbons, F. X. (1986). Social comparison and depression: Company's effect on misery. *Journal of Personality and Social Psychology, 51*, 140–148.
Gibbons, F. X., & Gerrard, M. (1989). Effects of upward and downward social comparison on mood states. *Journal of Social and Clinical Psychology, 8*, 14–31.
Goethals, G. R. (1986). Social comparison theory: Lost and found. *Personality and Social Psychology Bulletin, 12*, 261–278.
Goethals, G. R., & Darley, J. (1977). Social comparison theory: An attributional approach. In J. M. Suls & R. M. Miller (Eds.), *Social comparison processes: Theoretical and empirical perspectives* (pp. 259–278). Washington, DC: Hemisphere.
Greenwald, A. G. (1980). Fabrication and revision of personal history. *American Psychologist, 35*, 603–618.
Gruder, C. L. (1971). Determinants of social comparison choices. *Journal of Experimental Social Psychology, 7*, 473–489.
Hakmiller, K. L. (1966). Threat as a determinant of downward comparison. *Journal of Experimental Social Psychology, 2*(Supplement 1), 32–39.
Harter, S. (1985). The need for a developmental perspective in understanding child and adolescent disorders. *Journal of Social and Clinical Psychology, 3*, 484–499.
Heath, L. (1984). Impact of newspapers crime reports on fear of crime: Multimethodological investigation. *Journal of Personality and Social Psychology, 47*, 263–276.
Hornung, C. A., & McClullough, B. C. (1981). Status relationships in dual-employment marriages: Consequences for psychological well-being. *Journal of Marriage and the Family, 43*, 125–141.
Kiesler, S. B. (1966). Stress, affiliation and performance. *Journal of Experimental Research in Personality, 1*, 227–235.
Kuiper, N. A., MacDonald, M. R., & Derry, P. A. (1983). Parameters of a depressive self-schema. In J. Suls & A. G. Greenwald (Eds.), *Psychological perspectives on the self* (Vol. 2, pp. 191–217). Hillsdale, NJ: Lawrence Erlbaum Associates.
Latane, B. (1966). Studies in social comparison: Introduction and overview. *Journal of Experimental Social Psychology, 2*(Supplement 1), 1–5.
Lazarus, R. S., & Folkman, S. (1984). *Stress, appraisal and coping*. New York: Springer.
Levine, J. M., & Green, S. M. (1984). Acquisition of relative performance information: The roles of intrapersonal and interpersonal comparison. *Personality and Social Psychology Bulletin, 10*, 385–393.
Lewicki, P. (1983). Self-image bias in person perception. *Journal of Personality and Social Psychology, 45*, 384, 393.
Marks, G. (1984). Thinking one's abilities are unique and one's opinions are common. *Personality and Social Psychology Bulletin, 10*, 203–208.

Marks, G., & Miller, N. (1987). Research on the false-consensus effect: An empirical and theoretical review. *Psychological Bulletin, 102*, 72–90.

Markus, H., & Kunda, A. (1986). Stability and malleability of the self-concept. *Journal of Personality and Social Psychology, 51*, 858–866.

Miller, D. T., Turnbull, W., & McFarland, C. (1988). Particularistic and universalistic evaluation in the social comparison process. *Journal of Personality and Social Psychology, 55*, 908–917.

Pyszczynski, T., & Greenberg, J. (1987). Self-regulatory preservation and the depressive self-focusing style. *Psychological Bulletin, 102*, 122–138.

Pyszczynski, T., Greenberg, J., & LaPrelle, J. (1985). Social comparison after success and failure: Biased search for information consistent with a self-serving conclusion. *Journal of Experimental Social Psychology, 21*, 195–211.

Sande, G. N., Goethals, G. R., & Radloff, C. E. (1988). Perceiving one's own traits and others': The multifaceted self. *Journal of Personality and Social Psychology, 54*, 13–20.

Sanders, G. S., & Suls, J. (1982). Social comparison, competition, and marriage. *Journal of Marriage and the Family, 44*, 721–730.

Schachter, S. (1959). *The psychology of affiliation.* Stanford, CA: Stanford University Press.

Schulz, R., & Decker, S. (1985). Long-term adjustment to physical disability. *Journal of Personality and Social Psychology, 48*, 1162–1172.

Segal, A. V. (1988). Appraisal of the self-schema construct in cognitive models of depression. *Psychological Bulletin, 103*, 147–162.

Sherman, S. J., Presson, C. C., & Chassin, L. (1984). Mechanisms underlying the false consensus effect: The special role of threats to the self. *Personality and Social Psychology Bulletin, 10*, 127–138.

Sherman, S. J., Presson, C. C., Chassin, L., & Agostinelli, G. (1984). The role of evaluation and similarity principles in the false consensus effect. *Journal of Personality and Social Psychology, 47*, 1244–1262.

Singer, J. E. (1966). Social comparison: Progress and issues. *Journal of Experimental Social Psychology, 2*(Supplement 1), 103–110.

Smith, R. H., & Insko, C. A. (1987). Social comparison choice during ability evaluation. *Personality and Social Psychology Bulletin, 13*, 111–122.

Strube, M. J., & Roemmele, L. A. (1985). Self-enhancement, self-assessment, and self-evaluative task choice. *Journal of Personality and Social Psychology, 49*, 981–993.

Suls, J. M. (1986). Notes on the occasion of social comparison theory's thirtieth birthday. *Personality and Social Psychology Bulletin, 12*, 289–296.

Suls, J. M., & Miller, R. L. (1977). *Social comparison processes: Theoretical and empirical perspectives.* Washington, DC: Hemisphere.

Suls, J., & Wan, C. K. (1987). In search of the false-uniqueness phenomenon: Fear and estimates of social consensus. *Journal of Personality and Social Psychology, 52*, 211–217.

Swallow, S. R., & Kuiper, N. A. (1988). Social comparison and negative self-evaluations: An application to depression. *Clinical Psychology Review, 8*, 55–76.

Swann, W. B., Jr., Griffin, J. J., Jr., Predmore, S. C., & Gaines, B. (1987). The cognitive-affective crossfire: When self-consistency confronts self-enhancement. *Journal of Personality and Social Psychology, 52*, 881–889.

Tabachnik, N., Crocker, J., & Alloy, L. B. (1983). Depression, social comparison, and the false consensus effect. *Journal of Personality and Social Psychology, 45*, 688–699.

Taylor, S. E., & Brown, J. D. (1988). Illusion and well-being: A social-psychological perspective on mental health. *Psychological Bulletin, 103*, 193–210.

Thompson, S. C. (1985). Finding positive meaning in a stressful event and coping. *Basic and Applied Social Psychology, 6*, 279–295.

Watson, D., & Tellegen, A. (1985). Toward a consensual structure of mood. *Psychological Bulletin, 98*, 219–235.

Weiner, B. (1985). An attributional theory of achievement motivation and emotion. *Psychological Review, 92*, 548–573.

Wheeler, L. (1966). Motivation as a determinant of upward comparison. *Journal of Experimental Social Psychology, 2*(Supplement 1), 27–31.

Wheeler, L., Koestner, R., & Driver, R. E. (1982). Related attributes in the choice of comparison others: It may be there, but it isn't all there is. *Journal of Experimental Social Psychology, 18*, 489–500.

Wheeler, L., Shaver, K. G., Jones, R. A., Goethals, G. R., Cooper, J., Robinson, J. E., Gruder, C. L., & Butzine, K. W. (1969). Factors determining the choice of comparison others. *Journal of Experimental Social Psychology, 5*, 219–232.

Wills, T. A. (1974, April). *Happiness, Thanatos, social comparison theory, the gambler's fallacy, and death on the highway*. Colloquium presented to Department of Psychology, University of Oregon, Eugene, OR.

Wills, T. A. (1981). Downward comparison principles in social psychology. *Psychological Bulletin, 90*, 245–271.

Wills, T. A. (1983). Social comparison in coping and help-seeking. In B. M. DePaulo, A. Nadler, & J. D. Fisher (Eds.), *New directions in helping (Vol. 2). Help-seeking* (pp. 109–141). New York: Academic Press.

Wills, T. A. (1986). Discussion remarks on social comparison theory. *Personality and Social Psychology Bulletin, 12*, 282–288.

Wills, T. A. (1987). Downward comparison as a coping mechanism. In C. R. Snyder & C. Ford (Eds.), *Coping with negative life events: Clinical and social-psychological perspectives* (pp. 243–268). New York: Plenum.

Wills, T. A. (in press). Social comparison processes in coping and health. In C. R. Snyder & D. R. Forsyth (Eds.), *Handbook of social and clinical psychology*. New York: Pergamon.

Wilson, S. R., & Benner, L. A. (1971). The effects of self-esteem and situation on comparison choices during ability evaluation. *Sociometry, 34*, 381–397.

Wood, J. V., Taylor, S. E., & Lichtman, R. R. (1985). Social comparison in adjustment to breast cancer. *Journal of Personality and Social Psychology, 49*, 1169–1183.

4 Changing Patterns of Comparative Behavior as Skills Are Acquired: A Functional Model of Self-Evaluation

Diane N. Ruble
New York University

Karin S. Frey
University of Washington

Festinger's (1954) original statement of social comparison emphasized the concept of uncertainty. According to this formulation, people are motivated to compare with others in order to resolve uncertainties about themselves when information available from more objective standards is inadequate. This formulation portrays the potential social comparer as an active seeker and constructor of meaning, strategically selecting information to maximize diagnostic value. Such a formulation is consistent with many theories that portray fundamental human nature as intrinsically driven toward mastery of the environment (Berlyne, 1966; Deci & Ryan, 1985; Harter, 1981; Piaget, 1952; Veroff & Veroff, 1980; White, 1959), and with social developmental approaches that emphasize individual construction during periods of change (e.g., Kohlberg, 1966; Ruble, 1987; Stryker & Statham, 1985).

Certain core features of this depiction of social comparison and self-evaluation have recently been questioned, however. Goethals (1986), for example, argued that a key proposition—that there is a *drive* to evaluate one's opinions and abilities—remains unresolved. He suggested that research findings indicate that "there is more of a drive to think that our opinions are correct and that our abilities are good than to find out the truth" (p. 274). Similarly, Ross, Eyman, and Kishchuk (1986) argued that it is not clear how interested people really are in social comparison information. As Ross et al. suggested, rarely are individuals given a chance to indicate their motivation to acquire social comparison information in relation to other possible standards and in situations involving real life concerns.

The goal of this chapter is to re-examine these issues concerning the drive to self-define and evaluate, emphasizing the strategic and functional aspects of self-evaluation as it serves to maintain goal-directed behavior. Some recent reviews have similarly emphasized the importance of strategic factors, noting the impact of variations in individual goals on social comparison choices and behaviors (Dweck & Leggett, 1988; Nicholls, 1984; Taylor & Lobel, 1989; Tesser, 1986; Wood, 1989). Yet, they have largely neglected a variable that would seem to be critical to understanding when and why different kinds of goals and comparison choices prevail (i.e., level of knowledge and skill development in a particular domain). What one needs to extract from social comparison depends on what one already knows and can do in that domain. Amount of interest in evaluative standards and the form of comparison preferred is likely to be quite different when one is defining a new dimension of the self (e.g., competence as a novice golfer or new parent) than when one already has amassed considerable information relevant to competence in that dimension (Frey & Ruble, 1990).

Such issues have not been completely ignored in the literature. Most notably, in a series of elegant analyses, Trope (1983, 1986) has shown that uncertainty drives a search for diagnostic information, even if that information is likely to result in unflattering conclusions about one's competence. Previous analyses have also made related distinctions concerning forms of information seeking or evaluation in relation to different goals at different stages (Fazio, 1979; Mettee & Smith, 1977; Raynor & Brown, 1985; Veroff & Veroff, 1980). What we are arguing, however, is that the degree and nature of uncertainty change systematically in relation to an individual's emerging knowledge about each significant aspect of self-definition. This perspective leads us to a somewhat unconventional "developmental" analysis, one that operates at two levels: (a) phases in the emerging acquisition of skills—that is, within any given stage of life, people engage in novel tasks and go through distinct phases in acquiring requisite skills (e.g., novice to experienced golfer or reader); (b) stage of life—that is, different points in the lifespan tend to be particularly oriented to one or the other phase of skill acquisition (e.g., young children are likely to be novices at more things than the elderly). We attempt to integrate these two levels within a common framework and thus inform each through insights and research from the other.

In essence, we are applying a developmental analysis to phenomena that are often not considered in this way. In the present model, self-evaluation is conceptualized in dynamic rather than static terms. We suggest that self-evaluation involves different goals at different times, and that these goals change systematically across "development," defined both as skill acquisition and as stage of life. Predictable patterns and forms of assessment should occur in relation to developmental changes. Thus, what has been attributed to general interest or disinterest in social comparison and self-evaluation may be better interpreted in terms of the "fit" between the goals of different phases and the different forms of self-evaluation.

PHASES OF SELF-RELATED SKILL AND KNOWLEDGE ACQUISITION

We can identify four basic phases in skill acquisition that should influence interest in and use of self-evaluative information, including social comparison (see Fig. 4.1). First, initial task assessment involves task-definition goals (i.e., defining the nature of the dimension, learning what abilities and evaluative standards are involved, and adopting an orientation toward information that will foster improvement and mastery). Second, initial competence assessment occurs after the nature and meaning of the task has been constructed, and interest shifts from knowing what the task is to inferring one's capacities and limits. The third phase, maintenance of adaptive strategies, occurs after conclusions about competence have been reached. Maintenance efforts may include forming plans and sub-goals, self-monitoring, and selectively focusing on information relevant to outcomes (e.g., finishing a race or project) or process (e.g., enjoyment). Self-evaluation at this phase primarily entails monitoring progress toward goals rather than competence assessment. Completion of goals or extended periods of goal-outcome discrepancy will usher in the fourth phase, reassessment of competence level and goals, with a resumption of active interest in information relevant to competence appraisal.

This model assumes some level of initial commitment to the activity before this self-evaluative process is set into motion. Although not a formal part of the model, it is clear that, at least for adults, some form of pre-engagement assessment phase occurs before such a commitment is made. Before even trying a major new activity, people must determine whether there is an adequate person x situation match. For example, a 65-year-old competitive runner reported that she decided to start running after observing participants in a 10 km race. "I wanted to see if ladies my age could do it." In addition, individuals can make preliminary assessments of whether or not outcomes are likely to be satisfying based on assessments of competence on related activities.

A few additional qualifications about the model should be noted at the outset. The exact nature of each phase seems likely to vary somewhat with changing cognitive abilities and experiences of individuals at different levels

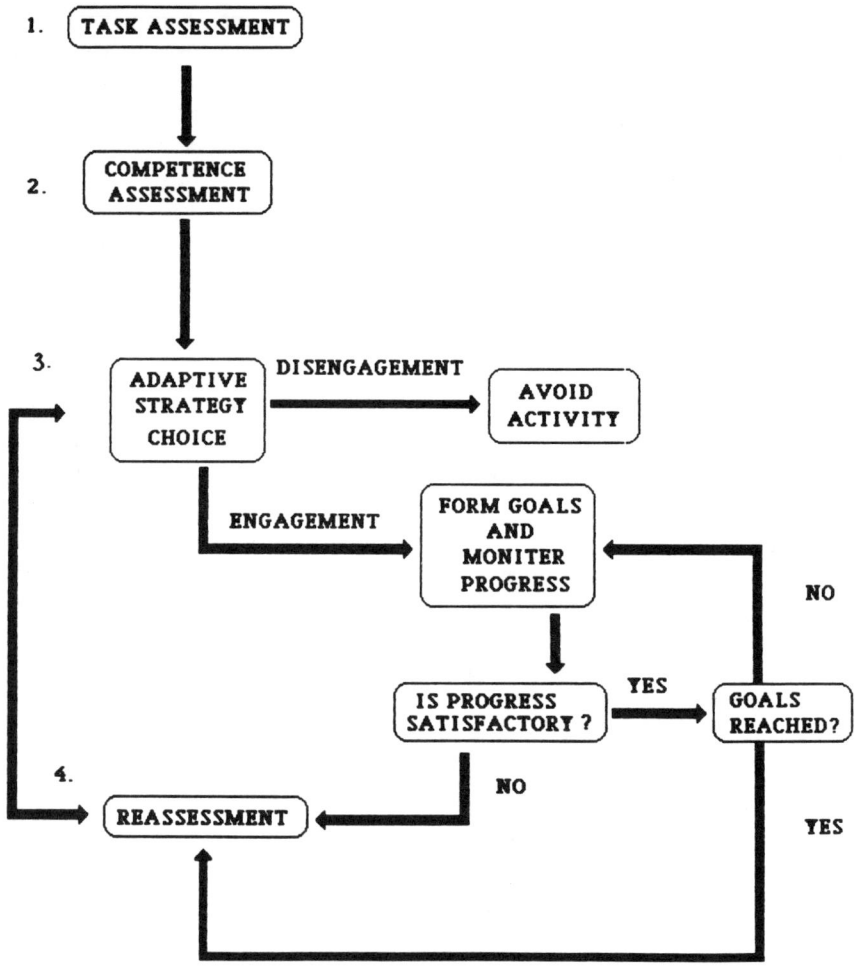

FIG. 4.1. Phases of self-related skill and knowledge acquisition.

of development, defined in terms of age. Very young children, for example, may lack a normative or differentiated concept of ability (Nicholls & Miller, 1984). Moreover, maintenance of goal-directed activity may require greater flexibility and inventiveness in older adults, as skills decline in relation to capabilities at younger ages (Frey & Ruble, in prep.).

Finally, the distinctions across phases are not likely to be as clearcut as portrayed here. There is little doubt that some level of competence assessment occurs in all phases, particularly if external reward structures (e.g., grades, grants, salaries) emphasize competition (Ames, 1986; Jagacinski & Nicholls, 1987). Moreover, there are individual differences in orientations relevant to these phases, such as orientations toward certainty versus uncertainty (Sorrentino & Short, 1986), fear of invalidity and need for cognitive structure (Kruglanski & Mayseless, 1987), autonomy versus control causality orientations (Deci & Ryan, 1987), and the importance accorded to competence assessment versus other goals (Dweck & Leggett, 1988). Nevertheless, we believe that the skill acquisition phase can explain a number of variations in evaluative behavior above and beyond these other influences. In order to illustrate such points, we restrict discussion of such qualifications in the presentation of the four phases.

Initial Task Assessment

What tasks confront an individual anticipating change such as learning a new skill (e.g., reading, playing piano, or golf) or undergoing a change in social circumstances (e.g., entering school, expecting a first baby, beginning a new job)? It seems highly unlikely that the first question posed by someone picking up a golf club for the first time would be "How good a golfer am I?" Instead, initial questions are likely to concern pragmatics (e.g., how hard to swing; how to get the ball in the air) or future orientation and improvement (e.g., "How far is it possible to hit the ball?"; "Will the second lesson go better than the first?").

A major prediction derived from our analysis is that level of interest in evaluative information should change over time. Because initial task assessment is a phase of considerable uncertainty, the need for information should be high as individuals engage in constructing personal meaning from the changes they anticipate and experience. In one study primiparous women showed peaks of information gathering for the specific topics corresponding to phases of childbearing (information concerning early pregnancy, labor and delivery, caring for a newborn), and the level of information seeking for all topics was considerably higher among pregnant women than among women desiring a child in the near future but not pregnant (Deutsch, Ruble, Fleming, Brooks-Gunn, & Stangor, 1988). Moreover, other findings suggested that women in the early stages of pregnancy were engaged in a particularly active search relative to those at other stages. Women at this stage attached the greatest importance to books, the one source of information that can only be obtained actively (information from other sources, such as friends, can be obtained passively). Such findings suggest that motivation to gain the specific information necessary for role acquisition changes quantitatively and qualitatively with movement into the role.

What form of information is likely to be sought during a construction phase? Several formulations have stressed the importance of temporal comparison during periods of rapid change. Albert (1977) suggests that comparison with self over time is advantageous during periods of transition for two reasons: (a) it provides a means of helping individuals to maintain a sense of personal stability by allowing them to evaluate and adjust to changes in self-definition over time; and (b) it provides an index of growth and improvement and a basis for predicting the future. Similarly, developmental analyses have suggested that temporal comparison precedes social comparison (Dweck & Elliott, 1983; Nicholls & Miller, 1984; Suls & Mullen, 1982; Veroff, 1969). Suls and Mullen (1982) argued that the use of temporal comparison is likely to be especially frequent for preschoolers because of developmental spurts occurring during this period, and associated large increments in improvement should make temporal comparison especially gratifying.

An analysis of the requirements of task assessment suggests that some forms of social comparison may be even more important than temporal comparison, at least at the beginning of Phase 1. One form of social comparison, observational learning, is widely recognized as important to learning and evaluating a performance (Bandura, 1986; Berger, 1977). We may look to others to evaluate our own behavior, as generally assumed, but we may also turn to social comparison to define the parameters of the task in question and to learn the techniques for acquiring relevant skills (Fazio, 1979; Ruble, 1983). A child's notion of what it means to play the piano may change after witnessing a peer actually playing a tune, instead of just pounding the keys. Such a demonstration may also illustrate critical aspects of skill acquisition, such as the role of musical notation in learning a composition.

Another form of social comparison, identifying the limits or boundaries of superior performance, is also essential to task definition. Novices may look to more experienced others, even those at the top, to set goals for themselves and imagine what is possible, as when Greg Louganis' $2\frac{1}{2}$ inward tuck dive is observed for the first time. Presumably, this function of social comparison is related to what Festinger meant by unidirectional drive upward. This idea has also been used recently to help explain some apparent anomalies in the study of social comparison among cancer victims—that people seek information about dissimilar others in more favorable circumstances, but appear to be little affected by comparisons with them (Wood, 1989). The explanation used in such cases is that upward comparison serves as a source of inspiration and not evaluation or competition. A 55-year-old runner, for example, maintained that she ran better in the company of older persons because it gave her "future running hope" (Frey & Ruble, in prep.).

Social comparison is also involved in two other goals during this phase. First, the value of learning an activity is strongly influenced by observing the preferences of others (e.g., "All of the other kids get to take ski lessons."). Second, observational learning may help define the standards

TABLE 4.1
Goals and Standards Associated with Phase 1—Initial Task Assessment

Goals	Standards
Define task parameters (e.g., range of possible performance; component skills)	Absolute standards
	Social comparison
Learn techniques for acquiring and improving skills	Observational learning
Define personal relevance and value	Social comparison
	Absolute comparison
Assess progress toward mastery	Absolute standards
	Temporal standards
Define standards relevant to assessing competent performance	Observational learning

of evaluation that are informative or customary for a particular endeavor (e.g., whether a child joining the swim team hears others emphasizing self-referenced standards—"personal best" finish times—or performance in competition). The availability of different standards available is constrained by the nature of the activity. For example, finish times are not informative to open-water rowers, who confront dramatically different current, wind and wave conditions across races. Accordingly, the words, "personal best," are not heard in the post-race conversations of ocean racers.

One other form of comparison, that involving absolute standards, may be utilized at this phase, singly or in combination with temporal or social comparison. The definition of some tasks and an assessment of whether one is learning the requisite skills may sometimes involve a relatively objective physical representation (e.g., staying upright on a bicycle). Temporal comparison may provide useful clues to what does not work (e.g., the handle bars cannot be turned too quickly), and social comparison may be an essential element in representing the absolute standard (riding down the street without wobbling). The activity the individual is primarily engaged in, however, may be better described as oriented toward reaching the absolute standard, rather than either temporal or social comparison.

In summary, initial task assessment involves several different goals and standards, which are listed in Table 4.1. Self-referenced autonomous standards (absolute and temporal comparison) appear to be key to assessing improvement, and somewhat less involved in defining the task and its personal value. Social comparison appears to have more wide-ranging impact, being involved in almost every aspect of this first phase, with the possible exception of assessing progress toward mastery. Although these Phase 1 functions typically do not involve social comparison in the sense of self-evaluation of competence, we do not mean to imply that such concerns are never involved. Social comparison of ability level is crucial, for example, to selecting a squash partner who will maximize enjoyment and minimize the discomfort of blatantly uneven matches. Similarly, a man being watched by his wife at his first golf lesson may be concerned about embarrassing himself. Other such self-presentational concerns may arise anytime one is aware of one's performance being evaluated by another, and other such contextual variations may make self-evaluative concerns relevant even when the dominant goal is task definition or improvement (Nicholls, 1984).

Competence Assessment

Once an individual knows how a dimension is defined and the basics of developing mastery, attention can shift to inferring one's likely capacity at the task. We suggest that this is the phase Festinger was referring to when self-evaluation was described as a drive. Uncertainty about competence levels remains high, as in the task assessment phase, but rate of improvement typically slows in this phase, resulting in a more reliable base for assessing competence. Consistent with views of individuals as motivated to understand and master puzzles and contradictions in their environment, we would argue that individuals need to reduce this uncertainty about competence if the particular area of self-knowledge is relevant to future functioning. As Festinger suggested, performance information based on absolute, objective standards is often insufficient and social comparison with similar others is required. Temporal comparison is still informative about improvement, and when coupled with social comparison might be highly diagnostic about competence by indicating how quickly one learns. By itself, however, it cannot provide the kind of information necessary to indicate certain key issues about competence (e.g., to allow sensible choices for the future, such as choice of major or occupation, or even predictions about likely grades). Accurate competence assessment is essential for optimizing outcomes in important endeavors (Trope, 1983).

One might expect to see a preoccupation with social comparison of ability at the competence assessment phase. Butler (1989c) showed a developmental change in reactions to competitive versus noncompetitive conditions that illustrate this point. Based on Nicholls' (1984) ideas that different situations elicit different goals, Butler predicted that noncompetition would lead to interest in mastery-related information (i.e., absolute standards), whereas competition would rouse interest in information relevant to competence assessment. In contrast to these predictions, the information search of younger (5 years) children suggested interest in mastery orientation in both conditions, whereas older (10 years) children seemed interested in ability appraisal in both conditions. To the extent that these age differences parallel phases of skill acquisition on school-related tasks (a not unreasonable assumption), such differences suggest that current goals and motivations may dominate search over and above the usual influences of variations in context.

Social comparison is not the only way individuals engage in competence assessment. Proximity to meeting more absolute standards also provides important information. For some domains, there may be little use for social comparison even in the competence assessment phase. If one is engaged in social services, social comparison would seem to be difficult to utilize as a standard of competence. One might attend to the relative number of clients being assisted, or the relative speed with which one completes a case. Such criteria seem at best tangential to competence assessment in this area, however. Instead, more absolute, personal standards (e.g., changing the life situation of the client in some way) may be relied on, and social comparison may be of most use in formulating alternative standards of self-assessment. Thus, comparisons with others might allow a young caseworker to assess what kinds of direct feedback to expect from clients or what strategies are most useful in different situations.

Regardless of the specific information used, the individual in this phase attempts to make realistic, rather than self-enhancing or validating self-assessments, because unrealistic goals are likely to lead to eventual failure. Moreover, because a conclusion has yet to be formed, the information search can remain relatively open, with information leading to both negative and positive conclusions being considered. There is considerable evidence in both the developmental and social psychological literatures that one's knowledge base influences information seeking and information processing (Bjorkland, 1987; Fiske & Taylor, 1984; Markus & Zajonc, 1985; Stangor & Ruble, 1990). The development of gender schemata, for example, is associated with a shift toward better memory for information consistent (vs. inconsistent) with gender stereotypes (Liben & Signorella, 1987; Ruble & Stangor, 1986; Stangor & Ruble, 1990).

Support for this idea with respect to competence assessment is provided in part by Trope's (1983, 1986) findings that uncertainty leads people to select the most diagnostic information, regardless of the likely implications of that information for self-esteem. A conclusion that one has low ability may be less painful if it is made prior to a commitment to pursue competitive goals, and perhaps experiencing multiple failures. With a realistic self-assessment, the individual can form attainable goals or choose to withdraw from the activity. Thus, realistic self-assessment at this phase may protect self-esteem in the long run, at least to the extent that the individual is free to choose future goals (Trope, 1983). If an individual cannot withdraw from an activity in which competence is perceived to be low, or if situational demands make it difficult to emphasize process or improvement goals over competitive ones, diagnostic information may best be avoided in the service of maintaining self-esteem. Instead, such conditions may lead to self-enhancing assessment, in which truly diagnostic information is avoided or deemphasized.

Self-enhancement is well documented when self-esteem or personal well-being are threatened. Considerable research suggests that individuals experiencing threat often make downward comparisons, presumably indicating attempts at self-enhancement (Levine & Green, 1984; Wills, 1981; Wood, 1989). A careful developmental analysis of such individuals may or may not indicate phases of accurate competence assessment. Longitudinal studies of cancer victims suggest that whereas a considerable amount of initial task assessment activity appears to occur (individuals prefer to spend time with victims who are doing better than they), when self-assessment activity does occur, it appears to involve downward comparison (Taylor & Lobel, 1989). Given the inability to withdraw from the situation, such apparently nonrealistic assessments may constitute the optimal adaptive approach. It may even be that under such circumstances, the initial competence assessment phase is bypassed in favor of validating a conclusion that makes optimism and continued effort possible. In this sense their apparently self-enhancing comparisons may represent behavior characteristic of the next stage.

Maintenance of Adaptive Strategies

Once an individual has defined task requirements and has attained competence at the activity, several alternative directions may ensue, as shown in Fig. 4.1. A critical deciding point is whether or not engagement in the activity will continue. Information about the demands or rewards of the task, taken together with inferences about likely competence and outcomes, are central to determining the most adaptive choice of action. If competence or reward potential is perceived as low, individuals may choose to discontinue participation and withdraw from further self-evaluation at this activity. If disengagement is desired but not possible, psychological disengagement may result. Carver and Scheier (1985) suggested that helpless behavior results from the thwarted desire to withdraw from an activity or situation. The characteristics of learned helplessness may represent a mental or psychological disengagement when actual disengagement is prevented. In this case, we might expect self-handicapping strategies (Jones & Berglas, 1978) and devaluation of the activity (Harter, 1986; Tesser, 1986) to be employed in the service of protecting self-esteem. The formation of school cliques whose members espouse antiacademic values (Ruble, Grosovsky, Frey, & Cohen, in press) is probably an illustration of such a goal.

Once an individual has chosen continued engagement, subgoals and plans to maintain the activity are formed (Carver & Scheier, 1981; Kirschenbaum, 1985). For example, a promising, young sculler may resolve to row three times a week for 2 months and take a wilderness rowing trip in preparation for his or her first open-water race. As shown in Fig. 4.1, evaluative activity is likely to emphasize self-monitoring of plans and progress rather than assessment of inherent capability. Moreover, individuals can optimize positive outcomes by strategically emphasizing particular goals and standards (Levine & Green, 1984; Masters & Keil, 1987; Tesser, 1986). Individuals who conclude they have low ability at a particular activity may choose continued participation but emphasize process goals, such as pure enjoyment or the accompanying social interaction. The benefits of a strategic choice of goals and standards are not limited to low ability individuals. One with high perceived competence may enhance self-esteem by emphasizing competitive performance evaluation and de-emphasizing other aspects of the endeavor.

As long as plans and subgoals are met with some regularity, the sense of certainty provided by initial competence assessment makes additional assessment efforts unnecessary. Support for this contention comes from several sources. Once a relatively certain conclusion is reached or a commitment made to a particular point of view, active information seeking (Frey, 1986) and interest in diagnostic assessment information (Trope, 1986) are both reduced. In fact, a continued emphasis on evaluation may distract from mastery efforts (Butler, 1989b; Nicholls, 1984) and prove counterproductive in terms of motivation. A person who focuses on possible inadequacies may jeopardize persistence and progress toward goals (Ahrens, 1987). At this phase, Goethals (1986) may have been correct in suggesting that there is little evidence supporting Festinger's proposed motive to engage in self-evaluation—that it occurs primarily when such information is forced upon the individual. Once initial uncertainty is reduced, self-assessment of ability (as opposed to self-monitoring of progress) may be largely passive and even avoided (Brickman & Bulman, 1977).

Competence assessment is often inescapable, however. For many activities, social comparison information is readily available and highly salient, such that comparative assessment may occur automatically, whether desired or not (Goethals, 1986). What is the nature of competence assessment at such times, given that the individual is likely to be somewhat committed to the self-assessment already made? Considerable evidence suggests that additional information will tend to be interpreted in ways that validate conclusions already formed (Higgins & Bargh, 1987). Interestingly, the latter process may occur even when conclusions about the self are negative and the subsequent feedback is positive (Swann, 1983).

Both cognitive and motivational mechanisms have been proposed as explanations for the tendency to validate conclusions already formed. It may represent standard schema-driven processing effects (Fiske & Taylor, 1984), in that strong expectations may serve as retrieval cues for congruent information (Srull, Lichtenstein, & Rothbart, 1985) and may lead individuals to ignore inconsistent information (Crocker, Hannah, & Weber, 1983).[1] There are also numerous indications that people tend to perceive themselves in more positive terms than objective evidence suggests is true (see Taylor & Brown, 1988, for a review). Selective information processing may take the form of downward comparison, as discussed earlier with respect to cancer victims, or it may take the form of distortions or attribution processes designed to make the new information *fit* with preconceptions (Ross & Fletcher, 1985). There may also be a built-in positive *drift*, such that performance feedback is perceived as somewhat more positive than it is. This is particularly likely to occur when individuals do not fully process information, as is often the case at this phase for both the cognitive and motivational reasons discussed previously.

This is a time when a more functional, strategic approach to evaluative information might be seen, with discrepant or negative information being ignored or discounted in order to maintain goal-directed activity. Because most social comparison studies involve adult subjects already quite experienced and knowledgeable about the tasks involved, such studies are probably tapping maintenance processes. Recent conclusions that people seem to exhibit highly strategic approaches to evaluation (i.e., to pick and choose different standards, to utilize them selectively, even sometimes to manufacture them; e.g., Suls, 1986; Wood, 1989) are consistent with this argument.

A cautionary note may be in order here. The emphasis of our model is on adaptive self-evaluation in the service of goal directed activity. Simply because adaptive strategies are possible during this phase does not mean they will necessarily be employed. As already mentioned, certain individual differences may make it difficult for some people to relinquish competence-assessment goals (Dweck & Leggett, 1988) even when they are no longer functional for mastery and satisfaction at the task.

---

[1] To illustrate, failure to evaluate oneself negatively on the basis of unflattering social comparison information (Ruble, Eisenberg, Feldman, & Higgins, in prep.; Stevens & Jones, 1976) may not be a motivated defensive bias, as usually assumed. Instead, because an ability schema in the relevant domain is already well established, the new information may not be incorporated into the existing schema and thus not fully processed or remembered.

Reassessment of Competence and Goals

Although maintenance processes may result in satisfaction with task engagement for many years, certain conditions may elicit a need to reassess one or more of the elements involved in maintaining engagement (see Fig. 4.1). First, a goal defined in absolute terms can be reached and thus no longer provides a basis for continued engagement. A golfer whose primary goal has been to beat his or her father or to break into the 80s will need to reassess plans and goals once these outcomes have been attained. Similarly, given that skill domains often consist of ordered levels, people will need to engage in reassessment of competence to decide whether to proceed from a lower to an upper level. In either of these cases, individuals have several options at this point. They may decide that competence is adequate and proceed to the next level; they may change goals to emphasize process (e.g., enjoying the beauty of the golf course setting) rather than outcome; or they may disengage and switch to alternative activities.

Second, consistent large discrepancies between goals, plans, and performance outcomes are likely to reintroduce uncertainty regarding competence. The necessity of reassessing goals and standards is clear if we consider performance stagnation. During the maintenance phase, even individuals of mediocre ability can gain pleasure from seeing signs of improvement via temporal comparison, whereas constant reminders of their relative incompetence via social comparison may be expected to undermine intrinsic motivation (Butler, 1989a; Nicholls, 1984). This conclusion contains an important presupposition, however: that the individuals are continuing to improve. What happens when asymptote is reached (e.g., when a golfer has reached his or her limit at a score of 85) or progress slows (e.g., a professor is no longer able to publish 10 articles per year)? In such cases, reassessment of goals and standards of competence assessment may be necessary to avert flagging motivation and declining self-esteem (Ahrens, 1987).

We tested this hypothesis recently in a questionnaire study of 153 male and 84 female runners participating in active competition (Frey & Ruble, in prep.). On the basis of self-reports, subjects were grouped into three *performance phases*: improving, stable, declining. As would be expected, runners whose performances were improving were more satisfied with their performance over the last year and in the last race than runners whose performances were stable or declining. More directly relevant to the present analysis, performance phase was associated with preferred goals and standards of evaluation. Improving runners were more likely than declining runners to refer to finish time as a standard of comparison but less likely to refer to a competitor. Similarly, declining runners were more likely to refer to satisfaction with competitive results than improving and stable runners, and less likely to cite changes in time as a source of satisfaction. Finally, when asked to rank the importance of racing and running program goals, runners with declining performance rated competition with similar others higher than those whose skills were stable or improving; and stable and declining runners ranked the importance of improving performance times lower than improving runners.

The reassessment phase contains elements of the first two phases, as appropriate standards of evaluation and true level of competence need to be reconsidered.[2] If the resulting decision is continued engagement, concerns will return to maintenance of goal-directed activity. This conceptualization is similar in many ways to the hierarchies of negative or discrepancy-reducing feedback loops proposed by Carver and Scheier (1981, 1985) to describe self-regulatory behavior. Our description has focused on the higher level *action programs* that decide which goals will be chosen to represent the self, as knowledge and skill level in a given domain develops. A developmental perspective suggests that these goals probably show similar changes across the lifespan, as well.

IMPLICATIONS FOR AGE-RELATED PREDICTIONS AND FINDINGS

We have suggested that the phases of skill acquisition should show parallels to age-related trends. In this section, we consider to what extent previous age-related analyses are consistent with the skill acquisition phases described here, and how well available data support such prediction.

Changes in Early Childhood

To our knowledge, every analysis of the development of orientations toward achievement activities and/or self-evaluation in young children (approximate age range: 3–10 years) suggests that initial orientations should be autonomous (absolute and temporal standards), and subsequent orientations should involve concern with competence and social comparison. These same predictions emerge even when there are quite different bases for suggesting them. Veroff (1969) suggested that because the young child is egocentric and has not yet encountered external pressures for social comparison, initial achievement strivings are based on internalized, au-

---

[2] Note, however, that an original assessment of incompetence is likely to endure if that assessment led to psychological or physical disengagement. As shown in Fig. 4.1, reassessment is stimulated by monitoring goal progress. Without goal-directed activity, reassessment is thus unlikely.

tonomous standards, turning to social comparison with any regularity only after 6–9 years of age. Suls and colleagues (Suls, 1986; Suls & Mullen, 1982; Suls & Sanders, 1982) suggested that in addition to such limitations, the rapid advance in skills evidenced by preschool children should make temporal comparisons particularly gratifying. During the early years of school, cognitive skills present by age 4, together with increased opportunities, pressures, and satisfactions should lead to increases in social comparison (cf. Masters & Keil, 1987). Finally, similar predictions are made on the basis of changing conceptions about competence (Butler, 1989c; Dweck & Elliott, 1983; Nicholls & Miller, 1984), often coupled with predictions concerning changes in the social context (Higgins & Parsons, 1983; Ruble, 1983; Stipek, 1984).

Social Comparison Standards. To what extent do existing data support these developmental predictions? There is considerable evidence that use of social comparison information for self-assessment of competence increases during the early years of school. When children younger than 7 years are presented with social comparison information about task performance, they show little or no use of this information in evaluating their own competence (Aboud, 1985; Butler, 1990; Ruble, Boggiano, Feldman, & Loebl, 1980; Ruble, Parsons, & Ross, 1976; Stipek & Tannatt, 1984), despite indications that they know who got more correct and can judge the outcome of another's performance on the basis of social comparison information (Ruble, Grosovsky, Frey, & Cohen, in press; Stipek, 1984).

Research from other paradigms shows a similar pattern. First, Veroff (1969) showed that younger children rarely select a task sufficiently challenging to demonstrate their competence when challenge is defined in social comparison terms, whereas by third grade over 50% do (see also Feld, Ruhland, & Gold, 1979). Second, children's assessments of their own relative performance in classrooms are quite unrealistic until after the early years of school (Nicholls & Miller, 1984; Stipek, 1984). Third, the importance of competitive success increases with age during the early school years (Butler, 1989a, 1989c, 1990; Feldman & Ruble, 1977; McClintock, Moskowitz, & McClintock, 1977).

Fourth, children's concern with social comparison revealed in fantasy increases until approximately 7 years of age (Feld et al., 1979).[3] Fifth, behaviors based on judgments of competence appear to be affected by social comparison for older children, even though younger children are affected by other sources of competence feedback (Boggiano & Ruble,

---

[3] In this study, the measure was not strictly defined in social comparison terms, as it involved reference to standards of excellence, such as grades, as well as competitive activity.

1979; Spear & Armstrong, 1978). Sixth, younger children rarely refer to social comparison as a reason for self-evaluative judgments, relative to older children (Harter & Pike, 1984; Ruble et al., in press), and are less likely to mention self-evaluation as a reason for engaging in social comparison (Butler, 1989c; Feldman & Ruble, 1977). Finally, there is an increase during the school years in seeking social comparison information (Butler, 1989c; Frey & Ruble, 1985; Ruble, Feldman, & Boggiano, 1976; Ruble & Flett, 1988).

Such findings do not imply, of course, that young children are uninterested in or never use social comparison. Preschool children exhibit considerable interest in peers doing similar work and in competition (Butler, 1989a, 1989c; Heckhausen, 1982; McClintock et al., 1977; Pepitone, 1972), and seem to want to make sure that they are getting their fair share of rewards (Masters, 1971). Similarly, kindergarten children use social comparison of performance as a basis for self-rewarding behavior (Smith, Davidson, & France, 1987). Preschool and primary grade children also make reference to social comparison in spontaneous verbalizations in a classroom (Mosatche & Bragonier, 1981), although the frequency of such comparison increases with age through first grade (Chafel, 1988; Frey & Ruble, 1985). Kindergarten children also appear to have reasonably accurate knowledge about some kinds of performance hierarchies, such as running skills (Morris & Nemcek, 1982). Children under 7 may even use social comparison for competence assessment (Levine, Snyder, & Mendez-Caratini, 1982; Ruble et al., in press) when the judgment involves specific performance outcome rather than general ability or social comparison is made highly salient (Ruble et al., in press; Ruble, Eisenberg, Feldman, & Higgins, in prep.; Suls, 1986).

Although the literature suggests little or no spontaneous use of social comparison for self-assessment of competence until 7–8 years of age, many studies show considerable interest in social comparison by younger children. How may this apparent contradiction across studies be explained? A few studies have suggested that the social comparison behavior of children at different ages is directed toward different goals (Butler, 1989a, 1989c; Frey & Ruble, 1985). Butler (1989c) showed quite clearly that what may appear to be the same social comparison behavior (glancing at peers) actually has quite different meaning and implications depending on the children's ages. For younger children, such information seeking seemed to reflect interest in learning the task (in our terms Phase 1 goals), whereas for older children, it indicated interest in competence assessment. In addition, younger children explained their interest in peers in terms of mastery goals, whereas older children gave ability assessment reasons.

Thus, social comparison among preschool children may indicate interest and awareness of such information, but not necessarily that they are basing self-evaluations of competence on comparative standards. A related argument has recently been proposed as part of a lifespan analysis of shifts in the forms of comparison processes by Suls and colleagues (Suls, 1986; Suls & Mullen, 1982). They make a compelling case that the importance of similar others for competence assessment will not be understood until after certain critical cognitive skills have developed at approximately 8–9 years. They argue that when social comparison occurs in children aged 5–8, it will be indiscriminate, as likely to involve adults as same-age peers. Because information from adults is at least as useful as that from same-age peers for meeting task definition and mastery goals, their emphasis on developmental changes in the form of comparison is compatible with the present emphasis on changing goals.

Consistent with a phase of skill acquisition analysis, there is also evidence that goals shift later in elementary school from competence assessment to more mastery-oriented standards. In an early analysis, Veroff (1969) suggested that after children had accommodated to social comparison motivations during the early to middle years of school, they would integrate autonomous with social comparison standards in a more flexible, adaptive achievement orientation. A series of recent studies provides evidence for this idea. When asked whether success in terms of social versus autonomous standards would provide greater pleasure, children younger than fourth grade select social comparison, whereas after this age there is a dramatic shift to autonomous comparison (Frey & Ruble, 1990). Similarly, older children sometimes show a greater impact of temporal as opposed to social standards in their self-evaluations (Ruble et al., in press). Finally, interest in self-assessment information shifts with age from social to autonomous comparison, especially for high ability children, and this shift is associated with greater certainty regarding competence level (Ruble & Flett, 1988). These findings support our prediction that children who have completed initial competence assessment will return to temporal and absolute standards, those most likely to maintain motivation and goal-directed activity in a population whose skills are improving.

In summary, there is considerable evidence concerning the development of comparative self-assessment of competence. With few exceptions, the data support the idea that interest in and use of social comparison increases during the early school years. Less evidence is available regarding a subsequent decrease, although what there is supports the proposed shift to an activity maintenance phase when self-assessment goals are less salient.

Autonomous Standards. The other part of the analysis—that young children's evaluations emphasize the temporal comparison and absolute standards typical of initial task assessment—receives inconsistent support. On the one hand, relative to older children, younger children are more likely to: (a) refer to autonomous standards and mastery goals (e.g., getting all problems correct) (Butler, 1989c; Feldman & Ruble, 1977), (b) use absolute standards for self-evaluation (Boggiano & Ruble, 1979; Heckhausen, 1984; Ruble, Parsons & Ross, 1976), and (c) engage in social comparison behavior relevant to task definition (Frey & Ruble, 1985). Consistent with the idea that young children's social comparisons are oriented toward task definition and improvement, engaging in social comparison is positively related to quality of performance in preschool children (Azmitia, 1988; Butler, 1989c, 1990; Morrison & Kuhn, 1983), but negatively associated for older children (Butler, 1989a, 1989c).

On the other hand, there is little support for the hypothesis that young children are particularly likely to rely on temporal standards. In contrast to predictions, two studies found no developmental decrease in autonomous motivation, as defined by children's preferences for challenging tasks, in relation to their own previous performance (Feld et al., 1979; Veroff, 1969). Indeed, Veroff found that autonomous motivation peaked at third grade and was lowest in kindergarten. Also, several studies found that preschool children make little use of feedback about prior performance in assessing their competence or likelihood of future success relative to older children (see Stipek, 1984; Stipek & MacIver, 1989, for reviews). Finally, direct comparisons of children's interest in or use of temporal versus social comparison standards also fail to support the developmental hypothesis. Young children were much more likely to refer to social than to temporal comparison when asked which kind of success would offer greater satisfaction and were no more likely to use temporal than social comparison feedback in their performance evaluations (Ruble et al., in press, in prep.).

In summary, the research generally supports the idea that younger children are especially responsive to absolute standards. The hypothesis that younger children are more responsive to temporal feedback because of its relevance to assessing improvement and mastery may need to be reevaluated, however. It may be that young children do not engage in any kind of systematic comparisons across performances for self-evaluation. Making temporal comparisons involves the same number of mental elements and type of integration (i.e., comparing another performance with one's present performance) as does social comparison (Higgins, 1989), which is not typically utilized for self-assessment of competence until fourth grade (Ruble et al., 1980). Thus, temporal standards may be developmentally appropriate Phase 1 standards for older but not younger children.

It is also possible that the research, failing to find greater use of temporal feedback relative to social feedback, does not measure Phase 1 task assessment. Some of the measures used are ones that may be quite familiar to kindergarten-age children, and they may be more concerned with competence assessment than with task definition and improvement. If so, why do we not see more evidence of competence assessment in kindergarten children? It may be that children use different criteria for competence assessment, such as effort or self-generated absolute assessments of performance (e.g., staying within the lines), and that researchers have overlooked these forms of competence assessment thus far.

We have previously suggested (Frey & Ruble, 1990) that social comparisons made by young children emphasize meeting developmental or age norms rather than placing high in a hierarchy of individual differences. Primary grade children do not have an accurate representation of classroom hierarchies, nor their own level within such hierarchies (Frey & Ruble, 1987; Nicholls & Miller, 1984; Stipek, 1984). In contrast, age differences are highly salient to young children (Edwards, 1984). Also, the cognitive requirements of assessments based on age norms are well within the grasp of preschool and kindergarten children, requiring only a judgment of like or not like rather than an understanding of seriation (Flavell, 1984). Indirect support for this hypothesis comes from evidence showing that preschool and kindergarten children make comparisons based on similarities between themselves and peers, whereas comparisons based on differences are common among first grade children (Frey & Ruble, 1985; Gottman & Parkhurst, 1980), becoming increasingly frequent with age.[4]

Using perceived age norms (being like the other kids) or other simple standards for self-evaluation, kindergarten children may have satisfied themselves regarding their competence, a satisfaction that evaporates as children develop a concept of ability based on individual differences. As each element of a mature ability concept develops, a new element of uncertainty is added regarding competence assessment. In effect, young children's performance standards change with their cognitions, resulting in an extended period of competence assessment.

Lifespan Analyses. The developmental framework we have sketched so far may also show some parallels to age-related changes in adulthood. For

---

[4] On the surface, Suls' (1986) suggestion that indiscriminate rather than similarity comparison occurs at this age seems to conflict with this evidence of "similarity" comparisons. There is a conceptual distinction between these two forms of similarity judgments, however. The first concerns whether or not an individual or group shares common features, whereas the second is the goal of the comparison: to evaluate similarities or differences. The former is typically what is referred to in the social comparison literature, and the nature of that original choice is assumed to determine the nature of the subsequent comparison (e.g., a comparison with Jack Nicklaus is referred to as one of dissimilarity, whereas a comparison with a comparable duffer is one of similarity) (Atkinson, 1986). We would argue, however, that, in general, mature forms of comparisons of ability all involve dissimilarity, to a greater or lesser extent. Adults compare with similar others to determine if they are performing better or worse. Young children, however, compare to assure themselves that they are the "same."

areas of self-knowledge that emerge in childhood, such as school-related abilities, the motivational processes characteristic of the maintenance and reassessment phases should predominate. For areas of self-knowledge that emerge in adulthood, such as job-related competence or parenting, young adulthood should be characterized somewhat more frequently by initial task assessment and middle adulthood by maintenance and reassessment with competence assessment occurring in between. Job-related competence in the later adult years is likely to be characterized by maintenance processes that deemphasize temporal comparison and/or stagnation. Any new activities undertaken during this period will involve initial task assessment and initial competence assessment. The individual's enthusiasm may accordingly be higher for these new activities than for later activities.

There have been few theoretical and empirical analyses relevant to addressing such hypotheses. Suls and colleagues (Suls, 1986; Suls & Mullen, 1982) have proposed a lifespan model of comparison, suggesting that relative preferences for similarity rather than indiscriminate social comparison and for temporal comparison may be more or less functional at different points in the lifespan. According to this analysis, after 8 years social comparison will tend to be with similar (same-age) others: This orientation continues through young adulthood, an assertion supported by a large number of studies with college students. For later stages, Suls and his colleagues propose a return to indiscriminate social comparison and then to temporal comparison. Although this description applies well to some activities (Suls, 1986), it does not seem to represent others fully (Frey & Ruble, in prep.). We suggest that the comparative standards preferred by adults will probably depend on a number of factors (e.g., the phase of skill acquisition, the availability of different types of comparative information, the implications of each type for self-esteem, and the importance the particular activity holds for the individual).

There is one other line of relevant research and analysis: that concerned with stage of life changes in motivations and goals. First, theories of personal growth, such as those of Maslow and of Rogers, suggest that there are changes in orientations and standards, as one matures. A fully functioning person is characterized as moving beyond immediate needs and socialization demands toward self-based standards and intrinsic goals. Maslow, for example, argued that once basic needs of self-esteem and confidence are met, needs shift to self-fulfillment and a full development of one's capacities (see Ryff, 1985, for a review). In our terms, such changes would occur with respect to different tasks throughout the lifespan once the individual had completed needs for competence assessment and entered a phase of maintenance and adaptation.

Second, there are a few analyses specifically concerned with developmental changes in achievement-related goals and feelings. Veroff and Smith

(1985), argued that individuals show changes in their value systems and feelings about their life circumstances over the course of five age groupings during the adult years. With respect to a man's life course, these shift from feelings of uncertainty about future accomplishments in the young adult, to feelings of confidence in middle age, to feelings of vulnerability and search for new challenges and social belonging in seniors.

Such descriptions are generally consistent with the kinds of orientations that would be predicted from a phase of skill acquisition analysis in relation to a long-term self-definitional experience, such as one's work or career. The initial stages are characterized by uncertainties with respect to task definition and competence assessment that are likely to carry through the young adult years for an issue of this magnitude. Middle age should represent the maintenance stage, where competence assessment has been completed and choices made that maximize feelings of accomplishment and pleasure. Subsequent activities seem characteristic of reassessment, involving attempts to deal with declining powers or a need for new challenges when many of the goals of early adulthood have either been reached or discarded. This would seem to be an adaptive shift for most seniors, and one that is compatible with some of the trends found in the study of runners (Frey & Ruble, in prep.). Although a few individuals had been running for 40 or 50 years, most senior runners had started running when in their 50s and 60s, a time when Veroff and Smith (1985) suggested the individual looks to leisure activities as alternative sources of accomplishment.

It is noteworthy that Veroff and Smith found it much harder to describe the trends for women, in part it appears, because of more diverse interests and goals. Assertive interests later in life were associated with adjustment, as if a shift to new challenges helped buttress losses associated with the end of a parenting role. Such unclear age trends are not surprising, in our view, because a lifespan examination of fulfillment must consider phase of developmental tasks, as well as age. Indeed, in a final section, these authors appear to come to similar conclusions: " . . . we are impressed with how much the context of a person's adult developmental status has a bearing on how motivational orientations affect the way he or she adapts to his or her life" (p. 49). Interestingly, their interpretation of context is remarkably similar to the present analysis, referring to the amount of time a person is in a role, such as job or parenting, and how that affects perceptions of life circumstances and degree of gratification or frustration.

In summary, the logic of the skill acquisition phase analysis suggests that life stages may be characterized by predictable changes in standards and motivations, at least for some activities. To the extent that the acquisition of skills is sufficiently prolonged, the phases may show parallels to life stages. These suggestions must be viewed with caution, however. Relevant evidence is scarce, and even the parallels we have previously noted are highly speculative.

MOTIVATIONAL IMPLICATIONS

Do the changing goals and standards associated with skill acquisition phases affect the desire to engage in a particular activity or the outcomes of performing it? Several recent analyses have suggested that such differences may have profound affective and motivational consequences (Higgins, Strauman, & Klein, 1986; Levine & Moreland, 1987; Masters & Keil, 1987). Concern with competence assessment is associated with less enjoyment, lowered quality of performance, and maladaptive responses to failures relative to an orientation toward learning or mastering the task (Ames, 1986; Boggiano et al., 1989; Butler, 1989a; Deci & Ryan, 1987; Dweck & Leggett, 1988; Harter, in press; Nicholls, 1984; cf. Harackiewicz, Abrahams, & Wageman, 1987). For example, Elliott and Dweck (1988) experimentally manipulated ability level and performance versus learning goals (by orienting subjects more toward demonstrating ability or more toward the value of the skill to be learned). They found that when oriented toward skill acquisition, children's competence level was irrelevant to their choices and behaviors; all children displayed a mastery-oriented, adaptive pattern of responses to failure feedback. In contrast, when children were oriented toward skill evaluation, only children with high perceived competence showed these adaptive responses under conditions of failure. Experimentally induced perceptions of low ability led children oriented toward competence assessment to show the same maladaptive attributions, negative affect, and strategy deterioration given failure feedback that, in earlier research, had characterized the behavior of children with a longstanding history of helplessness (Diener & Dweck, 1978). Other studies have shown similar effects of manipulations of competition versus individualistic goal structures, which appear to elicit competence assessment versus mastery orientations, respectively (Ames, 1986; Butler, 1989a; Nicholls, 1984).

Do comparable motivational and behavioral changes occur concurrently with the different orientations associated with skill acquisition phases? Specifically, orientations toward task definition and learning during initial task assessment may foster intrinsic motivation, feelings of mastery, and persistence in the face of failure. During competence assessment, task selection may be most strongly influenced by the diagnostic potential of the task, rather than opportunities for learning. Task engagement may not elicit feelings of mastery and pleasure, except in individuals who receive feedback that they are highly competent at the task. One way to interpret the Elliott and Dweck (1988) findings is in these acquisition phase terms. Their manipulation of learning goals oriented subjects toward acquiring new skills, thereby eliciting the motivational characteristics of initial task assessment.

Support for this parallel between the first two skill acquisition phases and learning versus performance goals is also available from studies of age changes in young children. Preschool and primary-grade children show impressive resilience in the face of failure; they maintain persistence, self-confidence, and expectations of success on future trials (Parsons & Ruble, 1977; Stipek, 1984). By midelementary school, however, such optimism and positive response to failure has largely disappeared. Moreover, concomitant changes in intrinsic motivation occur, with increasing disinterest in school-related activities appearing as children progress through elementary school (Harter, 1981). Finally, Butler (1989a) found that social comparison was associated with enhanced subsequent task interest in young children, but decreased in older children. This is the pattern that would be predicted if social comparison was utilized for observational learning of technique by younger children and for competence assessment by older children. Interpreted in the present terms, the learning and mastery-oriented use of social comparison feedback, characteristic of task assessment, enhanced interest, whereas the competence assessment use of social comparison feedback decreased interest.

In spite of the apparent parallels, a skill acquisition analysis raises some additional issues and questions that suggest certain limitations in the analysis of motivational implications of task orientations. We highlight two, in particular: (a) possible variations in the effects of competence assessment orientations; and (b) alternative conceptions of the origins of individual differences in task orientations.

Competence Assessment Goals

There is an important distinction between forms of self-evaluative goals that previous motivational analyses may not have adequately considered: that between the desire to appear competent (self-presentation and self-enhancement) versus the desire to obtain accurate competence feedback. When self-evaluation concerns are shown to diminish mastery and pleasure, such concerns have generally been communicated in self-enhancement terms, for example, "documenting the adequacy of ability" (Dweck & Leggett 1988, p. 263). Given the possible disclosure of inadequate ability, failure might well lead to a slackening of effort and task avoidance. It is less intuitively obvious that an accurate competence assessment orientation should always have similar consequences. Rather than decreasing effort or abandoning the task, a person who is unsure of the accuracy of negative feedback may well increase effort and persistence to make sure that a tentative conclusion of incompetence is, in fact, correct (Trope, 1986).

Dweck and Leggett (1988) acknowledged the adaptive potential of self-evaluative goals—that an accurate assessment of areas of competence and incompetence may be essential to effective learning and that problems arise when there is an over-emphasis on demonstrating competence. We suggest that in addition to differing emphases on competence assessment, there may be different functions. During Phase 2 a competence assessment orientation is in the service of development and adaptation, whereas, at other phases, it is not. As Higgins and Trope (in press) argued, the intrinsic versus extrinsic motivational implications of any particular aspect of an activity cannot be assessed without knowing the individual's primary identification of that activity (e.g., as something to master vs. a way to assess competence). The potentially different motivational implications of competence assessment goals at different phases warrant further empirical analysis. Veroff (1969) made a related point in referring to the motivational implications of the informational versus normative functions of social comparison.

Individual Differences

The acquisition phases analysis stimulates a developmental perspective regarding the origins of different task orientations and patterns of achievement behavior. Although much of this literature discusses situational factors influencing achievement goals (e.g., Ames, 1986; Nicholls, 1984), there is also evidence of relatively enduring individual differences in orientations influencing the goals adopted in specific achievement situations (Dweck & Leggett, 1988; Veroff & Veroff, 1980). What is the source of these individual differences in achievement goals? One answer concerns individual differences in fundamental conceptions of the nature of competence, as something that is not fixed but is subject to continuing improvement (Dweck & Leggett, 1988). The answer is incomplete, however, because the question of the origins of these conceptions still remains open.

One possibility is that competence assessment versus mastery goals are derived from conclusions drawn during earlier acquisition phases of a particular task or set of tasks. The definition of the task and what constitutes improvement and excellence are constructed during the task assessment phase. These serve as standards of competence for the next phase, and together with the context in which competence assessment occurs, determine whether perceived competence is high or low. To illustrate, consider the impact of the classroom environment at the competence assessment phase. In school environments emphasizing social comparison standards and competition, children are likely to define academic competence in these terms. Given such standards, many will inevitably come to the conclusion that they are not highly competent and exhibit signs of extrinsic motivation and learned helplessness. This point about the likely impact of features of classroom environment on student orientations and competence has been noted by several previous investigators (Ames, 1986; Nicholls, 1984) and has now been reasonably well documented empirically (Boggiano et al., 1989; Eccles, Midgley, & Adler, 1984; Harter, in press; Ryan & Grolnick, 1986).

Our phases of skill acquisition analysis suggest a further point. Definitions of standards and competence formed during the first two phases should resist change during the maintenance phase. These initial definitions may continue even when children shift to new classrooms using different kinds of standards, representing an individual difference in achievement orientations. Major shifts in definitions of standards and competence should only occur when new task definitions are required, as in school transitions. Developmental evidence suggests that changes in perceived competence and corresponding motivational orientations are most marked when children first enter school and again as they begin junior high school (Eccles et al., 1984; Harter, in press). Harter has also shown similar changes in competence assessment and motivation as part of another type of transition: entering a special program for the gifted.[5] Similar processes may also explain sometimes dramatic changes in learning and motivation shown in creative new programs for children with learning problems (e.g., King, Griffin, Diaz, & Cole, in press).

This kind of analysis may extend considerably beyond an academic context, as illustrated by a study of parents of disabled children (Frey, 1987). Shortly after a child has been diagnosed as impaired, parents engage in a period of intense information gathering, involving their child's prognosis and other children with disabilities. Years later, this information serves as potent standards for evaluating developmental progress and, presumably, the efficacy of their childrearing efforts (Frey & Ruble, 1990). Of course, perceived competence will vary dramatically depending on whether standards involve social comparison with normal children, as opposed to temporal comparison of progress or social comparison with other disabled children. Although competence assessments based on normal children are essential for making future plans regarding the child's care and potential for independence, they pose an evaluative standard that is unattainable. If parents were to continue to focus on such standards after competence assessment is complete, we would expect them to show the same signs of negative affect shown by subjects in "helplessness" inducing experiments.

---

[5] These data seem to suggest a direct, positive association between perceived competence and indices of intrinsic or more mastery oriented motivational orientations. The present analysis implies that such a correspondence is not necessary, depending instead on personal standards and goals (Butler, 1989b) and or freedom to make choices (Deci & Ryan, 1987). It may be that the academic context utilized by most research does not allow sufficient flexibility to observe the adoption of mastery standards and goals (e.g., temporal comparison and improvement) among children low in perceived competence.

In our study, a minority of parents were notable for their failure to make enhancing temporal or disability comparisons about their child ("Look at her. They said she'd never walk"), even though the children were functionally equivalent to those of the other parents. Indeed, these parents, who were likely to spontaneously compare their children to normal ones, exhibited more symptoms of depression, anxiety and hostility, and reacted more negatively to the demands of rearing a special child than the enhancing parents.

We have argued elsewhere (Frey & Ruble, 1990) that the particular goals and standards chosen in the maintenance phase may be less important for enhancing long-term effort than the ability to be flexible, changing goals as necessary to provide encouragement and positive feedback. Parents must make a dramatic, unanticipated shift in task definition, goals and evaluative standards after discovering their child is disabled. Most of the parents in our study seemed to have succeeded in making that shift.

Similar conclusions can be drawn from our study of runners (Frey & Ruble, 1989). The results suggest that those runners who were no longer improving had maintained their motivation to train by accommodating their standards to their changing capabilities. The disparity in numbers between improving ($n = 123$), stable ($n = 61$), and declining ($n = 35$) runners may in part reflect the attrition of those unwilling or unable to shift goals and standards. Although adults have lost the prospect of continued improvement that children enjoy, stagnation may not be an insurmountable handicap. Adults are better able to choose adaptive strategies for maintaining motivation than children. They have more freedom to select their activities and establish priorities among them. In addition, increased metacognitive knowledge of motivational influences may make adults more attentive to conditions that foster motivation and enhance self-esteem.

CONCLUSIONS

Self-evaluation is a central and continuing part of daily life, and trying to understand how it occurs has been a preoccupation of many scientific careers. Although there has never been any question that social comparison is a crucial part of this process, its exact role has remained elusive with social comparison findings marked by puzzle and contradiction. Why do individuals presumably interested in self-evaluation first select information about the highest performing others when similar others provide a better chance for accurate self-assessment (Wood, 1989)? How can both upward and downward comparisons exist simultaneously in the same people without engendering any contradictions (Taylor & Lobel, 1989)? Why are there such mixed conclusions about whether or not children under 7–8 years of age engage in social comparison (Ruble, 1983)?

Recent considerations of such questions have come to similar conclusions: social comparison shows such widely varying forms and patterns because it serves different functions. Individuals seek information about the top scorers on a task in order to familiarize themselves with the distribution of the underlying skill dimension, rather than as accurate self-assessment (Wood, 1989). Downward comparison bolsters self-esteem, whereas upward comparison provides information relevant to improvement and inspiration (Taylor & Lobel, 1989). Young children engage in social comparison when it can fulfill mastery goals, rather than the self-assessment goals characteristic of older children (Butler, 1989c). Thus, there is now fairly wide consensus that the need for accurate knowledge about one's abilities (Festinger, 1954) is only one of several reasons to engage in social comparison, such that observations across studies and forms of comparison can result in apparent contradictions.

We have attempted to push this line of analysis one step further. We have argued that not only does social comparison serve different goals, but these goals emerge systematically as part of a single, dynamic self-evaluative process. Level of knowledge and experience with a particular skill determine which goals are paramount. Thus, individuals seek to determine the dimension of a skill before engaging in similarity comparison because they need to define key parameters of the task before accurate competence assessment is even possible. Young children may tend to emphasize task assessment and mastery goals because they are at early stages of skill acquisition for most skill domains. Drivelike, diagnostic properties of social comparison may rarely be seen because they are time-delimited. Indeed, the competence assessment phase may be brief or even skipped entirely if the individual is not able to choose freely between engagement and disengagement goals. In young school children, however, this phase may extend over several years as children's understanding of criteria for evaluating competence changes.

Similarly, the present analysis provides an additional perspective to understanding why apparently conflicting comparisons may exist simultaneously in the same people with respect to a single domain. Taylor and Lobel (1989) noted that cancer victims engage both in upward contacts and downward comparisons. In cases such as this, the domain being considered is quite complex, involving a number of discrete elements and skills that may provide useful information based on social comparison. These apparently discrepant forms of comparison may involve different phases of self-evaluation for each element and skill. The downward comparisons may primarily concern assessment or maintenance processes with respect to an aspect of the disease that has already been defined, whereas the upward contacts may involve an attempt at understanding and inspiration with respect to aspects of the disease that remain to be defined.

This developmental perspective on social comparison findings builds on some current trends in the literature other than the recent recognition of divergent goals. First, implicit in some goals analyses has been an assumption of natural orders of progression: that in most circumstances one type of goal usually precedes another. Fazio (1979) described the need to construct a definition of the task before validating one's opinions or competence at it (see also Olson, Ellis, & Zanna, 1983). Similarly, Wood (1989) used the idea of familiarity to resolve the puzzle of why people seek information about the extremes of a dimension in apparent violation of the similarity principle. She argued that on unfamiliar dimensions, a first step toward self-evaluation is to learn the distribution of others' standings. In contrast to the present perspective, these previous considerations of dynamic processes have been limited to only a few select issues or to resolving apparent contradictions in the literature; they have not incorporated an awareness that self-evaluation is always a process in transition.

Second, the present analysis contributes to the growing trend of examining naturally occurring self-evaluative processes as they occur, for example, in people facing unexpected life crises (Taylor & Lobel, 1989), transitions into new situations such as school and parenting (Deutsch et al., 1988; Frey & Ruble, 1985), and changes in real life circumstances during normal maturation and aging (Suls, 1986). Because a dynamic view of self-evaluation is clearly central to such situations, it seems important now to begin to develop theories about the nature and process of changes in self-evaluation over time.

This emphasis on individual goals and their natural emergence during the acquisition of knowledge and skills, limits the meaning and applicability of social comparison in some ways and broadens it in others. Social comparison may not be the optimal approach to meeting certain goals. As discussed earlier, goals characteristic of task assessment and maintenance phases may be best served by temporal or absolute standards. Moreover, for some domains, there may be little use for social comparison even in the competence assessment phase. As discussed earlier with respect to social services, social comparison may be more useful in helping construct appropriate absolute standards than as a standard of competence, in its own right. A similar line of reasoning is used by Ross et al. (1986) to help understand why people assessing their own real life satisfaction rarely refer to social comparison. They suggest that comparative standards may be central to formulating the goals that are mentioned as reasons for inferring satisfaction.

This last example leads directly to the alternate point: that the present perspective, in the end, broadens, rather than limits, the meaning and applicability of social comparison in self-evaluation. Although the phase of accurate competence assessment emphasizing social comparison may be brief in many domains, the functions social comparison serves at other phases are integral to the self-evaluative process. Assessing the demands of the task, its usefulness to one's values and goals, whether and how to maintain motivation at the task are essential components of self-evaluation and social comparison is central to them. Indeed, it may be used even more frequently to fulfill some of these other goals than it is used in the more limited definition of self-evaluation usually ascribed to Festinger's original statement.

ACKNOWLEDGMENTS

We are grateful to Ruth Butler, Francine Deutsch, Denise Nelesen, Jerry Suls, Yaacov Trope, and Tom Wills for many probing and insightful comments and suggestions on an earlier version of this chapter. Preparation of this chapter was supported by a research grant (MH 37215) and a Research Scientist Development Award to the first author (MH 00484), both from the National Institute of Mental Health.

REFERENCES

Aboud, F. E. (1985). Children's applications of attribution principles to social comparisons. *Child Development, 56*, 682–688.

Ahrens, A. H. (1987). Theories of depression: The role of goals and the self-evaluative process. *Cognitive Therapy and Research, 11*, 665–680.

Albert, S. (1977). Temporal comparison theory. *Psychological Review, 84*, 485–503.

Ames, C. (1986). Conceptions of motivation within competitive and noncompetitive goal structures. In R. Schwarzer (Ed.), *Self-related cognitions in anxiety and motivation* (pp. 229–245). Hillsdale, NJ: Lawrence Erlbaum Associates.

Atkinson, M.L. (1986). The perception of social categories: Implications for the social comparison process. In J. M. Olson, C. P. Herman, & M. P. Zanna (Eds.), *Relative deprivation and social comparison: The Ontario Symposium* (Vol. 4, pp. 117–134). Hillsdale, NJ: Lawrence Erlbaum Associates.

Azmitia, M. (1988). Peer interaction and problem solving: When are two heads better than one? *Child Development, 59*, 87–96.

Bandura, A. (1986). *Social foundations of thought and action.* Englewood Cliffs, NJ: Prentice-Hall.

Berger, S. M. (1977). Social comparison, modeling, and perseverance. In J. M. Suls & R. L. Miller (Eds.), *Social comparison processes: Theoretical and empirical perspectives* (pp. 209–234). Washington, DC: Hemisphere.

Berlyne, D. E. (1966). Curiosity and exploration. *Science, 153*, 25–33.

Bjorklund, D. F. (1987). How age changes in knowledge base contribute to the development of children's memory: An interpretive review. *Developmental Review, 7*, 93–130.

Boggiano, A. K., Main, D. S., Flink, C., Barrett, M., Silvern, L., & Katz, P. (1989). A model of achievement in children: The role of controlling strategies in helplessness and affect. In R. Schwarzer, H. M. Van der Ploeg, & C. Spielberger (Eds.), *Advances in test anxiety research* (Vol. 6, pp. 13–26). Berwyn, PA: Swets North America, Inc.

Boggiano, A. K., & Ruble, D. N. (1979). Competence and the overjustification effect: A developmental study. *Journal of Personality and Social Psychology, 37*, 1462–1468.

Brickman, P., & Bulman, R. J. (1977). Pleasure and pain in social comparison. In J. M. Suls & R. L. Miller (Eds.), *Social comparison processes: Theoretical and empirical perspectives* (pp. 149–186). Washington, DC: Hemisphere.

Butler, R. (1989-a). Interest in the task and interest in peer's work in competitive and noncompetitive conditions: A developmental study. *Child Development, 60*, 562–570.

Butler, R. (1989-b). On the psychological meaning of information about competence: A reply to Ryan & Deci's commentary on Butler (1987). *Journal of Educational Psychology, 81*, 269–272.

Butler, R. (1989-c). Mastery versus ability appraisal: A developmental study of children's observations of peer's work. *Child Development, 60*, 1350–1361.

Butler, R. (1990). The effects of mastery and competitive conditions on self-assessment at different ages. *Child Development, 61*, 201–210.

Carver, C. S., & Scheier, M. F. (1981). *Attention and self-regulation: A control-theory approach to human behavior*. New York: Springer.

Carver, C. S., & Scheier, M. F. (1985). A control systems approach to the self-regulation of action. In J. Kuhl & J. Beckman (Eds.), *Action control: From cognition to behavior* (pp. 237–265). Berlin: Springer.

Chafel, J. A. (1988). The effects of two types of play settings on young children's use of social comparison. *Early Child Development and Care, 40*, 53–75.

Crocker, J., Hannah, D. B., & Weber, R. (1983). Person memory and causal attribution. *Journal of Personality and Social Psychology, 44*, 55–66.

Deci, E. L., & Ryan, R. M. (1985). *Intrinsic motivation and self-determination in human behavior*. New York: Plenum.

Deci, E. L., & Ryan, R. M. (1987). The support of autonomy and the control of behavior. *Journal of Personality and Social Psychology, 53*, 1024–1037.

Deutsch, F. M., Ruble, D. N., Fleming, A., Brooks-Gunn, J., & Stangor, C. S. (1988). Information seeking and maternal self-definition during the transition to motherhood. *Journal of Personality and Social Psychology, 55*, 420–431.

Diener, C. I., & Dweck, C. S. (1978). An analysis of learned helplessness: Continuous changes in performance, strategy, and achievement cognitions following failure. *Journal of Personality and Social Psychology, 36*, 451–462.

Dweck, C. S., & Elliott, E. S. (1983). Achievement motivation. In E. M. Hetherington (Ed.), *Handbook of child psychology: Vol. IV, Social and personality development* (pp. 643–691). New York: Wiley.

Dweck, C. S., & Leggett, E. L. (1988). A social-cognitive approach to motivation and personality. *Psychological Review, 95*, 256–273.

Eccles, J., Midgley, C., & Adler, T. F. (1984). Grade-related changes in the school environment: Effects on achievement motivation. In J. G. Nicholls (Ed.), *The development of achievement motivation* (pp. 283–332). Greenwich, CT: JAI Press.

Edwards, C. P. (1984). The age group labels and categories of small children. *Child Development, 55*, 440–452.

Elliott, E. S., & Dweck, C. S. (1988). Goals: An approach to motivation and achievement. *Journal of Personality and Social Psychology, 54*, 5–12.

Fazio, R. H. (1979). Motives for social comparison: The construction-validation distinction. *Journal of Personality and Social Psychology, 37*, 1683–1699.

Feld, S., Ruhland, D., & Gold, M. (1979). Developmental changes in achievement motivation. *Merrill-Palmer Quarterly, 25*, 43–60.

Feldman, N. S., & Ruble, D. N. (1977). Awareness of social comparison interest and motivation: A developmental study. *Journal of Educational Psychology, 69*, 579–585.

Festinger, L. (1954). A theory of social comparison processes. *Human Relations, 7*, 117–140.
Fiske, S. T., & Taylor, S. E. (1984). *Social cognition*. Reading, MA: Addison-Wesley.
Flavell, J. H. (1984). *Cognitive development* (2nd ed.). Englewood Cliffs, NJ: Prentice-Hall.
Frey, D. (1986). Recent research on selective exposure to information. In L. Berkowitz (Ed.), *Advances in experimental social psychology* (pp. 41–80). New York: Academic Press.
Frey, K. S. (1987). Coping responses of parents of disabled children. *Unpublished data*.
Frey, K. S., & Ruble, D. N. (1985). What children say when the teacher is not around: Conflicting goals in social comparison and performance assessment in the classroom. *Journal of Personality and Social Psychology, 48*, 550–562.
Frey, K. S., & Ruble, D. N. (1987). What children say about classroom performance: Sex and grade differences in perceived competence. *Child Development, 58*, 1066–1078.
Frey, K. S., & Ruble, D. N. (1990). Strategies for comparative evaluation: Maintaining a sense of competence across the lifespan. In R. J. Sternberg & J. Kolligian (Eds.), *Perceptions of competence and incompetence across the lifespan* (pp. 167–189). New Haven, CT: Yale University Press.
Frey, K. S., & Ruble, D. N. (in prep.). *Differences in preferred evaluative standards among runners 20 to 77 years of age: A function of age and improvement phase*. Manuscript in preparation, University of Washington, Seattle, WA.
Goethals, G. R. (1986). Social comparison theory: Psychology from the lost and found. *Personality and Social Psychology Bulletin, 12*, 261–278.
Gottman, J., & Parkhurst, J. (1980). Developmental theory of friendship and acquaintanceship process. In W. A. Collins (Ed.), *Minnesota symposium on child psychology* (Vol. 14, pp. 155–195). Hillsdale, NJ: Lawrence Erlbaum Associates.
Harackiewicz, J. M., Abrahams, S., & Wageman, R. (1987). Performance evaluation and intrinsic motivation: The effects of evaluative focus, rewards, and achievement orientation. *Journal of Personality and Social Psychology, 53*, 1015–1023.
Harter, S. (1981). A model of mastery motivation in children: Individual differences and developmental change. In A. Collins (Ed.), *Minnesota symposium on child psychology* (Vol. 14, pp. 215–255). Hillsdale, NJ: Lawrence Erlbaum Associates.
Harter, S. (1986). Processes underlying the construction, maintenance, and enhancement of the self-concept in children. In J. Suls & A. G. Greenwald (Eds.), *Psychological perspectives on the self* (Vol. 3, pp. 123–159). Hillsdale, NJ: Lawrence Erlbaum Associates.
Harter, S. (in press). The relationship between perceived competence, affect, and motivational orientation within the classroom: Processes and patterns of change. In A. K. Boggiano & T. Pittman (Eds.), *Achievement and motivation: A social-developmental perspective*. New York: Cambridge University Press.
Harter, S., & Pike, R. (1984). The pictorial scale of perceived competence and social acceptance for young children. *Child Development, 55*, 1969–1982.
Heckhausen, H. (1982). The development of achievement motivation. In W. W. Hartup (Ed.), *Review of child development research* (Vol. 6, pp. 600–668). Chicago: University of Chicago Press.
Heckhausen, H. (1984). Emergent achievement behavior: Some early developments. In J. G. Nicholls (Ed.), *The development of achievement motivation* (pp. 1–32). Greenwich, CT: JAI Press.
Higgins, E. T. (1989). Continuities and discontinuities in self-regulatory and self-evaluative processes: A developmental theory relating self and affect. *Journal of Personality, 57*, 407–444.
Higgins, E. T., & Bargh, J. A. (1987). Social cognition and social perception. *Annual Review of Psychology, 38*, 369–425.

Higgins, E. T., & Parsons, J. E. (1983). Stages as subcultures: Social-cognitive development and the social life of the child. In E. T. Higgins, D. N. Ruble, & W. W. Hartup (Eds.), *Social cognition and social behavior* (pp. 15–62). New York: Cambridge University Press.

Higgins, E. T., Strauman, T., & Klein, R. (1986). Standards and the process of self-evaluation: Multiple affects from multiple stages. In R. M. Sorrentino & E. T. Higgins (Eds.), *Handbook of motivation and cognition* (pp. 23–63). New York: Guilford.

Higgins, E. T., & Trope, Y. (in press). Identification processes in intrinsic and extrinsic motivation. In E. T. Higgins & R. M. Sorrentino (Eds.), *Handbook of motivation and cognition* (Vol. 2), New York: Guilford.

Jagacinski, C. M., & Nicholls, J. G. (1987). Competence and affect in task involvement and ego involvement: The impact of social comparison information. *Journal of Educational Psychology, 79*, 107–114.

Jones, E. E., & Berglas, S. (1978). Control of attributions about the self through self-handicapping strategies: The appeal of alcohol and the role of underachievement. *Personality and Social Psychology Bulletin, 4*, 200–206.

King, C. A., Griffin, P., Diaz, S., & Cole, M. (in press). A model systems approach to reading instruction and the diagnosis of reading disabilities. In R. Glaser (Ed.), *Advances in instructional psychology*. Hillsdale, NJ: Lawrence Erlbaum Associates.

Kirschenbaum, D. S. (1985). Proximity and specificity of planning: A position paper. *Cognitive Therapy and Research, 9*, 489–506.

Kohlberg, L. (1966). A cognitive-developmental analysis of children's sex-role concepts and attitudes. In E. E. Maccoby (Ed.), *The development of sex differences*. Stanford: Stanford University Press.

Kruglanski, A. W., & Mayseless, O. (1987). Motivational effects in the social comparison of opinions. *Journal of Personality and Social Psychology, 53*, 834–842.

Levine, J. M., & Moreland, R. L. (1987). Social comparison and outcome evaluation in group contexts. In J. C. Masters & W. P. Smith (Eds.), *Social comparison, social justice, and relative deprivation* (pp. 105–127). Hillsdale, NJ: Lawrence Erlbaum Associates.

Levine, J. M., & Green, S. M. (1984). Acquisition of relative performance information: The roles of intrapersonal and interpersonal comparison. *Personality and Social Psychology Bulletin, 10*, 385–393.

Levine, J. M., Snyder, H. N., Mendez-Caratini, G. (1982). Task performance and interpersonal attraction in children. *Child Development, 53*, 359–371.

Liben, L. S., & Signorella, L. S. (1987). *Children's gender schemata*. San Francisco: Jossey-Bass.

Markus, H., & Zajonc, R. B. (1985). The cognitive perspective in social psychology. In G. Lindzey & E. Aronson (Eds.), *Handbook of social psychology* (Vol. 1, pp. 137–230). New York: Random House.

Masters, J. C. (1971). Social comparison by young children. *Young Children, 27*, 37–60.

Masters, J. C., & Keil, L. J. (1987). Generic comparison processes in human judgment and behavior. In J. C. Masters & W. P. Smith (Eds.), *Social comparison, social justice, and relative deprivation* (pp. 11–54). Hillsdale, NJ: Lawrence Erlbaum Associates.

McClintock, C. G., Moskowitz, J. M., & McClintock, E. (1977). Variations in preferences for individualistic, competitive, and cooperative outcomes as a function of age, game, class, and task in nursery school children. *Child Development, 48*, 1080–1085.

Mettee, D. R., & Smith, G. (1977). Social comparison and interpersonal attraction: The case for dissimilarity. In J. M. Suls & R. L. Miller (Eds.), *Social comparison processes: Theoretical and empirical perspectives* (pp. 69–102). Washington, DC: Hemisphere.

Morris, W. N., & Nemeck, D. (1982). The development of social comparison motivation among preschoolers: Evidence of stepwise progression. *Merrill-Palmer Quarterly, 28*, 413–425.

Morrison, H., & Kuhn, D. (1983). Cognitive aspects of preschoolers' peer imitation in a play situation. *Child Development, 54*, 1041–1053.
Mosatche, H. S., & Bragonier, P. (1981). An observational study of social comparison in preschoolers. *Child Development, 52*, 376–378.
Nicholls, J. G. (1984). Achievement motivation: Conceptions of ability, subjective experience, task choice, and performance. *Psychological Review, 91*, 328–346.
Nicholls, J. G., & Miller, A. T. (1984). Development and its discontents: The differentiation of the concept of ability. In J. G. Nicholls (Ed.), *Advances in motivation and achievement: The development of achievement motivation* (Vol. 3, pp. 185–218). Greenwich, CT: JAI Press.
Olson, J. M., Ellis, R. J., & Zanna, M. P. (1983). Validating objective versus subjective judgments: Interest in social comparison and consistency information. *Personality and Social Psychology Bulletin, 9*, 427–436.
Parsons, J. E., & Ruble, D. N. (1977). The development of achievement-related expectancies. *Child Development, 48*, 1075–1079.
Pepitone, E. (1972). Comparison behavior in elementary school children. *American Educational Research Journal, 9*, 45–63.
Piaget, J. (1952). *The origins of intelligence in children*. New York: International Universities Press.
Raynor, J. O., & Brown, E. T. (1985). Motivation at different stages of striving in a psychological career. In D. A. Kleiber & M. L. Maehr (Eds.), *Advances in motivation and achievement* (Vol. 4, pp. 64–87). Greenwich, CT: JAI Press.
Ross, M., Eyman, A., & Kishchuk, N. (1986). Determinants of subjective well-being. In J. M. Olson, C. P. Herman, & M. P. Zanna (Eds.), *Relative deprivation and social comparison: The Ontario Symposium* (Vol. 4, pp. 79–93). Hillsdale, NJ: Lawrence Erlbaum Associates.
Ross, M., & Fletcher, G. J. O. (1985). Attribution and social perception. In G. Lindzey & E. Aronson (Eds.), *Handbook of social psychology* (Vol. 2, pp. 73–123). New York: Random House.
Ruble, D. N. (1983). The development of social comparison processes and their role in achievement-related self-socialization. In E. T. Higgins, D. N. Ruble, & W. W. Hartup (Eds.), *Social cognition and social development: A socio-cultural perspective* (pp. 134–157). New York: Cambridge University Press.
Ruble, D. N. (1987). The acquisition of self-knowledge: A self-socialization perspective. In N. Eisenberg (Ed.), *Contemporary topics in developmental psychology* (pp. 243–270). New York: John Wiley & Sons.
Ruble, D. N., Boggiano, A. K., Feldman, N. S., & Loebl, J. H. (1980). Developmental analysis of the role of social comparison in self-evaluation. *Developmental Psychology, 16*, 105–115.
Ruble, D. N., Eisenberg, R., Feldman, N. S., & Higgins, E. T. (in prep.). *Evaluating performance and ability: Developmental changes as a function of both target and standard of evaluation.*
Ruble, D. N., Feldman, N. S., & Boggiano, A. K. (1976). Social comparison between young children in achievement situations. *Developmental Psychology, 12*, 192–197.
Ruble, D. N., & Flett, G. L. (1988). Conflicting goals in self-evaluative information seeking: Developmental and ability level analyses. *Child Development, 59*, 97–106.
Ruble, D. N., Grosovsky, A. H., Frey, K. S., & Cohen, R. (in press). Developmental changes in competence assessment. In A. K. Boggiano & T. Pittman (Eds.), *Achievement and motivation: A social-developmental perspective*. New York: Cambridge University Press.
Ruble, D. N., Parsons, J. E., & Ross, J. (1976). Self-evaluative responses of children in an achievement setting. *Child Development, 47*, 990–997.

Ruble, D. N., & Stangor, C. (1986). Stalking the elusive schema: Insights from developmental and social analyses of gender schemas. *Social Cognition, 4*, 227–261.

Ryan, R. M., & Grolnick, W. S. (1986). Origins and pawns in the classroom: Self-report and projective assessments of individual differences in children's perceptions. *Journal of Personality and Social Psychology, 50*, 550–558.

Ryff, C. D. (1985). Adult personality development and the motivation for personal growth. In D. A. Kleiber & M. L. Maehr (Eds.), *Motivation and adulthood* (pp. 55–92). Greenwich, CT: JAI Press.

Smith, W. P., Davidson, E. S., & France, A. C. (1987). Social comparison and achievement evaluation in children. In J. C. Masters & W. P. Smith (Eds.), *Social comparison, social justice, and relative deprivation* (pp. 55–80). Hillsdale, NJ: Lawrence Erlbaum Associates.

Sorrentino, R. M., & Short, J. C. (1986). Uncertainty orientation, motivation, and cognition. In R. M. Sorrentino & E. T. Higgins (Eds.), *Handbook of motivation and cognition* (pp. 379–403). New York: Guilford.

Spear, P., & Armstrong, S. (1978). Effects of performance expectancies created by peer comparison as related to social reinforcement, task difficulty, and age of child. *Journal of Experimental Child Psychology, 25*, 254–266.

Srull, T. K., Lichtenstein, M., & Rothbart, M. (1985). Associative storage and retrieval processes in person memory. *Journal of Experimental Psychology, 11*, 316–345.

Stangor, C., & Ruble, D. N. (1989). Strength of expectancies and memory for social information: What we remember depends on how much we know. *Journal of Experimental Social Psychology, 25*, 18–35.

Stangor, C., & Ruble, D. N. (in press). Effects of gender schemas and gender constancy on children's information gathering and behavior. *Social Cognition*.

Stevens, L., & Jones, E. E. (1976). Defensive attribution and the Kelley cube. *Journal of Personality and Social Psychology, 34*, 809–820.

Stipek, D. J. (1984). The development of achievement motivation. In R. E. Ames & C. Ames (Eds.), *Research on motivation in education* (Vol. 1, pp. 145–174). New York: Academic Press.

Stipek, D., & MacIver, D. (1989). Developmental changes in children's assessment of intellectual competence. *Child Development, 60*, 521–538.

Stipek, D. J., & Tannatt, L. M. (1984). Children's judgments of their own and their peer's academic competence. *Journal of Educational Psychology, 76*, 75–84.

Stryker, S., & Statham, A. (1985). Symbolic interaction and role theory. In G. Lindzey & E. Aronson (Eds.), *Handbook of social psychology* (Vol. 1, pp. 311–378). New York: Random House.

Suls, J. (1986). Comparison processes in relative deprivation: A life-span analysis. In J. M. Olson, C. P. Herman, & M. P. Zanna (Eds.), *Relative deprivation and social comparison: The Ontario Symposium* (Vol. 4, pp. 95–116). Hillsdale, NJ: Lawrence Erlbaum Associates.

Suls, J., & Mullen, B. (1982). From the cradle to the grave: Comparison and self-evaluation across the life-span. In J. Suls (Ed.), *Psychological perspectives on the self* (Vol. 1, pp. 97–125). Hillsdale, NJ: Lawrence Erlbaum Associates.

Suls, J., & Sanders, G. S. (1982). Self-evaluation through social comparison: A developmental analysis. *Review of Personality and Social Psychology, 13*, 171–197.

Swann, W. B. (1983). Self-verification: Bringing social reality into harmony with the self. In J. Suls & A. G. Greenwald (Eds.), *Psychological perspectives on the self* (Vol. 2, pp. 33–66). Hillsdale, NJ: Lawrence Erlbaum Associates.

Taylor, S. E., & Brown, J. D. (1988). Illusion and well-being: A social psychological perspective on mental health. *Psychological Bulletin, 103*, 193–210.

Taylor, S. E., & Lobel, M. (1989). Social comparison activity under threat: Downward evaluation and upward contacts. *Psychological Review, 96*, 569–575.

Tesser, A. (1986). Some effects of self-evaluation maintenance on cognition and affect. In R. M. Sorrentino & E. T. Higgins (Eds.), *Handbook of motivation and cognition* (pp. 435–464). New York: Guilford.

Trope, Y. (1983). Self-assessment in achievement behavior. In J. Suls & A. G. Greenwald (Eds.), *Psychological perspectives on the self* (Vol. 2, pp. 93–121). Hillsdale, NJ: Lawrence Erlbaum Associates.

Trope, Y. (1986). Self-enhancement and self-assessment in achievement behavior. In R. M. Sorrentino & E. T. Higgins (Eds.), *Handbook of motivation and cognition: Foundations of social behavior* (pp. 350–378). New York: Guilford.

Veroff, J. (1969). Social comparison and the development of achievement motivation. In C. P. Smith (Ed.), *Achievement-related motives in children* (pp. 46–101). New York: Russell Sage.

Veroff, J., & Smith, D. A. (1985). Motives and values over the adult years. In D. A. Kleiber & M. L. Maehr (Eds.), *Advances in motivation and achievement* (Vol. 4, pp. 51–83). Greenwich, CT: JAI Press.

Veroff, J., & Veroff, J. B. (1980). *Social incentives: A life-span developmental approach.* New York: Academic Press.

White, R. W. (1959). Motivation reconsidered: The concept of competence. *Psychological Review, 66,* 297–333.

Wills, T. A. (1981). Downward comparison principles in social psychology. *Psychological Bulletin, 90,* 245–271.

Wood, J. V. (1989). Theory and research concerning social comparisons of personal attributes. *Psychological Bulletin, 106,* 231–248.

5 Emotion in Social Comparison and Reflection Processes

Abraham Tesser
Institute for Behavioral Research
University of Georgia

Social comparison theory has come a long way since its original formulation (Festinger, 1954). The original statement of the theory treated uncertainty as an independent variable and social information seeking as a dependent variable. It suggested that people have a need to evaluate their opinions and abilities and that they do this by comparing themselves to others, preferably similar others. Shortly afterwards, we learned that people also have a need to evaluate their emotions (Schachter, 1959; Taylor, Buunk, & Aspinwall, 1990). Over the years we have learned more about the meaning of *similar others* (e.g., Goethals & Darley, 1977; Miller, Turnbull, & McFarland, 1988; Wood, 1989) and that being with others or seeking information about others may serve a variety of functions (Taylor & Lobel, 1989; Wrightsman, 1960).

The original statement of the theory also posited a unidirectional drive upward in the case of abilities. It wasn't long until investigators began exploring the role of social comparison in self-esteem processes (Hakmiller, 1966; Thornton & Arrowood, 1966; Wills, 1981; 1987). This domain of social comparison research has become the major contemporary focus and we see aspects of it in research on ingroups–outgroups (e.g., Crocker & Schwartz, 1985), adjustment to illness (Wood, Taylor & Lichtman, 1985), depression (Alloy & Ahrens, 1987), and interpersonal relationships (Salovey & Rodin, 1984), to name a few. It is this, the self-evaluation maintenance aspect of the theory, with which the present chapter is concerned.

According to most social comparison theory accounts, another's better performance is a threat to self-esteem (Brickman & Bulman, 1977; Festinger, 1954; Wills, 1981). The self-evaluation maintenance (SEM) model suggests that this account tells only half the story; another's better performance can also have positive consequences for the self in that we sometimes bask in the reflected glory of another's good performance. Most social comparison theories have not focussed on emotion. The story to be told in this chapter features emotion as a leading character. Emotion plays three roles in this story. First, it serves as a marker. Its presence provides information about whether social comparison and reflection processes are engaged. Second, emotion is featured as a subjective, qualitative experience accompanying comparison and reflection processes. Finally, we consider the possibility that one aspect of emotion, arousal, may play a meditational role in causing the behaviors triggered by social comparison and reflection processes.

THE SELF-EVALUATION MAINTENANCE (SEM) MODEL

The story begins with a couple of commonsense assumptions. We assume that people want to feel good about themselves. That is, that they want to evaluate themselves positively. We also assume that the way in which people feel about themselves is at least partially determined by the social context in which they find themselves. An important part of the context is the quality of the performance exhibited by others in that context. We have all had the experience of meeting someone for the first time and having to listen to them tell us about their cousin who is the first violin in the Cleveland Symphony or their next door neighbor who actually shook hands with the President of the United States. Their descriptions of these events make it appear as if they, who have had nothing to do with these accomplishments, are somehow gaining stature by their association with these outstanding people. We have termed this process the *reflection process* (Cialdini, et al., 1976; Cialdini & Richardson, 1980).

If we were to analyze this process for a moment we would see that two things are necessary for someone to bask in the reflected glory of another. First, the other's accomplishments have to be very good. If the other's accomplishments are mediocre there would be very little for the self to gain by pointing out the association. One doesn't say, "Let me tell you about my cousin, the violinist, who couldn't make the Cleveland Symphony." The second necessary condition is that there must be some psychological connection between the self and the good performing other. We have termed this psychological connection *closeness*. Closeness is like Heider's (1958) notion of unit relatedness. "Briefly, separate entities comprise a unit when they are perceived as belonging together . . . For example, members of a family are seen as a unit." (p. 176.) Various kinds of physical and psychological similarity and spatial contiguity are further examples of variables that induce unit formation and increase psychological closeness.

One thing people can do to feel good about themselves is to build themselves up by basking in the reflected glory of another. In order to do this they must seek or construct relationships with good performing others or they must do whatever they can to bolster the performance of persons to whom they are already close. There is a danger in doing this, however. The juxtaposition of self and a good performing, similar other can make the self pale by comparison. This is the more commonly discussed effect of social comparison on self-esteem. Interestingly, the same variables that increase the potential positive outcomes via the reflection process also increase the potential negative outcomes via the comparison process. The threat of comparison increases to the extent that the other's performance is better than one's own. Thus, relative performance is important. At the same time comparisons are more likely to be drawn as the psychological closeness to the other increases. This shows that closeness is also important. If one were to focus only on the comparison process one would advise persons interested in feeling good about themselves to increase their psychological distance to others who perform particularly well and/or to hinder the performance of close others.

The reflection process and the comparison process are clearly antagonistic. The former suggests that the good performance of someone close to us can raise our self-evaluation. The latter suggests that the good performance of someone close to us can threaten our self-evaluation. The self-evaluation maintenance model deals with this contradiction by assuming that the two processes are not always equally important. It suggests that one's own definition of self plays a crucial role in the differential weighting of these processes.

All of us aspire to excellence in some areas. Some of us want to be lawyers. Others aspire to excellence in art. Still others have aspirations on the baseball field. All of us can recognize outstanding performance in each of these domains but our own aspirations are limited and do not cover all domains. Our self-identity consists, in part, of those domains in which we have aspirations to excellence. Another's performance is relevant to the extent that it represents one of those self-definitional domains. Following Festinger (1954), relevance is also partially determined by the level of the other's performance. If the other's performance is too discrepant from our own, comparisons will be difficult to make and relevance will be low. J. M. Suls (personal communication, April 1989) suggests that this aspect of relevance may be one of the boundary conditions which separates classical social comparison theory from SEM processes. However, it has received relatively little research attention in our own empirical work.

It is the relevance of another's performance that determines the importance of the reflection and comparison processes. To the extent that another's performance is relevant to our own self-definition the comparison process will be more important than the reflection process. On the other hand, if the other's performance is in a domain that has little relevance to our self-definition, the reflection process will be more important.

I have argued that people behave so as to maintain a positive self-evaluation. We have also indicated at least some of the ways in which one's sense of self can be affected by the performance of those around him or her. An example might be helpful in showing how these processes might play themselves out in everyday life. Suppose for John, playing baseball is very important. He comes to college and rooms with Jim. Both John and Jim try out for the baseball team. Jim is chosen to start at second base, John gets a slot on the second string team and does little more than warm the bench. Since baseball is important to John, Jim's performance is relevant to his self-definition. When relevance is high the comparison process is more important than the reflection process. Thus, John's self-evaluation is threatened by Jim's performance. What can John do? From the perspective of the SEM model, there are several possibilities. First, John can reduce his closeness to Jim. If he were to move out of his room he wouldn't be confronted by Jim as often and comparisons would be reduced. Second, John can attempt to change the performance differential. He can hide Jim's glove, he can keep Jim awake the night before the big game and so on. John could also operate on his own performance, such as trying to improve his batting. If he were able to reduce the performance differential the threat would also be reduced. A third possibility for John is to alter the relevance of baseball to his self-definition. Suppose John decides that baseball is a great game but it's not for him; chess is much more intellectual, important, and now, more self-defining. By reducing the relevance of Jim's performance to his own self-definition, he can change the weighting of the two processes and might begin to bask in the reflected glory of Jim's stellar performance on the diamond.

Some Comments on the Model

SEM versus "Classical" Social Comparison Theory. The social comparison process associated with the SEM model differs from the social comparison process outlined by Leon Festinger (1954) in several ways. Perhaps the most important difference is that the comparison process shares equal billing with the reflection process in the SEM model. Indeed, the SEM model could not make any predictions without the presence of the reflection process. There simply is no analog to the reflection process in classical social comparison theory. Classical social comparison theory emphasizes social comparison as a means of gaining cognitive clarity about opinions and abilities, although Festinger recognized a "unidirectional drive upward" for abilities. On the other hand, the motivational emphasis in the present approach is not on reducing uncertainty but rather on maintaining or enhancing self-evaluation. According to the classical theory, people seek out comparisons with slightly better others (to reduce uncertainty) and the results of such comparisons are, presumably positive. The present view is that comparison with someone who is better can sometimes be aversive (threaten self-evaluation) and lead to negative affect. The research paradigms are also different. Classical social comparison theory is often concerned with desire for information about performance differentials whereas the present formulation is more concerned with the *results* of performance differentials on emotions, self-definition, closeness and subsequent performance. (See Tesser, 1988 for a fuller discussion of some of these points).

Classical social comparison processes are said to be facilitated by the presence of a similar other. The present formulation suggests that the results of comparison should be stronger with a close than a distant other. Closeness in the present formulation maps roughly onto what Heider (1958) terms a *unit relationship* and hence includes similarity. While the similarity of classical social comparison and the closeness of the present formulation are often overlapping, they are not the same construct. One way of thinking about this difference recently has been articulated by Miller, Turnbull & McFarland (1988; see also Berger, 1977; Parsons, 1949) who distinguish between " . . . *universalistic evaluation*: people determining their standing relative to other people in general . . . [and]. . . *particularistic evaluation*: people determining their standing relative to others with whom they identify or feel a bond." (Miller et al., 1988, pp. 908–909.) Similarity from the perspective of classical social comparison theory is associated with universalistic evaluation and is often operationalized in terms of shared attributes related to the performance dimension (Goethals & Darley, 1977; Suls, Gastorf & Lawhon, 1978). The closeness construct of the SEM model has a greater affinity to particularistic evaluation and has been operationalized in a variety of ways that increases the "we-ness" among actors.

Miller et al. (1988) report five creative studies demonstrating the importance of particularistic evaluation for the classic social comparison concern: desire for information concerning another's performance. That is, people preferred performance information about others who were similar regarding a unique self attribute even though that attribute had nothing to do with performance. One of our own early studies showed the importance of particularistic evaluation for SEM functioning. The SEM model predicts that when self is outperformed by another on a specific dimension, especially a close other, the relevance of that dimension to the self should decrease. Tesser & Campbell (1980) manipulated closeness by leading subjects to believe that they were either similar or dissimilar to a confederate with respect to personality, school major, year in school and family background. After completing some pre-tests, subjects were told that both performed at about the same level but poorly ("below average") on one task. Each was told that they both did better on a second task although the confederate ("above average") outperformed the subject ("average") on that second task. If a universalistic evaluation is important, then subjects should say that the second task, the one on which the self did better, is more relevant to their self-definition. But, if a particularistic evaluation is important (i.e., subjects don't want to be outperformed by another on a self-relevant task) the first task should be judged as more relevant to the self. The results were consistent with the SEM model and the particularistic orientation: The first task became more relevant to the self, particularly when the confederate was close[1].

Self-Evaluation versus Self-Esteem. Thus far I have used the terms self-evaluation and self-esteem interchangeably. However, I prefer the term self-evaluation for the central construct of the model for a variety of reasons. First, the term self-esteem has a set of features which are incompatible with the present usage. When people speak of self-esteem they are usually referring to a chronic, individual difference variable. Self-evaluation, on the other hand, is subject to moment to moment fluctuations rather than being chronic. It is affected by changes in situations rather than being associated with individual differences. Further, when people think of self-esteem, they tend to think of a variable that is measurable through self-report. Self-evaluation, on the other hand, is a hypothetical construct whose validity is not necessarily assumed to be reflected in self-report. Indeed, I believe people are often unaware of changes in self-evaluation. Changes in self-evaluation may be very fleeting and therefore difficult to capture in self-report. Finally, self-esteem has been used in so many different ways and has acquired so much surplus meaning that it is difficult to restrict its meaning when using it in the context of a particular model. Self-evaluation, on the other hand, is defined in terms of the specific model described herein.

The SEM Model is Systemic. Most social psychological theories are linear with a recursive causal structure. The SEM model is systemic. There are no independent or dependent variables in the usual sense. Each of the

---

[1] Although the universalistic versus particularistic distinction was not at issue when the study was designed, closeness appears to have been manipulated along particularistic lines, i.e., nonperformance related dimensions. If this is the case, the results concerning this manipulation further testify to the importance of the particularistic orientation. However, we have no checks on this aspect of the manipulation.

5. EMOTION IN COMPARISON AND REFLECTION 121

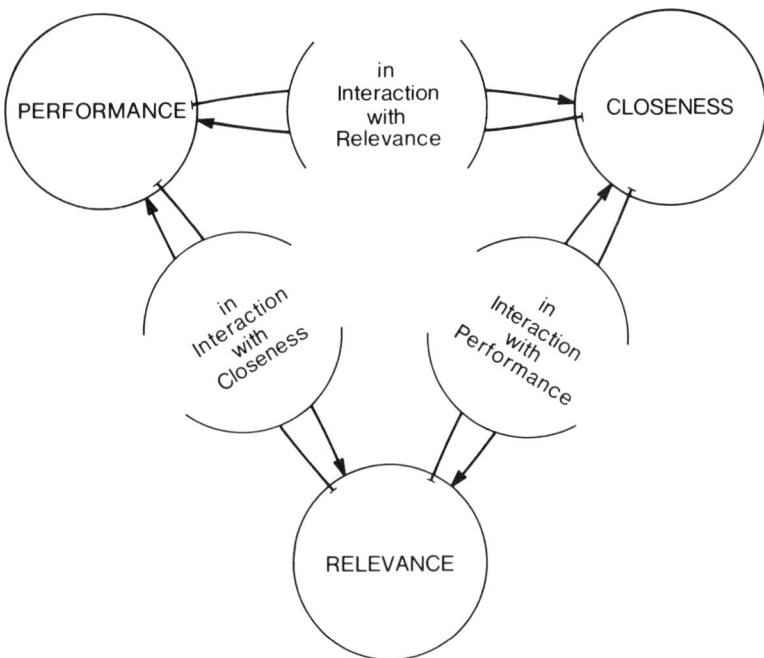

FIG. 5.1. Schematic illustration of the systemic nature of the self-evaluation maintenance model. (From Tesser, 1988.)

important model variables (relevance, closeness, and performance) are causes and, at the same time, consequences. As can be seen in Fig. 5.1, the SEM model is a little like Boyle's law relating temperature, pressure, and volume when describing the dynamics of gas. The arrows in the figure indicate causal direction. Performance (in interaction with relevance) should affect closeness: When relevance is high, the better another's performance the lower the closeness; when relevance is low, the better the other's performance the greater the closeness. Or, closeness (in interaction with performance) affects relevance. When another's performance is high, the closer the other, the lower the relevance. This relationship should disappear when the other's performance is not particularly good. To complete the circle, relevance (in interaction with closeness) should affect performance. When relevance is high, the closer the other the more we should attempt to interfere with or derogate the other's performance; when relevance is low, the closer the other the more we would expect to facilitate the performance of the other. Fig. 5.1 can be read going around the circle in the opposite direction. That is, performance (in interaction with closeness) affects relevance; relevance (in interaction with performance) affects closeness; closeness (in interaction with relevance) affects performance.

The model is nonlinear and its effects are interactive and causally bi-directional. Obviously, given a system like this, it is very difficult to do field studies in which it is unambiguously possible to identify causal direction. However, laboratory manipulations do permit such unambiguous inferences. Each of these hypotheses has been subject to laboratory test and each has been supported. In doing these tests, we have been careful to obtain both behavioral and cognitive measures of each of the variables. Since many of these studies have been reviewed elsewhere (e.g., Tesser, 1986), I will not review them again here but merely attempt to give the reader a feel for the kind of research that has been done.

To test the hypothesis that performance in interaction with relevance affects closeness, Pleban and Tesser (1981) measured how close subjects sat to a confederate who had either outperformed or performed at the same level as the subject in a kind of "college bowl" question and answer task. For half the subjects the topic of the quiz was high in relevance; for the remaining subjects the topic of the quiz was low. When relevance is high comparison is presumed to be important and the subject should attempt to distance oneself from the better performing confederate. When relevance is low reflection is assumed to be important and the subject should attempt to increase closeness to the better performing confederate. The predicted interaction emerged. When relevance was high the subject sat further away from the better performing confederate and when relevance was low the subject sat closer.

Tesser and Paulhus (1983) were interested in relevance as a dependent variable. Subjects were given feedback regarding their performance on "Cognitive Perceptual Integration," (CPI) a fictitious trait. Half the subjects were led to believe that they performed better while the remainder were led to believe that they performed more poorly than another. In addition, some subjects were led to believe that the other was similar to them (close) while others were led to believe that the other was dissimilar (distant). The relevance of CPI was measured by a paper-and-pencil questionnaire, by interview, and by surreptitiously recording how much time subjects spent reading biographies of people whom they believed to be high in CPI. Each of the measures of the relevance of CPI showed the same effect. Consistent with the SEM model, the better the self performed vis-a-vis the other, the more relevant was CPI. This was particularly true when the other was close.

Tesser and Smith (1980) examined the circumstances under which subjects would facilitate or interfere with the performance of others. Subjects participated with a friend (close other) and strangers (distant others) on a word identification task. Half of the subjects were led to believe that the task measured skills that were relevant to their self-identity and the remainder were led to believe that the task did not measure relevant skills.

Each participant had a chance to identify the target word from a series of clues. The clues were provided by the other participants from a list of clues that were graded in difficulty. If a subject wanted to prevent the identifier from performing well he could provide difficult clues; if a subject wanted to facilitate the identifier's performance he could provide easy clues. According to the SEM model, when relevance is high, one will suffer by comparison to the better performance of another, particularly a close other; when relevance is low, one can bask in the reflection of the better performance of a close other. Tesser and Smith (1980) found that when relevance was low subjects facilitated the performance of their friends more than that of the strangers by giving their friends easier clues. But, when relevance was high, subjects actually gave harder clues to their friends than to the strangers.

Emotion as a Marker, a Mediator and a Subjective Experience in the Self-Evaluation Maintenance Processes

As previously noted, a number of SEM predictions concerning behavior have been tested and supported. This provides some validation for the hypothesized reflection and comparison processes. The validation, however, is relatively distal. If comparison results in a threat to self-evaluation, a consequence of this threat that is more immediate than a change in behavior ought to be an emotional response, presumably a negative one. If reflection results in a boost to self-evaluation, it, too, should result in emotion. In this case a positive emotion. Thus, compared to behavior, emotion can serve as a relatively proximal marker of SEM processes. At the same time, these emotions ought to register themselves in qualitative, subjective experiences. That is, people should experience characteristic emotions under circumstances that produce the threat of comparison, e.g., jealousy, the promise of reflection, or pride in the other. Finally, we wish to see if the role of emotion in self-evaluation maintenance functioning is causal. That is, do emotions mediate the changes in behavior that have been observed in previous research.

EMOTION AS A MARKER OF SEM PROCESSES

The SEM model posits two processes. A comparison process and a reflection process. Each of the processes consists of the interaction of closeness and performance. When relevance is high, the comparison process is in place. Threat should be maximal when self is outperformed by a close other. Under these circumstances we should observe arousal² to be high. When relevance is low, the reflection process is in place. The highest level of augmentation to self is associated with being outperformed by a close other. Thus, when relevance is low we might also expect arousal to be highest when self is outperformed by a close other. Notice that the model predicts similar effects on arousal, regardless of relevance. (Relevance has a crucial effect on whether this emotion is positive or negative but arousal registers intensity of emotion not its direction.)

A Study on Arousal

Arousal is a hypothetical entity and not directly observable. It leaves its signature on behavior. That is, arousal tends to facilitate performance on well learned, simple tasks but tends to interfere with performance on complex tasks where the correct response is not dominant. If our theorizing about the SEM processes is correct we would expect to see high levels of arousal when the self is outperformed by another, particularly a close other (regardless of relevance of performance). We should observe that being outperformed by a close other facilitates performance on a simple task and interferes with performance on a more complex task.

This set of hypotheses was recently tested (Tesser, Millar, & Moore, 1988, Study 1). Subjects reported to the laboratory with a friend. They were given a number of computer administered trials in which they performed on either a social sensitivity task or a creativity task. (For some subjects creativity was more relevant than social sensitivity; for others, the opposite). After each trial, subjects were given feedback about how their friend, a close other, or a stranger, someone they had just met, performed on that trial. On half the trials the subject learned that they had performed better than the other person. On the remaining trials they learned that the other person had performed better than they. Following the feedback on each trial, subjects completed a secondary task. Performance on this task served as our indicant of arousal. Subjects were given a five digit number to enter into the computer as fast as they could. On half the trials this number represented a simple task. Each of the digits were identical (e.g., 55555). On the remaining trials the number represented a complex task. The five digits were a random sample of digits (e.g., 10344). The dependent variable was the amount of time subjects took to enter these digits into the computer.

---

[2] From the present perspective, arousal refers to a hypothetical level of energization of the organism. Arousal may reveal itself physiologically with changes in autonomic nervous system function, or it may reveal itself behaviorally by differentially affecting the performance of well and poorly learned responses (Zajonc, 1965).

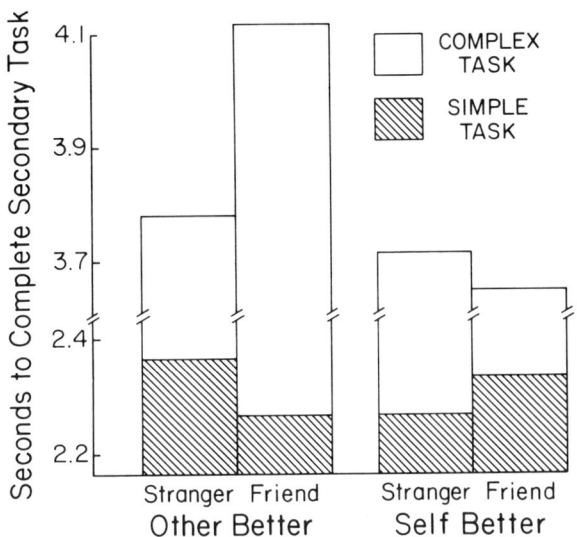

FIG. 5.2. Time taken (in seconds) to complete simple and complex secondary tasks as a combined function of performance feedback (self better vs. other better) and closeness of other (friend vs. stranger). (This figure originally appeared in Tesser, 1988.)

As can be seen in Fig. 5.2 the results were consistent with the hypotheses. There was a three factor interaction involving relative performance (self better vs. other better), closeness (friend vs. stranger), and complexity of the task. When self was outperformed by a close other arousal seemed to be present. Performance on simple tasks were facilitated (shorter latencies), whereas performance on complex tasks were debilitated (longer latencies). If the threat of comparison generates more arousal than the promise of reflection the pattern of behavior we observed and illustrated in Fig. 5.2 would be affected by relevance. The pattern would be exaggerated when relevance is high (and the comparison process is important) and attenuated when relevance is low (and the reflection process is important). There were no effects of relevance in this study. This indicates that both the reflection and comparison processes were of approximately equal magnitude. In sum, arousal appears to mark the SEM processes.

Affect: The Polarity of Emotion

Arousal is not the only aspect of emotion that can be used to mark the operation of reflection and comparison. Perhaps a more telling, more specific index of emotion is that of affect, the positive or negative aspect of emotion. Whereas the comparison and reflection processes make identical predictions concerning arousal, they make mirror image predictions concerning affect. When relevance is high and the comparison process is important the better performance of a close other ought to produce negative affect. In contrast, when relevance is low and the reflection process is important, the better performance of a close other ought to produce positive affect.

Previous Research. Several studies have obtained results consistent with the SEM hypotheses about the direction of affect. Nadler, Jazwinski, Lau & Miller (1980) varied the closeness of pairs of male college students using an attitude similarity manipulation. Subsequently, an attractive female confederate of the experimenter opted for or against the subject's partner (rather than the subject) to work with her. Finally, subjects filled out an affective reactions or "feeling" scale. Although Nadler et al. (1980) did not manipulate relevance, we would suggest that being chosen or rejected by an attractive co-ed was quite relevant to the self-definition of these male college-age subjects. Hence, the comparison process should be important. The interaction between closeness (similarity) and performance (rejection by the co-ed) predicted by the comparison process emerged: Being outperformed by a close other produced the most negative affect.

Salovey & Rodin (1984) manipulated relevance and performance. They gave subjects feedback that they had done well or poorly on a dimension that was either high or low in relevance to their self-definition. They also told subjects that another had done either well or poorly on the high or the low relevant dimension. As anticipated by the model, their subjects reported the most anxiety and depression and least positivity of mood when self did poorly and other did well on the highly relevant dimension.

At least two studies in which affect was measured can be interpreted as having manipulated all three variables: relevance, performance and closeness. Nadler, Fisher, & Ben-Itzhak (1983) asked their subjects to solve a mystery. Relevance was manipulated by telling some of the subjects that the solution required important skills and the remaining subjects that the solution was based on luck. After finding his own solution was wrong, the subject was given a clue from either a friend (close other) or a stranger (distant other). Thus, the other outperformed the self and this happened once or twice. Consistent with the prediction of the SEM model, the condition in which relevance was high and help was received from the friend on two occasions generated the most negative affect.

Vanyur (1980) manipulated the closeness of female subjects to a target other using feedback regarding attitude similarity. Relevance and performance were manipulated in an interview which the subject watched via closed circuit TV. In the interview, the target revealed notable success or failure (the performance manipulation) in either academics or their stamp collection (high vs. low relevance to the subject). Following the interview subjects gave a report of their mood. The pattern of data closely matched the SEM predictions. Although the overall three factor interaction was not significant, a planned comparison among the close other conditions revealed an interaction such that, relative to the other's failure, the other's success produced a better mood when relevance was low than when relevance was high. This interaction was not present among the distant other conditions.

Although several studies have produced results which are consistent with the SEM hypotheses concerning the direction of affect, none of them were designed explicitly to test the SEM model. Thus, their support for the model depends upon our *post hoc* interpretation. Further, each of the previous studies rely on self-reports of affect. From a construct validation perspective it would be useful to have an index of affect which did not share method variance (Campbell & Fiske, 1959). If we can observe similar effects with different methods then we know that the results are not due to an idiosyncracy of the method that has nothing to do with the hypotheses. For these reasons we decided to run our own studies specifically designed to study affect as a marker of the SEM processes.

The Reflection Process and Affect. Since most researchers who deal with social comparison and self-evaluation concern themselves with the threatening aspects of another's better performance we decided to focus first on the reflection process. The reflection process is important when relevance is low. Under these conditions the better performance of a close other ought to produce positive affect.

Our (Tesser, Millar, & Moore, 1988, Study 2) female subjects reported to the experiment with a friend. After filling out a questionnaire intended to measure the relevance of a number of knowledge areas to their self-definition, subjects from one friendship pair were introduced to subjects from another friendship pair. Then each subject was taken to a separate room where she responded to 30 computer administered items from the domain she had previously indicated was the least relevant to her self-definition. Prearranged feedback varied closeness and performance: The subject learned that either a close other (the friend she had brought with her) or a distant other (one of the subjects she had just met) had performed equal to or better than she had. Finally, subjects were asked to rate the pleasantness of a number of unfamiliar words (e.g., catarrh, obol, perdol). The average pleasantness rating served as an indirect index of subjects' affect[3] (Clark & Isen, 1982; Isen & Shalker, 1977).

---

[3] Subjects also responded to self-report measures of affect on a postexperimental questionnaire. These reports did not show the predicted effects. Perhaps the emotional responses are relatively transient or perhaps subjects are not aware of them.

The usual social comparison approach suggests that another's, particularly a close other's, better performance is threatening and, hence, should be associated with negative affect. The SEM model, on the other hand, suggests that when relevance is low there is the possibility of basking in the reflected glory of another's better performance, particularly if the other is psychologically close. The interaction predicted by the SEM model emerged. Using the pleasantnes ratings of the unfamiliar words as a measure of affect, the close other–better performance condition was associated with the most positive affect as predicted by the SEM model rather than the least positive affect as predicted by the more usual approach.

Comparison and Reflection Processes: The Facial Expression Study. Our next study (Tesser, Millar & Moore, 1988, Study 3) looked simultaneously at both the reflection and comparison processes and used facial expressions to index positive and negative affect.

Again, subjects were asked to report to the laboratory and again, they brought a friend along with them. Once again, each subject interacted with a computer. The computer presented a number of trials, some dealing with esthetic judgement, the remainder dealing with logical thinking. (For some subjects, logical thinking was more relevant than esthetic judgement; for other subjects esthetic judgement was more relevant than logical thinking.) Again, at the end of each trial, subjects were given feedback about how well they performed vis-a-vis the friend they had brought with them or a stranger. On half the trials they found that they had outperformed the other; on the remaining trials they found that the other person outperformed them.

In order to measure affective responses, subjects' faces were surreptitiously videotaped. (A signal was put onto the tape indicating for the judge the point at which subjects were getting feedback.) Finally, the tapes were viewed by judges who were blind to the independent variables. Judges used a simple seven point, graded scale anchored with the words "pleasant" and "unpleasant" for scoring facial responses. These ratings turned out to be quite reliable with a mean, per subject coefficient alpha of .81.

Recall our expectations. If the SEM model is correct, we expect a three factor interaction. When relevance is high, closeness and performance ought to interact to produce the most unpleasant expression with a close other outperforming the self. When relevance is low, closeness and performance ought to interact to produce the most pleasant expression when a close other outperforms self.

The theoretically crucial three factor interaction was indeed significant and in the appropriate direction. We illustrate this interaction in terms of closeness effects: the difference in positivity of facial affect between responses to a close and distant other. These data are presented in Fig. 5.3.

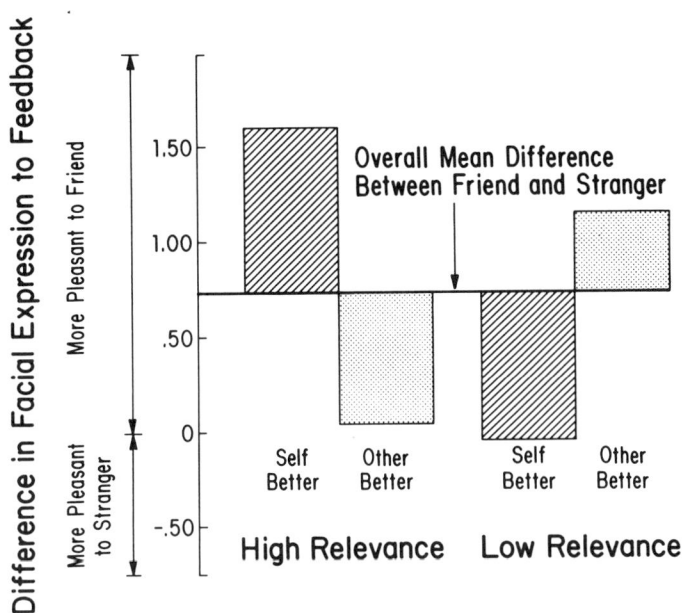

FIG. 5.3. Difference in pleasantness of facial expression to close (friend) and distant (stranger) other as a combined function of performance feedback, (self better vs. other better) and relevance of task to subjects' self definition. (From Tesser, Millar, & Moore, 1988.)

What is immediately apparent in this figure is that the overall mean difference is positive, indicating that facial expressions are more positive given feedback about a friend than feedback about a stranger. More interesting, though, are the relative differences around this overall mean.

When relevance is high and the other outperforms self there is a threat due to comparison, particularly with a close other. The closeness effect for other performs better should be less positive than for self performs better. This difference is apparent in the figure. Further, when relevance is low (and the reflection process is important) if the self outperforms the other, one cannot bask in the other's good performance. The closeness effect when the other performs better should be more positive than the closeness effect when the self performs better. Again, a review of the figure reveals that this is the case.

Not all the effects predicted by the model emerged in this study. Regardless of closeness, we expected more positive affect when other outperformed self on a high relevance dimension rather than a low relevance dimension. This effect was not significant. Although the study did not support the model in its entirety, it did provide support for some of the more subtle predictions, predictions not easily explained by other models. Thus, the results are encouraging.

We have suggested that emotion may serve as a proximal marker of the operation of reflection and comparison. To explore this suggestion we examined two aspects of emotion. Arousal, an index which increases with either positive or negative emotion; and affect, a directional index of emotion. In the studies we reviewed, emotion was inferred from overt behavior (the facilitation of simple responses and the interference with complex processes), from self-reports of affect, from indirect measures of affect (the ratings of unfamiliar words) and from physiological measures (facial expressions). Taken as a whole these measures seem to mark the operation of both comparison and reflection processes. Not only are people threatened by the good performance of a close other (when relevance is high) but (when relevance is low) they also seem to be positively affected by the good performance of a close other. (See Collins, Taylor, & Dakoff, 1989, for a discussion of other conditions under which being outperformed by another can be positive and outperforming another can be negative.)

THE EMOTIONAL EXPERIENCE OF COMPARISON AND REFLECTION PROCESSES

We have seen how aspects of emotion can be used to mark or document the operation of social comparison and social reflection processes. The aspects of emotion that were used to do this were arousal and affect. These components are perhaps the easiest to measure and appear to be important components in many behavioral systems. As such, they are quite useful. However, they fail to provide much insight into subjective experiences such as the negative emotions we all feel when confronted with being outperformed by someone, or the particular kind of pleasure of seeing a loved one succeed. These relatively rich subjective experiences are best documented through self-reports. Although there have been attempts to distinguish such emotions physiologically (Ax, 1953; Cacioppo & Petty, 1981; Hager & Ekman, 1983; Schwartz, Weinberger, & Singer, 1981) and those attempts appear to hold some promise, they cannot provide the kind of richness obtainable in a personal account.

Some Intuitive Hypotheses

What kind of subjective experiences should we expect people to report during the SEM processes? While the model itself is not helpful in providing the answer, we can make some guesses. Let us focus first on the comparison process. When a performance dimension is high in relevance to the self and we are confronted by another, particularly a close other, who outperforms us, our feelings might be labeled jealously or envy. (Although psychologists and philosophers have distinguished between jealousy and envy, e.g., Bryson, 1977, previous research has indicated that lay persons do not, e.g., Salovey & Rodin, 1986. We treat these two emotions as synonymous).

Salovey & Rodin (chapter 10, this volume) have identified similar conditions as causal in producing what they term social comparison jealousy (which they distinguish from other forms of jealousy). In a study intended to test these ideas, they (Salovey & Rodin, 1984) manipulated relative performance, similarity to another and relevance of the performance dimension. They found the most jealousy when subjects role-played being outperformed by a similar other on a relevant dimension. If being outperformed by a close other on a relevant dimension produces jealousy, what does outperforming a close other on a relevant dimension produce? My intuition suggests that the mirror image of jealousy is pride. Unfortunately, I know of no studies in which variables were manipulated and in which pride was measured.

The SEM model suggests that positive feelings are associated with the reflection process. The nature of those feelings seems to be a kind of pride–in–the–other. I find it interesting that I have not been able to locate any single word in the English language which captures this feeling of positivity when a close other does well. Other languages do have such a concept. For example, in Yiddish there are two words that capture this feeling: *Nachas* (transliteration) is a noun which names the feeling and *kvell* (transliteration) is a verb which describes experiencing this feeling. The words *orgullo* and *orghullo* in Spanish and Portuguese, respectively, refer to similar feelings. Although, we have no word for it in English, we would suggest that people do experience pride–in–the–other under the appropriate conditions.

In order to test our hypotheses about jealousy–envy, pride, pride–in–the–other and other subjective emotions, we (Tesser & Collins, 1988) interviewed people about their emotional experiences in each of the eight prototypical SEM situations. For each situation subjects were asked to recall a circumstance in which they and another, either a close or distant other were performing something either important or unimportant to their self-definition. The instance they were to recall had to be one in which the respondent either outperformed or was outperformed by the other. For each of these eight combinations the respondent was asked to describe in some detail the incident and then to focus on and describe his or her feelings. After freely describing their feelings associated with each incident, respondents rated the extent to which they experienced a number of specific emotions taken from Smith & Ellsworth (1985): happiness, sadness, fear, anger, boredom, challenge, interest, hope, frustration, contempt, disgust, surprise, pride, shame, and guilt. They also rated our hypothetical emotions: jealousy, envy, and pride–in–the–other's accomplishments.

We focus first on the emotions associated with our intuitive hypotheses. Jealousy and envy are presumed to be manifestations of the comparison threat. Such threats should be highest when self is outperformed by a close other on a relevant dimension. Closeness did not have a significant effect, but performance and relevance interacted in affecting jealousy and envy. As can be seen in Fig. 5.4A, this interaction is consistent with our intuitions. Jealousy and envy rise when the other outperforms the self. Further, the effect of other's performance is greater when the performance dimension is relevant to the self.

We hypothesized that pride would be the mirror image of jealousy. As can be seen in Fig. 5.4B, this expectation was also realized. Again, closeness had no systematic effect.[4] But, relevance and performance interacted to affect pride. Pride is higher when self outperforms the other than vice versa. This effect is more pronounced on a high relevance dimension than on a low relevance dimension. Jealousy–envy and pride are presumed to be manifestations of the comparison process. It is noteworthy that there is more action on these emotions (i.e., the effect of performance is greater when relevance is high).

Pride–in–the–other was the only specific emotional experience called to mind when thinking about the reflection process. Again, the predicted three factor interaction, closeness × relevance × performance was not significant. But, the relevance by performance interaction and closeness by performance interactions were significant. The means for these interactions are illustrated in Figs. 5.4C and 5.4D. As expected, pride–in–the–other is greater when other outperforms self than when self outperforms other. Pride–in–the–other is the subjective experience of the reflection process. The reflection process is important when relevance is low. It is heartening to note that the action for pride–in–the–other, (i.e., the performance effect) is greater in the low rather than in the high relevance conditions (Fig. 5.4C). Closeness also had an effect on pride–in–the–other. Not surprisingly, the close other generated greater pride–in–the–other than the distant other. Moreover, the impact of relative performance was greater for the close, rather than the distant, other (Fig. 5.4D). Thus, pride–in–the–other appears to be a subjective concomitant of the reflection process.

---

[4] It is not clear why closeness failed to have the expected effects on these self-reported emotions. Perhaps persons find it difficult to recall situations in which the other party was someone with whom they had little or no association. Perhaps subjects are reconstructing their emotions on the basis of their own naive theories of emotion rather than directly recalling their emotions, and those naive theories inaccurately discount the importance of closeness.

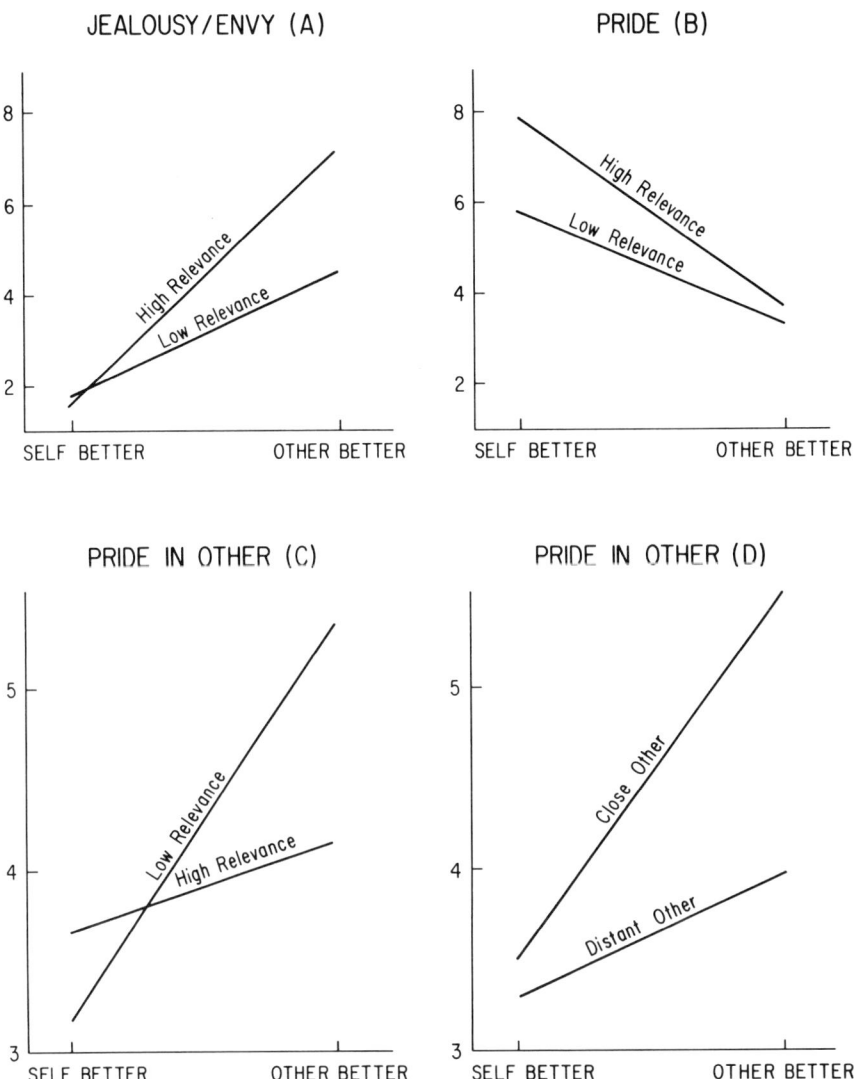

FIG. 5.4. The comparison emotions of envy, jealousy (averaged) and pride are displayed as a joint function of relevance and performance. (Panels A and B.) The reflection emotion of pride in other is displayed as a joint function of relevance and performance in Panel C and as a joint function of closeness and performance in Panel D. (From Tesser & Collins, 1988.)

Some Exploratory Analyses of Subjective Experiences

Recall that each of our respondents rated 18 different subjective emotional experiences for each of the eight SEM situations. We had intuitive hypotheses about only a small subset of these experiences. Since intuition can take us only so far, we decided to learn what we could from the remaining ratings and the free descriptions of these experiences. We focus first on the ratings.

Which particular emotions best distinguish the eight SEM situations from one another? In order to answer this question we used a statistical procedure known as multiple discriminant analysis (Dixon & Brown, 1979, Program P7M). This procedure finds the best linear combinations of emotion ratings that maximally discriminate the SEM situations from one another. The application of this procedure to the present data indicated that all the usable information necessary for discriminating among the eight situations could be captured in a set of only six emotions: SEM situations which are high in relevance and in which the self outperforms the other are associated with the emotional experiences of pride and happiness; situations which are also high in relevance but in which the other outperforms the self are associated with sadness and jealousy; situations which are low in relevance and in which the other outperforms the self are associated with pride-in-the-other; finally, the low relevance situations in which the self outperforms the other are associated with boredom.

The analysis does not do a very good job of discriminating among the SEM situations that differ only on the close–distant dimension. Further, the intuitively identified emotions; jealousy, pride, pride-in-the-other, constitute three out of the six emotions deemed important by the analysis. (Two of the remaining three emotions are relatively general, i.e., sadness, happiness.) The new information provided by this analysis is in the specification of boredom. Although it is not surprising that boredom characterizes low relevance situations, it did not come to mind in our intuitive analysis.

Subjects' free descriptions of their emotional reactions to the SEM situations were content analyzed. Several hints about SEM emotions emerged from this analysis. For example, specific mentions of jealousy, anger, and frustration come up only when the self is outperformed by the other and particularly when the task is highly relevant. All three of the SEM variables (closeness, relevance and performance) seem to interact in determining mentions of pride and guilt: Pride and guilt seem to be mentioned most frequently in connection with situations in which the self outperforms a close other on a relevant dimension.

The relevance of the SEM situation appears to be quite consequential. High relevance situations have more emotional action associated with them than low relevance situations. Low relevance situations produced 32 specific mentions of lack of affect, whereas high relevance produced only one. In fact, the ratio of specific mentions of emotion words for high to low relevance situations is about 2 to 1. The closeness of the SEM situations seems to affect the extent to which people mention the other. For close as compared to distant others, respondents are more likely to mention empathy and feeling good for the other when the other does well and feeling bad for the other when self does better.

The variables that define the operation of social comparison and social reflection processes seem to be associated with quite different subjective experiences. In line with intuition, social comparison processes affect emotions like jealousy–envy and pride, whereas social reflection processes affect such subjective experiences as pride in the other and empathy. High levels of relevance tend to produce more in the way of salient emotional experiences. Situations involving close others result in greater empathic feelings and what Ortony, Clore, & Collins (1988) call "the fortunes of others" emotions.

EMOTION AS A MEDIATOR OF SEM BEHAVIOR

We have seen that aspects of emotion, such as arousal and affect, can be used to mark the operation of social comparison and reflection processes. We have also seen that these processes have particular subjective experiences associated with them. The questions we wish to address concern the causal role of emotion in the unfolding of subsequent behavior. Do the emotional concomitants of SEM processes mediate subsequent behavior or are they merely epiphenomonal; a by-product of the threat or promise to self-evaluation inherent in the SEM situations? Parsimony would favor the by-product interpretation: The SEM model does a reasonable job of predicting behavior without emotion mediating those behaviors. Why complicate things by putting them in?

My own bias is to assume that if the emotional response is there, it is there for a functional reason. The most obvious reason is that it mediates subsequent behavior. How might it do so? One could focus either on the subjective emotional experience or the affect/arousal. A number of theorists (Ableson, 1983; Clore & Ortony, 1984; DeRivera, 1977; Roseman, 1984, Scherer, 1982; Smith & Ellsworth, 1985) suggest that our subjective emotions result from the construal of situations with respect to a number of emotion dimensions and that emotion cannot be divorced from such meaning analysis. Weiner (1986), for example, is concerned with the construal of situations in terms of attributions of causality as determinants of emotional experience. The kind of meaning analysis underlying the experience of emotion can provide direction for subsequent behavior. For example, if John knows that he harmed Jim for no good reason he ought to experience guilt. This same information, however, would suggest that John should compensate Jim. Thus, the emotional information is also the information on which subsequent reparation behavior is based. This is one way in which the information underlying the emotion could mediate subsequent behavior.

There is, however, another tradition based on the experience of arousal and/or affect. There are a variety of approaches in social psychology which assume that various response domains are somehow controlled by the experience of arousal. Blascovich and Katkin (1982) have described a number of such theories. These include cognitive dissonance theory (Cooper & Fazio, 1984), helping behavior (Pilliavin, Pilliavin, & Rodin, 1975), aggression (Berkowitz, 1969), social facilitation (Zajonc, 1965), interpersonal affiliation (Schachter, 1959), and attributional egotism (Stephan & Gollwitzer, 1981). This is the direction that has been taken in the SEM work.

My view of emotion in SEM functioning is similar to Cooper & Fazio's (1984) view of the role of arousal in cognitive dissonance processes and Stephan & Gollwitzer's (1981; Gollwitzer, Earle, & Stephan, 1982) view of the role of affect in attributional egotism. I assume a two step causal sequence. A change in external circumstances triggers the SEM processes which result in arousal. Increased arousal leads to a cognitive search (e.g., Berscheid, 1983; Mandler, 1975) resulting in behavior intended to eliminate or reduce the potential pain of comparison or to maintain or increase the potential pleasure of reflection. If this line of reasoning is correct then the presence of the SEM pattern of behavior should vary with emotional arousal.

There are three facets to this hypothesis. The *arousal facet* implies that the SEM pattern of behavior should be clear when arousal is high and become fuzzy or disappear when arousal is low. The *misattribution facet* implies that the SEM pattern should also dissolve if the arousal that is present is misattributed to some irrelevant source (e.g., Cooper & Fazio, 1984; Schachter, 1964; Stephan & Gollwitzer, 1981). The *interactive facet* implies that arousal and misattribution interact such that if arousal is low the SEM pattern of behavior will dissolve regardless of attribution or if there is a tendency to misattribute the arousal the SEM pattern of behavior will dissolve regardless of level of arousal.

Misattribution of Arousal and SEM Behaviors

Our first experiment on the mediational role of emotion (Tesser, Pilkington, & McIntosch, 1989, Study 1) examined the misattribution facet of the mediational hypothesis. In order to pursue this test we needed a paradigm which had generated the SEM pattern of behavior in the past. A successful test of the emotional mediation hypothesis would show that the SEM pattern of behavior is replicated where persons do not misattribute their

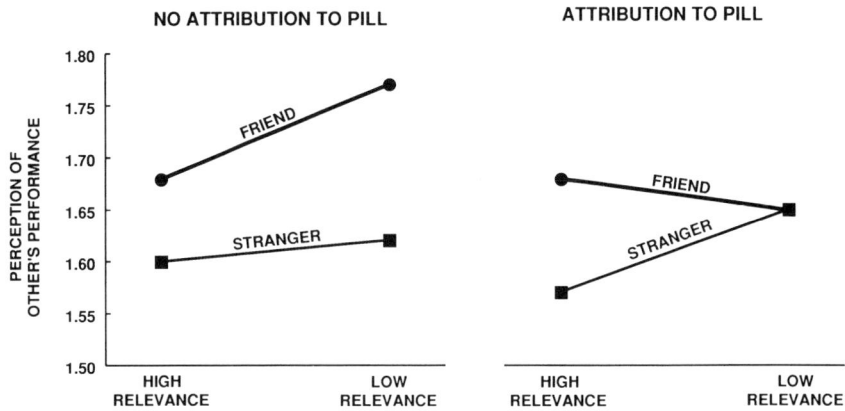

FIG. 5.5. Perception of the performance of another plotted as a function of closeness (friend vs. stranger), relevance to self and whether arousal is attributed to the vitamin C pill. (From Tesser, Pilkington, & McIntosch, 1988.)

arousal (i.e., under control conditions) but that the pattern dissolves when persons do misattribute their arousal.

A paradigm that meets these requirements was devised by Tesser & Campbell (1982). They had subjects perform on items from two dimensions that differed in personal relevance. After receiving feedback regarding their own performance on each item, subjects were asked to guess the performance of either a friend (close other) or a stranger (distant other). The results were entirely consistent with the SEM model: Subjects were more positive in their perception of a friend's performance on a low relevance task (the effect of relevance disappeared for the stranger); subjects were more charitable in their perception of their friend's performance than of the stranger's performance on the low relevance task (but the friend's advantage disappeared on the high relevance task.)

To test the misattribution hypothesis we duplicated the Tesser & Campbell (1982) conditions and added an attribution factor: All subjects were given a Vitamin C pill before completing any of the tasks. (Subjects were told that we were interested in seeing if Vitamin C would affect accuracy of perception.) Control subjects were told that the pill should have no physical effects: Misattribution subjects were told that the pill may produce "increased heartrate, sweaty palms, a nervous feeling in your stomach, a 'pumped up' feeling and that these feelings may come and go." Again, if emotion plays a mediational role, the SEM effect should be attenuated under conditions in which subjects are induced to attribute their arousal (emotion) to an external source, such as the Vitamin C capsule.

As can be seen in Fig. 5.5, the pattern of means closely conforms to the hypothesis. Let us focus first on the control conditions where we expect to find the SEM pattern of results. According to the SEM model the more relevant the performance, the less charitable one's view of another's performance, particularly that of a close other. Specifically, to replicate the previous Tesser & Campbell (1982) study, persons should be more charitable toward a friend on a low relevance task and this effect should be attenuated for strangers. The performance of a friend should be seen as more positive than the performance of a stranger on a low relevance task and the friend's advantage should be smaller on the high relevance task. All of these expectations were realized in one global comparison which was highly significant.

If emotion is an important mediator of SEM effects the SEM effects should disappear if the emotion is externally attributed, as it is in the misattribution conditions. Fig. 5.5 reveals this to be the case as well. The overall planned comparison reflecting the SEM expectations was not significantly different from zero and was significantly smaller than the comparison in the control conditions.

The results clearly confirm the misattribution hypothesis. In the control conditions, where emotion is not misattributed, the predicted SEM pattern emerges and nicely replicates Tesser & Campbell (1982). On the other hand, these effects disappear when emotional symptoms are attributed to the Vitamin C pill.

Arousal and Misattribution: Their Joint Effects

As noted previously, the emotion mediation hypothesis has other implications: Higher arousal should be associated with a clearer pattern of behavior than lower arousal. Further, arousal and (mis)attribution should interact in their effects on behavior. We expect to see a clear SEM pattern only when arousal is relatively high and the arousal is not misattributed.

We examined these implications in a second study by (Tesser et al., 1988, Study 2). Again, the conditions of the Tesser & Campbell (1982) study were replicated: Subjects were given feedback about their own performance on both high and low relevance tasks. They were asked to predict how a friend or a stranger would perform on them. Arousal and (mis)attribution were measured rather than manipulated. Subjects were exposed to noise during the session. They were categorized into "noise" (misattribution) and "no noise" conditions on the basis of a median split of responses to the question, "If you felt at all nervous or aroused, to what extent do you think it was due to the noise you were listening to?" The index of arousal that produced the most easily interpretable results was based on a median split of pre to post change in blood pressure (BP).

The partitioning of subjects into attribution to noise versus no noise groups provided a conceptual replication of the first study (attribution to pill vs. control). Although the results were of borderline significance, the pattern of means replicated, thereby confirming the attributional aspect of the emotional mediation hypothesis again.

More interesting are the effects of arousal, alone and in interaction with attribution. Subjects with relatively high arousal should show the SEM pattern more strongly than subjects with lower arousal. Subjects with increasing BP show the SEM pattern while subjects with decreasing BP do not. That is, in contrast to decreasing BP subjects, for increasing BP subjects the effect of relevance was more negative for a close other and the effect of closeness was more positive at low relevance.

To test the interaction facet of the emotional mediation prediction, subjects were joint classified according to both attribution (noise vs. no noise) and arousal (increasing vs. decreasing BP). Again, the results are quite consistent with the emotional mediation hypothesis (see Fig. 5.6). The SEM pattern of behavior emerged only when arousal was high and was not attributed to the noise. Where arousal was low or attributed to the noise, the pattern of behavior predicted by the SEM model did not manifest itself. Further, the pattern of behavior generated by the high arousal–no external attribution group is significantly closer to the predicted pattern than the patterns generated by the other groups.

The studies reviewed here provide support for the idea that emotion plays a mediational role in the unfolding of SEM behaviors. They suggest that arousal must be present (or not attributed to an irrelevant source) in order to observe at least some SEM behavior patterns.

Some Notes on the Mediational Role of Emotion

We have examined the role of arousal in SEM behavior and found that such behaviors follow predictions of the model only when arousal is present and it is not misattributed. The finding that misattribution plays a role suggests that cognitive factors may be important. Earlier I suggested a two stage process: (a) Potentially consequential circumstances lead to arousal and this arousal, in turn, (b) causes a search for behaviors that will minimize threat and/or maximize the promise to self-evaluation. The result of an arousal–search process is the SEM pattern of behaviors. Such a sequence of events accounts for the observed finding.

The two step model also suggests that not all arousal leads to SEM behaviors. We find Cooper and Fazio's (1984) treatment of dissonance and dissonance motivation to be a useful analog. Dissonant circumstances produce arousal but that arousal doesn't turn into dissonance motivation unless it is attributed to inconsistency. If it is attributed elsewhere dissonance reduction will not be observed. Similarly, if arousal generated from some other source is experienced but erroneously attributed to dissonant cir-

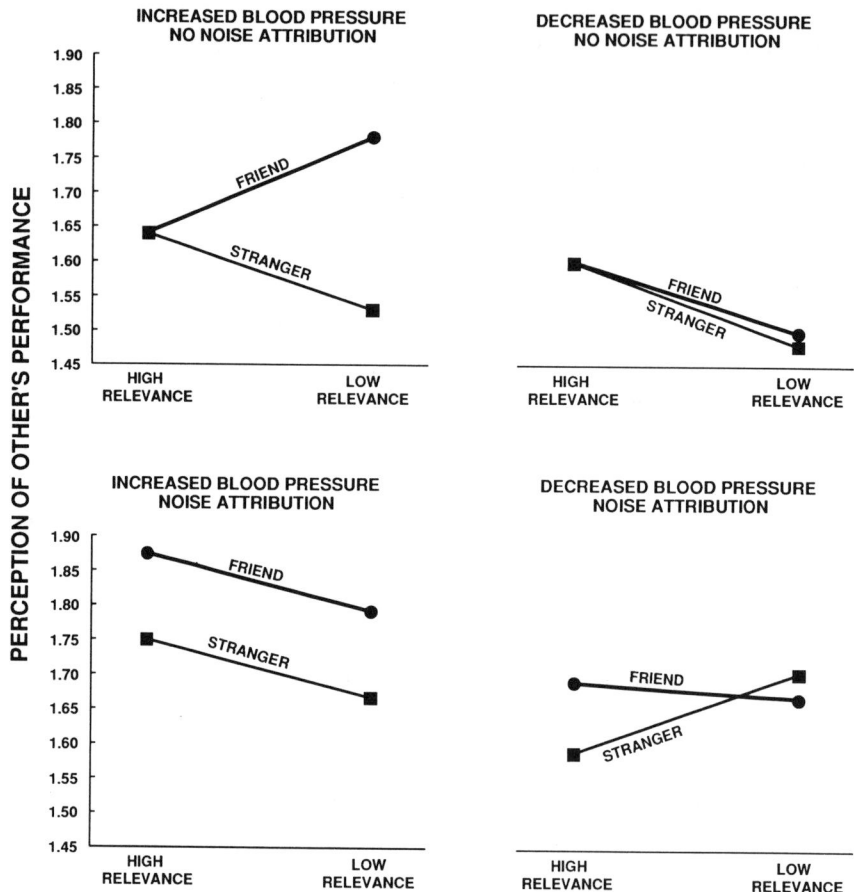

FIG. 5.6. Perception of the performance of another plotted as a function of closeness (friend vs. stranger), relevance to self, attribution to noise and change in blood pressure. (From Tesser, Pilkington, & McIntosh, 1988.)

cumstances, an increase in dissonance reduction will be observed. Perhaps similar processes operate with respect to self-evaluation maintenance behaviors. If a set of antecedent conditions, such as being outperformed by a close other, produces arousal, and if it is correctly attributed, we might expect to observe some shifts in the relevance of the performance dimension. If, on the other hand, this arousal is misattributed, it will not become SEM motivation and we will not observe the change in relevance. By the same token, if people are aroused in some way, such as through exercise, and they are lead to misattribute that arousal to another's performance, that misattribution will turn the arousal into SEM motivation and we will begin to observe changes in relevance. In a recently completed study, Tesser, Achee, & Pilkington (1990) found that for some people an irrelevant source of arousal, exercise, enhanced SEM functioning compared to a nonarousal group.

SUMMARY

In this chapter I have sketched a model in which social comparison can lead to a threat to self-evaluation and social reflection can lead to a boost in self-evaluation. The model is systemic. It is based on the mutual and interactive causal effects of relevance, relative performance and psychological closeness to a co-acting other. The aspect of the model that we focused on was it's emotional concomitants. We looked at arousal and affect as markers of the SEM processes and found that measures of these variables behaved in a way which was consistent with the operation of comparison and reflection processes. We then turned to the subjective experiences associated with such processes. Here we found variations in jealousy/envy and pride, pride–in–the–other, and boredom were able to distinguish the eight canonical SEM situations. Finally, we turned to the question of the mediational role of affect in self-evaluation maintenance functioning. In a series of studies we found that arousal appeared to play a causal role. Its presence facilitated behaviors predicted by the model and it's misattribution reduced the pattern of behaviors predicted by the model.

Research with the model is pursuing three threads. First, we are hoping to more carefully detail the mediational role of emotion in SEM functioning. Second, we are working on a series of explorations to locate the role of self-evaluation maintenance processes in the larger self system. In this connection we are asking the following questions: Are self-evaluation maintenance processes connected with self-affirmation (Steele, 1988), (i.e., Will subjects who are given an opportunity to affirm their important values show reduced SEM processes?). Are SEM processes related to dissonance reduction (Steele & Liu, 1983), (i.e., Will a boost to self-evaluation through reflection attenuate the tendency to reduce dissonance?). In general, is the self-system organized in such a way that successes in one sphere reduce defensiveness in another or are various spheres of self-functioning independent of one another. Finally, we are trying to use the model in a productive, applied way. Specifically, we are concerned with the conditions under which self-evaluation maintenance processes will lead to increased effort and productivity on the part of the self rather than derogation of or interference with the other. The work is exciting and challenging.

ACKNOWLEDGMENT

I am grateful for the support provided by NIMH Grant No. 1R01MH41487-01 in preparing this chapter.

REFERENCES

Abelson, R. P. (1983). Whatever became of consistency theory? *Personality and Social Psychology Bulletin, 9,* 37–54.
Alloy, L. B. & Ahrens, A. H. (1987). Depression and pessimism for the future: Biased use of statistically relevant information in predictions for self versus others. *Journal of Personality and Social Psychology, 52,* 366–378.
Ax, A. F. (1953). The physiological differentiation between fear and anger in humans. *Psychosomatic Medicine, 15,* 433–442.
Berger, S. M. (1977). Social comparison, modeling and perseverance. In J. M. Suls & R. L. Miller (Eds.), *Social comparison processes: Theoretical and empirical perspectives* (pp. 209–234). Washington, DC: Hemisphere.
Berkowitz, L. (Ed.). (1969). *Roots of aggression: A re-examination of the frustration-aggression hypothesis.* New York: Atherton.
Berscheid, E. (1983). Emotion. In H. H. Kelley, E. Berscheid, A. Christensen, J. Harvey, T. L. Huston, G. Levinger, E. McClintock, A. Peplau, & D. R. Peterson (Eds.), *Close Relationships* (pp. 110–168). San Francisco: Freeman.
Blascovich, J. & Katkin, E. S. (1982). Arousal-based social behaviors: Do they reflect differences in visceral perception? In L. Wheeler (Ed.), *Review of personality and social psychology* (Vol. 3) pp. 73–96. Beverly Hills: Sage.
Brickman, P., & Bulman, R. J. (1977). Pleasure and pain in social comparison. In J. Suls & R. L. Miller (Eds.), *Social comparison processes: Theoretical and empirical perspectives* (pp. 149–189). Washington, DC: Hemisphere.
Bryson, J. B. (1977 August). *Situational determinants of the expression of jealousy.* Unpublished paper presented at the annual meeting of the American Psychological Association, San Francisco.
Cacioppo, J. T., & Petty, R. E. (1981). Electromyograms as measures of extent and affectivity of information processing. *American Psychologist, 36,* 441–456.
Campbell, D. T. & Fiske, D. W. (1959). Convergent and discriminant validation by the multitrait–multimethod matrix. *Psychological Bulletin, 56,* 81–105.
Cialdini, R. B., Borden, R. J., Thorne, A., Walker, M. R., Freeman, S., & Sloan, L. R. (1976). Basking in reflected glory: Three (football) field studies. *Journal of Personality and Social Psychology, 34,* 366–375.
Cialdini, R. B., & Richardson, K. D. (1980). Two indirect tactics of image management: Basking and blasting. *Journal of Personality and Social Psychology, 39,* 406–415.
Clark, M. S., & Isen, A. M. (1982). Toward understanding the relationships between feeling states and behavior. In A. H. Hastorf & A. M. Isen (Eds.), *Cognitive social psychology* (pp. 73–108). New York: Elsevier.
Clore, G. L., & Ortony, A. (1984). Some issues for a cognitive theory of emotion. *Cahiers de Psychologie Cognitive, 4,* 53–57.
Collins, R. L., Taylor, S. E. & Dakoff, G. A. (1989). *The affective consequences of social comparison: Either direction has its ups and downs.* Unpublished manuscript, University of California, Los Angeles.
Cooper, J. & Fazio, R. H. (1984). A new look at dissonance theory. In L. Berkowitz (Ed.),

Advances in experimental social psychology. (Vol. 17, pp. 229–267). New York: Academic Press.
Crocker, J. & Schwartz, I. (1985). Prejudice and in-group favoritism in a minimal intergroup situation: Effects of self-esteem. *Personality and Social Psychology Bulletin, 11*, 379–386.
Darley, J. M. & Goethals, G. R. (1980). People's analyses of the causes of ability linked performances. In L. Berkowitz (Ed.), *Advances in experimental social psychology* (Vol. 13, pp. 1–37). New York: Academic Press.
DeRivera, J. (1977). A structural theory of the emotions. *Psychological Issues, 10*, (4, Monograph No. 40).
Dixon, W. J., & Brown, M. B. (Eds.), (1979). *BMDP-79: Biomedical computer programs, P-series.* Berkeley, University of California Press.
Festinger, L. (1954). A theory of social comparison processes. *Human Relations, 7*, 117–140.
Goethals, G. R., & Darley, J. M. (1977). Social comparison theory: An attributional approach. In J. M. Suls & R. L. Miller (Eds.), *Social comparison processes: Theoretical and empirical perspectives* (pp. 259–278). Washington, DC: Hemisphere.
Gollwitzer, P. M., Earle, W. B., & Stephan, W. G. (1982). Affect as a determinant of egotism: Residual excitation and performance attributions. *Journal of Personality and Social Psychology, 43*, 702–709.
Hager, J. & Ekman, P. (1983). The inner and outer meaning of facial expression. In J. T. Cacioppo & R. E. Petty (Eds.), *Social Psychophysiology: A Sourcebook* (pp. 287–306). New York: Guilford.
Hakmiller, K. L. (1966). Threat as a determinant of downward comparison. *Journal of Experimental Social Psychology, Suppl. 1*, 32–39.
Heider, F. (1958). *The psychology of interpersonal relations.* New York: Wiley.
Isen, A. M. & Shalker, T. E. (1977). *Do you "accentuate the positive, eliminate the negative" when you are in a good mood?* Unpublished manuscript, University of Maryland, Baltimore County, Catonsville, MD.
Mandler, G. (1975). *Mind and emotion.* New York: Wiley.
Miller, D. T., Turnbull, W. & McFarland, C. (1988). Particularistic and universalistic evaluation in the social comparison process. *Journal of Personality and Social Psychology, 55*, 908–917.
Nadler, A., Jazwinski, C., Lau, S., & Miller, A. (1980). The cold glow of success: Responses to social rejection as affected by attitude similarity between the rejected and chosen individuals. *European Journal of Social Psychology, 10*, 279–289.
Nadler, A., Fisher, J. D., & Ben-Itzhak, S. (1983). With a little help from my friend: Effect of single or multiple act aid as a function of donor and task characteristics. *Journal of Personality and Social Psychology, 44*, 310–321.
Ortony, A., Clore, G. L., & Collins, A. (1988). *The cognitive structure of emotions.* New York: Cambridge University Press.
Parsons, T. (1949). *Essays in sociological theory.* New York: Macmillan
Pilliavin, I., Pilliavin, J. A., & Rodin, J. (1975). Costs, diffusion, and the stigmatized victim. *Journal of Personality and Social Psychology, 32*, 429–438.
Pleban, R., & Tesser, A. (1981). The effects of relevance and quality and another's performance on interpersonal closeness. *Social Psychology Quarterly, 44*, 278–285.
Roseman, I. (1984). Cognitive determinants of emotion: A structural theory. In P. Shaver (Ed.), *Review of personality and social psychology* (pp. 11–36). Beverly Hills: Sage.
Salovey, P., & Rodin, J. (1984). Some antecedents and consequences of social-comparison jealousy. *Journal of Personality and Social Psychology, 47*, 780–792.
Salovey, P., & Rodin, J. (1986). The differentiation of social-comparison and romantic jealousy. *Journal of Personality and Social Psychology, 50*, 1100–1112.

Schachter, S. (1959). *The psychology of affiliation: Experimental studies of the sources of gregariousness.* Stanford, CA: Stanford University Press.

Schachter, S. (1964). The interaction of cognitive and physiological determinants of emotional state. In L. Berkowitz (Ed.), *Advances in experimental social psychology* (Vol. 1, pp. 49–79). New York: Academic Press.

Scherer, K. R. (1982). Emotion as process: Function, origin, and regulation. *Social Science Information, 21,* 555–570.

Schwartz, G. E., Weinberger, D. A., & Singer, J. A. (1981). Cardiovascular differentiation of happiness, sadness, anger, and fear following imagery and exercise. *Psychosomatic Medicine, 43,* 343–364.

Smith, C. A., & Ellsworth, P. C. (1985). Patterns of cognitive appraisal in emotion. *Journal of Personality and Social Psychology, 48,* 813–838.

Steele, C. M. (1988). The psychology of self-affirmation: Sustaining the integrity of self. In L. Berkowitz (Ed.), *Advances in experimental social psychology* (Volume 21, pp. 261–302). New York: Academic Press.

Steele, C. M. & Liu, T. J. (1983). Dissonance processes as self-affirmation. *Journal of Personality and Social Psychology, 45,* 5–19.

Stephan, W. & Gollwitzer, P. M. (1981). Affect as a mediator of attributional egotism. *Journal of Experimental Social Psychology, 17,* 442–458.

Suls, J. M., Gastorf, J., & Lawhon, J. (1978). Social comparison choices for evaluating a sex- and age-related ability. *Personality and Social Psychology Bulletin, 4,* 102–105.

Taylor, S. E. & Lobel, M. (1989). Social comparison activity under threat: Downward evaluation and upward contacts. *Psychological Review, 96,* 569–575.

Taylor, S. E., Buunk, B. P., & Aspinwall, L. G. (1990). Social comparison, stress, & coping. *Personality and Social Psychology Bulletin, 16,* 74–89.

Tesser, A. (1986). Some effects of self-evaluation maintenance on cognition and action. In R. M. Sorrentino & E. T. Higgins (Eds.), *The handbook of motivation and cognition: Foundations of social behavior* (pp. 435–464). New York: Guilford.

Tesser, A. (1988). Toward a self-evaluation maintenance model of social behavior. In L. Berkowitz (Ed.), *Advances in experimental social psychology* (Vol. 21, pp. 181–227). New York: Academic Press.

Tesser, A., Achee, J., & Pilkington, C. (1990). *On the role of arousal in self-evaluation maintenance processes.* Unpublished manuscript, University of Georgia, Athens, GA.

Tesser, A., & Campbell, J. (1980). Self-definition. The impact of the relative performance and similarity of others. *Social Psychology Quarterly, 43,* 341–347.

Tesser, A., & Campbell, J. (1982). Self-evaluation maintenance and the perception of friends and strangers. *Journal of Personality, 50,* 261–279.

Tesser, A. & Collins, J. (1988). Emotion in social reflection and comparison situations: Intuitive, systematic, and exploratory approaches. *Journal of Personality and Social Psychology, 55,* 695–709.

Tesser, A., Millar, M., & Moore, J. (1988). Some affective consequences of social comparison and reflection processes: The pain and pleasure of being close. *Journal of Personality and Social Psychology, 54,* 49–61.

Tesser, A., & Paulhus, D. (1983). The definition of self: Private and public self-evaluation maintenance strategies. *Journal of Personality and Social Psychology, 44,* 672–682.

Tesser, A., Pilkington, C., & McIntosh, W. (1989). Self-evaluation maintenance and the mediational role of emotion: The perception of friends and strangers. *Journal of Personality and Social Psychology, 57,* 442–456.

Tesser, A., & Smith, J. (1980). Some effects of friendship and task relevance on helping: You don't always help the one you like. *Journal of Experimental Social Psychology, 16,* 582–590.

Thornton, D. A. & Arrowood, A. J. (1966). Self-evaluation, self-enhancement, and the locus of social comparison. *Journal of Experimental Social Psychology, 2,* (Suppl. 1), 40–48.

Vanyur, J. M. (1980). *Reactions to the success or failure of a liked or disliked other as a function of the relevance of the other's success or failure.* Unpublished master's thesis, University of Maryland, College Park, MD.

Weiner, B. (1986). Attribution, emotion, and action. In R. M. Sorrentino & E. T. Higgins (Eds.), *Handbook of motivation and cognition* (pp. 281–312). New York: Guilford.

Wills, T. A. (1981). Downward comparison principles in social psychology. *Psychological Bulletin, 90,* 245–271.

Wills, T. A. (1987). Downward comparison as a coping mechanism. In C. R. Snyder & C. Ford (Eds.), *Clinical and social-psychological perspectives on negative life events.* (pp. 19–50). New York: Academic Press.

Wood, J. V. (1989). Contemporary social comparison theory. *Psychological Bulletin 106,* 231–248.

Wood, J. V., Taylor, S. E., & Lichtman, R. R. (1985). Social comparison in adjustment to breast cancer. *Journal of Personality and Social Psychology, 49,* 1169–1183.

Wrightsman, L. S. (1960). Effects of waiting with others in level of felt anxiety. *Journal of Abnormal and Social Psychology, 61,* 216–222.

Zajonc, R. B. (1965). Social facilitation. *Science, 149,* 269–274.

II SOCIAL COGNITION AND SOCIAL COMPARISON

The chapters in this section are concerned with particular social cognition phenomena that have an important bearing on aspects of comparison theory. In chapter 6, George Goethals, David Messick, and Scott Allison describe their program of research for the *uniqueness bias*, which refers to the tendency to underestimate the proportion of people who can or will perform socially desirable actions. The authors propose that people make these biased estimates of consensus through a mentally constructed social comparison. This is distinct from the self-assessment comparison described by Festinger, in which selection of an actual comparison person presumably occurs. In constructed comparisons, people may manufacture social consensus in their heads as part of a more self-serving process.

Chapter 7, by Norman Miller, Sharon Gross, and Rolf Holzer, examines whether social projection increases attitudinal certainty. Festinger hypothesized that people's confidence in their opinions will be increased through comparisons with others of like mind. Miller et al. examine this issue in the arena of consensus perceptions, standing the idea on its head. They consider whether attributing one's opinion to one's ingroup increases certainty in one's position. That is, by assuming similarity among relevant others, is certainty manufactured? The research program reported here provides important insights about whether projection can serve as a stand-in for more direct comparison.

Riia Luhtanen and Jennifer Crocker, in chapter 8, note that ingroup bias and favoritism can be observed even in the absence of competition or conflict over resources. They describe a model of intergroup relations suggesting that biased ingroup comparisons are the result of social comparison motives, based on individual needs for self-enhancement. In testing these arguments, they consider whether self-esteem influences ingroup bias in a laboratory paradigm, and distinguish between personal self-esteem and collective self-esteem as possible determinants of bias. Their discussion raises some interesting questions as to how social comparison theory may be involved in phenomena of prejudice and intergroup relations.

6 The Uniqueness Bias: Studies of Constructive Social Comparison

George R. Goethals
Williams College

David M. Messick
University of California, Santa Barbara

Scott T. Allison
University of Richmond

In this chapter we report a number of studies of what we call *the uniqueness bias*, the tendency for people to underestimate the proportion of people who can or will perform socially desirable actions. Past research has found that people underestimate the proportion of people who will play a prisoner's dilemma game cooperatively, and this underestimation is characteristic of both cooperators and competitors (Goethals, 1986a). Both groups see cooperative behavior as socially desirable and as considerably more unusual or unique than it actually is. That is, cooperative people see their own cooperative behavior as special or unique at the same time that competitors see cooperation in others as rare and their own competitive behavior as the norm. As a consequence of the uniqueness bias people see their own behaviors as either uniquely or unusually good, or in the worst case, as no worse than the behaviors of others. The uniqueness bias reflects our tendency to see ourselves as somewhat better than average (Myers & Ridl, 1979), a tendency that has been observed in a wide variety of domains including vulnerability to major life events (Weinstein, 1980), driving ability (Svenson, 1981), responses to victimization (Taylor, Wood, & Lichtman, 1983), perceptions of fairness (Messick, Bloom, Boldizar, & Samuelson, 1985) and goodness (Allison, Messick, & Goethals, 1989). The studies just cited, and those reported in the present chapter, indicate that the uniqueness bias is robust and pervasive. At the same time, we will show that it is constrained for particular kinds of behavior, specifically where the motivation to see oneself as better than others is low or where one's standing on the behaviors at issue are easily reality-tested.

We begin by laying out our basic hypotheses, showing how they not only grow out of social comparison theory but also suggest some extensions of social comparison theory, and explaining their relation to other research on perceptions of consensus.

We assume that people want to view themselves positively (e.g., Steele, 1988; Tesser, 1988). We also assume that, as a consequence of this desire and a number of other psychological processes, people generally manage to view themselves positively. More specifically, they do so to the maximum extent that reality, social or otherwise, permits. We also suggest that biased estimates of consensus for their own behaviors are critical in enabling or supporting people's perceptions of themselves as better, or no worse than, their peers. We hypothesize that people make these biased estimates through *constructive social comparison*. Constructive social comparison is social comparison "in the head," with little regard for actual social reality, and is comprised of a number of processes, including the manufacturing of self-serving consensus estimates.

SOCIAL COMPARISON THEORY AND PERCEPTIONS OF SOCIAL REALITY

Recent research on social comparison theory has changed it tremendously. The original theory has been supported in a number of specific respects. It has also been clarified and extended, and the general assumptions that guide more recent social comparison research envision a social comparer very different from the one suggested by Festinger's (1954) original statement of the theory (Goethals, 1986b; Taylor, Buunk, & Aspinwall, 1990; Wood, in press). For example, research and theory published after 1954 emphasized the self-enhancement or self-validation motive (e.g., Singer, 1966), and social comparison in regard to one's physical or psychological well-being (Taylor & Brown, 1988; Wood, Taylor, & Lichtman, 1985). We first consider Festinger's work on social comparison and show how his approach stopped short of treating errors in perceiving social reality. Later we will discuss how subsequent work, including some of Festinger's most important, suggests the importance of understanding constructive social comparison.

Festinger's Social Comparison Theory

Festinger's (1954) original paper on "A Theory of Social Comparison Processes" is typically treated as the starting point for the modern study of social comparison. While there is important work that precedes that paper, especially early work on reference groups (Hyman, 1942; Kelley, 1952), and Festinger's own work on level of aspiration and informal social communication (Festinger, 1950; Hertzman & Festinger, 1940), the 1954 *Human Relations* paper is typically regarded as the source. What does it say or imply about the way people perceive social reality and make estimates of consensus?

Festinger's social comparison theory made clear that perceptions of social reality, in particular one's standing relative to others, are at the heart of social comparison. Social comparison in turn, is an enormously important aspect of self-understanding. Regarding the importance of social comparison, Festinger made clear that people's drives to evaluate themselves is often satisfied through comparison with others and that the drive to compare is strong enough to affect dramatically a wide range of social processes, including affiliation tendencies, influence processes, coalition formation, feelings of hostility, and efforts to compete. In addition, while Festinger discussed self-evaluation as if it were an essentially objective process it is clear that he considered the psychologically important stake people have in the outcome of comparisons. That is, doing well in comparison with others has important motivational consequences. For example, in his discussion of the "unidirectional drive upward" Festinger made it clear that the desire to have the higher or more desirable performance score is a motive which is equal in strength to the desire to achieve ability uniformity in groups, an outcome which is essential for the purposes of social comparison. In his discussion of group formation and societal structure Festinger noted that "the subjective feelings of correctness in one's opinions and the subjective evaluation of adequacy of one's performance on important abilities are some of the satisfactions that persons attain in the course of these associations with other people." (pp. 135–136). In other words, people want to do well in social comparison. They want social comparison information to confirm the correctness of their opinions and the high level of their abilities. Social comparison theory states that a positive self-evaluation is important, and, as is implicit in this discussion, one derives such an evaluation by noting how one compares with others.

But what did Festinger actually say about the way people perceive social comparison or consensus information? It is the central hypothesis of this chapter that people perceive social reality badly, that they have highly self-serving perceptions of whether or not people agree with them and of whether other people are as talented or moral as they. Does Festinger's social comparison theory accommodate this view? Neither the 1954 social comparison theory nor Festinger's earlier 1950 theory of informal social communication said very much to indicate that people might misperceive social reality. However, in his early work on dissonance theory, written just a few years after the social comparison paper, Festinger (1957) made clear that perceptions of consensus are not only motivationally important but that they may be inaccurate. He argued that with respect to opinions, values, and beliefs, "what others think" may be an important reality and that discrepancy of opinion "if perceived . . . certainly produces cognitive dissonance." He also argued that cognitions do not "*always* correspond" to reality and that "one of the important consequences of the theory of dissonance is that it will help us understand some circumstances where the cognitive elements do not correspond with reality" (p. 11). Indeed in his earliest treatment of dissonance, Festinger (Festinger, Riecken, and Schachter, 1956) argued that people could simply forget cognitions that are in dissonant relationship. This clearly implies that people could distort dissonant cognitions about consensus on opinions or abilities, or, more to the point perhaps, create consonant ones. In other words in Festinger's early theorizing on both social comparison and dissonance, there was a recognition that other people's opinions affect our own feelings of correctness and that it is dissonant to have other people disagree. Furthermore, there was at least the suggestion that people might reduce dissonance by misperceiving other people's opinions. It is important to note that while Festinger did not emphasize misperceiving other people's opinions and levels of performance he did emphasize that changing their opinions and performance levels is an important social comparison process. It is not much of a leap from this hypothesis to suggesting that perceiving them as different is an easy substitute for making them different.

Dissonance and Extensions of Social Comparison Theory

We have suggested that Festinger's original social comparison theory can be extended, especially by using some of the concepts of dissonance theory, to account for the uniqueness bias and other forms of misperception of consensus. Let us be more explicit about such an extension. What does a social comparison theory that accounts for errors in consensus estimates, and reflects research that has been generated since 1954 look like?

Our basic thesis is that had Festinger devised social comparison theory two years after cognitive dissonance theory rather than two years before, he would have devised a social comparison theory informed by some of the insights of dissonance theory, and the result would have been quite different. We suggest the basic structure of a social comparison theory that is informed not only by dissonance theory and research, but also some of the principal theoretical and empirical extensions of social comparison theory since 1954. We note both the central principles of the original formulations of dissonance theory (Festinger, 1957; Festinger, Riecken, & Schachter, 1956) and the key extensions of social comparison theory that together might inform a revision of social comparison theory.

First and foremost, cognitive dissonance theory provides the key idea of self-justification. Although the 1957 book on dissonance did not highlight self-justification, Festinger's later discussions of the origins of dissonance theory (Festinger, 1975) and treatments of the theory by Aronson (1988) made clear that at the heart of the theory is the idea that people generate cognitions to fit, and therefore justify, their feelings and behavior. Second is the idea that people construct cognitions in the service of self-justification. For example, dissonance theory specifically proposes that people generate frightening perceptions of reality to justify fears and consonant cognitions about their own attitudes to justify behavior. Third, dissonance theory states that people seek out information that promises to reduce dissonance and avoid information that promises to increase dissonance. In this regard it also suggests that people will "set up quick defensive processes" to prevent dissonant cognitions "from ever becoming firmly established" (Festinger, 1957, p. 137). A social comparison theory incorporating these insights would hold that people construct social reality in ways that support self-enhancing appraisals of their opinions and abilities and seek out information that bolsters those positive appraisals while avoiding or distorting information that threatens them.

There have been a number of key extensions of social comparison theory in the decades following its 1954 formulation. We mention several of them and consider how they combine with the propositions of dissonance theory to point the way to an expanded statement of social comparison theory. Of central importance for the present formulation is the extension discussed by Hakmiller (1966), Latané (1966), Singer (1966), and Wheeler (1966) in the 1966 *Journal of Experimental Social Psychology* (JESP) supplement on social comparison, as well as by Wills (1981) in his important paper on downward social comparison. That is the need for self-enhancement. People often engage in social comparison with an eye toward validating a positive assessment of their opinions, abilities, or other personal characteristics. People prefer social comparison information, as other cognitions about self, reality, and others, to reflect well on the self. A second key extension is the idea that people often prefer not to engage in social comparison (Brickman & Bulman, 1977). There is pleasure and pain in social comparison, and as dissonance theory suggests, people are happy to receive comparison information that is consonant with high self-esteem, but try to avoid comparison information that is dissonant. A third important extension is the idea that we compare with other people who are salient or available, or with whom we interact often, whether we want to or not. That is, social comparison is often forced (Allen & Wilder, 1977; Mettee & Smith, 1977; Miller, 1983). A fourth extension is that people use principles of attribution to interpret social comparison information (Goethals & Darley, 1977). If consensus for their opinions or performances is high, attribution is external. The opinion reflects the entity judged and success or failure reflects the ease or difficulty of the task attempted. Conversely, if consensus is low the opinion or performance is attributed to the person. Furthermore, people will often make biased attributions in the interests of generating esteem-maintaining explanations for their relative performances (Darley & Goethals, 1980). A social comparison theory incorporating these ideas would be highly compatible with the one suggested by dissonance theory. People will seek comparison information that is self-enhancing; they will avoid, if they can, comparison information that threatens self-esteem, and they will work actively on whatever social comparison information they receive to generate positive causal attributions explaining that information.

Realistic and Constructive Social Comparison Processes

With these principles in mind we propose two different types of social comparison be distinguished. We refer to these as *realistic social comparison* and *constructive social comparison*. Realistic social comparison entails self-appraisal based on using and analyzing actual information about social reality. Constructive social comparison entails self-appraisal based on "in the head" social comparison based on guess, conjecture, or rationalization concerning social reality, often believed, and often self-serving. We further purpose that people use either realistic or constructive social comparison depending on what is in their interest, and that they move back and forth between the two, flexibly and fluidly, as their perceptions of their interests change. Sometimes people will feel their interests are best served by realistic social comparison. In other instances they may prefer constructive social comparison. It is possible that people will inaccurately appraise their own interests, and will engage in realistic social comparison when they might have been better served by engaging in constructive social comparison, and vice-versa. Students might look at a distribution of test scores with a goal of bolstering their view of themselves as being smarter than other students in the class. The information they receive may cause problems for that self-appraisal, and constructive processes may quickly be engaged to limit or reverse the damage. They may recall how little time they had to study for the exam. Some of their friends, in comparison, seemed to have spent days at the library studying just before the test.

The idea of constructive social comparison builds on a number of closely related concepts and discussions. Suls (1986) argued that self-generated comparison information may sometimes short-circuit actual social comparison. People will sometimes use what is in their heads rather than actual social reality to make comparative appraisals of the self. Orive (1988) proposed a reformulation of theory regarding the social comparison of opinions based on the idea of social projection. Like Suls, he discusses "implicit comparison" based on self-generated consensus. Taylor, Buunk, and Aspinwall (1990), reviewing work by Taylor, Wood, and Lichtman (1983), Wills (1987), and Wood, Taylor, and Lichtman (1985), concluded that "when a comparison target who makes the self appear better is not readily available, . . . people have the cognitive capacity to manufacture a less fortunate other. . . ." Similarly, Wood (1989; Wood et al., 1985) extended Goethals' (1986a) idea of fabricating and ignoring social reality and suggests that "social comparison often may be a process of *construction*" which may not involve comparison with real people. The present concept of constructive social comparison is entirely consistent with these ideas, holding that in the interests of self-enhancement people generate their own comparison information, ignore or distort real but threatening information, and make biased attributions about the causes of both their and other people's opinions and performances.

In general, *realistic social comparison* occurs when people are interested in self-evaluation rather than self-enhancement or self-validation. This is the kind of social comparison discussed almost exclusively in Festinger's 1954 statement of the theory, the unidirectional drive upwards notwithstanding. It involves actual comparison with other people's opinions, performances, etc., often with those who are similar, but sometimes with those who define the ends of the continuum on which one is trying to locate oneself. When engaging in realistic social comparison people may compare upward or downward and will typically engage in rational attribution processes to determine the correctness of their opinions and the level of their abilities.

People are also likely to engage in realistic social comparison, at least initially, when they are forced to by salient, but not necessarily sought after, comparative information. People may cross the line into constructive social comparison if this unsought information has dissonant implications. In addition, people are likely to engage in realistic social comparison when they are motivated to support a positive self-appraisal, or a specific social comparison conclusion, such as one that proves their group is being relatively deprived, and they expect comparison information to be consonant with what it is they are trying to show about themselves or their group.

Constructive social comparison is most likely to occur when people do not need, are not flattered by, would prefer to avoid, or wish to explain away, real social comparison information. It can be defined as the process of generating cognitive constructions of social reality that occurs when people have no need accurately to evaluate their opinions and abilities but for some other reason desire a definition of social reality. It is typically engaged when people want to devise esteem-maintaining views of social reality. Depending on the motivation and the situation, there are a variety of forms such constructions may take. They vary in their complexity, the effort needed to devise them, and the danger that they will conflict with conclusions suggested by realistic social comparison processes.

The most basic constructive social comparison process is the one that concerns us. That is fabricating constructions of social reality by making up consensus estimates regarding opinions and abilities. People should want to view their opinions as entity-caused and will do this by making up large, agreeing estimates of consensus (Goethals, Allison, and Frost, 1979). At the same time, due to the unidirectional drive upwards, they should want to view their successful performances as person-caused and will do this by estimating that a small proportion of people can perform as well (Goethals, 1986a). As Marks (1984) has shown, people will think that their opinions are common and that their abilities are unique. In addition, because people will want to fabricate self-serving consensus estimates of personal characteristics other than just opinions and abilities, we can propose more generally that people will construct small estimates of consensus for all their socially desirable behavior, including successful performances and moral actions, and that they will construct large estimates of consensus for thoughts, feelings, or behaviors that are of uncertain or negative social value, including opinions, performance failures, and moral lapses.

Generating self-enhancing estimates of consensus may be quite simple in many instances. Often there is an absence of information about consensus and people have a large field in which to grow estimates that validate their opinions or abilities. When there is available information about social reality that does not support these self-serving estimates, there is likely to be dissonance, and more complex constructive processes may be engaged to reduce the dissonance and maintain positive views of one's opinion or ability. Festinger et al. (1956) suggested that people can simply forget dissonant cognitions. Research reported in Goethals (1986a) suggests that in many circumstances people can and do simply forget that others disagree. A study by Stone and Kamiya (1957) showed that people make errors in consensus estimates following group discussion that are comparable to those made without discussion. If information about others' opinions are dissonant, it seems simply to be ignored.

If people cannot ignore the magnitude of disagreeing consensus for opinions, or the proportion of other people who can perform various tasks as well as or better than they do, more elaborate constructions may be devised. People may reject such others or render them noncomparable (Festinger, 1950; 1954; 1957). Or, they may engage in attributional analyses of their disagreeing opinions or superior performances which render those opinions and performances less threatening (Darley and Goethals, 1980; Goethals & Darley, 1977). For example, college students could decide that others who performed better on an exam were advantaged by having superior standing on related attributes such as amount of sleep before the test, how much they learned about the subject in high school, or how much they wanted to please their parents with a good grade. People seem to be endlessly inventive in these constructions.

In conclusion, principles of constructive social comparison theory suggest that when people are interested in self-validation rather than self-evaluation they will invent estimates of consensus that support a view of their opinions as correct and their ability levels as high. Specifically, they will overestimate consensus for opinions and failures while underestimating consensus for moral actions and successful performances. We would expect these tendencies to be strongest when information about actual consensus is the least available or accessible.

There have been a variety of approaches to explaining errors in consensus estimates. We believe the current approach, rooted in the concept of constructive social comparison, gives the most coherent account not only of the range of existing findings which demonstrate both overestimation and underestimation of consensus but also the studies of the uniqueness bias reported here.

STUDIES OF PERCEIVED CONSENSUS: OVERESTIMATIONS AND UNDERESTIMATIONS

The recent history of research on consensus estimates begins with Ross' work on the false consensus effect (Ross, 1977; Ross, Greene, & House, 1977). Before discussing his work, it is important to note that there are a number of early studies which show the sort of misperception of social reality that we have discussed above. There are a large number of studies indicating that people assume more consensus for their opinions than exists. The earliest, to our knowledge, was Hayes' 1936 study of the predictive accuracy of voters. The explanation of this finding has been cast in a number of terms, differing in varying degrees from Allport's (1924) early concept of social projection. Allport, in his discussion of the *illusion of universality* hypothesized that people often assume that others are responding to given situations in the same way as they and imagine that their own response is universal. Some authors (especially Gilovich, Jennings, & Jennings, 1983) have put forth highly similar ideas. Others have suggested markedly different ones, to which we shall return.

There are a few studies showing that people underestimate the extent to which others perform at the same level as themselves, are as moral as themselves, or, in general, stand as high on desirable social characteristics as they do. Studies by Brown (1965), Hinds (1962), Levinger and Schneider

(1969), and Wallach and Wing (1968) all suggested that people imagine that others are less risky than they actually are. A study by Jellison and Riskind (1970) showed that people think others have a lower probability of succeeding when attempting ability-linked risky behaviors than they have. More recent studies by Campbell (1986), Goethals (1986a), and Marks (1984) suggested that people underestimate the extent to which others behave as skillfully or as morally as they do themselves. We resemble the children in Lake Wobegone. The vast majority of us feels that we are above average.

As previously noted, Ross et al. (1977) study of the false consensus effect was a landmark in the study of errors and biases in estimating consensus. It rekindled interest in the problem of consensus estimates and tied data on this problem to recent concerns in attribution and social cognition. They showed that in a variety of behavioral domains people who perform an action have a higher estimate of the number or proportion of people who perform that action than do people who do not perform it. This does not necessarily mean that the performers of an action overestimate their numbers, just that they have a higher estimate of their numbers than do nonperformers. A meta-analysis by Mullen et al. (1985) showed that this effect is quite robust.

Marks and Miller (1987) reviewed a number of explanations for this effect. These included selective exposure and cognitive availability, salience and focus of attention, logical information processing, and motivational processes. Importantly, the motivational processes they discuss included gaining of social support and self-esteem maintenance. The two motivational processes advanced by Marks and Miller as possible explanations of the false consensus effect, gaining social support and maintaining self-esteem, are central parts of the social comparison processes we have been discussing. It is also the case that while all of Marks and Miller's explanations are applicable to overestimations of consensus, only self-esteem maintenance accommodates instances of consensus underestimation.

The earlier research on consensus estimates and perceptions of relative probability of success, and the more recent research on the false consensus effect is a starting point providing a context for our work on the uniqueness bias. The research already noted, as well as other work on consensus estimates, can, we believe, generally be summarized as follows: First, there is a reliable false consensus effect for a range of opinions and behaviors. People give higher estimates of the proportion of their peers that think and act as they do than do the people who do not. For example, in our research, people who commit themselves to giving blood give a higher estimate of the number of people who will give blood than do people who decline. Second, where there are values attached to behavioral choices, those who perform the positively valued action underestimate consensus whereas those who perform the negatively valued action overestimate consensus. For example, those who give blood underestimate the proportion that does likewise while those who decline overestimate the proportion that also declines. This latter pattern has also been demonstrated meta-analytically in a paper by Mullen and Goethals (in press). They showed that people tend to be fairly accurate in estimating consensus for behaviors with a neutral value. Effects associated with behaviors of varying value are independent of effects showing majorities underestimating and minorities overestimating consensus, as previously reported in Mullen and Hu (1988). With these findings in mind let us attempt to define the uniqueness bias precisely and begin to consider the research supporting it.

THE UNIQUENESS BIAS: ON BEING BETTER THAN AVERAGE

The false consensus effect is calculated by comparing two estimates of the frequency of a behavior, opinion, or attribute. One is the estimate given by the subgroup that possesses the attribute and the other is that given by the subgroup that does not. The difference between these estimates is the empirical measure of the false consensus effect. For example, in one of our studies a subgroup of 80% of high school juniors queried said they could "come up with an original solution to a difficult problem." This subgroup estimated that 38% could come up with the solution. The subgroup of 20% that said they could not solve the problem estimated that 29% could come up with the solution. The difference between the 38% estimated by the subgroup that said they could solve the problem and the 29% estimated by the subgroup that said they could not solve the problem is the measure of false consensus, in this case 9%.

The uniqueness bias, on the other hand, is calculated on the basis of the total group, not subgroups. It is measured by difference between the actual frequency of the attribute or opinion in the group, and the average estimated frequency given by all members of the group. In the example just mentioned, 80% is the proportion of the group that said that they could come up with the original solution. The overall estimate of the proportion that could do so, combining subjects who said they could solve the problem and subjects who said they could not is 36%. Thus the uniqueness bias is the difference between 80% and 36%, in this case 44%. (See Fig. 6.1 for a graphical representation of the false consensus effect and uniqueness bias).

As noted, the uniqueness bias is calculated using the consensus estimates of both those who perform a certain behavior and those who do not. It refers to a bias that, in this example, is shared by both subgroups. Both

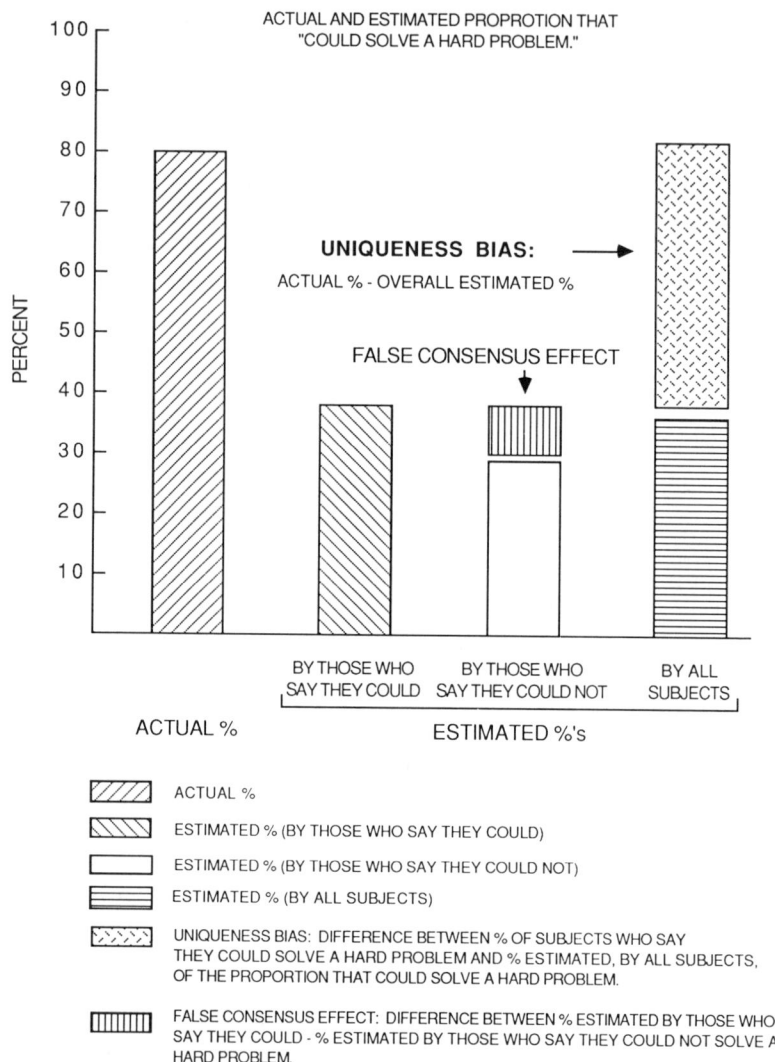

FIG. 6.1. The uniqueness bias: a graphical representation.

the subgroup that says it can solve a hard problem and the subgroup that says it cannot are biased toward underestimating the proportion that can. Both underestimates are self-serving and may reflect Festinger's unidirectional drive upwards. In the case of the people who can, the bias allows them to feel relatively unique. In the case of the people who cannot, it allows them to feel that they are no worse off than most others. Thus the uniqueness bias in any specific instance is a term that refers to an underestimation bias shared by both "can do" and "cannot do" subgroups, and is accordingly measured by combining the consensus estimates of all members of the group, regardless of the subgroup to which they belong.

We introduce our research on the uniqueness bias by describing a preliminary study that grew out of an experiment by Allison, Messick, and Goethals (1989). Allison et al. showed that when subjects responded to short one-paragraph vignettes about a hypothetical person considering whether to perform a socially desirable action they indicated a higher probability of themselves doing it than of their peers doing it. While this study did not assess consensus estimates it was similar to studies reported in Goethals (1986a) that had, with the latter studies, served as a basis for our initial study of the uniqueness bias. In this study, conducted at the University of California, Santa Barbara, subjects were asked whether they and their peers would or could perform a variety of behaviors involving moral choices (termed *would* items) or academic, athletic, creative, or interpersonal skills (termed *could* items). The behaviors listed included "could answer 60 percent of the questions in a Trivial Pursuits game," "would clean up the table after eating at McDonald's," "could win a joke-telling contest," "would report a person seen shoplifting," or "could follow the logic in a complex philosophical argument regarding the existence of God." All subjects were asked whether they would or could perform the behaviors and to indicate the percentage of their peers at UCSB that could perform them.

Statistical analyses of subjects' own responses and their consensus estimates included the between–subject variable of gender of the subject and the within–subject variables of behavior type, would versus could items, and the target rated, self or UCSB students. There were a number of interesting results. The largest was a main effect for target ($p < .001$) indicating that percentage of subjects saying they would or could perform all the socially desirable behaviors (M = 65%) was higher than the percentage estimated for UCSB students (M = 45%), yielding an average uniqueness bias (UB) of 20%. Another significant effect was a behavior type x target interaction ($p < .013$) indicating that the self-other differential was larger for the would items (UB = 22%) than it was for the could items (UB = 18%). There was also a behavior type x target x gender interaction ($p < .002$) indicating that men differentiated themselves from their peers more on could items than would items, while women did the opposite.

Two other features of the study should be mentioned briefly. First, order of measurement, self or UCSB students, was an additional between-subjects variable. In this and other studies discussed which all manipulated order, there were no consistent findings involving the order variable. Second, another group of subjects in this study was asked to indicate the probability that they or the average UCSB student would or could perform each of the behaviors. The probability results were very similar to the consensus results in all respects. Subjects believed they had a higher probability of performing the behaviors than the average UCSB student.

The results of this study show a number of things. First, as many other studies have shown, there is a strong self-serving bias, specifically, a uniqueness bias in consensus estimates. The proportion of people indicating that they would or could perform socially desirable behaviors is higher than the proportion people estimate would or could perform them.

Second, this first study shows that would items, dealing with a variety of moral choices, produce more self-other differentiation than could items, dealing with a variety of ability-linked performances. This latter finding is consistent with the *Muhammad Ali effect* found in the studies reported in Allison et al. (1989). Those studies showed that people are likely to think they are better than others in the sense of being fairer and more helpful but they do not think they are more intelligent than others. Recall that Muhammad Ali, when asked whether he had deliberately faked a low score on an army intelligence test to avoid armed service, responded, "I only said I was the greatest, not the smartest." (Ali, 1975, p. 129). While Ali may have been joking, our subjects seemed to be serious in claiming more exceptional moral virtue than exceptional competence. However, since the could items in this study covered a range of activities—intellectual, creative, athletic, and interpersonal—it isn't clear whether people differentiate self from others less on all ability-linked items or just items dealing with behaviors linked to intelligence. This question will be discussed in light of data from studies reported below.

Third, this study suggests there might be a variety of interesting differences in the ways men and women differentiate themselves from others, and to the extent that these differentiations support a high level of self-esteem, the sources of high self-esteem for men and women. This question was explored in the studies examined later.

REALITY-CONSTRAINED SELF-DECEPTION: THE ROLE OF BEHAVIORAL SPECIFICITY IN THE UNIQUENESS BIAS

The Muhammad Ali effect and the finding in the first study showing that the uniqueness bias is stronger for would than could behaviors may both be explained in terms of reality constraints on self-serving biases. Although we cannot be certain why people think they are more likely to be fair or helpful than others but not more likely to act intelligently, one possible explanation is that people's estimates of how intelligent they are compared to others are much more constrained by reality. They know what kinds of grades they have received compared to others, or what percentile they and to some extent others have scored on the SAT. There is much less hard information about their comparative level of moral performance. A similar argument can be made about would versus could items in the first study. Estimates of how much more likely one is to perform moral behaviors may be less constrained by reality than estimates of how much more likely one is to perform behaviors requiring ability.

The explanation above is supported by an additional finding from the first study. There were a number of could items which asked about a behavior that was defined in very general terms, the performance of which could not be easily measured or verified. For example: "could learn to use an unfamiliar computer." In contrast to these general items there were more specific ones where success or failure could be measured in very precise terms. For example, "could parallel park a car within 6 inches of the curb." The results of the study showed that the uniqueness bias was stronger for the general items than for the specific. Indeed, for the specific items there was virtually no uniqueness bias. Is such a phenomenon replicable and, if so, what does it mean?

Our view, based on the concept of the unidirectional drive upwards and the idea of constructive social comparison is that people wish to perceive themselves as superior to others, and that they will in fact construct perceptions of themselves and social reality that support this wish to the maximum degree that physical and social reality permit. Thus, when people are asked to appraise their performances in either absolute or relative terms they will view them reasonably objectively when there are relevant and salient objective standards to apply to them. People who bowl will appraise their performances in terms of how many pins they knock down and how that number compares to the number that salient others knock down. Thus their appraisal of their bowling ability is likely to be relatively accurate or objective, that is *reality-constrained*. Consequently, if we ask such people if they could bowl an average of 200 points a game they are likely to give a relatively honest answer. If asked to estimate the number of their peers that could average 200 they will be inclined to give a reasonably objective estimate. Their responses will be constrained by actual information they possess, or by what they could imagine to be the likely outcome in a specific, well-defined setting where performance level can be precisely calibrated.

On the other hand, when people are asked about their own and others' performance in a less precisely measured domain, such as planning a party or solving a problem, they have an open field. They are free to imagine themselves performing at a very high level where the performance itself or the standard by which it is judged is defined imprecisely. Here they can imagine themselves excelling. Thus, a large number might be likely to claim that they can do well, but estimate that relatively few of their peers could do the same.

Based on these considerations we predicted that the uniqueness bias would be greater when the behaviors presented were general and less easily measured. In order to test this reality-constrained self-deception hypothesis, a series of studies (Freilicher and Goethals, 1988) was conducted by Nancy A. Freilicher at Williams College. The subjects in the first study were undergraduates at that school who were asked to consider a total of 45 behaviors. They were asked about performances linked to intellectual, athletic, and creative ability and to moral choices. Within each of these four behavioral categories were listed some behaviors that were very specific and some that were more general. There were 5 or 6 behaviors within each behavioral type x specificity category. For example, an athletic-general item was "could bike on hilly terrain." A moral-specific item was "would give up one's seat on a crowded bus for a pregnant woman."

As in the previous study subjects were asked to indicate whether they would or could perform each behavior and the percent of Williams students they thought would or could perform them. In order to validate the manipulation of the specificity of the listed behaviors and to collect further data on subjects' perceptions of these items an additional group of subjects was asked to rate each of the 45 behaviors on three different 7-point scales. They were asked to indicate for each behavior how "easily one's performance of the behavior can be measured (i.e., how general or specific is it)," "how hard you think it would be to perform this behavior," and "how positively you would evaluate someone who performed this behavior."

The behaviors classified as specific were rated as much more specific than the ones classified as general ($p < .001$). It is important to note that the specific behaviors were not rated as more or less difficult to perform or more or less desirable than the general items. The specificity variable was manipulated, as planned, without confounding it with difficulty or desirability.

The major results of the study replicated the UCSB results. A strong target effect ($p < .001$) replicated the uniqueness bias from the earlier study. Overall, 66% of the subjects indicated they would or could perform the various listed behaviors. In contrast, they indicated that 55% of their peers at Williams would or could perform them (UB = 11%). In addition, we found that the magnitude of the uniqueness bias varied considerably according to the type of behavior being rated ($p < .016$). The degree of self-other differentiation was greatest for the athletic items (UB = 14%), then the moral (UB = 12%), creative (UB = 11%), and finally, intellectual (UB = 7%) items. The tendency for Williams students to differentiate less on the intellectual items than on the moral or athletic and creative items replicates the Muhammad Ali effect and shows that it is intellectual behaviors in particular, not all ability-related items, for which there is a weaker uniqueness bias among the subjects in our studies.

In support of the notion of reality-constrained self-deception we find that the self-other differentiation is greater for general items than for specific items ($p < .007$). This effect is qualified by an interaction ($p < .001$) indicating that for creative and intellectual items the self-other differential is considerably larger for general items than specific items, for athletic items it is about the same, and for moral items it is actually the case that the self-other differential is greater for the specific items than the general ones.

What do these results suggest about the existence and shape of the uniqueness bias? First, we find a strong uniqueness bias, so that we have evidence of its existence among college students from two quite different student populations, one a large state university in the West, the other a small private liberal arts college in the East. Second, we find evidence that people are less likely to differentiate themselves from their college peers on intellectually-based performances than they are on others. It is interesting that they differentiate themselves on athletic abilities more than they do on any of the other three behavioral domains; creative, moral, or intellectual. Perhaps college students are aware that other students around them are bright and so differentiate less on intelligence. They see themselves as having more ability than their peers in things such as athletics, because being athletic is not a necessary condition of going to college and may not be as salient a characteristic as intelligence. It is interesting to recall that when Muhammad Ali said he was the greatest, he meant that in an athletic sense. Our students' self-perceptions track his closely. They think they are markedly better than their peers athletically, but not so intellectually.

Third, the data support the idea of reality-constrained self-deception. When people judge the likelihood of performing specific, easily measured behaviors they do not differentiate themselves from their peers as much as they do in open field situations where behaviors are defined in very general terms. With the latter kind of behaviors subjects are freer to imagine a high degree of relative excellence. It should be noted that this is reminiscent of Perloff and Fetzer's (1986) finding that people perceive themselves as uniquely invulnerable in comparison to vague, abstract targets more than specific, concrete targets.

We note, however, that the specificity effect was reversed in the moral domain. Perhaps because moral behaviors are not typically measured as carefully as ability-related behaviors, people do not constrain egoistic claims as much when considering them as opposed to specific ability-linked behaviors. But why would there actually be a reversal? We suggest that subjects may actually be motivated to differentiate self from others more on specific behaviors. Specific behaviors may be highly vivid and salient and there may be more psychological gain from differentiation on them. This gain can easily be realized with moral behaviors. In the case of ability-linked behaviors specificity also provides a check. People have to be modest in their claims or risk loss of face. Goffman (1955) eloquently discussed the brakes that fear of loss of face put on claims about desirable abilities.

THE UNIQUENESS BIAS IN OTHER POPULATIONS

A frequent criticism of many studies in social psychology is an overreliance on college students as subjects (Sears, 1986). Our concern with this issue led us to investigate the uniqueness bias and several other findings related to it in other subject populations. We comment on the findings for a few of these groups separately.

Second, Fourth, and Sixth Graders

A study (Phillips, 1988) was conducted with second, fourth, and sixth graders by Elise D. Phillips, the results of which we summarize. A major departure from the usual procedures was that all 120 subjects tested were run individually. When asked about their peers, subjects were shown ten lollipops and asked to imagine that they represented ten of their classmates. Then they were asked to actually place some of the lollipops into a yes circle and some into a no circle for each question, indicating how many of their peers would or could perform each behavior. This procedure was devised to make the questions about peers easy for the second graders to answer. The older children were asked to follow this procedure as well. All consensus means are multiplied by ten for easy comparison to the earlier studies.

The results were comparable to those of the previous studies. First, there was a highly significant target effect ($p < .001$). Seventy three percent of the subjects indicated that they would or could perform the behaviors while the subjects estimated that 56% of their peers could perform them (UB = 17%). Second, there was a target x specificity interaction ($p < .001$) indicating that the self-other differential was greater for the general items than the specific items. (The items had previously been rated on a general versus specific scale by college students. The specificity manipulation was highly successful.) The target x specificity interaction was not qualified by the behavior type variable. In this respect the results were different from those of Williams students. Third, there was a target x behavior type interaction (p < .017) indicating that self-peer differentiation was strongest on moral items (UB = 21%) followed by intellectual (UB = 17%) and athletic (UB = 14%) items. Finally, while there was no overall interaction of subjects' grade (second, fourth, or sixth) with target, there was an interesting target x behavior x grade interaction suggesting developmental differences which are beyond the scope of this chapter. In brief, the data suggested that as children move from second through sixth grade they differentiate themselves less on intellectual items and more on moral items.

Eleventh Graders

A study was conducted at a regional high school in Williamstown, Massachusetts. The study was administered in the U.S. history classes required of all high school juniors. The sample included two advanced placement classes and two regular classes. As in the Williams study, general and specific questions were asked about intellectual, athletic, creative, and moral domains.

The results for the study were similar in many important respects to the results of the UCSB and Williams studies described previously. However, there were interesting differences as well. There was a strong main effect for target (p < .001). On average 64% of the students claimed they would or could perform the various behaviors while estimating that 43% of their peers would or could do likewise (UB = 21%). In addition, there was a significant, though not markedly strong, target x behavior interaction indicating that the self-other differential varied according to behavioral domain. Unlike the studies showing the Muhammad Ali effect, the high school students showed greater differentiation on the intellectual items (UB = 26%) than they did on the athletic (UB = 17%), creative (UB = 20%), or moral items (UB = 20%).

The effect supporting the reality-constrained self-deception hypothesis was replicated (p < .002). Self-other differentiation was stronger for general behaviors versus specific behaviors. As in the Williams study, this effect was qualified by a target x specificity x behavior interaction (p < .001). For all three ability domains—intellectual, creative, and athletic—self-other differentiation was stronger for general items than specific items, while in the moral domain it was stronger for specific items. Clearly the notion of reality-constrained self-deception operates differently for ability-related behaviors than it does for moral choices.

Another finding in the data for these subjects is a target x class level interaction (p < .001) indicating that the advanced placement students showed a stronger uniqueness bias than the students in regular U.S. history classes. There is also a target x class level x behavior interaction (p < .004) indicating that while the self-other differentiation was greater for advanced placement students in all four behavioral domains, the disparity in self-other differentiation between the two class levels was greatest on the intellectual items (UB = 39% for advanced placement versus UB = 13% for regular), less on the creative items (UB = 25% for advanced placement vs. UB = 14% for regular), and least on the athletic (UB = 20% for advanced placement vs. UB = 13% for regular) and moral (UB = 23% for advanced placement vs. UB = 17% for regular) items. It is not at all surprising that the uniqueness bias should be stronger for advanced placement students in the intellectual, and perhaps even creative, domain. It is less predictable that there should also be greater self-other differentiation on athletic and moral items. Perhaps the students in the prestige high school classes have a greater sense of self-esteem than those in less prestigious classes.

Middle Management Bankers

The final subject population on which we report is a group of bankers, median age 34, who participated in a two-week summer training program on current banking practices, hosted at Williams College. In a final evaluation session the bankers were asked to complete two questionnaires asking whether they or their banking peers would or could perform behaviors in the moral, intellectual, and athletic domains. The results revealed a familiar pattern. There was a reliable target effect ($p < .001$) showing the uniqueness bias. There was a target x behavior type interaction ($p < .043$) showing the greatest degree of self-other differentiation on the moral items (UB = 20%), next most on athletic items (UB = 18%), and least on intellectual items (UB = 13%). This finding indicates that the Muhammad Ali effect, which had disappeared in our study of high school students, is alive and well among adult bankers. The specificity variable was not manipulated in this study.

GENDER AND UNIQUENESS

In all of the studies we conducted there were significant effects involving the gender of the subjects. In most of the studies there was an overall target x gender interaction, indicating that, generally, men show more self-other differentiation than women. In all studies there was a target x gender x behavior interaction showing that males and females differentiate themselves from their peers differently in different behavioral domains. We review some of these effects briefly.

In the Williams data there is a very strong overall gender effect. The disparity between male and female self-other differentials is especially marked for athletic behaviors and is also considerable for intellectual and creative behaviors. However, for the moral behaviors women differentiate themselves more than men.

In the high school sample the overall gender difference is extraordinary. Men differentiate considerably more, though there is a modest reversal in the case of moral behaviors. The sample of second, fourth, and sixth grade students also showed an overall gender difference and an interaction showing boys differentiating more than girls on athletic and intellectual items while girls differentiated more on the moral items.

The data from our middle management bankers showed a highly significant overall gender difference and a familiar pattern of findings within each behavior domain. The self-other differential for men was greater than for women on athletic and intellectual items. The differentiation on the moral items was the same for men and women.

Across the studies, men consistently think that they are smarter than their peers but women think so much less markedly and reliably. On the other hand, females almost always show more self-other differentiation than males on moral items. The latter finding is remarkably consistent, with the exception of the bankers data. One way of characterizing these findings is to say that the Muhammad Ali effect seems to be especially strong among females. They clearly think they are better, in the moral sense, than their peers, but in many instances they show very little, if any, differentiation on intellectual items. Perhaps women's modesty in their intellectual claims is most dramatic among Williams women, an exceedingly intellectually talented group. While their male counterparts at Williams show a uniqueness bias of 17% on intellectual items, the women do so by only 1%. In conclusion, our data show that men have a more pronounced uniqueness bias than women, and that women are relatively modest in their self-perceptions in the intellectual domain but claim more for themselves than men in the moral domain. We must not overlook the fact that males differentiate themselves from others more than females on athletic items with great consistency, even though we made every effort to choose athletic items, such as soccer and biking, in which women have as much opportunity to participate as men.

THE LINK TO SELF-ESTEEM AND DEPRESSION

The theoretical position with which we started is that people construct estimates of consensus that allow them to view themselves positively relative to others and thereby maintain a high level of self-esteem. Festinger (1954) suggested that people who are unable to view themselves positively with respect to others on abilities would suffer "deep experiences of failure and feelings of inadequacy with respect to abilities" (p. 137). We would expect that if people view themselves positively with respect to others, that is, if they have a uniqueness bias, this bias should support a high level of self-esteem and prevent feelings of depression. We would expect individuals who show high degrees of uniqueness bias to have higher levels of self-esteem and lower levels of depression.

This hypothesis was tested in the sample of Williams College students discussed earlier. A perceived uniqueness score was calculated for each subject by taking the difference between the percentage of the 45 behaviors each of them indicated they would or could perform and their average consensus estimate across these behaviors. Thus, high scorers are people who claim that they could or would perform many of the behaviors, but think that only a small proportion of their peers could also perform them.

These scores were correlated with subjects' self-esteem scores as measured by the Texas Social Behavior Inventory (Helmreich, Stapp, & Ervin, 1974) and depression scores as assessed by the Beck Depression Inventory (Beck, 1967). Uniqueness scores were significantly correlated with self-esteem ($r = .31$, $p < .011$). The correlation was virtually identical for both men and women. Uniqueness scores were also significantly correlated, in a negative direction, with depression scores, ($r = -.29$, $p < .020$). The correlation was significant for women ($r = -.32$, $p < .034$) but not for men ($r = -.12$, n.s.).

Considering the two scores that are used to derive uniqueness scores for each subject we find that the percentage of items the subjects claimed they would or could perform was correlated positively with self-esteem and negatively with depression for females but not males. We also find that subjects' average consensus estimates were not correlated with depression scores for either males or females but were correlated in an interesting way with self-esteem scores. For women there was a nearly significant positive correlation between self-esteem scores and consensus estimates ($r = .28$, $p < .052$). Women who had high self-esteem thought many of their peers would or could do desirable things. For men the correlation between self-esteem and consensus estimates tended to be negative ($r = -.28$, $p < .111$). Men with high self-esteem thought relatively few of their peers would or could do desirable things. The correlations for men and women were significantly different from each other ($z = 1.97$, $p < .049$).

The data show that self-esteem is correlated with the uniqueness bias for both men and women. As predicted both sexes enjoy higher self-esteem when they have high uniqueness scores. The data also suggest that women's self-esteem is supported both by seeing themselves as performing a high percentage of desirable behaviors and by seeing a high percentage of their peers performing such behaviors. Women who perform well and perceive their peers as doing likewise feel good about themselves. In contrast, men's self-esteem is supported more through perceptions of other people's performances than their own. Men who see themselves as performing a high percentage of desirable behaviors do not have higher self-esteem than those who perceive themselves as performing a lower percentage. The key to men's self-esteem is their perception that few of their peers perform desirable behaviors. The less positively men view their peers, the higher their self-esteem.

CONSTRUCTIVE SOCIAL COMPARISON AND THE UNIQUENESS BIAS

We began with the hypothesis that people will devise self-esteem maintaining constructions of social reality. Specifically, they will construct social reality in a way that allows them to perceive themselves as comparing well to others. Often this means they will view other people as less likely to be willing and able to do good things than they actually are. This allows people to see their own positive behaviors as relatively unusual, reflecting their positive personal qualities. Their own negative behaviors are seen as not at all unusual, reflecting the situations the environment forces them to respond to.

The hypothesis of constructive social comparison grows out of basic principles of cognitive dissonance theory and key extensions of social comparison theory. It is consistent with other studies of self-serving biases (cf. Greenwald, 1980). Our data on the uniqueness bias support this hypothesis. Let us review our main findings briefly and outline what they seem to suggest about the processes that produce the uniqueness bias.

The most consistent finding is the uniqueness bias itself. In studies of college students, high school students, elementary school students, and adult bankers there were invariable tendencies for people to claim that they can or will do good things more frequently than their peers can or will. People tend to think more of their moral than of their intellectual superiority. This is what we have elsewhere called Muhammad Ali effect. People think they are better in a moral sense, and sometimes in an athletic sense, but their sense of being smarter is relatively muted. This tendency to think better of oneself in the moral domain is more characteristic of females than males. Males show more of the uniqueness bias than females and, relative to women, they show considerably more of it in the intellectual arena but slightly less of it in the moral arena. Finally, there is evidence, particularly for ability-related behaviors, of reality-constrained self-deception. People differentiate themselves from others more on specific, clearly defined behaviors than generally defined and less easily measured behaviors. Perhaps when people consider vaguely defined behaviors they imagine ones on which they can do well and tend to think they are superior to others in performing these behaviors. A fifth grade girl asked us what we meant when we asked if she "could solve a hard problem." She inquired, "Do you mean a math problem?" When she was told that the question asked about whatever she thought was a hard problem, she looked reassured, and smiled, and briskly checked "Yes." Her estimate of her capacity to succeed was not constrained by an imposed image of a specific, real, hard-to-solve problem.

An important finding is that the uniqueness bias correlates with self-esteem. Furthermore, it does so equally well for both men and women. In contrast, one's perception of one's own level of performance on the various behaviors, and one's estimates of other people's degree of success in performing them, do not correlate as consistently. It is the difference between what one can or will do and what others can or will do that is reliably related to self-esteem. Males and females support high self-esteem in different ways, but their general tendency to think well of themselves is well-indexed by their degree of self-other differentiation. Consistent with the finding that self-esteem correlates with the uniqueness bias is our finding in the high school sample that the uniqueness bias is greater for advanced placement students than students in regular classes. Students whose self-esteem is supported by being in a prestigious position in the school system enjoy positive assessments of their relative ability and morality.

What is it that produces the uniqueness bias? Why do people think they are more likely than their peers to do good things? Why do more of them think they can do good things than people in general? We think very early in life people develop a desire to think well of themselves. Praise for good performance is likely to be associated with important benefits such as safety, comfort, and affection. Since good performance is most often measured in relative terms people want to think of themselves as standing better than their peers. This wish seems to lead to constructive social comparison which generates perceptions of relative good standing, especially when people can consider how they stand on somewhat vaguely defined behaviors. That is, people want to see themselves as better than others and use constructive social comparison to do so unless a clear reality makes such self-perceptions dissonant with the facts. In short, we think, very simply, that people perceive themselves the way they want to perceive themselves by constructing esteem-maintaining perceptions of others. Wishes, like expectations, are powerful determinants of perceptions, and when levels of performance are somewhat ambiguous, people create their own reality.

More research is needed to identify the cognitive processes that translate the wish to see oneself positively into the reality of the uniqueness bias. We think a number of such processes are important. People's good behaviors are extremely available to cognition, more so than other people's

(Ross & Sicoly, 1979). Self-esteem probably depends on making one's own triumphs highly accessible. Also, when asked about general behaviors people probably construct images of themselves in situations where it is relatively plausible for them to excel. Furthermore, once people adopt a generally positive self-image on the basis of positive feedback from parents and teachers or early good performances, biases in schema-congruent perception, recall, and attribution will continue to maintain and enhance a richly differentiated positive self-image. Recent research on depressive realism (Alloy & Abramson, 1979) suggested that a host of cognitive biases serve to shield the average person from the fact that he or she is average, and support a high self-esteem based in large measure on the perception that one is better than average in a variety of interesting and important ways.

Clearly we do not know all the motivational or cognitive factors that contribute to constructive social comparison and weave their way into the uniqueness bias. But it does seem evident that people have a strong desire to see themselves positively, and have the wit to find ways to do so.

ACKNOWLEDGMENTS

The authors would like to thank Brian Mullen and Jerry Suls for extremely helpful comments on earlier drafts of this chapter.

REFERENCES

Ali, M. (1975). *The greatest: My own story*. New York: Random House.
Allen, V. L., & Wilder, D. A. (1977). Social comparison, self-evaluation, and conformity to the group. In J. M. Suls & R. L. Miller (Eds.), *Social comparison processes: Theoretical and empirical perspectives* (pp. 187–200). Washington, DC: Hemisphere.
Allison, S. T., Messick, D. M., & Goethals, G. R. (1989). *On being better but not smarter than others: The Muhammad Ali effect*. Unpublished manuscript, Williams College, Department of Psychology, Williamstown, MA.
Alloy, L. B., & Abramson, L. Y. (1979). Judgment of contingency in depressed students: Sadder but wiser? *Journal of Experimental Psychology: General, 108*, 441–485.
Allport, F. H. (1924). *Social psychology*. Cambridge, MA: Riverside Press.
Aronson, E. (1988). *The social animal* (5th ed.). New York: Freeman.
Beck, A. T. (1967). *Depression: Clinical, experimental, and theoretical aspects*. New York: Harper & Row.
Brickman, P., & Bulman, R. J. (1977). Pleasure and pain in social comparison. In J. M. Suls & R. L. Miller (Eds.), *Social comparison processes: Theoretical and empirical perspectives* (pp. 149–186). Washington, DC: Hemisphere.
Brown, R. (1965). *Social psychology*. New York: Free Press of Glencoe.
Campbell, J. D. (1986). Similarity and uniqueness: The effects of attribute type, relevance, and individual differences in self-esteem and depression. *Journal of Personality and Social Psychology, 50*(2), 281–294.

Darley, J. M., & Goethals, G. R. (1980). People's analyses of the causes of ability-linked performances. In L. Berkowitz (Ed.), *Advances in experimental social psychology* (pp. 1–37). New York: Academic Press.
Festinger, L. (1950). Informal social communication. *Psychological Review*, 57, 271–282.
Festinger, L. (1954). A theory of social comparison processes. *Human Relations*, 7, 117–140.
Festinger, L. (1957). *A theory of cognitive dissonance*. Stanford, CA: Stanford University Press.
Festinger, L., Riecken, H., & Schachter, S. (1956). *When prophecy fails*. Minneapolis, MN: University of Minnesota Press.
Festinger, L. (1975). *An interview with Leon Festinger*, Charles Harris (Ed.). [Audio tape]. Scranton, PA: Harper & Row Media Program (Distributor).
Freilicher, N. A., & Goethals, G. R. (1988, April). *Reality constrained and unconstrained self-deception*. Paper presented at the meeting of the Eastern Psychological Association, Buffalo, NY.
Gilovich, T., Jennings, D. L., & Jennings, S. (1983). Causal analysis and estimates of consensus: undermining the false consensus effect. *Journal of Personality and Social Psychology*, 45, 550–559.
Goethals, G. R. (1986a). Social comparison theory: Psychology from the lost and found. *Personality and Social Psychology Bulletin*, 12(3), 261–278.
Goethals, G. R. (1986b). Fabricating and ignoring social reality: Self-serving estimates of consensus. In J. M. Olson, C. P. Herman, & M. P. Zanna (Eds.), *Relative deprivation and social comparison: The Ontario symposium* (Vol. 4) (pp. 135–157). Hillsdale, NJ: Lawrence Erlbaum Associates.
Goethals, G. R., Allison, S. J., & Frost, M. (1979). Perceptions of the magnitude and diversity of social support. *Journal of Experimental Social Psychology*, 15, 570–581.
Goethals, G. R., & Darley, J. M. (1977). Social comparison theory: An attributional approach. In J. M. Suls & R. L. Miller (Eds.), *Social comparison processes: Theoretical and empirical perspectives* (pp. 259–278). Washington, DC: Hemisphere.
Goffman, E. (1955). On face-work: An analysis of ritual elements in social interaction. *Psychiatry: Journal for the Study of Interpersonal Processes*, 18, 213–231.
Greenwald, A. G. (1980). The totalitarian ego: Fabrication and revision of personal history. *American Psychologist*, 35, 603–613.
Hakmiller, K. L. (1966). Threat as a determinant of downward comparison. *Journal of Experimental Social Psychology*, (Suppl. 1), 32–39.
Hayes, S. P., Jr. (1936). The predictive ability of voters. *Journal of Social Psychology*, 7, 183–191.
Helmreich, R., Stapp, J., & Ervin, C. (1974). The Texas social behavior inventory (TSBI): An objective measure of self-esteem or social competence. *JSAS Catalog of Selected Documents in Psychology*, 4, 79 (ms. no. 681).
Hertzman, M., & Festinger, L. (1940). Shifts in explicit goals in a level of aspiration experiment. *Journal of Experimental Psychology*, 27, 439–452.
Hinds, W. C. (1962). *Individual and group decisions in gambling situations*. Unpublished master's thesis, Massachusetts Institute of Technology, School of Industrial Management.
Hyman, H. H. (1942). The psychology of status. *Archives of Psychology*, No. 269.
Jellison, J. M., & Riskind, J. (1970). A social comparison of abilities interpretation of risk-taking behavior. *Journal of Personality and Social Psychology*, 15(4), 375–390.
Kelley, H. H. (1952). The two functions of reference groups. In G. E. Swanson, T. M. Newcomb, & E. E. Hartley (Eds.), *Readings in social psychology* (2nd ed.). New York: Holt Rinehart & Winston.
Latané, B. (Ed.). (1966). Studies in social comparison: Introduction and overview. *Journal of Experimental Social Psychology*, (Supp. 1), 1–5.

Levinger, G., & Schneider, D. J. (1969). Test of the "risk is a value" hypothesis. *Journal of Personality and Social Psychology 11*, 165–169.

Marks, G. (1984). Thinking one's abilities are unique and one's opinions are common. *Personality and Social Psychology Bulletin, 10*, 203–208.

Marks, G., & Miller, N. (1987). Ten years of research on the false consensus effect: An empirical and theoretical review. *Psychological Bulletin, 102*, 72–90.

Messick, D. M., Bloom, S., Boldizer, J. P., & Samuelson, C. D. (1985). Why we are fairer than others. *Journal of Experimental Social Psychology, 21*, 480–500.

Mettee, D. R., & Smith, G. (1977). Social comparison and interpersonal attraction: The case for dissimilarity. In J. M. Suls & R. L. Miller (Eds.), *Social comparison processes: Theoretical and empirical perspectives* (pp. 69–101). Washington, DC: Hemisphere.

Miller, D. T. (1983, October). Presentation given at the Ontario Symposium on Relative Deprivation and Social Comparison. London: Ontario.

Mullen, B., & Goethals, G. R. (in press). *Short note: Social projection, actual consensus and valence*. British Journal of Social Psychology, Williamstown, MA.

Mullen, B., & Hu, L. (1988). Social projection as a function of cognitive mechanisms: Two meta-analytic integrations. *British Journal of Social Psychology, 27*, 333–356.

Mullen, G., Atkins, J. L., Champion, D. S., Edwards, C., Hardy, D., Story, J. E., & Vanderklok, M. (1985). The false consensus effect: A meta-analysis of 115 hypothesis tests. *Journal of Experimental Social Psychology, 21*, 262–283.

Myers, D. G., & Ridl, J. (1979). Can we all be better than average? *Psychology Today, 13*, 89–92.

Orive, R. (1988). Social projection and social comparison of opinions. *Journal of Personality and Social Psychology, 54*(6), 953–964.

Perloff, L. S., & Fetzer, B. K. (1986). Self-other judgments and perceived vulnerability to victimization. *Journal of Personality and Social Psychology, 50*(3), 502–510.

Phillips, E. D. (1988). *The uniqueness bias: A developmental approach to self-serving biases*. Unpublished master's thesis, Williams College, Williamstown, MA.

Ross, L. (1977). The intuitive psychologist and his shortcomings: Distortions in the attribution process. In L. Berkowitz (Ed.), *Advances in Experimental Social Psychology, 10*, 173–220. New York: Academic Press.

Ross, L., Greene, D., & House, P. (1977). The "false consensus effect": An egocentric bias in social perception and attribution processes. *Journal of Experimental Social Psychology, 13*, 279–301.

Ross, M., & Sicoly, F. (1979). Egocentric biases in availability and attribution. *Journal of Personality and Social Psychology, 37*, 322–336.

Sears, D. O. (1986). College sophomores in the laboratory: Influences of a narrow data base on social psychology's view of human nature. *Journal of Personality and Social Psychology, 51*(3), 515–530.

Singer, J. E. (1966). Social comparison-progress and issues. *Journal of Experimental and Social Psychology*, Supplement *1*, 103–110.

Steele, C. M. (1988). The psychology of self-affirmation: Sustaining the integrity of the self. *Advances in Experimental Social Psychology, 21*, 261–302.

Stone, P., & Kamiya, J. (1957). Judgments of consensus during group discussion. *Journal of Abnormal and Social Psychology, 55*, 171–175.

Suls, J. (1986). Notes on the occasion of social comparison theory's thirtieth birthday. *Personality and Social Psychology Bulletin, 12*(3), 289–296.

Taylor, S. E., & Brown, J. D. (1988). Illusion and well-being: A social psychological perspective on mental health. *Psychological Bulletin, 103*, 193–210.

Taylor, S. E., Buunk, B. P., & Aspinwall, L. G. (1990). Social comparison, stress, and coping. *Personality and Social Psychology Bulletin, 16*, 74–89.

Taylor, S. E., Wood, J. V., & Lichtman, R. R. (1983). It could be worse: Selective evaluation as a response to victimization. *Journal of Social Issues, 39,* 19–40.

Tesser, A. (1988). Toward a self-evaluation maintenance model of social behavior. In L. Berkowitz (Ed.), *Advances in Experimental Social Psychology* (Vol. 21, pp. 181–227). New York: Academic Press.

Wallach, M. A., & Wing, C. W., Jr. (1968). Is risk a value? *Journal of Personality and Social Psychology, 9,* 101–106.

Weinstein, N. D. (1980). Unrealistic optimism about future life events. *Journal of Personality and Social Psychology, 39,* 806–820.

Wheeler, L. (1966). Motivation as a determinant of upward comparison. *Journal of Experimental Social Psychology* (Supplement 1), 27–31.

Wills, T. A. (1981). Downward comparison principles in social psychology. *Psychological Bulletin, 90,* 245–271.

Wills, T. A. (1987). Downward comparison as a coping mechanism. In C. R. Snyder & C. Ford (Eds.), *Coping with negative life events: Clinical and social psychological perspectives.* New York: Plenum.

Wood, J. V. (1989). Theory and research concerning social comparisons of personal attributes. *Psychological Bulletin, 106,* 231–248.

Wood, J. V., Taylor, S. E., & Lichtman, R. R. (1985). Social comparison in adjustment to breast cancer. *Journal of Personality and Social Psychology, 49,* 1169–1183.

7 Social Projection and Attitudinal Certainty

Norman Miller and Sharon Gross
University of Southern California

Rolf Holtz
Lamar University

The process by which a person becomes more extreme in attitudinal position and more certain about the correctness of a belief has long been of interest to social psychologists. When studied within attitude change paradigms, it seems natural that explanations predominantly stress the effects of message content and cognitive process, such as judgmental assimilation and contrast effects.

Social comparison theory (Festinger, 1954) emphasizes instead a motivational perspective. It is predicated on "the existence of a drive to determine whether or not one's opinions were 'correct'" (p. 118). Because an objective measure for evaluating one's opinions and abilities is not available, this drive instigates comparison with others. Correctness or certainty is a continuum. Its degree or level depends on the consensus one observes for an opinion. Thus, the relation between attitude conviction and social comparison stems from Festinger's notion that uncertainty or ambiguity about one's correctness is an unstable state. In support of this postulate he cites Hochbaum (1953), who manipulated subjects' ability to make correct judgments about a discussion topic. Those made to feel they had poor judgment changed their opinions more to conform with group consensus than did those who felt they had good judgment. Similarly, subjects informed that most others in the group disagreed with them felt less confident about the correctness of their opinion (Festinger, Gerard, Hymovitch, Kelley, & Raven, 1952). When uncertain, one bolsters the certainty of one's belief by collecting information about the opinions of persons who are similar to self on related attributes, and becomes more certain as a consequence of the homogeneity of opinion implicit in this selection process.

Two primary aspects of social comparison have long been noted: its informational function and its normative function (e.g. Shaver, 1987). The informational function provides location information—Where am I on the dimension, relative to others. The normative function serves validation or self-esteem maintenance needs—Is my position a good or valid one?

Although most theoretical discussions emphasize comparison of self with similar others as the preferred mode of uncertainty reduction (e.g. Goethals & Darley, 1977; Wheeler, 1966), it also may be useful to seek out comparison others who are dissimilar (e.g. Suls, 1986). With respect to location information, although similar others are the ones whose positions one cares about, dissimilar others can provide information on the full range of positions on the issue (Wheeler, et al., 1969). With respect to normative concerns, as when one hopes to gain group acceptance, comparison both to dissimilar as well as similar others may again be useful. Knowledge of the positions held by those in a valued group may provide a sense of certainty about the correctness of one's similar view, or provide information relevant for instrumental adjustment of one's own position in order to gain acceptance (Sanders & Baron, 1977). Knowledge about the position of dissimilar groups, however, should also serve these functions. Hearing my own position disavowed by a well-hated outgroup should make me more certain of its correctness and more certain of my acceptability to my own ingroup.[1]

AN UNSPOKEN HALF OF SOCIAL COMPARISON THEORY: SOCIAL PROJECTION AS A SOURCE OF CERTAINTY

Social comparison applies to situations in which a person can successfully collect information about the view of others, either by direct question, observation, or inference from their actions. In other situations, however, this may not be possible, yet a person may still desire sufficient certainty

---

[1] With respect to conviction displayed in response to normative pressures, however, it is important to distinguish compliance from internalized certainty. When opinion formation or adoption is merely instrumental for initial acceptance into a group, although overt statements within the presence of group members may suggest that one is highly certain about the correctness of group-relevant beliefs, such initial compliance may not reflect an internalized attitude. Internalized certainty may only develop as a psychological consequence of maintaining one's membership in the group.

of belief to act in one direction or another. In such instances, (unconscious) social projection may serve a function that parallels that of social comparison. By assuming similarity between self and relevant others, the perception of consensual validation that ordinarily augments certainty can be manufactured (Allport, 1924).

Past experience may confirm the validity of such projected consensus. The selective exposure interpretation of projected similarity (Marks & Miller, 1987; Ross, Greene, & House, 1977) points to the biased sample of views to which the actor exposes oneself when engaging in social comparison. Thus, one might assume that if (the self-selected) others typically agreed with me in the past, they are likely to agree in this instance, too. In the many circumstances in which people avoid comparison (Brickman & Bulman, 1977), projecting opinion similarity to augment certainty may be preferable to seeking actual information. People may rather assume they are correct than risk collecting discrepant information (Goethals, 1986; Suls, 1986).

In the preceding discussion, projection, like social comparison, functions as a mediating variable that intervenes between antecedent events that elicit it, and subsequent expression of opinion extremity or conviction. The models in Fig. 7.1 show the social comparison process and alternative social projection processes. By projecting attitudinal similarity onto favorable targets, opinion certainty and self-appraisal are augmented. In the third model (Social Projection 2), certainty, not uncertainty, is the antecedent for projection. Breaking the process into its components, projection can be viewed as a dependent variable to be assessed in response to antecedent manipulations, or as an independent variable, the manipulation of which should affect opinion certainty. From the first perspective, just as a feeling of uncertainty might instigate comparison between self and others, it might also elicit projection of opinion similarity between self and others. When viewed as an independent variable, as when an experimenter directly attempts to manipulate the projective process that might underlie augmented opinion certainty, the experimental operations would consist of procedures that cause the subject to think about the opinion positions of others. Thus, subjects might be instructed to estimate the opinion of a specific person or group in order to examine the effect on their conviction.

As noted, comparison of self to dissimilar as well as similar others might function to increase certainty. Similarly, in the case of projection, wherein it is conceptualized as consisting of experimental procedures designed to elicit thought about the opinions of some target person or group, both dissimilar and similar others might serve important functions. Thinking about the opinions of similar others might imply consensual support. Thinking about those of a dissimilar outgroup might imply attack. This elicits distancing and increased conviction.

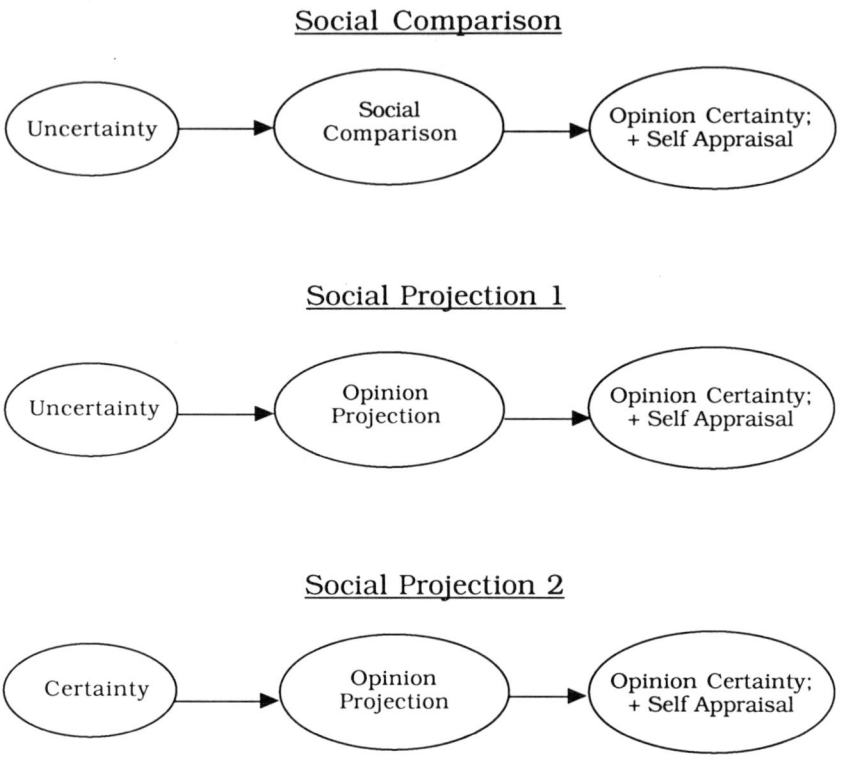

FIG. 7.1. Models of self-appraisal and opinion certainty.

We explore the concept of social projection and its relation to opinion certainty. We first place the concept of projected opinion similarity/dissimilarity within the broader literature on projection. We then compare three theoretical orientations toward it: interpersonal, intragroup, or intergroup process. We then report a series of studies that address the processes that underlie the relation between projection and opinion certainty. We conclude by considering the theoretical implications of our research outcomes.

Throughout, though we focus on opinion certainty, we view it along with opinion extremity, strength, or crystalization, as tapping a common underlying trait of conviction. Raden's (1985) review of strength-related attitude properties reported moderate correlations among the trio of *certainty*, *intensity*, and *generalized attitude strength*, suggesting an underlying factor for these measures even though other potential strength measures appear unrelated to it.[2] In addition, he claimed substantial relations between these three measures in his own work. Krosnick and Schuman (1988) also reported data consistent with the concept of an underlying latent variable. In 28 of 32 comparisons, measures of attitude intensity, certainty, and importance exhibited common response-scale distributions. Additionally, convergent validity (of no response effects) was found in separate meta-analyses of certainty, intensity, and importance. Thus a measure of attitudinal certainty will probably assess what is generally meant by conviction or strength of belief.

Social Projection and Other Related Terms

Discussion of projection extends back to the beginnings of scientific thought and may reflect early interest in the camera obscura as a device for projecting an image on a screen (Campbell, Miller, Lubetsky, & O'Connell, 1964). Such analogical thinking clearly is evident in Francis Bacon's (1853) discussions of the psychology of bias. Among the many he considered was projecting one's own world view onto others. The visual after-image, wherein the form of a previously inspected object is seen on the blank wall, implies this similarity projective mechanism. A previous internal experience is mistakenly projected onto reality. Yet, when considered with respect to color after-images, the analogizing might imply a contrast mechanism. The after-image of a red object is green. Bacon also spoke of such a contrast bias—the exaggeration of differences. The notion of projecting internal central nervous system events onto external reality was also present in James (1890) who cited others' prior use of the term. Contemporary pop psychology and other current usage, however, typically associate the term with Freud.

Most interpreters see Freud as having espoused similarity projection, especially with respect to its use as a defense mechanism—the unconscious attribution of own negative traits onto others (Freud, 1937). For love–hate, the most basic dimension of human interaction, however, a complementary mechanism—the attribution of that which justifies own behavior, makes the same prediction about own and attributed trait as does similarity projection (Campbell, et al., 1964). One who misperceives another as hostile would, as a consequence of that misperception, feel justified in feeling hostile toward that other. Only with respect to more specific traits can the distinction between the two mechanisms be made clear. In Murray's

---

[2] No studies reported correlations between generalized attitude strength and intensity.

(1933) classic study, after the experimenter told them scary ghost stories, the frightened girls saw the photographs of strange men as more threatening or frightening than they previously had, not as frightened like themselves. In Freud's discussion of latent homosexuality as underlying paranoid projection, a complementary mechanism is particularly clear. The paranoid does not see the world filled with other benign passive homosexuals like himself, but rather, filled with sexually aggressive homosexuals who, when present, would justify paranoid fears of attack.

In research on projection, which concerns individual traits far more than opinions or attitudes, there is a proliferation of names for its underlying mechanisms. Excluding response biases that reflect stable individual differences, as few as three basically distinct processes may suffice (Campbell et al., 1964). These are: (a) similarity: the attribution of one's own attribute to others, e.g. self guilty, other guilty; (b) contrast: the attribution of the opposite of one's own attribute, e.g. self stingy, other generous; (c) complementarity: the attribution of that which justifies one's own characteristic, e.g. self guilty, other accusing and punitive.

With respect to stereotypes, Allport (1954) favored complementary projection as characterizing outgroup depiction but also allowed that contrast projection might occur. Campbell (1967) also seemed to favor a contrast relation between the mutual stereotypes of related or spatially adjacent groups, but may also have advocated complementarity. Were our own research to focus on traits or stereotypes instead of opinions, it might be important to distinguish among projective mechanisms. However, given (a) our concern with attitudes and opinions associated with group membership, (b) the strong relevance of the love–hate dimension to ingroup–outgroup relations, (c) the well-established empirical links between liking and similarity (e.g. Byrne, Clore, & Smeaton, 1986) or dislike and dissimilarity (Rosenbaum, 1986), (d) the convergence among similarity, complementarity, and reactivity mechanisms for predictions regarding the basic dimension of love and hate, and (e) the melding of similarity and contrast projection into a single dimension of distance when operations for determining the zero-point of no-projection or actual similarity–dissimilarity are absent, we can justify our focus on relative similarity–dissimilarity. We thereby avoid the complicated issue of accuracy (Cronbach, 1955, 1958; Funder, 1987; Kenny & Allbright, 1987). At the same time, the work we report should not be viewed as providing discriminant validity for one or another of the various projective mechanisms. In our concluding discussion we return to the distinctions among them.

Theoretical Orientations Regarding Projection-Augmented Opinion Certainty

Consensual Support. Implicit in most models of social influence is the notion that consensual support increases opinion certainty (e.g. Latané,

1981; Tanford & Penrod, 1984). Also, attitude or value extremity correlates with perceived consensus (Crano, 1983; van der Pligt, Ester, & van der Linden, 1983). This suggests that projection onto a single, broad, nonspecific target group will confer greater certainty than projection onto a smaller, more specific target group or onto a single person. Seeing myself as holding a belief similar to that of most Americans, rather than most Alabamians, would confer greater certainty of belief. It is not the nature of the projection target or the fact that it is a group that confers certainty, but instead, the number of others to whom one has attributed similarity. Thus, it is neither an intra- nor intergroup process; it is merely interpersonal.

Intragroup Projection. Alternatively, a theoretical orientation that emphasizes group identity (Turner, 1987), perceived co-orientation of beliefs, values, or goals between self and other (Gerard & Orive, 1987) and selective exposure (e.g. Sherman, Chassin, Presson, & Agostinelli, 1984) anticipates a greater increment in certainty from projecting onto one's ingroup as opposed to either a single specific target or a more numerous array that does not function as an ingroup. If membership in the ingroup and direct interaction with its members not only provides a social identity, but also fulfills social comparison functions with respect to opinion certainty, then ingroup members should function as the projection targets that can best serve these functions in situations in which direct information about specific ingroup opinion positions and values cannot be obtained. Consequently, projecting own opinion onto ingroup members, by serving group identity or social support needs, should best confer opinion certainty.

In an elegant model of the cognitive dynamics that underlie individual opinion formation, Gerard and Orive (1987) took this perspective. Their theoretical emphasis argued that projection of own opinion onto other group members will be more likely when one knows that they are similar to self in important values. Knowledge of such general similarity presumably facilitates attribution of own position on the specific issue at hand, which in turn augments the attitudinal extremity of own position by augmenting perceived support for it. The perception that others are similar to self on the relevant opinion issue is also said to be augmented by action imminence. For instance, the sooner a debate will occur, the greater the perception that other group members hold views similar to one's own.

Intergroup Projection. An alternative conceptualization of the dynamics of opinion certainty emphasizes the relation between groups. Framing social comparison as an intergroup (ingroup–outgroup) process (Tajfel & Turner, 1985), rather than merely as a self-intragroup process (Gerard & Orive, 1987), implicitly calls attention to special functions of dissimilar others.

When projection is reframed as an intergroup phenomenon in which an actor engages in (imagined) opinion comparison with outgroup members, the nature of the goal structure that links the two groups becomes relevant. A competitive goal structure implies a winner and loser, being right or wrong. Within this context intergroup comparison implies disagreement. Likewise, projection of outgroup opinions, that is, thought about or estimation of them, implies disagreement with own position. Thus, thinking about outgroup opinions should promote differentiation of ingroup from outgroup, attitudinal polarization, and increased attitudinal certainty. On the other hand, cooperative goal structures increase the degree to which participants take the perspective of the outgroup members with whom they are cooperating (e.g. Orbell, van de Kragt, & Dawes, 1988). Consequently, when groups relate under a cooperative goal structure, both direct social comparison and thought about outgroup positions should decrease attitudinal polarization and certainty (Hong & Harrod, 1988).

RESEARCH ON THE EFFECTS OF SOCIAL PROJECTION

In line with the preceding discussion of intra and intergroup processes, we assumed in our own research that instructing a person to engage in the task of projecting onto an ingroup increases attitudinal certainty by making membership in that group salient, which in turn primes views relevant to that group and previously expressed by its members. When group membership is salient, its function in fulfilling social identity needs and providing social support is also salient. Consequently, projected opinion should exhibit a similarity bias and should increase opinion certainty. Likewise, a direct manipulation of the salience of ingroup membership should elicit the same processes that projection does and thereby similarly increase attitudinal certainty. The nature of the opinion issues, however, should moderate these effects. Perhaps the confidence-inducing effects of projection should be stronger on important or central dimensions (Suls, 1986).[3]

Finally, our discussion of projection as an interpersonal, intragroup, or intergroup effect, emphasizes respectively three conceptually independent sources of effect: (a) numerical size of the target whose position one is asked to think about, (b) the consequences of thinking about the positions of ingroup members, and (c) the consequences of thinking about the positions of outgroup members. As argued, increased thought about an issue

---

[3] The failure to make distinctions between types of attitudinal issues may account for the absence of target effects in research on social projection (e.g. Mullen et al., 1985).

is implicit in any instruction to estimate the position of a target person or group. The effect of simply thinking about an issue should, by itself, increase certainty (Tesser, 1978). However, the greater social support implicit in thinking about the position of a large ingroup compared either to a smaller one or to a single individual, may moderate the effect of such thought. Whereas the instruction to estimate ingroup positions should increase certainty (Hong & Harrod, 1988), the effect of thinking about the position of an outgroup is not as straightforward. In some circumstances it might reduce certainty by inducing one to experience the perspective of the outgroup, or similarly, by increasing both the salience and credibility of opposing views and arguments. In other circumstances, as when outgroup category salience is high, when the outgroup is combative or threatening, or when one is in competition with the outgroup for scarce resources the more likely effect is increased attitudinal certainty.

These ideas led us to conduct a series of studies that in different combinations factorially manipulated opinion projection, the target of opinion projection, and ingroup salience in order to examine their effects on attitudinal certainty regarding important and unimportant issues.

The Effect of Projection Target: Ingroup Versus Outgroup

In Holtz and Miller (1985), under the guise of preparing an article for the campus daily newspaper, we interviewed two groups of students; those who commuted to campus and did not belong to a fraternity and those who belonged to and resided in a fraternity. For the members of each group we made their group identity salient by reporting the contents of an alleged article in the student newspaper that had found differences in the attitudes, values, and behavior of the two groups. After assessing subjects' own attitudes on an array of issues, they were assigned one of four projection conditions in a between-groups design: asking commuter students and fraternity residents to estimate the opinion positions of other ingroup members (other commuter students and fraternity residents respectively); asking commuter students and fraternity residents to estimate the opinion positions of relevant outgroup members (fraternity residents and commuter students respectively); asking both groups to estimate the position of an irrelevant outgroup (veterans at an old folks home); and a no projection control condition that omitted any opinion estimation task. Thus, the three projection manipulations instructed the subjects to estimate the opinions of a particular target group with respect to the same attitude issues on which subjects had reported their own attitude. The key dependent measure was their opinion certainty on an array of issues.

Assumed Similarity. The results showed that both groups assumed greater similarity (a smaller absolute difference) between their own and ingroup positions than those of relevant or irrelevant outgroups.

Certainty. Of greater interest is the effect of the projection task on opinion certainty. Whereas projection onto the ingroup augmented certainty, projection onto the outgroup did not. Instead, compared to the no-projection control group, an outgroup projection target produced a directional effect of less certainty. These outcomes were primarily due to the important issues which included ingroup-related items.

The Effect of the Goal Structure Linking Groups: Cooperation Versus Competition

In a laboratory study, Holtz and Miller (1989) arbitrarily formed groups of six same-gender strangers into two 3-person groups, allegedly on the basis of their relative preference for the works of Klee and Kandinsky. Members of each group received badges that identified their membership and, in separate rooms, worked as a group to evaluate a painting by each artist on 11 artistic dimensions. The groups never interacted.

The 2x3 factorial design manipulated the reward structure linking the groups (competitive versus cooperative) and the projection target (ingroup members, outgroup members, or none). The key dependent measure was attitudinal certainty with respect to 10 items concerning various aspects of art and life factors that might contribute to artistic quality. Subjects also rated the importance of each item. The manipulation of cooperation and competition rested on the nature of subsequent group rewards. Under cooperation, both groups would be eligible for a monetary prize only if the average performance of all group members in both groups reached a predetermined standard on the 2-painting evaluation task. Under competition, only the group whose individual members had the higher average score would be eligible for the prize. The projection manipulation instructed subjects to estimate the positions of other ingroup members, the members of the other group in the session, or in the control condition, no one.

Assumed Similarity. Group members assumed greater similarity between self and their ingroup than between self and the outgroup. In addition, the interaction between goal structure and projection target reflected the fact that assumed similarity to ingroup members was equally high under the cooperative and the competitive goal structures, whereas there was greater distancing of the outgroup under the competitive as opposed to the cooperative condition.

Certainty. Our major concerns were the effects of projection and reward structure on certainty. Underlying the main effect of greater certainty about important issues under competition was an interaction between goal structure and projection target. Competition induced uniformly high certainty across the three projection conditions, whereas under cooperation, it varied across them and was lowest under outgroup projection.

It is instructive to think about the disjunction between the certainty effects and the levels of assumed similarity elicited by the experimental conditions. Competition produced strong differences in perceptions of similarity to ingroup and outgroup members and uniformly high certainty on important issues irrespective of projection target. On these same issues, cooperation reduced ingroup and outgroup differentiation but produced differences in certainty as a function of the projection target, with greater certainty occurring after projection onto the ingroup target.

Projection as an Operation for Making Ingroup Identity Salient

In Holtz and Miller (1985) we induced high salience of group identity among all subjects, varied the target of projection, and obtained increased certainty after projection onto ingroup members. In contrast, in Marks and Miller (1985) projection failed to increase opinion certainty. After they reached a decision about a court case, the projection task required subjects to attribute jury verdicts to unique persons from a broad array of categories (e.g. best friend, favorite actor). Not only was no social identity made salient, but also the nature of the projection task was unlikely to elicit any feeling of group membership or social identity.

To better understand these different outcomes we undertook a series of three studies that manipulated ingroup projection and salience of social identity. As previously indicated, we assumed that projecting onto an ingroup makes one's membership in the ingroup more salient, and in doing so primes related views and issues previously discussed by ingroup members. If the certainty inducing consequences of social projection function by priming ingroup membership, a direct manipulation of its salience should elicit the same processes and consequently, similarly increase attitudinal certainty. Even in the absence of specific instructions to engage in a projection task, increasing the salience of ingroup identity should spontaneously elicit (unmeasured) projection. We viewed these two manipulations as alternative operationalizations of a common underlying process and expected them to combine additively.

We thought the effects should be moderated by the opinion dimensions being considered. Our previous research had not separated group related and important issues. Consideration of the distinction between social and

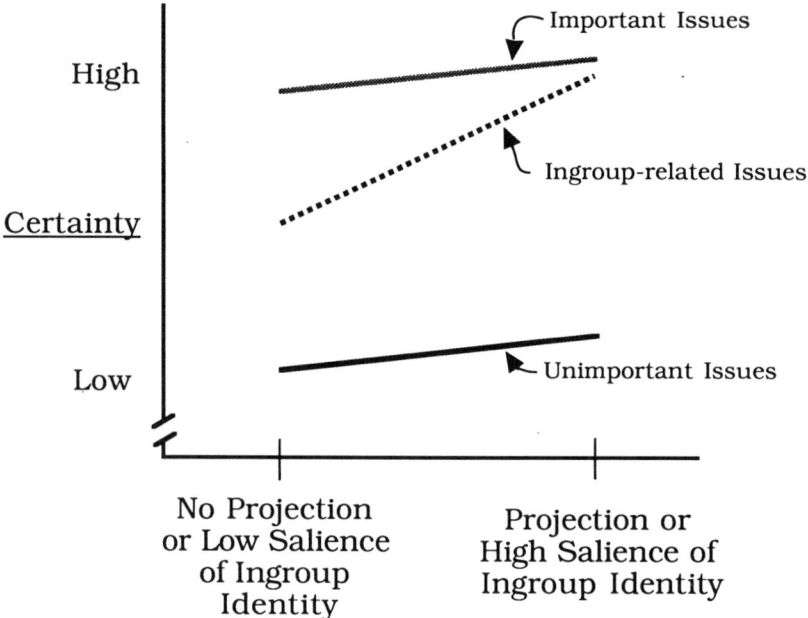

FIG. 7.2. Predicted interaction between projection, item type, and opinion certainty.

individual identity led us to think that ingroup projection and heightened ingroup salience should less strongly affect extremely important attitudes, namely, those that serve as core personal values. Being a component of individual identity, a feeling of correctness about them might be relatively independent of group membership. Instead, our predictions might find strongest support on dimensions relevant to the ingroup. Finally, being unrelated either to group or individual identity, we expected little effect on certainty about unimportant issues (see Fig. 7.2).

Procedure of Study 1. Seventy-six male Caucasian commuter students participated in the 2 (ingroup salience) × 2 (task) × 3 (issue type) mixed factorial design. They were either primed or not primed about their ingroup identity. After indicating their own position on each of 18 attitude items, they either projected (estimated the attitudes of other ingroup members) or did not. Using 9-point fully labelled scales, all subjects indicated their opinion certainty and their perception of issue importance on each item among the three types previously selected on the basis of pilot test: important (e.g. Students should become more involved in presidential elections.), unimportant (e.g. Daylight savings time should be instituted year round in this state.), and ingroup-related (commuter student) issues of middling importance (e.g. Commuter students exceed Row students in their comparative awareness of world affairs.). Six issues of each type appeared in a constant random order across all conditions and measures.

The high-salience manipulation primed ingroup identity by telling the commuter students about existing differences (e.g. class time preference, alumni power) between commuter students and fraternity members. Low-salience subjects were interviewed about individual school-related activities, without mention of any reference group, thereby controlling for amount of interaction with the experimenter.

Procedure of Study 2. In Study 1, to avoid priming commuter identity in the low-salience condition, the projection target differed between the high- and low-salience conditions (high: other commuters; low: other university students). Though two studies (Crano, 1983; Mullen et al., 1985) suggested no consequence of variation in the target, we thought it important to assess this potential confound. In Study 2 we recruited 107 male and female university apartment dwellers in their residence and randomly assigned them to the four cells of Study 1 and added a low-salience projection cell (high: other apartment dwellers; low: other university students; low: other apartment dwellers).

To induce high-salience of group identity, we described differences between apartment dwellers and fraternity or sorority house residents. In the low-salience conditions we told subjects that the survey concerned the attitudes of apartment dwellers. Other procedures replicated Study 1 except that the ingroup-related issues compared apartment dwellers to fraternity or sorority house residents.

Procedure of Study 3. A total of 223 male and female commuter students from four California universities participated in this 2 (salience of group identity) × 3 (task) × 2 (order) × 3 (issue type) mixed factorial design. Only issue type was manipulated within subjects.

Post hoc consideration of subject selection in Study 1 (asking them all if they were commuters) and Study 2 (approaching them in their residence) suggested that we may have undercut our salience manipulation by inadvertently priming group identity within both levels. Therefore, in Study

3, a commuter identifying question was embedded among an array of questions. Only such surreptitiously identified commuters qualified as subjects. Additionally, in the high-salience conditions the manipulation was strengthened by inducing a behavioral commitment relevant to their ingroup identity. We told subjects that the student senate was polling interest among various subpopulations on campus in order to represent more adequately student body needs. We then asked whether they would like to add their name to those of other commuters on a partially filled petition signature form for "*COMMUTERS* interested in receiving a newsletter." No one refused.

To avoid the target difference confounded with the salience manipulation of Study 1, we maintained a common target across the projection conditions. Finally, to better understand processes mediating increments in attitudinal certainty, we included additional experimental conditions that interpolated a memory task prior to, and a judgment task (degree of difficulty in indicating own attitude on each opinion issue) instead of the projection task.

Target Effects. Study 2 yielded a target difference. Contrary to the numerical consensual support hypothesis, comparison of the two low salience projection conditions shows that projection onto the smaller ingroup (student apartment dwellers) yielded greater assumed similarity ($M_A = 1.22$, $SD_A = .72$; $M_U = 1.74$, $SD_U = .91$) and greater certainty ($M_A = 6.85$, $SD_A = 1.09$; $M_U = 6.51$, $SD_U = 1.13$) than did projection onto the more superordinate ingroup category (University of Iowa students).

Projection and Ingroup Salience Effects. Diffuse tests (Rosenthal, 1984) show that despite differences across studies in experimenters, universities, ingroups, targets of projection, gender and ethnic make-up of subjects, the projection manipulations produced remarkably similar effects on attitudinal certainty. So too, did the ingroup salience manipulation, though its effects differed substantially from those of projection. This cross-study consistency strongly suggests a meta-analytic summary of results.

Table 7.1 shows the relation between projection and attitudinal certainty ($r = .16, p < .001$) across studies. Projection increased certainty, primarily on the ingroup-related issues ($r = .27, p < .001$). In contrast, as seen in Table 7.1, ingroup salience is unrelated to attitudinal certainty ($r = .01$, n.s.).

Tests of the Specific Theoretical Interactions. We had hypothesized that both heightening ingroup salience and engaging in the projection task would function in parallel fashion to augment subjects' identity as commuter students, which in turn might increase certainty on all types of issues,

TABLE 7.1
The Meta-Analytic Effect of Projection and Salience of Ingroup Identity on Attitudinal Certainty

Study	N	d.f.	Projection Effect F[1]	Projection Effect effect size (r)	Salience Effect F	Salience Effect effect size
			Highly important issues[3]			
1	76	1,74	0.33(+)	0.07	0.02(−)	0.02
2	102	1,100	0.07(+)	0.03	1.67(+)	0.13
3	145	1,143	0.05(+)	0.02	1.28(+)	0.09
Combined across studies[2]				*0.04*		*0.07*
			Ingroup-related issues			
1	76	1,74	4.37(+)	0.24	0.64(−)	0.09
2	102	1,100	7.31(+)	0.26	0.82(+)	0.09
3	145	1,143	6.41(+)	0.21	0.12(−)	0.03
Combined across studies				*0.23**		*−0.01*
			Unimportant issues			
1	76	1,74	1.57(+)	0.14	0.26(−)	0.06
2	102	1,100	1.00(+)	0.10	0.05(+)	0.02
3	145	1,143	1.05(+)	0.09	2.19(−)	0.12
Combined across studies				*0.11*		*−0.05*
			Pooled across issues			
1	76	1,74	2.28(+)	0.17	0.33(−)	0.07
2	102	1,100	3.04(+)	0.17	1.14(+)	0.11
3	145	1,143	2.85(+)	0.14	0.08(−)	0.02
Combined across studies				*0.16**		*0.01*

Notes: [1]Positive sign indicates greater certainty in the projection conditions.
[2]When effect sizes are combined using weighted sample sizes, they deviate from the unweighted values by ±.01.
[3]Effect size significance levels: * = $p < .001$.

but especially on those relevant to ingroup membership. This not only implies salience and projection main effects, but separate, parallel, two-way interactions between each and the within-subject factor of item type. Though the meta-analytic integration confirmed the projection main effect, it primarily is due to the consistent finding within each of the three studies that certainty increased on the ingroup-related items (p's associated with the F statistic <.05, .01, & .05 respectively across studies 1, 2, and 3), but especially so in the high salience conditions. Though confirming our predicted interaction between item type and projection, the meta-analytic results fail to confirm the predicted interaction between salience, item type, and certainty.

TABLE 7.2
The Meta-Analytic Effect of Ingroup Salience on Assumed Similarity to Ingroup

Study	N	d.f.	F[1]	effect size (r)[4]
Highly important issues[4]				
1	38	1,36	6.91(+)	0.40*
2[2]	51	1,49	0.27(−)	−0.07
3	64	1,62	1.65(+)	0.16
Combined across studies[3]				*0.17**
Ingroup-related issues				
1	38	1,36	3.61(+)	0.30
2	51	1,49	0.92(+)	0.14
3	64	1,62	3.18(+)	0.22**
Combined across studies				*0.22*
Unimportant issues				
1	38	1,36	1.26(+)	0.18
2	51	1,49	0.03(−)	−0.02
3	64	1,62	0.89(+)	0.12
Combined across studies				*0.09*
Pooled across issues				
1	38	1,36	5.87(+)	0.37*
2	51	1,49	0.00(+)	0.00
3	64	1,62	2.61(+)	0.20
Combined across studies				*0.20**

Notes: [1]Positive sign indicates more similarity in the high salience condition.
[2]The two low salience conditions of study 2 were pooled.
[3]When effect sizes are combined using weighted sample sizes, the range of deviation from the unweighted value is +0.0 to −0.02.
[4]Effect size significance levels: * = $p < 0.05$; ** = $p < 0.01$.

To provide as sensitive a test as possible, we applied the a priori weights implicit in our theorizing to test the planned interactions within each study separately. All three tests of the planned interaction between projection, item type, and attitudinal certainty upheld our expectations. In contrast, consistent with meta-analytic outcome, none confirmed an interaction between ingroup salience, item type, and attitudinal certainty.

Though it made sense to assume so, salience of ingroup identity cannot be considered conceptually isomorphic with projection. Even the most sensitive tests failed to support our theorizing. Lest one think that despite our care we failed to manipulate salience effectively in all three studies, the assumed similarity data counters this view (see Table 7.2). Meta-analytic combination across studies shows that subjects who received the high salience induction assumed greater attitudinal similarity to their ingroup than those who did not ($r = .20$, $p < .05$).

Exposure and Thought as an Explanation of Projection Effects

The failure to find ingroup salience effects that paralleled those found for projection led us to question the theoretical role of group identity in the obtained projection effects and to examine more carefully specific operations that comprised the projection manipulation. In Holtz and Miller (1985), all our effects for attitudinal certainty were perfectly mirrored when attitude extremity was used as a response measure, suggesting that a change in one's attitudinal certainty can be viewed as attitudinal polarization. Tesser (1978) has shown that polarization can occur from mere thought. On complex issues for which one has personal commitment, thought will increase attitudinal extremity. On highly novel issues that involve simple schema, however, it will increase extremity in the absence of commitment (Millar & Tesser, 1986).[4]

To apply these ideas to our three-study series, we reanalyzed the data. Although our sets of attitude issues, as well as the individual items within sets, may have varied in level of novelty or complexity, it is doubtful that any were highly novel. They clearly differ, however, with respect to commitment. Commitment should be lowest on unimportant issues (e.g. Bus fares are very reasonably priced.) and higher on important (e.g. The government and university should provide more financial aid to those who qualify for it.) and ingroup-related issues (of intermediate importance). The latter gain commitment as a consequence of their relation to ingroup

---

[4] Another way of thinking about the certainty differences between the item types is offered by Chaiken, Liberman, & Eagly (1989). They propose that "People cannot know with complete certainty that their attitudes (or other judgments) are correct, but they can hope to achieve some reasonable or sufficient level of confidence" (pp. 221). They offer the *sufficiency principle* which holds that "people will exert whatever effort is required to attain their *sufficiency threshold* (italics ours)" (pp. 221). This threshold (i.e. criterion point of sufficient confidence on a confidence continuum) can vary from person to person and situation to situation. This suggests that, whereas the sufficiency threshold was originally low on the ingroup-related items, requiring subjects to perform additional tasks on them raised the criterion point. Chaiken et al. describe personal relevance and task importance as motivating variables that can affect the sufficiency threshold. From this perspective, the projection task increased the personal relevance with respect to the ingroup-related issues, thereby raising the sufficiency threshold via systematic (as opposed to heuristic) processing. Asking subjects to project is, using their definitions, a systematic (more effortful) cognitive process. A difficulty with this explanation arises, however, when the results of the filler task are examined. How does rating the ease or difficulty in rating one's own attitude alter the personal relevance of the issues?

TABLE 7.3
Mean Certainty Compared Across Studies as a Function of the Number of Interpolated Tasks

Study	Number of Tasks			d.f.	F	p
	1	2	3			
Important and Ingroup-Related Issues						
1	6.83(1.01)	7.28(1.02)		1,72	1.64	0.21
2	6.81(0.93)	7.13(0.81)		1,98	4.81	0.03
3	6.26(1.25)	6.61(1.36)	6.92(1.01)	2,217	3.77	0.03
Combined (Unweighted)						0.001
Combined (Weighted by sample size)						0.002
Unimportant Issues						
1	6.28(1.64)	6.74(1.55)		1,72	1.26	0.22
2	6.03(1.16)	6.26(1.11)		1,98	1.51	0.22
3	5.78(1.10)	5.64(1.28)	5.86(1.01)	2,217	0.81	0.45
Combined (Unweighted)						0.064
Combined (Weighted by sample size)						0.136

Notes: [1]Higher means indicate greater certainty (range = 1–9).
[2]Numbers in parentheses are standard deviations.

identity and the fact that they all explicitly contrast subjects' own social category with a salient outgroup (e.g. Compared to Greek students, Commuters are more aware of University activities.). The experimental conditions varied in terms of the number of times they required subjects to think about the issues. After indicating own attitude, conditions differed with respect to the number of measurement tasks interpolated before the certainty measure (viz. projection, memory, importance, ease of indicating attitude). Thus, a reordering of the conditions in terms of the number of interpolated tasks allows an assessment of the effects of thought on attitudinal certainty.

Extrapolating from Millar and Tesser, we theorized that thought and commitment should interact to increase certainty. Table 7.3 bears out this expectation. On the highly important and ingroup-related issues (those with known commitment), certainty increased monotonically as a function of the number of times subjects performed some rating task on the items. On the unimportant issues there was no effect. The nature of the task, whether rating importance or ease of indicating own attitude, projecting onto an ingroup, or memory recognition, was not a source of variation.

Importance. In contrast to the preceding interpretation, the certainty results could have been mediated by importance. Knowing that an issue is important to a person increases the extremity of attitude attributed to that person (Mackie & Gastardo-Conaco, 1988). Using a Bemian, self-perception extrapolation, if self-attributions function in a parallel fashion, anything that increases one's perception that an issue is important might similarly lead one to attribute to oneself a more extreme or certain position on it. Thus, if either directly or via effort justification, the performance of more tasks with respect to the issues increased their perceived importance, certainty might have been increased commensurately.

The analysis of importance ratings, however, counters this interpretation. Neither projection nor number of tasks affected overall perceived issue importance. Further, whatever directional augmentation of importance did occur as a function of the number of tasks appeared on the unimportant items, the set on which certainty effects were absent.

Summary and Discussion

Our three-study series showed that augmenting the salience of one's social category increased assumed attitudinal similarity to other ingroup members, but did not increase certainty about those attitudes. That is, projected similarity did not confer conviction. However, when issues are important, increased thought about them did. These latter results, which conceptually reinterpret the projection task as a manipulation of amount of thought about the issues, sit well with Tesser's studies of induced thought or with a salience or focus of attention interpretation of certainty (Fiske & Taylor, 1984). It is not surprising that our obtained thought-induced increases in opinion certainty were not mediated by increases in the perceived importance of the issues as a consequence of induced thought about them. Bemian self-perception effects primarily occur when commitment and issue importance is low, conditions that do not apply to the important and group-related issues on which the certainty effects were obtained (Bem, 1972).

In further support of the confirmation of these cognitive effects, even in our studies in which we aroused motivational concerns more manifestly than we may have with our manipulation of the salience of ingroup membership, as in our manipulation of competitive and cooperative goal structures (Holtz & Miller, 1989), there was a disjunction between between-condition differences in projected opinion similarity and opinion certainty. Thus, our failure to find projection-mediated increases in opinion certainty do not seem attributable to a failure to engage motivational systems.

Our outcomes, antithetical to our initial thinking, also contradict the theoretical model of Gerard and Orive (1987).[5] In their model, projected

---

[5] A possible explanation for our failure to uphold the model of Gerard and Orive (1987) may lie in the nature of our experimental paradigms. In their theorizing, they state ". . . only if P judges that O shares a similar vantage point will P project his opinion onto O; this attributed opinion, which appears to P as eminating from O, acts back reciprocally on P as a confirmation of P's opinion . . ." (p. 189). Thus, their theorizing emphasizes the projection

similarity is a pivotal ingredient for polarization of opinion. They argue that its elicitation should increase opinion extremity and certainty. Likewise, in further contradiction to our results, they dismiss issue-focused thought as the underlying cause of opinion polarization.

Two points need to be made about the bearing of their data and theorizing on our outcomes. First, their supporting research does not provide strong measures of the mediating process events. Their global measure of perceived similarity to other group members seems more like a check on the successful manipulation of similarity of group members' values than confirmation that projection did occur. Second, even if their subjects did project opinion similarity onto other group members, as they clearly did in our studies, such projection may not have functioned to mediate their obtained polarization or certainty effects. Both links to the mediator require independent confirmation. Put differently, their manipulated variables may have directly polarized opinion rather than having been mediated by a projection process.[6]

Finally, although we did not systematically study the effect of the numerical size of the projection target, our target effects counter a simple model of greater certainty as a function of numerical size of the projection target. Instead, projection onto a smaller ingroup yielded greater opinion certainty than projection onto a larger superordinate category. Although models of monotonic increase as a function of numerical consensus find support with respect to conformity or influence (Gerard, Wilhelmy, & Connolley, 1968; Latané, 1981; Tanford & Penrod, 1984), it is worth noting that the studies on which they rest do not induce intergroup processes.

THE EFFECTS OF ATTITUDINAL CERTAINTY ON PROJECTION

The preceding discussion treated attitudinal certainty as a dependent variable. In this section we consider the opposing direction of effect and ex-

---

of reciprocal projection from the similar others in the setting whereas most of our paradigms compare conditions in which others are not physically present. It is conceivable that the physical presence of one's ingroup members might strengthen this reciprocation feature of their model. The results of Holtz and Miller (1989), however, suggest not. There, the ingroup was directly present and the outgroup, though not in view, was present in the setting. Nevertheless, there was no correspondence between variation in projected opinion similarity across conditions and degree of attitudinal certainty.

[6] For instance, they manipulate action imminence, which is said to augment projection by varying the temporal closeness of an impending debate. They interpret this operationalization as a manipulation of importance, which is said to be the more general conceptual variable that underlies immediacy. The closeness of the impending debate, however, may instead be a manipulation of anxiety and/or threat. Although threat and anxiety increase group cohesiveness (Dion, 1979), of which perceived similarity to other group members is symptomatic, it may directly polarize opinion and increase certainty of belief.

amine how certainty affects projection. In Marks and Miller (1985), we manipulated opinion certainty by giving subjects biofeedback that allegedly indexed conviction. Those made to feel they were more certain of their position on a jury case projected more similarity onto their fellow students than those made to feel uncertain. One line of theorizing views projected opinion similarity as a response motivated by opinion uncertainty (e.g. Gerard & Orive, 1987). This view suggests that induced uncertainty will augment projected similarity. The results of Marks and Miller counter this motivational view. Similarly, in the three-study series of the preceding section, another motivational manipulation, the heightening of ingroup salience and the arousal of concern about outgroup threat, also failed to augment certainty. There, thinking about issues, a more cognitive as opposed to motivational induction, increased certainty. In Marks and Miller, the induction of high certainty in subjects led them to infer consensus, again, seemingly a more cognitive than motivational process.

Anchoredness

In much research concerned with similarity attributions between self and others, self-enhancement or self-protection motivation offers a likely explanation of the effects. Individuals often see themselves as most similar to the best target, namely, the most attractive, (e.g. Marks, Miller, & Maruyama, 1981) the most admired (e.g. Kinder, 1978) and most well-liked (e.g. Sherman, et al., 1984) individual within an array of comparison persons. Greater perceived similarity to ingroup as opposed to outgroup members can be interpreted within this self-enhancement perspective. Such self-enhancement might be constrained when one compares self to other on a dimension on which one's own position is firmly anchored in reality.

In Marks and Miller (1988) each subject read descriptions of four target persons who differed in the favorability of their location on either an anchored (i.e., annual income or educational attainment) or an unanchored (i.e., likability or common sense) dimension. Other attributes ascribed to them were fully counterbalanced, making them irrelevant to subjects' projected attitude similarity to each target. Thus, type of dimension was manipulated between subjects whereas each target's favorability on the critical dimension was a within-subject variable. Subjects then estimated the attitudinal similarity between self and each of the four targets on twelve irrelevant issues. In agreement with previous studies, when own location on the critical dimension was not anchored in the external environment, subjects saw greater general attitudinal similarity between self and target as a direct function of the favorability of the targets' location on the critical dimension. This was not the case, however, when targets' favorability varied on dimensions on which the subjects' own location was anchored in reality and hard to distort without appearing to lie, namely, level of educational attainment and income. When targets differed on these latter dimensions, subjects perceived greatest attitudinal similarity to the middle targets who were, in fact, objectively closest to the subjects' own location on them.

In studies in which the comparison conditions differ in multiple ways, it is always possible that some feature other than the one pinpointed by the researcher is critical for obtaining the reported effect. Our design in Marks and Miller (1988) is vulnerable to this criticism in that the anchored and unanchored dimensions differ in numerous ways. Therefore, we conceptually replicated the study by experimentally manipulating anchoredness of subject's score on dot estimation ability (Gross & Miller, 1987). After asking subjects to estimate the number of dots shown briefly on slides, unanchored subjects were shown with a visual aid that their middling score of 22 fell within a large central range on the scale. The anchored subjects were shown a scale of equal range and shown that their score of 22 indicated that they were definitely average and that it fell within a small middle range delineated on the scale. Each subject then read descriptions of three company employees. Within the context of the study's purpose, the relevant dimension among the several that differentiated the three was their score on an employment test of perceptual acuity: one employee was definitely above average, one definitely below, and the third definitely average. Assumed similarity scores, the absolute difference between each subject's own attitudinal position on an array of general attitude statements and their estimate of the attitudinal stance of each target on these same issues, replicated Marks and Miller (1988).[7] The unanchored subjects assumed greatest attitudinal similarity to the best target (M = 1.65, SD = .58), whereas the anchored-middle subjects assumed the least attitudinal similarity (M = 1.95, SD = .85) to this target (t_{86} = 2.10, p = .04) and greater similarity to the middling target (M = 1.72, SD = .73).

Summary

The results of Marks and Miller (1985) ran counter to motivationally-based projection of similarity as a means of alleviating attitudinal uncertainty. Certainty, not uncertainty, increased general projection of attitudinal similarity. Our studies on anchoredness show that one type of certainty induction, anchoring a person's position on a dimension, can act to reduce projection in the service of self-enhancement motives. At the same time it increases projection of general opinion similarity to a target similar to oneself on an experimentally salient dimension.

---

[7] Data from the anchored high and low conditions is omitted from this report (cf. Boden, Marcus-Newhall, Gross, & Miller, 1990).

THE RELATION BETWEEN PROJECTION AND SOCIAL COMPARISON PROCESSES

In this section we discuss the relation between projection and social comparison processes and for each, the implications of our outcomes. A central core of social comparison theory concerns the collection of information about other and self. Such information establishes either confidence about a veridical view of self (location information) or confidence about a psychologically valued view of self (validation information). The answers one forms will depend on the comparisons one makes. Whereas traditional approaches to social comparison processes often center on the choice of a comparison other (e.g. Goethals & Darley, 1977; Gruder, 1977), in everyday life comparison is not totally controlled by volition. Daily experience thrusts it on us regardless of our normally preferred choices. Nonselected comparison information, as well as that obtained from self-selected comparison persons, bears on the two informational needs.

We initially theorized that projection could function as a process that complements social comparison processes. We thought that others could serve not only as a source of information, but also as targets who, by dint of an attribution, could help satisfy these two needs. As with social comparison, projection targets, too, can either be self-selected or externally imposed. Though apparently similar to other attributional phenomena such as stereotyping, impression formation, opinion estimation, or the social evaluation of individuals or groups, in that they too involve attributions or perceptions, projection differs from them. Like social comparison it has two ingredients, self and other. Implicit in the term projection is a lawful relation between these components, whether or not similarity, contrast, or complementarity best represents the nature of such lawfulness. In another sense it is unlike social comparison. In social comparison, after strategic selection of a comparison target, one makes an inference about self, thereby making other the causal impetus. In contrast, projection places the self-attribute in the primary causal role.

With our focus on the relation between projection and opinion certainty our research manifestly concerns the first comparison function, location or correctness. Admittedly, in studies that involve intergroup relations, unmeasured validation functions are also particularly likely to operate. In order to test the idea that projected as well as collected information augments opinion certainty, we examined projection from two perspectives, both as dependent and as independent variables. In some studies we manipulated projection. We either asked or did not ask subjects to estimate the attitudinal positions of a target group or person, and then assessed its effect on certainty. In others, we manipulated opinion certainty to study its effects on projection. This bidirectional strategy was necessary because theoretical analysis positioned projection as a mediator of opinion certainty. Finally, in all of our studies, the projection target was imposed rather than self-selected.

The Effects of Projection on Conviction

Perhaps our most striking finding is that projected similarity does not increase attitudinal certainty. A heightened awareness of ingroup membership did effectively increase attitudinal similarity to the ingroup, yet this clearly evidenced projection did not augment conviction. Instead, thinking about the attitude issue was the critical mediator of certainty effects. Thinking about ingroup related issues increased certainty about own position on those issues. The effects of thinking about the outgroup's position on ingroup-related issues, however, was more complicated. When the outgroup was not immediately present in the setting, thinking about their position reduced certainty of own position relative to thought about the ingroup's position, but not relative to not thinking about the issues. On the other hand, when present and in direct competition with them, certainty was equally high irrespective of whether one thought about ingroup or outgroup members' positions, or received no projection task. These latter outcomes suggest the obvious: that what one thinks about and not just thinking per se, is critical (Wilson, Dunn, Kraft, & Lisle, 1989). The ingroup and outgroup projection tasks presumably trigger different thoughts. Similarly, the thoughts triggered by an outgroup projection task will vary as a consequence of other situational variables such as whether the ingroup is linked to the outgroup by a cooperative or competitive goal structure.

These outcomes, counter to our initial theorizing, provide little help to any theorizing (e.g. Allport, 1924; Gerard & Orive, 1987) in which projected opinion similarity functions as a motivational dynamic for augmenting conviction. They challenge the relevance of the postulated underlying process events. Similarly, they mean that projection, viewed as linking a self-attribute to an attribute ascribed to another, does not function as a substitute social comparison that augments conviction. Mere thought is not projection in that it does not imply a link between own and other's attributes, but projection is an example of additional thought. The fact that mere thought or cognitive elaboration does moderate certainty, however, leads us to consider the relation between our work and Abelson's model of attitude conviction.

Abelson (1987) argues that attitudinal conviction has three underlying factors: Emotional Committment, Ego Preoccupation, and Cognitive Elaboration. Items such as "My beliefs express the real me.", "I can't imagine ever changing my mind.", "My beliefs are based on the moral sense of the way things should be.", and "I think my view is absolutely correct.", all load on the Emotional Committment factor. The second and third factors he identifies are Ego Preoccupation and Cognitive Elaboration. The Ego Preoccupation factor is an importance dimension, e.g. "My belief is important to me.", "I am extremely concerned about the issue.". The third, Cognitive Elaboration, reflects the richness of ideation associated with the attitude, e.g. "Several other issues could come up in a conversation about it.", "It's easy to explain my views".

The three components of Abelson's factor analytic model of conviction can be mapped onto our independent variables and dependent measures. Our certainty or response extremity measures seem to correspond to Abelson's first factor, an emotional committment or belief certitude factor. Although we have not used measures that manifestly imply emotional intensity, the previously reported parallel outcomes we obtained when we substituted attitude extremity for our certainty measures, support this correspondence and the interpretation of certainty as an intensity measure.

Our projection manipulation, an instruction to think about attitude issues, appears to correspond to the Cognitive Elaboration factor, albeit over a short duration. Specific to the immediate experimental situation, it amounted to a short time span of induced thought. It primarily shows its effect on the group-related issues which only attained their importance from the context of the experiments. It seems unlikely that our commuter subjects even considered themselves a group, or thought much about the ingroup-related issues prior to reading about them in our attitude items. Although we have done little to assess the implied consequences of elaborated thought with relevant response measures such as memory or thought listing procedures, this should be a theoretically fruitful direction for additional research. Finally, our manipulations of issue importance by selecting and comparing item types; important, group related, and unimportant issues, corresponds to the second factor, Ego Preoccupation. The highly important issues, though not ones that are likely to preoccupy subjects' attention on a day-to-day basis, were certainly more likely to have been thought about recurrently during their lives than were the unimportant issues; the group related items rose to a state of temporary preoccupation as a result of our experimental manipulations. It is interesting that in Abelson's (1987) analyses, the role of social support, which conceptually corresponds to projected consensus, mirrored our own outcomes. Just as manipulations that augmented assumed similarity (perceived opinion agreement or consensual support for own opinion) did not augment certainty in our own studies, Abelson found that the social support factor made little contribution to conviction.

Projection and Validation

Despite our lack of evidence for any projection effect with respect to the location function of social comparison, the tenacity of this concept in the history of psychology, as well as the steady sprinkling of supportive results (e.g. Holmes, 1978), urges further search for its potential role. This in turn implies turning attention to the validation function. Research showing differentiation (Kernis, 1984) or false uniqueness (e.g. Goethals, 1986; Marks, 1984) is supportive in that it emphasizes validation-oriented motivational effects in attribution, as do studies that show attributional differences as a function of differences in subjects' chronic levels of self-esteem (e.g. Campbell 1986). Examination of instances of seeming confirmation of a projective process suggests the necessity of strong and specific motivational antecedents (Bramel, 1962; Edlow & Kiesler, 1966; Murray, 1933; Pepitone, 1964; Steiner, 1968). In the absence of arousal of specific affective states and appropriate state-related targets, confirmation is elusive (e.g. Campbell et al., 1964). Of the two major needs served by social comparison, validation is the motivationally hotter one. In retrospect, support of a role for a projective process that functions as a substitute for social comparison processes seems more likely to occur with respect to validation than to certainty needs.

In the search for such confirming evidence, in addition to the potential importance of specific arousal, it also may be important to allow for the possibility that different types of projective mechanisms operate with respect to different types of motivational arousal. Three distinct needs can be identified: social support, justification, and uniqueness. A need for social support or social acceptance is fulfilled by knowledge of similar others. A need for justification is satisfied by an explanation. A need for uniqueness motivates differentiation and is quelled by evidence of distinctiveness. Each may respectively elicit similarity, complementary, and contrast projection. At the interpersonal level, attack of a specific self component when accepted as valid, and when self-esteem is low, may elicit similarity projection. (Bramel, 1963; Markus & Kunda, 1986). When attacked by a specific person or group with whom one is interacting or expects to interact in the future, and when self-esteem or group status is high, complementary projection, which explains the self-attribute by attributing to the attacker a nasty attribute that elicited the self-attribute, may occur. Induced high self-esteem, coupled with an absence of any threat, while perhaps eliciting general perceptions of similarity as a consequence of the increased sociability caused by positive affect (Isen, 1987), is at the same time likely to augment uniqueness concerns. When distinction between the ingroup and outgroup are sharply drawn and relative status is evaluatively favorable to the ingroup, its members are likely to seek positive differentiation from the group (Mackie & Cooper, 1984). When examined within the ingroup context, contrast projection is likely. Additionally, because projective processes build on a self-attribute, they may be more likely to occur in settings in which self-schema are highly salient (Kernis, 1984), or when objective self-awareness is high.

Efforts to study the relation between the validation function and projection call for self-esteem measures and manipulations as relacements for our certainty measures and manipulations. We emphasize that direct evidence of change in self-esteem or ingroup evaluation as a function of projection, and change in projected similarity, complementarity, or uniqueness as a function of manipulated self-esteem, are needed to tie the theoretical link between projection and validation needs. Alternatively, one could design comparison choices, administered subsequent to the projection activity, that specifically tap self (or ingroup) enhancement (e.g. Gruder & Dichtel, 1975, cited in Gruder, 1977). Without such measures one may merely be studying parallel aspects of person perception or trait inference about self and other with the key social comparison ingredient being absent. The discovery of self-other similarity may merely reflect appropriate cognitive inferences about the beliefs held by members of a social category, but may not speak on any projection process. To illustrate, it is implicit in the selective exposure interpretation of false consensus effects (Marks & Miller, 1987) that groups tend to consist of similar individuals. When social identity is activated and the category distinctiveness of one's group is made salient, the assumption of homogeneity of ingroup opinion also becomes particularly salient. One component of that overall homogeneity is a similarity between own opinion and that of other group members. Thus, an observed similarity between self-description and attribution may merely reflect these correlated inferences. Whether such parallel inferences serve any additional function, such as fulfilling validation needs, remains a separate question. In Marks and Miller (1987) and Marks et al. (1981) we discuss such parallel judgment process at the interpersonal level, as do Sherman et al. (1984).

Despite our negative outcomes regarding a role for projection in the service of social comparison needs, we have suggested circumstances in which future research may find more supportive results, specifying when an attributional bias directly linked to an actor's perceived self-attribute might function to improve the actor's self-view. At the same time, however, and more in line with our reported outcomes, we are not highly optimistic about our suggestions. The main reason for our pessimism is that the cognitive processes involved in projection, requiring attention both to self and to other's attribute, are more complex than other, more primitive devices. Projection is constrained by the reality both of actor and target's true traits. One must ask, why would an actor prefer a projective mechanism for self-enhancement purposes when simple mechanisms, such as the fundamental (Ross, 1977) or ultimate (Pettigrew, 1979) attribution error, direct self-bolstering (e.g. Dion & Earn, 1975) and denial or scapegoating (Allport, 1954) are available?

Certainty, Projection, and Social Comparison

Do our findings contradict any well established social comparison processes such as the normative (e.g. Cotton & Baron, 1980) and informational (e.g. Burnstein, 1982) influences that operate within groups to polarize opinion, and the important influence of observed consensus on judgments or beliefs (e.g. Sherif, 1936)? We do not think so. They do, however, question whether the dynamic of the theory—uncertainty reduction—operates with respect to projection. The theory proposes that uncertainty motivates an intervening comparison process which in turn produces certainty. Applied to opinion projection, uncertainty should induce projection which in turn should augment certainty. Instead, we find (Marks & Miller, 1985) that certainty induces projected opinion similarity and that it does so with respect to similar as opposed to dissimilar others (Gross & Miller, 1987). Spears and Manstead (1989) elaborate this certainty-induced projection effect within the false consensus paradigm and show how that on important issues, for those who hold the normative view, projection increases as a function of attitude certainty or strength. This effect is moderated, however, by the existing consensus for the position, being weaker if not largely absent among those who hold an antinormative position. These latter findings, in consonance with our own work, draw attention to the role of intergroup processes and the dynamics of power in affecting perceptions of consensus or opinion similarity between self and others. Perhaps too, they provide a hint to circumstances that might induce motivational effects in projection.

CONCLUSION

Finally, although we are pessimistic about whether projection routinely functions as a stand-in for the social comparison processes that fulfill the major human needs, it can nevertheless be studied in its own right. For those interested in opinion projection, false consensus, or opinion similarity, a full understanding will require consideration of three sources of effect: (a) the psychophysics of estimates, that is, whether in consensus estimates the perception of the difference between 10 and 20% equals that between 80 and 90% (Duncan, 1984; Stevens, 1975); (b) the psychology of cognitive inference, with consideration of factors such as knowledge of base rates (Dawes, 1989; Spears & Manstead, 1989) and other cognitive heuristics such as framing or availability (Kahneman, Slovic, & Tversky, 1982); and (c) the dynamics of motivated distortion in the attributions that are made to explain social facts (e.g. Borgida & Howard-Pitney, 1983; Goethals, 1986; Pettigrew, 1979; Pyszczynski & Greenberg, 1987) and the particular circumstances in which self attributes may prompt such attributions (e.g. Steiner, 1968).

To our knowledge, research on opinion projection and false consensus has not considered the bearing of work on the psychophysics of stimulus magnitude estimates. Though our starting point concerned the dynamics of motivated projection, our outcomes mainly emphasize the role of cognitive factors in inferring others' opinions. Finally, though one aspect of our work—the different effects of cooperative and competitive goal structures on opinion projection and certainty—may be interpreted as invoking motivational processes, the theoretically anticipated links between projected opinion similarity–dissimilarity and opinion conviction remain elusive. If projective processes play a role in the fulfillment of social comparison goals, we conclude that they are more likely to do so for validation than for conviction needs, but remain skeptical about the generality of this possibility too.

ACKNOWLEDGMENTS

This work was supported, in part, by Grant BSN-8719439 from the National Science Foundation to Norman Miller. Portions of this work have been presented at the 95th annual convention of the American Psychological Association, and the 65th, 67th, and 69th annual conventions of the Western Psychological Association.

We thank Brian Mullen, Diane Mackie, and the editors of this book for their helpful advice in the preparation of this chapter.

REFERENCES

Abelson, R. P. (1987). Conviction. *American Psychologist, 43*, 267–275.
Allport, F. H. (1924). *Social psychology*, Boston, MA: Houghton Mifflin.
Allport, G. W. (1954). *The nature of prejudice*. Menlo Park, CA: Addison–Wesley.
Bacon, F. (1853). *The physical and metaphysical works of Lord Bacon* (J. Dewey, Trans.) London: Bohn.
Bem, D. J. (1972). Self-perception theory. In L. Berkowitz (Ed.), *Advances in experimental social psychology* (Vol. 6, pp. 1–62). New York: Academic Press.
Boden, J. A., Marcus-Newhall, A., Gross, S. R., & Miller, N. (1990, April). *Social-outlook theory as an explanation for anchored high subjects*. Poster presented at the 70th annual convention of the Western Psychological Association, Los Angeles, CA.
Borgida, E., & Howard-Pitney, B. (1983). Personal involvement and the robustness of perceptual salience effects. *Journal of Personality and Social Psychology, 45*, 560–570.
Bramel, D. (1962). A dissonance theory approach to defensive projection. *Journal of Abnormal and Social Psychology, 64*, 121–129.
Bramel, D. (1963). Selection of a target for defensive projection. *Journal of Abnormal and Social Psychology, 66*, 318–324.

Brickman, P., & Bulman, R. (1977). Pleasure and pain in social comparison. In J. M. Suls & R. L. Miller (Eds.), *Social comparison processes: Theoretical and empirical perspectives* (pp. 149–186). Washington, DC: Hemisphere.

Burnstein, E. (1982). Persuasion as argument processing. In H. Brandstatter, J. H. Davis, & G. Stocker-Kreichgauer (Eds.), *Group decision-making* (pp. 103–124). London: Academic Press.

Byrne, D., Clore, G. L., & Smeaton, G. (1986). The attraction hypothesis: Do similar attitudes affect anything? *Journal of Personality and Social Psychology, 51*, 1167–1170.

Campbell, D. T. (1967). Stereotypes and the perception of group differences. *American Psychologist, 22*, 812–829.

Campbell, D. T., Miller, N., Lubetsky, J., & O'Connell, E. J. (1964). Varieties of projection in trait attribution. *Psychological Monographs, 78*, 1–33.

Campbell, J. (1986). Similarity and uniqueness: The effects of attribute type, relevance, and individual differences in self-esteem and depression. *Journal of Personality and Social Psychology, 50*, 281–294.

Chaiken, S., Liberman, A., & Eagly, A. H. (1989). Heuristic and systematic information processing within and beyond the persuasion context. In J. S. Uleman & J. A. Bargh (Eds.), *Unintended thought* (pp. 212–252). New York: Guilford.

Cotton, J. L., & Baron, R. S. (1980). Anonymity, persuasive arguments, and choice shifts. *Social Psychology Quarterly, 43*, 391–404.

Crano, W. D. (1983). Assumed consensus of attitudes: The effect of vested interest. *Personality and Social Psychology Bulletin, 9*, 597–608.

Cronbach, L. J. (1955). Processes affecting scores on "understanding of others" and "assumed similarity." *Psychological Bulletin, 52*, 177–193.

Cronbach, L. J. (1958). Proposals leading to analytic treatment of social perception scores. In R. Tagiuri and C. Petrullo (Eds.), *Person perception and interpersonal behavior* (pp. 353–379). Stanford, CA: Stanford University Press.

Dawes, R. M. (1989). Statistical criteria for establishing a truly false consensus effect. *Journal of Experimental Social Psychology, 25*, 1–17.

Dion, K. L. (1979). Intergroup conflict and intergroup cohesiveness. In W. G. Austin & S. Worchel (Eds.), *The social psychology of intergroup relations* (pp. 211–224). Monterey, CA: Brooks/Cole.

Dion, K. L. & Earn, B. M. (1975). The phenomenology of being a target of prejudice. *Journal of Personality and Social Psychology, 32*, 944–950.

Duncan, O. D. (1984). *Notes on social measurement: Historical and critical.* New York: Russell Sage Foundation.

Edlow, D., & Kiesler, C. (1966). Ease of denial and defensive projection. *Journal of Experimental Social Psychology, 2*, 56–69.

Festinger, L. A. (1954). A theory of social comparison processes. *Human Relations, 7*, 117–140.

Festinger, L., Gerard, H. B., Hymovitch, B., Kelley, H. H., & Raven, B. (1952). The influence process in the presence of extreme deviates. *Human Relations, 5*, 327–346.

Fisk, S. T., & Taylor, S. E. (1984). *Social cognition.* New York: Random House.

Freud, A. (1937). *The ego and the mechanisms of defense.* London: Hogarth Press.

Funder, D. C. (1987). Errors and mistakes: Evaluating the accuracy of social judgment. *Psychological Bulletin, 101*, 75–90.

Gerard, H. B., & Orive, R. (1987). The dynamics of opinion formation. In L. Berkowitz (Ed.), *Advances in experimental social psychology* (Vol. 20. *pp. 171–202*). San Diego, CA: Academic Press.

Gerard, H. B., Wilhelmy, R. A., & Connolley, E. S. (1968). Conformity and group size. *Journal of Personality and Social Psychology, 8*, 79–82.

Goethals, G. R. (1986). Fabricating and ignoring social reality: Self-serving estimates of consensus. In J. Olson, C. P. Herman, & M. P. Zanna (Eds.), *Relative deprivation and social comparison: The Ontario Symposium on Social Cognition*, (Vol. 4, pp. 135–157). Hillsdale, NJ: Lawrence Erlbaum Associates.

Goethals, G. R., & Darley, J. M. (1977). Social comparison theory: An attributional approach. In J. M. Suls & R. L. Miller (Eds.), *Social comparison processes: Theoretical and empirical perspectives* (pp. 259–278). Washington, DC: Hemisphere.

Gross, S. R., & Miller, N. (1987, April). *The effect of anchoredness on perceived similarity of opinion*. Paper presented at the 67th annual convention of the Western Psychological Association, Long Beach, CA.

Gruder, C. L. (1977). Choice of comparison persons in evaluating themselves. In J. M. Suls & R. L. Miller (Eds.), *Social comparison processes: Theoretical and empirical perspectives* (pp. 21–41). Washington, DC: Hemisphere.

Gruder, C. L. & Dichtel, M. (1975). Behavioral consequences of social comparison. Unpublished manuscript, University of Illinois at Chicago Circle.

Hochbaum, G. M. (1953). *Certain personality aspects and pressures to uniformity in social group*. Unpublished doctoral thesis, University of Minnesota, Minneapolis, MN.

Holmes, D. S. (1978). Projection as a defense mechanism. *Psychological Bulletin, 85*, 677–688.

Holtz, R., & Miller, N. (1985). Assumed similarity and opinion certainty. *Journal of Personality and Social Psychology, 48*, 890–898.

Holtz, R., & Miller, N. (1989). *Intergroup conflict, assumed similarity, and opinion certainty*. Unpublished manuscript, University of Southern California, Los Angeles.

Hong, O. P., & Harrod, W. J. (1988). The role of reasons in the ingroup bias phenomenon. *European Journal of Social Psychology, 18*, 537–545.

Isen, A. M. (1987). Positive affect, cognitive processes, and social behavior. In L. Berkowitz (Ed.), *Advances in experimental social psychology* (Vol. 20, pp. 203–253). New York: Academic Press.

James, W. (1890). *The principles of psychology*. New York: Holt.

Kahneman, D., Slovic, P., & Tversky, A. (1982). *Judgment under certainty: Heuristics and biases*. New York: Cambridge University Press.

Kenny, D. A., & Allbright, L. (1987). Accuracy in interpersonal perception: A social relations analysis. *Psychological Bulletin, 102*, 390–402.

Kernis, M. H. (1984). Need for uniqueness, self-schemas, and thought as moderators of the false consensus effect. *Journal of Experimental Social Psychology, 20*, 350–362.

Kinder, D. R. (1978). Political personal perception: The asymmetrical influence of sentiment and choice on perceptions of presidential candidates. *Journal of Personality and Social Psychology, 36*, 859–871.

Krosnick, J. A., & Schuman, H. (1988). Attitude intensity, importance, and certainty and susceptibility to response effects. *Journal of Personality and Social Psychology, 54*, 940–952.

Latané, B. (1981). The psychology of social impact. *American Psychologist, 36*, 343–356.

Mackie, D., & Cooper, J. (1984). Attitude polarization: Effects of group membership. *Journal of Personality and Social Psychology, 46*, 575–585.

Mackie, D. M., & Gastardo-Conaco, M. C. (1988). The impact of importance accorded an issue on attitude inferences. *Journal of Experimental Social Psychology, 24*, 543–570.

Marcus-Newhall, A., Gross, S. R., & Miller, N. (1989, April). *Perceptions of attitudinal similarity: Self-enhancement as an explanation*. Poster presented at the 69th annual convention of the Western Psychological Association, Reno, NV.

Marks, G. (1984). Thinking one's abilities are unique and one's opinions are common. *Personality and Social Psychology Bulletin, 10*, 203–208.

Marks, G., & Miller, N. (1985). The effect of certainty on consensus judgments. *Personality and Social Psychology Bulletin, 11*, 165–177.

Marks, G., & Miller, N. (1987). Ten years of research on the "False Consensus Effect": An empirical and theoretical review. *Psychological Bulletin, 102,* 72–90.
Marks, G., & Miller, N. (1988). Perceptions of attitude similarity: Effect of anchored versus unanchored positions. *Personality and Social Psychology Bulletin, 14,* 92–102.
Marks, G., Miller, N., & Maruyama, G. (1981). Effect of targets' physical attractiveness on assumptions of similarity. *Journal of Personality and Social Psychology, 41,* 198–206.
Markus, H., & Kunda, Z. (1986). Stability and malleability of the self-concept. *Journal of Personality and Social Psychology, 51,* 851–866.
Millar, M. G., & Tesser, A. (1986). Thought-induced attitude change: The effects of schema structure and commitment. *Journal of Personality and Social Psychology, 51,* 259–269.
Mullen, B., Atkins, J. L., Champion, D. S., Edwards, C., Hardy, D., Story, J. E., & Vanderlok, M. (1985). The false consensus effect: A meta-analysis of 115 hypothesis tests. *Journal of Experimental Social Psychology, 21,* 262–283.
Murray, H. A. (1933). The effect of fear upon the estimates of the maliciousness of other personalities. *Journal of Social Psychology, 4,* 310–329.
Orbell, J. M., van de Kragt, A. J. C., & Dawes, R. M. (1988). Explaining discussion-induced cooperation. *Journal of Personality and Social Psychology, 54,* 811–819.
Pepitone, A. (1964). *Attraction and hostility.* New York: Atherton.
Pettigrew, T. F. (1979). The ultimate attribution error: Extending Allport's cognitive analysis of prejudice. *Personality and Social Psychology Bulletin, 5,* 456–476.
Pyszczynski, T., & Greenberg, J. (1987). Toward an integration of cognitive and motivational perspectives on social influence: A biased hypothesis-testing model. In L. Berkowitz (Ed.), *Advances in experimental social psychology* (Vol. 20, pp. 297–340). New York: Academic Press.
Raden, D. (1985). Strength-related attitude dimensions. *Social Psychology Quarterly, 48,* 312–330.
Rosenbaum, M. E. (1986). Comment on a proposed two-stage theory of relationship formation: First, repulsion; then attraction. *Journal of Personality and Social Psychology, 51,* 1171–1172.
Rosenthal, R. (1984). *Meta-analytic procedures for social research.* Beverly Hills, CA: Sage.
Ross, L. D. (1977). The intuitive psychologist and his shortcomings: Distortions in the attribution process. In L. Berkowitz (Ed.), *Advances in experimental social psychology,* (Vol. 10, pp. 173–220). New York: Academic Press.
Ross, L., Greene, D., & House, P. (1977). The "false consensus effect": An egocentric bias in social perception and attributional processes. *Journal of Experimental Social Psychology, 13,* 279–301.
Sanders, G. S., & Baron, R. S. (1977). Is social comparison irrelevant for producing choice shifts? *Journal of Experimental Social Psychology, 13,* 303–314.
Shaver, K. G. (1987). *Principles of social psychology* (3rd ed). Hillsdale, NJ: Lawrence Erlbaum Associates.
Sherif, M. (1936). *The psychology of social norms.* New York: Harper & Row.
Sherman, S. J., Chassin, L., Presson, C. C., & Agostinelli, G. (1984). The role of the evaluation and similarity principles in the false consensus effect. *Journal of Personality and Social Psychology, 47,* 1244–1262.
Spears, R., & Manstead, A. S. R. (1990). Consensus estimation in social context. In W. Stroebe and M. Hewstone (Eds.), *European review of social psychology.* (Vol 1, pp 81–109). Chichester: Wiley.
Steiner, I. D. (1968). Reactions to adverse and favorable evaluations of one's self. *Journal of Personality, 36,* 553–563.
Stevens, S. S. (1975). *Psychophysics.* New York: Wiley.
Suls, J. (1986). Notes on the occasion of social comparison theory's thirtieth birthday. *Personality and Social Psychology Bulletin, 12,* 289–296.

Tajfel, H., & Turner, J. C. (1985). The social identity theory of intergroup behaviour. In S. Worchel & W. G. Austin (Eds.), *Psychology of intergroup relations* (pp. 7–24). Chicago: Nelson-Hall.

Tanford, S., & Penrod, S. (1984). Social influence model: A formal integration of research on majority and minority influence processes. *Psychological Bulletin, 95,* 189–225.

Tesser, A. (1978). Self-generated attitude change. In L. Berkowitz (Ed.), *Advances in experimental social psychology,* (Vol. 11, pp. 290–338). New York: Academic Press.

Turner, J. C. (1987). *Rediscovering the social group: A self-categorisation theory.* Oxford: Blackwell.

van der Pligt, J., Ester, P., & van der Linden, J. (1983). Attitude extremity, consensus and diagnosticity. *European Journal of Social Psychology, 13,* 437–439.

Wheeler, L. (1966). Motivation as a determinant of upward comparison. *Journal of Experimental Social Psychology,* (Suppl. 1), 27–31.

Wheeler, L., Shaver, K., Jones, R. A., Goethals, G., Cooper, J., Robinson, J., Gruder, C. L., & Butzine, K. (1969). Factors determining the choice of a comparison other. *Journal of Experimental Social Psychology, 5,* 219–232.

Wilson, E. D., Dunn, B. S., Kraft, D., & Lisle, D. J. (1989). Introspection, attitude change, and attitude-behavior consistency: The disruptive effect of explaining why we feel the way we do. In L. Berkowitz (Ed.), *Advances in experimental social psychology,* (Vol. 22, pp. 287–343). New York: Academic Press.

8 Self-Esteem and Intergroup Comparisons: Toward a Theory of Collective Self-Esteem

Riia Luhtanen and Jennifer Crocker
State University of New York at Buffalo

Over the last several years, there have been episodes of racist graffiti, jokes, anonymous hate notes or brawls at 175 campuses, including top private colleges like Brown University, Smith College, and Colby College, as well as at public universities like Michigan and Wisconsin (Berger, 1989). The incidents have ranged from the racist hate notes received by four black women at Smith college, to racial jokes broadcast on the university radio station at the University of Michigan, to an attack on a black student at the University of Massachusetts. These incidents seem to reflect an increase in prejudice and racism on college campuses in the U.S. Prejudice and discrimination are not limited to college campuses, however; they are pervasive aspects of social existence. Antipathy between groups of all sorts, from collegiate fraternities to racial and religious groups, is commonplace.

The increase in racial incidents on college campuses has sparked a renewed interest in the causes of prejudice and discrimination. A great deal of research over the past three decades has demonstrated the existence of prejudice. A vast number of studies have demonstrated people's tendency to discriminate against outgroups and in favor of ingroups in a wide range of intergroup situations (see Brewer, 1979, for a review). However, the causes of prejudice and discrimination are still not fully understood (see Dovidio and Gaertner, 1986, for some recent approaches.).

One explanation is that prejudice results from real conflicts between groups. According to the realistic group conflict theory (Campbell, 1965), prejudice and discrimination against outgroup members are consequences of realistic competition between groups over scarce resources, including not only material resources, but also political power, prestige, and moral superiority. In a groundbreaking study demonstrating the effects of competition on intergroup relations, Sherif and his colleagues (Sherif, Harvey, White, Hood and Sherif, 1961) divided the boys in a summer camp into two teams. In the initial stages of the study, relations between the two teams were smooth. When the experimenters introduced a competition between the two teams, however, outbreaks of hostility and antipathy toward the outgroup became common. The smooth intergroup relations were restored only when the researchers induced cooperation between the teams by giving them a common goal.

Realistic group conflict theory would explain the increase in racial incidents on college campuses in terms of competition over some resources such as jobs or admission to graduate schools. Competition alone cannot adequately explain the rise in campus racism, however, because the percentage of black students at predominantly white four year colleges has been declining in the last few years.

Indeed, research has shown that although competition clearly exacerbates prejudice and discrimination between groups, it is not a necessary precondition. Numerous studies have demonstrated intergroup bias and discrimination in the so-called *minimal intergroup situation*, even in the absence of explicit competition between two groups (e.g., Locksley, Ortiz & Hepburn, 1980; Tajfel, 1970; Tajfel & Billig, 1974; see Brewer, 1979, and Tajfel & Turner, 1986).

The minimal intergroup situation involves arbitrary division of subjects into groups, no interaction among subjects, anonymity of group memberships, and a task (a response measure) that is unconnected to the basis for group categorization. The task requires subjects to allocate points, money or other resources to ingroup and outgroup members, or to evaluate the ingroup and outgroup members (Tajfel, Billig, Bundy & Flament, 1971). Because the self is excluded from these allocations or evaluations, self-interest cannot provide a basis for responding to the task. Ingroup bias under these conditions has been demonstrated repeatedly (see Brewer, 1979; Hinkle & Schopler, 1986).

What underlies this tendency toward ingroup bias or favoritism, even in the absence of explicit competition or conflict over resources? Several theorists have argued that biased intergroup comparisons are often motivated by individuals' need for self-esteem or self-enhancement. In this chapter we examine the role of self-esteem in intergroup behavior, and describe our program of research on this topic.

The Role of Self-Esteem in Prejudice and Intergroup Comparisons: Review of Theories

The idea that prejudice may be related to personality characteristics has been around for a long time. In recent years, the specific role of the self-concept in prejudice has received renewed attention. The notion that attitudes toward others in general, and ethnic prejudice in particular, are linked to attitudes toward the self was proposed by Ehrlich (1973). According to Ehrlich, "positive self-attitudes provide the base for the acceptance of others; negative self-attitudes, for the rejection of others" (p. 130). Ehrlich suggested several reasons why self-attitudes and prejudice might be related, two of which are particularly relevant here. First, the person may generalize self-attitudes to others. This type of generalization has been demonstrated in the *false consensus effect* (Ross, Greene & House, 1977), in which people overestimate the extent to which their opinions, preferences, and attributes are shared by others. Through a similar process, people who have low regard for themselves may assume that others, including members of outgroups, are also unworthy of regard. Second, Ehrlich suggested that the deprecation of others may enhance self-attitudes. That is, one consequence of prejudice may be to enhance the self. The difference between these two possibilities lies in the direction of causality that is assumed. In the first case, a person's level of self-esteem is assumed to be causally prior to evaluations of outgroups, whereas in the second case, one's level of self-esteem is assumed to be a consequence of derogation of others.

A second and related perspective is Wills' (1981) theory of downward comparison. Wills proposed that people are motivated to maintain and enhance their subjective well-being. One way of increasing subjective well-being is to compare oneself with a less fortunate other, because favorable comparisons between the self and a less fortunate other enable one to feel better about the self and one's own situation. One can passively engage in downward comparison by identifying others who, in fact, are worse off than the self, or actively derogate or cause harm to another person or group of people. Wills argues that downward comparisons tend to be directed toward safe targets: groups of people who are lower in status and whom the dominant culture considers relatively acceptable to derogate. Thus, Wills considers prejudice and ingroup bias to be a downward comparison process, motivated by individuals' need to have a positive view of themselves.

Wills argues that people are most likely to engage in downward comparison when their self-esteem is low, or their subjective well-being is threatened. In other words, when their self-esteem is temporarily lowered by a failure experience or negative feedback from others, people may try to restore their self-esteem by comparing downward. Biased intergroup comparisons may therefore be motivated by the need to restore self-esteem following threat. In addition, those who are chronically low in self-esteem will engage in downward comparisons, because they live in a state of chronic threat to the self-concept. It follows that chronically low self-esteem individuals who have further received a situational threat to their self-esteem should be the most in need of self-enhancement, and thus the most likely to compare downward by, for example, derogating members of outgroups.

A third perspective on self-esteem and prejudice is provided by social identity theory (e.g., Tajfel, 1982; Tajfel & Turner, 1979, 1986; Turner, 1975). Like downward comparison theory, social identity theory assumes that people are motivated to maintain or enhance their self-esteem. While Wills (1981) conceptualizes self-esteem in very personal or individualistic terms, social identity theory differentiates between two parts of the self-concept: personal identity and social identity. Personal identity denotes specific attributes of the individual such as feelings of competence, psychological traits, and personal values. Social identity, on the other hand, is defined as "that part of the individuals' self-concept which derives from their knowledge of their membership of a social group (or groups) together with the value and emotional significance of that membership" (Tajfel, 1981, p. 255). Social identity theory argues that people are not just motivated to maintain or achieve a positive personal identity, but also a positive social identity. The latter is achieved from the positive distinctiveness of one's ingroup(s) relative to other groups (e.g., Tajfel & Turner, 1979, 1986; Turner, 1975, 1982). In other words, one's social identity is determined by the outcome of social comparisons between the ingroup and an outgroup. Even in the absence of conflict or competition over resources, people are motivated to show ingroup bias in intergroup comparisons. Both personal and social identity may contribute to general self-esteem.

A Paradox of Self-Esteem and Ingroup Bias

Both downward comparison theory and social identity theory make two important predictions. The first is that ingroup bias or successful intergroup discrimination will enhance self-esteem (in social identity theory, by enhancing social identity). The second is that chronically low or temporarily threatened self-esteem (or social identity) will promote ingroup bias because of the need to maintain or enhance self-esteem (or positive social identity). Consistent with both of the directions of causality suggested by Ehrlich, self-esteem is thus hypothesized as both an independent variable (a motivating force) and a dependent variable (a product) in intergroup comparisons and discrimination (cf. Abrams & Hogg, 1988).

These two predictions present something of a paradox. If ingroup bias enhances self-esteem, and low self-esteem individuals are more likely to engage in ingroup bias, then why are some people chronically low in self-esteem? Presumably, people who are low in self-esteem should be able to ameliorate their negative affective state through ingroup bias (and other types of downward comparison). One possibility is that ingroup bias is an ineffective strategy for enhancing subjective well-being, and may even lower self-esteem. Wills (1981) notes that people are ambivalent about engaging in downward comparison, because it is not a socially admired behavior to enhance oneself at the expense of others. Perhaps low self-esteem individuals are caught in a vicious cycle of self-derogation, derogation of others, and more self-derogation.

A second resolution of the paradox might be that low self-esteem individuals do not engage in more downward comparison than do high self-esteem individuals. Indeed, research suggests the opposite. A large and growing body of research suggests that people who are high in self-regard or low in depression are particularly likely to engage in a variety of self-serving or self-enhancing strategies, such as taking credit for success but denying responsibility for failure, overestimating their control over events, overestimating how positively they are viewed by others, and making overly optimistic predictions about the future. People who are low in self-esteem typically do not show such self-enhancing strategies (see Taylor and Brown, 1988, for a review).[1] If downward comparison in general, and ingroup bias in particular, is a self-enhancement strategy, these findings suggest that it may be high, rather than low self-esteem individuals who engage in ingroup bias. The paradox would be resolved, because high self-esteem individuals may gain or maintain their self-esteem by engaging in ingroup bias, whereas low self-esteem individuals may be low in self-esteem precisely because they fail to use this and other self-enhancing strategies.

Surprisingly few studies have tested these hypotheses by directly assessing and/or manipulating self-esteem in research on intergroup comparisons. We will consider evidence on each part of the paradox: First, we will examine whether ingroup bias enhances self-esteem, and second, we will examine whether low self-esteem individuals are more likely to engage in ingroup bias.

Effects of Intergroup Comparisons on Self-Esteem

One study that examined the effects of ingroup bias on self-esteem was conducted by Oakes and Turner (1980). Using the minimal intergroup paradigm, they divided subjects into two groups, ostensibly on the basis

---

[1] We do not mean to imply that people who are low in self-esteem are totally unconcerned about their self-evaluation. Considerable research indicates that low self-esteem individuals will engage in a variety of strategies to avoid negative evaluations. In a recent paper, Baumeister, Tice and Hutton (1989) have suggested that whereas high self-esteem individuals are concerned with enhancing the self and emphasizing their successes, low self-esteem individuals are concerned with self-protection and avoiding failure. It seems possible that downward comparison may at times lead to self-enhancement, and thus be more prevalent among high self-esteem individuals, and at other times lead to self-protection, and thus be more prevalent among low self-esteem individuals.

of their preferences for paintings (but, in reality, randomly). There was no interaction between subjects, and group assignments were anonymous. The experimental subjects then completed a task allocating points between an ingroup and an outgroup member (only identified by subject numbers and group memberships), while the control subjects read copies of newspaper articles. Both groups then completed measures of self-esteem. Results from the point allocation task showed that the experimental subjects displayed ingroup favoritism. More importantly, and consistent with both social identity and downward comparison theory, experimental subjects subsequently reported higher self-esteem than did control subjects, suggesting that ingroup bias does enhance self-esteem. The authors note an alternative explanation, however; the allocation task could have made group memberships more salient to the experimental subjects, and this salience itself could have raised subjects' self-esteem (perhaps by strengthening their typically positive identity). Another possibility is that the greater importance of the allocation task, compared to reading irrelevant newspaper articles, resulted in relatively higher self-esteem independent of the opportunity to discriminate (cf. Abrams & Hogg, 1988; Lemyre & Smith, 1985).

Self-esteem was also measured in an experiment by Turner and Spriggs (1982, cited in Lemyre & Smith, 1985). Subjects in their study were instructed to be either cooperative or competitive, and were either categorized according to painting preferences and asked to allocate points between ingroup and outgroup members, or were not explicitly categorized and were asked to allocate points between themselves and another person. While subjects showed ingroup favoritism in all conditions, it was greater in the competition than in the cooperation conditions, as well as in the group than the individual conditions. Self-esteem was also higher in the competitive conditions than in the cooperative conditions, as well as under individual conditions than under group conditions. While these results are consistent with the hypothesis that ingroup bias heightens self-esteem, one could argue that rather than discrimination itself raising self-esteem in this study, it was the competitive instructions that caused an increase in both ingroup bias and self-esteem.

Lemyre and Smith (1985) conducted an experiment that enabled them to assess whether ingroup bias (intergroup discrimination) results in higher self-esteem more than does mere categorization or completion of a significant experimental task. Using the minimal intergroup paradigm, they assigned subjects to one of eight different conditions that varied on the following three parameters: (a) categorization into groups versus no categorization, (b) type of point allocation task, and (c) the order of the point allocation and self-esteem tasks. If intergroup discrimination has a positive effect on self-esteem, the critical conditions in which subjects were categorized and completed ingroup—outgroup matrices before filling out self-esteem measures should show higher self-esteem than other conditions. In one of these critical conditions the ingroup—outgroup matrices were constructed in a way that forced subjects to make discriminatory point allocations in favor of an ingroup member; in another, subjects were free to choose either discriminatory or nondiscriminatory point allocations. In support of the hypotheses, subjects in these two conditions showed higher postexperimental self-esteem than subjects in other conditions, including categorized subjects who did not have the opportunity to show ingroup bias (because they allocated points between two outgroup members, or two ingroup members, or completed matrices that forced them to be fair), and noncategorized subjects who completed a similar task (allocating points between two noncategorized individuals) before the self-esteem measures.

Lemyre and Smith's results are consistent with social identity theory in that engaging in ingroup bias or intergroup discrimination had a positive effect on self-esteem relative to merely being categorized, or completing a meaningful task. However, noncategorized subjects who completed the self-esteem measures before their point allocation matrices showed self-esteem levels equivalent to subjects in the two critical conditions, suggesting that categorization decreased self-esteem (for reasons that are unclear), and discrimination against the outgroup subsequently restored it to its original level. Thus, while this study suggests that discrimination against outgroup members may be an effective strategy to restore self-esteem that has been lowered by categorization, it is unclear whether ingroup bias is a generally effective strategy for enhancing self-esteem following other types of threat, or whether ingroup bias would enhance self-esteem when the categorization is a longstanding one, rather than one newly created in the laboratory.

In general, these studies have provided some evidence for the prediction of downward comparison theory and social identity theory that outgroup discrimination serves to maintain or enhance self-esteem (but see Wagner, Lampen and Syllwasschy (1986) for an exception). As noted earlier, both downward comparison theory and social identity theory argue that self-esteem is not only a product of favorable intergroup comparisons, but also is a determinant of ingroup bias.

Effects of Self-Esteem on Intergroup Comparisons

According to the theories we have reviewed, ingroup bias is, at least in part, a function of the need to maintain or enhance self-esteem. Low self-esteem individuals should be more prejudiced than those high in self-esteem, because of their greater need for self-enhancement. Correlational evidence is consistent with this view. Self-esteem is positively correlated with evaluations of other people and negatively correlated with ethnic prejudice (see Ashmore & DelBoca, 1976; Ehrlich, 1973; Wylie, 1979). Furthermore, racial prejudice is strongest among persons of lower socioeconomic status, who tend to be low in self-esteem (Brewer & Campbell, 1976). Yet it is important to distinguish between negative evaluations of outgroups (*prejudice*) and negative evaluations of outgroups relative to ingroups (*ethnocentrism or ingroup favoritism*). Although low self-esteem individuals are more negative about others than high self-esteem individuals (i.e., more prejudiced), it is not clear if this also reflects greater ingroup favoritism, or if low self-esteem individuals just show greater negativism about everyone, including themselves and their ingroups. Downward comparison and social identity theories both specify that it is the favorable comparison between self and others or ingroup and outgroup that satisfies the need for self-enhancement.

To investigate whether low self-esteem individuals in fact show greater ingroup bias than those high in self-esteem, Crocker and Schwartz (1985) conducted an experiment using the minimal intergroup paradigm. Subjects first filled out the Rosenberg (1965) self-esteem inventory, and were then arbitrarily divided into two groups. They then indicated their expectations of the personality characteristics of members of the two groups by rating each subject, identified only by a group assignment, on five positive and five negative traits, after which they were debriefed and dismissed.

Overall, high self-esteem subjects rated both groups more favorably than did low self-esteem subjects. In addition, the results indicated that both high and low self-esteem subjects rated their ingroup better than the outgroup. High and low self-esteem individuals did not differ in the extent to which they showed ingroup bias; high self-esteem subjects were simply more positive about the two groups overall. In other words, although low self-esteem subjects were more prejudiced in the sense of giving lower ratings of outgroups compared to high self-esteem subjects, there was no evidence for greater ethnocentrism or ingroup favoritism. These results do not support the predictions of downward comparison theory and social identity theory that ingroup bias in the minimal intergroup situation would be motivated by the greater need of low self-esteem individuals for self-enhancement. Instead, they seem consistent with the possibility suggested by Ehrlich (1973), that attitudes toward outgroups are generalized from self-attitudes.

Given the arbitrary nature of the group boundaries in the minimal intergroup situation, subjects in the Crocker and Schwartz (1985) study may have had little self-enhancement to gain by derogating outgroup members. Perhaps ingroup favoritism is related to one's need for self-enhancement only when the group membership has more evaluative implications; that is, when it has positive or negative implications for one's personal attributes. Crocker, Thompson, McGraw and Ingerman (1987) conducted two studies to investigate this possibility. The interactive effects of self-esteem and threats to self-esteem were also investigated to test the prediction derivable from downward comparison and social identity theories that self-enhancement need should be the highest for low self-esteem individuals who have recently received a further threat to their self-esteem (e.g., negative feedback) and should be reflected in increased ingroup bias by these individuals.

In their first study, Crocker et al. (1987) divided their subjects into two groups (A and B) following the minimal intergroup paradigm. Subjects filled out the Rosenberg (1965) self-esteem inventory, and were then given the Social–Cognitive Aptitude Test (SCAT), which they were told was a valid and reliable measure of their interpersonal and intellectual competence. Subjects were randomly given either success feedback, failure feedback, or no feedback on the SCAT (see Crocker et al. for a more detailed description of the test administration and feedback). They then rated how true eight positive and eight negative traits were of themselves, the average student at their university, members of Group A, members of Group B, above-average scorers on the SCAT, and below-average scorers on the SCAT.

The results indicated that when the targets were As and Bs, subjects rated their ingroup higher than the outgroup. Low self-esteem subjects were more negative about both As and Bs than were high or moderate self-esteem subjects. Feedback on the SCAT had no effect on ratings of As and Bs. Thus, the findings replicated the ingroup favoritism effect obtained in many previous studies, as well as the pattern of results obtained by Crocker and Schwartz (1985) showing that all subjects showed ingroup favoritism, and that while low self-esteem subjects were overall more negative in their ratings than others, they did not show greater ingroup favoritism. These results were again contradictory to the predictions of downward comparison and social identity theories that ingroup bias in the minimal intergroup situation is motivated by needs for self-enhancement due to low trait self-esteem and transient threats to self-esteem.

A different pattern of results was obtained on ratings of below-average and above-average scorers on the SCAT. Here the group boundaries are based on test performance and thus may be more meaningful and have more evaluative implications than the arbitrary division into As and Bs. Based on what subjects knew about the SCAT, one would expect them to rate about-average scorers more positively than below-average scorers, and they did. However, this effect depended on subjects' level of self-esteem, and performance on the SCAT. High self-esteem subjects who received failure feedback rated below-average scorers (their in-group) more positively and above-average scorers (their outgroup) more negatively than did subjects who received success or no feedback (See Table 8.1). High self-

TABLE 8.1
Evaluations of Above-Average and Below-Average Scorers as a
Function of Subject's Personal Self-Esteem and Own Performance
(Crocker, Thompson, McGraw & Ingerman, 1987)

Personal Self-esteem	Individual performance feedback		
	Success	None	Failure
High			
Above-Avg.	32.88	27.16	21.33
Below-Avg.	3.78	−5.10	18.00
Low			
Above-Avg.	22.36	23.05	22.31
Below-Avg.	1.36	−5.47	3.18

Note. Higher numbers indicate more positive evaluations. Copyright by the American Psychological Association, 1987.

esteem subjects who failed were the only subjects who did not rate above-average scorers significantly more positively than below-average scorers. In other words, it was the high self-esteem subjects who responded to threats to self-esteem by altering their ratings of below-average and above-average scorers; low self-esteem subjects consistently rated above-average scorers positively than below-average scorers, regardless of how they themselves had performed. Only high self-esteem subjects showed ingroup favoritism in this context, a finding contrary to downward comparison and social identity theories, but consistent with studies indicating that high self-esteem and nondepressed individuals engage in a variety of self-serving illusions and biases (see Brown, 1986; Taylor & Brown, 1988).

In a second study, Crocker et al. (1987) investigated ingroup favoritism in naturally occurring groups in a field setting, namely, in campus sororities. Membership in a sorority is likely to contribute to one's social identity, and to the extent that one's sorority holds a low status compared to other sororities on campus, that membership should constitute a threat to the self-concept. Subjects in this study belonged to two high-status and two low-status sororities. They completed the Rosenberg (1965) self-esteem inventory and ratings of the typical member of several different sororities, including their own, on attributes such as attractive, snobbish, talented, and boring.

On the average, these subjects showed ingroup bias, by rating ingroup members more positively than outgroup members. Low self-esteem subjects and members of low status sororities were more negative overall in their ratings of both ingroups and outgroups. More interestingly, for subjects high in self-esteem ingroup bias were greater among those who belonged to a low-status sorority than those who belonged to a high-status sorority. For low self-esteem subjects, ingroup bias was unaffected by ingroup status. These results again suggest that it is high self-esteem people who respond to a threat to the self-concept by showing ingroup favoritism when the group boundaries have evaluative implications for the self.

These studies suggest that ingroup bias may be one strategy that high self-esteem people use to maintain their positive self-concepts when threatened. Thus, the paradox of social comparison we have proposed may be resolved by revising the prediction that low self-esteem individuals are more likely to engage in downward comparison than are high self-esteem individuals. Although these results are contrary to the initial predictions derived from downward comparison and social identity theories, they do indicate that self-esteem does sometimes play a role in intergroup comparisons.

Personal or Collective Self-Esteem

Self-esteem as operationalized in these studies may not have been appropriate to test social identity theory's predictions regarding the role of self-esteem in intergroup comparisons. Social identity theory distinguishes between personal and social identities, and predicts that ingroup bias is moderated, not by personal self-evaluations or threats to personal self-concept, but by social identity and threats to social identity. It is possible that the minimal intergroup paradigm represents a manipulation of social, not personal, identity, while categorization into groups on the basis of an evaluative test clearly implicates personal identity. Thus, the absence of self-esteem effects on ingroup favoritism in the minimal intergroup paradigm may be due to our focus on personal self-esteem and threats to private self-regard rather than social identity and threats to that part of the self-concept. In the minimal intergroup context, the issue may not be enhancement of personal self-esteem but enhancement of social identity.

In order to test this possibility, we needed a measure of the positivity of social identity. Existing self-esteem measures (e.g., Coopersmith, 1967; Janis & Field, 1959; Rosenberg, 1965; see Wylie, 1974) assess individuals' evaluations of themselves based on their individual characteristics. Although the domain of self-esteem assessed by these measures varies (including the self in academic and social situations, for example), they all assess individual differences in the evaluation of personal rather than social identity. Positivity of one's social identity is a function of how one evaluates ingroups with which one identifies, and how others evaluate those groups (e.g., Tajfel, 1982; Tajfel & Turner, 1979, 1986; Turner, 1975).

We developed a measure of collective self-esteem to assess the positivity of social identity (Luhtanen & Crocker, 1989). Our goal was to assess global, relatively stable levels of collective self-esteem, parallel to existing

TABLE 8.2
Items in the Collective Self-Esteem Scale

Private Collective Self-Esteem

I often regret that I belong to some of the social groups I do.[a]
In general, I'm glad to be a member of the social groups I belong to.
Overall, I often feel that the social groups of which I am a member are not worthwhile.[a]
I feel good about the social groups I belong to.

Public Collective Self-Esteem

Overall, my social groups are considered good by others.
Most people consider my social groups, on the average, to be more ineffective than other social groups.[a]
In general, others respect the social groups that I am a member of.
In general, others think that the social groups I am a member of are unworthy.[a]

Importance to Identity

Overall, my group memberships have very little to do with how I feel about myself.[a]
The social groups I belong to are an important reflection of who I am.
The social groups I belong to are unimportant to my sense of what kind of a person I am.[a]
In general, belonging to social groups is an important part of my self-image.

Membership Self-Esteem

I am a worthy member of the social groups I belong to.
I feel I don't have much to offer to the social groups I belong to.[a]
I am a cooperative participant in the social groups I belong to.
I often feel I'm a useless member of my social groups.[a]

Note. See Luhtanen and Crocker (1989) for the scale instructions.
[a]Item was reversed for scoring.

scales (e.g., Rosenberg, 1965) that measure global, relatively stable levels of personal self-esteem. The scale assesses four aspects of collective self-esteem, including private collective self-esteem (one's own evaluations of one's ingroups), public collective self-esteem (one's judgments of how other people evaluate one's social groups), the importance of one's group memberships to one's identity, and membership collective self-esteem (evaluation of one's role as a group member). The items included on each subscale are presented in Table 8.2. A more complete explanation of the subscales and the rationale for including them is presented in Luhtanen and Crocker (1989).

In completing the scale, subjects are asked to focus on memberships in several ascribed groups such as their race, religion, gender and ethnicity rather than achieved groups (such as membership in Phi Beta Kappa) to avoid confounding social identity with personal identity and to capture a general, cross-group tendency to have a positive social identity. The correlations between our Collective Self-Esteem Scale and other scales assessing personal self-esteem range from .33 to .38, suggesting that although collective and personal self-esteem are related, the two constructs are relatively distinct empirically as well as conceptually (see Luhtanen & Crocker, 1989, for more detail on the scale properties).

To test the possibility that ingroup bias is a function of collective rather than personal self-esteem needs, we conducted a study in which we assessed subjects' collective self-esteem as well as their personal self-esteem (Crocker & Luhtanen, 1990). Threats to collective self-esteem were manipulated by giving subjects group feedback. The design of this study was essentially the same as that of Crocker et al. (1987), except for the nature of the feedback. Subjects were again arbitrarily divided into two groups (As and Bs), and were administered the Social-Cognitive Aptitude Test (SCAT). Subjects were given information about the average score for their group (A or B), with their own score excluded from the calculations, to assure that threat to collective self-esteem and not personal self-esteem was manipulated. In actuality, subjects randomly received either group success or group failure feedback.

After the feedback, subjects rated themselves, Group A, Group B, above-average scorers, and below-average scorers on the SCAT on 16 adjectives, and completed some manipulation checks. Self-ratings were unaffected by the group feedback, suggesting that the feedback manipulated a threat to collective and not personal self-esteem (see Crocker & Luhtanen, 1990, for further discussion on the threat manipulation).

Analyses of subjects' ratings of ingroup and outgroup based on the minimal intergroup manipulation (i.e., division to As and Bs) showed that high collective self-esteem subjects gave higher ratings for both groups than did low collective self-esteem subjects and the ingroup was rated more positively than the outgroup. Although group success feedback subjects rated their ingroup more positively than did group failure feedback subjects, the feedback manipulation did not affect ratings of the outgroup. This pattern of results was the same when subjects were split on personal instead of collective self-esteem. Once again we did not find evidence for the prediction that ingroup bias in the minimal intergroup paradigm is moderated by self-esteem needs.

Analyses of subjects' ratings of above-average and below-average scorers, however, yielded a pattern similar to that of Crocker et al. (1987). Recall that in the earlier study, high personal self-esteem subjects showed biased evaluations of above-average and below-average scorers when they had received negative personal feedback. In this study (Crocker & Luhtanen, 1990), we manipulated threats to collective, rather than personal, self-esteem by giving group rather than personal feedback, and found that collective self-esteem interacted with group feedback in a similar manner

TABLE 8.3
Evaluations of Above-Average and Below-Average Scorers as a Function of Collective Self-Esteem and Group Performance (Crocker & Luhtanen, 1990)

Collective Self-Esteem	Group Performance	
	Success	Failure
High		
Above-Avg.	92.50	82.25
Below-Avg.	65.44	73.00
Low		
Above-Avg.	83.24	82.80
Below-Avg.	62.76	62.67

Note. Higher numbers indicate more positive evaluations. Copyright by the American Psychological Association, 1990.

(more specifically, private collective self-esteem showed this effect). As Table 8.3 shows, low collective self-esteem subjects were not responsive to threats to collective self-esteem; they rated above-average scorers better than below-average scorers regardless of whether their group had failed or succeeded. High collective self-esteem subjects, however, altered their ratings of above-average and below-average scorers as a function of the group threat manipulation. Highs who received group success feedback rated above-average scorers better and below-average scorers worse than did highs who received group failure feedback.

Consider the ratings of As and Bs together with the ratings of above and below average scorers. High collective self-esteem subjects whose group failed were no less willing to acknowledge the negative feedback when rating As and Bs than were low collective self-esteem (SE) subjects. Although they acknowledged that their group had done poorly on the test, they rated below-average scorers more positively, and above-average scorers more negatively than low collective SE subjects, suggesting that they were minimizing the significance of this poor group performance. In other words, high collective SE subjects appeared to defend against this threat to their collective self-esteem by minimizing the differences between above-average and below-average scorers. Reanalysis of these ratings with a median split on personal, rather than collective, self-esteem did not show this effect, indicating that collective threat (group feedback) only interacted with collective self-esteem. This further supports the argument that collective and personal self-esteem are relatively distinct aspects of identity. The interaction between self-esteem and threat thus appears to be specific to the type of self-esteem and type of threat; in the Crocker et al. (1987) study, subjects high in personal self-esteem responded to threats to personal self-esteem (i.e., negative individual feedback) by biasing their ratings of below-average and above-average scorers, and in the Crocker and Luhtanen (1990) study, high collective self-esteem subjects responded to threats to collective self-esteem (negative group feedback) in a similar manner.

Our research thus far has not supported the arguments of downward comparison theory and social identity theory that ingroup bias in the minimal intergroup situation is related to chronically low levels of personal or collective self-esteem, or self-esteem needs due to threats to personal or social identity. The arbitrariness of group assignments in the minimal intergroup situation may leave little to be gained with regard to any type of self-enhancement needs via enhancement of the ingroup. Further research should investigate what factors other than self-esteem needs cause biased intergroup comparisons in the minimal intergroup situation (cf. Abrams and Hogg, 1988). On the other hand, our results indicate that given more evaluative and/or meaningful group boundaries or group contexts, self-esteem and threats to self-esteem have an effect on ingroup bias. Thus, social identity theory does not seem to provide an adequate explanation for ingroup bias in the minimal intergroup situation, although it may account for at least some instances of ingroup bias when the basis for categorization is more evaluative. It appears, however, that it is high rather than low self-esteem individuals who exhibit biased intergroup comparisons following threat.

Unresolved Issues

Our research is consistent with recent evidence showing that high self-esteem people engage in self-enhancing or self-serving biases, whereas low self-esteem people fail to show these biases (see Taylor and Brown, 1988, for a review). Others have proposed that both high and low self-esteem individuals engage in self-serving biases, but the specific form of their biases may differ.

Brown, Collins and Schmidt (1988) have suggested that both high and low self-esteem individuals are motivated to enhance their self-images but engage in different forms of self-enhancement. They argue that low self-esteem individuals are doubtful of their ability to defend a positive identity and thus tend to engage in indirect forms of self-enhancement, whereas high self-esteem individuals, having higher expectations of their abilities, tend to engage in direct forms of self-enhancement. According to these authors, direct self-enhancement refers to self-enhancement biases that occur when the self is directly associated with positive outcomes and identities, and indirect self-enhancement refers to biases that occur when the self is indirectly linked to positive outcomes and identities through one's association with others. Brown et al. (1988) present data from two studies that are consistent with their hypothesis.

Although the notion that high self-esteem subjects are directly self-enhancing whereas low self-esteem subjects are indirectly self-enhancing is intriguing, it does not appear to be consistent with the results of our studies. In the study by Crocker and Luhtanen (1990), subjects were directly associated only with their ingroup based on the arbitrary division into As and Bs, and indirectly associated with either above-average or below-average scorers, depending on whether their group had performed well or poorly on the SCAT. It thus appears that high collective self-esteem subjects engaged in more indirect ingroup-enhancement than low self-esteem subjects, contrary to Brown et al.'s hypothesis. More research is needed to resolve the issue of whether high and low self-esteem subjects engage in different forms of self-enhancement or ingroup-enhancement. A clearer specification of what constitutes direct versus indirect self-enhancement would be useful in this regard.

Another issue concerns whether the distinction between above-average scorers and below-average scorers constitutes a group boundary. One could argue that the finding that high self-esteem subjects respond to negative feedback on a test by evaluating above-average scorers and below-average scorers more evenhandedly than when they receive positive feedback has little to do with intergroup comparisons. Rather, because of their expectations of performing well and their tendency not to accept negative feedback as being self-descriptive (cf. McFarlin & Blascovich, 1981; Shrauger, 1975), this effect is simply due to high self-esteem subjects dismissing the test as invalid after receiving negative feedback. Our data argue against this explanation in two ways. First, this argument implies that unlike high self-esteem subjects, those low in self-esteem did accept the test as valid because they did not alter their ratings of above-average and below-average scorers. If this was true, we would expect low self-esteem subjects' self-ratings to reflect the feedback they received on the test in the Crocker et al. (1987) study, but this was not the case. High and low self-esteem subjects did not differ in their self-ratings as a function of the feedback—both types of subjects rated themselves more negatively following failure than following success feedback. Second, if high, but not low, self-esteem subjects dismissed the test as invalid, it should have been reflected in the manipulation check measures. Our results indicate, however, that high self-esteem subjects are no less likely than lows to indicate that they would have liked themselves or their ingroup to score higher, that they were not satisfied with their or their ingroup's performance, or that the test was accurate.

In a more subtle way, however, this point may be well-taken. Given the large number of studies which show that high self-esteem individuals engage in self-enhancing strategies, it seems likely that the ingroup bias we have observed among high self-esteem subjects who are threatened is not an intergroup phenomenon per se, but part of a more general pattern of self-enhancement among high self-esteem individuals, which happens to be manifested in certain intergroup situations. Thus, concerns with self-enhancement may be one of many variables that can influence intergroup behavior.

The question then becomes, in which intergroup situations will self-esteem play a role? We can only speculate on this point, but on the basis of the larger pattern of our results, we would suggest that self-esteem will play a role when the group boundaries are explicitly evaluative, such as when the group boundaries define winners and losers, successes and failures, or villains and victims. In such cases, we would predict that high self-esteem individuals will attempt to maintain self-esteem by finding some way to dissociate themselves from the negative implications of their group membership, just as they tend to dissociate themselves from any failure experience. Of course, their strategy for maintaining self-esteem will be limited by the need to be a reasonable person. In other words, it is unlikely that high self-esteem individuals will self-enhance in ways that directly contradict known facts. Rather, they will attempt to alter the meaning or implications of those facts. In our studies, for example, high self-esteem subjects who were told that their group had failed rated that group more negatively than did subjects told their group had succeeded, acknowledging the feedback provided by the experimenter. However, high self-esteem subjects rated failing individuals less negatively, softening the negative implications of this feedback.

Toward a Theory of Collective Self-Esteem

Although our research on the role of collective self-esteem in intergroup relations began only recently, there are some interesting hypotheses and theoretical questions that can be posed.

Collective versus Personal Self-Esteem. Our findings (Crocker & Luhtanen, 1990; Luhtanen & Crocker, 1989) so far suggest that collective and personal self-esteem are conceptually and empirically distinct yet also in some ways related. We have found that while the Collective Self-Esteem Scale correlates significantly with personal self-esteem scales, these correlations are relatively low (in .30s) and much lower than correlations among different measures of personal self-esteem. Our results also indicate that collective and personal self-esteem are relatively distinct in that threats to collective self-esteem, at least under some conditions, interact with chronic levels of collective, but not personal, self-esteem. Yet our results also show that the pattern of interaction between collective self-esteem and threats to collective self-esteem is closely parallel to the pattern of interaction between personal self-esteem and threats to personal self-esteem. Furthermore, we have found that both collective and personal self-esteem are related to higher overall evaluations of different targets. These results suggest that while personal and collective self-esteem are relatively distinct, there may be a core component of self-esteem which is common to both personal and collective aspects of identity.

One interesting hypothesis that arises from the above analysis is that the role of collective self-esteem in mental health may parallel that of personal self-esteem. Taylor and Brown (1988) recently reviewed literature indicating that high self-esteem is related to a variety of self-serving biases and illusions, which they argue, promote several aspects of mental health, such as happiness, productivity, and caring about others. For example, compared to depressed and/or low self-esteem individuals, nondepressed and high self-esteem individuals have been found to be more likely to rate positive attributes as more descriptive and negative attributes as less descriptive of self than of others (e.g., Brown, 1986); to evaluate their abilities as rare and distinct and their opinions as common and correct (e.g., Campbell, 1986; Tabachnik, Crocker & Alloy, 1983); to make self-serving causal attributions (e.g., Seligman, Abramson, Semmel & von Baeyer, 1979); and to show illusions of personal control (e.g., Alloy & Abramson, 1979). Parallel to these findings, compared to low collective self-esteem individuals, those high in collective self-esteem may be more likely to rate ingroups better than outgroups on various attributes (at least when the group boundaries are meaningful or evaluative), especially when faced with collective threats; to engage in biased causal attributions on a group level, such that positive ingroup outcomes are attributed to characteristics of the ingroup while negative ingroup outcomes are attributed to external factors; and to exhibit greater optimism for the future of their ingroups.

Which type of self-esteem is a more important determinant of subjective well-being and exactly how are collective and personal self-esteem connected are intriguing questions for future research. Our prediction is that, at least in cultures where individual accomplishments are emphasized, such as the United States, level of personal self-esteem tends to be more important to most individuals than is level of collective self-esteem. Triandis and his colleagues (e.g., Triandis, Bontempo, Villareal, Asai & Lucca, 1988; Triandis, Leung, Villareal & Clack, 1985) have distinguished between the cultural dimension of collectivism versus individualism (the extent to which cooperation is a dominant pattern of social behavior and a dominant value orientation in different cultures) and the psychological dimension of allocentrism versus idiocentrism (the extent to which individuals emphasize their ingroup's vs. their personal goals, views, needs and beliefs). In line with these authors' distinctions, there may be cultural differences in the extent to which collective aspects of self-esteem tend to be emphasized over personal self-esteem, yet within any culture, there may also be individual differences in the extent to which one's level of collective self-esteem is more significant to one's well-being than is personal self-esteem.

Whether people tend to choose strategies that enhance personal self-esteem or those that enhance collective self-esteem may vary not only across cultures but also across individuals. Considering the findings that high self-esteem individuals are especially likely to engage in strategies that help maintain or enhance their positive self-concepts, one possibility is that given a discrepancy between levels of personal and collective self-esteem, people tend to choose strategies that protect or further enhance the type of self-esteem in which they are higher. For example, a student with a more negative personal than social identity might boast about their school's football team, or exaggerate the academic prestige of the school (called "basking in reflected glory" by Cialdini, Borden, Thorne, Walker & Freeman, 1976), whereas a student with a more positive personal than social identity might boast about their grade on a midterm or exaggerate their athletic skill. A further question concerning the connection between personal and collective self-esteem is whether enhancement of one produces an increase in the other. This is possible, considering the positive correlation between the two and the previously reviewed findings that intergroup discrimination (which should be more linked to social than personal identity) appears to increase personal self-esteem (e.g., Lemyre & Smith, 1985; Oakes & Turner, 1980). Future research should attempt to delineate the relationship between personal and collective self-esteem.

There may also be situational determinants that make one or the other types of self-esteem needs more salient. Tajfel and Turner (1979), for example, have noted an interpersonal–to–intergroup continuum in social behavior. At the interpersonal end of the continuum, individuals' interactions with one another are determined by their personal attributes, while at the intergroup extreme, people's interactions are largely determined by group memberships. Thus, contexts where group memberships rather than individual characteristics are salient or emphasized (e.g., team sports; interdepartmental or interorganizational meetings; interracial, ethnic, or international events) are likely to make social identity needs especially salient. Perhaps the more interpersonal the setting, the more likely it is that personal self-esteem will predict behavior, and the more intergroup the setting, the more likely it is that collective self-esteem will predict behavior.

Collective Self-esteem as a Moderator of the Use of Strategies to Enhance Social Identity. Tajfel and Turner (1986) have outlined several strategies that people may use when faced with a negative or threatened social identity. One is individual mobility, referring to people's attempt to leave, or dissociate themselves from, a low-status ingroup. Both collective and personal self-esteem may moderate the use of this strategy. Because it is an individualistic strategy, people high in personal self-esteem may be more likely than those low in personal self-esteem to disidentify themselves from negatively valued ingroups in order to protect their self-concept. Collective self-esteem may also, in some cases, moderate the tendency to adopt this strategy; high collective self-esteem individuals, when entering a new group which they come to devalue (e.g., a low-status organization, or an experimentally created group which is devalued), may be more likely than low collective self-esteem individuals to try to leave the group in order to protect their social identity. On the other hand, in situations where membership in one's ingroup is personally meaningful or dissociation is impossible, high collective self-esteem persons may tend to adopt other, more group-oriented, strategies to protect or enhance their social identity. For example, individuals high in collective self-esteem may be more active in causes and activities involving the enhancement of their ingroup's status in the society (e.g., civil rights movements). In other words, these individuals may be especially sensitive and responsive to what Runciman (1966) has termed fraternalistic deprivation, or the perception that the ingroup's position in society is disadvantaged in comparison to other groups (see Olson, Herman & Zanna, 1986, for recent contributions to the relative deprivation and social comparison literatures).

Collective self-esteem may be a more important moderator than personal self-esteem of the several group-oriented strategies to protect and enhance social identity discussed by Tajfel and Turner (1986). One of these strategies is direct competition with the outgroup in order to improve the status or objective location of the ingroup in the social hierarchy. In studies of intergroup behavior, this is often signified by discriminatory allocation of points or resources between the ingroup and the outgroup (see e.g., Brewer, 1979; Tajfel & Turner, 1986).

High collective self-esteem individuals may also be more likely than lows to use strategies that do not involve direct competition, which Tajfel & Turner (1986) group under the heading of social creativity. One is to compare one's ingroup to an outgroup on some new dimension when comparison on a different dimension yields a negative outcome for the ingroup. For example, individuals in organization A may receive lower pay than those in organization B, but, given that there is little members of organization A can do to alter this situation, they may choose to compare their benefits or supervisor-subordinate relationships to those of organization B. Another strategy is to "change the values assigned to the attributes of the group, so that comparisons which were previously perceived as negative are now perceived as positive" (Tajfel & Turner, 1986, p. 20). In other words, individuals may come to value attributes that the ingroup possesses (and perhaps devalue those on which the ingroup fares poorly; cf. Crocker & Major, 1989). "Black is beautiful" and "Gay Pride" are examples of this. Finally, individuals may change their comparison target by ceasing to compare their ingroup to a superior outgroup and selecting a new outgroup with which the ingroup compares favorably. Avoidance of comparisons that are likely to yield negative outcomes and thus have a damaging effect on self-esteem has been discussed on an individual rather than intergroup level by Brickman & Bulman (1977), but their arguments are easily transferred to group level. In Wills' (1981) terms, individuals may engage in passive downward comparisons between the ingroup and an outgroup that is objectively worse off. People high in collective self-esteem may be more likely than lows to select a worse-off outgroup with which to compare in order to protect or enhance a threatened social identity, provided that more suitable strategies of ingroup-enhancement are unavailable and some choice of comparison targets is available.

Campus Racism: The Role of Personal and Collective Self-Esteem

What can this research on self-esteem and intergroup comparisons tell us about campus racism? It suggests that one contributing factor in campus racism may be the need to protect or enhance self-esteem. Our research suggests that when group boundaries have evaluative implications, ingroup bias is particularly likely among people who are high in self-esteem who have received a threat to the self-concept.

What threat to the self-concept might elicit racism among privileged, intelligent white college students? An analysis of campus racism by Shelby Steele (1989) which appeared in the popular press suggests one possibility. He argues that the history of racism against blacks in the United States has imposed a burden of guilt on whites. This sense of guilt for past injustices may threaten one's self-concept as a fair, just, and good person. In other words, it may pose a threat to self-esteem. To the extent that students feel the boundary between white and black connotes a distinction between racist and victim, one strategy to maintain self-esteem is to reevaluate the implications of being racist. Just as high self-esteem students in our studies who were told they failed a test said that below-average scorers were not so bad, so may college students, particularly those who are high in self-esteem, cope with accusations of racism by rationalizing their antiblack sentiment. This may be easier for the current generation of college students, born after the civil rights movement, because they needn't feel personally responsible for injustices that occured before they were born.

At the same time, the declining numbers of blacks on college campuses may make racial identity particularly salient for those blacks who remain.

Black students may feel a collective vulnerability or threat as a consequence of their declining numbers and the increase in campus racism. Among black students, then, those who are high in collective self-esteem or black pride may be particularly likely to react to this collective threat, using the strategies identified by Tajfel and Turner (1986) for maintaining a positive social identity.

We do not wish to claim that efforts to enhance or protect the self-concept are the only, or even the major factors in campus racism. However, an increasing body of research has demonstrated the importance of the self-concept in a variety of social behaviors. Our research suggests that self-esteem may play an important role in racism and other intergroup comparisons.

ACKNOWLEDGMENTS

Preparation of this chapter was supported by National Science Foundation Grant BNS 8520693 to Jennifer Crocker, and BNS 8706153 to Brenda Major and Jennifer Crocker.

REFERENCES

Abrams, D., & Hogg, M. A. (1988). Comments on the motivational status of self-esteem in social identity and intergroup discrimination. *European Journal of Social Psychology, 18,* 317–334.

Alloy, L. B., & Abramson, L. Y. (1979). Judgment of contingency in depressed and nondepressed students: Sadder but wiser? *Journal of Experimental Psychology: General, 108,* 441–485.

Ashmore, R. D., & DelBoca, F. K. (1976). Psychological approaches to understanding intergroup conflict. In P. Katz (Ed.), *Towards the elimination of racism* (pp. 73–123). New York: Pergamon Press.

Baumeister, R. F., Tice, D. M., & Hutton, D. G. (1989). Self-presentational motivations and personality differences in self-esteem. *Journal of Personality, 57,* 547–579.

Berger, J. (1989, May 22). Racial strains show two perspectives on inequality. *New York Times,* Section A1, p. 1.

Brewer, M. B. (1979). Ingroup bias in the minimal intergroup situation: A cognitive-motivational analysis. *Psychological Bulletin, 86,* 207–324.

Brewer, M. B. & Campbell, D. T. (1976). *Ethnocentrism and intergroup attitudes: East African evidence.* New York: Halsted.

Brickman, P., & Bulman, R. (1977). Pleasure and pain in social comparison. In J. M. Suls and R. L. Miller (Eds.), *Social comparison processes: Theoretical and empirical perspectives* (pp. 149–186). Washington, DC: Hemisphere.

Brown, J. D. (1986). Evaluations of self and others: Self-enhancement biases in social judgments. *Social Cognition, 4,* 353–376.

Brown, J. D., Collins, R. L., & Schmidt, G. W. (1988). Self-esteem and direct versus indirect forms of self-enhancement. *Journal of Personality and Social Psychology, 55,* 445–453.

Campbell, D. T. (1965). Ethnocentric and other altruistic motives. In D. Levine (Ed.), *Nebraska symposium on motivation* (Vol. 13). Lincoln, NE: University of Nebraska Press.

Campbell, J. D. (1986). Similarity and uniqueness: The effects of attribute type, relevance, and individual differences in self-esteem and depression. *Journal of Personality and Social Psychology, 50,* 281–294.

Cialdini, R. B., Borden, R. J., Thorne, A., Walker, M. R., & Freeman, S. (1976). Basking in reflected glory: Three (football) field studies. *Journal of Personality and Social Psychology, 34,* 366–375.

Coopersmith, S. (1967). *The antecedents of self-esteem.* San Francisco, CA: Freeman.

Crocker, J., & Luhtanen, R. (1990). Collective self-esteem and ingroup bias. *Journal of Personality and Social Psychology, 58,* 60–67.

Crocker, J., & Major, B. (1989). Social stigma and self-esteem: The self-protective properties of stigma. *Psychological Review, 96,* 608–630.

Crocker, J., & Schwartz, I. (1985). Prejudice and ingroup favoritism in a minimal intergroup situation: Effects of self-esteem. *Personality and Social Psychology Bulletin, 11,* 379–386.

Crocker, J., Thompson, L. J., McGraw, K. M., & Ingerman, C. (1987). Downward comparison, prejudice, and evaluations of others: Effects of self-esteem and threat. *Journal of Personality and Social Psychology, 52,* 907–916.

Dovidio, J. F., & Gaertner, S. L. (Eds.). (1986). *Prejudice, discrimination, and racism.* New York: Academic Press.

Ehrlich, H. J. (1973). *The social psychology of prejudice.* New York: Wiley.

Gerald, H. B., & Hoyt, M. F. (1974). Distinctiveness of social categorization and attitude toward ingroup members. *Journal of Personality and Social Psychology, 29,* 836–842.

Hinkle, S., & Schopler, J. (1986). Bias in the evaluation of in-group and out-group performance. In S. Worchel & W. G. Austin (Eds.), *Psychology of intergroup relations* (2nd ed., pp. 196–212). Chicago: Nelson-Hall.

Janis, I. L., & Field, P. B. (1959). A behavioral assessment of persuasibility: Consistency of individual differences. In C. Hovland & I. L. Janis (Eds.), *Personality and persuasibility* (pp. 29–54). New Haven, CT: Yale University Press.

Lemyre, L., & Smith, P. M. (1985). Intergroup discrimination and self-esteem in the minimal group paradigm. *Journal of Personality and Social Psychology, 49,* 660–670.

Locksley, A., Ortiz, V., & Hepburn, C. (1980). Social categorization and discriminatory behavior: Extinguishing the minimal intergroup discrimination effect. *Journal of Personality and Social Psychology, 39,* 773–783.

Luhtanen, R., & Crocker, J. (1989). *A collective self-esteem scale: Self-evaluation of one's social identity.* Unpublished manuscript.

McFarlin, D. B., & Blascovich, J. (1981). Effects of self-esteem and performance on future affective preferences and cognitive expectations. *Journal of Personality and Social Psychology, 40,* 521–531.

Oakes, P. J., & Turner, J. (1980). Social categorization and intergroup behaviour: Does minimal intergroup discrimination make social identity more positive? *European Journal of Social Psychology, 10,* 295–301.

Olson, J. M., Herman, C. P., & Zanna, M. P. (Eds.). (1986). *Relative deprivation and social comparison: The Ontario symposium* (Vol. 4). Hillsdale, NJ: Lawrence Erlbaum Associates.

Rosenberg, M. (1965). *Society and the adolescent self-image.* Princeton, NJ: Princeton University Press.

Ross, L., Greene, D., & House, P. (1977). The "false consensus effect:" An egocentric bias in social perception and attribution processes. *Journal of Experimental Social Psychology, 13,* 279–301.

Runciman, W. G. (1966). *Relative deprivation and social justice: A study of attitudes to social inequality in twentieth-century England.* Berkeley, CA: University of California Press.

Seligman, M. E. P., Abramson, L. Y., Semmel, A., & von Baeyer, C. (1979). Depressive attributional style. *Journal of Abnormal Psychology, 88,* 242–247.

Sherif, M., Harvey, O. J., White, B. J., Hood, W. R., & Sherif, C. W. (1961). *Intergroup conflict and cooperation: The Robbers Cave experiment.* Norman, OK: University Book Exchange.

Shrauger, J. S. (1975). Responses to evaluation as a function of initial self-perceptions. *Psychological Bulletin, 82,* 581–596.

Steele, S. (February, 1989). The recoloring of campus life: Student racism, academic pluralism, and the end of a dream. *Harper's Magazine.*

Tabachnik, N., Crocker, J., & Alloy, L. B. (1983). Depression, social comparison, and the false consensus effect. *Journal of Personality and Social Psychology, 43,* 688–699.

Tajfel, H. (1970). Experiments in intergroup discrimination. *Scientific American, 223,* 96–102.

Tajfel, H. (1981). *Human groups and social categories: Studies in social psychology.* Cambridge, England: Cambridge University Press.

Tajfel, H. (1982). Social psychology of intergroup relations. *Annual Review of Psychology, 33,* 1–39.

Tajfel, H., & Billig, M. (1974). Familiarity and categorization in intergroup behavior. *Journal of Experimental Social Psychology, 10,* 159–170.

Tajfel, H., Billig, M., Bundy, R., & Flament, C. (1971). Social categorization and intergroup behavior. *European Journal of Social Psychology, 1,* 149–178.

Tajfel, H., & Turner, J. C. (1979). An integrative theory of intergroup conflict. In W. G. Austin and S. Worchel (Eds.), *The social psychology of intergroup relations* (pp. 33–48). Monterey, CA: Brooks–Cole.

Tajfel, H., & Turner, J. C. (1986). The social identity theory of intergroup behavior. In S. Worchel & W. G. Austin (Eds.), *Psychology of intergroup relations* (2nd ed., pp. 7–24). Chicago, IL: Nelson–Hall.

Taylor, S. E., & Brown, J. D. (1988). Illusion and well-being: A social psychological perspective on mental health. *Psychological Bulletin, 103,* 193–210.

Triandis, H. C., Bontempo, R., Villareal, M. J., Asai, M., & Lucca, N. (1988). Individualism and collectivism: Cross-cultural perspectives on self-ingroup relations. *Journal of Personality and Social Psychology, 54,* 323–338.

Triandis, H. C., Leung, K., Villareal, M. J., & Clack, F. L. (1985). Allocentric versus idiocentric tendencies: Convergent and discriminant validation. *Journal of Research in Personality, 19,* 395–415.

Turner, J. C. (1975). Social comparison and social identity: Some prospects for intergroup behaviour. *European Journal of Social Psychology, 5,* 5–35.

Turner, J. C. (1982). Towards a cognitive redefinition of the social group. In H. Tajfel (Ed.), *Social identity and intergroup relations* (pp. 15–40). Cambridge, England: Cambridge University Press.

Turner, J. C., & Spriggs, D. (1982). *Social categorization, intergroup behaviour and self-esteem: A replication.* Unpublished manuscript.

Wagner, U., Lampen, L., & Syllwasschy, J. (1986). In-group inferiority, social identity and out-group devaluation in a modified minimal group study. *British Journal of Social Psychology, 25,* 15–24.

Wills, T. A. (1981). Downward comparison principles in social psychology. *Psychological Bulletin, 90,* 245–271.

Wylie, R. C. (1974). *The self-concept* (Vol. 1). Lincoln, NE: University of Nebraska Press.

Wylie, R. C. (1979). *The self-concept* (Vol. 2). Lincoln, NE: University of Nebraska Press.

III SPECIFIC MODELS OF COMPARISON

The chapters in this section present innovative approaches to specific questions, showing how social comparison theory may provide insights into particular phenomena. In chapter 9, Brenda Major, Maria Testa, and Wayne Bylsma focus on the consequences of social comparison. They describe how the relevance of personal attributes to self-esteem and control over one's status determine reactions to comparison with persons either better off or worse off than the self. Among other predictions, the authors' model suggests that upward comparison need not have unpleasant consequences even though a person learns about others who are better off. The critical issue is whether it is possible for the individual to improve. That is contingent in part on perceptions of control and whether the dimension in question is central to feelings of self-worth. Major et al. provide a catalogue of possible moderators of the consequences of upward and downward comparison, providing a lengthy agenda for future researchers.

In chapter 10, Peter Salovey uses social comparison theory to understand the common emotions of envy and jealousy. Salovey's chapter emphasizes the importance of unfavorable comparison in interpersonal relationships, and considers how factors such as self-centrality of an attribute, or similarity of the comparison other, influence reaction to discrepant outcomes. He introduces a topic not covered by other authors (but anticipated by Festinger) in discussing how cultural beliefs and norms may influence the way in which persons pursue social comparison. Salovey also provides an intriguing discussion of factors that may determine whether comparison envy results in relatively benign outcomes or in violent and destructive behavior.

In the final chapter of this section, Dale Miller and Cathy McFarland provide an analysis of the *pluralistic ignorance* phenomenon, whereby people believe that their private thoughts and feelings are different from those of others, even though everyone's public behavior is identical. For example, bystanders who are unsure about the seriousness of a situation often assume that other bystanders, despite acting similarly to themselves, are confident that the situation is not an emergency. Miller and McFarland present a variety of data demonstrating that the nature of the social comparison process in these cases is what is responsible for the mistaken perception of personal deviance.

9   Responses to Upward and Downward Social Comparisons: The Impact of Esteem-Relevance and Perceived Control

Brenda Major
Maria Testa
Wayne H. Bylsma
State University of New York at Buffalo

A number of theories of human behavior share the assumption that we learn about and evaluate ourselves, our potentials, and our circumstances in life in part by social comparisons, that is, through comparing our abilities, opinions, emotions, and outcomes with those of others. Theory and research focussed on social comparison processes (Festinger, 1954; Suls & Miller, 1977) has, for the most part, addressed the question of which others people select for comparison purposes. This emphasis on choice of comparison other is reflected in early research investigating when people choose to compare themselves with similar versus dissimilar others (e.g., Wheeler et al., 1969; Zanna, Goethals & Hill, 1975), and contemporary research on downward social comparisons (Wills, 1981; 1987), and choice of comparisons among people coping with victimization (e.g., Wood, Taylor & Lichtman, 1985).

The current chapter, in contrast, addresses the question of how social comparisons affect the individual comparer. Specifically, this chapter focusses on factors that moderate the affective, cognitive, and behavioral consequences of upward and downward comparisons. In taking this perspective, we follow in the footsteps of several other authors, most notably Brickman and Bulman (1977) and Tesser and his colleagues (Tesser, 1988; Tesser & Campbell, 1983) by beginning at the point where past research on social comparison has typically ended—when an individual knows how he or she compares to another. Our analysis of the consequences of social comparisons also borrows from and extends seminal work on the consequences of relative deprivation (cf. Crosby, 1976; Mark & Folger, 1984).

In his influential theory of social comparison processes, Festinger (1954) focussed on the use of comparisons with others for purposes of self-evaluation. His model of the social comparer was one of a rational information seeker attempting to gain an accurate assessment of his or her abilities or opinions. The central proposition of Festinger's theory was the *similarity hypothesis* which predicted that individuals prefer to compare themselves with similar others since they provide the best means of gaining an accurate picture of oneself. The ensuing emphasis on the use of social comparisons for purposes of self-evaluation has given way recently to an emphasis on social comparisons motivated by other goals, most notably self-enhancement and self-improvement (Wood, 1989), and a corresponding shift in focus from similar versus dissimilar comparisons to upward versus downward comparisons.

A major factor in this shifting focus was an influential paper by Wills (1981) in which he argued that: (a) "people can increase their subjective well-being through comparisons with a less fortunate other" and (b) "downward comparison is evoked by a decrease in subjective well-being." A number of studies have supported his assertion that people under threat prefer to compare themselves with worse-off others (Friend & Gilbert, 1973; Hakmiller, 1966; Wood, Taylor & Lichtman, 1985; see Wills, 1987 for a review), and several suggest that under some circumstances downward comparisons can indeed increase subjective well-being (Crocker & Gallo, 1985; Gibbons, 1986; Morse & Gergen, 1970).

Upward comparisons, in contrast, usually have been regarded as an unpleasant, if not painful experience. This assumption is supported by much of the literature on relative deprivation and inequity distress, indicating that people frequently express anger and resentment when they discover that similar others are better-off than themselves (cf. Crosby, 1976; Martin, 1986; Walster, Walster & Berscheid, 1978). Upward comparisons are avoided following failure (Pyszczynski, Greenberg & LaPrelle, 1985) and upward comparisons in ability domains have been shown to result in negative affect (Pleban & Tesser, 1981) and jealousy (Salovey & Rodin, 1984).

A cursory overview of the literature on the consequences of upward and downward comparisons might tempt one to conclude that downward comparisons are good for the self and upward comparisons are bad. Such a conclusion, however, would be an oversimplification. The consequences of upward comparisons are not always negative, and are in many cases positive. Learning that someone is better-off than oneself is a double-edged sword. On the one hand it indicates that you are not as well off as others, but on the other hand it also indicates that it is possible for you to be better off (Brickman & Bulman, 1977). Furthermore, another's success can be a source of pride and inspiration as well as a guide as to how you too might achieve their level (Bandura, 1977; 1986; Tesser, 1988). Similarly, there is growing evidence that the consequences of downward comparisons are not always positive and are, in many cases, negative. Learning that someone is worse-off that oneself not only reveals that you are not as badly off as others, but also suggests that it might be possible for things to get worse. Thus, downward comparisons may make one feel threatened and vulnerable rather than comforted. Furthermore, downward comparisons may lower one's own expectations and aspirations (Brown & Inouye, 1978). A critical problem for social comparison theory is to predict when upward and downward comparisons will have these different consequences.

We propose that two factors are key determinants of the consequences of upward and downward social comparisons: (a) the *esteem-relevance* of the social comparison, and (b) the degree of *perceived control* the comparer feels over his or her status relative to the comparison other on the dimension under evaluation. Each of these factors is, in turn, determined by two additional factors. The esteem-relevance of a social comparison is determined by: (a) the similarity of the comparison other on dimensions surrounding the comparison dimension, and (b) the self-relevance, or importance, of the dimension under evaluation. In particular, comparisons with similar others on self-relevant dimensions are most esteem-relevant, that is, have the most psychological impact on the comparer (Tesser, 1988). The degree of control the comparer perceives over his or her status relative to the comparison other is also jointly determined by two factors: (a) the comparer's expectancies regarding the general stability or alterability of the comparison dimension, and (b) the comparer's expectancies regarding his or her personal ability to maintain or change his or her relative status on the comparison dimension.

In addition, we propose that esteem-relevance and perceived control interact to predict three major categories of responses to social comparisons: *self-directed* responses, *dimension-directed* responses, and *comparison–other–directed* responses. Self-directed responses involve changes in feelings, cognitions, and behaviors with respect to the self, such as elevated or depressed mood, changes in self-esteem, self-efficacy expectations, and self-improvement efforts. Dimension-directed responses involve affect, cognition, or behavior directed toward the dimension of comparison, or alternative dimensions. Altering the self-relevance or perceived value of a comparison dimension, increased or decreased striving with regard to a particular dimension, or changing the dimension along which comparisons are made to one more favorable to the self are examples. Comparison–other–directed responses are responses directed toward the comparison other, and include increased or decreased liking for the comparison other, approaching versus distancing oneself from the comparison other, changing one's comparison other, and avoiding or seeking further social comparisons.

Within each of these categories, possible responses may be further described as affective (e.g., self-esteem, anger, feelings of inequity distress), cognitive (e.g., self-efficacy, attributions, self-relevance, entitlement), and behavioral (e.g., persistence, withdrawal, interpersonal closeness, aggression). This distinction among types of responses is important since most studies have looked at only one category of response (e.g., only affective or only behavioral), thus hampering a full understanding of the complex reactions that social comparisons may engender. Indeed, Nadler and Fisher (1986) suggest that affective and behavioral responses to upward comparisons are not congruent. They suggest that upward comparisons even on controllable dimensions may lead to temporary negative affect while also leading to improved effort and persistence. A similar analysis might apply to responses to downward comparisons on controllable dimensions. While such comparisons may lead to more positive affect, they may also lower performance or outcome expectations and decrease subsequent striving.

A schematic drawing of the framework we propose is presented in Figure 9.1 for the case of upward comparisons and in Figure 9.2 for the case of downward comparisons. Although presented as dichotomous variables, we believe that perceived similarity, self-relevance, changeability, and perceived control are all continuous variables. Thus, a particular comparison other may be perceived as more or less similar, a dimension of comparison may be more or less self-relevant, one's relative status on a comparison dimension may be perceived as more or less changeable, and potential change may be perceived as more or less under one's personal control. Differences in the extent to which various responses to comparisons are elaborated in these figures reflect the degree to which certain types of responses have been either studied or ignored in existing research. Some of the responses articulated in these figures are based on prior research, others are more speculative.

It should be noted that the various responses we have described are not mutually exclusive; individuals may engage in several simultaneously in efforts to maintain or enhance their self-esteem. Like Tesser, we believe that the likelihood of any of these responses occurring increases as social comparisons become more esteem-relevant. Furthermore, social comparisons, perceived similarity between self and comparison other, self-relevance of the comparison dimension, perceived alterability of a comparison dimension, and personal control are part of a system and do not necessarily occur in the temporal order we have described. For example, individuals may respond to esteem-threatening social comparisons by changing their comparison other, decreasing the perceived similarity between themselves and the comparison other, decreasing the self-relevance of the comparison dimension and/or selecting other dimensions for comparison. Social comparisons also provide information about personal control. To the extent

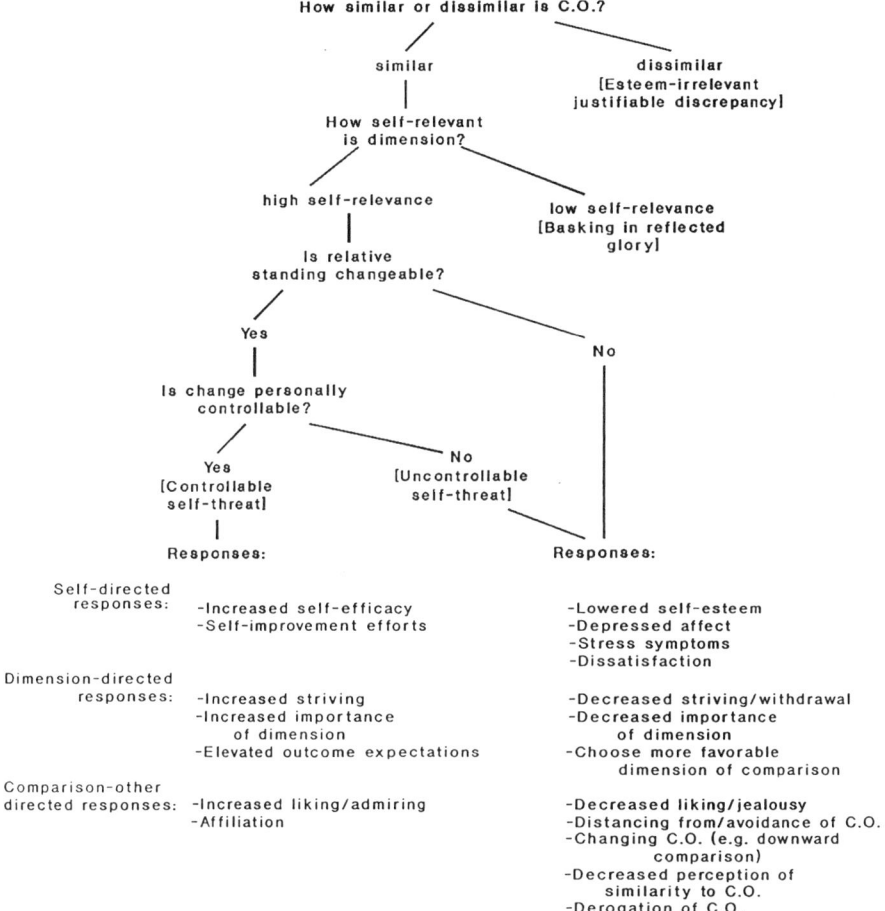

FIG. 9.1. Moderators of responses to upward comparisons. Note: C.O. = Comparison Other.

that others like myself achieve some level of performance or obtain some level of outcomes, this implies that I might too might expect a similar fate (e.g., DeVellis, DeVellis & McCauley, 1978).

In the following sections we elaborate our theoretical framework and review research on the consequences of upward and downward social comparisons within this framework.

Esteem-Relevant Social Comparisons

Consistent with the framework developed by Tesser and his colleagues (Tesser, 1988; Tesser & Campbell, 1983), we believe that the perceived

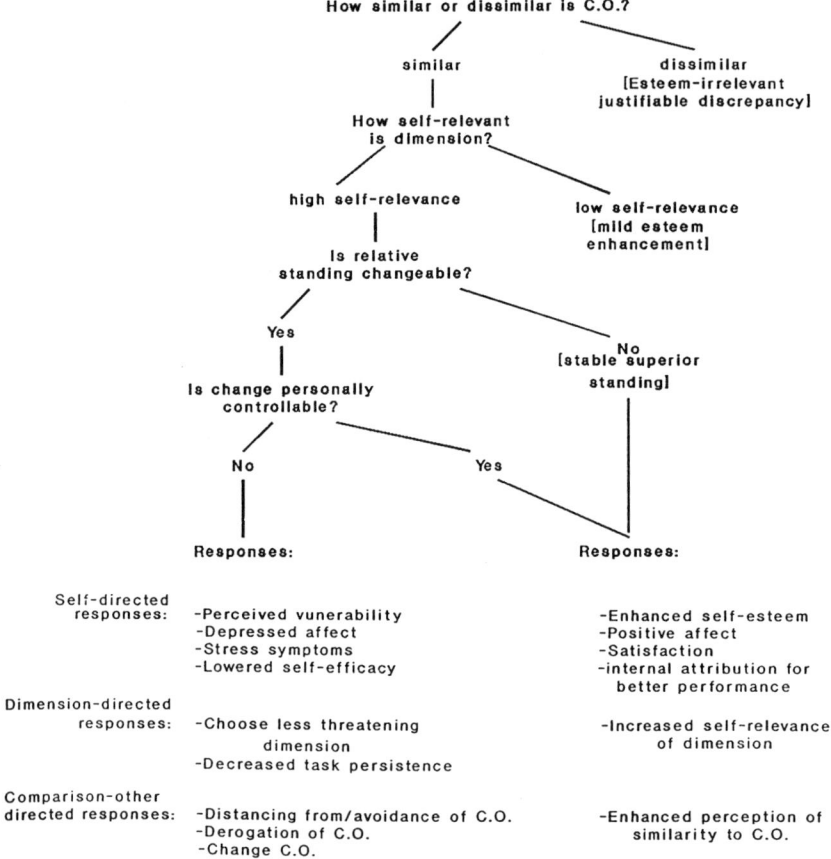

FIG. 9.2. Moderators of responses to downward comparisons. Note: C.O. = Comparison Other.

similarity of the comparison other and the self-relevance (importance) of the dimension of comparison interact to determine the psychological impact of upward and downward social comparisons. Adapting the coping framework developed by Lazarus and Folkman (1984; Folkman & Lazarus, 1980), we propose that the direction of the comparison and these two factors jointly influence the *primary appraisal* of a given social comparison as esteem-threatening, esteem-irrelevant, or esteem-enhancing.

Similarity of the Comparison Other. Consistent with Festinger's assertion that when comparison others are too different "one merely ceases to compare oneself with those persons" (1954; p. 128), a substantial amount of research indicates that comparisons with dissimilar others have less impact on the self than do comparisons with others who are perceived as similar to the self (see Wood, 1989, for a review). For example, individuals whose outcomes and life circumstances are poorer than those of others are unlikely to report feelings of dissatisfaction or relative deprivation if they regard those others as dissimilar to themselves (Crosby, 1976; Martin, 1986). Wood, Taylor, & Lichtman (1985) found that breast cancer patients regarded "supercopers," famous women who were presented in the media as coping extremely well, as dissimilar to themselves and thus irrelevant to their own situation. Seta (1982) found that subjects' performance on a task improved if a comparison other's performance was slightly better than their own, but was unaffected when the other's performance was highly discrepant from their own. Nadler and Fisher (1986) report that the self-esteem of recipients of help suffers more when the helper has similar attitudes rather than dissimilar attitudes or when the helper is a friend versus a stranger.

As Wood (1989) has pointed out, comparisons with similar others appear to have more impact regardless of whether the similarity is on dimensions related or unrelated to the dimension under evaluation. For example, subjects' judgements of personal entitlement are more affected by information about the pay received by same-gender others than cross-gender others whether or not gender is described as related to performance and hence pay (Bylsma, Major & Cozzarelli, 1990). Consistent with this view, Tesser (1988; Tesser & Campbell, 1983) has conceptualized similarity in terms of closeness on a variety of dimensions, including age, gender, family ties, proximity, etc, and has demonstrated in a variety of studies that comparison others who are close to the self on any one of these dimensions have more impact than do those who are not close. Similarly, Miller, Turnbull and McFarland (1988) demonstrated that comparisons with individuals who share distinctive attributes with oneself have more affective impact than do comparisons with individuals who share nondistinctive attributes.

It is important to note that perceived similarity between self and a comparison other can be distorted for self-enhancement purposes (Brickman & Bulman, 1977). For example, you may decide after being beaten at tennis that your partner is really not all that similar because she practices every day, whereas you play only once a month. Similarly, the woman who discovers that she makes two-thirds the salary of a similarly qualified male may decide that he really is not a relevant comparison because his job is not comparable to hers. As these examples illustrate, perceived similarity is a key determinant of whether or not an upward or downward comparison is regarded as justifiable. To the extent that another's superior performance or outcomes are seen as due to legitimate reasons, they may have less impact on the self. For example, Martin (1986) found that feminist secretaries were more distressed by gender-based occupational segregation and job discrimination than secretaries with a more traditional orientation.

This latter group presumably felt that their treatment was justifiable given the differences they perceived between themselves and (relatively advantaged) male comparisons.

Self-Relevance of the Comparison Dimension. Perceived similarity between oneself and a better-off or worse-off other, however, does not necessarily mean that a social comparison will have psychological impact. Upward comparisons on self-relevant dimensions are potentially more esteem-threatening, and downward comparisons on self-relevant dimensions are potentially more esteem-enhancing, than comparisons on irrelevant dimensions.

Tesser (1988) has observed that if a similar or close other is better-off than oneself on a dimension irrelevant to the self, one may bask in the reflected glory of her success, since it is not threatening to one's own self-evaluation. In contrast, if a similar other is better-off on a self-relevant dimension, then one's own self-evaluation may be decreased. A number of studies support these assertions (see Nadler & Fisher, 1986; Tesser, 1988 for reviews). Evidence that people are more threatened by upward comparisons with competitors than noncompetitors (cf. Brickman & Bulman, 1977; Mettee & Smith, 1977) may also be interpreted within this framework. When one is competing with another, the dimension in which they are competing becomes self-relevant by virtue of the competitive situation.

A similar analysis may be made of the impact of downward comparisons. Downward comparisons with similar others on dimensions irrelevant to the self should have less impact on the self than downward comparisons on dimensions relevant to the self. For example, if one does not care about one's mechanical skills, discovering that someone else's mechanical skills are worse than one's own should have relatively little impact on one's affective state. Self-relevance may, however, be less influential in predicting responses to downward comparisons than to upward comparisons (Pleban & Tesser, 1981).

Perceived Control over Comparison Discrepancies

We propose that an individual's responses to social comparison information are determined not only by the extent to which the comparison is appraised as esteem-relevant, but also by the extent to which the comparer perceives control over his or her standing relative to the comparison other on the comparison dimension. The degree of perceived control comparers feel they have over their status vis-à-vis a comparison other alters the meaning and significance of the comparison information and hence responses to it. Again adapting the coping framework of Lazarus and Folkman (1984), we propose that the direction of esteem-relevant comparisons and perceived control over comparison discrepancies influence the *secondary appraisal process*, that is, the comparer's assessment of his or her coping resources and options, and his or her subsequent responses.

Although the issue of control has played a central role in theories of coping with victimization and negative life events (cf. Abramson, Seligman & Teasdale, 1978; Bulman & Wortman, 1977; Lazarus & Folkman, 1984), it has not been integrated into the literature on social comparison processes. Several prior theorists have noted the importance of perceived control for understanding comparison processes. Wills (1981) noted that "Downward comparison theory addresses situations in which frustration or misfortune has occurred that is difficult to remedy through instrumental action" (p. 245), in other words, situations in which perceived control is low. Crosby (1976) and Singer (1981) noted that the effects of relative deprivation or inequity are mediated by the extent to which a comparer perceives personal control over his or her outcomes. Crosby speculates that stress symptoms result when a relatively deprived person either has low personal control or has high personal control but perceives his opportunities to attain a desired outcome as blocked. In contrast, self-improvement efforts result when a person perceives both high personal control and open opportunities. Also relevant is Nadler and Fisher's (1986) model of recipient's reactions to help. They argue that when an individual receives help from an another, an implied upward comparison has occurred. Furthermore, how the recipient responds depends on the interaction of self-threat and perceived control. Perceived control is defined in their framework as whether or not the recipient expects to have control over subsequent outcomes. They propose that controllable self-threat elicits short-term psychological distress (e.g., negative affect, unfavorable self- and other-evaluations) but instrumental behavioral responses. In contrast, uncontrollable self-threat is proposed to elicit a cluster of negative affective reactions and to lead to continued dependency over time.

Determinants of Perceived Control over Comparison Discrepancies. Within our framework, two types of expectancies contribute to perceived control over ones' standing relative to a comparison other. The first is the comparer's expectancy regarding the degree to which the standing relative to the comparison other is alterable, by anyone. Comparisons on some dimensions may be seen as relatively changeable (e.g., ones' health or tennis playing might improve or deteriorate). Comparisons along other dimensions may be seen as relatively stable and hence unlikely to change (e.g., discrepancies in intelligence or beauty). In addition, some comparison dimensions may be seen as under the control of external agents (e.g., wages) and hence relatively unalterable. These perceptions of the general alterability or stability of a comparison dimension are similar to what Bandura (1977) has termed "outcome expectancies." The second type of expectancy that contributes to perceived control over comparison discrepancies is the comparer's expectancy regarding the ability to successfully execute the behaviors required to elevate or maintain standing relative to the comparison other. Even though a comparer might feel it is possible to earn as high a salary as a comparison other (i.e., that the dimension is alterable), the comparer might not feel personally able to perform the behaviors necessary to do so. This type of expectancy is similar to what Bandura (1977) has called an "efficacy expectancy."

Both types of control-related expectancies can be affected by the nature of the dimension being evaluated, particular features of the situation, and individual difference factors. Although there is evidence that most people maintain the belief that they have control over their outcomes (cf. Alloy & Abramson, 1979; 1982; Langer, 1977), some dimensions of comparison are generally regarded as more or less alterable and personally controllable than others. Changes in effort, persistence, practice, and coping efforts are typically seen as more under one's personal control than are changes in abilities, personality characteristics, disease state, or outcomes such as pay. Some situations allow for the possibility of change and/or evoke greater feelings of control than do others. For example, some laboratory situations provide the possibility of future improvement or explicit guidelines for future improvement, and hence suggest the possibility that one's position relative to a comparison other might change and that one can exert control over this change (cf. Nadler, Ben-Itzhak, & Fisher, 1983; Testa & Major, 1990). Others provide no opportunities for improvement or change (e.g., Pleban & Tesser, 1981; Tesser & Paulhus, 1983). Individuals also differ in the degree to which they expect to have control and in the degree to which they expect things to improve. While the up and coming young executive may feel capable of increasing his status and salary, and hence find upward pay comparisons inspirational, the middle-aged or minority worker may feel incapable of improving his situation and hence find such comparisons demoralizing. Individual difference factors that may be especially influential in determining responses to upward comparisons include self-esteem, depression, optimism–pessimism, and locus of control. People who are high in self-esteem, nondepressive, optimistic, or who have an internal locus of control may chronically have more positive expectancies and perceive greater control over their environment than do those who are low in self-esteem, depressed, pessimistic, or who have an external locus of control.

Perceived Control and Responses to Social Comparisons. Perceived control over comparison discrepancies alters the meaning and significance of these discrepancies and the comparer's responses to them. Applying Lazarus and Folkman's (1984) framework, in the case of an esteem-relevant upward comparison, if the comparer perceives this threat as alterable and personally controllable, *problem-focussed coping efforts* (i.e., management of the problem that is causing distress) are more likely. In contrast, when the comparer perceives the threat engendered by upward comparison as unalterable and/or not personally controllable, *emotion-focussed coping efforts* (i.e., regulation of the emotional distress) are more likely (Folkman, 1984). Likewise, in the case of an esteem-relevant downward comparison, if the comparer feels that the position of advantage relative to another in the future is potentially changeable and that one has no control over this change (e.g., "There but for the grace of God, go I."), downward comparisons will be appraised as threatening and increases in perceptions of vulnerability and decreases in subjective well-being will occur. Under these conditions the individual may fear that the negative event that has befallen the comparison other may befall the self as well and engage in emotion-focussed strategies designed to reduce perceived vulnerability.

When an esteem-relevant upward comparison occurs, the perception that one is unable to alter one's inferior status, either because the dimension is unchangeable, is under the control of some external agent, or because one is personally unable to execute the behaviors necessary to alter one's status, implies that positive outcomes on self-relevant dimensions are attainable for similar others, but not for the self. If the comparer feels that nothing can be done to alter the discrepancy, either by oneself or anyone else, feelings of universal helplessness may result, accompanied by affective, cognitive, and motivational deficits (Abramson, Seligman, & Teasdale, 1978). If the comparer makes an internal attribution (blames oneself) for the inferior (and unchangeable) standing relative to the comparison other, the discrepancy is likely to be particularly threatening and debilitating, and feelings of personal helplessness may result, accompanied by lowered self-esteem as well as affective, cognitive, and motivational deficits (Abramson et al., 1978). Esteem-relevant upward social comparisons that are perceived as unchangeable and attributed to the influence of an external agent are particularly likely to lead to anger (Weiner, 1986) and to externally oriented change efforts such as aggression (cf. Crosby, 1976). In contrast, esteem-relevant upward comparisons that are accompanied by the belief that one's relative position is changeable and that one can personally control this change imply to the comparer that one may achieve better outcomes or better performance. Hence, upward comparisons paired with high perceived control over the ability to alter one's relative standing are apt to increase self-efficacy and inspire and motivate performance rather than induce helplessness or anger.

Perceived control over one's relative standing also affects the secondary appraisal of esteem-relevant downward social comparisons and hence their meaning and significance. The extent to which the comparer feels what will happen in the future is controllable with regard to the comparison dimension is particularly important. Downward comparisons with similar others on self-relevant dimensions may enhance positive affect when the comparer feels the position of relative advantage can be maintained, either because the dimension of comparison is relatively stable or because there is personal control over change on the dimension of comparison. For example, comparing one's own publication rate with that of a close but less prolific colleague may increase subjective well-being as long as one believes that one's own higher productivity is likely to continue, either because the comparison discrepancy is stable (e.g., is due to differences in intelligence) or is due to factors under one's personal control (e.g., effort). Enhanced self-esteem and pride are particularly likely to occur when the comparer makes an internal attribution for relative superiority (Weiner, 1986).

In contrast, esteem-relevant downward comparisons are likely to be threatening and increase perceptions of personal vulnerability when the comparer feels there is little control over whether the relative position on the dimension changes. For the cancer victim who feels little control over whether his or her condition improves or deteriorates, comparisons with worse-off others are likely to be frightening rather than esteem-enhancing. Brickman and Bulman (1977) were the first to suggest that downward comparisons might have painful affective consequences. They described the impact of interviews with paraplegics and quadriplegics on the second author's own perceptions of vulnerability. Rather than make her feel good that she was in better health, she instead felt vulnerable and fearful that such a random negative event might befall her as well. This notion has also been discussed by Coates and Winston (1983) who claim that support groups may have a negative impact when they lead cancer patients to learn through talking to others that cancer might return, or lead rape victims to fear that rape might happen again. Wood, Taylor, and Lichtman (1985) also found that for a certain group of breast cancer patients downward comparisons were threatening because they suggested that things could get worse. Freak accidents, cancer, and rape are all relatively uncontrollable occurrences that could happen to anyone, hence downward comparisons on these dimensions would be more likely to have esteem-threatening consequences.

Learning that similar others have experienced misfortune is threatening because it implies that the self is vulnerable to similar negative outcomes (Coates, Wortman & Abbey, 1979). Individuals may deemphasize the similarity between themselves and the less fortunate comparison other in order to render the information less threatening. Cook and Curtin (1987) claim that members of the mainstream in society derogate and emphasize their dissimilarity to the underclass in an attempt to justify their unequal status, prevent feelings of guilt, and to make the possibility of poverty seem unlikely. Lerner and Miller (1976) review considerable evidence that the occurrence of apparently random negative events is threatening and results in attempts to restore faith in a just world by blaming and derogating the victim. People also may avoid interactions with less fortunate others such as cancer patients (e.g. Wortman & Dunkel-Schetter, 1980), even if they are victims themselves (e.g., Molleman, Pruyn & van Knippenberg, 1986), as a way of reducing the threat such uncontrollable comparisons imply. Downward comparisons accompanied by attributions to uncontrollable factors are also likely to evoke pity for the comparison other (Weiner, 1986).

We have proposed that individuals' reactions to information that another is better-off or worse-off than themselves are determined by: (a) the degree to which the comparison is appraised as esteem-relevant, and (b) the amount of perceived control comparers feel they have over maintaining or changing their relative standing on the comparison dimension. If an upward comparison is appraised as esteem-relevant, the degree to which the comparer feels that the relative status on the comparison dimension is changeable and can be controlled affects the appraisal of the threat and responses to it. Similarly, if a downward comparison is appraised as esteem-relevant, assessments of changeability and personal control over the comparison discrepancy are critical determinants of the comparer's response. In the following sections we review research on the consequences of upward and downward social comparisons within the framework outlined. Because perceived control has been explicitly manipulated or measured in only a few of these studies, in our following discussion we have inferred the probable degree of control comparers perceived over change in their relative standing in each study described.

REVIEW OF RELEVANT RESEARCH

When Upward Comparisons Hurt or Downward Comparisons Help. Many studies demonstrating the negative consequences of upward social comparisons or the beneficial consequences of downward comparisons have measured affective responses and have employed designs which provide the comparer with little sense that the individual's position relative to the comparison other is changeable. In many laboratory studies, individuals are informed that their performances or outcomes are better or worse than those of a partner. They are then given no second chance for their relative performances or outcomes to improve or deteriorate. Individuals in these studies should perceive little likelihood that their position relative to the comparison other will change on the dimension of comparison. Other studies have assessed responses to comparison dimensions that are relatively immutable (e.g., physical attractiveness). In these types of situations or with these dimensions, individuals exposed to upward comparisons should feel it is unlikely that they will be better-off, or as good as, the comparison other, whereas those exposed to downward comparisons should feel it is unlikely than they will be worse-off, or as bad as, the comparison other.

When esteem-relevant upward comparisons occur under these conditions, we would expect the comparer to engage in self-directed responses such as more negative affect and lowered self-esteem, and/or to engage in a variety of dimension-directed and comparison other-directed responses designed to maintain self-esteem. Examples include devaluing the dimension of comparison or distancing oneself from or derogating the comparison other. When esteem-relevant downward comparisons occur under these conditions, we would expect the comparer to engage in self-directed responses such as more positive affect and elevated self-esteem, and/or to engage in responses designed to enhance self-esteem, such as valuing the dimension of comparison and seeking further (downward) comparison information. Unfortunately, as most of the studies reviewed did not incorporate a control condition in which no comparison information was provided, these studies can inform us only about the relative consequences of upward versus downward comparisons.

Several studies using an experimental design in which no change in standing relative to the comparison other was possible have been conducted by Tesser and his colleagues. In general, these studies indicate that unalterable, esteem-relevant upward comparisons are threatening for the self. For example, Pleban & Tesser (1981) found that after an esteem-relevant upward comparison with a confederate, participants sat further way from the confederate, indicated less desire to work with the confederate in the future and rated the confederate as generally more dissimilar to themselves than did participants who had performed better than their competitor. Similarly, Tesser and Paulhus (1983) found that when subjects performed worse than a partner, they rated the comparison ability as less self-relevant than when they had performed better than their partner, especially if the partner had been described as similar. In addition, Tesser, Millar and Moore (1988, Experiment 3) found that subjects displayed more negative affect if a friend did better than themselves on a self-relevant dimension than if a friend did worse on a self-relevant dimension. Results of a study by Salovey and Rodin (1984) also are consistent with the hypothesis that esteem-threatening upward comparisons that are unchangeable generate negative affect and distancing from the comparison other. Subjects who were informed that another student had performed better than they on a self-relevant dimension reported more envy, jealousy, depression, and anxiety, and disparaged the comparison other more, than did subjects in any other condition.

Another response to upward comparisons that are perceived as unchangeable is to avoid additional threatening information or to seek self-enhancing comparison information. For example, Hakmiller (1966) found that most subjects wanted to see the score of someone whom they believed scored even worse than they on a measure of hostility toward one's parents. Similarly, Pyszczynski, Greenberg and LaPrelle (1985) found that students who had been told they performed poorly on a social sensitivity test requested more comparison information when they expected it (the test) to reveal that they had performed better than most. They requested less information when they expected it to show they had performed more poorly than most. Testa and Major (1990) showed this same pattern, but only among subjects who believed that they could not improve upon (change) their initially poor performance.

Physical appearance is a comparison dimension likely to be perceived as relatively unchangeable. Two studies have examined the relative impact of appearance-related upward versus downward comparisons on self-evaluations. Cash, Cash and Butters (1983) found that women exposed to upward comparisons (i.e., who were asked to rate pictures of attractive others) rated themselves as less attractive than did women who were exposed to downward comparisons (i.e., who were asked to rate pictures of unattractive women). Morse and Gergen's (1970) classic "Mr. Clean, Mr. Dirty" study also showed the negative impact of appearance-related upward comparisons compared to downward comparisons on self-evaluations. Participants in this study experienced a significant decrease in self-esteem after encountering the well-groomed and self-confident "Mr. Clean" on a job interview and an increase in self-esteem after encountering the dazed and inappropriately dressed "Mr. Dirty."

Several field studies also provide suggestive evidence that greater exposure to better-off others relative to worse-off others can have detrimental effects on aspects of the self-concept. Davis (1966) found that compared to similarly qualified students at small, less prestigious colleges, students in large, prestigious colleges had lower career aspirations, presumably because the latter were "small fish in a big pond" rather than "big fish in a small pond." Marsh and Parker (1984) found that students attending schools which had a high average socioeconomic status had lower academic self-concepts than did students attending poorer schools.

Other recent studies suggest that individuals differ in their affective response to upward versus downward social comparisons. Crocker and Gallo (1985) found that low self-esteem subjects who failed exhibited more positive mood and greater life satisfaction if they subsequently engaged in downward comparisons (i.e., listed groups they were glad they were not a member of) as opposed to upward comparisons (i.e., listed groups they wished they were a member of). In contrast, high self-esteem subjects who failed exhibited higher subjective well-being if they made upward rather than downward comparisons. We would interpret these results as suggesting that high self-esteem subjects had higher perceived control and/or more optimistic outlooks and thus were more likely than low self-esteem subjects to perceive that they could become members of desired groups. Gibbons (1986) found that exposure to downward comparisons (negative personal stories written by other college students) elevated the mood of depressed but not nondepressed students. Thus, these studies provide some evidence for the relatively self-enhancing effects of downward comparisons but only among subjects who are low in self-esteem or depressed.

In each of the studies mentioned we assumed that comparers perceived little control over, or ability to change, their standing on the relevant comparison dimension, either because they had no opportunity to perform the task again, were given no instructions as to how they might improve, or perceived the dimension as relatively immutable (e.g., beauty, intelligence). In Morse and Gergen's (1970) study, although the comparison dimension (grooming) was not uncontrollable, the job applicants participating in this study clearly could not alter their relative appearance prior to their interview. Thus, it is reasonable to assume that these job-seekers perceived their status relative to the comparison other as unchangeable. Collectively, these studies suggest that when people perceive little likelihood of changing their standing relative to the comparison other, they respond to esteem-relevant upward versus downward comparisons with more negative affect and lowered self-evaluations and/or by engaging in dimension- or comparison-directed self-evaluation maintenance strategies. Our assumption that people perceived little control in these studies, however, is clearly post hoc. Only two studies have directly examined the impact of high and low perceived control on the consequences of upward or downward comparison information (Nadler, Ben-Itzhak, & Fisher, 1983; Testa & Major, 1990). These studies are unique in that they measured behavioral as well as affective responses to comparisons.

Participants in Testa and Major's (1990) study experienced an initial failure on an essay-writing task and were then exposed to either upward or downward social comparison information. Participants were also led to believe that it was either possible (high control) or impossible (low control) for them to improve (change) their performance on a second test. Results revealed that individuals who believed they had little control and who were exposed to upward comparisons exhibited greater depressive and hostile affect and less persistence on a subsequent task than did subjects in all other conditions. In contrast, individuals who were exposed to upward comparisons but who believed it was possible to improve exhibited affective and behavioral responses comparable to individuals exposed to downward comparisons. There were no differences in affect or persistence among individuals exposed to downward comparison information according to whether they believed or did not believe they could improve. Results of this study are consistent with our hypothesis that upward comparisons are more affectively distressing and behaviorally debilitating than downward comparisons only when people feel they have little possibility of changing their (inferior) status.

The impact of perceived control on reactions to upward comparisons also was examined by Nadler, Ben-Itzhak, & Fisher (1983) in an experiment on recipients' reactions to aid. They argue that receiving aid is a form of upward comparison since it implies that someone else is more competent or better-off than the self. In their experiment, subjects who initially performed poorly on an ego-relevant task subsequently received help from either a friend or a stranger. In addition, subjects were either given specific suggestions for how to improve on a subsequent task (high control) or no suggestions for future improvement (low control). Subjects engaged in the most self-help (expended the most effort preparing for the impending task) when they received help from a friend (esteem-threatening comparison) and believed that there were things they could do to improve their performance. The most negative affect and least liking for the helper was displayed by subjects who received help from a friend but who received no suggestions for how to improve. This latter group of subjects also attributed their poor performance more to lack of ability than did subjects in other conditions. Thus, results of this study are consistent with those of Testa and Major in suggesting that esteem-relevant upward comparisons are affectively distressing only when the perceived possibility of improving one's inferior status is low. This study suggests that esteem-relevant upward comparisons paired with high perceived control lead to increased attempts to improve performance.

When Upward Comparisons Help and Downward Comparisons Hurt. The studies reviewed demonstrate the expected finding that upward comparisons are bad for the self, e.g., more esteem-threatening and downward comparisons are good for the self, e.g., more esteem-enhancing. A small but growing body of research, however, suggests that this is not always the case. Studies which have demonstrated the positive benefits of upward comparisons have, for the most part, examined behavioral rather than affective responses. Furthermore, these studies have employed dimensions which were either implicitly or explicitly perceived as more under ones personal control or ability to change (e.g., coping efforts).

Bandura and his colleagues have conducted a number of studies with people attempting to change problem behaviors (e.g., phobias, smoking). By seeking treatment, these individuals at least implicitly believe that their behavior is changeable. Results of these studies indicate that exposure to positive models who are successfully performing the desired behavior (upward comparisons) increases self-efficacy and leads to behavioral improvement (e.g., Bandura, Adams & Beyer, 1977; Bandura, Reese & Adams, 1982). Models who are perceived as more similar to the self have a stronger and more positive impact than do models who are less similar (e.g., Meichenbaum, 1971; Schunk & Hanson, 1985). Meichenbaum found that snake phobics who are exposed to coping models (people who also were afraid of snakes but who overcame their fear) showed less fear, more self-efficacy, and greater approach behavior than did phobics exposed to mastery models (people who had no fear at all). A similar beneficial effect of exposure to positive models was found by Zastowny, Kirschenbaum and Meng (1986) with children facing surgery. Children exposed to similar models (peers) using effective coping strategies exhibited fewer maladaptive behaviors before, during, and after surgery than did children in a control group or in an anxiety reduction treatment group.

Seta (1982) also observed the beneficial behavioral consequences of upward comparisons when subjects are given an opportunity to perform over several trials. In his first study, subjects performed a pattern recognition task in the presence of a coactor whose performance was inferior, identical, or slightly superior to the subject's. Subjects who participated with a slightly superior coactor showed superior performance relative to those working with either an identical or inferior other. In a second study, subjects participated either alone or with a coactor whose performance was either inferior, identical, or either slightly, moderately, or very superior to the subject. Subjects who participated with a moderately superior other exhibited the best performance of all the groups.

Whereas these studies demonstrated the beneficial effects of exposure to successful models (upward comparisons), Brown and Inouye (1978) demonstrated the detrimental effects of exposure to failing models (downward comparisons) on self-efficacy expectations and task persistence. Subjects in their study were led to believe that they were either similar to or more competent than a same-gender coworker (a confederate), or were given no similarity feedback about the confederate. Subjects in these conditions then watched the confederate fail at an anagram task prior to doing the task themselves. Subjects in a fourth control group were not exposed to an unsuccessful model. Results revealed that subjects who believed they were similar to the confederate had lower performance expectations and persisted less on the subsequent task than did subjects in other conditions.

Collectively, the research reviewed suggests the beneficial consequences of exposure to upward comparisons, especially with similar others, in situations where improved performance is perceived as possible. Under these conditions upward comparisons raise perceptions of self-efficacy and motivate task persistence. Exposure to downward comparisons with similar others under these conditions, in contrast, lowers perceptions of self-efficacy and inhibits subsequent performance. These effects occur, we argue, because social comparisons with similar others in situations where change is possible provide information about what might and can occur for the self. Seeing similar others succeed or cope successfully with a problem transmits the belief that "If she can do it, I can do it too,"; seeing similar others fail or cope unsuccessfully conveys the belief that "What happened to him can happen to me as well."

The research reviewed focused on the cognitive and behavioral consequences of upward and downward comparisons in situations where change in one's status is possible. A study by Collins, Taylor, and Dakof (1989) demonstrates that downward comparisons may also have a negative influence on affective responses when perceived control is low. They examined the correlation between belief that coping with cancer was controllable and negative affect following downward comparison. They found a negative correlation such that those patients who believed they had little control over the course of their disease experienced more negative affect following exposure to downward comparison information about other cancer patients than did those who believed they had more control. The correlation between perceived control and affect, however, was not significant among those patients exposed to upward comparisons.

In the only studies to directly demonstrate more positive affective responses to upward than downward comparisons, the dimension of comparison was potentially changeable and under personal control. Taylor, Aspinwall, Dakof & Reardon (1989) exposed distressed individuals to either positive or negative stories about others suffering from similar problems. Their first study revealed that cancer patients rated stories about other cancer patients who were coping successfully as being more helpful than stories about cancer patients who were not coping well. Their second study revealed that stressed college students rated stories about other students who were coping successfully with their problems as more helpful than stories about college students who were not coping well. In addition, students felt happier and less depressed after exposure to upward comparisons (positive stories) than after exposure to downward comparisons (negative stories). Unfortunately, neither study contained a control condition in which subjects received no comparison information. Thus, it is impossible to determine whether the differences observed were the result of elevated affect in the upward condition or depressed affect in the downward condition.

SUMMARY AND CONCLUSIONS

In the current chapter we have outlined a framework for predicting when upward versus downward social comparisons will have beneficial versus detrimental effects for the comparer and have reviewed a number of studies within this framework. We have proposed that perceived similarity or closeness between self and comparison other, self-relevance or importance of the comparison dimension, the perceived changeability of the comparison dimension and the degree of personal control comparers perceive over changing or maintaining the comparison discrepancy are important determinants of how individuals respond to social comparisons. Comparisons with similar others on self-relevant dimensions are most esteem-relevant, and hence have the most potential to be either esteem-threatening or esteem-enhancing. We further propose that how individuals respond to esteem-relevant social comparisons is determined by the degree to which they perceive change or maintenance of their relative position as possible and controllable.

Upward social comparisons produce a variety of responses indicative of threats to self-esteem when individuals perceive that their inferior standing relative to a close comparison other on an important comparison dimension is unlikely to change. These responses include: more negative affect, lowered self-evaluations, increased attributions to lack of ability, distancing from or derogation of the comparison other, diminished self-relevance of the comparison dimension, avoidance of additional upward comparison information, and decreased self-help. This pattern of results is consistent with the self-evaluation maintenance model proposed by Tesser and his colleagues, and with the affective, cognitive, and motivational deficits postulated by learned helplessness theory.

In contrast, when individuals believe their inferior status on the comparison dimension is potentially changeable and that they have control over this change, upward comparisons with similar others have been shown to produce higher self-efficacy expectations and positive behavioral consequences, including increased persistence and better performance. Under these conditions, it is inspiring to learn that others who are like oneself are doing well since this suggests that it may be possible for the self to achieve these positive outcomes, too. Individuals who learn that a similar other has better performance or outcomes than themselves and who believe that they have the ability to change their relative standing may also be more likely to attribute their poorer standing to internal temporary causes such as lack of effort or inadequate preparation. Such attributions have been linked to improved performance on subsequent tasks (e.g., Dweck & Repucci, 1973). The nature of affective responses to upward comparisons on controllable dimensions is less clear. Although Nadler and Fisher (1986) speculate that the immediate affective response to such comparisons is negative, recent research suggests that the affective reaction to upward comparisons under conditions of perceived control is comparable to (Testa & Major, 1990) or more positive than (Taylor et al., 1989) reactions to downward comparisons.

Responses to downward comparisons with similar others on self-relevant dimensions also are determined by the extent to which people believe they have control over maintaining their advantaged status relative to the comparison other. When one is better-off than another and perceives that, due either to the nature of the situation or the perceived controllability of the dimension of comparison one will continue to enjoy this state, responses indicative of enhanced well-being occur. These responses include increased positive affect, elevated self-evaluations, greater satisfaction with one's outcomes, and increased self-relevance of the comparison dimension. These results are compatible with Wills (1981) hypothesis that "people can increase their subjective well-being through comparisons with a less fortunate other." In contrast, we have argued that downward comparisons with similar others increase perceptions of vulnerability when they are accompanied by little perceived control over the maintenance of one's relatively advantaged status. Downward comparisons under these conditions are threatening to self-esteem and evoke attempts to maintain self-esteem. Responses include more negative affect, lowered self-efficacy, decreased task persistence, enhancing the dissimilarities between self and comparison other, derogating the comparison other, and avoiding the comparison other.

Although our review has focused primarily on responses to social comparisons about abilities or performances, we believe that a similar framework can be fruitfully applied to social comparisons of other types of attributes, such as pay. A careful consideration of the influence of esteem-relevance of the attribute and perceived control over comparison discrepancies may help to refine when feelings of relative deprivation or inequity distress will and will not result from relative discrepancies in perceived inputs and outcomes. The framework we have outlined also helps to clarify previous inconsistencies in the literature on responses to social comparison information and highlights areas where further research is needed, such as research on affective reactions to controllable upward comparisons, and cognitive and behavioral responses to downward comparisons. In addition, since few studies have included a no comparison control condition, the absolute rather than relative impact of upward versus downward comparisons is as yet undetermined.

Finally, although a number of studies are consistent with the framework presented in this chapter, it must still regarded as speculative until confirmed by direct tests. Nevertheless, the bulk of the evidence reviewed here illustrates that answers to the question: "Which is better: upward or downward comparisons?" depend on comparers' assessment of the extent to which comparison discrepancies are changeable and controllable.

REFERENCES

Abramson, L. Y., Seligman, M. E. P., & Teasdale, J. D. (1978). Learned helplessness in humans: Critique and reformulation. *Journal of Abnormal Psychology, 87,* 49–74.

Alloy, L. B., & Abramson, L. Y. (1979). Judgment of contingency in depressed and nondepressed students: Sadder but wiser? *Journal of Experimental Psychology: General, 108,* 441–485.
Alloy, L. B., & Abramson, L. Y. (1982). Learned helplessness, depression, and the illusion of control. *Journal of Personality and Social Psychology, 42,* 1114–1126.
Bandura, A. (1977). Self-efficacy: Toward a unifying theory of behavioral change. *Psychological Review, 89,* 191–215.
Bandura, A. (1986). *Social foundations of thought and action: A social cognitive theory.* Englewood Cliffs, NJ: Prentice-Hall.
Bandura, A., Adams, N. E., & Beyer, J. (1977). Cognitive processes mediating behavioral change. *Journal of Personality and Social Psychology, 35,* 125–139.
Bandura, A., Reese, L., & Adams, N. E. (1982). Microanalysis of action and fear arousal as a function of differential levels of self-efficacy. *Journal of Personality and Social Psychology, 43,* 5–21.
Brickman, P., & Bulman, R. J. (1977). Pleasure and pain in social comparison. In J. M. Suls, & R. L. Miller (Eds.), *Social comparison processes: Theoretical and empirical perspectives* (pp. 149–186) Washington, DC: Hemisphere.
Brown, I., Jr., & Inouye, D. K. (1978). Learned helplessness through modeling: The role of perceived similarity in competence. *Journal of Personality and Social Psychology, 36,* 900–908.
Bulman, R. J., & Wortman, C. B. (1977). Attributions of blame and coping in the "real world": Severe accident victims react to their lot. *Journal of Personality and Social Psychology, 35,* 351–363.
Bylsma, W. H., Major, B., & Cozzarelli, C. (1990). Group differences in personal entitlement: The impact of social comparisons and procedural fairness. Manuscript under review.
Cash, T. F., Cash, D. W., & Butters, J. W. (1983). "Mirror, mirror, on the wall . . . ?": Contrast effects and self-evaluations of physical attractiveness. *Personality and Social Psychology Bulletin, 9,* 351–358.
Coates, D., & Winston, T. (1983). Counteracting the deviance of depression: Peer support groups for victims. *Journal of Social Issues, 39,* 169–194.
Coates, D., Wortman, C. B., & Abbey, A. (1979). Reactions to victims. In I. H. Frieze, D. Bar-Tal, & J. S. Carroll (Eds.), *New approaches to social problems* (pp. 21–52). San Francisco, CA: Jossey-Bass.
Collins, R. L., Taylor, S. E., & Dakof, G. A. (1989). *The affective consequences of social comparison: Either direction has its ups and downs.* Unpublished Manuscript.
Cook, T. D., & Curtin, T. R. (1987). The mainstream and the underclass: Why are the differences so salient and the similarities so unobtrusive? In J. C. Masters & W. P. Smith (Eds.), *Social comparison, social justice, and relative deprivation* (pp. 217–264). Hillsdale, NJ: Lawrence Erlbaum Associates.
Crocker, J., & Gallo, L. (1985, August). The self-enhancing effect of downward comparison. In T. A. Wills (Chair), *Self-esteem maintenance: Theory and evidence.* Symposium conducted at the meeting of the *American Psychological Association,* Los Angeles, CA.
Crosby, F. (1976). A model of egoistical relative deprivation. *Psychological Review, 83,* 84–113.
Davis, J. A. (1966). The campus as a frog pond: An application of the theory of relative deprivation to career decisions of college men. *American Journal of Sociology, 72,* 17–31.
DeVellis, R. F., DeVellis, B. M., & McCauley, C. (1978). Vicarious acquisition of learned helplessness. *Journal of Personality and Social Psychology, 36,* 894–899.
Dweck, C. S., & Repucci, N. D. (1973). Learned helplessness and reinforcement responsibility in children. *Journal of Personality and Social Psychology, 25,* 109–116.

Festinger, L. (1954). A theory of social comparison processes, *Human Relations*, 7, 117–140.
Folkman, S. (1984). Personal control and stress and coping processes: A theoretical analysis. *Journal of Personality and Social Psychology*, 46, 839–852.
Folkman, S., & Lazarus, R. S. (1980). An analysis of coping in a middle-aged community sample. *Journal of Health and Social Behavior*, 21, 219–239.
Friend, R. M., & Gilbert, J. (1973). Threat and fear of negative evaluation as determinants of locus of social comparison. *Journal of Personality*, 41, 328–340.
Gibbons, F. X. (1986). Social comparison and depression: Company's effect on misery. *Journal of Personality and Social Psychology*, 51, 140–148.
Hakmiller, K. L. (1966). Threat as a determinant of downward comparison. *Journal of Experimental Social Psychology*, (Suppl. 1), 32–39.
Langer, E. J. (1977). The psychology of chance. *Journal for the Theory of Social Behavior*, 7, 185–208.
Lazarus, R. S., & Folkman, S. (1984). *Stress, appraisal, and coping*. New York: Springer.
Lerner, M. J., & Miller, D. T. (1976). Just world research and the attribution process: Looking back and ahead. *Psychological Bulletin*, 85, 1030–1051.
Mark, M. A., & Folger, F. (1984). Responses to relative deprivation: A conceptual framework. In P. Shaver (Ed.), *Review of personality and social psychology*, (Vol. 5, pp. 192–218). Beverly Hills, CA: Sage.
Marsh, H. W., & Parker, J. W. (1984). Determinants of students' self-concept: Is it better to be a relatively large fish in a small pond even if you don't learn to swim as well? *Journal of Personality and Social Psychology*, 47, 213–231.
Martin, J. (1986). Tolerance of Injustice. In J. M. Olson, C. P. Herman & M. P. Zanna (Eds.), *Relative Deprivation and Social Comparison: The Ontario Symposium* (Vol. 4, pp. 217–240). Hillsdale, NJ: Lawrence Erlbaum Associates.
Meichenbaum, D. H. (1971). Examination of model characteristics in reducing avoidance behavior. *Journal of Personality and Social Psychology*, 17, 298–307.
Mettee, D. R., & Smith, G. (1977). Social comparison and interpersonal attraction: The case for dissimilarity. In J. M. Suls & R. L. Miller (Eds.), *Social comparison processes: Theoretical and empirical perspectives* (pp. 69–101). Washington, DC: Hemisphere.
Miller, C. (1987). Social comparison and coping. Unpublished Manuscript. University of Vermont. Burlington.
Miller, D. T., Turnbull, W., & McFarland, C. (1988). Particularistic and universalistic evaluation in the social comparison process. *Journal of Personality and Social Psychology*, 55, 908–917.
Moleman, E., Pruyn, J., & van Knippenberg, A. (1986). Social comparison processes among cancer patients. *British Journal of Social Psychology*, 25, 1–13.
Morse, S., & Gergen, K. J. (1970). Social comparison, self-consistency, and the concept of self. *Journal of Personality and Social Psychology*, 40, 624–634.
Nadler, A., Ben-Itzhak, S. B., & Fisher, J. D. (1983). *Perceived control and threat to self-esteem as determinants of self-help*. Unpublished Manuscript. Tel-Aviv University. Tel-Aviv, Israel.
Nadler, A., & Fisher, J. D. (1986). The role of threat to self-esteem and perceived control in recipient reaction to help: Theory development and empirical validation. In L. Berkowitz (Ed.), *Advances in experimental social psychology*, (Vol. 19, pp. 81–121). Orlando, FL: Academic Press.
Pleban, R., & Tesser, A. (1981). The effects of relevance and quality of another's performance on interpersonal closeness. *Social Psychology Quarterly*, 44, 278–285.
Pyszczynski, T., Greenberg, J., & LaPrelle, J. (1985). Social comparison after success and failure: Biased search for information consistent with a self-serving conclusion. *Journal of Experimental Social Psychology*, 21, 195–211.

Salovey, P., & Rodin, J. (1984). Some antecedents and consequences of social comparison jealousy. *Journal of Personality and Social Psychology, 47*, 780–792.

Schunk, D. H., & Hanson, A. R. (1985). Peer models: Influence on children's self-efficacy and achievement. *Journal of Educational Psychology, 77*, 313–322.

Singer, E. (1981). Reference groups and social evaluations. In M. Rosenberg & R. H. Turner (Eds.), *Social psychology: Sociological perspectives*. (pp. 66–93). New York: Basic Books.

Seta, J. (1982). The impact of comparison processes on coactors' task performance. *Journal of Personality and Social Psychology, 42*, 281–291.

Suls, J. M., & Miller, R. L. (Eds.). (1977). *Social comparison processes: Theoretical and empirical perspectives*. Washington, DC: Hemisphere.

Taylor, S. E., Aspinwall, L. G., Dakof, G. A., & Reardon, K. K. (1989). *Storytelling, social comparison and social support: Reactions to stories of similar others undergoing stressful events*. Unpublished Manuscript, University of California, Los Angeles.

Taylor, S. E., Wood, J. V., & Lichtman, R. R. (1983). It could be worse: Selective evaluation as a response to victimization. *Journal of Social Issues, 39*, 19–40.

Tesser, A. (1988). Toward a self-evaluation maintenance model of social behavior. In L. Berkowitz (Ed.), *Advances in experimental social psychology*. (Vol. 21, pp. 181–227). San Diego, CA: Academic Press.

Tesser, A., & Campbell, J. (1983). Self-definition and self-evaluation maintenance. In J. Suls & A. G. Greenwald (Eds.), *Psychological perspectives on the self* (Vol. 2, pp. 1–31). Hillsdale, NJ: Lawrence Erlbaum Associates.

Tesser, A., Millar, M., & Moore, J. (1988). Some affective consequences of social comparison and reflection processes: The pain and pleasure of being close. *Journal of Personality and Social Psychology, 54*, 49–61.

Tesser, A., & Paulhus, D. (1983). The definition of self: Private and public self-evaluation strategies. *Journal of Personality and Social Psychology, 44*, 672–682.

Testa, M., & Major, B. (1990). The impact of social comparison after failure: The moderating effects of perceived control. *Basic and Applied Social Psychology, 11*, 205–218.

Walster, E., Walster, G. W., & Berscheid, E. (1978). *Equity: Theory and research*. Boston: Allyn & Bacon.

Weiner, B. (1986). Attribution, emotion, and action. In R. M. Sorrentino and E. T. Higgins (Eds.), *Handbook of motivation and cognition: Foundations of social behavior*, (pp. 281–312). New York: Guilford.

Wheeler, L., Shaver, K. G., Jones, R. A., Goethals, G. R., Cooper, J., Robinson, J. E., Gruder, C. L., Butzine, K. W. (1969). Factors determining choice of a comparison other. *Journal of Experimental Social Psychology, 5*, 219–232.

Wills, T. A. (1981). Downward comparison principles in social psychology. *Psychological Bulletin, 90*, 245–271.

Wills, T. A. (1987). Downward comparison as a coping mechanism. In C. R. Snyder, & C. E. Ford (Eds.), *Coping with negative life events: Clinical and social psychological perspectives* (pp. 243–267). New York: Plenum.

Wood, J. V. (1989). Theory and research concerning social comparisons of personal attributes. *Psychological Bulletin, 106*, 231–248.

Wood, J. V., Taylor, S. E., & Lichtman, R. R. (1985). Social comparison in adjustment to breast cancer. *Journal of Personality and Social Psychology, 49*, 1169–1183.

Wortman, C. B., & Dunkel-Schetter, C. (1979). Interpersonal relationships and cancer: A theoretical analysis. *Journal of Social Issues, 35*, 120–155.

Zanna, M. P., Goethals, G. R., & Hill, J. F. (1975). Evaluating a sex-related ability: Social comparison with similar others and standard setters. *Journal of Personality and Social Psychology, 11*, 86–93.

Zastowny, T. R., Kirschenbaum, D. S., & Meng, A. L. (1986). Coping skills training for children: Effects on distress before, during, and after hospitalization for surgery. *Health Psychology, 5*, 231–247.

10 Social Comparison Processes in Envy and Jealousy

Peter Salovey
Yale University

Although social comparison theory has inspired social psychological research for nearly four decades, until recently very little explicit attention has been paid to the emotional consequences of social comparison processes (but see Tesser, chapter 5, this volume). This neglect of the emotional consequences of comparison finds its roots in Festinger's (1954) predominant concern with the selection of comparison objects and the informative value of comparison feedback rather than its more affective repercussions. In the past, a fairly undifferentiated pleasant or unpleasant affect has been thought to accompany positive or negative comparisons (e.g., Brickman & Bulman's, 1977, "pleasure and pain" of social comparison), but the precise quality of these reactions has not been of primary concern. The only affective consequence of social comparison that has been focused upon systematically by investigators is change in self-evaluation, but not the specific emotions that accompany such appraisals.

Certain specific emotional states do, however, accompany social comparison. These are most likely to include what Ortony, Clore, and Collins (1988) labeled the *appreciation emotions* (e.g., admiration, awe, respect), the *reproach emotions* (e.g., contempt, disdain, indignation), and the *resentment emotions* (e.g., envy, jealousy). This chapter will focus on the resentment emotions, envy and jealousy in particular. I will describe first some of the ways in which envy and jealousy have been characterized and studied, argue for the usefulness of a situational rather than a dispositional or phenomenological perspective in understanding jealousy and envy, and then summarize some of the specific social comparison processes possibly underlying these states.

Envy and jealousy are emotions with cross-cultural, legendary significance. Even in the Old Testament jealousy played an important role in defining the relationship between humans and the Lord. In the Book of Genesis, it is written, "I am a jealous God," proclaiming that God would not tolerate the Israelites sharing their attention, praise, and trust with any other. Mark Twain (1938/1962) recognized the importance of such a blanket admonition for the Judeo–Christian ethic by noting, ". . . jealousy, do not forget it, keep it in mind. It is the key . . . all through history it is present and prominent. It is the blood and bone of His disposition, it is the basis of His character. How small a thing can wreck His composure and disorder his judgments if it touches the raw of His jealousy!" (p. 27). Twain is a bit tongue–in–cheek here; yet it is certainly true that jealousy is deeply ingrained in our culture. For relationships among humans, Ovid described jealousy as "the surest means of rekindling" tepid love, and we are all familiar with Shakespeare's metaphor of the green-eyed monster.

References to envy abound as well and have been compiled articulately by Sabini and Silver (1982). Cain murdered Abel because he believed that Abel's sacrifice would be more pleasing to God. An Islamic prophet is held to have said, "Envy devours faith as fire devours wood." And, St. Thomas Aquinas labeled envy as one of the seven deadly sins, so evil that it spawns other sins. Surprisingly, envy may be the only sin that has no pleasure associated with it (Fairlie, 1978; Wilson, et al., 1962).

The availability of wise quotations does not in itself justify the psychological study of a phenomenon. We need only consider the pervasiveness of these phenomena and the relative paucity of theoretically motivated investigations of them (Salovey & Rodin, 1989). Although social comparison theory has not been used explicitly to predict envious and jealous reactions to social situations, it may provide a useful framework from which to understand the available literature. Before turning to a view of envy and jealousy guided by social comparison theory, it may be helpful to contrast it with the other dominant perspectives in this area of study.

Envy and Jealousy as Dispositions, Feelings, and Situations

The investigation of envy and jealousy has been guided by several competing frameworks. The dispositional approach focuses especially on individual differences in the propensity to experience envy and jealousy. The phenomenological approach involves isolating the variables that define what an individual experiences and labels as envy and jealousy. A situational view emphasizes those aspects in the social environment that produce feelings labeled as envy or jealousy in most individuals. After reviewing some of the findings in each of these areas, I describe in more detail a situational view rooted in social comparison processes.

Semantic Roots. The word *jealous* is derived from the same Greek root as that for *zealous*, *zelos*. Zeal is the fervent devotion to and promoting of some person or object. Jealousy refers to the belief or suspicion that what has been promoted is in danger of being lost. *Envy* is derived from *invidere*, Latin for looking upon another with malice. In this sense, envy represents a desire for the possessions or attributes of another person in the context of a discontent with or begrudging of the other person for having such possessions or attributes (Bryson, 1977). By comparison, rivalry derives from the Latin *rivalus*, one who uses the same stream as you. Your rival is the person who competes for access to the same water supply as you do.

The Oxford English Dictionary reflects these classic roots by defining jealous as "troubled by the belief or suspicion or fear that the good which one desires to keep for oneself has been or may be diverted to another; resentful towards another on account of known or suspected rivalry." Envy is defined as feelings of "displeasure and ill-will at the superiority of (another person) in happiness, success, reputation, or the possession of anything desirable; to regard with discontent another's possession of some superior advantage which one would like to have for himself."

As is clear, envy and jealousy have been distinguished by the locus of possession of some desired attribute or relationship. When one possesses this quality or relationship and is concerned that it could be threatened by another, jealousy is said to result. Envy, on the other hand, is the term reserved for the begrudging of another's possession of an attribute or relationship that one would like to have for oneself. Surprisingly, common usage of these terms often ignores this distinction. Jealousy is sometimes used to describe both situations. For example, a movie reviewer might note that the theme of *Amadeus* is Salieri's intense jealousy of Mozart. Envy really is the more precise term. Later in this chapter, I will discuss why many interpersonal situations that result in jealousy also engender envy, possibly accounting for the confusion in usage.

Dispositional Conceptualizations. A dispositional approach to envy and jealousy argues that individuals differ in their sensitivity to envy- or jealousy-provoking situations and in their propensity to experience or at least report these emotions. A number of scales have been developed to measure such individual differences in the jealousy domain (e.g., Bringle, Roach, Andler, & Evenbeck, 1979; Buunk, 1978; Hupka & Bachelor, 1979; Mathes & Severa, 1981; Tipton, Benedictson, Mahoney, & Hartnett, 1978; White,

1981a). Surprisingly, little effort has been devoted to discovering stable individual differences in the propensity to experience envy or even in sensitivity to social comparison or competitiveness. The dominant approach among investigators within this framework has been to examine associations among propensity–to–experience jealousy scales and various personality characteristics such as self-esteem, attitudes toward women, arousability, and locus of control (for reviews see Bringle, 1981; Bringle & Buunk, 1985). The magnitude of these correlations has been fairly modest and, at times, surprisingly inconsistent, although some stable associations between jealousy and attitudes toward exclusivity, arousability, and sometimes self-esteem have been reported.

Phenomenological Conceptualizations. A phenomenological perspective deems it important to identify the specific thoughts and feelings that characterize an individual's experience of envy and jealousy. Investigators working within this paradigm have most commonly tried to establish differences in the feelings associated with envy versus jealousy. Results of such efforts have been somewhat inconsistent, underscoring the difficulties inherent in this perspective. In particular, studies of the experience of envy and jealousy in this tradition have been forced to rely on verbal self-reports, with all of their limitations. For example, envy and jealousy are more easily distinguished among verbally facile individuals than those with less ability to articulate the contents of introspection.

If envy and jealousy cannot be distinguished reliably on the basis of the feelings and thoughts they each evoke, perhaps a phenomenological perspective is not especially helpful to us. Theorists, however, have long held that jealousy and envy must be phenomenologically distinct. For example, Spielman (1971) proposed that jealousy is a stronger feeling state than envy because it involves more hate. Envy, it is claimed, is an unhappiness caused by feelings of inferiority rooted in possessions or attributes of another person that one would like to have for oneself. Jealousy is thought to be an apprehension and suspicion generated by the loss or potential loss of a highly valued possession of one's own. As another example, Gellert (1976) believed that jealousy could be reduced to the combination of anger and fear of abandonment, and that envy's "prime factors" are anger, sadness, and self-pity.

The empirical study of the phenomenology of envy and jealousy, and, especially their differentiation, has not yielded consistent results. In a pilot study for some of our work (Salovey & Rodin, 1986), we asked college students to list synonyms for the word *jealousy*. Seventy-four distinct terms were generated, and the most frequent were envy, coveting, and wanting. Other classes of terms included: (a) hate, anger, (b) hurt, deprivation, sadness, (c) rivalry, possessiveness, and (e) insecurity, low self-esteem, and self-blame. The range of synonyms generated probably reflects the great range of individual experiences of jealousy. More importantly, jealousy was often reported in conjunction with envy.

While studying the phenomenology of jealousy and envy in the laboratory (Salovey & Rodin, 1986), we found that subjects could reliably distinguish these two states on the basis of their prototypic eliciting conditions (threats to valued social relationships versus social comparison failures). However, both envy-provoking and jealousy-provoking situations generated similar affective reactions, mostly involving anger, sadness, and some anxiety. Specific feelings did not differentiate envy and jealousy. Rather, differences between jealousy and envy were better characterized by comparing the intensity of overall emotional reactions. When presented with either envy- or jealousy-provoking stimuli, subjects reported the same angry, sad, and anxious emotions, but, they reported more of these feelings for jealousy than for envy. Envy and jealousy, however, did not differ in terms of categorically different emotional reactions.

The finding that jealousy and envy result in a phenomenological state that differs in intensity rather than quality has not gone unchallenged. Parrott and Smith (1987) argued that it is just this intensity difference that obscures the ability to find categorical differences in the feelings associated with envy and jealousy. After equating the intensity of subjects' responses to experiences involving envy and jealousy, some distinguishing characteristics of the feelings associated with them emerged (e.g., jealousy involved fear, distrust, self-doubt and anxiety, but envy produced greater feelings of inferiority and guilt). Moreover, when subjects were asked to generate situations that produced strong envy or strong jealousy, other qualitative differences emerged. Jealousy was consistently experienced as more intense than envy (Smith, Kim, & Parrott, 1988), and unless these differences in intensity were controlled for, clear phenomenological distinctions between the two states were difficult to find.

Situational Conceptualizations. A situational perspective on jealousy and envy argues that these emotion terms can best be thought of as labels for particular situations or predicaments in which individuals find themselves, rather than as specific blends of feelings (Hupka, 1981, 1984). We have argued that the situational antecedents of envy and jealousy lend themselves easily to a traditional analysis involving a P–O–X triad in which P is the individual experiencing the emotional state, O is another person, and X is a third person or desired object (Salovey & Rodin, 1989).

As depicted in Fig. 10.1 (based on Bryson, 1977), jealousy, envy (and, for comparison, rivalry) can be discriminated on the basis of whether there is a previously established sentiment or unit relationship (Heider, 1958) between two elements in the triad. Jealousy is the consequence of P's belief

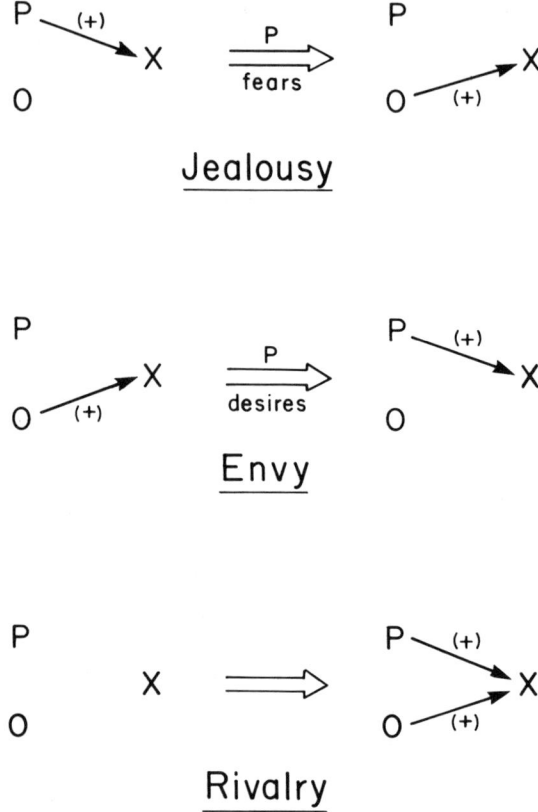

FIG. 10.1. The differentiation of jealousy, envy, and rivalry (after Bryson, 1977).

that his or her previously established unique relationship with X is threatened by real or imagined attempts between O and X to form an equivalent relationship. When O has a previously established relationship with X (and X can be a person, object, personal attribute, possession, etc.), attempts by P to replace O in that relationship with X and to denigrate the O–X relationship can be considered envy. Rivalry is simply the situation in which neither P nor O has a previous emotionally-based relationship with X but both desire one (Bryson, 1977). The elegance of such P–O–X definitions of envy and jealousy suggests that it might be especially useful to define jealousy and envy in terms of the situations that elicit these feelings rather than by specifically trying to clarify the feelings themselves.

Of course, situational antecedents to envy or jealousy may exert their power by interacting with intrapersonal variables. White's (1981b) model of romantic jealousy posits two kinds of potential losses that are necessary to trigger jealousy: loss of anticipated relationship rewards (a situational variable) and loss of self-esteem (an intrapersonal variable). Indeed, it appears that jealousy is triggered by both of these threats, and that individuals high in jealousy propensity may be especially sensitive to them (Mathes, Adams, & Davis, 1985).

Social comparison theory may provide a useful framework around which a situational approach to envy and jealousy might be integrated. Envy- or jealousy-provoking situations often involve esteem threatening comparisons with others. Traditionally, social comparison theory attempted to understand situations in which individuals deliberately seek comparison information as a source of self-knowledge (Festinger, 1954) or, in more recent versions of the theory, self-enhancement (Wills, 1981). The theory should also be useful in explicating situations in which comparison is not deliberately sought but occurs nonetheless (Wood, 1989). I argue for the particular importance of unfavorable comparisons that have esteem threatening consequences. More than another person merely becoming more fortunate than the self, there must also be threat to the individual's public or private self-image. For this and other reasons, not all negative comparisons engender envy.

Reconciling Alternative Conceptualizations. Inconsistencies in the results of studies attempting to determine the dispositional correlates of envy and jealousy and to discriminate the feelings associated with them may result from the fact that jealousy-provoking situations are also laden with envy-provoking characteristics. When one compares oneself with another and does not measure up, one experiences envy as one ponders the superior characteristics of the rival. When the rival also threatens a relationship one has with another person, jealousy is experienced as one also imagines the loss of that relationship and envisages the superior characteristics of the rival that have allowed this to happen. In this sense, envy is experienced as a part of many jealousy-provoking situations (Salovey & Rodin, 1986). This irony was not lost on Baruch Spinoza:

> If I imagine that an object beloved by me is united to another person by the same or by a closer bond of friendship than that by which I myself alone held the object, I shall be affected with hatred toward the beloved object itself, and shall envy that other person.... This hatred toward a beloved object when joined with envy is called 'jealousy,' which is therefore nothing but a vacillation of the mind springing from the love and hatred both felt together, and attended with the idea of another person whom we envy. (1675/1949, *Ethics*, Part 3, Proposition XXXV, pp. 153–154)

In equally graceful terms, "If my lover runs away with another man, I might be jealousy of him . . . I might be envious also if his *savoir faire* in seducing my lover highlights my lack of it (Sabini & Silver, 1982, p. 15).

This part–whole relationship between envy and jealousy highlights the common social comparison processes in both of these states. Jealousy is the whole, envy the part. In envy there is threat to self-evaluation through negative social comparison. In jealousy this same threat arises in the context of a challenged relationship with another person. Because of this relationship between envy and jealousy they often can be discussed together. The remainder of this chapter focuses specifically on the situational conditions that give rise to these unfortunate social comparisons.

Social Comparison and Self-Definition: The Antecedents of Envy and Jealousy

We believe that the type of social comparison situation most likely to engender envy or jealousy is one in which individuals receive some esteem threatening feedback relative to another person who is similar to them and when such feedback is especially self-relevant or on a self-defining dimension (Salovey & Rodin, 1983, 1984). When such a comparison situation involves a threat to a stable relationship, jealousy is provoked. Otherwise, the consequence of such a situation is envy. In the next section of this chapter, I will describe the basis for these three eliciting conditions: (a) negative feedback (b) in a self-relevant domain that (c) involves comparison to a similar other.

Negative Feedback. We may desire the possessions of another person or become anxious about hypothetical threats to our relationships, but we only experience envy and jealousy when the characteristics or behaviors of others threaten our senses of self-worth. Although popular self-help books like to link envy and jealousy to low self-esteem, global self-esteem is not what is meant here by a threat to self-worth. In fact, trait self-esteem inconsistently correlates with the propensity to experience jealousy and envy (compare Aronson & Pines, 1980; Bringle, 1981; Hupka & Bachelor, 1979; Jaremko & Lindsey, 1979; and Manges & Evenbeck, 1980, with Buunk, 1982; Mathes & Severa, 1981; and White, 1977; 1981b; 1981c). Rather, envy and jealousy are likely to result when one's present self-evaluation is threatened by social comparison. What seems particularly important are threats to self-evaluation that result from loss of status relative to comparison others.

In an analysis of envy influenced by both Festinger (1954) and Goffman (1959), Sabini and Silver (1982) noted that envy is likely when one experiences an eroding of one's social position. In particular, the behaviors that we associate with envy (e.g., derogating the rival) may be motivated as an attempt to prevent self-diminution. Interestingly, the envious response only seems to make matters worse: "Since an attribution of envy presupposes that the actor's self has been diminished, or at least that he perceives this to be the case, to be seen as envious is doubly damaging. Not only has he committed a transgression, but he has tacitly acknowledged his lessened worth" (p. 25).

The important point is that envy is more likely to be ascribed to an actor when he or she seems to be taking antisocial actions in order to stave off a blow to self-evaluation. In such a situation, if the person whose status is diminished belittles the character of the successful person, or undercuts his or her success, envy is perceived.

Silver and Sabini (1978) tested these hypotheses by having subjects view videotapes depicting four actors describing their successes and failures regarding medical school applications. Several versions of the scenario were constructed in which one actor usually achieved this goal and another did not. After viewing a tape, subjects were asked to complete a questionnaire regarding how the characters felt toward each other. Most subjects stated that the unsuccessful character would feel "envious" or "jealous" toward the successful character in all conditions. For example, in a standard version of the scenario, 92% of the subjects thought the unsuccessful character would be envious or jealous. When the relative achievement of the successful actor was lessened, 86% of the subjects still reported envy or jealousy. Envy was less expected after viewing other kinds of scenarios: 59% reported envy when one of the actors boasted, 55% when the unsuccessful actor wept, 54% when both actors obtained equal success, but only 36% when the unsuccessful actor expressed admiration for the successful one. Silver and Sabini (1978) interpreted these results as reflecting that the perception of envy is a recognition of two social comparison factors: (a) that actor X has greater success than actor Y, and (b) that Y has acted inappropriately, inconsiderately, or disrespectfully toward X in order to bolster Y's threatened self-esteem.

Social comparison theory's first cousin, interdependence theory (Thibaut & Kelley, 1959), may provide important predictions regarding the conditions under which negative, esteem-threatening feedback relative to comparison others is especially likely to instigate emotions such as envy. Working within this perspective, Smith and Diener (1986) suggested that envy does not result from all absolute differences in outcomes relative to comparison others. They claim that an important determinant of envy may be that the individual's own outcomes are evaluated without regard to the outcome difference itself. Instead, outcomes are evaluated against personal standards or comparison levels. Smith and Diener demonstrated that envy is evoked when an encounter with a successful other results in an individual's outcomes falling below this standard of comparison. However, they underscored the idea that the attribute differences that produce envy are those that are most likely to affect self-evaluation because they are important or self-relevant for the individual.

Self-Relevancy of Feedback Domain. Although the provocation of envy or jealousy is likely, individuals prefer comparisons with people on dimensions that are relevant or central to their self-definition (Miller, 1984). Wood (1989) interpreted this finding as reflecting a motive for subjects to evaluate themselves on dimensions that are central to their identities rather than on the arbitrary dimensions (such as those often provided by social comparison investigators). Festinger (1954), too, noted that dimensions may vary in terms of their importance and that desire for accurate self-evaluation would be felt most acutely on especially important dimensions.

The most systematic attention to the special consequences of comparison on self-defining dimensions has been that of Tesser and his colleagues (Tesser, 1986; Tesser & Campbell, 1982, 1983; see also chapter 5 in the present volume). Tesser developed a model that views positive self-evaluation as a primary motive of most individuals. Positive self-evaluation is achieved through two, at times competing, processes: reflection and comparison. Reflection occurs when the successes of close others make us feel good about ourselves; we "bask in reflected glory" (Cialdini et al., 1976). Under some conditions, however, high quality performances of close others can threaten our self-evaluations. Tesser labels such situations as ones that invoke the comparison process. The critical variable that determines whether the successes of close others make us feel good about ourselves (reflection) or have the opposite effect (comparison) is the relevance of the other's success or personal qualities to our self-definition. Reflection results when the other's performance is in a nonself-definitional domain.

Because we are motivated to maintain high self-evaluation, we bask in the reflected glory of our friends' successes so long as they do not threaten our self-evaluation. But when personal relevance is high, we maintain positive self-evaluation by engaging in other kinds of behavior such as: (a) changing our self-definition to reduce the relevance of the other's performance, (b) reducing the closeness of the relationship with the other person, or (c) reevaluating the quality of the other person's performance or actually preventing it from happening (Tesser & Campbell, 1983).

These thoughts and behaviors seem to describe common reactions to various envy- and jealousy-provoking situations quite well (Salovey & Rodin, 1983). We tend to be attracted to others who perform well, as long as their superior performances are on dimensions not highly self-defining. We envy, those who perform highly in self-definitional domains because envy arises when our self-evaluation is threatened by the performance of others. Additionally, we jealously protect those aspects of ourselves that are particularly important to maintaining self-definition and self-evaluation (including attributes, possessions, close relationships). Finally, we perceive another person as envious or jealous when we see him or her inappropriately demean a third person in order to maintain self-worth (Silver & Sabini, 1978).

Some of our empirical work in recent years underscores the importance of the self-relevancy of comparison feedback in the experience of envy and jealousy. Data supporting this view can be found in a reader survey on envy and jealousy conducted for *Psychology Today*, from which we received nearly 25,000 responses (Salovey & Rodin, 1985). Although limited by its self-selected subject sample, this study did afford us the opportunity to investigate relationships among self-relevant feedback, self-regard, envy, and jealousy with a larger and more diverse population than is found typically in Introductory Psychology subject pools.

In constructing this survey, we hypothesized that jealousy and envy would be reported in situations particularly salient to one's self-definition. These situations should be especially likely to produce jealousy or envy when a large discrepancy exists between one's idealized view of oneself and one's actual view of oneself in the domain. This discrepancy should lead to lowered self-evaluation in contexts in which the self-definitional dimension is made salient. Lowered self-evaluation should trigger attempts by the individual to raise it, and the behaviors engaged in to accomplish this goal should be easily identifiable as inspired by envy or jealousy. Based on these ideas, we asked respondents what attributes were particularly important to them, how they would ideally like to perform on these attributes, and how they actually perceived themselves. We measured self-evaluation using five items from the Rosenberg Self-Esteem scale, and then obtained respondents' reports of the frequency that they have actually engaged in a variety of jealous and envious behaviors. We also asked participants to indicate from a list of hypothetical situations those that they thought would most likely incite their jealousy or envy.

Envy and jealousy, as well as a variety of specific envious and jealous behaviors, were predicted most consistently by large discrepancies between actual and ideal ratings on the most highly valued, self-definitional (i.e., important) attribute. These large real–ideal discrepancies were related to lower self-evaluation, and both the degree of discrepancy and lower self-evaluation were associated with expectations of intense envy and jealousy. This association was strongest in the most self-defining (important) areas. The single best predictor of envy or jealousy in a domain was that domain's importance to the self. For example, a subject with a large real–ideal discrepancy for personal wealth and who reported wealth as very important to her self-definition was likely to report great envy if her neighbor won the state lottery or great jealousy if her husband flirted with a wealthy woman at a party (more so than if her husband flirted with a woman with different attributes like fame, attractiveness, or popularity).

Similarity of Comparison Other. Similarity has been the variable of traditional interest to social comparison theorists. Festinger's (1954) similarity corollary (IIIA) stated that comparisons with another are most likely when that other person is similar to the self in terms of ability or attitudes. Whether or not similarity had to be on dimensions relevant to comparison or not has been a source of considerable debate (Latané, 1966; Suls, 1977). Certainly, the usefulness of comparison feedback improves when comparison is with a relatively similar other (Radloff, 1966; Wheeler, Koestner, & Driver, 1982; Wilson, 1973), and it is of little consequence in cases of extreme dissimilarity (France-Kaatrude & Smith, 1985). Individuals appear most sensitive to comparison feedback from others whose similar characteristics are relevant to the domain of comparison (Goethals & Darley, 1977; Suls, Gastorf, & Lawhon, 1978; Wheeler & Zuckerman, 1977). As discussed earlier, Tesser (1986) and his colleagues have noted that closeness is a required precondition for self-relevant feedback to have an impact on self-evaluation. Individuals often become close to us because they are similar (Byrne, 1971).

As an example of a study demonstrating the importance of similarity, Dakin and Arrowood (1981) examined the situational conditions under which individuals will engage in one of three types of social comparison, competition (perhaps resulting in envy), cooperation, or conformity. They predicted that competition, and, perhaps, envy should be most likely when two individuals are similar in ability and when one is clearly more successful than the other on a task. To test this hypothesis, subjects competed in pairs on a reaction-time task in which false feedback concerning the participant's success and failure was given after each trial. As predicted, competitive tendencies were related to interpersonal proximity. That is, competition was more likely when subjects were close in ability. There was also a tendency for competition to increase when subjects were comparing themselves to superior others. Thus "competition is greatest when P and O are similar and when P is losing" (Dakin & Arrowood, 1981, p. 105).

Social comparison theorists have discussed on occasion whether comparisons are motivated by a desire to be similar to relevant others or to exceed them. Festinger (1954) described a unidirectional drive upward whereby in Western cultures individuals not only try to evaluate their abilities accurately but to improve on them relative to others. Emotions theorists see an important distinction between *coveting* and *envy*. Coveting is the strong desire to have what similar others have. Envy, however, includes strong resentment that others have what they do and is combined with a desire to obtain it for oneself and, simultaneously, see the other deprived of it. If we envy the genius in the office next door, we both wish we were as smart as he is but, perhaps secretly, wish he were not quite so smart. If we do not begrudge him his intellect, however, we may only be covetous rather than envious. Envy seems to be rooted in a sense of deprivation relative to the other, more so than simply a unidirectional drive for self-improvement. The envious person wants to have more and also would like others to have less. In fact, individuals experiencing envy seem better able to simulate mentally the removal of desired attributes from others more so than they can imagine the transfer of those attributes to themselves. Envy seems a function of the urge to compare oneself invidiously (as opposed to admiringly) with others (Schoeck, 1969). A goal of the envious person may be to be distinctive rather than similar to all others, as similarity can imply mediocrity (Brickman & Bulman, 1977; Fromkin, 1972). Clearly, individuals experiencing envy are not always the rational seekers of accurate self-appraisals described by Festinger (1954; see also Wood, 1989, for a more thorough discussion of this issue).

Putting It All Together. Based on the analysis described above, Salovey and Rodin (1984) proposed that envy or *social-comparison jealousy* would be reported under three eliciting conditions: (a) negatively valenced information about oneself relative to another person, (b) high self-relevance of this information, and (c) high similarity to or a close personal relationship with the comparison person. Under these conditions, individuals should experience a transient threat to positive self-evaluation, and engage in subsequent behaviors to bolster their threatened self-worth.

In an experiment designed to examine these antecedents of envy, subjects received false positive or negative feedback regarding aptitude that was either relevant to their self-definition or not relevant. Subjects were recruited based on their expressed career commitments for a study that they expected to be about personality and career choice. After completing a *personality inventory*, the participants were given bogus feedback relevant to likely success, either in their career domain or another one. Subjects then thought they would interact with a successful other person whose career interests were described as similar or dissimilar to theirs. As another *personality test*, they were asked to make judgments about the characteristics of this person after having read an essay purportedly written by him or her.

Individuals reported the most envy when they received negative, self-relevant feedback and subsequently thought they would associate with a similar, successful other person, as depicted in Fig. 10.2. Anticipated meetings with this comparison other were greeted with feelings of depression and anxiety. Most interestingly, this situation had a profound impact on behavior. Subjects expressed diminished desire for the other person's friendship, and they disparaged him or her on a variety of trait scales used to evaluate the person based on the essay. These consequent behaviors most likely served to diminish the relative status of the comparison person and thus reduce the likelihood that he or she would be viewed as a relevant source of comparison feedback. These results regarding envy and dero-

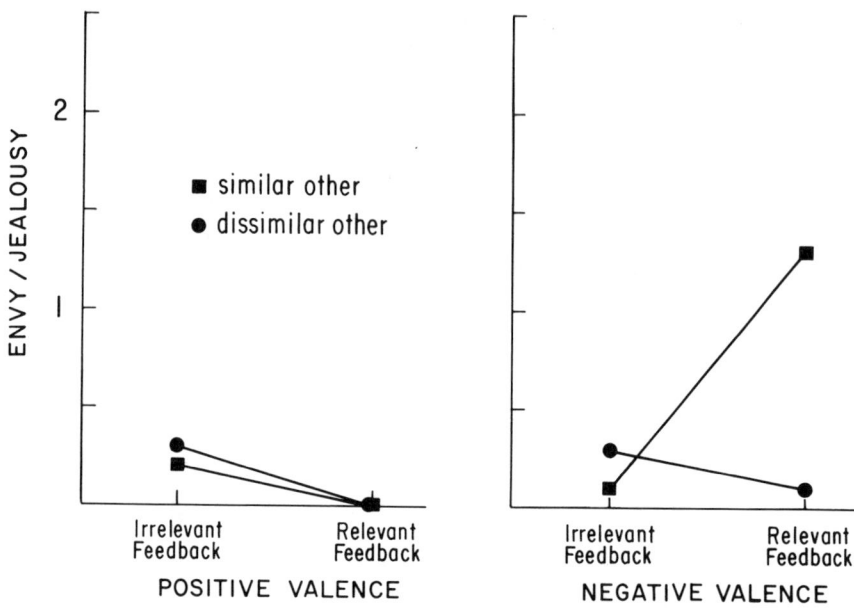

FIG. 10.2. Amount of envy reported in eight different feedback conditions (data from Salovey & Rodin, 1984).

gation were consistent with those reported by Silver and Sabini (1978), described earlier.

Social Consequences of Envy and Jealousy

When confronted with situations engendering envy or jealousy, individuals will behave so as to reduce potential social comparison and/or bolster threatened self-evaluation. Among the possible actions that such individuals can take are: (a) altering their self-definition to reduce the relevance of comparison feedback, (b) changing the nature of the relationship with the comparison person, (c) derogating the comparison person, (d) reappraising the performance of the comparison person, or (e) acting violently toward the source of comparison feedback. Each of these behavioral consequences of envy and jealousy is examined in the next section of this chapter.

Changing Self-Definition. One way in which individuals can minimize envy and jealousy resulting from implicit or explicit comparisons in which they do not measure up to a rival in a self-defining domain is to reduce the self-relevance of the comparison domain. Social comparison feedback is less likely to result in envy or jealousy if the attribute or relationship in question is no longer thought to be important. In fact, a coping style that we labeled *selective ignoring*, which involved reducing the importance of a comparison domain, was moderately effective in preventing the experience of envy and jealousy in the face of situations that could provoke these emotions (Salovey & Rodin, 1988). This coping strategy was clearly more effective in reducing the pain of comparison than was one involving bolstering self-worth by thinking about one's positive qualities. Because situations that promote envy and jealousy make the self-attributes on which one falls short so obvious, stimulus- as opposed to self-focused coping strategies may be especially effective.

In a similar vein, Tesser and Campbell (1980) asked subjects to rate the importance of a performance domain in which they were successful but still outperformed by another person. As compared with dimensions on which they performed equally well as close others, subjects rated the dimensions (e.g., social sensitivity, aesthetic judgment) on which they were outperformed as less important to them. In a conceptual replication of this finding (Tesser & Paulhus, 1983), subjects rated the pseudo-attribute, *cognitive-perceptual integration* as more important to their self-definitions when they received better performance feedback on it than did a close other. When the other was described as similar to them in terms of age, college major, and personality profile, the relationship between relative performance and perceived importance was especially strong.

A change in self-definition instigated by envy-producing comparisons may also facilitate a shift from upward to downward comparisons. That is, after not measuring up, envious individuals may decide that it is more relevant to their self-definitions to compare themselves to others who are also inferior or disadvantaged (Wills, 1981). When threatened with unfavorable comparison, there is some evidence that individuals will select inferior others for subsequent comparison (Friend & Gilbert, 1973; Levine & Green, 1984; Wilson & Benner, 1971).

Reducing Relevance of Comparison Person Through Relationship Distancing. Recall that in a study described earlier (Salovey & Rodin, 1984), individuals who received negative performance feedback on a relevant dimension relative to a similar comparison person expressed less interest in befriending the comparison person than did subjects who received other combinations of feedback. One way individuals can attempt to terminate envy-provoking experiences is to minimize the amount of contact or potential contact with their rivals. Better yet, individuals can decide that they do not like their rivals at all or decide that their rivals are in no way similar to them (Brickman & Bulman, 1977) and remove them as relevant objects of social comparison. Similarly, it is rare in a situation engendering romantic jealousy that one befriends the rival for one's lover's attention.

In an experiment framed as a "College Bowl" trivia competition, Pleban and Tesser (1981) varied the performance feedback that subjects received in several different domains (e.g., football, rock music). At the end of the experiment, subjects rated a confederate who had outperformed them as less similar to themselves when the performance was in a self-relevant domain. Although performance comparisons had no direct influence on ratings of how much subjects liked the confederate, when outperformed in a relevant domain, subjects felt that the comparison other probably did not have much in common with themselves, they were less willing to work with him, and they sat farther away from him. Similarly, when outperformed by a sibling who was close in age, Tesser (1980) found that respondents reported less closeness in their relationship with that sibling. Similarity and closeness can also be reduced by derogating competitors, a consequence of social comparison envy and jealousy that I will turn to next.

Derogation of Rivals. One common consequence of negative social comparison or the threat of negative comparison is the derogation of successful rivals (Cialdini & Richardson, 1980; Crocker, Thompson, McGraw, & Ingerman, 1987). When the comparison dimension is self-relevant, we are especially likely to underestimate the performance quality or characteristics of comparison others (Campbell, 1986; Marks, 1984). In the experiment described earlier, subjects who received negative, self-relevant information were likely to evaluate negatively a similar but successful rival (Salovey & Rodin, 1984). And, based on their study described previously, Silver and Sabini (1978) considered the derogation of rivals when self-evaluation is threatened the defining feature of envy. In this sense, envy serves a self-protective function. We try to short-circuit self-diminution by undercutting the performance or attributes of successful others (Sabini & Silver, 1982). The self-esteem bolstering function of rival derogation has long been recognized (Freud, 1955). We also might focus on their negative attributes so as to tarnish their superior standing on the comparison dimension.

In an excellent analysis of rival derogation in situations involving romantic jealousy, Schmitt (1988) noted that the rival serves as the ideal target for denigration. First, obviously, it is the rival who most directly threatens the envious or jealous person's self-worth. Second, in the romantic jealousy situation, the rival is seen as an intruder into a predictable relationship, a destabilizing force. Third, the jealous person often knows little about the rival and easily conjures up a negative image of him or her. Finally, the jealous person would prefer to derogate the rival rather than the beloved because continuing the relationship with the beloved is often desired.

Schmitt also notes that this situation places the jealous person in an ironic situation. The rival is clearly threatening a desired relationship as well as the self-evaluation of the jealous person, which can be protected via derogation. However, if the person loved by the jealous individual is attracted to the rival, the rival must have some redeeming characteristics. In the context of the romantic relationship, the characteristics of the jealous individual that are most relevant to his or her self-definition (Tesser, 1986; Tesser & Campbell, 1983) are those that the partner values and perhaps formed the basis of the partner's attraction to the person in the first place.

As relationships mature, the characteristics that are important to one's partner become extremely self-relevant. In two experiments, Schmitt (1988) demonstrated that it is just these attributes on which the rival is derogated by the jealous person. Individuals experiencing jealousy evaluated their rivals negatively on dimensions that they considered to be important to their partners, but they judged their rivals to be as attractive as themselves on dimensions that they believed were less relevant to their partners. It is interesting that jealous individuals selectively derogate attributes of their rivals. One might think that they should hate any and all aspects of such an individual. Perhaps in order to be able to present a credible argument to the lover (and to themselves) about why the original relationship should be maintained, such individuals may be willing to acknowledge irrelevant strengths in their rivals but act as if they had particular sensitivity when it comes to self-relevant dimensions. The threatened individual would like to create an impression in the lover that he or she is a sensitive, rational person rather than a completely naysaying misanthrope.

Traditionally, social comparison, whether it is in the context of a romantic relationship or not, is thought to be motivated by either a lack of a general standard on which one can assess oneself or in order to maintain a positive view of oneself. Schmitt (1988) noted that in circumstances involving romantic jealousy, we are motivated to compare ourselves to rivals and potential rivals who we may not know and whose only similarity to ourselves is that they are attracted to the same person to whom we are. Hence, social comparison in the context of romantic relationships may be motivated not just by a desire to obtain veridical information about the self or to bolster self-evaluation but also as an attempt to understand those characteristics of value to one's partner. Thus, we may be simultaneously repulsed and intrigued by our rivals.

Re-Attributing the Source of the Other's Success. We often conclude that another is envious or jealous when we see him or her demean the performance, attributes, or relationships of another person. "Sour grapes" is a common consequence of situations in which the successes of others challenge one's self-worth. We can decide that the success was due to luck rather than skill, or that the individual succeeded due to an unfair advantage (e.g., friends in high places). Moreover, individuals may make active efforts to interfere with another person's esteem-threatening accomplishments. For example, individuals refused to provide helpful clues that would enable a close friend to solve problems when the domain of the problem was self-definitionally important (Tesser & Smith, 1980). In fact, subjects in this experimental condition actually hindered their friends' performance by deliberately providing difficult clues.

Violence. Occasionally, the accomplishments of others or their threats to our relationships result in violence against them or their property. The relationship between envy, jealousy, and violence has been studied most systematically in the romantic domain. The psychiatric literature is the source of a variety of studies of murderers, with the typical finding that many experienced intense jealousy immediately preceding the killing. Several in depth case studies have been described by Lehrman (1939) and Cuthbert (1970), and in an analysis of reported homicides, Psarska (1970) found that in nearly one-fourth, nondelusional jealousy was a causal factor. In these 38 cases, 16 involved actual unfaithfulness and the remaining 22 cases comprised situations where longstanding marital conflicts developed into jealousy. Further, morbid (i.e., delusional) jealousy has been reported to be one of the leading motives of murderers judged insane (Mowat, 1966).

Similarly, envy may lead to violence when individuals perceive their failure to attain desired possessions or other attributes as the result of arbitrary or discriminatory forces. Resentment of others is greatest when individuals do not have something desirable but similar others are perceived as having it (Crosby, 1976). Violence in these instances seems most likely, as desirable qualities and possessions are attained, or almost so. Riots, for example, are not likely when one group is extremely deprived, but rather when these conditions have improved to the point that the social and economic distance between privileged and deprived groups is relatively minimal (Crosby, 1976; Pettigrew, 1967).

Social Comparison, Envy, and Jealousy in Sociocultural Context

Envy. Envy, jealousy, and other emotions based on social comparison can also be understood at a sociocultural level of analysis. For example, in an influential volume, Schoeck (1969) claimed that envy motivates socioeconomic progress in Western societies, facilitating social and industrial development. In the developing world, however, Schoeck believed that envy functions as a form of social control that helps to maintain the status quo and inhibits economic development by defining clear limits of acceptable achievement for members of a social group.

In traditional cultures, envy is aroused when one group member receives something that others lack. Members of such societies fear arousing the envy of others so as not to become victims of their rage, destroy the close fabric of intragroup relationships, or increase social distance among subgroups (J. A. Davis, 1959). Such a fear of arousing envy tends to inhibit change and development in the group. Thus, even though social comparison and envy might provide incentives for achievement and innovation, it poses a threat to social order by arousing anger and suspicion. This fear of envy was captured eloquently by Foster (1972): "Sensing the ever-present threat of envy to himself and to his society, man fears: he fears the consequences of his own envy, and he fears the consequences of the envy of others. As a result, in every society people use symbolic and nonsymbolic cultural forms whose function is to neutralize, or reduce, or otherwise control the dangers they see stemming from envy, and especially their fear of envy." (p. 165)

In cultures where envy is believed to cause such great harm, rituals and other protective devices have developed to inhibit behaviors that might arouse envy in self or others. Most notable in these cultures is a strong belief in the evil eye (reviewed by Stiles, 1987; see also Schoeck, 1969). The evil eye could bring one considerable misfortune, and in the 67 cultures who believe in it (Roberts, cited in Bush, 1977), individuals make substantial efforts to avoid attracting its stare. In nearly all these cultures, the evil eye is thought to be tempted easily by bragging about one's successes and showing off good fortune. For example, mothers may be unwilling to show new babies in public or advertise pregnancies lest they attract the evil eye. Conversely, sharing one's wealth through charity is often thought to be an effective prophylactic. The underlying theme in these cultures is that arousing the envy of others can bring harm, disease, and other misfortunes to oneself. Local myths tell of individuals who aroused envy and then suffered some misfortune. Such envy myths serve the purpose of regulating the economic activities acceptable to the culture. In contrast, Western culture, especially American society, has been criticized as being fueled by envy as way of maintaining a capitalist economy (Cohen, 1986; Fairlie, 1978), although the direction of causality is not always clear. In this view, individuals are encouraged—mostly through media advertising—to view any attribute that can be purchased as relevant to the self. More importantly, added relevance is ascribed to possessions or attributes owned by one's neighbors but not oneself. In capitalist cultures, the intrinsic satisfaction of receiving a better reward than one's neighbor seems to compensate for the blow to interpersonal harmony, especially when the reward is scarce or valuable (J. A. Davis, 1963).

Jealousy. By way of contrast, the sociocultural roots of jealousy seem to be norms regarding sexual "property" (K. Davis, 1936). Such norms (and therefore jealousy) serve to protect relationships valued by the community. According to this view, a given culture defines which relationships are particularly valued and guides an individual's interpretation of events threatening these valued relationships. Further, cultures also prescribe behaviors that protect these relationships. This view may also apply to valued relationships that are not sexual in nature. Strong norms prohibiting threats to close friendships and family relations also emerge.

Hupka (1981) identified several characteristics that differentiate jealous from non-jealous cultures. Cultures low in jealousy discourage individual property rights, view sexual gratification and companionship as easily available, but do not engender in their members a desire for sex as a pleasurable pastime. Such cultures place little value on personal descendants or the need to know whether the children in the family are one's own progeny. Marriage is not required for economic survival, companionship, or recognition of the individual as a competent member of the society.

Whitehurst (1977) proposed that jealousy thrives in cultures with rigidly prescribed sex roles. In these cultures, sex role sanctioned divisions of labor lead to a sense of inadequacy in which one spouse (usually the wife) may feel uneasy about her role relative to the other, and this anxiety is expressed as jealousy. Similarly, in rigid sex role prescribed relationships, jealousy is used to gain power and control, to generate self-righteousness, to excuse one for vicious or physically abusive behavior, or to justify withdrawal from a relationship (Clanton & Smith, 1977).

CONCLUSIONS

Envy and jealousy are commonly experienced affective states. They can be considered from a dispositional, phenomenological, or situational perspective. In the present chapter, some of the situational antecedents of envy and jealousy have been highlighted along with some of their consequences for social interaction. The role of social comparison processes in the experience of these affects should be clear. Envy and jealousy are often the result of comparisons of one sort or another involving feedback that is threatening to self-evaluation in a self-defining (or relevant) domain. The intrapersonal and antisocial consequences of envy and jealousy are often attempts by the individual to bolster threatened self-evaluation. Although social comparison theory originally accounted for situations in which individuals compare themselves with others quite deliberately for its information value, it is still a useful framework for understanding the emotional consequences of less intentional comparisons, especially when the self-relevancy of the feedback information is taken into account.

I began by noting that investigators working in the tradition of social comparison theory have neglected the specific emotional consequences of comparisons (although Brickman & Bulman, 1977, was a nice start in this direction). On the other hand, investigators of complex, social emotions such as envy and jealousy have ignored social psychological theory, in general, as a way of anchoring their study of these emotions. In fact, the study of envy and jealousy has proceeded rather atheoretically and, for the most part, descriptively. Because the psychological literature on jealousy and envy per se is only a bit more than a decade old, this descriptive stance is probably not unwarranted. However, there is now a sufficient corpus of empirical work on these emotions so that a more theoretically motivated approach to their study would certainly be useful. The present chapter discusses some of the ways in which ideas from social comparison theory might help us to understand situations that provoke envy and jealousy. It does not provide a social comparison theory of envy and jealousy. Such a goal may be the logical next step for investigators in this area. In 1967, Pettigrew provided an exemplary theoretical integration (that he called social evaluation theory) as way of understanding, among other things, relations among individuals of different races. Future investigators of envy and jealousy may want to model Pettigrew's approach in trying to find a theoretical blend that will motivate subsequent empirical work. This chapter, I hope, suggests that social comparison theory might provide a good jumping off point.

ACKNOWLEDGMENTS

Please address correspondence concerning this manuscript to Peter Salovey, Department of Psychology, Yale University, Box 11A Yale Station, New Haven, CT 06520-7447. I would like to thank John D. Mayer, Jerry Suls, and Thomas Wills for their comments on an earlier draft of this chapter. Preparation of this chapter was facilitated by NIH Biomedical Research Support Grant S07 RR07015 and funding from the National Center for Health Statistics, National Cancer Institute, and Presidential Young Investigator program of the National Science Foundation.

REFERENCES

Aronson, E., & Pines, A. (1980, April). *Exploring sexual jealousy.* Paper presented at the annual meeting of the Western Psychological Association, Honolulu, HI.
Brickman, P., & Bulman, R. J. (1977). Pleasure and pain in social comparison. In J. M. Suls & R. L. Miller (Eds.), *Social comparison processes: Theoretical and empirical perspectives* (pp. 149-186). Washington, DC: Hemisphere.
Bringle, R. G. (1981). Conceptualizing jealousy as a disposition. *Alternative Lifestyles, 4,* 274-290.

Bringle, R. G., & Buunk, B. (1985). Jealousy and social behavior: A review of person, relationship, and situational determinants. In P. Shaver (Ed.), *Review of Personality and Social Psychology* (Vol. 6, pp. 241–264). Beverly Hills, CA: Sage.

Bringle, R. G., Roach, S., Andler, C., & Evenbeck, S. (1979). Measuring the intensity of jealous reactions. *Catalog of Selected Documents in Psychology, 9*(2), 23–24.

Bryson, J. B. (1977, September). *Situational determinants of the expression of jealousy.* Paper presented at the annual meeting of the American Psychological Association, San Francisco, CA.

Bush, S. (1977). The evil eye—A stare of envy. *Psychology Today, 11,* 154–155.

Buunk, B. (1978). Jaloezie 2. Ervaringen van 250 Nederlanders. *Intermediair, 14,* 43–51.

Buunk, B. (1982). Anticipated sexual jealousy: Its relationship to self-esteem, dependency, and reciprocity. *Personality and Social Psychology Bulletin, 8,* 310–316.

Byrne, D. *The attraction paradigm.* New York: Academic Press.

Campbell, J. D. (1986). Similarity and uniqueness: The effects of attribute type, relevance, and individual differences in self-esteem and depression. *Journal of Personality and Social Psychology, 50,* 281–294.

Cialdini, R. B., Borden, R. J., Thorne, A., Walker, M. R., Freeman, S., & Sloan, L. R. (1976). Basking in reflected glory: Three (football) field studies. *Journal of Personality and Social Psychology, 34,* 366–375.

Cialdini, R. B., & Richardson, K. D. (1984). Two indirect tactics of impression management: Basking and blasting. *Journal of Personality and Social Psychology, 39,* 406–415.

Clanton, G., & Smith, L. G. (Eds.). (1977). *Jealousy.* Englewood Cliffs, NJ: Prentice–Hall.

Cohen, B. (1986). *The Snow White syndrome: All about envy.* New York: MacMillan.

Crocker, J., Thompson, L. L., McGraw, K. M., & Ingerman, C. (1987). Downward comparison prejudice and evaluation of others: Effects of self-esteem and threat. *Journal of Personality and Social Psychology, 52,* 907–916.

Crosby, F. (1976). A model of egoistical relative deprivation. *Psychological Review, 83,* 85–113.

Cuthbert, T. M. (1970). A portfolio of murders. *British Journal of Psychiatry, 116,* 1–10.

Dakin, S., & Arrowood, A. J. (1981). The social comparison of ability. *Human Relations, 34,* 89–109.

Davis, J. A. (1959). A formal interpretation of the theory of relative deprivation. *Sociometry, 22,* 280–296.

Davis, J. A. (1963). Structural balance, mechanical solidarity, and interpersonal relations. *American Journal of Sociology, 68,* 444–462.

Davis, K. (1936). Jealousy and sexual property. *Social Forces, 14,* 395–405.

Fairlie, H. (1978). *The seven deadly sins today.* Washington: New Republic.

Festinger, L. (1954). A theory of social comparison processes. *Human Relations, 7,* 117–140.

Foster, G. (1972). The anatomy of envy: A study in symbolic behavior. *Current Anthropology, 13,* 165–202.

France-Kaatrude, A., & Smith, W. P. (1985). Social comparison, task motivation, and the development of self-evaluative standards in children. *Developmental Psychology, 21,* 1080–1089.

Freud, S. (1955). Some neurotic mechanisms in jealousy, paranoia, and homosexuality. In J. Strachey (Ed. and Trans.), *The standard edition of the complete psychological works of Sigmund Freud* (Vol. 18, pp. 221–234). London: Hogarth Press. (Original work published 1934.)

Friend, R. M., & Gilbert, J. (1973). Threat and fear of negative evaluation as determinants of locus of social comparison. *Journal of Personality, 41,* 328–340.

Fromkin, H. L. (1972). Feelings of interpersonal undistinctiveness: An unpleasant affective state. *Journal of Experimental Research in Personality, 6,* 178–185.

Gellert, S. (1976). Mixed emotions. *Transactional Analysis Journal*, 6, 129–130.
Goethals, G. R., & Darley, J. M. (1977). Social comparison theory: An attributional approach. In J. M. Suls & R. L. Miller (Eds.), *Social comparison processes: Theoretical and empirical perspectives* (pp. 259–278). Washington, DC: Hemisphere.
Goffman, E. (1959). *The presentation of self in everyday life.* Garden City, NY: Anchor.
Heider, F. (1958). *The psychology of interpersonal relations.* Hillsdale, NJ: Lawrence Erlbaum Associates.
Hupka, R. B. (1981). Cultural determinants of jealousy. *Alternative Lifestyles*, 4, 310–356.
Hupka, R. B. (1984). Jealousy: Compound emotion or label for a particular situation? *Motivation and Emotion*, 8, 141–155.
Hupka, R. B., & Bachelor, B. (1979, April). *Validation of a scale to measure romantic jealousy.* Paper presented at the annual meeting of the Western Psychological Association. San Diego, CA.
Jaremko, M. E., & Lindsey, R. (1979). Stress coping abilities of individuals high and low in jealousy. *Psychological Reports*, 44, 547–553.
Latané, B. (1966). Studies in social comparison: Introduction and overview. *Journal of Experimental Social Psychology*, Suppl. 1, 1–5.
Lehrman, P. R. (1939). Some unconscious determinants in homicide. *Psychiatric Quarterly*, 13, 605–621.
Levine, J. M., & Green, S. M. (1984). Acquisition of relative performance information: The roles of intrapersonal and interpersonal comparison. *Personality and Social Psychology Bulletin*, 10, 385–393.
Manges, K., & Evenbeck, S. (1980, April). *Social power, jealousy, and dependency in the intimate dyad.* Paper presented at the annual meeting of the Midwestern Psychological Association, St. Louis, MO.
Marks, G. (1984). Thinking one's abilities are unique and one's opinions are common. *Personality and Social Psychology Bulletin*, 10, 203–208.
Mathes, E. W., Adams, H. E., & Davis, R. M. (1985). Jealousy: Loss of relationship rewards, loss of self-esteem, depression, anxiety, and anger. *Journal of Personality and Social Psychology*, 48, 1552–1561.
Mathes, E. W., & Severa, N. (1981). Jealousy, romantic love, and liking: Theoretical considerations and preliminary scale development. *Psychological Reports*, 49, 23–31.
Miller, C. T. (1984). Self-schemas, gender, and social comparison: A clarification of the related attributes hypothesis. *Journal of Personality and Social Psychology*, 46, 1222–1228.
Mowat, R. R. (1966). *Morbid jealousy and murder: A psychiatric study of morbidly jealous murderers at Broadmoor.* London: Tavistock Publications.
Ortony, A., Clore, G. L., & Collins, A. (1988). *The cognitive structure of emotions.* New York: Cambridge University Press.
Parrott, W. G., & Smith, R. H. (1987, August). *Differentiating the experiences of envy and jealousy.* Paper presented at the annual meeting of the American Psychological Association, New York.
Pettigrew, T. F. (1967). Social evaluation theory: Convergences and applications. In D. Levine (Ed.), *Nebraska Symposium on Motivation*, (Vol. 15, pp. 241–311). Lincoln, NE: University of Nebraska Press.
Pleban, R., & Tesser, A. (1981). The effects of relevance and quality of another's performance on interpersonal closeness. *Social Psychology Quarterly*, 44, 278–285.
Psarska, A. D. (1970). Jealousy factor in homicide in forensic psychiatric material. *Polish Medical Journal*, 6, 1504–1510.
Radloff, R. (1966). Social comparison and ability evaluation. *Journal of Experimental Social Psychology*, Suppl. 1, 6–26.
Sabini, J., & Silver, M. (1982). *Moralities of everyday life.* Oxford: Oxford University Press.

Salovey, P., & Rodin, J. (1983, April). *A self-esteem maintenance model of envy.* Paper presented at the annual meeting of the Eastern Psychological Association. Philadelphia, PA.

Salovey, P., & Rodin, J. (1984). Some antecedents and consequences of social-comparison jealousy. *Journal of Personality and Social Psychology, 47,* 780–792.

Salovey, P., & Rodin, J. (1985). The heart of jealousy. *Psychology Today, 19*(9), 22–25, 28–29.

Salovey, P., & Rodin, J. (1986). Differentiation of social-comparison jealousy and romantic jealousy. *Journal of Personality and Social Psychology, 50,* 1100–1112.

Salovey, P., & Rodin, J. (1988). Coping with envy and jealousy. *Journal of Social and Clinical Psychology, 7,* 15–33.

Salovey, P., & Rodin, J. (1989). Envy and jealousy in close relationships. In C. Hendrick (Ed.), *Close relationships: Review of Personality and Social Psychology* (Vol. 10, pp. 221–246). Newbury Park, CA: Sage.

Schmitt, B. H. (1988). Social comparison in romantic jealousy. *Personality and Social Psychological Bulletin, 14,* 374–387.

Schoeck, H. (1969). *Envy: A theory of social behavior.* New York: Harcourt Brace & World.

Silver, M., & Sabini, J. (1978). The perception of envy. *Social Psychology, 41,* 105–117.

Smith, R. H., & Diener, E. (1986). *The role of comparison level and alternative comparison domains in the perception of envy.* Unpublished manuscript, University of Illinois, Urbana.

Smith, R. H., Kim, S. H., & Parrott, W. G. (1988). Envy and jealousy: Semantic problems and experiential distinctions. *Personality and Social Psychology Bulletin, 14,* 401–409.

Spielman, P. M. (1971). Envy and jealousy: An attempt at clarification. *Psychoanalytic Quarterly, 40,* 59–82.

Spinoza, B. (1949). *Ethics.* (J. Gutmann, Ed. and Trans.). New York: Hafner Publishing Co. (Original work published in 1675).

Stiles, C. (1987). *Envy and the evil-eye.* Unpublished manuscript, Yale University, New Haven, CT.

Suls, J. M. (1977). Social comparison theory and research: An overview from 1954. In J. M. Suls & R. L. Miller (Eds.), *Social comparison processes: Theoretical and empirical perspectives* (pp. 1–19). Washington, DC: Hemisphere.

Suls, J. M., Gastorf, J., & Lawhon, J. (1978). Social comparison choices for evaluating a sex- and age-related ability. *Personality and Social Psychology Bulletin, 4,* 102–105.

Tesser, A. (1980). Self-esteem maintenance in family dynamics. *Journal of Personality and Social Psychology, 39,* 77–91.

Tesser, A. (1986). Some effects of self-evaluation maintenance on cognition and action. In R. M. Sorrentino & E. T. Higgins (Eds.), *Handbook of motivation and cognition* (pp. 435–464). New York: Guilford.

Tesser, A., & Campbell, J. (1980). Self-definition: The impact of the relative performance and similarity of others. *Social Psychology Quarterly, 43,* 341–347.

Tesser, A., & Campbell, J. (1982). Self-evaluation maintenance and the perception of friends and strangers. *Journal of Personality, 50,* 261–279.

Tesser, A., & Campbell, J. (1983). Self-definition and self-evaluation maintenance. In J. Suls & A. Greenwald (Eds.), *Social psychological perspectives on the self* (Vol. 2, pp. 1–31). Hillsdale, NJ: Lawrence Erlbaum Associates.

Tesser, A., & Paulhus, D. (1983). The definition of self: Private and public self-evaluation management strategies. *Journal of Personality and Social Psychology, 44,* 672–682.

Tesser, A., & Smith, J. (1980). Some effects of task relevance and friendship on helping: You don't always help the one you like. *Journal of Experimental Social Psychology, 16,* 482–590.

Thibaut, J. W., & Kelley, H. H. (1959). *The social psychology of groups*. New York: Wiley.
Tipton, R. M., Benedictson, C. S., Mahoney, J., & Hartnett, J. J. (1978). Development of a scale for the assessment of jealousy. *Psychological Reports, 42*, 1217–1218.
Twain, M. (1962). *Letters from the Earth*. (Edited by B. DeVoto). New York: Harper & Row. (Original work published 1938).
Wheeler, L., Koestner, R., & Driver, R. E. (1982). Related attributes in the choice of comparison others: It's there, but it isn't all there is. *Journal of Experimental Social Psychology, 18*, 489–500.
Wheeler, L., & Zuckerman, M. (1977). Commentary. In J. M. Suls & R. L. Miller (Eds.), *Social comparison processes: Theoretical and empirical perspectives* (pp. 335–357). Washington, DC: Hemisphere.
White, G. L. (1977, September). *Inequity of emotional involvement and jealousy in romantic couples*. Paper presented at the annual meeting of the American Psychological Association, San Francisco, CA.
White, G. L. (1981a, August). *Coping with romantic jealousy: Comparison to rival, perceived motives, and alternative assessment*. Paper presented at the annual meeting of the American Psychological Association, Los Angeles, CA.
White, G. L. (1981b). A model of romantic jealousy. *Motivation and Emotion, 5*, 295–310.
White, G. L. (1981c). Some correlates of romantic jealousy. *Journal of Personality, 49*, 129–147.
Whitehurst, R. N. (1977). Jealousy and American values. In G. Clanton & L.G. Smith (Eds.), *Jealousy* (pp. 136–140). Englewood Cliffs, NJ: Prentice–Hall.
Wills, T. A. (1981). Downward comparison principles in social psychology. *Psychological Bulletin, 90*, 245–271.
Wilson, A., Sitwell, E., Connolly, C., Fermor, P. L., Waugh, E., Sykes, C., & Auden, W. H. (1962). *The seven deadly sins*. London: Sunday Times Publications.
Wilson, S. R. (1973). Ability evaluation and self-evaluation as types of social comparison. *Sociometry, 36*, 600–607.
Wilson, S. R., & Benner, L. A. (1971). The effects of self-esteem and situation upon comparison choices during ability evaluation. *Sociometry, 34*, 381–397.
Wood, J. V. (1989). Theory and research concerning social comparison of personal attributes. *Psychological Bulletin, 106*, 231–248.

11 When Social Comparison Goes Awry: The Case of Pluralistic Ignorance

Dale T. Miller
Princeton University

Cathy McFarland
Simon Fraser University

Most of us have participated in, or at least witnessed, the following classroom dynamic. The sequence begins when the professor pauses during a complex lecture to ask the students if they have any questions. At this point, the bewildered but outwardly composed students furtively try to gauge their classmates's reactions. Despite widespread confusion, no hands are raised. This aspect of the dynamic is not surprising—students can hardly be blamed for not wishing to embarrass themselves in front of their professor and peers. The surprise comes with the next step in the sequence. Students misinterpret the silence and demeanor of the other students, inferring that their classmates understand the lecture and that they alone are confused.

The students in this scenario are experiencing *pluralistic ignorance*, a state characterized by the belief that one's private thoughts, feelings, and behaviors are different from those of others, even though one's public behavior is identical. Floyd Allport (Katz & Allport, 1928; Schanck, 1932) is credited with coining the term pluralistic ignorance, over sixty years ago, to describe the situation in which virtually all members of a group privately reject group norms, yet believe that virtually all other group members accept them. Allport introduced the concept of pluralistic ignorance to account for a puzzle: widespread public conformity to social norms in the absence of widespread private support. Allport contended that it is not necessary for the majority to support a social norm for it to be perpetuated. The perpetuation of the status quo can occur even if no one believes, as long as everyone believes that everyone else believes (Krech, Crutchfield & Ballachey, 1962).

Investigators following Allport's lead have linked pluralistic ignorance to the perpetuation of privately unpopular social norms in a wide variety of social settings (e.g. Kauffman, 1981; Matza, 1964; O'Gorman, 1975; Packard & Willower, 1972; Wheeler, 1961). This is but one of the many faces of pluralistic ignorance, however. In the classroom scenario with which we began, it is not the perpetuation of a group norm that results from the mistaken perception of personal deviance but rather a decrease in self-esteem. In another well-known illustration of pluralistic ignorance, Latané and Darley (1970) linked the concept to the hesitancy of bystanders to intervene in emergency situations. According to Latané and Darley, bystanders, who are themselves unsure about the seriousness of a situation, often assume that other bystanders, despite acting similarly to themselves, are confident that the situation is not an emergency. Bystanders in emergency situations are like the characters in Hans Christian Anderson's story of the *The Emperor's New Clothes*. They act similarly to others but assume that their perceptions must be different.

THE PUZZLE OF PLURALISTIC IGNORANCE

Any phenomenon that plays a role in the perpetuation of unpopular social practices, the hesitancy of bystanders to intervene on a victim's behalf, and the lowering of self-esteem, is of obvious practical and social import. It is also of considerable theoretical interest because of its resistance to easy explanation. Indeed, the phenomenon of pluralistic ignorance stands in sharp relief to a voluminous literature documenting the tendency of people to overestimate their similarity to others (Mullen et al., 1985; Ross, Green & House, 1977). Many mechanisms have been proposed to contribute to what has come to be known as the *false consensus effect* (Marks & Miller, 1987; Sherman, Presson, & Chassin, 1984). The question this raises for the pluralistic ignorance literature is clear: What is special about those circumstances in which pluralistic ignorance, rather than false consensus, emerges?

One obvious place to look for the answer to this question is that research which does not find the false consensus effect. Studies that report the underestimation of self-other similarity are relatively rare, but some do exist (e.g. Campbell, 1986; Goethals, 1986; Marks, 1984; Suls & Wan, 1987). The most popular accounts of the systematic underestimation of self-other similarity, or the *false uniqueness effect*, emphasize motivational factors.

The need to be unique, and see oneself as distinct from others, is at the center of one motivational account of false uniqueness effects (Snyder &

Fromkin, 1980). This account assumes that people are motivated to underestimate their similarity to others so as to satisfy their need to feel unique. Although the need for uniqueness may bias perceptions of self-other similarity in some contexts, we can discern nothing in those contexts that seem to serve as breeding grounds for pluralistic ignorance that could be expected to arouse this motive. True, the students who infer that they are more confused than their classmates can derive whatever satisfaction comes from standing apart from the herd, but the psychic price for being able to do so hardly seems a bargain. The individuals who experience pluralistic ignorance in the situations we have described do not just feel different from others, they feel deviant. And it is difficult to understand how they could be made to feel better about themselves by generating this illusion of deviance.

There are times, of course, when deviance implies superiority, and in these circumstances false uniqueness effects are not difficult to understand. A series of studies conducted by Goethals (1986) demonstrates this point. In one illustrative study, students indicated whether or not they were willing to donate blood and then estimated the percentage of other students who would act similarly. Those students who volunteered actually comprised the majority (60%), but they predicted that they would be in the minority (making up less than 40%). Goethals suggested that the volunteer students' perceptions were motivated by their desire to enhance their self-esteem. The fewer others there are who engage in a socially desirable act, the more laudatory such behavior becomes. The plausibility of Goethals' motivational account is strengthened by the estimates of those who refused to volunteer (presumably a socially undesirable act). These students overestimated the percentage of others who would act as they did by almost 25%.

The desire for self-enhancement undoubtedly plays a role in many instances of false uniqueness but not, we think, in the cases of pluralistic ignorance we have described. It is difficult to see how the tendency of bystanders to think they are more confused than the other bystanders is psychologically comforting. The classroom example is even clearer on this point. How could a student's self-esteem be enhanced by characterizing him or herself as less knowledgeable than other students?

PLURALISTIC IGNORANCE AND THE SOCIAL COMPARISON PROCESS

A comparison of the situations that spawn pluralistic ignorance reveals many differences and a number of interesting similarities. One of the similarities is that all of the situations seem fertile ground for social comparison.

For example, the classroom and bystander contexts we described both confront the actor with a situation that is at once ambiguous and anxiety-provoking. Individuals in these situations lack the *cognitive clarity* (Schachter, 1959) necessary to make stable evaluations of either themselves or their situations. Because there are no objective criteria for arriving at such evaluations, they must rely on the *social reality* conveyed by the reactions of others (Festinger, 1950; 1954). So far, so good; but now a problem occurs. The *fix on reality* that the social comparison process provides them with in these situations is a grievously distorted one. True, the evaluations that the individuals hold following the social comparison process may be more stable, but stable or not, they are also less accurate. Consider the case of bystanders confronted with a potential emergency. The bystanders, having compared their reactions to others, may indeed be more confident in their revised evaluation of the situation, but their evaluation is now seriously inaccurate. Thus, in both the bystander and the classroom context, the social comparison process poorly serves the participants. Any cognitive clarity the individuals have gained through the social comparison process is illusory.

To state our argument boldly, the phenomenon of pluralistic ignorance appears to be an instance of the social comparison process gone awry. We know from previous research that people often fabricate a distorted social reality in the absence of social comparison information (Goethals, 1986). But from our analysis of pluralistic ignorance, it appears that a distorted social reality can also arise in the presence of, and because of, social comparison information. Interestingly, this observation contrasts sharply with previous analyses of pluralistic ignorance. In one of the most influential analyses of the phenomenon Merton (1957) offered the following generalization, "This is a frequently observed condition of a group which is so organized that mutual observability of its members is slight" (p. 377). In our view, Merton's generalization is fundamentally wrong. Pluralistic ignorance does not arise among the students in the classroom, or among bystanders in emergency situations, because "mutual observability . . . is slight." Mutual observability is very high in these contexts. Indeed, the pluralistic ignorance that manifests itself in these contexts appears to arise precisely because of *mutual observability*. Without mutual observability, and the social comparison it affords, there would be no pluralistic ignorance in these contexts. Consider the case of a single bystander confronted with an emergency situation. Based on the false consensus literature, we have every reason to believe that this single bystander would assume that his or her perceptions and concerns would be shared by the majority of others. Similarly, we suspect that it is extremely unlikely that a single student listening to an incomprehensible lecture would assume that other students, if present, would have a superior understanding of it. The latter inference, we contend, will emerge only following a period of social comparison. If individuals were denied the opportunity to compare with others in these and other pluralistic ignorance situations, we suspect that they would be more likely to arrive at the correct interpretation of the situation (e.g. the lecture is incomprehensible or the victim needs help) even if they were less confident in that interpretation. The opportunity to compare with others may leave them more confident in their interpretation, but, if it does, the price they pay for this gain in confidence is a loss in accuracy. In short, the source of pluralistic ignorance lies not with the nature of the stimulus (e.g. an injured victim or an incomprehensible lecture) but with the social comparison process that occurs in the presence of the stimulus.

THE BREEDING GROUNDS FOR PLURALISTIC IGNORANCE

The contexts that spawn pluralistic ignorance may be ones that subvert the social comparison process but how exactly do they accomplish this?

When the Appearance of Unconcern is Interpreted as Lack of Concern

Consider once again the pluralistic ignorance that arises in the emergency and classroom scenarios we described. Examination of these examples reveals that in addition to producing uncertainty and anxiety the situational press in both contexts leads participants to dissemble and act inauthentically. In the classroom scenario, students conceal their confusion as they try to gauge the reactions of their classmates. Bystanders also endeavor to mask their internal confusion and uncertainties as they survey the reactions of others. In both of these situations, the participants present a facade because they fear that presenting their authentic self could lead to embarrassment. Latané and Darley (1970) described the public image anxieties of the bystander this way:

> No member of a crowd wants to be the first to fly off the handle, the one to cry "Wolf!" when no wolf may really be present. Too great a show of concern may in itself be embarrassing, and it also may prematurely commit the bystander to a course of action he has not had a chance to think through. Until he decides what to do, each member of a crowd, however truly concerned he may be about the plight of a victim, may try to maintain a calm demeanor, an unruffled front. (p. 40)

The facades that the individuals in these situations present to one another are so effective that they actually convince one another of the authenticity of their facades. Pretence becomes reality. Although the actors recognize that their own bravado and nonchalance is the stuff of impression management posturing, they assume that the bravado and nonchalance of others is genuine. The general truth about the social comparison process revealed here is that in seeking social reality individuals also convey social reality. The more particular truth revealed here is that when the search for information is accompanied by dissembling and misrepresentation, collective distortion can result.

When Lip Service Masquerades as Conviction

Another general class of circumstances in which people dissemble also seems conducive to pluralistic ignorance. This is the situation in which people take a public position on a social issue that misrepresents their private position. Pluralistic ignorance arises here because individuals erroneously perceive the public expressions of others to represent faithfully their private positions. There are three circumstances in which people take public positions that belie their private ones that seem particularly likely to foster pluralistic ignorance.

One of these circumstances was described by Schanck (1932) in his study of social attitudes in the pseudonymously named community of Elm Hollow. The Baptist church was one of the most powerful institutions in this community and no member of this congregation was more zealous in adherence to the teachings of the church than "Mrs. Salt," the daughter of the former Baptist minister. Mrs. Salt enjoyed considerable status in the community and was rarely challenged. The majority of the church's members publicly acquiesced to her pronouncements, even though they held private views that were considerably less conservative than hers. Expressing polite approval of the pronouncements of a high status and venerated person may not, in an of itself, seem to be a phenomenon requiring careful psychological analysis. The dynamic becomes more curious, however, when we see its consequence. Schanck's interviews revealed that the church members assumed that the other members held private views that were much closer to those of Mrs. Salt than were their own.

A second circumstance in which people may take public positions that misrepresent their private one's occurs when the positions involve values that are central to the doctrine, code, or identity of the individual's institution. This circumstance also was observed by Schanck (1932). He found repeatedly, over a great range of issues, that members of both Mrs. Salt's Baptist church and the Methodist church supported the teachings of their respective churches more strongly in public than they did in private. For example, members of the Methodist church opposed card games much more strongly in public than they did in private. By itself, this latter finding is not surprising since the Methodist church officially opposed card playing. And, after all, discrepancies between what people practice and what they preach are hardly uncommon. What Schanck also discovered, however, was that the church members believed that the gap between public words and private actions was narrower in the case of their fellow church members than it was in their own case. The church members assumed that the others actually practiced what they preached.

Goffman (1961) has proposed that people's public behavior generally reflects their institution's attitudes more closely than does their private behavior. In his words, "when the individual presents himself before others, his performance will tend to incorporate and exemplify the officially accredited values of the society, more so, in fact, than does his behavior as a whole." (p. 35). The tendency to idealize one's group's values in one's public behavior provides an opening for pluralistic ignorance. If the institution's members do not recognize the extent of the gap between the *on stage* and *off stage* behavior of their peers, they may mistakenly perceive themselves to be deviant, a phenomenon amply demonstrated by a variety of studies about institutions.

Prisons constitute one institutional climate that seems particularly conducive to pluralistic ignorance. As numerous studies show, members of the prison culture (guards and inmates) tend to assume that their peers endorse their subculture's values more strongly than they do themselves. In one of the earliest studies of prison life, Wheeler (1961) found that both prison guards and inmates systematically underestimated the similarity of their attitudes to those of their peers, each assuming that their own position was more sympathetic toward the outgroup than was the position of their peers. Kauffman (1981) also found that the private attitudes of prison guards were significantly more liberal than those they attributed to their fellow guards. For example, the majority (78%) of the prison guards in her study approved of an officer defending an accused inmate in the formal setting of a disciplinary board hearing, but less than half (44%) of these guards assumed that their view would be shared by other guards. Similarly, Klofas and Toch (1982) found that whereas only 37% of guards agreed with the position that "the best way to deal with inmates is to be firm," almost 70% believed that their fellow guards would agree with this statement. Toch and Klofas (1984) suggest that pluralistic ignorance arises in these circumstances because pressure to defend the ingroup's values results in prisoner's and guard's onstage behavior being less sympathetic to the outgroup than their private views would dictate: "One knows oneself to be—or suspects oneself of being—tender minded, naive, vulnerable, and pro-social. One evolves a tough facade to avoid being ridiculed. . . . Some of one's peers—a clear minority—are *truly* tough; others—like the person himself—are " 'facade tough'." (Toch & Klofas, 1984, p. 136).

Pluralistic ignorance presumably occurs in this setting because the individuals interpret the facade toughness of their peers to reflect genuine toughness.

Packard and Willower (1972) found a similar pattern of pluralistic ignorance in their investigation of the attitudes of school teachers. These researchers were most interested in assessing teacher support for a *custodial pupil control ideology* (an emphasis on the maintenance of order, distrust of pupils, and a moralistic approach to pupil control). Although only a small minority of the teachers indicated that they actually supported this position, Packard and Willower found most teachers believed that the majority of their peers embraced it. They explained this case of pluralistic ignorance as follows:

> Norms enjoining strictness toward students and the maintenance of social distance typically appear to mark the student subculture, and pressures for faculty members to exhibit a united front to guard against organizational problems resulting from pupil control breakdowns seem substantial. Thus, on stage behavior is likely to indicate support for the prevailing collective even if off stage behavior may reveal personalistic tendencies contrary to consensual social requirements. Teachers "may feel obligated to represent their views on pupil control so that they appear to support prevailing norms." (p. 80)

From this brief review, we see that those situations that conspire to make the on stage behavior of actors more consistent with their institution's values than with their private beliefs appear to be fertile ground for pluralistic ignorance. In these circumstances the on stage behavior of others tends to be taken at face value and, as such, contrasts with the off stage behaviors and views of the self.

There is a third circumstance in which people both publicly misrepresent their private beliefs and assume that the public behavior of others corresponds to their private beliefs. The sequence begins with members of a vocal minority creating the illusion that that they are the majority. The members of the *silent majority*, thinking they are in the minority, then conform to what they mistakenly perceive to be the majority position (Noelle-Neumann, 1986). Finally, pluralistic ignorance emerges among the conforming majority as they assume that their dissembling peers are acting in accordance with their genuine convictions. The illusion of personal deviance that begins by misinterpreting the representativeness of a vocal minority is thus perpetuated by a misinterpretation of the conformity of an isolation-fearing majority. One example of this sequence is provided by Alexis de Tocqueville's (1856/1955) account of the decline of the French church in the middle of the 18th century: "Those who retained their belief in the doctrines of the Church because of being alone in their allegiance and, dreading isolation more than error, professed to share the sentiments of the majority. So what was in reality the opinion of only a part . . . of the nation came to be regarded as the will of all and for this reason seemed irresistible, even to those who had given it this false appearance" (p. 155).

As this example illustrates, a minority position advocated strongly and visibly can induce conformity in an isolation-fearing majority, one consequence of which is that the dissembling members of the majority may interpret the dissembling of their peers to confirm their fears that they are in the minority.

Wheeler's (1961) study of prison inmates also found that minority positions (i.e. antiadministration opinions) received more visible public expression than the beliefs of the majority. He explained this circumstance as follows, ". . . much of the strength of the inmate culture may reside in the ability of antistaff oriented inmates to attain positions of high visibility within the inmate system, thereby generating and reinforcing the image of a culture marked in conflict with the values of the administration." (p. 291) Klofas and Toch (1982) similarly found that those guards and prisoners with the most hard-line positions (subculture custodians in their terms) were inclined to adopt self-appointed roles as spokesman for their respective constituencies. Packard and Willower (1972) also acknowledged that the pluralistic ignorance they observed among school teachers may have been triggered by witnessing custodial behavior in places of high visibility within the school.

Pluralistic Ignorance Versus False Uniqueness

In the previously described studies it is possible that the comparison of the self to an unrepresentative sample of one's social group, in and of itself, could have led to the mistaken perception of personal deviance. If the observed false sense of uniqueness was acquired in this manner, it would not qualify as pluralistic ignorance as we have defined the term. We reserve the latter term for the phenomenon wherein people interpret the similar behavior of the self and others differently. To clarify the distinction, consider a study that reports results that constitute evidence of false uniqueness but not necessarily pluralistic ignorance (Korte, 1972). This study found that Vassar students perceived themselves to be less liberal than the majority of their peers on a number of social and political issues. Whereas only 36% of the students agreed with the statement "Religious beliefs are essentially self-deluding and false," the average student estimated that as many as 55% would agree with this liberal sentiment. To interpret this bias it is necessary to realize that the ethos or institutional norm at Vassar at the time of the study was decidedly liberal and those who embodied liberal values may well have been particularly prominent and conspicuous on campus. Korte (1972) offers the following general summary of this process, ". . . the side of an issue representing a cultural (or subcultural) value is more prominent, more frequently and loudly advocated by its adherents. From the point of view of the individual, this source of bias constitutes an unrepresentative sampling of the relevant population" (p. 586).

Korte's analysis of the situation existing at Vassar is buttressed by Newcomb's (1943) earlier study of Bennington students in which he found that students who espoused Bennington's tradition of liberalism tended to be popular and prominent in positions of leadership.

The illusion of uniqueness reported by Korte (1972) appears to be borne of the social comparison process. The individuals correctly recognize the difference between their attitudes and those of their comparison others but they err by assuming that those with whom they are comparing themselves are representative of their social group. Although the bias found in this study surely qualifies as an instance of false uniqueness, it is not necessarily an instance of pluralistic ignorance. Pluralistic ignorance is a state of uniqueness that arises when individuals misinterpret the similar behavior of similar others, not when they generalize inappropriately from the dissimilar behavior of dissimilar (unrepresentative) others. Of course, these two errors can occur simultaneously. The mistaken perception that one is deviant may arise initially in those special cases where a minority position is more prominently expressed than a majority position. This perception may then be perpetuated when it leads to widespread public conformity to the minority position and, in turn, to pluralistic ignorance and the misperception of deviance. What begins because of a silent majority can continue because of a conforming majority.

TOWARD A THEORY OF PLURALISTIC IGNORANCE

We have defined pluralistic ignorance as a group phenomenon. It occurs when individuals compare themselves to similarly acting others and infer that their own internal states (ie. beliefs, perceptions, feelings) are different than those of their peers. Our review reveals that it arises most commonly when people publicly misrepresent their private beliefs, feelings, and perception. At first glance, it might not seem surprising that pluralistic ignorance develops under conditions in which there is widespread misrepresentation of private feelings and behavior. Why not take other people's behavior at face value? Why not interpret the composed manner of other bystanders to suggest that they have decided that the situation confronting them is not an emergency? Why not interpret the conservative rhetoric of your peers to suggest that they hold conservative convictions? If the victims of pluralistic ignorance were merely observing the group's behavior, their correspondent inferences certainly would be justified. But the victims of pluralistic ignorance are not observers, they are participants in the group dynamic who know that their own behavior belies their internal state and cannot be taken at face value. To unlock the mystery of pluralistic ignorance we must explain why individuals—who realize that their behavior is a facade and an inaccurate reflection of their real feelings—do not assume that this is probably true of others as well. We must explain why they do not assume that the causes underlying their behavior also underly the behavior of the similarly acting (dissembling) others.[1]

Social comparison theory suggests one way of addressing these questions. This theory, especially Goethals and Darley's (1977) restatement of it, does not predict that similar behavior on the part of the self and others will invariably lead to inferences of similar ability or opinions. It is not only where the self and comparison others stand on behavior or performance that determines the self-evaluation made, but also where the self and comparison others stand on those attributes relevant to the behavioral or the performance domain. For example, an individual's score on a test may reflect high or low ability, depending on whether it is higher or lower than the scores of people who are similar to the individual on attributes predictive of performance. An additional implication of their model, however, is that people can justifiably see themselves as deviants even if they act or perform similarly to others if they believe they occupy a different standing than the comparison others on a related attribute. Individuals who view themselves as possessing an intense fear of flying might justifiably feel that they demonstrated a unique degree of courage following an interval of inflight turbulence in which they displayed a degree of nervousness no greater than that of the other passengers.

Following this line of reasoning, we can speculate that pluralistic ignorance may arise when people mistakenly believe that they differ from others on a dimension that is causally related to the actions they have performed. More than this, our review allows us to speculate that the

---

[1]Note that pluralistic ignorance is not simply a manifestation of the well-known tendency of actors and observers to offer divergent causal accounts for the actor's behavior (Jones & Nisbett, 1971). The self-other differences in causal attributions that emerge in pluralistic ignorance do not arise because individuals attribute their own behavior to situational factors and the behavior of others to their dispositions. They emerge because the individuals locate the cause of their own behavior and that of others in different dispositional factors. Furthermore, the actor-observer bias, by itself, would not seem sufficient to produce pluralistic ignorance. For example, students may provide situational accounts for their choice of major and dispositional accounts for the choices of other students (Nisbett, Caputo, Legant, & Maracek, 1973) but this would not necessarily lead them to infer that they like their major either more or less than other students.

dimension on which individuals focus in pluralistic ignorance contexts is social inhibition. People misrepresent their behavior in these contexts because they fear embarrassing themselves. If people believe that fear of embarrassment is a more potent determinant of their own behavior than the behavior of others, it follows that behavior attributed to fear of embarrassment, when engaged in by the self, might be attributed to different factors when engaged in by others. In short, pluralistic ignorance may arise because of an attributional divergence that has its origins in a self-other divergence in the perception of personality traits.

EMPIRICAL EVIDENCE

Study 1: Predicting the Behavior of Others in Embarrassing Situations

If people believe that they possess a greater degree of a particular trait than does the average other, it seems reasonable for them also to expect that their behavior in situations that engage that trait would be different than that of the average other. This was the rationale underlying the first study we conducted (Miller & McFarland, 1987). The experimental context we chose was modeled on the classroom situation we described earlier. According to our theoretical analysis, pluralistic ignorance occurs in this situation because students believe that fear of embarrassment is influencing their behavior more than the behavior of the other students. The students' belief that fear of embarrassment is insufficient cause for the behavior of their classmates leads them to search for alternative accounts for the behavior of others. The termination of this search is the inference that the others possess a superior grasp of the material. Thus, a chain of causal inferences creates a state of pluralistic ignorance in which each student assumes that he or she possesses less knowledge than the other students.

If our analysis of this situation is correct, it is misleading to say that students conclude that they are more confused than the other students despite the fact that the others respond similarly to themselves. Rather, they do this precisely because the others respond similarly. Pluralistic ignorance depends upon the students examining their behavior in light of the behavior of the other students. Only when they have compared their behavior with that of the other students does pluralistic ignorance occur. The others' facades are not assumed to be facades, and thus the students infer that the others must not be as confused as they are. Our first study tests a critical assumption of this reasoning: that individuals will underestimate the percentage of others who will attempt to avoid embarrassing themselves in a situation similar to the classroom setting we have described.

Subjects were 22 undergraduates who participated in the experiment individually. Subjects were told that the purpose of the study was to investigate laypersons' theories of the self-concept and that they were to take part in a tape recorded discussion with other students later in the session. The experimenter explained that because the arrivals of participants had been staggered, the other discussion-group members were currently working in other rooms. For the alleged purpose of preparing them for the discussion, subjects were then asked to read an article addressing theoretical perspectives on the self. The article was written in a purposively obtuse manner and was virtually incomprehensible to individuals without expertise in the area. The experimenter explained to subjects that she would leave them alone to read the article while she did some work in her office. Before leaving, she announced that if they ran into "any really serious problems in understanding the paper," they could come and ask her for help. Presumably because of the high risk of embarrassing themselves, no subjects actually sought her out (DePaulo & Fisher, 1980). On her return, the experimenter asked subjects to complete a questionnaire designed to assess participants' reactions to experimental procedures.

To disguise the purpose of the questionnaire, subjects were presented with a number of filler items. The critical dependent measures asked subjects to indicate: (a) what percentage of other people in the study they thought would go to ask the experimenter questions regarding the article before the discussion, (b) the degree to which they personally understood the article, and (c) the degree to which the average other participant would understand the article. Following the completion of this questionnaire, subjects were fully debriefed.

Subjects were expected to overestimate the number of other people who would seek clarification from the experimenter. This hypothesis was confirmed. Subjects estimated that 37% of other subjects would ask the experimenter questions, when in actuality none of the subjects asked the experimenter questions.

It is possible that subjects' tendency to overestimate the percentage of others who would approach the experimenter may have reflected the belief that the others would understand the material less well than they did rather than their belief that the others would be less inhibited than they were. Consistent with our analysis, however, subjects estimated their own level of understanding to be no different than that of the other participants.

Study 2: Interpreting the Behavior of Others in Embarrassing Situations

Subjects in our first experiment indicated that they expected a sizeable proportion of students to ask an experimenter to clarify a difficult essay even though they themselves did not. How might they respond when they could actually compare their behavior to that of others and discovered that others also did not seek out the experimenter? One possibility is that subjects would revise their view of how generally fearful others are of embarrassing themselves. A second possibility, suggested by our analysis, is that they would revise their view of how confused the others were relative to themselves. Specifically, they might draw the inference from the inaction of others that these others actually understood the essay better than they themselves did. This latter prediction should only obtain, however, when people attribute their own inaction to social inhibition. No self-other differences in comprehension should be expected when subjects attribute their own behavior to a factor that is believed to affect the self and others equally (e.g. experimental instructions). Our next experiment (Miller & McFarland, 1987) tested this reasoning.

Subjects were 32 undergraduate volunteers. Up to the point at which the experimenter departed for the alleged purpose of completing some work in her office, the procedure was identical to that of Study 1, except for the fact that subjects took part in groups of 3–8. In the constrained condition, the experimenter explained as she left that subjects could not come to ask for clarification (for purposes of experimental control). In the unconstrained condition, the experimenter indicated that subjects could ask questions, although the procedure for doing so required that they risk embarrassing themselves. They were told that if they "had any really serious problems in understanding the article," they could approach her in her office several doors away. The experimenter then departed, leaving subjects to read the article. No subjects in either condition sought out the experimenter.

When the experimenter returned, she explained to subjects that they were to complete a brief background information questionnaire before the group discussion. The alleged purpose of the questionnaire was to assess factors that might influence the course of the discussion. Several measures devised to assess pluralistic ignorance were included. The three critical questions asked of the subjects were to indicate on 3-point scales: (a) how well they understood the ideas in the article relative to the average other participant (1 = I understand less well, 2 = I understand equally well, 3 = I understand better than others), (b) how much knowledge regarding the self-concept they possessed relative to the average other participant (1 = less knowledge, 2 = the same knowledge, 3 = more knowledge), and (c) how well they would do relative to the average other participant if they had to write an essay on the topic of the self-concept (1 = I would perform less well, 2 = I would perform the same as, 3 = I would perform better). Upon completion of this questionnaire, subjects were fully debriefed.

We expected that ratings of the self relative to the average other would be more negative in the unconstrained than in the constrained condition. This prediction followed from the assumption that the subjects in the unconstrained condition would attribute their failure to seek out the experimenter to their uniquely high fear of embarrassment, whereas the subjects in the constrained condition would attribute both their behavior and the behavior of others to the experimental instructions. The results supported the prediction. On an index that averaged responses to the three measures, subjects in the unconstrained condition evaluated themselves significantly more negatively relative to other (M = 1.56) than did subjects in the constrained condition (M = 1.98), $t(30) = 2.58$, $p < .02$.

It should be noted that the responses from subjects in the unconstrained condition of this experiment differed not only from the responses of subjects in the constrained condition but from those responses provided by subjects in Study 1. Subjects in the earlier study, deprived of social comparison information, assumed that other subjects, had they been present, would comprehend the essay neither better nor worse than themselves. Considering these sets of findings together, we find considerable support for our analysis of pluralistic ignorance. The phenomenon does not simply arise whenever people are inhibited from taking action, as was true of subjects in Study 1. Other, similarly inhibited individuals must also be present. But even this circumstance is not guaranteed to spawn pluralistic ignorance. It is also necessary for the individuals to attribute their own inhibition to fear of embarrassment.

Study 3: Perceived Self-Other Differences in Social Inhibition

Our analysis of pluralistic ignorance rests on the assumption that people believe they possess more of those traits that produce social inhibition than others do. Of course, once we posit the existence of such an illusion, we must explain it. One possible explanation emerges from a consideration of the evidential basis of traits associated with social inhibition. The presence of these traits is inferred primarily from internal, unobservable criteria such as thoughts and feelings (Funder, 1980; Kenrick & Stringfield, 1980). Two related predictions follow from this fact. First, the evidence pertaining to the existence of traits associated with social inhibition will be more directly accessible to the self than to others. Second, the greater access that individuals have to evidence of these traits will result in their actually having more evidence of their existence in the self than in others. We conducted a study to test these predictions (Miller & McFarland, 1987).

Two lists of 10 trait adjectives were selected from a list of 555 trait adjectives for which Anderson (1968) provided social desirability ratings.

The adjectives in one list represented traits defined primarily by internal referents (sympathetic, self-critical, sensitive, hesitant, bashful, choosy, self-conscious, inhibited, indecisive, and preoccupied); the adjectives from the second list represented traits defined primarily by external referents (poised, orderly, daring, quiet, aggressive, wordy, ungraceful, argumentative, submissive and sarcastic). The lists were created so that the average social desirability rating of the internal and external traits was equivalent. Social desirability was systematically varied within the two lists, however, with the first five traits in each list having higher social desirability ratings than the remaining five. A pretest involving 72 Simon Fraser University students established that: (a) the traits classified as internal were indeed perceived to be more internally based than the traits classified as external, and (b) the traits classified as socially desirable were indeed perceived to be more socially desirable than the traits classified as socially undesirable.

In the principal study, 116 Simon Fraser University undergraduates completed a questionnaire allegedly concerned with people's perceptions of the similarities between their own personality and that of the average other person. They were supplied with the 20 trait adjectives and asked to indicate on separate scales the extent to which each trait described them as well as the average other student (1 = not at all to 9 = extremely).

The trait ratings were analyzed in a 2 × 2 × 2 repeated measures analysis of variance (Target: Self vs. Other × Trait Desirability: Desirable vs. Undesirable × Trait Basis: Internal vs. External). We hypothesized that subjects would rate themselves higher than the average other on internal traits but not on external traits. A significant interaction between trait basis and target supported this prediction $F(1, 113) = 37.87, p < .001$.

Subjects assigned higher ratings to themselves (M = 5.83) than to the average other (M = 5.20) on internal traits, $t(113) = 6.49, p < .001$, but they did not differ in the level of external traits they ascribed to self (M = 5.16) and the average other (M = 5.14) ($t < 1$). The self-other differences that emerged on the internal traits occurred for both those traits that were judged (by two independent raters) to be most related to social inhibition (inhibited, self-conscious, bashful, sensitive, hesitant), $F(1, 115) = 31.86, p < .001$, and those traits that were judged to be least related to social inhibition (sympathetic, self-critical, choosy, indecisive, preoccupied, $F(1, 115) = 67.17, p < .001$.

The results of Study 3 support our contention that people believe that they possess a greater degree of traits that lead to social inhibition than does the average other. Presumably, this belief derives from the greater access they have to their own internal states. We proposed that it is people's belief that they are generally more bashful, self-conscious, and so on than the average other that leads them to infer the situationally specific differences between self and others that constitute pluralistic ignorance.

DISCUSSION

We have traced the origins of pluralistic ignorance to the social comparison process. Social comparison can serve two functions. First, it can facilitate self-evaluation; others can help us evaluate the goodness or badness of our abilities and the rightness or wrongness of our opinions (Festinger, 1954). Second, it can provide us with cognitive clarity concerning our environment (Schachter, 1959); others can help us decide whether a situation is dangerous, whether an exam is easy, and so on. The two functions served by comparisons with others are highly interrelated. When people discover that others found a test much easier than they did, they learn both that it was an easy test and that they are not as knowledgeable as their peers. Similarly, when people discover that others do not find a situation as threatening as they do they are led toward a modified view of not only the situation, but of themselves: "I guess I'm a bit paranoid."

In those circumstances in which pluralistic ignorance arises the social comparison process fails to fulfill either of its functions. People's situational interpretations, however confident, are illusory, as are their self-evaluations. The circumstances that produce pluralistic ignorance generally share two features. First, the individuals' public behavior in these circumstances misrepresents their true feelings. Second, the motive behind this misrepresentation is the individuals' fear that revealing their true selves would be embarrassing. Our review suggests that there are two broad classes of situations in which these conditions can be found.

In one circumstance, pluralistic ignorance yields the illusory belief that others hold the group's values more strongly than does oneself. This form of pluralistic ignorance arises because people do not realize that the idealized on stage behavior of others reflects a desire to appear to embody the institution's values and not a genuine commitment to those values. We saw instances of this type of pluralistic ignorance in institutions as diverse as schools (Packard & Willower, 1972), churches (Schanck, 1932), prisons (Kauffman, 1981), and mental institutions (Goffman, 1961). And it can arise in the context of broader cultural myths as well. One illustration of this fact was provided by Hill, Stycos, and Back (1957) in their study of family attitudes among Puerto Rican males. Although the Puerto Rican males interviewed showed considerable private support for the concept of small families, they believed that the desire for large families was shared by most other Puerto Rican males. There is no direct evidence in this study to suggest why pluralistic ignorance arose, but our analysis suggests one possibility. First, the desire to avoid appearing deviant may have led the Puerto Rican males to suppress their true beliefs and to pay lip service to the *macho* code which valued large families. Second, the assumption that they feared appearing deviant more than other males may have led them to interpret the lip service of others to be genuine.

The error that characterizes the pluralistic ignorance observed in the class of situations we have just described concerns the priority that the other members of the group are believed to place on a particular value or norm. In the second class of situations in which pluralistic ignorance arises, the individuals correctly identify the positive value that the group places on a particular position or characteristic, but fail to realize that the others are only pretending to have these characteristics. In the emergency situation, for example, the bystanders do not err by overestimating the value the others attach to "keeping cool" but in underestimating the strength of their motivation to avoid acting in a manner inconsistent with this value. Similarly, subjects in Miller and McFarland's (1987) experiment did not err by overestimating the value the others attached to being smart, but in underestimating the motivation the others had to avoid appearing stupid.

In both of the forms of pluralistic ignorance we have described, discrepancies exist between private beliefs and public behavior. More than this, the discrepancies are produced by fear of embarrassment. But there are other fears that could produce discrepancies of this type, and it is appropriate to ask whether their activation might not also lead to pluralistic ignorance. Perhaps people believe that they are motivated by all fears more than is the average person. This is possible but we doubt it. We doubt that hostages who are forced at terrorists' gun point to mouth antiAmerican rhetoric would assume that the pronouncements of fellow hostages were any more genuine than their own. Pluralistic ignorance may arise whenever fears of any type constrain behavior but we suspect that there is something special about the fear of social disapproval. For one thing, fear of embarrassment may be perceived to implicate the self more directly than other fears. Fear of a loaded gun may seem like a universal, biological reaction, whereas fear of looking foolish in front of strangers, however general a fear it might be, may seem to reflect more strongly one's unique history and personality. It may also be important that often the strongest evidence of our fear of embarrassment comes from realizing how powerful this fear is in relation to other fears. A teenage girl who is so embarrassed about discussing birth control with her partner that she knowingly risks becoming pregnant may feel she has highly compelling evidence of her fear of embarrassment, and find it hard to believe that her peers would be similarly influenced. A second, unique aspect of fear of embarrassment, that follows from the first, is that people might not share their experiences concerning this fear as widely as they do their experiences concerning other fears.

Consequences of Pluralistic Ignorance

Pluralistic ignorance can have consequences for the social group and the individual. At the group level, pluralistic ignorance can lead to the perpetuation of unpopular social norms. People will tolerate unjust social conditions, acquiesce to flawed decisions, and desist from advocating needed reforms all because they assume the majority of their peers disagree with them and believe that nothing, other than personal embarrassment, could be gained by revealing their true beliefs. Racial segregation, for example, may have persisted in various contexts in our society long after the majority opposed it because those who held antisegregation positions mistakenly believed they were in the minority (Breed & Ktsanes, 1961; Fields & Schuman, 1976; O'Gorman, 1975; O'Gorman & Garry, 1976). Similarly, dubious group decisions may be implemented simply because the decision-makers believe that their misgivings are not shared by others (Janis, 1982; Shaw & Blum, 1965). Pluralistic ignorance can also lead groups to take collective action that does not reflect the private values of the group. In this regard, Matza (1964) discusses how delinquent gangs will engage in actions that individual members disapprove of but go along with because they believe these actions are viewed as desirable by their fellow gang members. This occurs, according to Matza, because ". . . there is a system of shared misunderstandings, based on miscues, which lead delinquents to believe that all others situated in their company are committed to their misdeeds, (Matza, 1964, p. 52). Thus, even illusory peer pressure can lead adolescents to engage in behaviors they disapprove of, if it is sustained by pluralistic ignorance (see Chassin et al., 1981; Leventhal, Glynn & Fleming, 1987 for a similar analysis of smoking behaviors among adolescents).

Pluralistic ignorance can lead to changes in private attitudes and behaviors as well as in public behavior. Bystanders in emergency situations do not just pay lip service to the social construals they attribute to others, they accept them as their own. Pluralistic ignorance can facilitate social change by inducing private acceptance of a mythical position and not simply by inducing public conformity to it. One implication of this fact is that much pluralistic ignorance may go undetected because it so quickly leads to revisions in private attitudes. Consider the believers in Eighteenth century France described by de Tocqueville. It is conceivable that eventually these victims of pluralistic ignorance would have become nonbelievers, having been persuaded by the antichurch sentiments that were voiced by others and, indeed, by they themselves. Once this occurred, the opportunity to document pluralistic ignorance would have been lost. Illusion would have become reality.

Pluralistic ignorance may frequently play this catalytic role in belief formation and change. As an example, consider how this process might operate in the development of gender-typed beliefs among males. Initially, young boys may act or speak in a sexist manner around their peers because they do not wish to be embarrassed by not appearing appropriately masculine. They may not understand why a boy should not play girls' games or like girls' activities but they may act as though they do so as not to seem a deviant. Over time, however, they may internalize the gender-typed rhetoric to which they originally just paid lip service because they thought everyone else believed it. Pluralistic ignorance, thus, may shorten the road between compliance and internalization (Kelman, 1958).

The tendency to internalize a position erroneously assumed to be the majority position may account for why so many of the documented cases of pluralistic ignorance occur when a group or culture is in transition and the individual members hold social beliefs that are more progressive than those they attribute to their peers. During periods of social change, there may frequently be a relatively protracted phase in which the majority no longer holds an old view but thinks the old view is still held by the majority. The alternative transitional stage, in which the majority does not yet hold a new value but believes that the majority of their group does, may tend to be much shorter in duration and thus more difficult to measure. The public position of a group may be slower to catch up to the changing private opinions of the group members than the private positions of group members are to catch up to the changing public position of a group.

The group or societal consequences of pluralistic ignorance will often be accompanied by intrapersonal and interpersonal consequences. Among other things, pluralistic ignorance will often leave its victims feeling deviant and alienated from one another. Feelings of alienation can lead to lower group cohesion which, in turn, can have negative consequences for the group's functioning (Lott & Lott, 1965). The sense of deviance and alienation that accompanies the illusion of uniqueness may intensify with group size. As the number of others presumed to be dissimilar increases, the greater may be the sense of personal deviance. In fact, Allport's (1924; 1933) original discussion of pluralistic ignorance focused more on the consequences of the *illusion of universality* among the other group members than on the *illusion of deviance* that we have emphasized in our analysis.

Guilt and self-recrimination may often accompany the sense of deviance and alienation that victims of pluralistic ignorance experience. People may experience guilt when they believe they do not hold appropriate values or beliefs. People may also feel guilty about lacking the courage to act in accordance with their true beliefs. Pluralistic ignorance can lead its victims to hold distorted beliefs about both themselves and their peers. To illustrate, consider the case where a group of females are in the presence of a high status male who makes sexist comments. Even if the females disapprove of the comments it is conceivable that they would not confront him because of their hesitancy to create a scene. If this were to happen, how might the women interpret their behavior and that of the other women? If they attributed the behavior of the other women to the same desire to avoid a scene that guided their own behavior, they will neither perceive the other women as unenlightened, nor their own behavior as particularly cowardly. On the other hand, if the women think that their own behavior reflected their fear of embarrassment but that the behavior of the others reflected their lack of distress over the man's comments, they may be led to unfair inferences concerning both their own cowardice and the political correctness of the other women.

Another area in which pluralistic ignorance may have important consequences is that of reactions to negative life events. Various authorities have proposed that the dysphoria produced by negative life events is greater in people who believe that their reactions to these events differ from those of most other people (Coates & Peterson, 1982; Coates, Wortman & Abbey, 1979; Glick, Weiss & Parkes, 1974; Nisbett, Borgida, Crandall, & Reed, 1976; Strohmer, Biggs, & McIntyre, 1984; Valins & Nisbett, 1971; Wortman & Dunkel-Schetter, 1979). Some empirical support for this proposition comes from research that indicates that providing people with evidence of the commonness of their problems can influence their responses to such problems (Coates & Winston, 1983; Gibbons, 1986; Levy, 1976; Snyder & Ingram, 1983; Wilson & Linville, 1982). The present analysis suggests that one reason a false perception of uniqueness may arise in the context of negative life events is because the victim's fear of embarrassment may lead him or her to be hesitant to reveal fears, conflicts, and insecurities to similar others. This failure to disclose, coupled with the belief that fear of embarrassment is a greater inhibitory force on the self than on others, may lead the victim to infer that his or her emotional reactions are greater than those of others. This perception may, in turn, exacerbate the negative affect the victim is experiencing (Valins & Nisbett, 1971).

Preventing or Dissipating Pluralistic Ignorance

The negative consequences that pluralistic ignorance can have compel us to consider means of preventing or dissipating this phenomenon. In some contexts pluralistic ignorance will simply dissipate over time because of the difficulty of sustaining a facade. Newcomb's (1961) classic study of the acquaintance process among college students provides an interesting example of this phenomenon. One of the findings was that the majority of a group of 17 college males who had lived together for two days predicted that the majority of their housemates would endorse statements such as one should "try to become close friends with all the people you know . . ." and one should "let people know you trust them and want to be close friends . . ." even though they themselves endorsed statements that reflected a more cautious approach to the formation of friendships. Newcomb attributed the fact that the students thought they were more "standoffish" than their peers to the fact that everyone began the acquaintance process by displaying exemplary cordiality. The students knew their own cordiality was at least somewhat motivated by their desire to make a good impression but assumed that the cordiality of others was genuine. Follow-up interviews, however, showed that the illusion that the others were friendlier and less standoffish than the self soon dissipated. Presumably, the students found it difficult to maintain their on stage level of friendliness indefinitely and soon lapsed into more natural interaction patterns which permitted more accurate evaluations.

Pluralistic ignorance will not always dissipate over time, however, and intervention may well be necessary. Our analysis suggests a number of strategies to take in this regard, all of which involve facilitating the social comparison process. The first of these strategies involves encouraging people to act in accordance with their private beliefs and to publicly show their true feelings. The more exposure people have to one another's off stage behavior, the greater the likelihood that pluralistic ignorance will diminish. Of course, this presupposes that pluralistic ignorance has not precipitated internalization and actually modified off stage behavior. It also presupposes that people will generalize from their experience with their peers and friends to their beliefs about the larger social group. Generalization of this type apparently did not occur in the community of Elm Hollow. Residents knew that their friends and family had attitudes toward card playing and alcohol similar to their own, but they still thought that those of the broader community were different (see Perloff & Fetzer, 1986 for a similar finding). Another technique for precluding pluralistic ignorance involves altering the formal procedures that guide communication within a group. In his discussion of strategies for avoiding *groupthink*, Janis (1982) describes several techniques that might reduce the pluralistic ignorance that arises in group discussions. These include: (a) selecting a nondirective leader, (b) encouraging group members to play the role of devils' advocate and (c) inviting experts to challenge the viewpoints of group members.

Finally, the dissemination of social comparison information through reports of surveys may be particularly effective in diminishing pluralistic ignorance as Katz and Schanck (1938) noted in their discussion of the link between pluralistic ignorance and support for prohibition. They proposed that prohibition lasted as long as it did, at least partly, because people were hesitant to express their antiprohibition sentiments publicly. Once objective checks of private opinions were made public, however, "prohibition collapsed like a punctured balloon (p. 175)."

The important point is that for communication to decrease pluralistic ignorance it must be candid communication. If it is not candid, communication may actually facilitate pluralistic ignorance. This point is relevant to the functioning of support groups. Central to the concept of support groups is the assumption that the opportunity to share experiences with people in similar circumstances makes people better able to cope with their fates. This assumption is clearly compatible with our analysis of pluralistic ignorance. Without the forum of a support group, people's inhibitions against revealing their experiences to others, coupled with their belief that their inhibitions are greater than those of others, may lead them to feel unique and deviant. Support group leaders who encourage individuals to overcome their inhibitions may help dissipate this pluralistic ignorance. However, support groups can be expected to have this effect only to the extent that individuals actually do share their feelings and experiences. If individuals continue to be inhibited from sharing their true experiences and feelings with others, in spite of being urged to do so, pluralistic ignorance may even increase. Individuals may infer from the fact that others are not reporting feelings and thoughts corresponding to their own that the others do not have these thoughts and feelings. Support groups, therefore, could actually have an effect on adjustment opposite to the desired one, a possibility that may account for the mixed evidence on the effectiveness of such groups (Coates & Winston, 1983).

In encouraging people to be frank and open with one another, people should also be made aware of the influence that fear of embarrassment has on others. If people knew that fear of embarrassment was affecting the behavior of the others as much as it was their own, they could be expected to show less inhibition, or at least interpret the inhibited behavior of others appropriately.

Final Thoughts

We believe that our account of pluralistic ignorance can parsimoniously explain both the data we have presented and the literature we have reviewed. Nevertheless, we willingly acknowledge that our account may be incomplete. For one thing, the phenomenon may well be overdetermined, such that different processes may be sufficient to produce it in some conditions but not necessary in others. Consistent with this possibility, note that there are vast differences in the contexts in which pluralistic ignorance is found. For example, the bystander situation studied by Latané and Darley (1970) involved brief interactions among strangers who did not communicate with one another, whereas the situation studied by Shanck (1932) involved extended interaction among friends and neighbors who communicated extensively with one another.

One alternative, or supplementary, process that may be involved in some instances of pluralistic ignorance is what can be called the *differential-encoding* hypothesis. This hypothesis, in contrast to the *differential-interpretation* hypothesis that we have proposed, directs attention to the possibility that people in pluralistic ignorance situations fail to recognize that the behavior of the self and others is similar. Once again, consider bystanders in emergency situations. The differential-interpretation hypothesis assumes that the bystanders correctly recognize that they appear as calm and unconcerned as do the other bystanders but incorrectly infer that this similar public behavior reflects different internal states. The differential-encoding or *illusion of transparency* hypothesis suggests that the bystanders, in fact, do not realize that they appear as calm and unconcerned as the others do. That is, they do not realize the extent to which their public behavior masks or belies their internal state of concern and confusion. By this account, it is the bystanders' erroneous perception that there is a self-other difference in public behavior ("They do not look as confused or concerned as I do.") that leads them to the conclusion that the situation is not an emergency.

We know of no empirical support for this hypothesis; nor can this hypothesis account for the findings of our Study 2. (If a self-other encoding difference was responsible for subjects believing that the essay confused them more than the other subjects, this effect should have arisen in the constrained as well as the unconstrained condition.) Still, the hypothesis has intuitive appeal. For example, in anxiety-provoking situations it is often very difficult for people to believe that, despite feeling highly nervous, they do not appear highly nervous. In parallel fashion, it may be difficult for bystanders in emergency situations to believe that they actually look as calm and cool as they do, given their aroused internal state. At this point, all we can say with confidence is that what ever the definitive explanation of this fascinating phenomenon turns out to be, the social comparison process will surely be involved. For this reason, research and theory that illuminates the phenomenon of pluralistic ignorance can be expected to shed considerable light on the social comparison process as well.

ACKNOWLEDGMENTS

Preparation of this chapter was supported by National Institute of Mental Health Grant MH44069-01 to Dale T. Miller. We are grateful to E. E. Jones, D. Prentice, J. Suls and T. Wills for comments on an earlier draft.

REFERENCES

Allport, F. H. (1924). *Social psychology.* Boston: Houghton Mifflin.
Allport, F. H. (1933). *Institutional behavior.* Chapel Hill: University of North Carolina Press.
Anderson, N. H. (1968). Likableness ratings of 555 personality-trait words. *Journal of Personality and Social Psychology, 9,* 272–279.
Breed, W., & Ktsanes, T. (1961). Pluralistic ignorance in the process of opinion formation. *Public Opinion Quarterly, 25,* 382–392.

Campbell, J. D. (1986). Similarity and uniqueness: The effects of attribute type, relevance, and individual differences in self-esteem and depression. *Journal of Personality and Social Psychology, 50,* 281–294.

Chassin, L., Corty, E., Presson, C., Olshavsky, R., Bensenberg, M. & Sherman, S. J. (1981). Predicting adolescents' intentions to smoke cigarettes. *Journal of Health and Social Behaviors, 22,* 445–455.

Coates, D. & Peterson, B. A. (1982). Depression and deviance. In G. Weary & H. L. Mirels (Eds.), *Integrations of clinical and social psychology* (pp. 154–170). New York: Oxford University Press.

Coates, D. & Winston, T. (1983). Counteracting the deviance of depression: Peer support groups for victims. *Journal of Social Issues, 39,* 169–194.

Coates, D., Wortman, C. B., & Abbey, A. (1979). Reactions to victims. In I. H. Frieze, D. Bar-Tal, and J. S. Carroll (Eds.), *New approaches to social problems* (pp. 21–56). San Francisco: Jossey–Bass.

de Tocqueville, A. (1955). *The old regime and the French Revolution* (S. Gilbert, Trans.), New York: Doubleday/Anchor. (Original work published in 1856)

DePaulo, B. M. & Fisher, J. D. (1980). The costs of asking for help. *Basic and Applied Social Psychology, 1,* 23–35.

Festinger, L. (1950). Informal social communication. *Psychological Review, 57,* 271–282.

Festinger, L. (1954). A theory of social comparison processes. *Human Relations, 12,* 117–140.

Fields, J. M., & Schuman, H. (1976). Public beliefs and the beliefs of the public. *Public Opinion Quarterly, 40,* 427–448.

Funder, D. C. (1980). On seeing ourselves as others see us: Self-other agreement and discrepancy in personality ratings. *Journal of Personality, 48,* 473–493.

Gibbons, F. X. (1986). Social comparison and depression: Company's effect on misery. *Journal of Personality and Social Psychology, 51,* 140–148.

Glick, I. O., Weiss, R. S., & Parkes, C. M. (1974). *The first year of bereavement.* New York: Wiley.

Goethals, G. R. (1986). Fabricating and ignoring social reality: Self-serving estimates of consensus. In J. Olson, C. P. Herman, & M. P. Zanna (Eds.), *Relative deprivation and social comparison: The Ontario Symposium on Social Cognition* (Vol. 4, pp. 137–157). Hillsdale, NJ: Lawrence Erlbaum Associates.

Goethals, G. R., & Darley, J. (1977). Social comparison theory: An attributional approach. In J. Suls and R. L. Miller (Eds.), *Social comparison processes: Theoretical and empirical perspectives* (pp. 259–278). New York: Halsted.

Goffman, E. (1961). *Asylums: Essays on the social situation of mental patients and other inmates.* Garden City, NY: Anchor.

Hill, R., Stycos, J. M., & Back, K. (1957). *The family and population control: A Puerto Rico experiment in social change.* Chapel Hill, NC: University of North Carolina Press.

Janis, I. (1982). *Victims of group think: A psychological study of foreign-policy decisions and fiascos* (rev. ed.). Boston: Houghton–Mifflin.

Jones, E. E., & Nisbett, R. E. (1971). *The actor and the observer: Divergent perceptions of the causes of behavior.* Morristown, NJ: General Learning Press.

Katz, D. & Allport, F. H. (1928). *Student attitudes: A report of the Syracuse University research study.* Syracuse, NY: Craftsman Press.

Katz, D. & Schanck, R. L. (1938). *Social psychology.* New York: Wiley.

Kauffman, K. (1981). Prison officer attitudes and perceptions of attitudes. *Journal of Research in Crime Delinquency, 18,* 272–294.

Kelman, H. C. (1958). Compliance, identification, and internalization: Three processes of attitude change. *Journal of Conflict Resolution, 2,* 51–60.
Kenrick, D., & Stringfield, D. O. (1980). Personality traits and the eye of the beholder: Crossing some philosophical boundaries in the search for consistency in all of the people. *Psychological Review, 87,* 88–104.
Klofas, J., & Toch, H. (1982). The guard subculture myth. *Journal of Research in Crime and Delinquency, 19,* 238–254.
Korte, C. (1972). Pluralistic ignorance about student radicalism. *Sociometry, 35,* 576–587.
Krech, D., Crutchfield, R. S., & Ballachey, E. L. (1962). *Individual in society: A textbook in social psychology.* New York: McGraw–Hill.
Latané, B. & Darley, J. (1970). *The unresponsive bystander: Why doesn't he help?* New York: Appleton Century Crofts.
Leventhal, H., Glynn, K. & Fleming, R. (1987). Is the smoking decision an informed choice. *Journal of the American Medical Association, 257,* 3373–3376.
Levy, L. H. (1976). Self-help groups: Types and psychological processes. *Journal of Applied Behavioral Science, 12,* 310–322.
Lott, A. J. & Lott, B. E. (1965). Group cohesiveness as interpersonal attraction: A review of relationships with antecedents and consequent variables. *Psychological Bulletin, 64,* 259–309.
Marks, G. (1984). Thinking one's abilities are unique and one's opinions are common. *Personality and Social Psychology Bulletin, 10,* 203–208.
Marks, G., & Miller, N. (1987). Ten years of research on the false consensus effect: An empirical and theoretical review. *Psychological Bulletin, 102,* 72–90.
Matza, D. (1964). *Delinquency and drift.* New York: Wiley.
Merton, R. K. (1957). *Social theory and social structure* (rev. ed.). Glencoe, IL: Free Press of Glencoe.
Miller, D. T. & McFarland, C. (1987). Pluralistic ignorance: When similarity is interpreted as dissimilarity. *Journal of Personality and Social Psychology, 53,* 298–305.
Mullen, B., Atkins, J. L., Champion, D. S., Edwards, C., Hardy, D., Story, J. E. & Vanderlok, M. (1985). The false consensus effect: A meta-analysis of 115 hypothesis tests. *Journal of Experimental Social Psychology, 21,* 262–283.
Newcomb, T. M. (1943). *Personality and social change.* New York: Dryden Press.
Newcomb, T. M. (1961). *The acquaintance process.* New York: Holt, Rinehart & Winston.
Nisbett, R. E., Borgida, E., Crandall, R., & Reed, H. (1976). Popular induction: Information is not necessarily informative. In J. S. Carroll and J. W. Payne (Eds.), *Cognition and social behavior* (pp. 227–236). Hillsdale, NJ: Lawrence Erlbaum Associates.
Nisbett, R. E., Caputo, C., Legant, P., & Marecek, J. (1973). Behavior as seen by the actor and as seen by the observer. *Journal of Personality and Social Psychology, 27,* 154–164.
Noelle-Neumann, E. (1986). *The spiral of silence.* Chicago: University of Chicago Press.
O'Gorman, H. J. (1975). White and black perceptions of racial values. *Public Opinion Quarterly, 39,* 313–330.
O'Gorman, H. J., & Garry, S. L. (1976). Pluralistic ignorance—a replication and extension. *Public Opinion Quarterly, 40,* 449–458.
Packard, J. S. & Willower, D. J. (1972). Pluralistic ignorance and pupil control ideology. *Journal of Education Administration, 10,* 78–87.
Perloff, L. S., & Fetzer, B. K. (1986). Self–other judgments and perceived vulnerability to victimization. *Journal of Personality and Social Psychology, 50,* 502–510.
Ross, L., Greene, D., & House, P. (1977). The "false consensus effect": An egocentric bias in social perception and attribution processes. *Journal of Experimental Social Psychology, 13,* 279–301.
Schachter, S. (1959). *The psychology of affiliation.* Stanford, CA: Stanford University Press.

Schanck, R. L. (1932). A study of community and its group institutions conceived of as behavior of individuals. *Psychological Monographs, 43*(2), 1–133.

Shaw, M. E., & Blum, M. (1965). Group performance as a function of task difficulty and the group's awareness of member satisfaction. *Journal of Applied Psychology, 49,* 151–154.

Sherman, S. J., Presson, C. C. & Chassin, L. (1984). Mechanisms underlying the false consensus effect: The special role of threats to self. *Personality and Social Psychology Bulletin, 10,* 127–138.

Snyder, C. R., & Fromkin, H. L. (1980). *Uniqueness: The human pursuit of difference.* New York: Plenum.

Snyder, C. R., & Ingram, R. E. (1983). "Company motivates the miserable": The impact of consensus information on help seeking for psychological problems. *Journal of Personality and Social Psychology, 45,* 1118–1126.

Strohmer, D. C., Biggs, D. A., & McIntyre, W. F. (1984). Social comparison information and judgments about depression and seeking counselling. *Journal of Counselling Psychology, 31,* 591–594.

Suls, J., & Wan, C. K. (1987). In search of the false uniqueness phenomenon: Fear and estimates of social consensus. *Journal of Personality and Social Psychology, 52,* 211–217.

Toch, H., & Klofas, J. (1984). Pluralistic ignorance, revisited. In G. M. Stephenson and J. H. Davis (Eds.), *Progress in applied social psychology,* Vol. 2, New York: Wiley.

Valins, S., & Nisbett, R. E. (1971). *Attribution processes in the development and treatment of emotional disorders.* Morristown, NJ: General Learning Press.

Wheeler, S. (1961). Role conflict in correctional communities. In D. R. Cressey (Ed.), *The prison: Studies in institutional organization and change* (274–298). New York: Holt, Rinehart & Winston.

Wilson, T. & Linville, P. (1982). Improving the academic performance of college freshman: Attribution therapy revisited. *Journal of Personality and Social Psychology, 42,* 367–376.

Wortman, C. B., & Dunkel-Schetter, C. (1979). Interpersonal relationships and cancer: A theoretical analysis. *Journal of Social Issues, 35,* 120–155.

IV APPLIED MODELS OF SOCIAL COMPARISON

The three chapters in this section show how social comparison theory may be used to illuminate topics of applied importance. The focus of chapter 12, by Frederick X. Gibbons and Meg Gerrard, is on how people use downward comparison as a coping strategy to help them deal with personal problems such as eating disorders, smoking cessation, and depression. Downward comparison can take one of two forms: a passive form, in which the individual takes advantage of opportunities to compare with others who are worse off; or an active form, in which the status of the other is lowered, thereby creating a more favorable comparison. Drawing from their extensive research program, Gibbons and Gerrard demonstrate how active and passive downward comparison can influence mood states, optimism, perceptions of deviance, and social distancing in populations experiencing various kinds of threats to self-esteem.

In chapter 13, Donna Nagata and Faye Crosby consider the role of social comparison in perceptions of injustice. They discuss a phenomenon termed the *denial of personal disadvantage* in which people recognize that their reference group is discriminated against, but see themselves individually as exempt from discrimination. They then raise the question of whether an ethnic minority who emphasize group harmony, such as Japanese-Americans, are less willing to see themselves as differing from their group in terms of suffering. This question is put to test in several studies including data from the Sansei Research Project, where several hundred Japanese-Americans were interviewed about their feelings concerning their parents' internment during World War II. The results show considerable variability in the phenomenon, and suggest that cultural differences may place limits on the degree to which people engage in denial processes in comparison behavior.

Glenn Affleck and Howard Tennen, in chapter 14, discuss research on the use of social comparison among persons with serious medical problems. They consider research on persons with life-threatening illness, and report findings from their research program in medical settings. Three populations are discussed: arthritis patients, mothers of premature infants, and women with impaired fertility. Results regarding the benefits of downward comparison as a coping mechanism, the impact of comparisons directed by others, and the use of comparisons with oneself in the past are discussed. The authors also provide an insightful discussion of methodological challenges facing researchers who wish to study comparison processes in field settings.

12 Downward Comparison and Coping With Threat

Frederick X. Gibbons and Meg Gerrard
Iowa State University

People engage in social comparison for one reason, and that is to gain information. While that motive remains constant, the desire to obtain information as well as the type of information that is sought vary considerably depending on the person and the circumstances in which the comparison occurs. Certain types of situations or circumstances are much more likely than others to prompt an interest in obtaining useful information. When there is some ambiguity concerning a person's current status the motivation to seek out others for purposes of comparison will typically increase (Festinger, 1954; Schachter & Singer, 1962). The same is true when the person is facing some kind of problem or threat (Schachter, 1959). The current chapter concerns those types of situations and circumstances. More specifically, we will be examining how people use social comparison to help them cope with a variety of different kinds of threats.

We will look at populations as diverse as people with eating disorders and persons with mental retardation, smokers, cancer patients, and people who are depressed or have chronic low self-esteem. Each one of these groups is facing threat of one kind or another. In some instances that threat is psychological in nature (e.g., having a stigma or else the ego threat associated with a low opinion of oneself and one's abilities). In other instances the threat is physical. In each case, however, the threat affects the social comparison behavior of the person who is trying to cope. In particular, it steers that comparison in a downward direction. The focus of the chapter, then, will be on *downward social comparison* (DC) and its use as a coping strategy.

We will begin with a brief, general discussion of downward comparison, and a description of the two forms it can take: active and passive. The next section, the longest, comprises a discussion of the benefits of passive DC, followed by a discussion of DC and coping outcome. We will then describe active DC, including the process of social distancing, and finally we will summarize what we think are the advantages and disadvantages of this type of social comparison, when used as a method of coping.

Downward Comparison

There are three major developments in the social comparison literature that form the basis of the work we will be discussing. The first is Brickman and Bulman's (1977) chapter entitled "Pleasure and Pain in Social Comparison." These authors were the first to present in a concise statement what previous researchers had identified as an oversight in Festinger's (1954) reasoning. Festinger believed that comparison choice will typically be oriented toward superior others (i.e., *upward comparison*). The reason is that people who are doing better than the self on a particular dimension are most likely to provide information that will facilitate improvement on that dimension. Brickman and Bulman made a convincing argument, however, that comparison with others who are thought to be doing better, though potentially informative, can also be threatening. For this reason, such comparisons are often avoided, especially by persons who feel threatened. Instead comparisons with others who are thought to be worse off, or downward comparisons, are sought.

What eventually developed out of the Brickman and Bulman chapter (see also Gruder, 1977) was a major modification of social comparison theory. This modification (originally proposed by Singer, 1966) states that social comparison has two very different motives. One is a desire to self-evaluate, which is essentially what Festinger was describing. The other is a desire to self-enhance. The two motives are reflected in different social comparison strategies. Generally speaking, upward, or lateral comparison (i.e., with similar others) is associated with a desire to evaluate the self, and downward comparison with a desire to protect a vulnerable or besieged ego; in other words, self-enhancement.

The first clear theoretical statement of DC theory was presented by Wills (1981) in a paper that provides the second basis for our chapter. He suggested that DC is most common among people who are experiencing some kind of threat. In addition, he claimed that the result of DC, or at least the goal, is an increase in *subjective well-being*. Simply put, this basic principle of DC theory suggests that people should feel better about their own situation or about themselves if they find out there are others who are worse off. Although this sounds a bit cynical (and Wills acknowledges that), he claims that the phenomenon is pervasive, and is manifested in a wide variety of different behaviors ranging from the use of humor to aggression.

Active and passive downward comparison. An additional corollary of Wills' theory is relevant to our discussion. He draws a distinction between two different kinds of DC: active and passive. While the end result of each type is essentially the same, the process is different. According to Wills, passive DC refers to "taking advantage of available opportunities for comparison with a less fortunate other." Active DC, on the other hand, requires some kind of action. It may be psychological (i.e., derogation of another person) or it could be physical (causing harm to someone). In either case the goal is to lower the status of the other person, thereby facilitating a favorable comparison. Evidence of passive DC can be seen in research indicating that threatened persons do prefer lower status comparison targets (e.g., Hakmiller, 1966; Wilson & Benner, 1971). As examples of active DC, Wills discusses a number of projection and aggression studies (e.g., Berkowitz, & Green, 1962; Nickel, 1974), indicating that persons who have been harmed will subsequently either retaliate more against the person(s) who harmed them or displace aggression onto another person. Few of these studies provided direct evidence of Wills' basic principle of DC, however, which is the hypothesis that subjective well-being is improved as a consequence of DC. Since this hypothesis is at the core of DC theory (and this chapter), we will devote more attention to it later.

Social Comparison and Coping

The third basis for our discussion comes from research by Taylor and her colleagues. This research provided the first systematic investigation of DC outside of the laboratory, and it was conducted among people who were experiencing very real threat. Taylor, Wood and Lichtman (1983; see also Wood, Taylor & Lichtman, 1985) interviewed a number of women with breast cancer and their husbands in order to examine the psychological aspects of the strategies they were using in coping with their disease. Though somewhat unexpected, evidence of DC was quite apparent in this sample. When asked how well they were coping with their problems in comparison with other breast cancer victims, 80% of the women interviewed reported they were doing "somewhat" or "much" better than other women. Moreover, an analysis of the spontaneous comments they made during the interview indicated that the vast majority of them had engaged in some kind of DC with other cancer victims. No matter how serious these women's problems were, they believed that there were others who were worse off. And if they didn't know of a specific person who had been more seriously afflicted, they imagined others, or even fabricated a target. The same was true of their husbands. For example, when asked how well they were coping with their wife's illness, these men admitted having a lot of difficulty. However, more than a quarter of them also claimed that they were not having nearly as much trouble as many other men they knew—as one man put it "you know, those animals who leave their wives because of it." In fact, less than 4% of the marriages of the women in the sample actually broke up as a consequence of the cancer. Thus, the stereotype of the poor coper these men were comparing with, or at least their estimates of the prevalence of (stereotypical) bad copers, was apparently a figment of their imaginations. Taylor et al. referred to these fabricated DC targets as *mythical men*. They concluded that comparison with these targets in particular, and DC in general, somehow helped these men cope with their problems, perhaps, as Wills (1981) suggested, by allowing them to feel better about their own situation (cf. also Taylor & Lobel, 1989).

Taylor and Wood's research provided indirect evidence that individuals who are experiencing difficulty do engage in passive DC in terms of target choice, apparently as a means of coping with their particular problem. More direct evidence of passive DC can be seen in recent laboratory research by ourselves and others (e.g., Bell, 1978; Gibbons, 1986), and in research we have conducted in different types of support groups. In this support group research, described in more detail later, subjects with fairly serious problems (eating disorders in one case, Gerrard, Gibbons & Sharp, 1985; smoking in another, Gibbons, Gerrard, Lando & McGovern, in press) showed a preference for having (in their group) other group members who had more serious problems.

The results of these studies suggest that the social comparison tendencies of people who are under stress or experiencing threat differ from those of nonthreatened persons in at least two important ways: they are more likely to involve some form of passive DC, and they are less likely to include upward comparison. In regard to this latter point, Wright (1983) has suggested that the stereotype of the overachieving, highly competent physically handicapped person (i.e., the "supercrip" image of the nature of Helen Keller), which so permeates the media and entertainment industries, is offensive to many disabled persons. This is true in spite of the fact that these targets certainly have the potential to offer useful information on a variety of dimensions including coping with the handicap itself. Why upward comparison targets or role models of this nature are avoided is not hard to understand. The appeal of DC targets is somewhat less obvious, however, and is in many respects a theoretically and empirically more interesting issue. The research that we will discuss in the next section provides some evidence of why DC appears to be so prevalent, especially among threatened persons. Before discussing this research, however, we will briefly describe a model that outlines the benefits associated with DC. The research that follows will provide some support for each of the components of that model.

The Benefits of Downward Comparison

Undoubtedly the benefits associated with DC vary considerably from person to person and situation to situation, and there are a number of them. We would suggest, however, that those positive effects can be subsumed by two major categories: subjective well-being and coping effects.

Subjective well-being. The primary benefit of DC is an improvement in *subjective well-being* (Wills, 1981) or what might simply be called general satisfaction (cf. Emmons & Diener, 1985). Realizing or imagining that there are others with more severe problems is likely to have a positive effect on one's outlook when it suggests to the comparer that "things could be worse," but they are not and they are not likely to become so. In other words, the crucial component of DC is the information it provides. To be effective, that information must in some way be construed as favorable to the comparer. Within this general category there are four specific, related types of effects that can occur depending on the nature of the comparison. All of them can contribute to an improvement in subjective well-being. The first three involve self-enhancement and are unique to DC, the fourth is not:

1. Realizing that things could be worse (but aren't) will lead almost immediately to an improvement in *mood state.*
2. Realizing that there are others who either have it worse and have survived, or else do not appear to have the same level of coping skills, can be encouraging in terms of one's own prognosis; thus, downward comparison should have direct effects on *optimism.*
3. Downward comparison on behavioral dimensions, such as coping ability, can boost *self-esteem.*
4. Realizing that there are others who share the same fate reduces a personal sense of *deviance* (and is therefore also likely to improve mood). Certain types of lateral comparisons with similar (i.e., equally bad off) others may produce the same effect. In fact, research suggests people will often seek out the company of others who share the same bad fate (e.g., Bell, 1978; Schachter, 1959). Comparisons of this nature, with similar others, are likely to be informative and therefore may help satisfy the motive of self-evaluation (e.g., "Is my response appropriate?"). They are not likely to boost the ego, or satisfy the motive of self-enhancement, however, as is

the case with most types of downward comparison. (More generally, our discussion in this chapter will be limited to self-enhancement effects associated with DC.)

Downward comparison as emotion-focused coping. The second major benefit of DC has to do with *coping ability*. The improvement in subjective well-being, including any of the related benefits just mentioned, may eventually be accompanied by an enhanced sense of self-efficacy with regard to coping ability. This, in turn, may lead to more effective coping. However, because DC has its primary impact on subjective well-being and affects self-efficacy indirectly, it would be considered an example of what has been labelled *emotion-focused* coping. According to Lazarus and Folkman (1984), emotion-focused coping is a defensive tactic, the goal of which, as the name implies, is to reduce the emotional discomfort associated with stress or threat. It contrasts with *problem-focused* coping, which is a more active strategy representing an attempt by the individual to respond directly to the problem and overcome it. Like other forms of emotion-focused coping, DC is not likely to eliminate the cause of the problem, only some of its symptoms. Nonetheless, it can facilitate transition to active, problem-focused coping, and in many instances, may be a necessary step along the way.

DOWNWARD COMPARISON AND SUBJECTIVE WELL-BEING

Several correlational studies have provided evidence of a relation between DC and a general improvement in subjective well-being. Pearlin and Schooler (1978), for example, claim that people can create "congenial perceptions of problematic experiences" by comparing those experiences with similar or more severe experiences of other people. They call this process *positive comparison*, and suggest that it is common and effective, because it can reduce distress. More recently Schulz and Decker (1985) found evidence of a form of DC among spinal-cord injured persons several years after their injury. These people thought they were better off than nondisabled persons in many respects, because they tended to *selectively focus*, meaning that they chose to socially compare on attributes that made them appear relatively advantaged (e.g., intelligence instead of physical abilities). Similar selective focus on what were thought to be positive self-attributes was found among cancer patients in Taylor et al. (1983) and in Wood et al. (1985). Finally, Emmons and Diener (1985) found that a measure of social comparison was the best predictor of subjective well-being among college students. The measure assessed students' perceptions of how well they were doing relative to other students on 11 different life domains, including love life, grades and friends.

Mood States, Part I: Experimental Research

Attributing the positive mood effects in the Emmons and Diener (1985) research to DC is, of course, just an inference (in fact, that is the case in each of these correlational studies), but it is one that might logically be drawn given the wording of the question subjects were asked ("How are you doing relative to most students? . . . much worse or much better?"). There is, however, more direct evidence in several recent studies in which we have manipulated comparison experimentally. In the first of those studies (Gibbons, 1986), mildly depressed and nondepressed students were presented with information indicating that another person was very upset because of an incident that this person had been involved in. Prior to reading the information, subjects' mood states were assessed. After reading the statement, they were asked to evaluate their partner's mood states and fill out a second mood scale.[1] The dimension of comparison was negative affect, and both depressed and nondepressed subjects' reports indicated that they thought the target was worse off than they were on that dimension. Only the depressed subjects were affected by what they had read, however. They reported a significant increase in mood state immediately after reading the statement, whereas the nondepressed subjects' mood states remained essentially the same.

Problem severity versus coping success. In another study (Gibbons & Gerrard, 1989a) we explored the impact of social comparison information on the mood states of persons facing what might be considered a chronic threat—namely low self-esteem. The issue that we were concerned with had to do with the nature of the DC information provided by the target. Most researchers interested in the relation between DC and coping have not paid much attention to the particular dimension on which the target was thought to be worse off. For example, some of the women in Taylor et al. (1983) based their comparisons on disease severity or progress, such as their own lumpectomy versus another's radical mastectomy. Others, including a fair number of the husbands, based their comparisons on rel-

---

[1] Mood change was assessed in this study, as it has been in most of our other studies, via mood scales administered before and after the comparison manipulation. The first scale consisted of 3 positive items from the MAACL (Zuckerman and Lubin, 1965) and 3 negative items (e.g., happy and insecure), while the second scale consisted of the polar opposites of each of those 6 items (e.g., sad and secure). Comparison of the (positive–negative) sums of the two scales provided a good indication of subjects' mood change and did so in a manner that was not transparent to them.

ative coping success. Both types of focus were categorized as DC by Taylor et al. Although problem severity and coping success are certainly both adequate grounds for DC, and are logically linked together, they are different dimensions and therefore provide the comparer with different types of information. One might wonder how a person with lung cancer might react to an encounter with a similar victim whose disease is more severe and decline more evident, but who is also clearly coping very well (better) with the situation. In this regard, Thoits (1986) has argued that the most effective social support is provided by a similar person who has encountered serious problems, but has managed to cope with these problems successfully. Others have also suggested that observation of coping success by others facing similar, serious problems is helpful (Gottlieb, 1985a; Meichenbaum, 1977; Molleman, Pruyn & Van Knippenberg, 1986; Ringler, 1981; Vachon, Lyall, Rogers, Freedman-Letosky & Freeman, 1980).

To examine the problem severity versus coping success question we had subjects who were either high or low in self-esteem become members of one-time, 4-person simulated support groups. During the course of the study they were separated and asked to write a statement about coping strategies that they had used as well as difficulties they had encountered in adjusting to college. These statements were then supposedly swapped among group pairs. Actually each subject received one of three bogus statements indicating the author was either having few problems and very little difficulty adjusting (upward comparison condition), few specific problems but a lot of trouble adjusting in general (downward comparison condition), or, in what we called the severe problem condition, a lot of problems but also a good deal of success in coping with them. The primary dependent variable was the impact that the statements had on subjects' mood states. We assumed that the low self-esteem people would be more threatened by the topic (they did report having more difficulty adjusting), and therefore would be more affected by DC on this dimension. In contrast, high self-esteem persons should benefit little from realizing that there are others having problems. In general, people will not respond favorably to DC on dimensions that are not in some way threatening to them.

As expected, results in the DC target condition were very similar to those in Gibbons (1986): significant mood improvement after reading the statement occurred for the low self-esteem people and not for the high. Just the opposite pattern occurred in reaction to the upward target, however. Significant mood improvement occurred only among the high self-esteem people. Finally, the good coper–severe problem target proved to be generally beneficial for everyone; both groups of subjects reported mood improvement after reading that statement. The results provided answers for two of the questions that we had raised. The first is that DC based strictly on coping difficulties can be effective, even in the absence of any real problems. That was the case in the DC condition. The second is that comparison with a person who is coping well in spite of severe problems is helpful and that's true even for people with low self-esteem.

Mood States, Part II: Support Groups

The studies mentioned thus far that we conducted were run in our laboratory. Although they provided some indication of the effects of one-time comparison on the mood states of threatened subjects, they tell us little about the impact of social comparison over a longer term. To address this issue, we decided to examine social comparison in what we considered to be a more natural setting. We chose support groups for several reasons. One was simply popularity; these groups have definitely proliferated over the last 10–15 years. But the primary reason was because we assumed that, in many ways, social comparison is what these groups are all about (cf. Gottlieb, 1985b). People with a wide range of problems join them in order to obtain information about themselves, about their problems, and about other people; the way to do that is through social comparison, both upward and downward.

We chose as the focus of our first experimental groups (Gibbons & Gerrard, 1989b) eating disorders, a problem that had been quite prevalent on college campuses during the 1980s. College women who had indicated that they had moderate to severe symptoms of bulimia (as defined by the DSM III) were asked to come to our laboratory for a clinical interview. Based on the interview, 34 women, half with high self-esteem, half with low, were assigned randomly to five different groups. The groups were led by two trained psychology graduate students and met once a week for a total of five weeks. The women received research credit in exchange for their participation, and were well aware that the primary purpose of the groups was research and not therapy. Nonetheless, they were encouraged to talk about their problems as much as they wanted, and most of them had a good deal to say. The group facilitators, who were not aware of the hypotheses, indicated to us that there was ample opportunity for subjects to socially compare on a variety of dimensions.

We assessed changes in subjects' self-perceptions that occurred from the first session until the last one. We did this on three dimensions: problem severity (absolute and relative to others), self-efficacy, and optimism. In addition, we assessed mood change during each of the sessions. Our assumption was that subjects would find that there were others in the group whose problems were more severe than their own, and that they would, therefore, have at least an opportunity for DC. This being the case, we expected that the low self-esteem people would report the most benefit from the comparison opportunities, and that this would be reflected in increases in their mood states, as well as their levels of optimism and self-efficacy. Results generally confirmed our hypotheses. First of all, both high and low self-esteem subjects placed themselves somewhere close to the middle of the scale on the questions concerning problem severity and severity relative to others in the group. Thus DC targets did exist for them within the groups. More important, there was no evidence of mood improvement among the high esteem subjects, whereas the low self-esteem individuals reported significant improvement in four of the five sessions. In three of those four sessions, the amount of their improvement was significantly greater than that of the high self-esteem group.[2] Thus, the mood benefits associated with DC appeared consistently over the course of the group.

Increased Optimism

The general improvement in mood demonstrated by the low self-esteem subjects in this support group study was consistent with Wills' basic principle of DC. The model of DC processes that we have proposed, however, is more specific in terms of the benefits of DC. In order to illustrate these effects, it is necessary once again to consider the type of information provided by the comparison itself. Realizing that there are others whose problems in one way or another are more serious indicates to the comparer that the situation potentially could be worse but it is not (DC that suggests decline is likely is an entirely different issue, which we will discuss later). Likewise, recognizing that there are others who are persevering in spite of severe problems (as in the severe problem condition of the Gibbons & Gerrard, 1989a, study) is likely to have a favorable effect on the comparer's assessment of their own future. In short, one of the bases of the improvement in subjective well-being appears to be encouragement, or an increase in optimism.

We were able to explore this optimism hypothesis in three of our studies by looking at specific types of mood change. In the lab study we have already discussed (Gibbons & Gerrard, 1989a), the mood checklist included an optimism variable (i.e., the adjectives "hopeful" and "hopeless"). As

---

[2]In two of the three sessions in which low self-esteem people showed more mood improvement their initial mood scores were significantly lower than those of their high self-esteem counterparts, and thus they had more room for improvement. In the third session, however, the low self-esteem group actually started off with slightly more positive mood states, and still showed significantly more improvement. The high esteem group's mood states declined slightly in that session. In general, greater mood improvement by low self-esteem subjects in these studies cannot be attributed to lower initial mood scores. The high esteem subjects have had room for improvement as well (e.g., both high and low esteem groups improved in the severe problem condition of the Gibbons & Gerrard, 1989a study).

might be expected, the severe problem—good coper target induced the greatest overall improvement on this variable. In addition, improvement in the primary cell of interest (low self-esteem, DC target) was clearly strongest on the hope change variable. In our eating group study (Gibbons & Gerrard, 1989b), subjects were asked how likely they thought it was that they would still have their eating problem in a year. High and low esteem subjects started out with similar expectations on this measure. Consistent with the pattern of results on the mood items, however, only the low self-esteem people reported significant improvement in optimism. Finally, in a study recently completed in our laboratory (Gibbons & Boney McCoy, in press), low self-esteem subjects who had experienced failure, reported a significant overall improvement in mood after hearing a tape supposedly made by a fellow group member indicating that person was having trouble adjusting to college. This time the improvement was strongest on the adjective encouraged—discouraged, and only marginally significant on the other mood items. Although not conclusive, the converging pattern of results in these three studies does suggest that changes in optimism may be one factor mediating the effects that DC has on subjective well-being.

Self-Esteem

Wills (1981) suggested that low self-esteem people are generally more likely than high self-esteem persons to engage in DC, and there is some empirical evidence to support his claim (Friend & Gilbert, 1973; Wilson & Benner, 1971). One reason for this may be that low self-esteem people are generally threatened in terms of their own abilities. If this is the case, then one benefit for low self-esteem persons who engage in DC on behavioral dimensions should be an improvement in self-esteem (cf. Wills, 1981). To date, however, there have been very few empirical investigations of that question (cf. Morse & Gergen, 1970).

Social comparison of contraceptive behavior. One of our students, Theresa Reis, examined the impact of social comparison on a specific behavior that she assumed was the focus of some social comparison. In this study (Reis, Gibbons & Gerrard, 1989) sexually active women with either high or low self-esteem, who either were or were not using effective methods of contraception, were recruited to participate in a one-time discussion group on the topic of sexuality and contraception. Using essentially the same paradigm as in our previous studies, subjects received bogus information indicating that one of their group partners was also sexually active, and either was or was not using effective birth control (pill vs. inconsistent rhythm). Manipulation checks indicated that subjects knew that their own method was or was not effective, which meant that they had the opportunity to socially compare at one of three levels on the dimension of contraceptive behavior: upward or downward (i.e., self-effective/target ineffective, or vice-versa), or laterally (both self and target using effective or ineffective methods).

The primary measure that we were interested in was change in self-esteem as a function of the comparison opportunity, and results on this measure did follow the predicted pattern. The primary cell of interest was that consisting of the low self-esteem persons engaging in DC (self-effective/target ineffective). We assumed that this group, though not specifically threatened in the study, would be most affected by the DC opportunity. In fact, this group did improve in reported self-esteem after the comparison, and their improvement was significantly greater than that of any other group. Unexpectedly, these low self-esteem subjects did not report significant mood improvement after the comparison. One interpretation of this pattern of results is that different types of DC dimensions (e.g., behavior vs. affect or experience) may have differential effects on the self-perceptions of people who engage in them. Thus, some dimensions such as coping skills, may affect optimism, whereas comparison on other behaviors may have its primary impact on self-esteem. Still other dimensions, such as disease severity, may affect mood states rather than self-esteem. Further research is being planned to examine this question more carefully.

Social comparison and attitude change. One other variable in the Reis et al. study is relevant to a discussion of self-change. In mass-testing sessions held prior to the study, subjects were asked the extent to which they were likely to use birth control pills in the future (this was the method of choice of the effective target). They were then asked the same question again, after they heard about their partner's behavior. Comparing the two responses to the same question provided an indication of the attitude change, or what might be considered learning, that took place as a result of the comparison. Those who were already using the pill did not change their opinions, of course. Among the ineffective contraceptors, however, low and high self-esteem persons responded very differently to the upward and lateral comparisons. Low self-esteem people subjected to an upward comparison, with a pill user, reported a significant positive change in their likelihood of pill usage. The high self-esteem subjects, however, reported positive change after comparing with another equally ineffective user; their opinions of the pill became significantly more positive after this lateral comparison. When comparing with an effective user, the high self-esteem subjects actually showed some evidence of reactance. They tended to lower their reported intentions to use the pill, although not significantly.

One explanation for the results among the ineffective contraceptors is that those with low self-esteem attributed the error of the discrepancy between their behavior and that of the effective target (cf. Duval & Wicklund, 1972) to themselves, whereas their high self-esteem counterparts essentially dug in their heels when the comparison reminded them that they were behaving unwisely. These results appear to have a number of implications regarding the effects of social comparison on attitude change and learning—topics that have not as of yet received much empirical attention. Attitude change was not the primary focus of the Reis et al. study, however (nor of this chapter), so we will not speculate further. Nevertheless, the potential implications of this issue of attitude and behavioral intention change as a result of social comparison warrant further empirical attention.

Social Comparison and Deviance

The final benefit that we have suggested is associated with DC (and sometimes with lateral comparison) is its effects on perceptions of deviance. Once again support groups provide a good setting for a discussion of this topic. Two explanations for the recent proliferation of support groups are seen most frequently in the social psychological literature (cf. Coates & Winston, 1983). One is that contact with others who are facing similar problems reduces anxiety via a *shared stress* type of process (following from Schachter's 1959 work on fear and affiliation). This explanation relates back to the hypothesis that people with similar problems who have experienced some coping success are most effective at providing social support (cf. Schulz & Decker, 1983; Thoits, 1986). Evidence of this comes from research with quadriplegic psychotherapy clients (Rogers & Figone, 1979), spinal cord-injured persons (Rohrer et al., 1980), and people in wheelchairs (McKay, 1980). The other explanation is that participation in support groups reduces feelings of uniqueness or deviance (Levy, 1979). Ablon (1981), for one, claims that being around similar others allows dwarves to see themselves as less deviant. Along the same lines, the widows in Barrett's (1978) study, who had participated in support groups, reported having fewer feelings of "unique experience" after their support group was over.

Although a number of researchers have discussed the hypothesis that contact with similar others leads to lessened feelings of deviance, few have actually examined it empirically. One exception is a study by Coates and Winston (1983) who found that self-perceptions of deviance did decline among rape victims over the course of a support group. In discussing the topic, Coates and Winston suggested that people who have been victimized in some way suffer from a profound sense of uniqueness or deviance. The same perception has been detected among depressed persons (Coates & Peterson, 1983; Swallow & Kuiper, 1987). One reason for this, according to Coates and Peterson (1983), is that these people seldom have an opportunity to come in contact with others like themselves, and thus tend to see their own lot as more unusual than it actually is. Just seeing others around them who are experiencing some of the same difficulties allows them to feel less abnormal or deviant. Presumably the worse off those others are, the less deviant they will feel (i.e., DC should have more of an effect than lateral comparison). Given the small n of the Coates and Winston study (only 9 subjects completed the group), however, there is an obvious need to replicate the deviance reduction finding before any definitive conclusions can be drawn.

Prevalence estimates. Another way to examine the deviance reduction hypothesis would be to assess subjects' perceptions of the prevalence of their particular problem before and after support group participation. Presumably, the reduction in perceived deviance would be accompanied by an increase in participants' estimates of the number of people who share their problems. Along these same lines, Jemmott and his colleagues (e.g., Jemmott, Ditto & Croyle, 1986) have demonstrated that there is a negative relation between perceptions of disease prevalence and seriousness: the more common the disorder is, the less serious it is thought to be. Finally, a reduction in deviance could also be achieved by underestimating the prevalence of one's own positive attributes among one's peers (cf. Schulz & Decker, 1985; Suls, Wan & Sanders, 1988). In other words, there are two different ways in which downward comparison might reduce the discomfort of deviance. Both of them include some distortion of oneself or one's attributes vis-a-vis others'. One involves focusing on and emphasizing one's own positive traits (Wills, 1987), and the other, focusing on the problems of others, or more specifically, the prevalence of those problems.

DOWNWARD COMPARISON AND COPING OUTCOME

Self-Efficacy

Theoretically, one of the primary reasons why people choose to engage in DC is an unwillingness to accept the potentially ego-threatening implications of upward comparison. As we have suggested, DC is most prevalent among persons for whom negative affect, low self-esteem, or depression are severe enough that they are interfering with more active attempts to cope with their problems. For this reason we believe that passive DC, like other forms of emotion-focused coping (Lazarus & Folkman, 1984), may serve to facilitate coping in an indirect manner. By first reducing anxiety or increasing subjective well-being, DC may allow the individual to eventually attempt more active, and presumably more effective coping strategies.

Unfortunately the evidence relating DC in particular, and social comparison in general, to coping outcomes is very sketchy. Taylor and her colleagues did not report any data in their cancer research regarding the link between social comparison and coping success. Some indirect evidence is provided in two other studies, however. Affleck, Tennen, Pfeiffer, Fifield and Rowe (1987) examined social comparison behavior among persons with rheumatoid arthritis. They found that victims who thought their illness was less severe than that of other victims were rated by health care providers as more positively adjusted. This correlation was significant even when the effects of disease activity, duration, and functional status of the patients were partialled out. It would be difficult to argue that a person who thinks their disease is less severe than others' is more threatened by that disease. We would argue instead that while comparison target choice is directly related to perceived threat, simply believing that there are others who are worse off is likely to benefit almost anyone who is experiencing problems. More specifically, what this suggests is that a belief that one is relatively well off, which comes about through DC, is an important step along the way to satisfactory adjustment (cf. Emmons & Diener, 1985).

Additional evidence of a relationship between DC and enhanced self-efficacy can be seen in our eating group study (Gibbons & Gerrard, 1989b). The low self-esteem women in that study, who we assumed would be most likely to engage in DC and reported the most improvement in mood and optimism, also reported a significantly greater increase in self-efficacy for their eating problems than did their high self-esteem counterparts. Moreover, these improvements in self-efficacy were strongly related to the mood changes that we found; the correlations between mood change and increases in optimism and self-efficacy were .43 and .51, respectively.

Changes in Passive Downward Comparison

As we have suggested, the decision to engage in DC sometimes comes at the expense of valuable information that may be provided by lateral or upward social comparison. Extended reliance on DC, like other forms of emotion-focused coping, may soothe the ego. But it is not likely to facilitate coping in the long run, unless a more active strategy is adopted. Both Wills (1987) and Wood et al. (1985) have suggested that the need for DC may be strongest early in the process of adaptation to a negative event (when threat and/or dysphoria are at a peak), but may be less urgent after long term adaptation to the event has occurred. This is congruent with Schulz and Decker's (1985) finding that DC was not commonly reported by spinal-cord injured persons several years after their accident, when they had adapted to the injury. In the Wood et al. (1985) cancer study, interest in DC appeared to be strongest among breast cancer victims close in time to their surgery, when threat was presumably greatest, and it declined after that. In summary, DC is most useful when coping confidence is low, when the problem is most severe, or when threat is the greatest. As confidence increases, however, threat will decline, and the pattern of social comparison behavior will presumably change. Specifically, interest in passive DC should decrease, and this decline will usually be evidence of improvement.

We tested this hypothesis in a longitudinal study of support groups for people trying to quit smoking (Gibbons et al., in press). Each of the groups in this study consisted of 10–12 people and met a total of 16 times over the course of 9 weeks. All subjects agreed to quit smoking at the 8th session (called the quit date.) Data were collected at the first session, the quit date, the last (16th) session and again at a 6-month follow-up. Subjects' perceptions of their smoking problems were assessed in several ways, including perceptions of the seriousness of those problems (i.e., two questions: "How serious is your smoking problem?" and "How serious is your problem relative to other smokers?" combined to form a single index, which was our operational definition of threat). We also assessed social comparison processes. This included preferences for potential support group members ("What type of person would you like to have in the group?") according to two DC characteristics: severity of smoking problem and how much difficulty the person was having quitting—roughly equivalent to problem severity and coping success (cf. Gibbons & Gerrard, 1989a). As expected, there was a significant positive correlation between subjects' perceptions of how serious their smoking problem was and their preferences for DC targets. At the first session this correlation was significant but weak ($r = .17$); by the end of the group, however, the correlation was quite strong (.43). The increase in the strength of this relationship reflects the fact that change in perceived threat was correlated with change in (DC) target preference ($r = .43$). Specifically as subjects' perceived threat diminished, their interest in DC targets also declined considerably.

Approach and Avoidance of Downward Comparison Targets

Although we have spent some time reviewing research that has emphasized the appeal of DC targets, it would be inaccurate to conclude that threatened persons exclusively prefer others who are worse off for purposes of comparison. There are some circumstances under which DC can itself be threatening. In fact, avoidance of contact with potential DC targets has been demonstrated, primarily among cancer patients (Dakof, 1986; Dunkel-Schetter & Wortman, 1982; Molleman et al., 1986; Wood et al., 1985).

Indeed, in most of those cases the cancer victims indicated they often found contact with other cancer victims to be aversive. This, of course, contrasts with research we have already discussed in which a preference for contact with similar or worse off others has been detected among groups such as smokers trying to quit (Gibbons et al., in press), depressed women with eating disorders (Gerrard et al., 1985), and depressed students (Gibbons, 1986).

In reviewing these two sets of studies, there appears to be one important characteristic that discriminates between them. That characteristic has to do with the nature of the problem and the comparer's perceptions of its prognosis or outcome (cf. Taylor & Lobel, 1989). For example, Dunkel-Schetter and Wortman (1982) reported that many of the cancer patients in their study indicated they did not like to interact with other cancer patients in physicians' waiting rooms because the sight of someone else's deterioration was depressing for them. Molleman et al. (1986) found that cancer patients' interest in social comparison with similar others increased as their anxiety increased up to a moderate level. As anxiety continued to increase, however, to high or very high levels, the preference became much more pronounced for patients who were better off.

Cancer is a potentially fatal illness. Consequently, serious decline and even death are very real possibilities that people with this disease must face, and that puts a very different perspective on the DC process. When decline is inevitable, as with a degenerative disease such as rheumatoid arthritis, or when the person fears that decline is a real possibility, then contact with someone else whose illness has progressed further is not likely to be encouraging. On the contrary, most people would undoubtedly prefer to avoid clear reminders that there are worse times ahead. Even for terminal cancer patients, however, there is likely to be some solace in the realization that there are others who are also struggling with the disease and perhaps struggling even more. But that does not necessarily mean that they want to be in the physical presence of those people.

On the other hand, the women in Gerrard et al. (1985), the college students in Gibbons (1986), and the smokers in Gibbons et al. (in press) were all trying to cope with what were, essentially, behavioral problems. Decline for these people was certainly not inevitable, and they had every reason to believe that they could overcome the problem eventually (we suspect that some minimum level of optimism and self-efficacy is necessary before a person would consider joining support groups like these). Cancer is not a behavioral problem, and simply having it is not likely to lower one's self-esteem, at least not directly. The ability to cope with cancer will definitely affect self-esteem, however. Thus, a cancer victim may respond favorably, through DC, to the realization that their coping ability is better than others'. Such a comparison would definitely be self-enhancing, and would probably be sought out. In sum, to be effective, the DC information must give some indication that the person is better off than others on some important dimension, especially one that involves self-esteem, and that decline is not inevitable. Otherwise, DC will usually be avoided.

Cognitive Downward Comparison

Before turning our attention to active DC, we will conclude this section with a discussion of a different type of passive DC. Besides its pioneering effects in the study of applied social comparison, Taylor et al.'s (1983) research also had a significant impact on social comparison theory per se. One of their most important contributions is their discussion of what might be considered cognitive social comparison. That is, comparison with nonspecific or vague targets, often on dimensions that have been created by the comparer (cf. also Suls, 1986; Taylor & Lobel, 1989; and Wood et al., 1985). Taylor et al. (1983) suggested that cancer victims may sometimes manufacture normative standards of coping behavior for purposes of comparison in much the same way that they create images of "mythical" poor copers. Taylor et al. also suggest that people who are experiencing coping difficulty on one dimension may choose to emphasize or shift their attention to alternative dimensions on which they happen to feel that they are doing well. They call this choice process selective focus. Thus, the younger cancer victims in their study chose to focus on age as a point of comparison. Similarly, the disabled persons in Schulz and Decker's (1985) study saw themselves as better off than most disabled persons "by selectively focusing on attributes that made them appear advantaged (e.g., brain is more important than brawn.)" (p. 1171). Both examples provide evidence of the flexibility of the cognitive comparison process. Moreover, an obvious advantage of this type of comparison is that it is not fixed to any particular dimension or information. Consequently, the comparer has much more control over the entire process, including the dimensions being compared, the target of the comparison, and, ultimately, even the outcome of the comparison itself.

Selective recall. Some of our own data (Gibbons & Gerrard, 1987) suggest that low self-esteem persons may take a more active role (than high self-esteem persons) in the cognitive social comparison process, specifically selective focus. All subjects participated in a screening interview prior to joining our eating disorder groups (i.e., Gibbons & Gerrard, 1989b), during which they were asked to read four case histories of women with eating problems. The histories were abstracted from actual reports of previous group participants, and were intended to provide potential group members with information about the groups. At the end of the interview we assessed recall for some of the information presented in the histories, including the target's description of her problem, a (bogus) scale score of her coping success, and an assessment of the seriousness of her problem. For three of the cases the problem described was either moderate or severe, and the woman was having some difficulty coping with it. The fourth case presented a mild problem with which the woman was dealing quite well. Analyses indicated that the low and high self-esteem persons were equally accurate in recall for the three relatively severe cases. The low self-esteem persons, however (who reported more concern about their own eating problem), had considerably more difficulty recalling details of the successful coper's history than did the high self-esteem persons and they had much more difficulty recalling details about the successful coper than they did about the other three cases. Perhaps more important was the fact that the mistakes they made were in a downward direction. They underestimated the target's coping success and gave her a lower rating on the physical attractiveness dimension.

This type of distortion, in which others' situations are recalled as being worse than they actually were, is similar to the mythical men prevalence distortions demonstrated by some of the husbands in Taylor et al. (1983). It is also similar in some respects to what Lazarus and Folkman (1984) have called *cognitive reappraisals*, which refer to the reinterpretation of stressful situations in order to reduce the threat posed by them. In this case the information produced by the comparison is reinterpreted in such a way as to reduce the threat posed by it. Distortions of this nature could, of course, turn virtually any comparison into a DC. Whether this type of cognitive bias serves the same function as other forms of DC, in terms of effective coping, remains to be seen, however.

ACTIVE DOWNWARD COMPARISON AND SOCIAL DISTANCING

The threat for many of the cancer patients and other victims who have shown a desire to avoid DC targets is the possibility that they themselves may end up like those targets. Believing that one is very similar to a DC target is likely to be somewhat upsetting and may very well defeat what was the goal of the comparison in the first place. Whereas some perceived similarity is necessary for the comparison to have an effect (cf. Miller, Turnbull & McFarland, 1988), too much similarity to a DC target can itself be threatening. This would be especially true when the target represents a negative prototype of some kind—an image that the comparer may be trying to avoid or perhaps overcome. Consistent with this reasoning, there is some empirical evidence to suggest that people may seek out evidence of distinction between themselves and DC targets (Brickman & Bulman, 1977). Some examples from this research will help us illustrate a point that is relevant to coping behavior.

Invulnerability. Several programs of research, most notably those of Perloff (1987; Perloff & Fetzer, 1986) and Weinstein (1983; 1984; 1988) have indicated that people generally underestimate their own vulnerability to a variety of negative events such as divorce and disease. Both Perloff and Weinstein suggest that this *illusion of unique invulnerability* is the result, at least in part, of a social comparison process. They claim that when people estimate their own risk for developing a disease, cancer for example, they are likely to compare their own vulnerability with that of other people. The target that is chosen, however, is usually not just another average person, like oneself; rather, it is someone whose behaviors and attributes make them especially likely to develop the disease. In other words, it is clearly a worse off other, which is why Perloff (1987) suggests that the process is actually a form of DC. Choosing to compare with a high risk victim prototype is likely to leave the individual with a false sense of invulnerability. And this, in essence, is the basis of the illusion. Presumably, the less similar a person believes they are to the victim prototype, the safer that person will feel (and the less likely they are to take prophylactic actions; Janz & Becker, 1984).

Stigma and Downward Comparison

The notion of *prototype threat*, or actually the threat associated with similarity to a prototype, is a theme that has been evident for some time in literature in the area of stigma. In a study of formerly institutionalized mentally retarded persons, Edgerton (1967) reported that many of them were obsessed with a desire to avoid the retardation label and "pass" as nonretarded. This obsession was translated into avoidance of other retarded persons. In fact, numerous other examples can be found in this literature of attempts by mildly handicapped persons to avoid others who have a similar, but more severe handicap. That tendency has been noted among people with visual impairment (Criddle, 1953), overweight children (Richardson, 1983), and people who are mildly physically handicapped (Wright, 1983). Wright believes that this is due not so much to a desire to avoid specific individuals, but rather a desire to dissociate or distance oneself from the stigma of one's affliction.

Mental retardation and downward comparison. Additional empirical evidence of distancing from similar others comes from a series of studies that we conducted with persons with mental retardation. Our research was based on two assumptions: mildly retarded persons are aware of the negative prototype associated with mental retardation, and they view themselves more favorably than that prototype. The procedure that we used was fairly simple. Subjects were presented with pictures of unnamed target persons, some of whom were said to be retarded and some not. They were then asked to evaluate those target persons. In several of these studies (e.g., Gibbons, 1985; Gibbons & Kassin, 1982), mildly retarded persons showed a preference for the nonretarded target, as a roommate and workmate for example, and they also evaluated that person more favorably on dimensions such as social skills. In addition, the evaluations they gave themselves, on items such as intelligent and friendly, were surprisingly positive, being comparable to those given to the nonretarded target and more favorable than the retarded target.

In one of our studies (Gibbons, 1985), we compared the perceptions of retarded persons living in an institution with those living in the community (level of IQ was covaried to account for any differences). We found that both groups derogated the retarded target relative to themselves and the nonretarded target, but, as expected, this difference was strongest among the community women. This group also happens to have the most contact with nonretarded people (Kleinberg & Galligan, 1983) and, therefore, is most aware of and most likely to be threatened by the stigma (cf. Edgerton & Sabagh, 1962). In general, the results of these studies were congruent with what might be considered one of the earliest hypotheses of DC, presented by Edgerton and Sabagh a number of years ago. These authors suggested that mildly retarded persons living in institutions can self-aggrandize by comparing themselves with other retarded persons of lower intelligence.

Active and passive downward comparison. Evidence of both active and passive DC can be seen in the responses of these mentally handicapped subjects. On the one hand, their preference for the nonretarded target on the social distance questions appears to be a reflection of passive DC with more severely retarded targets; and the unexpectedly high self-evaluations are consistent with this interpretation. On the other hand, the evaluative data indicate that our subjects were engaging in active DC as well, by derogating the retarded target. We also found evidence of a potential negative consequence of active DC in this study. Since other retarded persons are by far their most frequent social contacts, it might be expected that a negative attitude toward the mental retardation prototype might have a negative effect on their relationships with some mentally retarded individuals. In fact, most of these subjects did maintain very pessimistic opinions with regard to their own social lives as well as those of their peers. In general, psychological distancing from a vague prototype may be beneficial, but it can conceivably become detrimental when physical distancing from certain members of the category represented by the prototype is not possible.

Social Distancing

The type of active DC demonstrated by these mildly retarded persons is once again similar to that displayed toward the so-called mythical man prototype by a sizable portion of the husbands of cancer victims in Taylor et al. (1983). Derogation of the hypothetical other creates distance between the self and the prototype, thereby facilitating the DC process and enhancing self-perception. In the same manner, distancing oneself from a *victim prototype* (Perloff, 1987) can reduce anxiety and foster a false sense of security. In each of these instances it would be safe to assume that the more distinct the person believes s/he is from the DC target, the more beneficial the comparison will be. Consistent with this reasoning, Perloff and Fetzer (1986) found that the amount of the invulnerability illusion varied as a function of the social distance of the target of comparison. When subjects were asked to compare their health risks with an unnamed, hypothetical other, the illusion was greatest; but it all but disappeared when the target was a close friend or someone the subjects knew well. It would appear that familiarity and similarity vis-a-vis the DC target interfere with the derogation and distancing processes.

Distancing and smoking cessation. This assumption led us to the specific hypothesis that people who are trying to overcome a threatening behavioral problem will psychologically distance themselves from the prototypical victim of that problem (Gibbons et al., in press). Moreover, this distancing should include some active DC in the form of derogation of the prototype. We chose smoking as the behavioral problem to focus on, but actually any one of a number of problems would fit the bill. As long as the affected person can conjure up an image of an appropriate prototype—for example, the typical alcoholic, or the typical spouse abuser—then he can actively distance himself from and derogate that image as part of his efforts to quit the behavior. In fact, even if the person is not successful in extinguishing the behavior, it may be reassuring to believe that he or she is not like, or actually not as bad off as, the typical offender.

In addition to indicating their social comparison target preferences (which we have already discussed), the subjects in our smoking cessation study were asked to evaluate the smoker prototype (i.e., the "typical smoker") on several dimensions, including similarity to the self, a series of descriptive adjectives (e.g., friendly, self-assured, considerate), and ability to quit smoking. They also evaluated members of their own cessation group on the same descriptive adjectives. These perceptions were assessed at four times: the start of the group, the quit date, the last group session, and at a 6-month follow-up. Our assumption was that these smokers would start off with a generally positive image of the typical smoker (they were, after all, fairly typical smokers themselves). We thought the distancing process would begin once they had quit smoking, that it would continue through the follow-up, and that it would be evident in two related dimensions: increasingly negative evaluations of the prototype and decreasing perceived similarity to him/her. The results were consistent with this pattern. When the smokers entered the groups they had positive perceptions of the prototype and thought s/he was similar to themselves. These evaluations became even more favorable by the quit date, but then declined noticeably from then on. By the follow-up, the decline on the similarity, adjective evaluations and ability to quit items was very pronounced (all $p < .006$). Moreover, this tendency was strongest among those who were still abstaining from smoking at the 6-month follow-up. Even those who had relapsed continued to derogate the prototype, however, which suggests that once the distancing process has begun it is hard to reverse (an example, perhaps, of the *perseverance effect*; cf. Ross, Lepper & Hubbard, 1975).

Active versus passive downward comparison. The pattern of results on the evaluation or active DC items contrasted sharply with that found on the passive DC questions. It may be recalled from our previous discussion that subjects' preferences for DC targets (i.e., smokers who were having difficulty quitting) declined noticeably as their perceptions of the seriousness of their smoking problem diminished. What this means is that the nature of the DC shifted over time among those subjects for whom smoking threat (i.e., problem seriousness) declined. Their interest in passive DC with worse off others decreased, while their active DC or distancing, which was reflected in their (negative) evaluations of the prototype, increased. Interestingly, the active DC that we detected applied only to the vague prototype outside of the group. Subjects' perceptions of their fellow group members were much more positive than those of the prototype, even though the other group members were probably also fairly typical smokers. In addition, those group member evaluations remained favorable while the prototype evaluations declined. We interpreted this to mean that active DC is much easier with a vague victim prototype than it is with a specific person (cf. Perloff & Fetzer, 1986), and therefore serves the purpose of distancing much more effectively.

Summary. The fact that the distancing process became stronger as perceived problem seriousness or threat declined, suggests that confidence may be an underlying factor in this transition. Early on the prototype may have been seen as too similar to the self for these smokers to feel comfortable derogating him/her. Over time, however, smokers became more confident that they were actually different from the typical smoker. As that happened, they felt less need for passive DC, and also were more willing to derogate the smoker prototype. By the same token, some level of confidence that they were different from the prototype was probably a prerequisite for subjects in our stigma research to derogate the typical mentally retarded person, or for the husbands in Taylor et al. (1983) to derogate the mythical man poor coper. Conversely, those who are not confident of the distinction will continue to engage in passive DC and seek out the company of worse off others, but they will not derogate that prototype nearly as much. Finally, the fact that the abstainers were still derogating the prototype six months after they had quit suggests that distancing may, in some way, help keep these people out of the smoker category, and thus facilitate maintenance of abstinence.

SUMMARY AND CONCLUSIONS

The Advantages and Disadvantages of Downward Comparison

We have outlined a number of benefits associated with the DC process, which illustrate the instrumental value of DC in facilitating coping. These benefits generally involve perceptions of one's own situation relative to that of others'—what we have called *general outlook*. Like other forms of emotion-focused coping, DC does little to directly alter the problem at hand. It can have an indirect effect, however, by placing the afflicted individual in a frame of mind whereby that person may eventually be able to consider more active and more direct coping behavior. To be effective, then, DC usually must be time-limited. Extended reliance on DC as a coping strategy is not likely to lead to improvement, and it may very well be harmful, because of the negative consequences associated with it. The most obvious disadvantage is the fact that DC usually does not provide useful coping information. In addition, passive DC may leave the comparer with some delusions regarding the seriousness of his or her problem or the need to adopt a different coping strategy (cf. Lazarus, 1966 discussion of *defensive reappraisal*). Comparison with a victim prototype, for example, may leave the "uniquely invulnerable" individual with the belief that precautionary steps are not necessary (Weinstein, 1988). Finally, as Wills (1987) has noted, most people are likely to experience some guilt or uneasiness about their positive reactions to the misfortunes of others, and this ambivalence may ultimately counteract the favorable effects of the passive DC.

There are additional potential difficulties associated with active DC. By definition, active DC involves derogation of or harm to a comparison target, and that certainly has the potential to be problematic. For example, the negative attitude toward the typical retarded person, reflected in the responses of the mildly retarded persons in our research, would be expected to interfere with their social interactions with one another. In fact, there was evidence of that in our data. To the extent that it does involve specific individuals or groups of individuals, distancing can cause problems and might even interfere with coping. Most of the research suggests, however, that distancing is more likely to be directed at vague or nonspecific targets, which seem to fit the bill as scapegoats much more effectively.

Implications for Psychotherapy

With the caveats that we have discussed in mind, there is some reason to believe that the judicious use of DC may constitute an effective technique in fostering behavior change in psychotherapy. Early on in the therapy process, when depression or dysphoria are primary obstacles to functional behavior, DC is most likely to be beneficial. For those people who can get better and expect to, information indicating that others are not coping as well will initially have a positive effect on mood states and/or self-esteem, and perhaps eventually on self-efficacy. By the same token, encouraging members of support or self-help groups to distance themselves from an undesirable prototype may very well promote behavioral change and improvement. In this sense the prototype may act as what Markus and Nurius (1986) have labelled a *negative possible self* (e.g., self as smoker or alcoholic), which the individual is trying to avoid becoming (or stop being). The therapist or group leader who makes certain that the prototype remains nonspecific can use this DC target to some advantage. The motivating potential of the undesirable prototype, as well as the distancing process, remain to be investigated; we think such research is likely to prove fruitful.

CONCLUSION

What is most remarkable about downward social comparison, in a coping context, is its range, or flexibility. The process does not require a specific target; one can be created. It doesn't have to involve specific behaviors, normative standards can be manufactured. The information doesn't have to be downward, or even factual, it can be forgotten or selectively recalled, or distorted in a downward direction. In short, there are many different forms that downward social comparison can take. That is one reason why it is so common, and perhaps why it is apparently so effective. We have touched on only a few of those forms in this chapter, and have only begun to identify some of the parameters of the process. It remains to be seen how extensive this paradoxical behavior is, and ultimately how effective a coping strategy it can be.

ACKNOWLEDGMENT

The writing of this chapter was facilitated by NSF Grant #BNS8718691.

REFERENCES

Ablon, J. (1981). Dwarfism and social identity: Self-help group participation. *Social Science and Medicine, 15*, 25–30.

Affleck, G., Tennen, H., Pfeiffer, C., Fifield, J., & Rowe, J. (1987). Downward comparison and coping with serious medical problems. *American Journal of Orthopsychiatry, 57*, 570–578.

Barrett, C. J. (1978). Effectiveness of widows' groups in facilitating change. *Journal of Consulting and Clinical Psychology, 46*, 20–31.

Bell, P. A. (1978). Affective state attraction and affiliation. *Personality and Social Psychology Bulletin, 4*, 616–619.

Berkowitz, L., & Green, J. A. (1962). The stimulus qualities of the scapegoat. *Journal of Abnormal and Social Psychology, 64*, 293–301.

Brickman, P., & Bulman, R. J. (1977). Pleasure and pain in social comparison. In J. M. Suls & R. L. Miller (Eds.), *Social comparison processes: Theoretical and empirical perspectives.* (pp. 149–186). Washington, DC: Hemisphere.

Coates, D., & Peterson, B. A. (1983). Depression and deviance. In G. Weary & H. L. Mirels (Eds.), *Integrations of clinical and social psychology.* (pp. 154–170). New York: Oxford University Press.

Coates, D. & Winston, T. (1983). Counteracting the deviance of depression: Peer support groups for victims. *Journal of Social Issues, 39*, 169–194.

Criddle, R. (1953). *Love is not blind.* New York: Norton.

Dakof, G. A. (1986). *Psychological and social adaptation to Parkinson's Disease.* Unpublished doctoral dissertation, University of California, Berkeley.

Dunkel-Schetter, C., & Wortman, C. (1982). The interpersonal dynamics of cancer: Problems in social relationships and their impact on the patient. In H. S. Friedman & M. R. DiMatteo (Eds.), *Interpersonal issues in health care.* New York: Academic Press.

Duval, S., & Wicklund, R. A. (1972). *A theory of objective self awareness.* New York: Academic Press.

Edgerton, R. G. (1967). *The cloak of competence: Stigma in the lives of the mentally retarded.* Berkeley: University of California Press.

Edgerton, R. B., & Sabagh, G. (1962). From mortification to aggrandizement: Changing self-conception in the careers of the mentally retarded. *Psychiatry, 25*, 263–272.

Emmons, R. A., & Diener, E. (1985). Factors predicting satisfaction judgments: A comparative examination. *Social Indicators Research, 16*, 157–167.

Festinger, L. A. (1954). A theory of social comparison processes. *Human Relations, 7*, 117–140.

Friend, R. M., & Gilbert, J. (1973). Threat and fear of negative evaluation as determinants of locus of social comparison. *Journal of Personality, 41*, 328–340.

Gerrard, M., Gibbons, F. X., & Sharp, J. (1985, August). Social comparison in a self help group for bulimics. Paper presented at the American Psychological Association Annual Meeting, Los Angeles.

Gibbons, F. X. (1985). Stigma perception: Social comparison among mentally retarded persons. *American Journal of Mental Deficiency, 90*, 98–106.

Gibbons, F. X. (1986). Social comparison and depression: Company's effect on misery. *Journal of Personality and Social Psychology, 51*, 1–9.

Gibbons, F. X., & Boney-McCoy, S. (in press). Self-esteem, similarity, and reactions to active and passive downward comparison. *Journal of Personality and Social Psychology.*

Gibbons, F. X., & Gerrard, M. (1987, August). Recall error as a form of downward comparison. Paper presented at the American Psychological Association Annual Meeting, New York.

Gibbons, F. X., & Gerrard, M. (1989a). Effects of upward and downward social comparison on mood states. *Journal of Social and Clinical Psychology, 8*, 14–31.

Gibbons, F. X., & Gerrard, M. (1989b). *The role of downward comparison in a support group for bulimic women.* Unpublished manuscript, Iowa State University, Ames.

Gibbons, F. X., Gerrard, M., Lando, H. A., & McGovern, P. G. (in press). Smoking cessation and social comparison: The role of the "typical smoker." *Journal of Experimental Social Psychology.*

Gibbons, F. X., & Kassin, S. M. (1982). Behavioral expectations of retarded and nonretarded children. *Journal of Applied Developmental Psychology, 3*, 85–104.

Gottlieb, B. H. (1985a). Theory into practice: Issues that surface in planning interventions which mobilize support. In I. G. Sarason & B. R. Sarason (Eds.), *Social support: Theory, research and applications* (pp. 417–437). The Hague, The Netherlands: Martinus Nijhof.

Gottlieb, B. H. (1985b). Social support and community mental health. In S. Cohen & L. Syme (Eds.), *Social support and health* (pp. 303–326). Orlando, FL: Academic Press.

Gruder, C. L. (1977). Choice of comparison persons in evaluating oneself. In J. M. Suls & R. L. Miller (Eds.), *Social comparison processes: Theoretical and empirical perspectives,* (pp. 21–41). Washington, DC: Hemisphere.

Hakmiller, K. L. (1966). Threat as a determinant of downward comparison. *Journal of Experimental Social Psychology, 2* (Suppl. 1), 32–39.

Janz, N. K., & Becker, M. H. (1984). The health belief model: A decade later. *Health Education Quarterly, 11*, 1–47.

Jemmott, J. B., Ditto, P. H., & Croyle, R. T. (1986). Judging health status: Effects of perceived prevalence and personal relevance. *Journal of Personality and Social Psychology, 50*, 899–905.

Kleinberg, J., & Galligan, B. (1983). Effects of deinstitutionalization on adaptive behavior of mentally retarded adults. *American Journal of Mental Deficiency, 88*, 21–27.

Lazarus, R. S. (1966). *Psychological stress and the coping process.* New York: McGraw–Hill.

Lazarus, R. S., & Folkman, S. (1984). *Stress, appraisal and coping.* New York: Springer.

Levy, L. H. (1979). Processes and activities in groups. In M. A. Lieberman & L. D. Borman (Eds.), *Self-help groups for coping with crisis* (pp. 234–271). San Francisco: Jossey-Bass.

Markus, H., & Nurius, P. (1986). Possible selves. *American Psychologist, 41*, 954–969.

McKay, J. (1980). The effect of rehabilitation counselor disability status on similarly disabled clients' perception of counselor social influence and empathy (Doctoral dissertation, The Florida State University, 1979). *Dissertation Abstracts International, 40*, 9-A, 4898.

Meichenbaum, D. (1977). *Cognitive-behavior modification: An integrative approach.* New York: Plenum.

Miller, D. T., Turnbull, W., & McFarland, C. (1988). Particularistic and universalistic evaluation in the social comparison process. *Journal of Personality and Social Psychology, 55*, 908–917.

Molleman, E., Pruyn, J., & Van Knippenberg, A. (1986). Social comparison processes among cancer patients. *British Journal of Social Psychology, 25,* 1–13.

Morse, S., & Gergen, K. J. (1970). Social comparison, self-consistency, and the concept of self. *Journal of Personality and Social Psychology, 16,* 148–156.

Nickel, T. W. (1974). The attribution of intention as a critical factor in the relation between frustration and aggression. *Journal of Personality, 42,* 482–492.

Pearlin, L. I., & Schooler, C. (1978). The structure of coping. *Journal of Health and Social Behavior, 19,* 2–21.

Perloff, L. S. (1987). Social comparison and illusions of invulnerability to negative life events. In C. R. Snyder & C. Ford (Eds.), *Coping with negative life events; Clinical and social-psychological perspectives.* (pp. 217–242). New York: Plenum.

Perloff, L. S., & Fetzer, B. K. (1986). Self-other judgments and perceived vulnerability to victimization. *Journal of Personality and Social Psychology, 50,* 502–510.

Reis, T., Gibbons, F. X., & Gerrard, M. (1989). *Social comparison and the pill: Effects of downward comparison on self-esteem.* Unpublished manuscript, Iowa State University, Ames.

Richardson, S. A. (1983). Children's values in regard to disabilities: A reply to Yuker. *Rehabilitation Psychology, 28,* 131–140.

Ringler, K. (1981). *Processes of coping with cancer chemotherapy.* Unpublished doctoral dissertation. University of Wisconsin, Madison.

Rogers, J., & Figone, J. (1979). Psychosocial parameters in treating the person with quadriplegia. *The American Journal of Occupational Therapy, 33,* 432–439.

Rohrer, K., Adelman, B., Puckett, J., Toomey, B., Talbert, D., & Johnson, E. W. (1980). Rehabilitation in spinal cord injury: Use of a patient-family group. *Archives of Physical Medicine and Rehabilitation, 61,* 225–229.

Ross, L., Lepper, M. R. & Hubbard, M. (1975). Perseverance in self-perception and social perception: Biased attribution processes in the debriefing paradigm. *Journal of Personality and Social Psychology, 32,* 880–892.

Schachter, S. (1959). *The psychology of affiliation.* Palo Alto, CA: Stanford University Press.

Schachter, S., & Singer, J. E. (1962). Cognitive, social and physiological determinants of emotional state. *Psychological Review, 69,* 379–399.

Schulz, R., & Decker, S. (1983). Social support, adjustment, and the elderly spinal cord injured: A social psychological analysis. In G. Weary & H. L. Mirels (Eds.), *Integrations of clinical and social psychology* (pp. 272–286). New York: Oxford University Press.

Schulz, R., & Decker, S. (1985). Long-term adjustment to physical disability: The role of social support, perceived control and self-blame. *Journal of Personality and Social Psychology, 48,* 1162–1172.

Singer, J. E. (1966). Social comparison—progress and issues. *Journal of Experimental Social Psychology,* Supplement 1, 103–110.

Suls, J. (1986). Notes on the occasion of social comparison theory's thirtieth birthday. *Personality and Social Psychology Bulletin, 12,* 289–296.

Suls, J., Wan, C. K., & Sanders, G. S. (1988). False consensus and false uniqueness in estimating the prevalence of health-protective behaviors. *Journal of Applied Social Psychology, 18,* 66–79.

Swallow, S. R., & Kuiper, N. A. (1987). The effects of depression and cognitive vulnerability to depression on judgments of similarity between self and other. *Motivation and Emotion, 11,* 157–167.

Taylor, S. E. & Lobel, M. (1989). Social comparison activity under threat: Downward evaluation and upward contacts. *Psychological Review, 96,* 569–575.

Taylor, S. E., Wood, J. V., & Lichtman, R. R. (1983). It could be worse: Selective evaluation as a response to victimization. *Journal of Social Issues, 39,* 19–40.

Thoits, P. A. (1986). Social support as coping assistance. *Journal of Consulting and Clinical Psychology, 54,* 416–423.
Vachon, M. L. S., Lyall, W. A. O., Rogers, J., Freedman-Letofsky, K., & Freeman, S. J. J. (1980). A controlled study of self-help intervention for widows. *American Journal of Psychiatry, 137,* 998–1002.
Weinstein, N. D. (1983). Reducing unrealistic optimism about illness susceptibility. *Health Psychology, 2,* 11–20.
Weinstein, N. D. (1984). Why it won't happen to me: Perceptions of risk factors and illness susceptibility. *Health Psychology, 3,* 431–457.
Weinstein, N. D. (1988). The precaution adoption process. *Health Psychology, 7,* 355–386.
Wills, T. A. (1981). Downward comparison as a coping mechanism. In C. R. Snyder & C. Ford (Eds.), *Coping with negative life events: Clinical and social-psychological perspectives.* (pp. 243–267). New York: Plenum.
Wills, T. A. (1987). Downward comparison as a coping mechanism. In C. R. Snyder & C. Ford (Eds.), *Coping with negative life events: Clinical and social-psychological perspectives* (pp. 243–268). New York: Plenum.
Wilson, S. R., & Benner, L. A. (1971). The effects of self-esteem and situation on comparison choices during ability evaluation. *Sociometry, 34,* 381–397.
Wood, J. V., Taylor, S. E., & Lichtman, R. R. (1985). Social comparison in adjustment to breast cancer. *Journal of Personality and Social Psychology, 49,* 1169–1183.
Wright, B. A. (1983). *Physical disability: A psychological approach.* New York: Harper & Row.
Zuckerman, M., & Lubin, B. (1965). *Multiple affect adjective checklist.* San Diego: Educational and Industrial Testing Service.

# 13 Comparisons, Justice, and the Internment of Japanese-Americans

Donna Nagata and Faye Crosby
Smith College

Comparisons are the stuff of social life. Everybody knows this intuitively, and since the days of Leon Festinger (1954), social psychologists have developed a formal knowledge of the operation of social comparisons in human interactions. Following Festinger's lead, the social comparison researchers investigated how comparisons with other people influence a person's attitudes and opinions, including the assessment of their own abilities (Goethals, 1986; Suls, 1977).

Early research relied heavily on the comparison–choice procedure (Gruder, 1971; Thornton & Arrowood, 1966; Wheeler 1966, Wheeler & Kiestner, 1984; Wheeler, Kiestner & Driver, 1982). In the procedure a subject is given some feedback—say, a grade on a test—and is allowed to see the grade of one other subject of one's choice. The researcher records whether the subject chooses another whose score is said to be, or is likely to be, better or worse than the subject's own score, and from this the researcher makes inferences about self-evaluation and self-enhancement.

Subsequent researchers moved away from the comparison–choice procedure to investigate how people engineer comparisons. Singer (1966) and Goethals and Darley (1977) noted that comparisons can be used to enhance self-esteem and that people typically avoid comparisons that are likely to threaten self-esteem. To paraphrase Goethals and Darley, people want to know how good they are but they also want to know that they are good. Downward comparisons—comparisons to worse-off others—can help people maintain the belief that they are functioning well (Taylor & Lobel, in press; Wills, 1981).

347

The avoidance of comparisons to advantaged others might also be an important ingredient in maintaining a sense of justice. Social comparison theorists have, by and large, not paid much attention to the role of comparison processes in the perception of social systems (Crosby, 1984a; Crosby & Gonzales-Intal, 1983), but it seems likely that comparisons which are not used to evaluate the self can be used to evaluate the social system. It seems possible, furthermore, that the kind of defensiveness that Wills (1981) and that Goethals (1986) described with respect to maintaining a positive view of the self can also operate when people are maintaining a positive view of the social system in which they live (Deutsch & Steil, 1988).

When the group to which a person belongs is disadvantaged, the person who is not ready to force social change faces a special dilemma. There are several possible solutions. The person can deny that the entire membership group is disadvantaged. A business woman might, for instance, deny that women are economically discriminated against. ("It's nice to have the doors held open; I don't know what these women's lib people are talking about.") The person can dissociate the self from the group. ("What I like about this business is that I am treated like a man.") Finally, the person can acknowledge the disadvantage of the group, express allegiance to the group but see the self as lucky. Some people recognize that their membership group is discriminated against but see themselves or their immediate family as exempt from discrimination.

Seeing oneself as exempt from the injustices that affect one's group has been called *the denial of personal disadvantage*. The phenomenon is of special interest to those who study social comparisons because it illustrates how people can avoid discomforting comparisons. The purpose of our chapter is to summarize the existing research on the denial of disadvantage and to extend the research by reporting findings from a study of how one ethnic minority has reacted to an instance of racial injustice. Because the denial of personal disadvantage was first documented in the context of relative deprivation research, the chapter narrates the history of relative deprivation research as a preamble to describing the findings on denial. The chapter closes by noting avenues for future research on the denial of disadvantage that might lead to an increased understanding of social comparison processes and of social status and change.

Relative Deprivation

During World War II, psychologists and other social scientists intensively studied American military personnel. The American soldier was observed, measured, and tested, and volumes were written about the factors that influenced human performance and motivation, so meticulously and minutely scrutinized on and off the battlefields. Two volumes, written under the direction of Samuel Stouffer bore the apt title: *The American Soldier* (Stouffer, Suchman, DeVinney, Star & Williams, 1949).

Among the numerous curiosities of Stouffer's research was the finding that men in the military police during the War were more satisfied with the promotion system than were men in the air corps. The finding struck many as odd because the military police was famous for the long tenure rank of its officers while the air corps was known as a place of extremely rapid advance. In explaining the anomalous findings, Stouffer et al. coined the term *relative deprivation*. People in the military police reasoned Stouffer, must have expected to forego promotions and so were satisfied with the promotional system. In the air corps, a number of individuals must have seen their buddies be promoted, anticipated rapid promotion and were then been disappointed (Vol. 1, pp. 251–253). Deprivations or dissatisfactions must have been felt relative to the group norm.

The concept of relative deprivation, invented to account for unexpected findings, might have been lost from social scientific view had it not been for the sociologist Robert Merton. In 1957 shortly after Festinger had written his germinal paper on social comparison processes, Merton, along with Alice Rossi published an important paper entitled "Contributions to the theory of reference group behavior." The paper arranged in a systematic way the various observations of Stouffer and his colleagues.

Merton and Rossi argued compellingly that people's feelings of dissatisfaction did not depend simply on objective reality, but rather, varied as a function of people's subjective standards. These, in turn, were at least partially dependent on people's reference groups. Merton and Rossi's work lent substance to the adage of Karl Marx (quoted in Useem, 1975, p. 53): "A house may be large or small; as long as the surrounding houses are equally small, it satisfies all social demands for a dwelling. But let a palace arise beside the little house, and it shrinks from a little house to a hut."

The proposition that deprivations are felt when people experience a discrepancy between their own situation and some subjective standard came in very handy after the racial unrest of the late 1960s. During the late 1960s and throughout the 1970s, social scientists and policy makers bent to the task of understanding all forms of Black activism, from urban riots to civil rights movements. The questions that intrigued many of the scholars represented variations on a central puzzle. Why, asked the scholars, should Black unrest occur in American just when the lot of blacks appeared to be improving throughout the nation (Useem, 1975)?

The answer, according to many, was that Black Americans were experiencing deprivation because changing social comparisons meant that aspirations and expectations were accelerating and improvements in Blacks' actual situations were not keeping pace with their aspirations and expectations. When the dissatisfied Blacks possessed skills and opportunities, their dissatisfaction took positive form and resulted in such constructive actions as civil disobedience against racism and racial injustice. When the opportunities for positive action were blocked, destruction—including self-destruction—seemed likely to occur (Crosby, 1976). Whether constructive or destructive, Black activism was analyzed in light of relative deprivation theory.

Of course, some scholars found the data more supportive of relative deprivation theory (RD) than did others. Leading the pro-RD faction was the social psychologist Thomas Pettigrew (1964, 1967, 1971; Vanneman & Pettigrew, 1972). Synthesizing survey data and historical accounts, Pettigrew argued that many Black people, especially in the North, compared their own underprivileged situations with the situations of a few privileged Blacks and that, furthermore, some Black people had come to compare their situations with those of White people. Once such comparisons were made, dissatisfactions were virtually guaranteed.

Prominent among the opposition scholars were sociologists, including McPhail (1971) and Spilerman (1971). Employing elaborate statistical analyses, these scholars argued that the urban riots resulted from structural, not psychological factors, such as the amount of time that Black male youths had on their hands. Comparisons to better-off others had little to do with generating unrest, said the structuralists.

One hallmark of the debates about Black social unrest and relative deprivation theory was the extent to which different scholars used the same terms to denote different concepts and different terms to denote similar concepts (Crosby 1979a, 1979b; Miller & Bolce, 1977; Miller, Bolce & Halligan, 1977). The interdisciplinary appeal of relative deprivation as a theory probably added to the confusion (Cook, Crosby, & Hennigan, 1977). Researchers in different disciplines conducted their work in different scholarly traditions with varying ideas of how to measure or infer anger and resentment.

By the late 1970s, there were several models of relative deprivation theory, each with its own particularly unique list of preconditions of felt deprivation (Berstein & Crosby, 1980). Most elaborate of the models was that of Crosby (1976). It proposed that feelings of dissatisfaction or deprivation occurred only when five preconditions had been met. According to Crosby, a person who lacked something (X) would feel upset about the lack only if the person: (a) wanted X; (b) felt entitled to obtain X; (c) saw others (including the self in the past) as possessing X; (d) thought it impossible to obtain X soon; and (e) did not blame the self to the current failure to possess X. Obviously, Crosby's model was quite elaborate. Obviously too, in Crosby's model (and in several other models of relative deprivation) comparisons to a better-off other constituted a necessary but not a sufficient precondition for felt deprivation.

The next phase in the research was characterized, at least in part, by two shifts. First, attention turned from Blacks to women (Crosby, Golding, & Resnick, 1983; Golding, Resnick & Crosby, 1983; Rhodebeck, 1981; Young, MacKenzie & Sherif, 1980). Second, new prominence was accorded the distinction, first articulated by W. G. Runciman (1966) between *egoistical deprivations* and *fraternal deprivations*. Egoistical deprivations are feelings of injustice that arise in people when they contemplate their own situation as it compares to the situation of specific other people within their reference group. Fraternal deprivations, in contrast, have to do with comparisons between groups.

Both shifts, but especially the latter, were evident in the work of Joanne Martin. In an early study Martin (1981) found subjects expressed the most dissatisfaction on behalf of a group (e.g., clerical workers) when pay inequalities within the group were small and pay inequalities between groups (e.g., between clerical workers and management) were large. Large inequalities between groups also served, said Martin and Murray (1983), to make people feel unjustly treated as an individual member of a recognizable group.

After further reflections on the conceptual distinctions between egoistical and fraternal deprivation (Martin, 1982; Martin & Murray, 1983), Martin focused on the connection between fraternal deprivation and collective action (Martin & Murray, 1984; Martin, Scully, and Levitt, 1987). Like other scholars (Guimond & Dube, 1983; Kinder, 1986; Pettigrew, 1978; Taylor & Dube, 1986; Walker & Mann, 1987), Martin proposed that injustices felt in connection with one's group membership are more likely to result in collective action than are injustices felt by an individual qua individual. The data from a laboratory experiment with 40 female subjects confirmed the prediction that feelings of fraternal deprivation correlated with a propensity toward collective action, in this case, a willingness to think about changes in the outcomes of an entire group (Martin, 1986; Martin, Brickman, & Murray, 1984).

The shift to focusing on women and on the distinction between individual and group dissatisfaction were evident in a survey study conducted in 1978 and 1979 in Newton, Massachusetts (Crosby, 1982, 1984a). The Newton study had two central purposes, one applied and one theoretical. At a theoretical level, the study tested the validity of all models of relative deprivation and cognate theories. To do so, it measured all of the attitudes that served as preconditions of felt deprivation proposed in any model (e.g., the attitude then was one of not obtaining what one deserves), feelings of deprivation (operationalized as feelings of grievance) and feelings of dissatisfaction. It then used structural modelling to see which of the preconditions (hypothesized by any model) actually predicted variations in felt deprivation or in dissatisfaction, either alone or in combination.

Attitudes demand an attitude object, and the models of relative deprivation had to be tested in specific attitude domains. The Newton study included 345 women and men who worked outside the home and 60 housewives, all white and all between the ages of 25 and 40. The employed respondents were asked about their job attitudes; the married respondents (with or without children) were asked about their home lives; and all of the respondents were asked about the situation of working women. Each model of relative deprivation was, thus, tested in three domains.

The second central purpose of the Newton study was to shed light on the paradox of the contented female worker. A large literature existed demonstrating gender inequities in the labor market. Yet, numerous studies had also shown females to be as contented as males with their jobs. Why were working women not upset? (It is interesting to note that this question, asked mostly by female investigators, is the inverse of the question asked, mostly by White male investigators, about Blacks.)

The results of the Newton study were both disappointing and gratifying. Concerning theory, all models of relative deprivation theory and cognate theories were found to be invalid. The researchers were forced to conclude that relative deprivation should best be construed as a heuristic concept (like love or emotion) that can facilitate discussions of complex phenomena but that does not strictly permit predictions (Crosby, 1982; Crosby, Muehrer, & Loewenstein, 1986).

If the findings of the Newton survey disappointed the model builder, they produced a rich yield for those interested in the paradox of the contented female worker. One interesting finding was that the working women who felt most dissatisfied with their own jobs were those who named males as the people to whom they compared themselves when trying to decide how good their jobs were (Zanna, Crosby, & Loewenstein, 1987). Such women were, however, in a minority. Most women used other females as their reference group, and most were content about their jobs. As males were better-off than females in the labor force, the discontented women were comparing themselves to others who were presumably better-off than they while the contented females were not.

The high level of job satisfaction among the female workers in Newton replicated earlier findings, with one vital addition: unlike earlier surveys, the Newton study contained precise information on the job characteristics of the respondents and their salaries. By design, half the working women sampled occupied high status jobs (e.g., physician; lawyer) and half low status jobs (e.g., clerk). The same split was, again by design, replicated among the working men in the study. The samples of working women and working men, exactly matched on ratings of occupational prestige (Hodge,

Siegel, & Rossi, 1964), were also matched on all other measured characteristics (e.g., hours worked per week; educational level) that are usually considered to be employment *inputs*. Equated on inputs, the males and females differed on employment outcomes: the employed men in Newton in 1979 earned $8000 a year more, on average, than did the employed women! It was hard to escape the conclusion that the women were the victims of discrimination.

Objectively at a disadvantage, but subjectively satisfied with all aspects of work, including pay, the employed women in the Newton study seemed to represent the reincarnation of Stouffer's military policemen or Pettigrew's pre-civil rights Black person. The question arose: Did the women's contentment arise from a general devaluing of females? More specifically: How did the women view the situation of most working women?

On six of eight measures, the employed women of Newton felt more upset and more concerned about the plight of female workers than did either the housewives or the employed men. Employed women in Newton, blind to their own personal disadvantage, had no problem perceiving the disadvantage of working women generally. They thought that the average working woman earned less than a comparable male and less than she was entitled to earn. They felt bitter and resentful about the situation. They shunned false optimism about sex discrimination in America generally.

DENIAL OF PERSONAL DISADVANTAGE

Having documented in Newton the existence of what has been called the denial of personal disadvantage, the next logical step was to investigate the generalizability of the phenomenon. Are White middle-class women living in suburban Boston the only ones to deny their personal disadvantage? Or is the tendency more general? If so, what are the conditions that influence and delimit the denial of personal disadvantage?

Beginning Research

At the time that the Newton study was published, indications already existed that the findings did not represent an isolated case. John d'Emilio, who had written an award-winning account of the early gay rights movement in America, claimed that even as they fought the oppression of homosexuals, many of the early activists denied that they themselves had been the victims of discrimination (Crosby, 1984b). Guimond and Dube (1983) had shown that Francophones in Canada minimized the extent to which the business community penalized them for their ethnicity. Black optimism was shown in at least one sample to correlate with fraternal, but not with of egoistical, deprivation (Abeles, 1976).

Recently two additional studies have tested the limits of phenomenon documented in Newton (Crosby, Pufall, Snyder, O'Connell, & Whalen, 1989). In one of the studies, two samples of lesbians from the middle- and professional-classes were asked about the experiences of lesbians in America and in their local community, and about themselves personally. Unlike the employed women in Newton, the respondents in the lesbian samples had a conscious and deliberate sense of themselves as people separate from, and in some ways at odds with, the mainstream of American society. Being politicized, the lesbians ought to have been more able than most to see how their personal destinies were linked to the destiny of their group (Crosby & Herek, 1986; Gurin, 1987). If they, like earlier groups, fell prey to the tendency to deny their own personal disadvantage, then one could have confidence that the phenomenon was quite entrenched in middle-class people.

The lesbians, like groups sampled earlier, denied their own personal disadvantage. They saw themselves as suffering less discrimination than lesbians in America generally and than other lesbians in the local community. It is logically possible that the lesbians in the studies lived in an especially tolerant area of the country and did suffer less discrimination than lesbians in America generally; but it is not logically possible that each woman in the sample suffered less than other homosexual women in the local community.

Not all of the lesbians were equally blind to the presence of discrimination in their lives. The more strongly a respondent identified herself with the lesbian community and with lesbian causes, the more likely was she to admit that she had been the victim of discrimination. Hostility toward the heterosexual world did not predict variations in willingness to acknowledge personal discrimination.

Given the robustness of the denial of personal disadvantage among middle-class Americans, even those middle-class American women with a problematic relationship to the dominant, heterosexual world, the need arose to examine the importance of social class in limiting the phenomenon. To do so, Crosby et al. (1989) distributed questionnaires to over 200 students at a technical college in Springfield, Massachusetts. The population of students at the college was almost entirely working-class. The sample included 106 Caucasian women, 80 Caucasian men, 24 minority women, and 12 minority men.

The 9-page questionnaire asked, among other things, the extent to which the respondent and the respondent's family had suffered discrimination in terms of employment, housing, and so on in the last year and ever. People did not distinguish between themselves and their families, but they did see themselves as having suffered more "ever" than in the last year. There were no differences between ethnic groups. Women and men were statistically similar on the ratings for the last year, but women did admit to greater discrimination when the questions related to one's life, ever.

The questionnaire also included two version's of Cantril's Ladder. In its original form, the instrument has respondents place themselves and other individuals or groups along an 11-rung ladder, imagining that the top rung represents the best possible life and the bottom rung represents the worst possible life (Cantril, 1965). Materials in the Springfield study included one version of the ladder with the original wording and another version of the ladder with anchors stating at one end, "a life which is free of discrimination" and, at the other, "a life which is full of discrimination."

Quite surprisingly, most people in the Springfield study claimed to have suffered as much or more discrimination than other people. Three-quarters of the men in the sample, for instance, believed they had experienced a life more filled with discrimination than most men, and a quarter also saw themselves as having suffered more than most women. Eighty-eight percent of the women saw themselves as having suffered more discrimination than most men and 60% more than most women.

These results suggest the way in which denial of discrimination operates may be influenced by class. Perhaps only middle-class people need to see themselves as exempt personally from the stresses and problems they know to exist for their group as a whole. Perhaps working-class people are more willing to admit how the system has mistreated them. Are working-class people also more willing than middle-class people to admit that they are not coping well with life's stresses? Absolutely not! The respondents in the Springfield study saw themselves as having far greater chances for success in life than most other people. Nearly three-quarters of the women saw their own chances of success as better than those of most women and 23.4% also saw themselves as better off than most men. It was as if the respondents in Springfield were claiming, in essence, that society might have dealt them personally an especially severe blow but that they were too powerful to be bested.

Taylor, Wright, and Moghaddam (1989) wondered if such findings might be due to a greater willingness on the part of people to see the group as more extreme than the self, no matter what the dimension. To test for the possibility, they also had subjects rate the degree of disadvantage and also the degree of privilege for themselves and for their groups. Subjects saw their group as more disadvantaged than themselves, as did Crosby's (1982). Taylor's subjects also saw themselves as more privileged than their groups, demonstrating that the phenomenon is not simply an artifact of a response bias toward group extremity.

Although not artifactual, the denial of personal disadvantage might come more from the exaggeration of group suffering than from the minimization of personal suffering. So suggested Taylor, Wright, and Moghaddam (1988). Consistent with their suggestion, questionnaire responses from Indian and Haitian women living in Canada showed that the women were willing to acknowledge moderate levels of personal discrimination and high levels of group discrimination.

Old Answers and New Questions

Social comparisons do, as Festinger proposed, serve several obvious functions. In some situations, comparisons are foisted on people; in others, people exercise a choice, comparing themselves and their outcomes to selected others but not to all others. Like other researchers (Goethals & Darley, 1977; Taylor & Lobel, in press; Wills, 1981) we find strong evidence that most people in most situations seek to protect the sense that they function as well or better than others. The accumulated research on relative deprivation theory and on the denial of personal disadvantage shows that many people, even those who are objectively disadvantaged, try to see their social world as one that permits (even if it does not facilitate) their own personal effectiveness.

While the general contours of the phenomenon appear robust, some variations do exist. The employed women in Newton who compared themselves to employed men were less prone to deny their own discrimination than were other women. The more developed the sense of identification as a lesbian, the less likely was a lesbian to ignore the presence of discrimination in her own life. In a working-class sample, respondents were less hesitant than earlier samples of middle-class people, to complain about mistreatment.

The documentation of variations raises questions about the phenomenon of denial. It is clear from the sweep of previous findings that denial is sometimes stronger and sometimes weaker. When, one wonders, would people be especially likely or especially unlikely to see themselves or their close associates as exemptions to the disadvantage that they acknowledge as characteristic of the larger reference group? Are there any disadvantaged groups that might be less likely than middle-class Caucasians to perceive themselves or their families as no more successful at coping with the stresses than are others? Are there, in other words, any special circumstances that reduce the tendency to see oneself as the lucky exception to the rule of disadvantage?

People who value group harmony above individual success might be less likely to deny personal disadvantage than mainstream Americans, with their commitment to the ideal of individualism (Sampson, 1977). Japanese-Americans are known to embrace the cultural ideal of group identification (Kitano, 1969). Japanese-Americans, then, whose sense of self includes connection rather than separateness might be less willing than most White Americans to see themselves as differing from the group in terms of suffering or coping (Markus, 1989).

Examining the extent of denial of personal disadvantage among Japanese-Americans provides a good check on the generalizability of previous findings. The Japanese-American community suffered a grave injustice during World War II, when 120,000 Japanese-Americans were stripped of their civil rights and interned without trial in concentration camps. Some of the people imprisoned in the camps were Issei or first-generation Japanese-Americans. Most were Nisei or second-generation Japanese-Americans. The movement for redress has been molded not only by the Nisei but also by the Sansei or third-generation Japanese-Americans who felt upset about the injustices of the camps. Would Sansei minimize the suffering of their own parents while acknowledging (or even exaggerating) the victimization of the reference group generally? If the results of the lesbian study were applicable, they might.

Then again, there were reasons to believe they would not minimize parental suffering. Three factors seemed to mitigate against the tendency to deny personal (including familial) disadvantage among third-generation Japanese-Americans. First, the Sansei are known to be angry about the abrogation of Japanese-American rights during the War. Second, middle-class Japanese-Americans are less likely to be individualistic than are white middle-class Americans. Finally, the internment represented an intense and unique trauma. Perhaps the dramatic quality of the internment would interrupt the tendency to see oneself and one's own family as free of the trials and attributions of one's ethnic group. Vivid episodes of injustice may galvanize people more readily than the slow and subtle accumulation of wrongs. Turning a blind eye to discomforting comparisons may not be as easy to do when the contrasts between what is and what ought to be explode in delimited time frame. Maybe it is only when people are motivated to maintain the illusion of a just world that they resist salient information that would make them upset. Given the Sansei's conviction that the internment was racially unjust, they might have no reason to deny personal disadvantage.

Sansei Project

How third-generation Japanese-Americans interpret and react to the internment experiences of their parents is the subject of the Sansei Research Project (Nagata, 1987, 1988, 1990). Data in the Sansei Research Project comes from two sources: a questionnaire completed by approximately 600 Sansei and intensive interviews with 32 Sansei. Data for the present analyses are drawn entirely from the questionnaire sample.

Methods. The questionnaire was distributed across the continental United States and Hawaii. All respondents included in the present analyses were born after World War II and had at least one parent who had been interned. Respondents were identified with the assistance of the Japanese American Citizens League (JACL), a national organization that has chapters in American cities where there exist large concentrations of Japanese-Americans. Additional surveys were sent to youth directors of the Young Buddhist Association and to individuals who requested to participate in the study. A total of 1250 surveys were sent. Sixty percent (740) were returned. Of these, 13 were omitted because they were incomplete or received too late for inclusion, and an additional 134 were omitted because they were returned by Sansei who themselves had been interned at a young age.

Fifty-one percent of the respondents were male and 49% were female. The average age of respondents was 32 years. Forty-two percent were married, 48% single, 3% remarried, and 7% divorced, separated, or widowed. The majority of participants came from California (44%), followed by the Midwest (18%), Northwest (17%), East (13%), Hawaii (4%), and Intermountain (3%) regions. Respondents reported an average personal income of between $25,000–$35,000. Thirty-one percent had completed college, while another 47% had received or completed some post-graduate education.

The 20-page survey contained over 100 fixed-choice questions covering a range of issues regarding Sansei perceptions of the internment. Of particular interest were questions in which respondents were asked to rate how much the Japanese-Americans had suffered from the internment on a five-point scale (where 1 meant very little suffering and 5 a great deal of suffering) and, later, how well Japanese-Americans had coped (where 1 meant very poorly and 5 meant very well). The Sansei also compared their own families to most interned Japanese-Americans in terms of suffering on a scale from 1 (much less than most) to 5 (much more than most) and in terms of coping (from 1 indicating that parents coped much worse than most to 5 indicating that parents coped much better).

Additional measures of attitudes allowed us to see whether perceptions of unusually low stress (or unusually competent coping) varied as a function of other factors. The attitude questions, selected for their possible relationship to the phenomenon of denial, focused upon the degree to which Sansei preferred associating with other Japanese-Americans over Caucasion-Americans, had open family communication about the internment experience, had an interest in the topic of the internment, maintained strong negative emotions about their parents' incarceration, and supported the movement seeking monetary redress for former internees.

Sansei responded to 27 attitude questions using a 7-point scale (where 1 meant strongly disagree and 7 meant strongly agree). A factor analysis of these statements revealed four main factors: (a) Barriers to Communication About the Internment; (b) Ethnic Preference; (c) Sense of Vulnerability; and (d) Likelihood to Resist Future Internments. For a listing of specific items within each factor, see Nagata (1990). These factors, along with 11 additional attitude questions and the suffering and coping scales provided the data for our analyses.

Findings: Parents As Possible Exceptions To The Rule. Our first concern was to see if the respondents would perceive that their parents had suffered less or coped better than most other Japanese-Americans during the War. We expected that the Sansei would not minimize parental suffering.

Our expectations were confirmed. The Sansei in the sample felt that the suffering of Japanese-Americans interned during World War II was substantial. On the five-point scale, the average response among the sample was 4.63. Sixty-eight percent of the sample rated the amount of suffering as 5, the highest possible score. When asked to compare their own parents' suffering with that of other internees, furthermore, the respondents acknowledged that their parents had suffered as much as others. The average score was 3.12 on the 5 point scale. The verbal designation that corresponded to a score of 3 on the questionnaire was "about the same as most."

What about coping? In the Springfield study, people who were willing to acknowledge that they had been discriminated against also perceived that they had coped with the discrimination far better than most. Would the same apply in the Sansei Project? Would the respondents imagine that their parents had coped far better than most of the Japanese-Americans interned during the War?

For coping, as for suffering, the respondents did not indulge in the illusion that their own parents had coped much better than other. However, the Sansei did differentiate between their parents and most other Japanese-Americans to a greater degree on the coping than on the suffering scale. Respondents averaged a score of 3.66 on the 1 to 5 scale. A score of 3 meant "about the same as most" and 4 meant "slightly better than most."

An examination of the overall distribution of scores for the parental suffering and coping scales also provided support for the hypothesis that, as Japanese-Americans, the Sansei would experience a press not to differ from the group. For both scales, but particularly on the suffering scale, respondents clustered at the midpoint, indicating that they perceived their parents' suffering as being about the same as other Japanese-Americans.

But there did emerge an interesting subgroup of Sansei who saw that their own parents had suffered less and/or coped better than most other internees, a group who had, it appeared, denied personal disadvantage. Would their responses to other attitude items also reflect this denial? Did this subgroup for example, also tend to minimize their affiliation with other

Japanese-Americans? Did they have less pronounced feelings of ethnic preference than others? Would they be less supportive of the redress movement, or report less communication with their parents around the topic of internment?

To find out, we first partitioned the sample into three groups on the basis of perceived parental suffering. One group included those respondents who saw their parents as having suffered less than most (N = 66). A second group were those respondents who saw their parents as having suffered about the same as others (N = 301); and the third group included respondents who saw their parents as having suffered more than most others (N = 209). These three groups were compared on the set of attitude measures.

A discriminant function analysis was performed using 15 attitude measures as predictors of membership in the three groups of suffering. Included as predictors were respondents' scores on the four attitude factors cited previously: Barriers to Communication About the Internment, Ethnic Preference, Sense of Vulnerability, and Likelihood to Resist Future Internments. Other predictors included: two items assessing current and past membership in Japanese-American groups, two items assessing past and current interest in the internment, two items on the average frequency and length of communication with parents about the internment, three items on the degree of support for, knowledge of, and activity in the redress movement, and two items evaluating respondents' level of anger and sadness in response to their parents' past internment.

Results from the discriminant analysis indicated an overall significant difference between the three groups of suffering, $[X^2(30, N = 576) = 68.2, p < .001]$. In order to identify the precise nature of this difference, a subsequent discriminant function was calculated comparing those who denied parental suffering with those who saw their parents as suffering about the same as others. The analysis also yielded a significant effect, $[X^2(15, N = 376) = 39.9, p < .001]$.

Table 13.1 presents the canonical loadings and means for each of the predictors in this analysis. Examination of the canonical loadings indicates that two predictor variables, Ethnic Preference and Length of Conversations With Parents, had loadings of .38 or above and distinguished between those Sansei who perceived parental suffering as less than most others and those who perceived parental suffering as being about the same as others. Sansei who saw less than average parental suffering reported a significantly lower level of preference for other Japanese-Americans, $[F(1,352) = 6.5, p < .05]$, as well as shorter conversations with their parents about the camps, $[F(1,352) = 8.4, p < .05]$. While not shown in the discriminant function, the two groups also differed in univariate analyses on their reported level of sadness about their parents' internment, $[F(1,352) = 4.3,$

TABLE 13.1
Results of Discriminant Function Analysis of Attitudinal Variables
for Perceived Parent Suffering

		Group Means		
Predictor Variables	Canonical Loadings	Suffered Less	Suffered the Same	Suffered More
Barriers to communication[a,b]	.291	−.202	.059	−.021
Ethnic preference[a,b]	.382	−.256	.045	.298
Sense of vulnerability[a,b]	.112	−.032	.035	−.238
Likelihood to resist internments[a,b]	.010	.017	−.016	.005
Support for redress movement	−.147	6.045	6.023	6.413
Knowledge of redress movement	−.030	4.379	4.385	5.037
Activity in redress movement	.070	2.576	2.591	3.165
Current activity in Japanese American groups	.140	.682	.698	.743
Past activity in Japanese American groups	−.066	.697	.684	.697
Current interest in internment[a]	.259	−.262	−.014	.186
Past interest in internment[a]	.234	−.322	−.070	−.023
Number of conversations with parents	.246	3.273	3.498	3.569
Length of conversations with parents	.444	2.061	2.475	2.642
Anger about parents' internment	.286	5.333	5.807	6.110
Sadness about parents' internment	.317	5.773	6.110	6.358

Canonical Correlation = .329
[a]Represents normalized factor scores
[b]Attitude factor score

$p < .05$], with respondents who saw less parental suffering reporting less sadness. No other univariate comparisons were statistically significant.

The finding that the Sansei who reported less parental suffering were also those who were less closely identified with other Japanese-Americans echoes the findings of earlier investigations of denial. Among the lesbians in a previous study, denial was attenuated when the woman had a strong, positive identification with lesbian women. The findings are also consistent with Gurin's (1987) suggestion that close bonds with their group help people become politically mobilized. While the discriminant function results are informative, caution must be used in their interpretation. No single canonical loading was higher than .444 and, as shown by the canonical correlation listed in Table 1, the discriminant function accounted for a small proportion of the variance.

From suffering, we turned to coping. We partitioned the sample in terms of coping, contrasting those Sansei who felt their parents had coped slightly or much better than most others ($N = 237$) with those who felt their parents had coped about the same as others ($N = 231$). (It was not possible to form a third group on this scale due to an inadequate number of respondents who rated their parents as coping worse than others). A discriminant function analysis was again performed using the same 15 predictor variables. No significant discriminant function emerged, indicating that the predictor variables did not discriminate between those Sansei who perceived parental coping as better than most others and those who saw parental coping as being about the same as others. In addition, the only significant univariate comparison occurred for the predictor Barriers to Communication About the Internment [$F(1,355) = 5.0, p < .05$]. Examination of the means for this factor suggested that those who saw their parents as coping better than others reported less barriers to communication.

Findings: Self Contrasted With Parents. Finally, we recognized that the Sansei data differed from previous studies in terms of the reference group to whom the respondents compared themselves. Earlier work on the denial of disadvantage contrasted the self with others in one's membership group. The Sansei data, in comparison, included contrasts between one's own family and one's membership group. Obviously, it would make no sense to ask Sansei who had no experience in the camps and often had not even been born until after the War how well they coped relative to others in their reference group. But it did make sense to ask the respondents to imagine how well they might have coped with the situation. One statement on the questionnaire read: "My parents have adjusted to life after the camps better than I could have." Seven response options were presented ranging from 1 (strongly disagree) to 7 (strongly agree). The numbers show that nearly 50% of the sample thought their parents coped better than they could have coped. Thirty percent were undecided. Only 10% of the sample imagined that they might have coped better than their parents. Here again, there is little evidence of a tendency to deny that the self is somehow exempt from the trials and tribulations of the disadvantaged membership group.

LESSONS

Social comparisons help people evaluate themselves and their social environment. Goethals and Darley (1977) proposed that comparisons are selected or avoided in a way that allows people to maintain a positive image of their own abilities and outcomes. Researchers like Taylor (Taylor & Lobel, in press) and Wills (1981) have documented the aptness of this observation.

The research on the denial of personal disadvantage growing out of the work on relative deprivation, has also demonstrated how people will construct and misconstruct comparative information in a way that allows them to maintain the illusion that they are personally exempt from the injustices that beset society. Deprivations felt on behalf of the self tend not to lead to collective social action (Pettigrew, 1978) probably because social solutions seem most appropriate for social problems. Unless people who feel personally deprived, particularly through comparisons (real or imagined) to better-off others, can see the personal as the political, even those deprivations that result almost wholly from one's membership in a disadvantaged social category are likely to masquerade as private woes. Problems that appear to be caused by idiosyncratic or personal situations but are in fact due to social conditions almost always fail to be solved by individualistic solutions. The difficulty of solutions can make a person want to avoid recognition of the problem altogether. Unless forced to make unpleasant comparisons, most people will avoid them. And, in a way that perpetuates the status quo, many people from disadvantaged groups engage in the denial of personal disadvantage.

How universal is the tendency toward denial? The data from the Sansei Research Project suggest that denial of personal disadvantage is not constant across all populations and situations. Like most phenomena in social psychology, the denial of personal disadvantage is partially a product of culture and is subject to modification (Gergen, 1973; Markus, 1989). Overall, the majority of Sansei did not perceive their own parents as suffering less than most other Japanese-Americans. Our guess is that several factors, including cultural norms, contribute to this finding. The cultural ethnic of group solidarity among Japanese-Americans was no doubt an important ingredient in the respondents' disinclination to separate their own parents from the wider ethnic group or to imagine themselves as possibly stronger or better than their parents. Anglo-Americans might show a greater strain toward individualism even in the face of injustices perpetrated because of racial identification.

While cultural values probably influenced the pattern of results, the Sansei Research Project data do not permit us to rule out other important factors. Especially noteworthy is the episodic and dramatic nature of the injustice of wartime internment. The incarceration of Japanese Americans in America during World War II provided a rallying point for the whole community. David Winter (1988) proposed that groups become socially or politically active only if they have a score to settle. When there is no dramatic event, what *is* appears synonymous with what *ought to be*. For this reason, says Winter, injustices that slowly and imperceptibly accumulate over time prove quite resistant to detection and correction. The existence of a dramatic event or set of events, on the other hand, allows individuals to link their own individual fates with the larger social system.

It is not possible for us to disambiguate the reasons why the majority of Sansei in our sample escaped the tendency to deny personal discrimination, but the different factors we have identified should be investigated by future researchers. It would be informative to study the perceptions of discrimination among American Indians. Some American Indian Tribes are characterized by the same valuing of group harmony as the Japanese-Americans display. Discrimination against American Indians may be more continual and less episodic than discrimination against Japanese-Americans.

Looking at the thoughts and feelings of American Indians is only one technique to separate reactions due to cultural values from reactions due to the episodic nature of the internment. Another technique would be to see how Anglo-Americans react to dramatic moments of injustice as compared to steady states of injustice. Whichever approach is used, it would serve researchers well to see how social comparisons that are forced on people (as is often the case in a moment of social drama) interact with the comparisons that people spontaneously select or avoid.

The Sansei data revealed that there can be important individual differences in the denial of personal disadvantage within a given cultural group. Not all Sansei were immune to denial. Some felt that their parents had suffered less than most others during the internment. While it is possible that this subgroup actually had parents who suffered less than the norm, the indignity of the internment as well as the harsh and impersonal physical conditions of the camps were experienced by all. The fact that these respondents also reported significantly less preference for associating with other Japanese-Americans than Sansei who did not deny parental suffering in relation to the group suggests the existence of a more pervasive phenomenon of denial worthy of further investigation. The emergence among the Sansei of the subgroup of deniers, despite the cultural press to rate personal disadvantage as being the same as others, points to the importance for social comparison researchers to examine "within group differences" along side "between group differences." Here, as elsewhere, the comparisons could be instructive.

ACKNOWLEDGMENT

We are thankful to Kathy Bartus, Cathy Hogan, Joanne Martin, Donald Taylor, and Janice Steil. We also want to thank Steven J. Trierweiler for his assistance.

REFERENCES

Abeles, R. (1976). Relative deprivation, rising expectations, and militancy. *Journal of Social Issues*, *32*(2), 119–137.

Bernstein, M., & Crosby, F. (1980). An empirical examination of relative deprivation theory. *Journal of Experimental Social Psychology*, *16*, 442–456.

Cantril, H. (1965). *The pattern of human concerns*. New Brunswick, NJ: Rutgers University Press.

Cook, T. D., Crosby, F., & Hennigan, K. M. (1977). The construct validity of relative deprivation. In J. M. Suls & R. L. Miller (Eds.), *Social comparison processes: Theoretical and empirical perspectives* (pp. 307–333), Washington: Hemisphere.

Crosby, F. (1976). A model of egoistical relative deprivation. *Psychological Review*, *83*, 85–113.

Crosby, F. (1979a). Relative deprivation revisited: A response to Miller, Bolce, and Halligan. *American Political Science Review*, *73*, 103–112.

Crosby, F. (1979b). Rejoinder. *American Political Science Review*, *73*, 822–825.

Crosby, F. (1982). *Relative deprivation and working women*. New York: Oxford University Press.

Crosby, F. (1984a). Relative deprivation in organizational settings. In B. Staw & L. L. Cummings (Eds.), *Research in organizational behavior: An annual series of analytical essays and critical reviews*, (Vol. 6, pp. 51–93). Greenwich, CT: JAI Press.

Crosby, F. (1984b, July). Selective vision. Why every woman thinks she's the great exception. *Working Woman Magazine*, 67–69.

Crosby, F., Golding, J., & Resnick, A. (1983). Discontent among male lawyers, female lawyers, and female legal secretaries. *Journal of Applied Social Psychology*, *13*, 183–190.

Crosby, F., & Gonzales-Intal, A. M. (1983). Relative deprivation and equity theories: Felt injustice and the underserved benefits of others. In R. Folger (Ed.), *The sense of injustice: Social psychological perspectives* (pp. 141–166). New York: Plenum.

Crosby, F., & Herek, G. M. (1986). Male sympathy with the situation of women: Does experience make a difference? *Journal of Social Issues*, *42*(2), 55–66.

Crosby, F., Muehrer, P., & Loewenstein, G. (1986). Relative deprivation and explanation: Models and concepts. In J. Olson, M. Zanna, & P. Herman (Eds.), *Relative deprivation and assertive action. The Ontario symposium* (Vol. 4, pp. 214–237). Hilldale, NJ: Lawrence Erlbaum Associates.

Crosby, F., Pufall, A., Snyder, R. C., O'Connell, M., & Whalen, P. (1989). The denial of personal disadvantage among you, me and all the other ostriches. In M. Crawford & M. Gentry (Eds.), *Gender and thought* (pp. 79–99). New York: Springer-Verlag.

Deutsch, M., & Steil, J. M. (1988). Awakening the sense of injustice. *Journal of Social Justice Research*, *2*, 3–23.

Festinger, L. (1954). A theory of social comparison processes. *Human Relations*, *7*, 117–140.

Gergen, K. (1973). Social psychology as history. *Journal of Personality and Social Psychology*, *26*, 309–320.

Goethals, G. R. (1986). Social comparison theory: Psychology from the lost and found. *Personality and Social Psychology Bulletin*, *12*, 261–278.

Goethals, G. R., & Darley, J. M. (1977). Social comparison theory: An attributional approach. In J. M. Suls & R. L. Miller (Eds.), *Social comparison processes: Theoretical and empirical perspectives* (pp. 259–278). Washington, DC: Hemisphere.

Golding, J., Resnick, A., & Crosby, F. (1983). Satisfaction as a function of gender and job status. *Psychology of Women Quarterly*, *7*(8), 286–290.

Gruder, C. L. (1971). Determinants of social comparison choices. *Journal of Experimental Social Psychology*, 7, 473–389.

Guimond, S., & Dube, L. (1983). Relative deprivation theory and the Quebec Nationalist Movement: On the cognitive-emotion distinction and the personal-group deprivation issue. *Journal of Personality and Social Psychology*, 44, 526–535.

Gurin, P. (1987). The political implications of women's statuses. In F. Crosby (Ed.), *Spouse, parent, worker: On gender and multiple roles* (pp. 165–196). New Haven: Yale University Press.

Hodge, R. W., Siegel, P. M., & Rossi, P. H. (1964). Occupational prestige in the United States, 1925–1963. *American Journal of Sociology*, 70, 286–302.

Kinder, D. R. (1986). The continuing American dilemma: White resistance to recall change 40 years after Myrdal. *Journal of Social Issues*, 42(2), 151–171.

Kitano, H. H. L. (1969). *Japanese Americans: The evolution of a subculture*. Englewood Cliffs, NJ: Prentice–Hall.

Markus, H. (1989, March). *Self and culture*. Paper presented at the meeting of the Eastern Psychological Association. Boston, MA.

Martin, J. (1981). Relative deprivation: A theory of distributive injustice for an era of shrinking resources. In L. L. Cummings & B. M. Staw (Eds.), *Research in organizational behavior: An annual series of analytical essays and critical reviews* (Vol. 3, pp. 53–105). Greenwich, CT: JAI Press.

Martin, J. (1982). The fairness of earning differentials: An experimental study of the perceptions of blue collar workers. *The Journal of Human Resources*, 17, 110–112.

Martin, J. (1986). The tolerance of injustice. In J. M. Olson, C. P. Herman, and M. P. Zanna (Eds.), *Relative deprivation and social comparison: The Ontario symposium* (Vol. 4, pp. 217–240). Hilldale, NJ: Lawrence Erlbaum Associates.

Martin, J., Brickman, P., & Murray, A. (1984). Moral outrage and pragmatism: Explanations for collective action. *Journal of Experimental Social Psychology*, 20, 484–496.

Martin, J., & Murray, A. (1983). Distributive injustice and unfair exchange. In K. S. Cook and D. M. Messick (Eds.), *Theories of equity: Psychological and sociological perspectives* (pp. 169–205). New York: Praeger.

Martin, J., & Murray, A. (1984). Catalysts for collective violence: The importance of a psychological approach. In R. Folger (Ed.), *The sense of injustice: Social psychological perspectives* (pp. 95–132). New York, NY: Plenum.

Martin, J., Scully, M., & Levitt, B. (1987). Revolutionary visions of injustice: Damning the past, excusing the present, and neglecting the future. *Social Science*, 72, 74–80.

McPhail, C. (1971). Civil disorder participation: A critical examination of recent research. *American Sociological Review*, 36, 1058–1073.

Merton, R., & Rossi, A. S. (1957). Contributions to the theory of reference group behavior. In R. Merton (Ed.), *Social theory and social structure* (pp. 279–333). New York: Free Press.

Miller, A. H., & Bolce, L. H. (1979). Reply to Crosby. *American Political Science Review*, 73, 818–822.

Miller, A. H., Bolce, L. H., & Halligan, M. (1977). The J–Curve theory and Black urban riots. *American Political Science Review*, 71, 964–982.

Nagata, D. K. (1987, August). *Long-term effects of the Japanese-American internment on the children of internees*. Paper presented at the meeting of the Asian American Psychological Association. New York.

Nagata, D. K. (1988, August). The long-term effects of victimization: Present-day effects of Japanese-American internment. In D. Nagata (Chair) *Varied forms of victimization during*

World War II. Symposium conducted at the meeting of the American Psychological Association. Atlanta, GA.

Nagata, D. K. (1990). The Japanese-American internment: Exploring the transgenerational consequences of traumatic stress. *Journal of Traumatic Stress, 3*(1), 47-69.

Pettigrew, T. F. (1964). *A profile of the Negro American*. Princeton, NJ: Van Nostrand.

Pettigrew, T. F. (1967). Social evaluation theory. In D. Levine (Ed.), *Nebraska symposium on motivation* (Vol. 15, pp. 241-318). Lincoln: University of Nebraska Press.

Pettigrew, T. F. (1971). *Racially separate or together?* New York: McGraw-Hill.

Pettigrew, T. F. (1978). Three issues in ethnicity: Boundaries, deprivations, and perceptions. In J. M. Yinger & S. J. Cutter (Eds.), *Major social issues: A multidisciplinary review* (pp. 241-318). New York: Free Press.

Rhodebeck, L. (1981). Group deprivation: An alternative model for explaining collective political action. *Micropolitics, 1*, 239-267.

Runciman, W. G. (1966). *Relative deprivation and social justice*. Berkeley: University of California Press.

Sampson, E. E. (1977). Psychology and the American ideal. *Journal of Personality and Social Psychology, 35*, 767-782.

Singer, J. E. (1966). Social comparison: Progress and issues. *Journal of Experimental Social Psychology, Suppl. 1*, 103-110.

Spilerman, S. (1971). The causes of racial disturbances: Tests of explanations. *American Sociological Review, 36*, 427-442.

Stouffer, S. A., Suchman, E. A., DeVinney, L. C., Star, S. A., & Williams, R. M. (1949). *The American soldier: Adjusting during army life* (Vol. 1). Princeton, NJ: Princeton University Press.

Suls, J. M. (1977). Social comparison theory and research: An overview from 1954. In J. M. Suls & R. L. Miller (Eds.), *Social Comparison Processes. Theoretical and empirical perspectives* (pp. 1-19). Washington, DC: Hemisphere.

Taylor, D. M., & Dube, L. (1986). Two faces of identity: The "I" and the "We." *Journal of Social Issues, 42*(2), 81-98.

Taylor, D. M., Wright, S. C., & Moghaddan, F. M. (1988 August). *The personal/group discrimination discrepancy: Perceiving my group, but not myself, to be a target for discrimination*. Paper presented at the Annual meeting of The American Psychological Association. Atlanta, GA.

Taylor, D. M., Wright, S. C., & Moghadden, F. E. (1989). The personal/group discrimination discrepancy: Testing for potential artifacts. Unpublished manuscript. McGill University, Montreal.

Taylor, S. E., & Lobel, M. (In Press). Social comparison activity under threat: Downward evaluation and upward contacts. *Psychology Review*.

Thornton, D. A., & Arrowood, A. J. (1966). Self-evaluation, self-enhancement, and the locus of social comparison. *Journal of Experimental Social Psychology* (Suppl. 1), 40-48.

Useem, M. (1975). *Protest movements in America*. New York: Bobbs-Merrill.

Vanneman, R. D., & Pettigrew, R. F. (1972). Race and relative deprivation in the urban United States. *Race, 13*, 461-486.

Walker, I., & Mann, L. (1987). Unemployment, relative deprivation, and social protest. *Personality and Social Psychology Bulletin, 13*, 275-283.

Wheeler, L. (1966). Motivation as a determinant of upward comparison. *Journal of Experimental Social Psychology* (Suppl. 1), 27-31.

Wheeler, L., & Kiestner, R. (1984). Performance evaluation: On choosing to know the related attributes of others when we know their performance. *Journal of Experimental Social Psychology, 20*, 263-271.

Wheeler, L., Kiestner, R., & Driver, R. E. (1982). Related attributes in the choice of comparison others: It's there but it isn't all there. *Journal of Experimental Social Psychology, 18,* 489–500.

Wills, T. A. (1981). Downward comparison principles in social psychology. *Psychological Bulletin, 90,* 245–271.

Winter, D. (1988 July). *Linking the personal to the political.* Paper presented at the Eleventh Annual Scientific Meeting of the International Society for Political Psychology. Secaucus, NJ.

Young, C. J., MacKenzie, D. L., & Sherif, C. W. (1980). In search of token women in academia. *Psychology of Women Quarterly, 4,* 508–525.

Zanna, M. P., Crosby, F., & Loewenstein, G. (1987). Male reference groups and job satisfaction among female professionals. In B. A. Gutek & L. Larwood (Eds.), *Pathways to women's career development* (pp. 28–41). Beverly Hills: Sage.

14 Social Comparison and Coping with Major Medical Problems

Glenn Affleck and Howard Tennen
University of Connecticut Health Center

Social comparison theory (Festinger, 1954) has long guided efforts to understand how people use social information to accurately evaluate their skills and abilities when objective indicators are lacking (Suls, 1977). More recently, it has stimulated research on how people distort, or even construct, information about others to enhance the self (Taylor & Lobel, in press; Wills, 1987). Cognitive biases in making self-other comparisons have been elucidated in a wide ranging series of studies on the role of adaptive illusions in mental health (See Taylor & Brown, 1988 for a review) and in coping with adversity (e.g., Burgess & Holstrom, 1979; Schulz & Decker, 1985; Taylor, 1983; Thompson, 1985). This research shows that under ordinary circumstances, people tend to evaluate their personal attributes more favorably than objective evidence would warrant, and that under threatening circumstances they are apt to compare themselves to less fortunate others, both real and imagined. This proclivity of nonvictims to make unrealistically positive self-other comparisons and of victims to make *downward social comparisons* (Wills, 1981) supplies the theme of this chapter on the role of comparison processes in coping with serious medical problems.

Serious medical problems provide a key setting for field studies of social comparison phenomena. First, seriously ill individuals often are unable to obtain clear information about the course of their disorder or the best way of controlling its outcome, making an objective self-evaluation difficult. Second, they encounter threats to self-esteem and social valuation, especially when they perceive themselves and are viewed by others as victims

(Taylor, Lichtman, & Wood, 1983). Third, they face times of emotional distress that may not be mitigated by problem-focused (Lazarus & Folkman, 1984) or primary control (Rothbaum, Weisz, & Snyder, 1982) coping strategies. These consequences of serious medical disorders: ambiguity and uncertainty, diminished self-esteem and stigmatization, and emotional distress that cannot always be reduced by direct behavioral action, may well prompt the search for comparisons that provide meaning, enhance self-esteem, undercut a sense of victimization, and engender feelings of well-being.

Taylor and her colleagues (Taylor, 1983; Taylor & Lobel, in press; Wood, Taylor, & Lichtman, 1985) initiated formal research on social comparisons in serious illness with a study of women with breast cancer. They found a preponderance of downward comparisons in these women's appraisals of themselves and their situation. These women appeared to have searched actively for comparisons concerning their illness and their coping abilities that helped them to feel relatively advantaged. Those who were in the earlier phases of contending with this problem were more likely to make downward comparisons, perhaps because these comparisons freed them from "being overwhelmed by new, frightening circumstances" (Wood et al., 1985, p. 1181).

We begin this chapter by summarizing additional research, largely our own, that builds upon Taylor's pivotal study. Specifically, we examine social comparison phenomena in three very different populations: individuals with rheumatoid arthritis, mothers of medically fragile infants, and women with impaired fertility. The many situational differences in these medical crises afford needed tests of the generalizability of social comparison activity across populations (Taylor & Lobel, in press). Second, we consider how people who are coping with these and other medical problems respond to support providers' efforts to supply social comparisons. Such comparisons may be communicated by helping professionals through their counseling and patient education practices and by well-meaning family members and friends who wish to provide a helpful framework for interpreting the significance of the problem. Third, we introduce evidence from our work that a broader conceptualization of comparison processes, involving temporal as well as social comparisons, merits scrutiny in studies of cognitive adaptations to serious medical problems. Finally, we enumerate methodological challenges in conducting comparison research in these populations.

SOCIAL COMPARISONS IN RHEUMATOID ARTHRITIS

Rheumatoid arthritis (RA) is a relatively common, chronic, and incurable disease. Its physical signs and symptoms include severe joint pain and stiffness, fatigue, and short of surgery, irreversible joint damage and immobility. Many affected individuals face increasing disability as the disease progresses. Still, a confident prognosis for most patients is difficult to make, and many patients experience fluctuating symptoms of disease activity, i.e., flares and remissions. The ambiguity of this illness and its many threats to self-esteem and well-being (Affleck, Tennen, Pfeiffer, & Fifield, 1987; Affleck, Pfeiffer, Tennen, & Fifield, 1988) make it a useful context in which to study social comparisons and other selective evaluations.

Our own research in this area began with an exploratory study of how individuals with RA compare themselves to other individuals with this illness (Pfeiffer, Affleck, & Tennen, 1986). Most patients compared themselves favorably to the typical patient with this illness. In justifying their positive self-other comparisons, our participants mentioned one or more of three major attributes: the severity of their illness, their degree of disability, and their ability to cope with the illness.

For our full study we recruited 129 individuals with RA, who represented 70% of eligible patients in a university-based rheumatology practice and a large community-based practice, who were invited to participate. Two-thirds of them were women, reflecting the higher prevalence of this illness in females. The average participant was 50 years old and had been living with the illness for ten years. In a first report on this sample (Affleck, Tennen, Pfeiffer, Finfield, & Rowe, 1987), we summarized the results of two inquiries into these patients' social comparisons. The first was a classification of spontaneous social comparison statements in patients' descriptions of the experience of living with this illness. The second was a structured assessment of patients' ratings of the severity of their illness and their ability to cope with the illness, compared to the average person with RA.

Downward social comparisons far outweighed upward comparisons in patients' unprompted descriptions of their illness. Fourteen percent compared their illness to that of other affected individuals, and all but two of these individuals stated that their illness was less severe than others'. One woman cautioned us even before we started the interview that she didn't think she would be a very good subject for our study: "After all, I've been so fortunate. Whenever I go to the clinic, I see people in the waiting room who are so much worse off than me . . . people on crutches who seem to be in such awful pain."

Replying to a structured interview question, participants also tended to rate their illness as being less severe than that of the average person with RA and their adjustment as being better than average. These conclusions parallel those that cancer patients make about their comparative health status and coping abilities (Taylor, Falke, Shoptaw, & Lichtman, 1986; Wood et al., 1985). Findings such as these would be less compelling if the subjects were, in fact, adjusting better and had less severe illnesses than modal members of the populations from which they were sampled. In our study, there were no significant differences between participants and nonparticipants in age, gender, and illness duration. Our medical school's human subjects guidelines prohibit the collection of clinical data on nonparticipants; thus, we were precluded from determining the equivalence of the two groups' illness severity and adjustment. Wood et al. (1985), however, were able to determine that participants did not differ from nonparticipants on several illness and treatment characteristics or on physicians' ratings of their patients' psychosocial adjustment.

Those RA patients who rated their illness as less severe than average most often cited less disability and less pain as the reasons. And those who thought they were coping better than average often mentioned their superior capacity to control negative emotions and thoughts, to maintain a hopeful, optimistic outlook, and to remain physically active. Several demographic and illness characteristics were inspected as correlates of the social comparison ratings. Measures of disease activity included pain and stiffness as measured by the Rapid Assessment of Disease Activity in Rheumatology (Mason & Meenan, 1983), and a measure of disability was supplied by the Modified Health Assessment Questionnaire (Pincus, Summey, & Soraci, 1983). Patients' rheumatologists, nurse practitioners, or both rated participants on the Global Adjustment to Illness Scale (Derogatis, 1975). The correlational analyses showed that patients who rated their illness as comparatively less severe actually had a less active disease than other patients in the sample. They had also been ill for a briefer time. Finally, they were judged by their care providers as adjusting better to their illness. These findings suggest that these social comparison ratings may have some degree of accuracy and may even signal differences in psychosocial adjustment to RA.

Associations between comparison ratings and adaptational outcomes are apt to be partially confounded by the severity of the illness itself. In a second report (Affleck, Tennen, Pfeiffer, & Fifield, 1988), we examined more directly (a) the accuracy of patients' responses to a social comparison questionnaire and (b) the specific association between their social comparison conclusions and their psychosocial adjustment as rated by health care providers. We reasoned that if patients' abilities to draw favorable conclusions about their comparative health status correlates with psychosocial adjustment independent of their actual health status or the accuracy of their comparisons, then we would have stronger confirmation of the hypothesis that downward social comparison conclusions are adaptive or at least reflect differences in adaptation.

Sixteen potential comparison attributes derived from our preliminary study were presented in questionnaire format. Respondents rated each item on five point scales; (1 = much worse that the average patient, 3 = about the same, and 5 = much better). Separate scores were calculated for disease activity, disability, and coping–adjustment comparisons. Their accuracy was examined by computing their intraclass correlations with the aforementioned criterion measures of disease activity, functional status, and psychosocial adjustment. Significant, but only modest, statistical agreement with criterion measures was found for the disease activity and disability comparisons but not for the coping–adjustment comparison. Multiple regression analyses showed that patients who expressed more favorable views of their comparative disease activity were rated as adjusting better to their illness, independent of their age, education, income, illness duration, actual disease activity, and the accuracy of their disease activity comparison.

Several interpretations of the latter finding are plausible. First, if patients were able to derive comfort from the belief that their illness was less severe than it might be, then this might aid their adjustment. A second explanation turns on the possibility that unmeasured dispositional characteristics mediate the relation between favorable self-other comparisons and positive adaptation. For example, people who are dispositionally optimistic are more likely to hold positive self-appraisals and cope better with adversity (Scheier & Carver, 1987). A third interpretation is that the social comparison questionnaire tapped other emotion-focused coping responses, including positive reappraisal and minimization (Wills, 1987), which could improve adjustment through the mitigation of distress.

Another program of research being carried out at the University of North Carolina complements our's by examining RA patients' use of social comparisons in their daily life and their preferences for information that could be used to make social comparisons. Blalock, DeVellis, and DeVellis (1989) examined RA patients' reported use of social comparisons under two conditions: when they were encountering difficulties in tasks involving manual dexterity and when they were setting standards for desired functioning in this area. Participants said that they more often compare themselves to other individuals with RA when they are encountering performance difficulties, but they tend to compare themselves to healthy individuals when they are setting performance standards. Those who were most likely to describe this contextual difference in social comparison were more satisfied with their ability to perform the manual tasks. Satisfaction, in turn, was related positively to emotional well-being.

In a second study, DeVellis et al. (in press) examined RA patients' preferences for information that could be used to make either a downward or an upward social comparison. In addition to summarizing their information preferences on a questionnaire, participants were also given the choice of selecting a folder in which they could read about a patient who was doing better or doing worse than they were.

Consistent with downward comparison theory (Wills, 1981), most participants preferred information on patients whose illness was more severe than their own. Nearly two-thirds of the sample chose to read about a patient who was more ill than they were. And over 90 percent of the patients wanted to know about others "whose pain is more than you experience" as opposed to others whose pain is less than their's. This pattern was reversed, however, for informational preferences concerning other patients' coping and adjustment to the illness. For example, three times as many patients wanted to learn about others with RA whose spirits are high more often than low as they did about others whose spirits are low more often than high, and nine times as many desired information about others who lead active lives with this illness as desired information about others who lead inactive lives.

One key to explaining this pattern of findings is that significantly more respondents preferred information about less fortunate others when the choice contained an *explicit* self-referent (e.g., pain that is worse than yours) as opposed to items which were phrased without self-referents. Unfortunately, the confounding of item type (presence versus absence of self-referent) with information type (illness severity versus adjustment) weakens the conclusion that these individuals preferred information about individuals who were sicker than, but coping better than they. This problem aside, there is no assurance that the information they desired about individuals making an exemplary adjustment to RA would prompt an upward social comparison. In fact, as Taylor and Lobel (in press) have demonstrated, the use of downward social comparisons for self-enhancement can, and does, coexist with the desire to interact with similar others who are contending admirably with the problem.

DeVellis et al. (in press) also constructed a measure of comparative self-evaluation from the differences between participants' ratings of themselves and the typical RA patient on 11 dimensions. Generally, they saw themselves as doing better than the typical patient, echoing our findings. In contrast however, these comparison conclusions did not correlate with adaptational measures once symptom severity was controlled statistically. One explanation of this discrepancy is that these investigators used participants' self-reports as indicators of both symptom severity and adaptation whereas we drew upon treating health professionals' judgments of their patients' adjustment. In our research with RA patients, we have found only modest correlations between treating clinicians' judgments of psychosocial adjustment and their patients' self-reported emotional well-being. This does not imply the superior validity of clinician-rated adaptational outcomes. But it does raise the possibility that controlling for symptom severity may lead to greater attenuation of the relation between comparison conclusions and adjustment indicators when all variables are measured solely by self-report.

SOCIAL COMPARISONS BY MOTHERS OF MEDICALLY FRAGILE INFANTS

The premature or hazardous delivery, intensive care, and homecoming of medically fragile infants are phases of an unfolding crisis for parents. Like individuals with RA, they face threats to self-esteem, confront an uncertain outcome, and find it difficult to obtain unambiguous information about the problem. What distinguishes our research with this population from our research in rheumatoid arthritis is its emphasis on the first weeks and months after the onset of the stressor and its focus on the longitudinal findings on social comparisons made by mothers of medically fragile infants.

One hundred and fourteen mothers, representing 72% of those who were invited to participate, were recruited into a prospective cohort before their infant was discharged from a regional newborn intensive care unit (NICU). They were older than 16, spoke English, were free of major psychopathology, and their children had each spent longer than ten days on the NICU and had at least one of 13 serious perinatal complications associated with subsequent health or developmental disorders. All but nine of these mothers were interviewed at hospital discharge and six months later.

We published results on 69 of these mothers' social comparisons before their infant was discharged (Affleck, Tennen, Pfeiffer, Fifield, & Rowe, 1987). During their baby's hospitalization, they had extensive opportunities for comparing their child with dozens of other children who were on the unit at the same time and with other parents who could be observed or approached when they were visiting. Mothers' social comparisons to other infants and parents were explored by two methods identical to those we had used in our study of RA patients: the classification of spontaneous comparison statements from their unprompted descriptions of the crisis of newborn intensive care and their ratings of their child's comparative medical status and their own comparative adjustment.

Approximately 20% of the mothers explicitly compared their own infant to other sick infants when describing the crisis of newborn intensive care. We consider this a high proportion in view of the range of topics that mothers were free to discuss. All of these mothers, except one, made downward comparisons. For several mothers, such as the two quoted next, a downward comparison appeared an immediate way of coping with their first visit to the NICU:

> The first time I saw my baby, he looked wonderful compared to some of the other babies on the unit. He was very tiny and attached to all these wires and tubes, but the other babies looked a lot worse. Their skin seemed transluscent, all full of blotches, and discolored.

> I remember standing at the door of the unit, worried to death about what my baby would look like. When I walked over to the isolette, I just fell apart completely. But then I looked around and saw several babies who were smaller than mine. And there was one baby whose head was bigger than his body. In a way, that helped calm me down.

Like women with breast cancer (Wood, et al., 1985) and individuals with rheumatoid arthritis, these mothers compared selectively on physical dimensions of the problem that made their infant's condition seem less serious than others'. Mothers of the smallest babies, for example, tended to compare their babies to those who needed more technological support to stay alive (e.g., less time on ventilator). Conversely, those whose babies were larger, but in some ways sicker, compared their infants to the infants who were smaller.

Fewer mothers, approximately 9%, made spontaneous comparisons to other parents of medically fragile infants. Yet, all of those who did, including the parents quoted below, made downward comparisons:

> Whenever I would visit the NICU, I would feel so much sympathy for some of the others. Some of them seemed so helpless, so unable to cope with all of this.

> I would carefully watch how other parents would react to bad news about their baby. I must have been better informed because they seemed not to be upset by the news. If you really knew what was happening, you would have to be upset!

The latter comment is noteworthy because it reveals how a potentially demoralizing upward comparison concerning a manifest behavior can be mitigated by making a downward comparison concerning its meaning or significance. That is, the salient feature of this mother's view of herself as being more distressed than other parents was that it reflected her exceptional understanding of the threatening aspects of this situation.

Many of our participants also volunteered that their infant's outcome was better than it could have been. Twenty-five percent of the mothers, when describing the intensive care experience, made this type of downward comparison, which lacks a specific comparison target and is labeled by Wood et al. (1985) a *dimensional* comparison. Not surprisingly, most of these mothers compared their infant's survival to his or her possible death. The tone of their comments did not leave us with the impression that this was always an afterthought—an obligatory attempt to remind themselves, as others often did, that things could have been worse. In fact, several added that their child had become more precious to them because he or she had been so close to death. Some, for example, said that they admired their baby's "fighting spirit" or ability to "beat the odds."

The greater prevalence of downward versus upward comparisons in mothers' descriptions of the newborn intensive care crisis paralleled their ratings of their child's and their own comparative status. Few parents saw their infant's medical condition as being worse than average or their own adjustment as being worse than that of the average parent in this situation. In justifying their conclusions, mothers most often claimed that their child seemed to be larger or to need less medical intervention and that they were better able to control negative emotions and thoughts, were more informed about their child's condition and treatment, and were developing a closer attachment to the baby.

We collected other data at NICU discharge and six months later that extend and elaborate upon these results. At hospital discharge, mothers rated how important it was for them to know how other babies and parents were doing. Paralleling our finding of more frequent social comparison statements about their baby than about themselves, mothers were significantly more interested in assessing the medical condition of other infants than the coping and well-being of other parents. Interestingly, those who were more interested in the medical status of other infants were more apt to make downward comparison statements about their child when they described the crisis of newborn intensive care. Thus, mothers who may have been searching more actively for social comparison information may have been more likely to derive downward comparisons from their observations.

The role of downward social comparison in mothers' coping with newborn intensive care was also mirrored in their active memories of their child's hospitalization, six months later. When asked at that time to describe their continuing remembrances of the NICU crisis, almost 20% of the mothers mentioned how the social comparisons they had made before discharge remain part of their recurring memories. For example,

> I have memories of that time when I look at the pictures of her then and begin to reflect on how small she was. Then I begin to remember all of the other babies and how many of them were even smaller.
>
> It's funny, but my memories aren't so much about how my baby was back then. Instead, I seem to be recollecting all the other babies who didn't make it or who probably didn't turn out as well as mine.
>
> Some days when I'm watching her sleep, I'll begin to remember what a rough time we had. I'll begin to wonder why this had to happen. And then I'll think how some of the other babies were worse off, and how lucky I really was.

At the six-month follow-up, we asked these mothers once again to compare their adjustment to that of the average parent caring at home for a medically fragile infant. As earlier, few rated their adjustment as poorer than average. There was a significant, but low, correlation between their social comparison conclusions at this time and those they had made six months earlier. Many of the comparison attributes they had cited at discharge they cited again six months later. But new opportunities for downward comparison emerged that were related to the assumption of full time care. These included perceptions of themselves as better than average caregivers and of their ability to normalize their child's care, as in avoiding the temptation to overprotect the child. Further, those who compared themselves favorably to other parents rated their child's temperament more positively on the Infant Characteristics Questionnaire (Bates, Freeland, & Lounsbury, 1979). Thus, there may be something about their child's characteristics, or at least mothers' perception of those characteristics, that buttresses a favorable evaluation of their own success as parents in this difficult situation.

Our findings further suggest that relations between social comparison ratings and indicators of well-being and adjustment may depend on the timing of the inquiry. Mothers' social comparison ratings at NICU discharge were not significantly correlated with either their self-reported mood or with nurses' ratings of their success in coping with their child's hospitalization, although the validity of the latter measure is questionable (Affleck, Tennen, Pfeiffer, Fifield, & Rowe, 1987). But mothers who reported more favorable comparison conclusions six months later did report more positive mood on the Profile of Mood States–B (Lorr & McNair, 1982) and less depression and a greater sense of competence on the Parenting Stress Index (Abidin, 1983), even controlling for their earlier social comparison conclusions and their infant's caretaking difficulty.

Though we did not formally assess mothers' comparisons of their infant's condition at six months, several volunteered downward social comparisons in the course of the follow-up interview. Downward comparisons were offered for the most part by mothers whose children were exhibiting developmental delays, recurring illnesses, or difficult temperament. For example, one mother of a physically handicapped child said: "I have faced the reality that she will be physically handicapped for life. But she'll probably only need braces and crutches, not the wheelchair that other children like her sometimes need."

Another, commenting on her child's delayed motor skills, said: "His motor skills aren't what they should be. But I'm very fortunate compared to other parents because he's such a happy baby."

Finally, a mother of a baby whose schedules of hunger and sleep were unpredictable and who was hard to soothe during frequent episodes of distress told us: "My nephew had cancer so this all seems so trivial. At least my child is healthy and she'll live. With cancer, you never know."

Whereas mothers of children who were doing well were more apt to reflect this fact in their social comparison ratings, those whose children were exhibiting problems seemed more likely to be relying on downward comparisons as a way of deriving comfort. In the section on methodological challenges, we will address this apparent contradiction.

Yet another source of evidence for social comparison comes from our inspection of mothers' reasons for desiring interaction with other parents of NICU-treated infants (Affleck, Tennen, Rowe, Walker, & Higgins, in press). They were asked whether and why they were or were not interested in making such contacts. Consistent with Wortman and Dunkel-Schetter's (1979) analysis of the benefits of mutual support, most mothers wanted contact with similar others in order to reduce their feelings of isolation and to compare their situation to that of other parents. Twenty percent said that they sought such contacts in order to compare themselves to other parents, and 17% in order to compare their child to other children who were on the unit. Yet, not all mothers wanted to engage other parents in order to make such comparisons. In fact, one in five mothers said that they desired no contact with other parents because their situation seemed to be too unique to allow any helpful comparisons.

Finally, brief mention should be made of these mothers' comparisons to the population at risk for this event. Perloff (1983; 1987) drew attention to the use of social comparisons in victims' and nonvictims' appraisals of their vulnerability for negative events, including serious illnesses. Both she and Wills (1987) hypothesize that victims may come to view their misfortune as a relatively commonplace occurrence. This reappraisal may be comforting because it substitutes a perception of "universal vulnerability" for a sense of "unique vulnerability" (Perloff, 1983). Our findings lend compelling support to these hypotheses (Affleck, Tennen, & Rowe, 1988). Our participants were asked to estimate the chances that they would encounter a recurrence of newborn intensive care if they should become pregnant again. As a group, mothers felt vulnerable for a recurrence; their average risk estimate was about four in ten, somewhat higher than the one in four chance of a recurrence of a premature delivery. Yet, only 60% of them believed that their current risk was greater than that of the "average mother about to have her first child." In estimating the risk facing the average first-time mother, the mean estimate was one in five, which is substantially higher than the actual incidence of newborn intensive care of 1 in 20 live births (Phibbs, Williams, & Phibbs, 1981). Almost 15% went so far as to say that the average mother faced a fifty-fifty chance of having her first baby being treated on a newborn intensive care unit. One interpretation of these findings can be derived directly from downward comparison theory: mothers may have constructed and compared themselves to a stereotyped image of the average mother as someone who takes little action to reduce her risk for this outcome (See Perloff & Fetzer, 1986).

SOCIAL COMPARISONS AMONG WOMEN WITH IMPAIRED FERTILITY

The crisis of infertility provides another useful context in which to examine the role of social comparison in contending with a medical disorder. The outcomes of infertility and its medical treatment are often ambiguous. This problem threatens self-esteem because it blocks a major developmental milestone—the transition to parenthood. An inability to conceive a child, like the birth of a medically fragile infant, invalidates one's expectancies of control over reproductive outcomes. The most obvious difference between these crises is that the birth of medically fragile infant is an undesirable event whereas infertility involves the failure to achieve a desired event.

We are studying a cohort of 65 infertile women who were interviewed twice, fourteen months apart. They were recruited from an infertility clinic, a local meeting of a national infertility organization, and from newspaper notices. All participants had been trying for at least one year to have a child, and the average woman had been trying unsuccessfully for three years. During each interview various appraisals of the problem were measured, including perceptions of personal control over its outcomes, acceptance of the problem, and the ability to find purpose or benefits in the situation, as well as social comparison tendencies.

Participants recorded their agreement with the downward comparison statement: "I think I'm fortunate compared to other people. I could have worse problems than infertility." As did participants in our other studies of rheumatoid arthritis and newborn intensive care, they also rated their coping success compared to other women with this problem. Both measures of social comparison were moderately stable over the fourteen-month period separating the interviews. Most women saw themselves as coping better than other women in this situation. Key dimensions on which these women compared themselves favorably to others included the ability to obtain social support, greater acceptance of the problem, the presence of fewer infertility-related medical problems, the capacity to distract oneself from the problem, and the availability of other opportunities to have nurturant relationships with children.

Wills' (1987) hypothesis that downward comparisons may overlap with other cognitive accommodations to stressful events is supported by our findings. After being unable to conceive during the fourteen months of their participation in our study, the women who agreed more with the downward comparison statement construed more benefits from their infertility and expressed greater acceptance of the prospect of not being able to bear a child (Tennen, Affleck, Mendola, McCann, & Fitzgerald, 1989).

Relations between the two comparison measures and women's recent mood as reported on the Profile of Mood States–B, their psychological symptomatology as reported on the SCL–90R (Derogatis, 1977), and their subjective stress as reported on the Impact of Event Scale (Horowitz, Wilner, & Alvarez, 1979) were also inspected. Much like our results with RA patients and mothers of sick infants after NICU discharge, the most consistent finding was a significant association between women's favorable evaluations of their comparative coping success and indicators of positive adaptation.

Directed Social Comparisons

The research reviewed to this point has emphasized the role of presumably self-generated social comparisons in coping with medical disorders. An important question for both theory and helping practices is how victims react to directed social comparisons, i.e., attempts by support providers to supply such comparisons. Comparison information may be communicated by professionals through their counseling and patient education practices and by family and friends who wish to provide a helpful framework for the patient's interpretation of one's own plight.

Preliminary evidence concerning the possible benefits and costs of directed comparisons is found in our research with RA patients (Affleck, Pfeiffer, Tennen, & Fifield, 1988) and mothers of medically fragile infants (Affleck, Tennen, Rowe, Walker, & Higgins, in press). We asked each group to describe what people had done or said that helped them to cope with their situation as well as what support gestures had added further strain to their coping. In describing a range of helpful support tactics, 9% of the RA patients said that they had appreciated it when others compared them favorably to others with RA. All of these directed comparisons emphasized the patient's superior coping skills, but none the patient's less severe illness. Moreover, none of these patients described other people's efforts to encourage social comparisons as being an unhelpful tactic.

When asked similarly to describe helpful support gestures, 19% of the mothers of infants at risk described comparisons that others had made for them during their child's hospitalization. None of the directed comparisons mentioned appeared to encourage a downward comparison. Rather, they were stories told about similar infants who thrived in their future health and development. But a smaller number of mothers (8%) described similar stores as an unhelpful support gesture. These mothers often added that they resented others' attempts to minimize the uniqueness of their baby's problems by equating them with those of other sick infants, however positive their outcomes might have been.

These findings underscore the robust individual differences that probably exist in victims' responses to directed comparisons. Clearly, much more research is needed to determine how the situation, the victim's own appraisals, and the identity of the support provider might combine to predict victims' responses to directed comparisons. The simple answer may be that those who are searching actively for helpful comparisons will most appreciate hearing them from others.

The available data tentatively suggest directed comparison strategies that support providers could adopt with varying chances of success. In our opinion, the safest approach would be to emphasize the ways in which the person is exhibiting comparatively good adjustment to the problem. We have no evidence from our extensive interviews to suggest that people would resent such a compliment. Providing information on others who are coping well with the problem may also be an effective strategy. DeVellis et al. (in press) showed that most RA patients prefer information on other affected individuals who are coping well, rather than coping poorly. Taylor and Lobel (in press) have also summarized research demonstrating that cancer patients want to hear about other patients who are adjusting well. They conclude that exposure to information about similar others who have overcome their difficulties does not necessarily prompt an upward social comparison. Rather, the apparent desire for upward contacts may coexist comfortably with, and not undercut, the use of downward comparisons in making self-evaluations.

More risky strategies, in our view, would be to offer downward comparisons about the severity of the medical problem, i.e., physical comparisons (Wood et al., 1985). We suspect that some individuals hearing this type of downward comparison might interpret it as an effort to minimize the unique burdens and challenges that have been and may still need to be overcome. A second reason for avoiding downward physical comparisons is especially compelling in the case of a chronic disease. Presenting these individuals with a worse case scenario might serve as a troubling reminder of what the future may hold. Cancer patients are upset by stories about other patients who deteriorated physically and are apt to question the motives of the storyteller (Taylor & Lobel, in press).

Finally, we have the impression from our interviews that social comparisons are more often supplied by family members and friends than by professionals. Professionals, on the other hand, appear more likely than informal support givers to discourage social comparisons. A few mothers of medically fragile infants noted that nurses and physicians in the NICU had advised them to avoid comparing their infant to other infants on the unit. One mother said: "I got this feeling that I was only supposed to look at my own baby. One day I remember reading the chart of another child who had the same birthweight and was informed abruptly that I shouldn't concern myself with how other children are doing."

This informal finding needs to be studied directly in order to clarify some of the assumptions that underlie care providers' implicit beliefs about the costs and benefits of social comparison. Some health professionals may see social comparison as a potential distraction that prevents the patient or family member from developing a realistic view of the problem, its course, and its treatment. This assumption may well derive from the care provider's clinical training, which emphasizes the unique characteristics of each case.

Temporal Comparisons

To this point, we have concerned ourselves exclusively with the phenomenon of social comparison: how people who are coping with medical problems compare themselves, or are encouraged or discouraged to compare themselves, to other real or imagined individuals. Albert (1977), Wills (1987), and Suls and Mullen (1982) drew attention to people's use of temporal comparisons in making self-evaluations and in coping with threatening circumstances. In this section, we briefly summarize evidence from our research for victims' use of downward temporal comparisons, which we define as a favorable comparison of the current situation to earlier aspects of the problem or earlier related events in one's life.

Rheumatoid Arthritis. To explore the importance of temporal comparisons in RA patients' illness experience, we analyzed their illness descriptions for evidence of statements comparing the present severity of their illness and their current coping ability to an earlier time in the course of the illness. More participants in our study offered temporal comparisons rather than social comparisons of their illness' severity (59% versus 14%). Approximately 10% made both upward and downward temporal comparisons, and another 10% would only a describe a time when their illness was comparatively less severe than it is now (an upward comparison). The largest proportion, almost 40%, made a downward temporal comparison, as is illustrated in this woman's comment: "It was very painful at first. For twelve years, I was miserable. Now it's like it doesn't exist. I have some pain now and then, but compared to what it was then, it's nothing."

Those who included downward temporal comparisons about the severity of their illness in their statements scored lower on measures of current disease activity, reporting less pain, joint swelling, and morning stiffness. The most parsimonious explanation is that those whose illness is in remission simply have more opportunities to make a downward temporal comparison and may be pleased enough with this change to highlight it in their illness descriptions.

Similarly, more patients volunteered downward temporal comparisons concerning their coping and adjustment (23% versus 2%). One man valued changes in his coping skills, perhaps even more so in the face of a worsening illness: "I think my arthritis has hit rock bottom. It's never been so painful. For a long time, I was just too unable to deal with it. But gradually, I've been learning how to cope with it, learning how to be more adaptable."

The Hospitalization and Home Care of Medically Fragile Infants. We uncovered two sources of evidence for temporal comparison in our prospective study of mothers of medically fragile infants. First, in describing the crisis of newborn intensive care, 12% of the sample spontaneously compared their infant's survival to the occurrence of earlier reproductive disappointments that are relatively common in this population, such as infertility, miscarriages, and stillbirths (Affleck, Pfeiffer, Tennen, Fifield, & Rowe, 1987). For example, one mother said: "My baby was born when I was six months pregnant. I was so happy and relieved that I hadn't miscarried, like I had in two earlier pregnancies. My parents and brother were so upset, but I couldn't understand why. This is no big deal compared to what I went through when I lost my other babies."

Second, downward temporal comparisons played a role in mothers' active memories of their child's intensive care (Affleck, Tennen, Rowe, & Higgins, 1990). Six months after discharge, two-thirds of the mothers said they were continuing to have memories of how sick or close to death their baby had been in the hospital. And nearly half of the mothers reporting this memory added a spontaneous downward temporal comparison concerning their child. For some mothers, such as the following, a downward temporal comparison seemed to interrupt the distress stemming from this painful memory: "Sometimes when I'm feeding him, I'll start feeling upset because I start to remember how difficult it was to feed him in the hospital. Then I find myself comparing that with how much he eats now, and that makes me feel better." "When I'm in a sad mood, I find myself picturing him so sick, seeing him with all the tubes, and remembering what awful things he had to go through. Then I start to think of how much better he's doing now, and I start feeling happy."

Infertility. Finally, in our study of infertile women, we discovered how social and temporal comparisons are intertwined. Several women, describing the basis upon which they had concluded that they were coping better than other women with this problem, answered with a downward temporal comparison. They replied, for example, that "I hit fewer low points than I used to.", "I look at the problem more realistically now than before.", and "I think I've come a long way in being able to cope with this.". What is important here is that these women were significantly more likely to report that they had had no actual contact with other infertile women. When asked about their social comparisons, they appeared to equate their own earlier ability to cope with this problem with the coping abilities of other women. This suggests how, in the absence of a clear picture of the plight of similar others, a downward temporal comparison can be used to make a downward social comparison.

Methodological Challenges

Two of the more pressing methodological challenges facing investigators of comparison processes in medical disorders and other threatening occurrences are: (a) the validity and convergence of methods of measuring comparisons and (b) the need for longitudinal studies that elucidate the changing meaning and significance of comparisons as the medical crisis unfolds.

Measurement Strategies. A review of the measurement strategies used by Wood et al. (1985) in their study of breast cancer patients, by Blalock et al. (1989) and DeVellis et al. (in press) in their research in rheumatoid arthritis, and by the present authors in studies of rheumatoid arthritis, newborn intensive care, and infertility, reveals few commonalities. The only approach common to these investigations was the direct request of participants to compare the severity of the disorder or their adjustment with that of others encountering the same problem. Even here, the comparison target was framed somewhat differently. Wood et al. asked women how they compared themselves to other women with breast cancer, we asked infertile women how they compared themselves to other women with this problem, DeVellis, et al. measured comparisons to the typical RA patient, and we asked for comparisons to the average RA patient or the average infant (or parent of an infant) being treated on an NICU.

In principle, being asked to compare oneself to others leaves more room to report a favorable self-evaluation than would be afforded by requests to compare oneself to the typical or average person facing the same problem. Whether or not the respondent would actually make such a distinction in drawing a comparison conclusion requires an empirical test. One would need to determine something about the respondents' portrayal of the average or typical other, in view of the fact that both victims (Wood et al., 1985) and nonvictims (Perloff & Fetzer, 1986) appear to have a distorted image of average comparison targets.

Both we (Affleck, Tennen, Pfeiffer, & Fifield, 1988) and DeVellis et al. (in press) went a step further by building questionnaires for measuring comparison conclusions by RA patients. DeVellis and colleagues asked their subjects to rate the typical patient and then one's self on 11 dimensions of the illness and coping. After difference scores were adjusted for each patient's illness severity, principal components analysis revealed a single seven-item factor that did have high internal consistency.

Our experiences raise a note of caution to investigators who would adopt this strategy. Our questionnaire provided 16 opportunities for making a self-other comparison. Respondents were also allowed to report that they had "no idea of how I compare to the average RA patient" on a given attribute. And, for some items, as many as 1 in 5 respondents checked this answer. This "don't know" response was rarely elicited when they were asked to compare themselves to the average patient on a vague attribute such as adjustment, perhaps because they have wide latitude to define that concept in their own ways.

As the comparison dimension becomes more specific, respondents may be forced to make comparisons that they have neither considered nor believe they have any basis to make. The items on which more respondents declined to make comparisons also tended to be relatively less accessible to observers, as in "the tendency to dwell on problems" and "the illness' harm on interpersonal relationships." Fewer declined to compare themselves on the more visible attributes, such as "the ability to get around" and "the amount of medication needed." The unanswered question is whether forcing respondents to make a reluctant comparison alters the meaning of the summary questionnaire score. The danger is that validity might be sacrificed for the sake of presumed reliability. Conversely, by offering respondents the option of declining a comparison, we could determine reliability coefficients only for those respondents who did supply a comparison for all of the items comprising a summary score. We also found that patients who were older and less educated checked the "don't know" option on significantly more items on the social comparison questionnaire. Why this is so is unclear, but it raises the possibility that subject characteristics can bias relations between questionnaire-derived comparison ratings and criterion variables. For example, elderly persons with RA may both be more disabled and be less able or willing to make a comparative self-evaluation of their disability.

A more fundamental question is the convergence among alternative measures of social comparison (Wood, in press). In addition to measuring comparison conclusions, investigators have classified statements emerging spontaneously in subjects' responses to a global question about the nature of the problem (Affleck, Tennen, Pfeiffer, Fifield, & Rowe, 1987; Affleck, Tennen, Pfeiffer, & Fifield, 1988) or across an entire interview (Wood et al., 1985); determined preferences for information that could supply an upward or downward comparison (DeVellis, et al., in press); and measured reported contacts with potential comparison targets (Wood et al., 1985).

A key distinction can be made on both conceptual and empirical grounds between the conclusions that individuals draw about their comparative status and their use of social comparison, or, comparison processes. As discussed previously, comparison conclusions indicate simply how victims see themselves or their situation in relation to others with the same problem. Comparison processes have been assessed through measures of information preferences, the use of downward comparison as a coping strategy, and their appearance in people's descriptions of their problem and their adaptation. From a logical standpoint, patients who report that their illness seems less severe than others' need not be actively comparing themselves to less fortunate others as a way of deriving comfort or finding meaning. As our research with RA patients suggests, some individuals with a less severe illness may simply be reporting a veridical conclusion. Others reporting the same conclusion may have been using cognitive strategies such as positive appraisal and minimization that lead to a more favorable self-other comparison. Still others may be optimists, who have such a rosy view of themselves and their problem that they have little need to make comparisons. This is not to suggest that the process of social comparison has little relevance for social comparison conclusions. But the ability to draw a favorable conclusion may be due to facts, appraisals, or personal dispositions that could even mitigate the use of social comparison as a coping strategy. In any event, there may be little about the tendency of seriously ill individuals to make favorable self-other comparison ratings that is not echoed in typical individuals' propensity to evaluate their personal attributes positively in comparison to others' (Taylor & Brown, 1988).

Our studies show that social comparison conclusions and comparison process variables are also statistically unrelated. For example, RA patients and mothers of fragile infants who made more downward comparison statements in their interview were not more likely to report more favorable views of the comparative severity of the problem or their comparative adjustment. Also, infertile women who agreed that they were fortunate compared to others did not see themselves as coping better than other women with this problem.

This basic distinction between comparison conclusions and comparison processes is also captured in their differing associations with indicators of well-being and adjustment. In our studies, the comparison conclusion measure has been related to adaptational outcomes. Participants who report more favorable comparison conclusions also report more positive mood, fewer psychological symptoms, and greater freedom from intrusive thoughts about the problem and have been seen by their care providers as adjusting better to the problem. Our findings with RA patients are especially important because they link illness comparison conclusions with care providers' adjustment ratings independent of sociodemographic characteristics, actual illness severity, and the accuracy of the conclusion itself.

In none of our studies, nor in DeVellis' study of RA patients, have the more process-oriented measures of social comparison correlated with positive adaptation. In fact, DeVellis and colleagues found just the opposite: that patients who wanted more information that could lead to a downward comparison were more depressed and had lower self-esteem. This could mean that those who are more depressed and have encountered greater threats to self-esteem have a greater need for information that can provide them with a downward comparison. If so, and in the absence of appropriate longitudinal data, any positive effects for this group of actually making a downward comparison would likely be obscured in the analysis. From the experimental literature, Gibbons (1986) has shown that depressed subjects report improved mood after acquiring downward comparison information.

Those planning investigations in this area would be well-advised to incorporate multiple comparison measures in their interview schedules. We also concur with Wood et al. (1985) that the most revealing data may come from comparison statements that emerge across the entire interview. As they suggest, these statements may reveal processes that are more central to the victim's experience than can be tapped by direct interview questions. In this regard, their method for classifying free responses deserves special consideration. Some variant of extant systems of classifying people's appraisals of events from verbatim material (e.g., the CAVE technique for assessing explanatory style: Peterson and Seligman, 1987) would be a timely development in measuring spontaneous comparisons.

The Need for Longitudinal Research. To our knowledge, our research on mothers of medically fragile infants and infertile women includes the only prospective analyses of social comparison variables. Although calls for longitudinal studies are an almost obligatory post script to discussions of coping with negative events, there are particularly important reasons for emphasizing their necessity in studying the meaning of comparisons in coping with medical disorders. Principally, social comparison may be an early phase coping response that declines in frequency and intensity as the problem unfolds or its meaning and significance become clearer (Festinger, 1954; Schacter, 1959). This is suggested by Wood et al.'s (1985) finding that downward comparison statements were more frequent in the interviews of women whose surgery for breast cancer was more recent. It is supported by our findings of more numerous social comparison statements in mothers' descriptions of newborn intensive care at the time of their infant's discharge than in RA patients' descriptions of their illness an average of 10 years after its diagnosis. It is suggested by the fact that RA patients with more recent diagnoses expressed more favorable conclusions about the comparative severity of their illness.

The ideal prospective study would, therefore, attempt to measure social comparison variables as soon after the onset of the problem as is practical. Even our earliest assessment at hospital discharge of medically fragile infants may have missed the time when social comparisons were most relevant for mothers. (Recall that some mothers mentioned how social comparison helped them cope with their first visit to the NICU.) If investigators have a reasonable picture of some of the transitional phases of the problem, repeated measurements of social comparison could be linked to periods at which increased ambiguity or threats to well-being and self-esteem could be anticipated. Examples from our research include when a diagnosis of a developmental disability is most likely to occur for a medically fragile child or when an infertility investigation fails to find evidence of a medically correctable defect.

Finally, our preliminary efforts at integrating social comparisons with temporal comparisons underscore the desirability of tracking both of these comparisons over time. An intriguing hypothesis is that a decline in active social comparisons parallels the increasing importance of temporal comparisons as the outcome becomes clearer or the individual learns to adapt to it. Our findings show only a modest degree of temporal stability in social comparison measures. This leaves room for detecting patterns of mutual change in social and temporal comparisons.

SUMMARY AND CONCLUSIONS

We have summarized new research findings concerning the nature and significance of social comparison in coping with three major medical problems: rheumatoid arthritis, newborn intensive care and its aftermath, and infertility. Together with the results of Wood et al.'s (1985) study of women with breast cancer, these findings show that downward social comparison is often used by victims of medical problems as a way of finding meaning in their plight and mitigating threats to self-esteem and psychological well-being. This conclusion is strengthened by the variability in the populations and methodologies of these studies. The participants include survivors of an acute, potentially fatal illness; individuals with a chronic disabling disease; parents of acutely ill infants who are at risk for subsequent health and developmental disorders; and individuals who are unable to conceive a child. They were studied from weeks to many years after the onset of the problem, some even prospectively. And, the evidence favoring the use of downward social comparison transcended differences in data collection procedures and measurement strategies.

The appeal of this overarching conclusion should not distract investigators from pursuing studies of between–group and within–group differences in the use of social comparison in coping with major medical problems. First, many features of serious medical problems were not represented in the studies we have reviewed. None of these participants were, at the time they were interviewed, facing their own or a loved one's likely or imminent death. Many mothers of sick infants mentioned avoidance of this worse alternative as a comforting feature of the intensive care crisis. Would those whose infants had died be less able to make a downward comparison? Or would even these parents see the avoidance of further suffering and pain as a preferable outcome? Second, sampling biases may have influenced the generalization of the findings to the full population contending with the problem. With the exception of the studies of rheumatoid arthritis, all of these investigations were limited to women. And, few of the participants in these studies were recruited from lower SES or ethnic minority groups. We know little about how gender roles or cultural factors might shape social comparison processes. Third, as we have already noted, differences in the use of social comparison may be sensitive to the timing of inquiry. All of the medical problems included in this review have complex courses and variable outcomes following the initial phases of recognition, diagnosis, and treatment, and the evidence points to the greater importance of social comparison in the early phase of coping with these problems. Both our inability to answer these questions about individual differences and, more important, some of our research participants' criticisms of directed social comparisons stand as notes of caution to professionals who would encourage their patients or their patients' family members to make downward comparisons.

We have also highlighted how temporal comparisons can serve much the same purpose as social comparisons in coping with a medical disorder. The individual with rheumatoid arthritis may feel better by concentrating on the ways in which his or her illness is less severe than someone else's. But the same comfort can be taken by recalling how the illness had once been more severe than it is now. Even in the face of a worsening illness, satisfaction may be derived from perceived changes in one's ability to cope with its effects. The anxiety of a mother of a baby being treated in a newborn intensive care unit may be allayed by noticing that her baby is less sick than others seem to be. But, later she can look back upon that experience as being worse than the problems she may now face in rearing her child. She can even compare her child's survival, however stressful the hospitalization, to greater disappointments in her reproductive history. Even the woman who remains infertile can reflect with satisfaction upon her gradual ability to accept this difficult reality.

Participants in these research programs have taught us and other investigators how misfortune is framed in the context of both interpersonal and intrapersonal comparison. These forays into the application of social comparison theory have been both rewarding and exciting. We hope that the initial enthusiasm for the rich potential of comparison theory for understanding people's cognitive adaptation to major medical problems will not be dampened as investigators attempt to meet the many methodological challenges that must be addressed in future research.

ACKNOWLEDGMENTS

The research summarized in this article was supported by National Institute of Disability and Rehabilitation Research grant G0084C0043 to the University of Connecticut Pediatric Research and Training Center, National Institutes of Health grant AM20262 to the University of Connecticut Multipurpose Arthritis Center, and the University of Connecticut Research Foundation. The contributions of Carol Pfeiffer, Jonelle Rowe, Judith Fifield, Lisa McCann, Terry Fitzgerald, Richard Mendola, Linda Walker, and Pamela Higgins to these studies are gratefully acknowledged. We also thank Robert DeVellis and Susan Blalock for their comments on an earlier version of this chapter.

REFERENCES

Abidin, R. (1983). *Parenting stress index*. Charlottesville, VA: Pediatric Psychology Press.
Affleck, G., Pfeiffer, C., Tennen, H., & Fifield, J. (1988). Social support and psychosocial adjustment to rheumatoid arthritis: Quantitative and qualitative findings. *Arthritis Care and Research, 1*, 71–77.
Affleck, G., Tennen, H., Pfeiffer, C., & Fifield, J. (1987). Appraisals of control and predictability in adapting to a chronic disease. *Journal of Personality and Social Psychology, 53*, 273–279.
Affleck, G., Tennen, H., Pfeiffer, C., & Fifield, J. (1988). Social comparisons in rheumatoid arthritis: Accuracy and adaptational significance. *Journal of Social and Clinical Psychology, 6*, 219–234.
Affleck, G., Tennen, H., Pfeiffer, C., Fifield, J., & Rowe, J. (1987). Downward comparison and coping with serious medical problems. *American Journal of Orthopsychiatry, 57*, 570–578.
Affleck, G., Tennen, H., & Rowe, J. (1988). Adaptational features of mothers' risk and prevention appraisals after the birth of high risk infants. *American Journal of Mental Retardation, 92*, 360–368.
Affleck, G., Tennen, H., Rowe, J., & Higgins, P. (1990). Mothers' remembrances of newborn intensive care: A predictive study. *Journal of Pediatric Psychology, 15*, 67–81.
Affleck, G., Tennen, H., Rowe, J., Walker, L., & Higgins, P. (in press). Mothers' interpersonal relationships and adaptation during the transition from hospital to home care of high risk infants. In R. Antonak & J. Mulick (Eds.), *Transitions in mental retardation* (Vol. 5). Norwood, NJ: Ablex Publishing.
Albert, S. (1977). Temporal comparison theory. *Psychological Review, 84*, 485–503.
Bates, J., Freeland, C., & Lounsbury, M. (1979). Measurement of infant difficulties. *Child Development, 50*, 794–803.

Blalock, S., DeVellis, B., & DeVellis, R. (1989). Social comparison among individuals with rheumatoid arthritis. *Journal of Applied Social Psychology, 19*, 665–680.

Burgess, A., & Holstom, L. (1979). *Rape: Crisis and recovery.* Bowie, MD: Brady.

Derogatis, L. (1975). *Global adjustment to illness scale.* Baltimore, MD: Clinical Biometrics Research Series.

Derogatis, L. (1977). *SCL-90: Administration, scoring and procedures manual for the revised version.* Baltimore, MD: Clinical Biometrics Research Series.

DeVellis, R., Holt, K., Renner, B., Blalock, S., Blanchard, L., Cook, H., Klotz, M., Mikow, V., & Harring, K. (in press). The relationship of social comparison to rheumatoid arthritis symptoms and affect. *Basic and Applied Social Psychology.*

Festinger, L. (1954). A theory of social comparison processes. *Human Relations, 7*, 117–140.

Gibbons, F. (1986). Social comparison and depression: Company's effect on misery. *Journal of Personality and Social Psychology, 51*, 140–148.

Horowitz, M., Wilner, N., & Alvarez, W. (1979). Impact of event scale: A measure of subjective stress. *Psychosomatic Medicine, 41*, 209–218.

Lazarus, R., & Folkman, S. (1984). *Stress, appraisal and coping.* New York: Springer.

Lorr, M., & McNair, D. (1982). *Profile of mood states-B.* San Diego, CA: Educational and Industrial Testing Service.

Mason, J., & Meenan, R. (1983). *Rapid assessment of disease activity in rheumatology.* Unpublished manuscript, Boston University School of Medicine, Boston, MA.

Perloff, L. (1983). Perceptions of vulnerability to victimization. *Journal of Social Issues, 39*, 41–61.

Perloff, L. (1987). Social comparison and illusions of invulnerability to negative life events. In C. R. Snyder & C. Ford (Eds.), *Coping with negative life events: Clinical and social psychological perspectives.* (pp. 217–242). New York: Plenum.

Perloff, L., & Fetzer, B. (1986). Self-other judgments and perceived vulnerability to victimization. *Journal of Personality and Social Psychology, 50*, 502–510.

Peterson, C., & Seligman, M. (1987). Explanatory style and illness. *Journal of Personality, 55*, 237–266.

Pfeiffer, C., Affleck, G., & Tennen, H. (1986, August). *Social comparison as a coping strategy in rheumatoid arthritis.* Paper presented at the annual meeting of the Arthritis Health Professions Association, New Orleans, LA.

Phibbs, C., Williams, R., & Phibbs, R. (1981). Newborn risk factors and costs of neonatal intensive care. *Pediatrics, 68*, 313–321.

Pincus, T., Summey, J., & Soraci, S. (1983). Assessment of patient satisfaction in activities of daily living using a modified Stanford health assessment questionnaire. *Arthritis and Rheumatism, 26*, 1346–1453.

Rothbaum, F., Weisz, J., & Snyder, S. (1982). Changing the world and changing the self: A two process model of perceived control. *Journal of Personality and Social Psychology, 42*, 5–37.

Schacter, S. (1959). *The psychology of affiliation.* Stanford: Stanford University Press.

Scheier, M., & Carver, C. (1987). Dispositional optimism and physical well-being: The influence of generalized outcome expectancies on health. *Journal of Personality, 55*, 169–210.

Schulz, R., & Decker, S. (1985). Long-term adjustment to physical disability: The role of social support, perceived control, and self-blame. *Journal of Personality and Social Psychology, 48*, 1162–1172.

Suls, J. (1977). Social comparison theory and research: An overview from 1954. In J. Suls & R. Miller (Eds.), *Social comparison processes: Theoretical and empirical perspectives* (pp. 1–20). Washington, DC: Hemisphere.

Suls, J., & Mullen, B. (1982). From the cradle to the grave: Comparison and self-evaluation across the life span. In J. Suls (Ed.), *Psychological perspectives on the self* (Vol. 1, pp. 97–125). Hillsdale, NJ: Lawrence Erlbaum Associates.

Taylor, S. (1983). Adjustment to threatening events: A theory of cognitive adaptation. *American Psychologist, 38,* 624–630.

Taylor, S., & Brown, J. (1988). Illusion and well-being: A social-psychological perspective on mental health. *Psychological Bulletin, 103,* 193–210.

Taylor, S., Falke, R., Shoptaw, S., & Lichtman, R. (1986). Social support, support groups, and the cancer patient. *Journal of Consulting and Clinical Psychology, 54,* 608–615.

Taylor, S., Lichtman, R., & Wood, R. (1983). It could be worse: Selective evaluation as a response to victimization. *Journal of Social Issues, 39,* 19–40.

Taylor, S., & Lobel, M. (in press). Social comparison activity under threat: Downward evaluation and upward contacts. *Psychological Review.*

Tennen, H., Affleck, G., Mendola, R., McCann, L., & Fitzgerald, T. (1989). *The vicissitudes of primary and secondary control beliefs: A longitudinal study of appraisals in coping with infertility.* Manuscript submitted for publication.

Thompson, S. (1985). Finding positive meaning in a stressful event and coping. *Basic and Applied Social Psychology, 6,* 279–295.

Wills, T. A. (1981). Downward comparison principles in social psychology. *Psychological Bulletin, 90,* 245–271.

Wills, T. A. (1987). Downward comparison as a coping mechanism. In C. R. Snyder & C. Ford (Eds.), *Coping with negative events: Clinical and social psychological perspectives* (pp. 243–268). New York: Plenum.

Wood, J. (in press). Theory and research concerning social comparisons of personal attributes. *Psychological Bulletin.*

Wood, J., Taylor, S., & Lichtman, R. (1985). Social comparison in adjustment to breast cancer. *Journal of Personality and Social Psychology, 49,* 1169–1183.

Wortman, C., & Dunkel-Schetter, C. (1979). Interpersonal relationships and cancer: A theoretical analysis. *Journal of Social Issues, 35,* 120–155.

15 Commentary: Neo-Social Comparison Theory and Beyond

Thomas Ashby Wills
*Ferkauf Graduate School of Psychology, and
Albert Einstein College of Medicine*

Jerry Suls
The University of Iowa

Our goal in this commentary is to suggest some common themes based on the chapters in this volume and show how social comparison theory has been enlarged by this work. In this discussion we draw linkages to other bodies of social-psychological theory and suggest possible directions for further research. The general question we address is: "How has the body of social comparison research been altered and expanded?"

We consider six issues that we think represent enduring problems for social comparison theory. Because an individual contributor's work often addresses several issues, a given chapter may be mentioned at several points in the discussion. We will outline the questions, and discuss the contributors' work with respect to these issues and our own theoretical orientations.

Similarity and Social Comparison

From the outset (Festinger, 1954) similarity between self and other was recognized as a crucial element in social comparison. Festinger's original postulate was that persons will prefer a comparison other who is highly similar to the self on the ability dimension that is the focus of comparison. Although there is support for this model, understanding of similarity has been broadened in several ways. Wheeler notes there is considerable evidence for choice of dissimilar others for comparison in several different experimental paradigms. Within the ability-evaluation paradigm, choice of comparison others at the extreme ranges of the ability continuum (i.e., range-seeking) is sometimes observed. Ruble and Frey suggest that this type of comparison will be characteristic during the early phase of skill acquisition, when persons are trying to define the range of possible performances before they proceed to a subsequent phase of comparison where they aim to determine their own personal potential.

In other paradigms there is evidence that persons will choose comparison with dissimilar others because self-enhancement is the dominant goal, hence unpleasant affective consequences of comparison are blunted when the comparison person is not highly similar to the self. This process is found in Tesser's work, which finds that comparisons with dissimilar others are preferred when a self-central dimension is the focus of comparison. This may be characteristic of situations where one's performance is highly salient and the bearing of the social comparison on one's self-concept is likely to be high.

Understanding of what *similarity* means has been altered in another way by the work of several contributors. For one, the model of related attributes (Goethals & Darley, 1977) outlines how ability comparisons depend on attributes related to the focal dimension of ability, so that people will prefer comparison others who are similar on several dimensions (such as practice or experience) in addition to the specific ability dimension. As discussed by Wheeler and Wood, there is considerable support for some aspects of this model, and several studies have shown that comparison has greater impact on self-evaluation when related-attributes information is available (e.g., Gastorf & Suls, 1978; Wheeler, Koestner, & Driver, 1982). At the same time, other studies have shown that people will select additional information even when it is not related to the ability or performance (e.g., Feldman & Ruble, 1981; C. Miller, 1982; Suls, Gaes, & Gastorf, 1979). This suggests that the related-attributes process is embedded within other concerns of social comparison, which may include assessment of competitive standing (essentially an intergroup process) or needs for protection of self-esteem, a more individual process.

Another view of similarity is that comparison choices are pursued primarily when there is a social bond that links the self and the other. Work by D. Miller, Turnbull & McFarland (1988) suggests that in addition to comparison with people in general, *universalistic comparison*, people attach importance to comparison others with whom they share a significant social bond, *particularistic comparison*. Tesser has defined similarity or closeness as in family relationships, where there is a bond because of kinship and intimacy. Tesser's work has shown that closeness may encourage social comparison, but may potentiate the unpleasant consequences of comparison if the dimension involves an attribute that is central to the individual's self-esteem. Recent work suggests that social comparison involves more than information about a specific ability; it also depends on the existence of a meaningful social connection with the comparison person.

When downward comparison is the dominant process, how is similarity involved? The model proposed by Wills suggests that there are several distinct types of similarity, which may have different effects on downward comparison. Personality similarity may have generally positive consequences because persons can gain improved subjective well-being through the knowledge that a similar other is also experiencing difficulties; but future similarity may have negative consequences if it suggests that the person's situation may become worse in the future. This model shifts the focus of downward comparison from a momentary impact on emotional state to a more elaborated process in which persons are aiming to assess the likelihood that their own state will improve in the future. It may be that downward comparison operates in both ways, that is, people will not eschew an opportunity that is spontaneously provided to compare with a worse-off other; but they may at times engage in processing of social information to aim for comparisons that suggest a better future is in store for themselves (see Major et al.'s chapter). The latter mechanism is more purposive and in a sense more cognitive, but may represent an important mode of downward comparison. Gibbons and Gerrard have provided some evidence for this type of downward comparison, suggesting that it has effects on optimism and confidence about future coping success.

To summarize, recent work has changed views of how similarity operates. One conclusion is that there are several distinct types of similarity: related attributes that may be employed as part of comparison information, and variables such as personality similarity and future similarity, which may have opposite effects on the outcome of the comparison. In addition, social bonding may determine the impact of particular comparisons. Another conclusion is that the operation of similarity is linked to the individual's comparison goals; when self-evaluation is the dominant goal then similarity may have positive effects, but when self-enhancement is the dominant goal then sometimes it can have negative effects.

How Do Comparison Goals Shift?

One of the developments represented in this volume is the recognition that social comparison may be motivated by several different goals, and accordingly, that different types of comparison will be employed depending on which goal is dominant. What principles can be used to predict how and when comparison goals will shift? The work of the contributors suggests several postulates about this question.

Ruble and Frey focus on skill acquisition in a model that has application both for children and for adults. The model outlines four discrete stages and the basic postulate is that comparison goals will be determined by phase. During task assessment, comparison goals focus on defining the nature of the task and the potential performances. The dominant type of comparison will be information gathering and range-seeking. During the competence assessment phase the dominant goal is determining one's personal competence. Comparison with similar others is employed because it provides a better appraisal of how one's eventual performance will compare with that of significant others (analogous to D. Miller's concept of particularistic comparison). Once a skill has been learned and the individual invests greater commitment and self-centrality to the performance, comparison goals may shift to focus on information that is self-enhancing, and unavoidable upward comparisons with reference others whose performance is much better may be avoided or balanced by comparisons with others whose performance is worse. The final phase in this model considers the period when asymptotic performance has been attained and absolute standards are relevant. Here new comparison dimensions may be introduced to maintain engagement in the activity, or salient absolute standards may be invoked to justify disengagement. This model has theoretical richness because it makes specific predictions about when comparison goals will shift, both as a function of cognitive development level during childhood, and as a function of life span development during adulthood.

Tesser's model considers shifts in comparison goals from a different perspective. It is assumed that self-esteem maintenance is a basic motivation and that in close relationships there will be unfavorable comparisons which are unavoidable because the relationship is a continuing one. Thus the focus is on responses which may include balancing unfavorable comparisons with reflection (identifying with close others' better performance on noncentral dimensions), altering the perceived importance of the comparison dimension, downward comparison (favorable comparison with distant others whose performance is worse), or perhaps even withdrawing from the activity. The specific prediction is that comparison choices shift in a way that helps to maintain self-esteem.

A different prediction concerns the shift from upward comparison to downward comparison. One model, discussed by Wood and Wills, suggests that a shift from upward to downward comparison will be evoked by threat because different comparison goals become dominant: self-evaluation is operative in the former case, self-protection or self-enhancement in the latter. The field studies discussed by the contributors complement laboratory data that are supportive of this model. Gibbons and Gerrard find that interest in downward comparison targets is high among persons who are distressed because of a personal problem, but reduces as the problem is resolved. Similarly, Affleck and Tennen observe a high prevalence of downward comparisons among individuals coping with medical problems, and their longitudinal data suggest that comparison-oriented coping is related to adjustment primarily during the early stages of coping with a disease. This model predicts that upward–downward shifts will be observed within person across dimensions (i.e., downward comparison for dimensions where performance is poor) and within dimension across time (as threat reduces for a given dimension). Another hypothesis suggested by Affleck and Tennen is that when persons are having problems on a given dimension, they may employ temporal information to provide a (favorable) comparison with previous, worse times.

Other models suggest some differences from this perspective. Major et al. focus on responses to unavoidable comparisons and predict that the controllability of the dimension affects responses to comparison; responses to upward comparison should be positive if the dimension is perceived as controllable, but negative if it is perceived as uncontrollable. Extension of this model might suggest that comparison choices would also be influenced by controllability of the target dimension. Affleck and Tennen outline a model of comparison among medical patients, proposing that patients may compare downward when evaluating their own adjustment, but may compare upward when setting goals for themselves. Comparative tests of these models in field settings would be informative (Taylor & Lobel, 1989; cf. Wood, Taylor, & Lichtman, 1985).

One factor implied in some work is the role of competition for shifting comparison goals. Although social comparison theory has usually been framed as a theory of individual self-evaluation or individual self-enhancement, comparison goals may also be linked to cooperative versus competitive orientations. One suggestion (Wheeler, Wood, Salovey) is that upward comparisons may produce negative outcomes when the comparison other is a competitor. Thus the dimension of similarity versus dissimilarity may sometimes be overshadowed by whether the comparison other is in a competitive versus cooperative relationship to the subject. Such thinking suggests that comparison goals may be shifted dramatically as a function of competitive orientation.

From construing social comparison with respect to individual competitive orientation, the Luhtanen and Crocker chapter extends social comparison constructs to the study of intergroup relations in laboratory settings. Their chapter discusses a model of how social perception may be influenced by motives derived from ingroup–outgroup distinction, which is typically assumed to be a competitive relation. Thus, pursuing a favorable comparison with a historical outgroup may be used in the service of self-enhancement comparison goals. Luhtanen and Crocker's review of evidence on the relation between social prejudice and self-enhancement suggests that ratings of targets may be influenced either by threats to individual self-esteem or by threats to group-based self-esteem. It remains to test the relative contributions of individual- and group-based esteem to subjective well-being, test social comparison hypotheses with real social groups and significant competitive differences, and determine the possible strategies that persons may use to cope with threats to group-based self-esteem.

A final issue in the study of comparison goals is the question of individual differences. Recent work has focused on trait self-esteem as a determinant of comparison strategies. The chapters by Wood, Luhtanen and Crocker, and Gibbons and Gerrard suggest that linkages of personality to comparison goals are observable. The general finding is that persons with low self-esteem are more likely to select worse-off others for comparison, a pattern that is consistent with self-enhancement comparison goals. At the same time, work by these investigators and by Goethals suggests that persons with high self-esteem are more likely to exaggerate their distinctive attributes or superior performance with the effect of increasing their comparative superiority to others. Hence, they achieve self-enhancement through a different mechanism. These findings indicate that self-esteem is an important predictor of comparison behavior, and suggests that self-enhancement goals are achieved through different mechanisms by low- and high-esteem persons. It would be interesting to study how other personality traits influence self-enhancing comparisons or self-evaluative comparison preferences.

Consequences of Comparison

In a *New Yorker* cartoon which appeared at a time when a Swedish movie star was prominently featured in the media, a woman reading the newspaper is remarking to her partner, "I'm sick and tired of hearing how perfect Liv Ullman is." Social comparison research has sometimes been criticized for giving little attention to the consequences of comparison (Wheeler, Wood, see also Brickman & Bulman, 1977; Suls, 1986). Recent work has addressed this imbalance, and in the present volume the chapters by Tesser, Salovey, Major et al., Miller and McFarland, Gibbons and Gerrard, Affleck and Tennen, and Nagata and Crosby provide various approaches to this question.

One development in comparison research has been specific tests of whether downward comparison has consequences for subjective well-being. Gibbons and Gerrard discuss this question for persons with psychological problems, while Affleck and Tennen discuss it for persons with medical problems. There is consistency in the research programs of these investigators and others, the general finding being that use of downward comparison as a coping mechanism is related to greater subjective well-being. This has been demonstrated in controlled laboratory studies and in field research. A noteworthy aspect of this evidence is findings from prospective field studies by Affleck and Tennen which show downward comparison related to increased subjective well-being over time. These findings suggest that comparison-oriented coping does have functional value for helping distressed persons to cope with problems (Wills, 1987).

Research by both Salovey and Tesser has addressed the issue of how unfavorable comparisons may produce distress, envy, or jealousy. Salovey's model is oriented toward competitive situations, where a valued resource may be awarded to a rival. So again comparison goals are related to other personal motives such as competition. Salovey's data emphasize the importance of self-centrality, as social comparison jealousy is highest when the resource is central to one's self-definition and when the other is highly similar to the self. Reactions to unfavorable comparisons include not only personal distress but also relationship distancing with the other, and derogation of the other's personal attributes on other dimensions. Finally, Salovey provides a discussion of individual and cultural factors that may produce aggression as a result of unfavorable comparisons, providing another linkage of social comparison to the theory of prejudice and aggression.

Tesser's model delineates several possible reactions to unfavorable comparison, which include reducing the perceived importance of the comparison dimension; reducing the closeness of the relationship with the other; or interfering with the other's performance. These reactions have been demonstrated with self-report and physiological measures. In addition, Tesser has collected data on the specific emotions associated with various types of comparison experiences. His data suggest that jealousy and sadness are highest when the self is outperformed by another on a central dimension; pride and happiness are elevated when own performance is better than the other; and pride–in–other was elevated when a close other performs better than the self on a noncentral dimension (i.e., reflection). Major et al. follow a similar line of thinking in considering how controllability of the dimension (as well as closeness and relevance) may affect reactions to upward and downward comparison. They suggest, for example, that upward comparison on an uncontrollable (but valued) dimension may evoke anger, resentment, and dissatisfaction. The question remaining from this work is that if social comparison produces so many negative affective responses, why would people pursue it at all? It would be plausible that if negative responses were frequent, people would just cease comparing or shift toward an exclusive focus on comparisons that prove satisfying.

A final issue in reactions to comparison is whether social comparison has undesirable consequences which have not been previously recognized. Work by two contributors has addressed this issue from somewhat different perspectives. Nagata and Crosby suggest that comparison processes operate in a way that encourages persons to deny personal disadvantage (by pursuing favorable comparisons at the individual level) while recognizing that their group as a whole is disadvantaged. They discuss data from several sources which provide somewhat mixed support for this model, as the basic phenomenon (perceiving individual disadvantage as less than group disadvantage) is observed in some studies but the reverse is found in other studies. This work suggests that social comparison may lead persons toward imbalanced perceptions of injustice in social systems. Further research seems important to investigate the generality of the proposed process, examine hypothesized mediators and causal pathways, and determine whether social comparison is related to persons' efforts to change social systems and eliminate discrimination.

Gibbons and Gerrard have suggested another negative consequence. They propose that use of downward comparison may encourage derogatory perceptions of social outgroups or even of one's own group (cf. Luhtanen and Crocker). Making ingroup–outgroup distinctions or derogating personality attributes of target groups may have a short-term effect for self-enhancement, but in the long run may reduce social relations with outgroup members and possibly result in distancing from similar others. As yet there is little direct evidence for this supposition, but research on this possible consequence of comparison seems indicated.

Do People Strive for Uniformity or Uniqueness?

Although Festinger derived the 1954 theory from his earlier theory of informal social communication, Wheeler points out there are important differences between the two. The earlier theory posited pressures toward uniformity among group members in order to attain group goals. It seemed to subscribe to Schopenhauer's view that "We forfeit three-quarters of ourselves to be like other people." (One can only guess how Schopenhauer arrived at the 3/4 rather than 2/3, 7/8, etc.). In comparison theory, uniformity is desired with respect to opinions but the unidirectional drive upward motivates one to be slightly better, and therefore different, than others with respect to ability. Despite the fact that comparison theory acknowledged distinctiveness and similarity, both advocates and critics of the theory in the 1950s and 1960s tended to emphasize the latter. The ambiguities associated with the original statement of the similarity hypothesis may have helped to perpetrate this one-sided interpretation. Also, in proposing that people want to be only slightly better, Festinger gave more weight to uniformity than distinctiveness.

The attributional reformulation of the theory recasts this issue. Seeking out others who are similar on related attributes (Goethals and Darley's (1977) term) or surrounding dimensions (Wood and Taylor's term) allows us to determine to what degree we are the same or different on the ability in question. According to this approach, the dynamic is not uniformity versus distinctiveness, but rather uniformity and distinctiveness, at least with respect to abilities. The pressure toward uniformity still applies to opinions, however.

The notion that both processes are operative runs through the chapters in this volume. N. Miller, Gross, and Holtz document that people attribute agreement to other members of the ingroup on important opinions. This tendency is so strong that it occurs even when ingroup feeling is based on relatively trivial issues. The consensus research of Goethals, Messick, and Allison indicates a striving toward uniqueness for positive attributes, but toward social consensus for negative attributes. Gibbons and Gerrard's work on downward comparison also suggests that recognizing that others share our fate reduces a personal sense of deviance. The suggested mechanism is that people enhance feelings of self-acceptance through the perception that they are distinctive on positive attributes, and enhance perceived other-acceptance because they have similar opinions. For negative attributes, perceived deviance is reduced through the perception that the negative attribute is relatively common (Jemmott, Ditto, & Croyle, 1986; Snyder & Ingram, 1983; Suls & Wan, 1987). Thus social perception can serve esteem-maintenance goals through several mechanisms. It is possible that people can have the best of both worlds by perceiving that their abilities are rare but their opinions are common (Marks, 1984; Marks & Miller, 1987).

Nagata and Crosby suggest that distinctiveness striving even occurs with respect to one's own ingroup. Women believe that on the average women are discriminated against, but as individuals they are not—the *denial of personal disadvantage*. The contribution of Nagata and Crosby's research is that this tendency appears to be tempered in some cultures, such as Japanese-Americans, who emphasize the cultural ideal of group identification. How culture influences the balance between striving for uniqueness versus uniformity is in need of further systematic examination. Interestingly, Festinger suggested that the unidirectional drive upward may operate differently in some cultures because of the emphasis placed on collective versus individualistic outcomes. Salovey's chapter carries on this line of thinking with a discussion of cultural influences on perceptions of envy and jealousy. Unfortunately, cross-cultural study of comparisons has not received the attention it deserves.

Most of the contributors perceive uniqueness as serving a self-enhancement function, but Miller and McFarland demonstrate that not all false beliefs about uniqueness are self-enhancing. When others' behavior is constrained by subtle external or internal factors, social comparison may produce the mistaken impression that one is different from others. This occurs because people have greater access to feelings of self-consciousness or shyness in oneself than in others, but may be hesitant to acknowledge them because it would reflect unfavorably on the self. Because cultures differ in their concern with public displays of emotion, pluralistic ignorance is a perfect subject for cross-cultural study. One need not look to foreign cultures. New York City taxi drivers can be considered a cultural subgroup for whom social inhibitions are minimal and may, therefore, test the ultimate limits of Miller and McFarland's theory.

A final comment on uniqueness: The book's contributors have defined distinctiveness in terms of other people, but there is another form of distinctiveness. In his essay "On Recognition," playwright Arthur Miller (1978) observed, ". . . it is finally not enough to be distinct from others; the time comes when you have to be distinct from yourself, too" (p. 239). In psychological terms, the implication is that temporal comparisons may be just as important for perceptions of distinctiveness as social comparisons are. Understanding how the two types of comparison are used in conjunction is an important question for future study.

To What Degree is Comparison Motivated by Uncertainty?

Festinger's theory posited that people engage in comparison when they are in a state of uncertainty about their ability standing or the correctness of their opinions. A major shift in emphasis, anticipated by Hakmiller (1966), Singer (1966), and Wheeler (1966), is shown in contemporary research. At times, people don't necessarily want to know what their relative position is but want reassurance that their position is a good one. From this perspective, the self-enhancement processes discussed in several chapters may not reduce uncertainty per se, but instead strengthen an already established belief. Here the focus is on what are termed *constructed comparisons*, which serve to provide confirmation that a desired belief is correct.

Some writers have suggested that the drive to think we are good or correct is the major one (Goethals, 1986, p. 274). Certainly contemporary researchers have given more attention to how people use comparison to confirm an established belief about the self than to arrive at an accurate assessment of their standing or correctness. The sheer number of pages in this volume devoted to uncertainty reduction as opposed to confirmation might lead one to conclude the latter is more important. Goethals, Messick, and Allison propose that people construct social norms in their heads to confirm an already existing or desired conclusion about the self. Biased projections, such as underestimating the prevalence of one's positive traits and overestimating the prevalence of one's negative traits, serve to reinforce existing positive views of the self. Similarly, Wood, Taylor, and

Lichtman (1985) have suggested that persons who feel threatened conceive of others with undesirable attributes, presumably to make one's own state of affairs seem more desirable. This research suggests that people have a strong idea about what they want to find, and through selective memory and other biases find support for the desired conclusion. Wills and Gibbons and Gerrard discuss this with reference to self-perceptions, and N. Miller et al. make a similar case with respect to attitudinal certainty.

Ruble and Frey contend that uncertainty is not required to instigate social comparison in ability evaluation; rather, comparison depends on the stage of skill acquisition. In the first stage, uncertainty is posited to be a primary motivation, but in later stages, confirmation of one's standing is posited to be the dominant force. Perhaps confirmation-seeking comparison is a more common experience, but during early stages of skill acquisition and in novel situations, uncertainty will lead to social comparison behaviors. Data from clinical populations, presented by Gibbons and Gerrard and by Affleck and Tennen, suggest that confirmation of one's own worth is a strong motivation, and this may be the major motivation for persons with a high level of psychological distress and uncertainty about their own prognosis.

In our view, Festinger's original theory has a more circumscribed domain than the recent efforts that Wheeler calls *neo–social comparison theory*. Festinger was concerned with specific abilities or opinions rather than self-esteem, while contemporary research is more oriented to general dimensions of the self. It would be surprising to find, except among children, that people are completely uncertain about their standing on traits and abilities with which they have a long history of practice. Furthermore, most new tasks are based on combinations of familiar skills. This enables the individual to make a good guess as to how he or she will likely perform. (This may be why laboratory experiments on social comparison go to great lengths to develop cover stories about various fictitious "abilities" to create uncertainty.) When people find themselves in truly unfamiliar settings, taking on novel tasks, or dealing with new opinion issues, the original theory seems on target. We don't find it surprising that early comparison research dealt with domains of just this kind, while recent work has been more concerned with self-dimensions with which the individual is already familiar.

Before concluding our discussion of uncertainty as a necessary condition for comparison, one implication of N. Miller and colleagues' research deserves mention. They find that opinion projection to the ingroup increases certainty about one's own opinion because it encourages more thinking about the opinion issue. Projected similarity per se did not increase feelings of certainty. These results seem to contradict the consensus estimation research of Goethals and others, but the inconsistency may be more apparent than real. Goethals did not study the confidence associated with consensus estimates, and also used only traits and abilities; N. Miller et al. considered only opinion issues. It remains to be seen whether Miller's findings have a parallel in the ability realm. One possible resolution is that people make self-enhancing consensus estimates, but the effect of this "in the head" approach is relatively weak in relation to comparison with a real target. As Miller observes, projection per se may not be able to step in for actual comparison.

One aspect of Goethals' results suggests that people are reluctant to be too carried away by their self-enhancing consensus estimates: Recall that the illusion of distinctiveness was shown for general, but not for specific behaviors. Goethals observes that people probably recognize that it is easy to relatively perceive oneself as unique when the referent is vague, but more difficult when the criterion is a very specific behavior ("I can bowl 200 points every game"). This has roots in Festinger's thinking, as he recognized that social comparison was more likely pursued for attributes that were not easily quantified; and in recent downward comparison research, which has found more evidence of self-enhancing comparison for vague targets (the average college student) than for specific persons such as close friends or relatives (Perloff & Fetzer, 1986). The lesson may be that constructive comparisons are common, but are tentative and subject to revision.

Do People Avoid Comparison?

Another New Yorker cartoon shows a fashionable couple conversing in their fashionable living room. One partner—wearing a wry grin—has just posed a question, and the other is responding acerbically, "No, I am not interested in knowing how you would rate me on a scale of one to ten." Another enduring problem concerns the avoidance of social comparison. Brickman and Bulman (1977) were the first to systematically describe the potential costs of comparison for the parties involved. The aversiveness of learning that one has inferior standing is well recognized. However, finding one has superior standing also has its costs; feelings of resentment, envy or embarrassment on the part of those who fared worse can be expected to make social interaction more difficult, and focus on superior status may result in an unpleasant level of self-consciousness. Equality may leave everyone feeling average and undistinguished. Perhaps this line of argument was what Cervantes had in mind when he wrote, "All comparisons are odious." Of course, Brickman and Bulman did not think that people always avoid comparison; rather they try to maintain a hedonic balance between its costs and benefits. The evidence on this important question, however, has been minimal, in part because it is always easier to demonstrate the occurrence of something than to demonstrate its absence.

Several of the contributors offer new evidence regarding avoidance of comparison. Moreover, they describe a third alternative: Rather than active avoidance, there may be situations in which comparison is viewed with disinterest. Ruble and Frey's functional model discusses both possibilities. Learning about a task or deciding about its personal relevance may require social comparison, but gaining personal satisfaction with mastery may be more appropriately gauged in terms of temporal standards (progress) and absolute criteria. In the mastery phase comparison is not actively avoided, but is simply less relevant because self-focus would interfere with immersion in the flow of activity (Czikszentmihalyi, 1975). On the other hand, in later stages of skill acquisition when competence assessment is over, if competence or potential for reward is low then individuals may discontinue the activity and/or further self-evaluation of the ability; in other words, people may avoid social comparison entirely.

Tesser's approach also discusses avoidance of comparison. The SEM (self-evaluation maintenance) model predicts that individuals will withdraw from an activity and hence avoid comparison if they learn that someone with whom they are close (such as a friend or relative) has outperformed them on a dimension that is tied to their self-definition. Disinterest in comparison should occur when someone with whom one is not close outperforms us on a dimension with which we have no investment. Similarly, Major et al.'s analysis suggests that people will prefer to avoid comparison with a better-performing other on a highly self-relevant dimension if they feel they have little control over whether their relative position on the dimension can change. They also suggest that people will avoid comparison with someone worse off if they feel they may come to have a similar fate. The consideration of perceived control as a moderator of comparison behavior begs for more study and suggests understanding of social comparison may be increased by giving more attention to the learned helplessness phenomenon (Crocker, Alloy, & Kayne, 1988).

Perhaps not immediately obvious, avoidance of comparison is also relevant to D. Miller and McFarland's analysis of pluralistic ignorance. The belief is thought to arise because of mutual observability, but the individual interprets the similar behavior of the self and other differently: "The others aren't raising their hands so they must understand the lecture"; "I'm not raising my hand because I'm too embarrassed to admit I don't understand." Miller and McFarland suggest the feeling that one is more bashful and inhibited results from such traits being more accessible to self than to others. Such inferences may also result from a reluctance or inability to actively compare on these dimensions. In fact, discerning one's relative standing regarding shyness and embarrassment is problematic because the nature of the trait itself discourages active social comparison.

NEW DIRECTIONS

Throughout this discussion we have discussed possibilities for future study. We now outline five directions, listed in no particular order, that we think research could take.

(1) Some researchers, such as Wood, Taylor, Gibbons and Gerrard, and Affleck and Tennen have studied naturalistic social comparisons with interviews or surveys. The limitation of such procedures is that they can only obtain retrospective accounts. This work needs to be supplemented with study of comparison processes in situ (Czikszentmihalyi & Graef, 1980; Stone & Neale, 1984). Using experience sampling methodologies to tap naturalistically occurring comparison behavior would be an important addition to the existing literature. Longitudinal studies are also necessary for determining causal directionality and investigating how comparison processes change over the course of a coping effort. The existing field studies have contributed at least as much to theory development as to applied concerns, and further efforts are warranted.

(2) A number of questions focus on the measurement of social comparison. These include the use of spontaneous comparisons versus comparative ratings, and the study of comparison target choices versus comparison dimension choices. Orthogonal to these issues is the need for multidimensional assessment of comparison outcomes, with attention not only to psychological dimensions (e.g., depression, anxiety, perceived deviance, self-esteem, efficacy, optimism), but also examining for possibly functional or dysfunctional consequences of comparison on personal and social competence. Finally, there is a question as to how social comparison is related to other coping and self-evaluational mechanisms. It is difficult to believe that people typically use only one coping mechanism in the course of a coping effort (e.g., Perri, 1985; Shiffman, 1985), and the question then is how social comparison is related to the use of other cognitive and behavioral strategies.

(3) Since the mid-1970s, theoretical and empirical developments in comparison study have been influenced chiefly by the intellectual currents of attribution, self-psychology, and social cognition. There are additional areas from which comparison theory may profit. For example, the study of comparison processes has never made full contact with social judgment theory (Sherif & Hovland, 1961) and psychophysics (Parducci, 1974), areas with which it shares similar interests. Kruglanski (in press) has described how the classic theory and current revisions may be further elaborated by recognizing that comparisons between people share similar dynamic comparisons of objects.

Atkinson (1986) and Sherman and his associates (Houston, Sherman, & Baker, 1989) have recently proposed how Tversky's (1977) theory of feature matching and similarity may be relevant to the comparison process. Specifically, perceived similarity depends on the direction the comparison takes place (e.g. How similar am I to you vs. How similar are you to me?) and the degree to which comparison objects share common features. The implications of feature-matching for self-evaluation have only just begun to be explored (see Holyoak & Gordon, 1983; Srull & Gaelick, 1983).

Comparison theory also needs to take into account *Norm theory* proposed by Kahneman and D. Miller (1986). They challenge the notion that ". . . norms are precomputed . . . [but instead] are constructed on the fly in a backward process that is guided by the characteristics of the evoking stimulus and by the momentary context" (p. 150). If each event or object brings its own frame of reference into being by recruiting specific representations, then what role do preexisting norms about members of the reference group play? It is just such existing norms that comprise the material of social comparison. The constructed or projected comparisons described by several of the contributors may be similar to norms created "on the fly," but much remains to be sorted out.

(4) The study of comparison processes still remains somewhat parochial. The self literature points out that temporal comparison, reflected appraisal, and self-perceptions also influence perceptions of capability and self-esteem. In 1977, Mettee and Smith observed that a comprehensive theory of self-evaluation would need to take into account all of these diverse sources of information. The beginnings of this pursuit can be discerned in the work of Higgins (1987), Masters and Keil (1987), and Ruble and Frey (chapter 4, this volume), but much more work is needed.

(5) With the exception of the chapter by N. Miller et al., there is a lack of attention devoted to opinion social comparison by contemporary researchers (with conspicuous exceptions: Gerard & Orive, 1987; Gorenflo & Crano, 1989; Kruglanski & Mayseless, 1987). Perhaps attitude comparison poses a dilemma because it is more complicated than ability comparison. The attributional approach posited that comparison operates differently for value versus belief opinions. Similar others provide validation for values, but persons with a dissimilar perspective provide validation for beliefs because of a triangulation-type process. Actually, beliefs and values are probably more appropriately conceived as the endpoints of a continuum and not as dichotomous categories. What happens at the edges when a belief shades into a value? Who becomes more important, a similar or a dissimilar other? Comparison research on personal attributes such as traits and abilities has dominated the agenda for the past decade. Perhaps it's time for opinions to take their place.

REFERENCES

Alicke, M. D. (1985). Global self-evaluation as determined by the desirability and controllability of trait adjectives. *Journal of Personality and Social Psychology, 49*, 1621–1630.

Atkinson, M. L. (1986). The perception of social categories: Implications for the social comparison process. In J. Olson, M. P. Herman, & M. Zanna (Eds.), *Relative deprivation and social comparison: The Ontario symposium* (Vol. 4, pp. 117–134). Hillsdale, NJ: Lawrence Erlbaum Associates.

Brickman, P., & Bulman, R. J. (1977). Pleasure and pain in social comparison. In J. M. Suls & R. M. Miller (Eds.), *Social comparison processes: Theoretical and empirical perspectives*. Washington, DC: Hemisphere.

Crocker, J., Alloy, L., & Kayne, N. T. (1988). Attributional style, depression, and perceptions of consensus for events. *Journal of Personality and Social Psychology, 54*, 840–846.

Czikszentmihalyi, M. R. (1975). *Beyond boredom and anxiety*. San Francisco: Jossey–Bass.

Czikszentmihalyi, M. R., & Graef, R. (1980). The experience of freedom in daily life. *American Journal of Community Psychology, 8*, 401–414.

Feldman, N. S., & Ruble, D. N. (1981). Social comparison strategies: Dimensions offered and options taken. *Personality and Social Psychology Bulletin, 7*, 11–16.

Festinger, L. (1954). A theory of social comparison processes. *Human Relations, 7*, 117–140.

Gastorf, J. W., & Suls, J. (1978). Performance evaluation via social comparison: Performance similarity vs. related-attributes similarity. *Social Psychology, 41*, 297–305.

Gerard, H. B., & Orive, R. (1987). The dynamics of opinion formation: An informational social comparison model. In L. Berkowitz (Ed.), *Advances in experimental social psychology* (Vol. 20, pp. 171–202). San Diego: Academic Press.

Goethals, G. R. (1986). Social comparison theory: Psychology from the lost and found. *Personality and Social Psychology Bulletin, 12*, 261–278.

Goethals, G. R., & Darley, J. (1977). Social comparison theory: An attributional approach. In J. M. Suls & R. M. Miller (Eds.), *Social comparison processes: Theoretical and empirical perspectives* (pp. 259–278). Washington, DC: Hemisphere.

Gorenflo, D. W., & Crano, W. D. (1989). Judgmental subjectivity/objectivity and locus of choice in social comparison. *Journal of Personality and Social Psychology, 57*, 605–614.

Hakmiller, K. L. (1966). Threat as a determinant of downward comparison. *Journal of Experimental Social Psychology, 2* (Suppl. 1), 32–39.

Higgins, E. T. (1987). Self-discrepancy: A theory relating self and affect. *Psychological Review, 94*, 319–340.

Holyoak, K., & Gordon, P. (1983). Social reference points. *Journal of Personality and Social Psychology, 44*, 881–887.

Houston, D. A., Sherman, S. J., & Baker, S. M. (1989). The influence of unique features and direction of comparison on preferences. *Journal of Experimental Social Psychology, 25*, 121–141.

Jemmott, J. B., Ditto, P., & Croyle, R. T. (1986). Judging health status: Effects of perceived prevalence and personal relevance. *Journal of Personality and Social Psychology, 50*, 899–905.

Kahneman, D., & Miller, D. T. (1986). Norm theory: Comparing reality to its alternatives. *Psychological Review, 93*, 136–153.

Kruglanski, A. (in press). Classic and current social comparison research: Expanding the perspective. *Psychological Bulletin*.

Kruglanski, A., & Mayseless, O. (1987). Motivational effects in the social comparison of opinions. *Journal of Personality and Social Psychology, 53*, 834–842.

Marks, G. (1984). Thinking one's abilities are unique and one's opinions are common. *Personality and Social Psychology Bulletin, 10*, 203–208.

Marks, G., & Miller, N. (1987). Ten years of research on the false-consensus effect: An empirical and theoretical review. *Psychological Bulletin, 102*, 72–90.

Masters, J. C., & Keil, L. J. (1987). Generic comparison processes in human judgment and behavior. In J. C. Masters & W. Smith (Eds.), *Social comparison, social justice, and relative deprivation: Theoretical, empirical, and policy perspectives* (pp. 11–54). Hillsdale, NJ: Lawrence Erlbaum Associates.

Mettee, D. R., & Smith, G. (1977). Social comparison and interpersonal attraction: The case for dissimilarity. In J. M. Suls & R. L. Miller (Eds.), *Social comparison processes: Theoretical and empirical perspectives* (pp. 69–102). Washington DC: Hemisphere.

Miller, A. (1972). *The theater essays of Arthur Miller.* New York: Viking Press.

Miller, C. T. (1982). The role of performance–related similarity in social comparison of abilities: A test of the related-attributes hypothesis. *Journal of Experimental Social Psychology, 18,* 513–523.

Miller, D. T., Turnbull, W., & McFarland, C. (1988). Particularistic and universalistic evaluation in the social comparison process. *Journal of Personality and Social Psychology, 55,* 908–917.

Parducci, A. (1974). Contextual effects: A range–frequency analysis. In E. C. Carterette & M. P. Friedman (Eds.), *Handbook of perception* (Vol. 7, pp. 127–141). New York: Academic Press.

Perloff, L., & Fetzer, B. (1986). Self-other judgments and perceived vulnerability to victimization. *Journal of Personality and Social Psychology, 50,* 502–510.

Perri, M. G. (1985). Self-change strategies for the control of smoking, obesity, and problem drinking. In S. Shiffman & T. A. Wills (Eds.), *Coping and substance use* (pp. 295–318). Orlando, FL: Academic Press.

Sherif, M., & Hovland, C. (1961). *Social judgment.* New Haven: Yale University Press.

Shiffman, S. (1985). Coping with temptations to smoke. In S. Shiffman & T. A. Wills (Eds.), *Coping and substance use* (pp. 223–242). Orlando, FL: Academic Press.

Singer, J. E. (1966). Social comparison: Progress and issues. *Journal of Experimental Social Psychology, 2,* (Suppl. 1), 103–110.

Snyder, C. R., & Ingram, R. E. (1983). The impact of consensus information on help-seeking for psychological problems. *Journal of Personality and Social Psychology, 45,* 1118–1126.

Srull, T. K., & Gaelick, L. (1983). General principles and individual differences in the self as a habitual reference point: An examination of self-other judgments of similarity. *Social Cognition, 2,* 108–121.

Stone, A. A., & Neale, J. M. (1984). A new measure of daily coping. *Journal of Personality and Social Psychology, 46,* 392–406.

Suls, J. (1986). Notes on the occasion of Social Comparison Theory's thirtieth birthday. *Personality and Social Psychology Bulletin, 12,* 289–296.

Suls, J., Gaes, G., & Gastorf, J. W. (1979). Evaluating a sex-related ability: Comparison with same-, opposite-, and combined sex norms. *Journal of Research in Personality, 13,* 294–304.

Suls, J., & Wan, C. K. (1987). In search of the false-uniqueness phenomenon: Fear and estimates of social consensus. *Journal of Personality and Social Psychology, 52,* 211–217.

Taylor, S., & Lobel, M. (1989). Social comparison activity under threat: Downward evaluation and upward contacts. *Psychological Review, 96,* 569–575.

Tversky, A. (1977). Features of similarity. *Psychological Review, 84,* 327–352.

Wheeler, L. (1966). Motivation as a determinant of upward comparison. *Journal of Experimental Social Psychology, 2* (Suppl. 1), 27–31.

Wheeler, L., Koestner, R., & Driver, R. E. (1982). Related attributes in the choice of comparison others: It may be there, but it isn't all there is. *Journal of Experimental Social Psychology, 18,* 489–500.

Wills, T. A. (1987). Downward comparison as a coping mechanism. In C. R. Snyder & C. Ford (Eds.), *Coping with negative life events: Clinical and social-psychological perspectives* (pp. 243–267). New York: Plenum.

Wood, J. V., Taylor, S. E., & Lichtman, R. R. (1985). Social comparison in adjustment to breast cancer. *Journal of Personality and Social Psychology, 49,* 1169–1183.

Author Index

A

Abbey, A., 248, *258*, 307
Abeles, R., 353, *365*
Abelson, R. P., 135, *142*, 200, 201, *205*
Abidin, R., 378, *391*
Ablon, J., 329, *342*
Aboud, F. E., 93, *107*
Abrahams, S., 100, *109*
Abrams, D., 214, 216, 225, *232*
Abramson, L. Y., 173, *173*, 228, *232*, *234*, 245, 246, 247, *257*, *258*
Achee, J., 141, *144*
Adams, H. E., 267, *283*
Adams, N. E., 254, *258*
Adelman, B., *344*
Adler, T. F., 103, *108*
Affleck, G., 29, *46*, 54, *74*, 331, *342*, 371, 372, 375, 378, 379, 380, 381, 384, 385, 386, *391*, *392*, *393*
Agostinelli, G., 55, *77*, 183, *208*

Ahrens, A. H., 41, *46*, 89, 91, *107*, 115, *142*
Albert, S., 83, *107*, 383, *391*
Alicke, M. D., 29, 44, *46*, 56, 71, *74*
Ali, M., 162, *173*
Allbright, L., 182, *207*
Allen, V. L., 153, *173*
Allison, S. T., 149, 156, 161, 162, *173*, *174*
Alloy, L. B., 41, *46*, 48, 68, 77, 115, *142*, 173, *173*, 228, *232*, *232*, *234*, 246, *257*, 407, *410*
Allport, F. H., 157, *173*, 179, 200, *205*, 287, 306, *310*, *311*
Allport, G. W., 203, *205*
Alvarez, W., 381, *392*
Amabile, T. M., 54, *74*
Ames, C., 82, 100, 102, 103, *107*
Amoroso, D. M., 53, 65, *74*
Anderson, E. A., 65, 71, *75*
Anderson, N. H., 301, *310*
Anderson, S., 71, *74*
Andler, C., 263, *282*

AUTHOR INDEX

Armstrong, S., 94, *112*
Aronson, E., 153, *173*, 268, *281*
Arrowood, A. J., 7, 9, 10, 18, *19*, *21*, 23, 26, 27, *46*, *49*, 115, *144*, 272, *282*, 347, *367*
Asai, M., 228, *234*
Ashmore, R. D., 218, *232*
Aspinwall, L. G., 115, *144*, 150, 155, *175*, 255
Atkins, J. L., *175*, *208*, *312*
Atkinson, J. W., 24, *46*
Atkinson, M. L., 97, *107*, 408, *410*
Auden, W. H., *285*
Ax, F., 130, *142*
Azmitia, M., 96, *107*

B

Bachelor, B., 263, 268, *283*
Back, K., 303, *311*
Bacon, F., 181, *205*
Baker, S. M., 408, *410*
Ballachey, E. L., 288, *312*
Bandura, A., 24, 27, 34, *46*, 86, *107*, 239, 246, 254, *248*
Bard, L., 10, *20*
Bargh, J. A., 89, *109*
Baron, R. S., 178, 204, *206*, *208*
Barrett, C. J., 329, *342*
Barrett, M., *107*
Bates, J., 378, *391*
Baumeister, R. F., 42, *46*, 215, *232*
Baumgardner, A. H., 55, *75*
Beck, A. T., 170, *173*
Becker, M. H., 336, *343*
Bell, P. A., 320, 321, *342*
Bem, D. J., 195, *205*
Ben-Itzhak, S., 126, 246, *143*, 252, 253, *259*
Benediction, C. S., 263, *285*

Benner, L. A., *21*, 37, 42, *49*, 53, 55, 68, *78*, 275, *285*, 319, 321, *345*
Benner, D. H., 10, 53, 65, *75*
Bensenberg, M., *311*
Berger, J., 211, *232*
Berger, S. M., 14, *19*, 27, *46*, 86, *107*, 119, *142*
Berglas, S., 88, *110*
Berkowitz, C., 58, *75*, 136, *142*, 319, *342*
Berlyne, D. E., 79, *107*
Berman, J. J., 26, *46*, 51, *75*
Bernstein, M., 350, *365*
Berscheid, E., 136, *142*, 238, *260*
Beyer, J., 254, *258*
Biggs, D. A., 307, *313*
Billig, M., 212, *234*
Binkley Gaus, U., *49*
Bjorklund, D. F., 87, *107*
Blalock, S., 54, *75*, 373, 385, *392*
Blanchard, L., *75*, *392*
Blascouich, J., 136, *142*, 226, *233*
Bloom, S., 149, *175*
Blum, M., 305, *313*
Boden, J. A., 198, *205*
Boggiano, A. K., 93, 94, 95, 100, 103, *107*, *111*
Bolce, L. H., 350, *366*
Boldizer, J. P., 149, *175*
Boney-McCoy, S., 327, *343*
Bontempo, R., 228, *234*
Borden, R. J., 229, *142*, *233*, *282*
Borgida, E., 204, *205*, 307, *312*
Bragonier, P., 94, *111*
Bramel, D., 202, *205*
Breed, W., 305, *310*
Brewer, M. B., 211, 212, 218, *232*
Brewin, C. R., 41, *46*
Brickman, P., 12, *19*, 26, 27, 31, 33, 37, 38, *46*, 51, 53, 65, 66, *75*, 89, *108*, 115, *142*, 153, *173*, 179, *206*, 231, *232*, 237,

238, 243, 244, 248, *258*, 261, 273, 281, *281*, 318, 336, *342*, 351, *366*, 400, 406, *410*
Bringle, R. G., 263, 264, 268, *281*
Brooks-Gunn, J., 83, *108*
Brown, E. T., 80, *111*
Brown, I., Jr., 239, 254, *258*
Brown, J. D., 24, 30, 39, 41, *46*, *48*, 55, 70, 71, *75*, 77, 90, *112*, *175*, 215, 220, 225, 226, 228, *232*, *234*, 387, *393*
Brown, M. B., 134, *143*
Brown, R., 157, *173*
Bryson, J. B., 131, *142*, 263, 265, 266, *282*
Bulman, R. J., 12, *19*, 27, 31, 33, 37, 38, *46*, 51, 66, *75*, 89, *108*, 115, *142*, 153, *173*, 179, *206*, 231, *232*, 237, 238, 243, 244, 245, 248, *258*, 261, 273, 175, 281, *281*, 318, 336, *342*, 400, 406, *410*
Bundy, R., 212, *234*
Burgess, A., 369, *391*
Burish, T. G., 53, 65, *75*
Burnstein, E., 15, *19*, *206*
Bush, S., 279, *282*
Butler, R., 86, 89, 91, 93, 94, 96, 100, 101, 103, 105, *108*
Butters, J. W., 251, *258*
Butzine, K. W., *21*, *49*, *78*, *209*, *260*
Buunk, B. P., 115, *144*, 150, 155, *175*, 263, 264, 268, *282*
Bylsma, W. H., 243, *258*
Byrne, D., 182, *206*, 272, *282*

C

Cacioppo, J. T., 130, *142*
Campbell, D. T., 127, *142*, 181, 182, 202, *206*, 211, 218, *232*, *233*

Campbell, J. D., 29, 30, 31, 37, 38, 41, 44, *46*, *49*, 56, 68, 71, *75*, 119, 137, 138, *144*, 158, *173*, 202, *206*, 228, *233*, 237, 241, 243, *260*, 270, 275, 276, 277, *282*, *284*, 288, *311*
Canon, L. K., 15, *20*
Cansler, D. C., 54, *75*
Cantril, H., 355, *365*
Caputo, C., 297, *312*
Carver, C. S., 88, 89, 92, *108*, 373, *392*
Cash, D. W., 251, *258*
Cash, T. F., 251, *258*
Castor, 16
Castore, C. H., 14, *19*
Chafel, J. A., 94, *108*
Chaiken, S., 193, *206*
Champion, D. S., *175*, *208*, *312*
Chassin, L., 36, *48*, 55, 77, 183, *208*, 288, 305, *311*, *313*
Cialdini, R., 116, *142*, 229, *233*, 270, 276, *282*
Clack, F. L., 228, *234*
Clanton, G., 280, *282*
Clark, M. S., 127, *142*
Clore, G. L., 135, *142*, *143*, 182, 261, *283*
Coates, D., 30, 47, 65, *75*, 248, *258*, 307, 309, *311*, 329, 330, *342*
Cohen, B., 279, *282*
Cohen, R., 89, 93, *111*
Cohen, S. J., 65, *75*
Cole, M., 103, *110*
Collins A., 135, *143*, 261, *283*
Collins, J., 131, *144*
Collins, R. L., 55, *75*, 130, *142*, 225, *232*, 255, *258*
Connolley, E. S., 196, *206*
Connolly, C., *285*
Cook, H., *75*, 392
Cook, T. D., 248, *258*, 350, *365*

AUTHOR INDEX

Cooper, J., 11, *19*, *21*, *49*, *78*, 136, 139, *142*, 202, *207*, *209*, *260*
Coopersmith, S., 221, *233*
Corty, E., *311*
Cotten, J. L., 204, *206*
Cottrell, N. B., 7, *19*, 30, *47*
Crandall, R., 307, *312*
Crano, W. D., 183, 189, *206*, 409, *410*
Criddle, R., 336, *342*
Crocker, J., 29, 41, 42, 44, 45, *47*, *48*, 55, 68, *75*, 77, 90, *108*, 115, *143*, 218, 219, 221, 222, 223, 224, 225, 227, 228, 231, *233*, *234*, 238, 251, *258*, 276, *282*, 407, *410*
Cronbach, L. J., 182, *206*
Crosby, F., 237, 238, 243, 245, 247, *258*, 278, *282*, 348, 350, 351, 352, 353, 354, 355, *365*, *368*
Croyle, R. T., 330, *343*, 403, *410*
Crutchfield, R. S., 288, *312*
Curtin, T. R., 248, *258*
Cuthbert, T. M., 278, *282*
Czikszentmihalyi, M. R., 407, 408, *410*

D

Dakin, S., 272, *282*
Dakoff, G. A., 130, *142*, 255, *258*, 332, *392*
Darley, J., 16, 18, *19*, 51, 73, *76*, 288, 291, 297, 309, *311*, *312*, 396, 402, *410*
Darley, J. M., 32, 34, *47*, 115, 119, *143*, 154, 156, *174*, 178, 199, *207*, 272, *283*, 347, 356, 362, *365*
Davidson, E. S., 94, *112*

Davis, J. A., 251, *258*, 267, 279, *282*
Davis, K., 280, *282*
Davis, R. M., *283*
Dawes, R. M., 184, *206*
Deker, S., 54, 77, 322, 329, 330, 331, 333, *344*, 369, *392*
Deci, E. L., 79, 83, 100, 103, *108*
DelBoca, F. K., 218 *232*
Dembo, T., 6, *20*
DeNinno, J. A., 14, 16, *19*
DePaulo, B. M., 299, *311*
DeRivera, J., 135, *143*
Dermer, M., 65, *75*
Derogatis, L., 372, 381, *392*
Derry, P. A., 67, *76*
de Tocqueville, A., 294, *311*
Deutsch, F. M., 83, 106, *108*
Deutsch, M., 6, *19*, 348, *365*
DeVellis, B., 54, *75*, 241, *258*, 373, *392*
DeVellis, R., 54, *75*, 241, *258*, 373, 382, 385, 386, *392*
DeVinney, L. C., 349, *367*
Diaz, P., 103, *110*
Dichtel, M., 10, *19*, 203, *207*
Diener, C. I., 100, *108*
Diener, E., 55, 65, *75*, 269, *284*, 321, 322, 323, 331, *342*
Dion, K. L., 196, 203, *206*
Ditto, P. H., 330, *343*, 403, *410*
Dixon, W. J., 134, *143*
Dovidio, J. F., 68, *75*, 211, *233*
Driver, R. E., 17 *21*, 26, *49*, 51, 73, *78*, 272, *285*, 347, *368*, 396, *411*
Dube, L., 351, 353, *366*, *367*
Duncan, O. D., 204, *206*
Dunkel-Schetter, C., 249, *260*, 307, *313*, 332, 333, *342*, 379, *393*
Dunn, R. S., 200, *209*
Duval, S., 329, *342*

Dweck, C. S., 80, 83, 84, 90, 93, 100, 101, 102, *108*, 256, *258*

E

Eagly, A. H., 193, *206*
Earle, W. B., 136, *143*
Earn, B. M., 203, *206*
Ebling, T., 17, *19*
Eccles, J., 103, *108*
Edgerton, R. G., 336, 337, *342*
Edlow, D., 202, *206*
Edwards, C., *175*, *208*, *312*
Edwards, C. P., 97, *108*
Ehrlich, H. J., 213, 218, *233*
Eisenberg, N., 58, *75*
Eisenberg, R., 90, 94, *111*
Ekman, D., 130, *143*
Elliott, E. S., 84, 93, 100, *108*
Ellis, R. J., 106, *111*
Ellsworth, P. C., 131, 135, *144*
Emmons, R. A. 55, *75*, 321, 322, 323, 331, *342*
Epley, S. W., 7, *19*, 30, *47*
Erickson, B. H., 27, *48*
Ervin, C., 170, *174*
Ester, P., 183, *209*
Evenbeck, S., 263, 268, *282*, *283*
Eyman, P., 79, *111*

F

Fabes, X., 58, *75*
Fairlie, H., 262, 279, *282*
Falke, R., 371, *393*
Fazio, R. H., 80, 84, 106, *108*, 136, 139, *142*
Feld, S., 93, 96, *108*
Feldman, N. S., 17, *19*, 51, 73, *75*, 90, 93, 94, 95, *108–111*, 396, *410*

Fermor, P. L., *285*
Festinger, L., 3, 4, 5, 6, 10, 15, 16, *19*, *20*, 23, 24, 25, 27, 29, 35, 45, *47*, 51, 52, 56, *76*, 79, 105, *109*, 115, 117, 118, *143*, 150, 151, 152, 155, 156, 169, *173*, 177, *206*, 237, 238, 242, *259*, 261, 267, 268, 270, 271, 272, 273, *282*, 290, 303, *311*, 317, 318, *342*, 347, *365*, 369, 388, *392*, 395, *410*
Fetzer, B. K., 36, *48*, 165, *175*, 308, *312*, 336, 338, 339, *344*, 379, 385, *392*, 406, *411*
Field, P. B., 221, *233*
Fields, J. M., 305, *311*
Fifield, J., 29, *46*, *74*, 331, *342*, 371, 372, 375, 378, 381, 384, 385, 386, *391*
Figone, J., 329, *344*
Fisher, J. D., 126, *143*, 240, 243, 244, 245, 246, 252, 253, 256, *259*, 299, *311*
Fiske, D. W., 127, *142*
Fiske, S. T., 87, 90, *109*, 195, *206*
Fitzgerald, T., 380, *393*
Flament, C., 212, *234*
Flavell, J. H., 97, *109*
Fleming, A., 83, *108*
Fleming, R., 305, *312*
Fletcher, G. J. O., 90, *111*
Flett, G. L., 94, 95, *111*
Flink, C., *107*
Folger, R., 237, *259*
Folkman, S., 67, *76*, 242, 244, 245, 247, *259*, 322, 330, 335, *343*, 370, *392*
Foster, G., 279, *282*
France, A. C., 94, *112*
France-Kaatrude, A., 272, *282*
Freedman-Letofsky, K., 324, *345*
Freeland, C., 378, *391*
Freeman, S., *142*, 229, *233*, *282*

AUTHOR INDEX

Freeman, S. J. J., 324, *345*
Freilicher, N. A., 164, *174*
Freud, S., 181, *206*, 276, *282*
Frey, D., 54, *75*, 89, *109*
Frey, K. S., 80, 82, 84, 89, 91, 93, 94, 95, 96, 98, 99, 103, 104, 106, *109*, *111*
Friend, R., 10, *19*, 26, 27, 37, 42, 43, 44, *46*, *47*, 53, 55, 68, *76*, *259*, 275, *282*, 327, *342*
Fromkin, H. L., 31, *47*, 273, *282*, 289, *313*
Frost, M., 156, *174*
Funder, D. C., 182, *206*, 301, *311*
Furnham, A., 41, *46*

G

Gaelick, L., 409, *411*
Gaertner, S. L., 68, *75*, 211, *233*
Gaes, G. G., 17, *20*, 396, *411*
Gaines, B., 71, *77*
Galligan, B., 337, *343*
Gallo, L., 29, *47*, 238, 251, *258*
Garry, S. L., 305, *312*
Gastardo-Condo, M. C., 194, *207*
Gastof, J., 119, *144*
Gastorf, J. W., 17, *19*, 27, 32, *47*, 51, 73, *75*, 272, *284*, 396, *410*, *411*
Gaus Binkley, V., 42, *49*
Gellert, S., 264, *283*
Gerard, H. B., 177, 183, 195, 196, 197, 200, *206*, *233*, 409, *410*
Gergen, K. J., 29, *48*, 238, 251, 252, *259*, 327, *344*, 363, *365*
Gerrard, M., 54, 55, 68, *76*, 320, 323, 325, 326, 327, 331, 332, 333, 334, *342*, *344*
Gibbons, F. X., 29, 42, *47*, 54, 55, 68, *76*, 238, 252, *259*, 307, *311*, 320, 323, 324, 325, 326, 327, 331, 332, 333, 334, 337, 338, *342*, *344*, 388, *392*
Gilbert, J., 10, *19*, 37, 42, 43, 44, *47*, 53, 55, 68, *76*, *259*, 275, *282*, 327, *342*
Gilouich, T., 157, *174*
Glazebrook, A. H., 54, *74*
Glick, I. O., 307, *311*
Glos, B., 10, *19*
Glynn, K., 305, *312*
Goethals, G. R., 15, 16, 17, 18, *19*, *20*, *21*, 32, 34, 35, 46, *47*, *49*, *50*, 51, 71, 73, *76*, *77*, *78*, 79, 89, *109*, 115, 119, *143*, 149, 150, 153, 154, 155, 156, 158, 159, 161, 164, *174*, *175*, 178, 179, 199, 202, 204, *206*, *207*, *209*, 237, *260*, 272, *283*, 288, 289, 290, 297, *311*, 347, 348, 356, 362, *365*, 396, 402, 404, *410*
Goffman, E., 166, *174*, 268, *283*, 303, *311*
Gold, M., 93, *108*
Golding, J., 351, *365*
Gollwitzer, P. M., 136, *143*, *144*
Gonzales-Intal, A. M., 348, *365*
Gordon, P., 409, *410*
Gorenflo, D. W., 409, *410*
Gottlieb, B. H., 324, 325, *343*
Gottman, J., 97, *109*
Graef, R., 408, *410*
Greenberg, J., 37, *48*, 54, 67, *77*, 204, *208*, 238, 251, *259*
Green, J. A., 319, *342*
Green, S. M., 54, *76*, 88, 89, *110*, 275, *283*
Greene, D., 157, *175*, 179, *208*, 213, *233*, 288, *321*
Greewald, A. G., 71, *76*, 171, *174*
Griffin, J. J., Jr., 71, *77*, 103
Griffin, P., *110*
Grolnick, W. S., 103, *112*

AUTHOR INDEX

Grosousky, A. H., 89, 93, *111*
Gross, S. R., 198, 204, *205*, *207*
Gruder, C. L., 10, *19*, *21*, 40, 41, 43, 45, *47*, *49*, 51, *76*, *78*, 199, 203, *207*, *209*, *260*, 318, *343*, 347, *366*
Guimond, S., 351, 353, *366*
Gurin, P., 354, 361, *366*

H

Hager, J., 130, *143*
Hakmiller, K. L., 9, 18, *19*, *20*, 29, 44, *47*, 53, 65, *76*, 115, *143*, 153, *174*, 238, 251, *259*, 319, *343*, 404, *410*
Halligan, M., 350, *366*
Hannah, D. B., 90, *108*
Hanson, A. R., 254, *260*
Harackiewicz, J. M., 100, *109*
Hardy, D., *175*, *208*, *312*
Harring, K., *75*, *392*
Harrod, W. J., 184, 185, *207*
Harter, S1, 54, *76*, 79, 88, 94, 100, 101, 103, *109*
Hartnett, J. J., 263, *285*
Harvey, O. J., 212, *234*
Hayes, S. P., Jr., 157, *174*
Heath, L, 54, *76*
Heckhausen, H., 94, 96, *109*
Heider, F., 116, 119, *143*, 265, *283*
Helmreich, R., 170, *174*
Hennigan, K. M., 350, *365*
Hepburn, C., 212, *233*
Herek, G. M., 354, *365*
Herman, C. P., 230, *233*
Hertzman, M., 151, *174*
Higgins, E. T., 89, 90, 93, 94, 100, *109*, *110*, *111*, 409, *410*
Higgins, P., 379, 381, 384, *391*
Hill, J., 16, *21*, 32, *50*, 237, *360*
Hill, R., 303, *311*

Hinds, H. H., 157, *174*
Hinkle, S., 212, *233*
Hochbaum, G. M., 177, *207*
Hodge, R W., 352, *366*
Hoffman, P. J., 7, *20*
Hogg, M. A., 214, 216, 225, *232*
Hoh, K., *75*, *392*
Holmes, D. S., 53, 65, *75*, 202, *207*
Holstom, L., 369, *392*
Holtz, R., 185, 186, 187, 193, 195, 196, *207*
Holyoak, K., 409, *410*
Hong, O. P., 184, 185, *207*
Hood, W. R., 212, *234*
Hornung, C. A., 73, *76*
Horowitz, M., 381, *392*
House, P., 157, *175*, 179, *208*, 213, *233*, 288, *312*
Houston, D. A., 408, *410*
Houston, B. K., 53, 65, *75*
Hovland, C., 408, *411*
Howard-Pitney, B., 204, *205*
Hoyt, M. F., *233*
Hu, L., 159, *175*
Hubbard, M., 339, *344*
Hupka, R. B., 263, 265, 268, 280, *283*
Hutton, D. G., 42, *46*, 215, *232*
Hyman, H. H., 150, *174*
Hymovitch, B., 177, *206*

I

Ingerman, C., 41, *47*, 68, *75*, 218, *233*, 276, *282*
Ingram, R. E., 307, *313*, 403, *411*
Inouye, D. K., 239, 254, *258*
Insko, C. A., 37, 42, *48*, 54, 55, 68, *77*
Isen, A. M., 127, *142*, *143*, 202, *207*
Israel, J., 14, *20*

J

Jacobson, E., 65, *75*
Jagacinski, C. M., 82, *110*
James, W., 181, *207*
Janis, I. L., 221, *233*, 305, 308, *411*,
Janoff-Bulman, R., 65, *75*
Janz, N. K., 336, *343*
Jaremko, M. E., 268, *283*
Jazwinski, C., 126, *143*
Jellison, J. M., 158, *174*
Jemmott, J. B., 330, *343*, 403, *410*
Jennings, D. L., 157, *174*
Jennings, S., 157, *174*
Johnson, E. W., *344*
Jones, E. E., *19*, 88, 90, *110*, *112*, 297, *311*
Jones, R. A., *21*, *49*, *78*, *209*, *260*

K

Kahneman, D., 36, *47*, 204, *207*, 409, *410*
Kamiya, J., 156, *175*
Kassin, S. M., 337, *343*
Katkin, E. S., 136, *142*
Katz, D., 287, 308, *311*
Katz, P., *107*
Kauffman, K., 288, 293, 303, *311*
Kaufman, C. M., 55, *75*
Kayne, N. T., 407, *410*
Keil, L, J., 89, 93, 100, *110*, 409, *410*
Kelley, H. H., 16, *20*, 150, *174*, 177, *206*, 269, *285*
Kelman, H. C., 306, *312*
Kenny, D. A., 182, *207*
Kenrick, D., 301, *312*
Kernis, M. H., 202, *207*
Kiesler, S. B., 53, 65, *76*, 202, *206*
Kim, S. H., 265, *284*

Kinder, D. R., 197, *207*, 351, *366*
King, C. A., 103, *110*
Kirschenbaum, D. S., 89, *110*, 254, *260*
Kishchuk, N., 79, *111*
Kitano, H. H. L. 356, *366*
Klein, R., 100, *110*
Kleinberg, J., 337, *343*
Klofas, J., 293, 295, *312*, *313*
Klotz, M., *392*
Koestner, R., 17, 18, *21*, 26, 27, 32, *49*, 51, 73, *78*, 272, *285*, 347, *367*, 396, *411*
Kohlberg, L., 79, *110*
Koltz, M., *75*
Korte, C., 295, 296, *312*
Korth, B., 10, *19*
Kraft, D., 200, *209*
Krauss, R. M., 6, *19*
Krech, D., 288, *312*
Krosnick, J. A., 181, *207*
Kruglanski, A., 83, *110*, 408, 409, *410*
Ktsanes, T., 305, *310*
Kuhn, D., 96, *111*
Kuiper, N. A., 41, *47*, 67, 72, *76*, 77, 329, *344*
Kunda, Z., 68, 71, *77*, 202, *207*

L

Lampen, L., 217, *234*
Lando, H., 320, *343*
Langer, E. T., 246, *259*
LaPrelle, J., 37, *48*, 54, *77*, 238, 251, *259*
Latané, B., 10, 11, *20*, 51, *76*, 153, *174*, 182, 196, *207*, 272, *283*, 288, 291, 309, *312*
Lau, S., 126, *143*
Lawhon, J., 17, *21*, 119, *144*, 272, *284*

Lawrence, D. H., *20*
Lazarus, R. S., 67, *76*, 242, 244, 245, 247, *259*, 322, 330, 335, 340, *343*, 370, *392*
Lepper, M. R., 339, *344*
Legant, P., 297, *312*
Leggett, E. L., 80, 83, 90, 100, 101, 102, *108*
Lehrman, P. R., 278, *283*
Lemyre, L., 216, 229, *233*
Lerner, M. J., 11, *20*, 249, *259*
Leung, K., 228, *234*
Leventhal, H., 305, *312*
Levine, J. M., 54, *76*, 88, 89, 94, 100, *110*, 275, *283*
Levine, L., 15, *21*
Levinger, G., 157, *175*
Levitt, B., 351, *366*
Levy, L. H., 307, *312*, 329, *343*
Levy, P. E., 55, *75*
Lewicki, P., 39, *47*, 68, 71, *76*
Lewin, K., 6, *20*
Liben, L. S., 87, *110*
Liberman, A., 193, *206*
Lichtenstein, M., 90, *112*
Lichtman, R. R., 29, *48*, *50*, 54, 78, 115, *145*, 149, 150, 155, *176*, 237, 238, 243, 248, *260*, 319, *344*, *345*, 370, 371, *393*, 399, 405, *411*
Lindsey, R., 268, *283*
Linville, P., 307, *313*
Lisle, D. J., 200, *209*
Liu, T. J., 141, *144*
Lobel, M., 80, 88, 104, 105, 106, *112*, 115, *144*, 320, 333, 334, *344*, 347, 356, 363, *367*, 369, 370, 374, 382, *393*, 399, *411*
Locksley, A., 212, *233*
Loebl, J. H., 93, *111*
Loewenstein, G., 352, *365*, *368*
Lorr, M., 378, *392*
Lott, A. J., 306, *312*
Lott, B. E., 306, *312*
Lounsbury, M., 378, *391*
Lubetsky, J., 181, *206*
Lubin, B., 323, *345*
Lucca, N., 228, *234*
Luhtanen, R., 221, 222, 223, 225, 226, 227, *233*
Lyall, W. A. O., 324, *345*

M

MacDonald, M. R., 41, *47*, 67, *76*
MacIver, D., 96, *112*
MacKenzie, D. L., 351, *368*
Mackie, D. M., 194, 202, *207*
Mahoney, J., 263, *285*
Main, S. K., *107*
Major, B., 231, *233*, 243, 246, 251, 252, *260*
Mandler, G., 136, *143*
Manges, K., 268, *283*
Mann, L., 351, *367*
Manstead, A. S. R., 204, *208*
Marcus-Newhall, A., 198, *205*
Marecek, J., 297, *312*
Mark, M. A., 237, *259*
Marks, G., 31, *47*, 56, 71, *76*, *77*, 156, 158, *175*, 179, 187, 197, 198, 202, 203, 204, *207*, *208*, 276, *283*, 288, *312*, 403, *410*
Markus, H., 68, 71, *77*, 87, *110*, 202, *207*, 341, *343*, 357, 363, *366*
Marsh, H. W., 251, *259*
Martin, J., 37, *47*, 238, 243, *259*, 351, *366*
Maruyama, G., 197, *208*
Mason, J., 372, *392*
Masters, J. C., 89, 93, 94, 100, *110*, 409, *410*
Mathes, E. W., 263, 267, 268, *283*
Matza, D., 288, 305, *312*

AUTHOR INDEX

Mayseless, O., 83, *110*, 408, 409, *410*
McCann, L., 380, *393*
McCaulwy, C., 241, *258*
McClintock, C. G., 93, 94, *110*
McClintock, E., 93, *110*
McClullough, B. C., 73, *76*
McFarland, C., 33, *48*, 58, 77, 115, *143*, 243, *259*, 298, 300, 301, 304, *312*, 335, *343*, 396, *411*
McFarlin, D. B., 24, *48*, 226, *233*
McGovern, P. G., 320, *343*
McGraw, K. M., 41, *47*, 68, *75*, 218, *233*, 276, *282*
McIntosh, W., 136, *144*
McIntyre, W. F., 307, *313*
McKay, J., 329, *343*
McNair, D., 378, *392*
McPhail, C., 350, *366*
Meenan, R., 372, *392*
Meichenbaum, D. H., 254, *259*, 324, *343*
Mendez-Caratini, G., 94, *110*
Mendola, R., 380, *393*
Meng, A. L., 254, *260*
Merton, E., 349, *366*
Merton, R. K., 290, *312*
Messick, D. M., 149, 161, *173*, *175*
Mettee, D. R., 11, *20*, *21*, 38, *47*, 80, *110*, 153, *175*, 244, *259*, 409, *411*
Michela, J.L., 42, *49*
Midgley, C., 103, *108*
Mikow, V., *75*, *392*
Millar, M., 30, 33, *49*, 124, 127, 128, *144*, 193, *208*, 250, *260*
Miller, A., 126, *143*
Miller, A., 404, *411*
Miller, A. H., 350, *366*
Miller, A. T., 82, 84, 93, 97, *111*

Miller, C. T., 17, 18, *20*, 32, 33, *47*, *259*, 270, *283*, 396, *411*
Miller, D. T., 33, *48*, 58, 61, 77, 115, 119, *143*, 153, *175*, 243, 249, *259*, 298, 300, 301, 304, *312*, 335, *343*, 396, 409, *410*, *411*
Miller, N., 56, 77, 158, *175*, 179, 181, 185, 186, 187, 193, 195, 196, 197, 198, 203, 204, *206*, *207*, *208*, 288, *312*, 403, *410*
Miller, R. L., 13, *20*, 33, 39, *48*, 51, *77*, 237, *260*
Moghadden, F. E., 355, 356, *367*
Molleman, E., 249, *259*, 324, 332, 333, *344*
Moore, J., 31 33, *49*, 125, 127, 128, *144*, 250, *260*
Moreland, R. L., 100, *110*
Morris, W. N., 94, *110*
Morrison, H., 96, *111*
Morse, S., 29, *48*, 238, 251, 252, *259*, 327, *344*
Mosatche, H. S., 94, *111*
Moskowitz, J. M., 93, *110*
Mowat, R. R., 278, *283*
Muehrer, P., 352, *365*
Mullen, B., 84, 93, 95, 98, *112*, 158, 159, *175*, 184, 189, *208*, 288, *312*, 383, *392*
Murray, A., 351, *366*
Murray, H. A., 181, 202, *208*
Myers, D. G., 149, *175*

N

Nadler, A., 126, *143*, 240, 243, 244, 245, 246, 252, 253, 256, *259*
Nagata, D. K., 357, 359, *366*, *367*
Natsoulas, T., 15, *21*

Neale, J. M., 408, *411*
Nelson, R. E., 15, *19*
Nemeck, D., 94, *110*
Newcomb, T. M., 307, *312*
Nicholls, J. G., 80, 82, 84, 86, 89, 91, 93, 97, 100, 102, 103, *110*, *111*
Nickel, T. W., 319, *344*
Nisbett, R. E., 297, 307, *311*, *312*
Nissen, H. W., 6, *20*
Noelle-Neumann, E., 294, *312*
Nosanchuk T. A., 27, *48*
Novak, D. W., 11, *20*
Nurius, P., 341, *343*

O

Oakes, P. J., 215, 229, *233*
O'Connell, E. J., 181, *206*
O'Connell, M., 354, *365*
O'Gorman, H. J., 288, 305, *312*
Olshausky, R., *311*
Olson, J. M., 106, *111*, 230, *233*
Orbell, J. M., 184, *208*
Orive, R., 154, *175*, 183, 195, 197, 200, *206*, 409, *410*
Ortiz, V., 212, *233*
Ortony, A., 135, *142*, *143*, 261, *283*

P

Packard, J. S., 288, 294, 295, 303, *312*
Parducci, A., 408, *411*
Parker, J. W., 251, *259*
Parkes, C. M., 307, *311*
Parkhurst, J., 97, *109*
Parrott, W. G., 265, *283*

Parsons, J. E., 93, 96, 101, *110*, *111*, 119
Parsons, T., 15, *20*, 119, *143*
Patchen, M., 15, *21*
Patchen, M. A., 16, *20*
Paulhus, D., 122, *144*, 246, 250, *260*, 275, *284*
Pearlin, L. I., 322, *344*
Penrod, S., 183, 196, *209*
Pepitone, A., 202, *208*
Pepitone, E., 94, *111*
Perloff, L. S., 36, *48*, 165, *175*, 308, *312*, 338, 339, *344*, 379, 382, *392*, 406, *411*
Perri, M. G., 408, *411*
Peterson, B. A., 307, *311*, 329, 330, *342*
Peterson, C., 388, *392*
Pettigrew, T. F., 203, 304, *208*, 278, 281, *283*, 350, 351, 363, *367*
Petty, R. E., 130, *142*
Pfeiffer, C., 29, *46*, *74*, 331, *342*, 371, 373, 375, 378, 394, 385, 386, *391*, *392*
Phibbs, C., 379, *392*
Phibbs, R., 379, *392*
Phillips, E. D., 166, *175*
Piaget, J., 79, *111*
Pike, R., 94, *109*
Pilkington, C., 136, 141, *144*
Pilliavin, I., 136, *143*
Pilliavin, J. A., 136, *143*
Pincus, T., 372, *392*
Pines, A., 268, *281*
Pleban, R., 30, 38, *48*, 122, *143*, 238, 244, 246, 250, *259*, 276, *283*
Predmore, S. C., 71, *77*
Presson, C. C., 36, *48*, 55, *77*, 183, *208*, 288, *311*, *313*
Pruyn, J., 249, *259*, 324, *344*

Psarska, A. D., 278, *283*
Puckett, J., *344*
Pufall, A., 354, *365*
Pyszczynski, T., 37, *48*, 54, 67, 77, 204, *208*, 238, 251, *259*

R

Raden, D., 180, *208*
Radloff, R., 10, *20*, 71, 77, 272, *283*
Raven, B., 177, *206*
Raynor, J. O., 24, *46*, *48*, 80, *111*
Reardon, K. K., 255, *260*
Reckman, R. F., 17, *20*
Reed, H., 307, *312*
Reese, L., 254, *258*
Reis, T., 327, *344*
Renner, B., 75, *392*
Repucci, N. D., 256, *258*
Resnick, A., 351, *365*
Rhodebeck, L., 351, *367*
Richardson, K. D., 116, *142*, 276, *282*
Richardson, S. A., 336, *344*
Ridl, J., 149, *175*
Riecken H., 152, *174*
Ringler, K., 324, *344*
Riskin, J., 11, *20*, 158, *174*
Roach, S., 263, *282*
Robinson, J. E., *21*, *49*, 78, *209*, *260*
Rodin, J., 38, *48*, 115, 126, 131, 136, *143*, 238, 250, *260*, 262, 264, 265, 267, 270, 271, 273, 275, 276, *284*
Roemmele, L. A., 71, *77*
Rogers, J., 324, 329, *344*, *345*
Rohrer, K., 329, *344*
Roseman, I., 135, *143*
Rosenbaum, M. E., 182, *208*

Rosenberg, M., 218, 219, 220, 221, 222, *233*
Rosenthal, R., 190, *208*
Ross, J., 93, 96, *111*
Ross, L., 157, 158, *175*, 179, *208*, 213, *233*, 288, *312*, *344*
Ross, L. D., 203, *208*
Ross, M., 79, 90, 106, *111*, 173, *175*
Rossi, A. S., 349, 353, *366*
Rossi, P. H., *366*
Rothbart, M., 90, *112*
Rothbaum, F., 370, *392*
Rowe, J., 29, *46*, *74*, 331, *342*, 371, 378, 379, 381, 384, 386, *391*
Ruble, D. N., 17, *19*, 51, 73, *75*, 79, 80, 82, 83, 84, 87, 89, 90, 91, 93, 94, 95, 96, 97, 98, 99, 101, 103, 104, 106, *108*, *109*, *111*, *112*, 396, *410*
Ruhland, D., 93, *108*
Runciman, W. G., 230, 351, *233*, *367*
Ryan, R. M., 79, 83, 100, 103, *108*, *112*
Ryff, C., 98, *112*

S

Sabagh, G., 337, *342*
Sabini, J., 262, 267, 268, 269, 270, 274, 276, *283*
Salovey, P., 38, *48*, 115, 126, 131, *143*, 238, 250, *260*, 262, 264, 265, 267, 268, 270, 271, 273, 275, 276, *284*
Sampson, E. E., 356, *367*
Samuelson, C. D., 149, *175*
Sande, G. N., 71, *77*

Sanders, G. S., 27, *47*, 73, *77*, 93, *112*, 178, *208*, 330, *344*
Schachter, S., 7, 8, *20*, 23, *48*, 51, 77, 115, 136, *144*, 152, *174*, 290, 303, *312*, 317, 321, 329, *344*, 388, *392*
Schanck, R. L., 287, 292, 303, 308, 309, *311*, *313*
Scheier, M. R., 88, 89, 92, *108*, 373, *392*
Scherer, K. R., 135, *144*
Schmidt, G. W., 55, *75*, 225, *232*
Schmitt, B. H., 276, 277, *284*
Schneider, D. J., 157, *175*
Schoeck, H., 273, 278, *284*
Schooler, C., 322, *344*
Schopler, J., 212, *233*
Schulz, R., 54, 77, 322, 329, 330, 331, 333, *344*, 369, *392*
Schuman, H., 181, *207*, 305, *311*
Schunk, D. H., 254, *260*
Schwartz, G. E., 130, *144*
Schwartz, I., 115, *143*, 218, 219, *233*
Scully, M., 351, *366*
Sears, D. O., 166, *175*
Sears, P. S., 6, *20*
Segal, A. V., 67, 77
Seligman, M. E. P., 228, *234*, 245, 247, *257*, 388, *392*
Semmel, A., 228, *234*
Seta, J., 27, *48*, 243, *260*
Severa, N., 263, 268, *283*
Shalker, T. E., 127, *143*
Sharp, J., 320, *343*
Shaver, K. G., *21*, *49*, *78*, 178, *208*, *209*, *260*
Shaw, M. E., 305, *313*
Sherif, C. W., 212, *234*, 351, *368*
Sherif, M., 204, *208*, 212, *234*, 408, *411*

Sherman, S. J., 36, 44, 45, *48*, 55, 56, *77*, 183, 197, 203, *208*, 288, *311*, *313*, 408, *410*
Shiffman, S., 408, *411*
Shoptaw, S., 371, *393*
Short, J. C., 83, *112*
Shrauger, J. S., 226, *234*
Sicoly, F., 173, *175*
Siegel, P. M., 353, *366*
Signorella, L. S., 87, *110*
Silver, M., 262, 267, 268, 269, 270, 274, 276, *283*
Silvern, L., *107*
Singer, E., 245, *260*
Singer, J. A., 130, *144*
Singer, J. E., 6, *20*, 23, 26, *48*, 73, 77, 150, 153, *175*, 317, 318, *344*, 347, *367*, 404, *411*
Sitwell, E., *285*
Sloan, L. R., *142*, *282*
Slovic, P., 204, *207*
Smeaton, G., 182, *206*
Smith, C. A., 131, 135, *144*
Smith, D. A., 99, *113*
Smith, G., 11, *20*, 38, 80, *110*, 153, *175*, 244, *259*, 409, *411*
Smith, J., 31, *49*, 122, 123, *144*, 278, *284*
Smith, L. G., 280, *282*
Smith, M., 38, *49*, 55
Smith, P. M., 216, 229, *233*
Smith, R. H., 37, 42, *48*, 54, 68, 77, 265, 369, *283*, *284*
Smith, S. P., 94, *112*
Smith, W. P., 272, *282*
Snyder, C. R., 288, 307, *313*, 403, *411*
Snyder, H. N., 94, *110*
Snyder, R. C., 354, *365*
Snyder, S., 370, *392*
Soraci, S., 372, *392*
Sorrentino, R. M., 83, *112*

Spear, P., 94, *112*
Spears, R., 204, *208*
Spielman, P. M., 264, *284*
Spilerman, S., 350, *367*
Spinoza, B., 267, *284*
Spriggs, D., 216, *234*
Srull, T. K., 90, *112*, 409, *411*
Stahlberg, D., 54, *75*
Stangor, C. S., 83, 87, *118*, *112*
Stapp, J., 170, *174*
Star, S. A., 349, *367*
Statham, A., 79, *112*
Steele, C. M., 141, *144*, 150, *175*
Steele, S., 231, *234*
Steil, J. M., 348, *365*
Steiner, I. D., 202, 205, *208*
Stephan, W., 136, *144*
Stephan, W. G., 136, *143*
Stevens, L., 90, *112*
Stevens, S. S., 204, *208*
Stiles, C., 279, *284*
Stiles, W. B., 54, *75*
Stipek, D. J., 93, 96, 97, 101, *112*
Stone, A. A., 408, *411*
Stone, P., 156, *175*
Story, J. E., *175*, *208*, *312*
Stotland, E., 15, *19*, *20*, *21*
Stouffer, S. A., 349, *367*
Strauman, T., 100, *110*
Stringfield, D. O., 301, *312*
Strohmer, D. C., 307, *313*
Strube, M. J., 71, *77*
Stryker, S., 79, *112*
Stycos, J. M., 303, *311*
Suchman, E. A., 349, *367*
Suls, J., 17, *19*, *20*, 27, 30, 32, 36, 44, *47*, 51, 55, 57, 69, 73, *75*, 77, 84, 90, 93, 94, 95, 97, 98, 106, *112*, 154, *175*, 178, 179, 184, *208*, 288, *313*, 330, 334, *344*, 347, *367*, 369, 383, *392*, 396, 400, 403, *410*, *411*
Suls, J. M., 10, 12, 13, 17, *20*, *21*, 26, 32, 39, *48*, 51, 77, 119, *144*, 237, *260*, 272, *284*, *367*
Summey, J., 372, *392*
Suenson, 149
Swallen, S. R., 67, 72, *77*, 329, *344*
Swann, W. B., Jr., 71, *77*, 90, *112*
Sykes, C., *285*
Syllwasschy, J., 217, *234*

T

Tabachnik, N., 41, *48*, 55, 68, 69, *77*, 228, *234*
Tajfel, H., 183, *209*, 212, 214, 221, 229, 230, *234*
Talbert, D., *344*
Tanford, S., 183, 196, *209*
Tannatt, L. M., 93, *112*
Taylor, D. M., 351, 355, 356, *367*
Taylor, K. L., 42, *49*
Taylor, S. E., 11, *21*, 24, 29, 35, 36, 38, 39, 40, *48*, *50*, 54, 71, *77*, *78*, 80, 87, 88, 89, 90, 104, 105, 106, *109*, *112*, 115, 130, 142, *144*, *145*, 149, 150, 155, *175*, *176*, 195, *206*, 215, 220, 225, 228, *234*, 237, 238, 243, 248, 255, 256, *258*, *260*, 319, 320, 322, 333, 334, 338, 340, *344*, *345*, 347, 356, 363, *367*, 369, 370, 371, 374, 382, 387, *393*, 399, 405, *411*
Teasdale, J. D., 245, 247, *257*
Teelegen, A., 65, *78*
Tennen, H., 29, *46*, *74*, 331, *342*, 371, 372, 375, 378, 379, 380, 381, 384, 386, *391*, *392*, *393*
Tesser, A., 10, 30, 31, 33, 35, 38, 39, *48*, *49*, 80, 88, 89, *113*, 122, 123, 124, 127, 128, 131, 136, 137, 138, 141, *143*, *144*,

150, *176*, 184, 193, *208*, *209*, 237, 238, 230, 241, 243, 244, 246, 250, *259*, *260*, 270, 275, 276, 277, 278, *283*, *284*
Testa, M., 246, 251, 252, 256, *260*
Thibault, J. W., 269, *285*
Thoits, P. A., 324, *345*
Thompson, L. L., 41, *47*, 68, *75*, 218, *233*, 276, *282*
Thompson, S., 369, *393*
Thompson, S. C., 54, *77*
Thorne, A., *142*, 229, *233*, *282*
Thorton, D., 9, 18, *21*, 23, 26, *49*, 115, *144*, 347, *367*
Tice, D. M., 42, *46*, 215, *232*
Tipton, R. M., 263, *285*
Toch, H., 293, 295, *312*, *313*
Toomey, B., *344*
Triandis, H. C., 228, *234*
Trope, Y., 24, 27, *49*, 80, 86, 87, 88, 89, 101, 102, *110*, *113*
Turnbull, W., 33, *48*, 58, *77*, 115, *143*, 243, *259*, 335, *343*, 396, *411*
Turner, J. C., 183, *209*, 212, 214, 215, 216, 221, 229, 230, *233*, *234*
Tversky, A., 36, *47*, 204, *207*, 408, *411*
Twain, M., 262, *285*

U, V

Useem, M., 349, *367*

Vachon, M. L. S., 324, *345*
Valins, S., 307, *313*
van de Kragt, A. J. C., 184, *208*
van der Linden, J., 183, *209*
van der Plight, J., 183, *209*

Vankerklok, M., *175*, *208*, *312*
van Knippenberg, A., 249, *259*, 324, *344*
Vanneman, R. D., 350, *367*
Vanyur, J. M., 126, *145*
Veroff, J., 79, 80, 84, 92, 93, 95, 96, 98, 99, 102, *113*
Veroff, J. B., 79, 80, 102, *113*
Villareal, M. J., 228, *234*
von Baeyer, C., 228, *234*

W

Wageman, R., 100, *109*
Wagner, U., 217, *234*
Walker, I., 351, *367*
Walker, L., 379, 381, *391*
Walker, M. R., *142*, 229, *233*, *282*
Wallach, M. A., 158, *175*
Walster, E., 238, *260*
Walster, G. W., 238, *260*
Walters, R. M., 53, 65, *74*
Wan, C. K., 30, 36, 44, 48, 55, *77*, 288, *313*, 330, *344*, 403, *411*
Watson, D., 65, *78*
Waugh, E., *285*
Weber, R., 90, *108*
Weinberger, D. A., 130, *144*
Weiner, B., 61, *78*, 135, *145*, 247, 248, 249, *260*
Weinstein, N. D., 36, *49*, *176*, 340, *345*
Weiss, R. S., 307, *311*
Weisz, J., 370, *392*
Whalen, P., 354, *365*
Wheeler, L., 8, 10, 15, 16, 17, 18, *20*, *21*, 26, 27, 32, 34, 37, *49*, 51, 73, *78*, 153, 178, *209*, 237, *260*, 272, *285*, 347, *367*, 368, 396, 404, *411*
Wheeler, S., 288, 293, 295, *313*

White, B. J., 212, *234*
White, G. L., 264, 266, 268, *285*
White, R. W., 79, *113*
Whitehurst, R. N., 280, *285*
Wicklund, R. A., 329, *342*
Wilder, D. A., 153, *173*
Wilhelmy, R. A., 196, *206*
Wilkins, P. D., 11, *20*
Williams, M., 71, *74*
Williams, R. M., 349, *367*
Williams, S., 379, *392*
Willower, D. J., 288, 294, 295, 303, *312*
Wills, T. A., 18, *21*, 29, 30, 41, 44, *49*, 52, 54, 58, 62, 66, 70, 73, 74, *78*, 88, *113*, 115, 116, *145*, 153, 155, *176*, 213, 214, 215, 231, *234*, 237, 238, 245, 257, *260*, 267, 275, *285*, 318, 321, 327, 330, 331, 340, *345*, 347, 348, 356, *368*, 369, 373, 374, 379, 380, 383, *393*, 401, *411*
Wilner, N., 381, *392*
Wilson, A., 262, *285*
Wilson, S. R., 10, 16, *21*, 37, 42, *49*, 53, 55, 68, *78*, 272, 275, *285*, 319, 327, *345*
Wilson, T. D., 200, *209*, 307, *313*
Wing, C. W., Jr., 158, *176*
Winston, T., 30, *47*, 248, *258*, 307, 309, *311*, 329, *342*
Winter, D. 363, *368*
Wood, J. V., 23, 24, 29, 31, 33, 34, 35, 36, 37, 39, 42, 43, 44, 46, 48, *49*, *50*, 54, 63, 64, *78*, 80, 84, 88, 90, 104, 105, 106, *113*, 115, *145*, 149, 150, 155, *176*, 237, 238, 243, 248, *260*, 267, 270, 273, *285*, 319, 322, 331, 332, 334, *344*, *345*, 370, 371, 372, 376, 382, 385, 386, 388, 389, *393*, 399, 405, *411*
Wortman, C. B., 245, 248, 249, 258, 307, *311*, *313*, 332, 333, *342*, 379, *393*
Wright, M., 320, 336, *345*
Wright, S. C., 355, 356, *367*
Wrightsman, L. S., Jr., 7, *21*, 115, *145*
Wylie, R. C., 218, 221, *234*

Y, Z

Young, C. J., 351, *368*

Zajonc, R. C., 87, *110*, 124, 136, *145*
Zander, A., 15, *19*, *21*
Zanna, M. D., 16, *21*, 32, *50*, 106, *111*, 230, *233*, 237, 352, *260*, *368*
Zastowny, T. R., 254, *260*
Zuckerman, M., 16, *21*, 26, *49*, 272, *285*
Zuckerman, M., 323, *345*

Subject Index

Attribution
  and social comparison, 16–18, 136–141, 153–155
  impact of jealousy on, 277–278
  in Pluralistic Ignorance, 297–298
BIRGing, 34, 116–117, 229
Cognitive development and social comparison, 95
Cognitive dissonnance and social comparison, 151–154, 156
Comparison choice
  dissimilarity of, *see also* Downward comparison; Upward comparison, 5–6, 10–13, 38
  imaginary, 35–37, 46
  similarity of, 5, 10, 12, 14–15, 24–38, 40, 92, 95, 97–98, 119, 122, 395–397
  on abilities, 6, 13–14, 16
  on attitudes, 13–14
  on dimension evaluated *see also* Comparison choice similarity on abilities; opinions; performance, 25–32
  effects on jealousy, 271–274
  effects on envy, 271–274
  on opinions, 6, 16
  on performance, 8–10, 16
  on personality, 59–61, 64–65, 68–69
  on related attributes, *see also* Comparison choice similarity on unrelated attributes, 16–18, 32, 34
  and uniformity drive, 5–8
  on unrelated attributes, *see also* S.E.M. model, 33–35, 38–40, 63–64, 119, 242–244
Competition
  and social comparison, 13–14, 58–100
Consensus bias, 155–158
  and prejudice, 213
Constructive social comparison, 150, 154–173
Coping, *see* Downward

429

comparison and; Temporal comparison and
Denial of personal disadvantage, 347–364
  in avoiding social comparisons, 353–364
  in relative deprivation, 348–353
Dimensional comparison, 38–40
Downard comparison, 9, 18, 28–32, 41, 51–74
  and affect, *see also* effects of esteem-relevance, 9, 11–13, 38, 54, 57–58, 321–327, 60, 65
  and coping, 66–70, 90, 319–322, 330–341, 370–391
  in forced comparisons, 381–383
  methodological concerns, 385–389
  effects of esteem-relevance, 249–255
  effects of perceived control, 244–248
  and prejudice, 213–214
  and self-esteem, 41–45, 55–74, 88, 327–329
False consensus effect, *see* Consensus bias,
Gender differences
  in lifestage determinants of self-evaluation, 99
  in uniqueness bias, 168–169
Generality of similarity schema, 15
Group uniformity, *see* Social comparison; Social communication
Imitation, *see* Modeling
Lateral comparison, 53, 56–57, 63, 73
Minimal Group Paradigm
  and ingroup bias, 212, 215–219

Mixed Elements in social comparison, 59–62
Modeling and social comparison, 7, 28, 34, 84–85, 101
  similarity of target, 14–16
Observational learning, *see* Modeling
Particularistic comparisons, 15, 58, 119–120, 396
Pluralistic Ignorance, 287–288
  social comparison influences on, 289–291, 297–304
  consequences of, 304–307
Psychological disengagement, *see also* S.E.M. model, 88
Rank-Order Paradigm, 8–11
Relative deprivation, 348–353
Self-concept, *see* S.E.M. model
Self enhancement, 9–10, 18, 24–25, 28–36, 40–46, 52–55, 57–61, 65–74, 88, 90 153, 197
  and consensus bias, 156–159
  and constructive social comparison, 150, 154–156
  and uniqueness bias, 172–173
Self esteem, *see also* S.E.M.; BIRGing, 24, 41–45, 55–74, 88, 120, 327–329
  collective self esteem, 221–225, 227, 231
  in prejudice, 231–232
  and ingroup bias, 212–227, 231
  in prejudice, 212–214
  and self enhancement, 24, 29–32, 41, 225–226
  in skill acquisition, 87–89, 91, 104
  and social projection, 197–198, 203
  and uniqueness bias, 169–171

SUBJECT INDEX

Self evaluation, *see also* social comparison of abilities; opinions, 9–10, 15, 24–28, 31, 33, 40, 41, 45–46, 64, 120
   developmental determinants of, 81–99, 101–107
      in life stage, 81–82, 92–99
      in skill acquisition, 81–92, 95, 99, 101–107
      and affect, 100, 103–104
      and motivation, 100–104
   S.E.M. model, 116–141
   and emotion, 123–141
Self handicapping, 88
Self Improvement, *see also* self evaluation in skill acquisition, 25, 27–29, 31, 33–34, 40, 66, 73
Self protection, 13, 37–38
Self relevance in social comparison, *see also* S.E.M. model, 30–32, 39–40, 194–105, 241–242
   and esteem-relevance, 244
   and jealousy 268–271, 274–275
Self validation, *see* self enhancement; self esteem
Social communication, 4–5
Social comparison, *see also* self evaluation; self enhancement, 5
   of abilities, 5, 6, 8–11, 13–14, 16, 24
   and affect, *see also* Downward comparison; self enhancement; self esteem, 12–13, 33, 116
      jealousy and envy, 268–278
   and affiliation, 7, 30
   of attitudes, 13–14
   avoidance of, 37–38, 232–234
   in Pluralistic Ingorance, *see also* Denial of personal disadvantage, 407
   motivation for, *see also* self evaluation; self enhancement, 5–6, 9, 12, 24, 79, 89, 119
   of opinions, 5–6, 16, 24
   and positive instance hypothesis, 8–9
   and unidirectional drive upward, 5–6, 8, 24, 27, 84, 119
   and uniformity, 5–8
Social perception, 55–56
Social projection, 179, 199–204
   and opinion certainty in social comparison, 182–199
   effects of perceived ingroup similarity, 185–186, 192–195
   effects of group salience, 187–195
   on group relevant issues, 184–191, 194
Temporal comparisons, 83–84, 91–93, 95–96
   and coping, 383–385
Uniqueness bias, 149, 156, 159–173
   in Pluralistic Ignorance, 288–290, 295–296
Universalistic comparisons, 15, 28, 119–120, 396
Upward comparison, 27–29, 34, 52, 66, 70, 73, 84
   and affect, 12–13, 38, 73, 249–255
   effects of esteem relevance, 249–255
   effects of perceived control, 244–249